CANYON COUNTRY EXPLORATIONS & RIVER LORE

The Remarkable Resilient Life of Kenny Ross

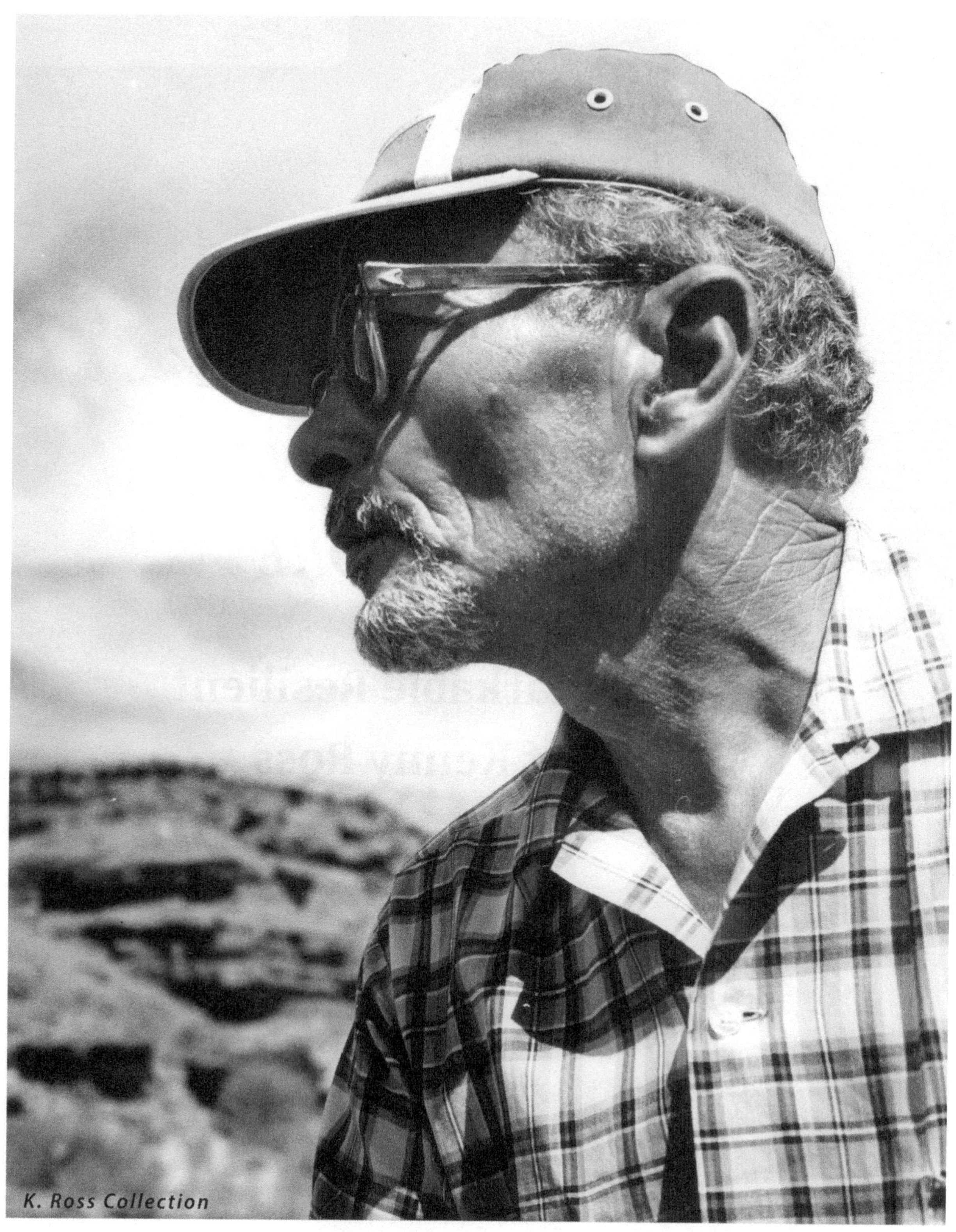

Frontispiece [Kenny Ross, 1969]

CANYON COUNTRY EXPLORATIONS & RIVER LORE

The Remarkable Resilient Life of Kenny Ross

By Gene M. Stevenson

ISBN: 9781793136039
Published by *Living Earth Studios, LLC*
Bluff, Utah 84512

Printed in the United States of America

Cover Photo: View of San Juan River as it cuts through Comb Ridge;
steeply dipping red beds on left define eastern flank of the Monument Upwarp;
Abajo Mountains in distance (G.M. Stevenson photo)

Dedicated
to
Don and Doug Ross

In fond memory of William R. "Big Bill" Dickinson

[finally got 'er done, Bill]

CONTENTS

ACKNOWLEDGMENTS

Writing a book about someone's life is a surreal experience. It's harder than I thought and more rewarding than I could ever imagine. None of this would have been possible without learning to listen to storytellers, like my father, my dear Uncle Mose and Grandpa Stevenson. But I want to mainly thank my parents who insisted that I learned to read and to comprehend! And to ask questions. Not being distracted by TV helped, particularly in expanding my imagination and observations. Learning to read opened the door to the world around me. Somewhere along the line I learned to enjoy researching specific subjects and to not stop with one source of information. Research led to finding loop holes in various arguments and if I looked long enough I was rewarded by filling in some of those holes. That's what I've tried to accomplish in writing this book – to *fill in the gaps* about what was known about Kenneth Irving Ross, a truly remarkable and resilient man.

I am forever indebted to Don Ross and Doug Ross for entrusting me with all their fathers photos and files and their seemingly endless stories about their father – "the old man." Their recollections from their earliest years growing up in Mancos and Bluff, their first river trips, the rough roads and long shuttle trips, the first time they got to run their own boat and memories of their mother, Mildred. Her incredible strength and support of her two boys and Kenny were indispensable. Every review of a draft of a chapter led them to add more depth and details. Doug's memories of the rapids on the lower San Juan below Copper Canyon and the side canyons in Glen Canyon were most helpful as he made many more trips through the Glen than Don. However, Don was particularly helpful in recalling the first years of Wild Rivers Expeditions camps in Bluff and in helping defer some of the costs for photo scanning, printing ink and paper.

Very special heartfelt thanks to Bill Dickinson, one of Kenny's first students who went on to become a world renowned geoscientist. The many letters that Bill shared between him and Kenny were incredibly useful. I was so looking forward to hearing more stories from him about Kenny, but he passed away suddenly before we had the chance.

Charlie DeLorme provided many insights into Kenny's later years and Susan DeLorme was most helpful in sharing her love and admiration of Mildred. Their review of an early draft and their continued encouragement to forge ahead are most appreciated. I would like to thank all those who have been a part of my efforts to get this story of Kenny into a book form: Herm Hoops' typescript of a taped oral interview of Kenny Ross in Mancos, CO in 1986 and his knowledge of inflatable boats; the great work by the folks at *FotoBridge* who scanned most of the print and slide photos; Lacey Hook for retyping [verbatim] all of Kenny's onion-skin carbon copies into readable form; Brad Dimock for the Bert Loper notes and encouragement; Harvey Leake for background information about John Wetherill; Andy Christenson for RBMV photos and related information (particularly nailing down Kenny Ross being on first RBMV river trip); Winston Hurst and Fred Blackburn for Bluff area history and archaeology; my neighbor Jerry Howell for people, businesses and place names in Bluff in the 1950s and 1960s; Martha Austin-Garrison at Diné College, Tsaile, AZ for correct Navajo spelling; Elizabeth Kahn and Allison Fischer-Olson for RBMV aerial pilot and camera information; Peekay Briggs, Archivist at Canyonlands NP in helping identify Explorers Arch as Castle Arch in Needles District; Mesa Verde NP Ranger Jill Blumenthal for diorama access; Sally Jo Leitner at Cortez, CO Public library for newspaper clippings of Jackson Reservoir and Four Corners monument dedication; June Head with the Montezuma County Historical Association and her stories of the Four Corners Motorcycle club, photos and insights into June Hall; LaVerne Tate with Blue Mountain Shadows articles and photos from the San Juan County Historical Society; Bill & Merrie Winkler for insights into Ansel Hall and the DUKW; Roger Hayes and Tim Leahy for identifying the 1938 airplane; Jon Frembling at the Amon Carter Museum of Art in trying to get information about Eliot Porter from his family; Mark Schwindt's phone conversation in 2016 about the 1970s vintage frames he made for two of Kenny's J-rigs and information about Mildred; Brandt Hart for San Juan River history and his article about the Swingin' Bridge; Jay Willian for USGS aerial photos and local history; Michael MacMillan, Archeologist at AHC Canyon of the Ancients NM regarding Cahone ruin; Silas Sparks, BLM Outdoor Recreation Planner for river statistical data; Stewart Aitchison and JR Lancaster for use of their photos; and Bill Frank at the Huntington Library. Thanks also to Rana Chan at the Georgia O'Keeffe Museum for permission to use a couple of photos of Georgia in 1961 and to Sam and Betsy at the Todd Webb Archives in Portland, ME for photos from the 1961 Eliot Porter/Georgia O'Keeffe rive trip.

Special thanks to: Ted Howard, CDOT; Mel Herrera, NMDOT; Mike Ellis and Elizabeth Giraud, UDOT; and Rusty Crerand, AZDOT for GIS help w/bridges and dates. Thanks also to Roy Webb who convinced me, Don and Doug to donate the "Kenny collection" to the Marriott Library at the University of Utah.

Finally, this book would have never made it to the finish line without the unwavering support and encouragement from my wife and illustrator - Theresa Breznau. She worked with me on all the maps and made the photos as clear as possible. Her assistance in editing and critiquing were most appreciated. Plus, the book would have never been completed without Theresa's uncountable hours in getting this manuscript into a publishable format.

Any mistakes and omissions are my fault and mine alone.

PREFACE

"When you come to the fork in the road, take it" – Yogi Berra

Most of us have experienced the old feeling that hindsight is 20/20. When I was a young boy I recall my paternal grandmother alluding to this phenomenon as she was telling me a story while reflecting on her life and how she came to meet and marry my grandfather. She said that as her daily life experiences passed by she didn't give much thought about the good things, or bad, that had happened. They just happened and she moved on through those life experiences. But then in hindsight, as she was nearing eighty years of age, she said it was like looking at a road map to her life. Things and situations when viewed in her reflections of her past seemed like they were *supposed* to happen. I didn't give much thought to that explanation as a nine year old kid, but now I can see exactly what she was talking about – at least as far as my own life experiences have progressed. Decisions that were made at certain periods in my life now look as though they were predetermined. Some may call it 'fate.'

My "Fork in the Road"

As best I can remember it was the spring of 1969, probably somewhere around the third weekend in March when I was a student participating in a geology class field trip. I was in my 5th class in geology having finally made the decision to major in Geology and try to finish my rather arduous time as a student at Fort Lewis College in Durango, Colorado. I had bounced around for two years taking required "core" courses while trying classes ranging from business law to the Bible as literature and for the most part not really liking what I had enrolled in. My solid "C minus" average reflected my lack of commitment. But other things had recently happened that were changing my direction in life. I had started my college days as a jock; I had gotten an athletic scholarship to play football at Fort Lewis in 1966, so for the first several semesters (trimesters at FLC) I was mainly there to play football, be a gym-rat, take some filler courses and have a good time. But by the end of football season in 1968 I could see that my interests had changed and I had finally found something I could sink my teeth into; and that was Geology. So here I was missing spring football practice for the first time in many years dating back to my junior high school days and I was taking part in a group field trip that would take three days out of my life – a first for me.

The group of geology students ranged from first year to advanced levels and consisted of ten guys and two girls. Four of us were good friends and had progressed through the geology program together. We were all utterly enthralled by the new geology professor Donald L. Baars, who had shown up in the fall semester of 1968 and lit a fire under me for sure. He quickly became my mentor and a life-long friend and colleague. However, at this juncture, he was the trip leader and we had driven in two college vehicles (International Carry-all) from Durango to Bluff, Utah. There we were to meet up with this old guy who had some boats that would take us down a river so that Professor Baars could point out some stuff we had studied in class. Prof. Baars was great at diagramming maps and cross-sections on the chalk board, or by pulling out the movie screen and showing us slides of what he was discussing. We had just finished a section in **stratigraphy** class where he had shown these limestone canyons and outcrops of a certain type of fossiliferous mound, or reef-like build-up. He explained that they were of a particular type of calcareous algae that was the principal reservoir for oil that had been produced from a nearby field called Aneth. The only realistic way to go and see these algal mounds was to access them by boat and Prof. Baars knew this old guy in Bluff that could take us down the river – the San Juan River.

The drive from Durango to Bluff took a long time and the roads got narrower and bumpier and the country changed from the forested mountains of Colorado to barren wasteland of Utah dotted with Navajo hogans and eventually some scattered oil pump jacks alongside the San Juan River. We drove up a switchback road and pulled out on an overlook where Prof. Baars waved his arms and said we were looking down on one of the largest oil fields in America. Unimpressed, we all shrugged our shoulders and he pointed out the river and said we wouldn't see it again until we got to our launch point near Bluff. We drove on and finally came down this narrow little canyon cut through cream-colored sandstone with cottonwood trees in the wash and pulled into an old cinder block garage of an abandoned gas station that had been converted into a boat shop. The name "Wild Rivers Expeditions" was painted across the top of the building, so we knew we had gotten to our destination. We all got out stretching our legs and needing to pee and Prof. Baars went inside to find the man who owned the boats that were lying outside the garage. We poked around looking at these semi-inflated World War II relics and wondered if these were what we were going to ride on down the river. We all were thirsty and dug into the ice chest in back of one of the Carry-all's and passed out beers or soda pop. After several minutes had gone by, we looked inside the garage and there sat Prof. Baars holding a can of beer and smoking a cigarette talking to this old man. The old guy was wearing a baseball cap, had a hunched back, gray scruffy beard and scraggly hair protruding from the sides of his cap and also smoking a cigarette and sipping on a can of beer – Hamm's beer! Yuk! Prof. Baars turned to us and then introduced us to Kenny Ross and said he was "the old man of the San Juan River" and would run one of the boats tomorrow. It was a bigger boat sitting outside on a big trailer and had an outboard motor dangling off the back but he spoke up and asked if any of us wanted to "row" one of the "7-man crafts" laying there on the ground? One of my buddies said "you bet" and the four of us were immediately delegated to "captain" the 7-man smaller black boat, even though I had no idea to what "7-man" was referring. Mr. Ross asked if any of us had ever rowed a boat before and we all lied and said yes we had; or at least I lied, sort of. I had rowed a small hard-hulled fishing boat on some small lakes and ponds, but never on moving water, but heck, how hard could that be? Look at this old man and he was going to run this twenty foot-long boat on a tiny motor. This river couldn't be that tough, I thought.

So we guzzled our drinks and after some further discussion, Prof. Baars said we should load up. We hardly drove a few hundred yards and then stopped again and got out and filled up some water jugs from a pipe sticking out of the ground with running water. Two buff-tan sandstone buttes towered over us now, and Baars pointed out they were called the "Navajo Twin Rocks" and he pointed to a small tilted toadstool of a rounded block of sandstone balanced on red shale and said it was called "Sunbonnet Rock." The water was cold and tasted great and we filled up the water jugs and drove through this little town of Bluff by zig zagging just about every block. My first impression of this *town* was that it looked mostly abandoned. We crossed a bridge over a dry wash and then we passed a café and trading post, a few trailers, a couple of gas stations and were immediately in the barren desert country headed west. We drove several more miles and turned off and drove down a steep hill and saw the river again. We went to a small cottonwood grove near the river and Baars said this was where we were going to camp tonight. We were at the Sand Island camping area and Prof. Baars said that the boats would be hauled down later and he pointed downstream as to where we would launch. We all walked down to the river and we weren't too impressed with it. The river was slowly moving, a murky greenish-brown color and didn't look like it was going to be very much of a challenge, even if we hadn't rowed a boat on a river before.

It wasn't all that late, but the March sun was beginning to set, so we unpacked our gear and then we all spread out to gather up some dry firewood for a campfire. Some guys had tents, but I only had an old cotton-fiber sleeping bag along with a military waterproof duffle bag I had borrowed from my girlfriend's dad. We sat on cottonwood logs and drank beer, ate some hotdogs & beans, drank some more beer before it was time to roll out the sleeping bag. Until now I hadn't noticed that the zipper was blown. With minimal ground cover I spent most of the night awake, and it was damn cold too. I recall lying there shivering most of the night and waiting for dawn. I was first up to light a fire and get a pot of coffee brewing. Others soon gathered for some sort of forgettable breakfast, and we watched as a truck came down the hill pulling a now fully inflated big boat with the smaller boat stacked on top. We went over and helped out as best we knew how, and finally got to putting on some life vests as Mr. Ross explained some stuff to which we didn't pay attention. It was time to board the boats and Prof. Baars got on the big boat with Captain Ross while my three cohorts and I jumped in the small black boat.

My friend John was first to grab the oars and Kenny Ross motored out in front of us. I remember these strange rolling waves immediately and wondered how they formed as there weren't any constriction of the river to form a rapid. After a few miles we stopped briefly at a big petroglyph site and made a couple more stops for Baars to arm wave and explain what we were looking at before we entered this big canyon to which he had alluded. The change in topography was obvious to us all. The relatively open terrain we had started in with nearly flat-lying layers of tan and red sandstone cliffs set back away from the river were now tilted at nearly 45 degree angles. A myriad of fractured slabs of red rock mixed with gray layers made a beguiling landscape and the river was now beginning to get enclosed into this tilted terrain. Somewhere in this early stretch it was my turn to navigate and I flailed away, but generally kept the boat on course. As we cut into this canyon, the river suddenly narrowed and picked up speed and then there were all sorts of large angular rocks to try to dodge. In a matter of minutes the world had changed before my eyes. We were now in a deep narrow canyon and the rock layers were again flat-lying but gray and green and alternating skyward in uncountable frequency. Only the upper reaches of the canyon maintained a reddish hue. We seemed to ship water every time we bumped a rock, or slid through a wave and we got pretty well soaked and still had seen nothing I'd call a rapid yet. I forget who was rowing when we got to Four-Foot Rapid, but we went through sideways, backwards, you name it, and got really drenched; and this March water was *cold*! But we were young and popping beers and having a great time flailing our way down this rocky little creek and glad it wasn't a big river. We finally reached our overnight destination in the afternoon and unloaded boats and then went for a short hike to see up close and in person these "algal mounds" that Prof. Baars had sketched on the chalk board earlier in the week emphasizing their importance to containing oil.

I must say, we were all agog with being at the bottom of a thousand foot deep canyon with shear vertical walls towering above us. Evening came and after we ate whatever it was, we sat around the driftwood fire and Baars and Kenny told stories of their times on this river or other rivers. When it was time to go to bed, I dug a trench in the sand and spread out some hot coals from the fire and then buried them with sand and threw my bag on top. It was too hot and I had to add more sand, but I finally got it just about right and had a toasty sleep that night. The next day we got up and my friend John rowed the 7-man boat through Eight Foot Rapid – the biggest rapid we were to negotiate on this trip. Other than getting thoroughly soaked again we made it through just fine and I got to navigate a smaller rapid or two before we stopped and walked over to an old drill pipe sticking out of the ground. There were all sorts of rusted and weathered iron pipe, a big round wheel with cogs and lots of rotten iron cable lying about. Baars collected a bunch of two-inch diameter cylindrical pieces of cored rock that he said had been recovered by drilling this well in 1928. He said the well didn't find any oil, but had encountered a large amount of carbon dioxide gas while drilling a big limestone layer. The well was drilled deep enough to hit Precambrian granite or "the basement" as he called it. He also pointed out the road that had been constructed to get the drilling equipment to this remote location and said that the road-building was actually a bigger feat than the drilling of this well. The place was called Soda Basin and the well was located directly on the crest of the Raplee Anticline, even though the structure had been seriously breached by the down-cutting of the river. The thousand feet of layers of rock bent sharply downstream in a spectacular fashion that became more picturesque once we got underway again. When we returned to the boats, I turned over the oars to someone else for the next rapid that ran right alongside a limestone ledge that we barely missed hitting. That seemed to be the last of the rapids, but we had some more of these strange little sets of waves to float through. Now the layers of gray-green colored rocks bent sharply downward and quickly gave way to tilted red layers similar to what we saw as we had entered the canyon the day before. Soon we were in relatively open country again – a land of red rock in all directions you looked. The tilted red and gray rocks made a dazzling image of zig-zag patterns similar to that seen in a woven Navajo rug and we wondered if this sight is what gave them their idea. It was an easy float from here on out, with some occasional wave trains to float over and, of course, the obvious balanced rock promontory for which Mexican Hat got its name.

We finally landed at a small graded out spot near the *town*, if you want to call it that, of Mexican Hat in the afternoon. We helped load the boats back onto the trailer, shook hands with Mr. Ross and thanked him and then we got in our vans that had been driven to the takeout by some folks from Bluff. We didn't wait for Kenny Ross and the boats because we had to get back to Durango as classes resumed the next morning. All I remember about Mexican Hat was one small trading post and some baby-sized oil pump jacks alongside the road as we headed back to Bluff.

Of course, a few miles after leaving the boat ramp we passed the Mexican Hat Rock again, this time on a paved road. Then Prof. Baars detoured left and took us out on a road that dead-ended at an overlook of the Goosenecks of the San Juan River. Now we were standing on the rim of the canyon looking down over a thousand feet above the river that seemingly wound around like a large snake. It was truly a spectacular site and Prof. Baars said these "entrenched meanders" were quite unusual and were incised just about on top of the huge Monument Upwarp. We could see the monuments in Monument Valley to the south and behind us, Cedar Mesa towered above us another thousand feet or more. The drive back to Bluff was spectacular, and seeing Comb Ridge for the first time looking east you could see what a wall it created and how near impossible it was for early pioneers to cross; the roadcut through the Comb cemented this thought in my mind – this is some tough country to get around in. We arrived in Durango late that evening tired and dirty, but exhilarated by the experience.

We split up and went our own ways but my life had been changed forever!

∞ ∞ ∞

Now, fifty years later, I sit at my home computer typing this manuscript realizing what a major effect that trip had on me. I continued with my geology studies at Fort Lewis and after graduating with a degree in Geology, I continued on to Flagstaff for a Master's degree in Geology and then spent the rest of my life – right up to this moment continuing to study the "earth and planetary sciences" as it is now called and have focused most of my time on furthering my understanding of the geologic intricacies of the Colorado Plateau and specifically the greater Four Corners region – the core of the province. And I also continued beyond that first river trip to become reasonably proficient at reading the river, running rapids and enjoying the splendors of the numerous canyons of the Colorado River system by either rowing or motoring any number of different sized water craft, all of which have been of the inflatable type. I've worked as a professional river guide for over thirty years, and a river runner enthusiast for all these fifty years having made trips from Grand Canyon to the Snake, but most of my time was spent here, on the old San Juan River. I suppose I know this river and the surrounding geology as well as most other folks with these two interests. It's as though there was never a fork in the road for me – I was destined to do what I have done.

My grandmother was right, everything that has happened in my life now just seems like they were *supposed* to happen, including writing about the rivers and canyons of the central Colorado Plateau that were explored by Kenny Ross.

∞ ∞ ∞

Why the book? After Kenny passed away in 1990 I worked a number of San Juan River trips with Doug Ross and he mentioned bits and pieces about "the old man" and how he was probably the first outfitter to run commercial trips in inflatable rubber boats following World War II. I had heard Doug tell stories of seeing the *real* lower San Juan River canyons and rapids that were by then drowned by lake water and silt. He spoke of his early times as a youth and his brother, Don, seeing Rainbow Bridge and hiking to the top before it was restricted. I saw some of the 35 mm slides from those days in the 1950s and early 1960s and asked when he was going to write all this up. But we were all busy boating and the subject just sort of languished (we are all such great procrastinators). He told me there were tons more photos and files at his brother's house and I should see them and talk to Don. For various reasons now unknown we three never got together about documenting Kenny's remarkable life's story until winter 2014.

By then I had written or co-authored a number of technical geological articles for professional periodicals and guidebooks, but I had never tackled researching and writing a book about anything or anyone that was non-scientific. Besides, I finally had time since my commercial boating days were seemingly over and my interest in writing about the river and Kenny got me to thinking – why not? So, I decided to give it a try as by then there was still little to no mention of Kenny Ross by river historians and what a pioneer in commercial river running he had been. I contacted Don Ross and went to his home and out came the boxes. Don brought out boxes and boxes of photographs, slides, negatives and movie reels. He had boxes of notes, files of communication with scores of individuals. And he had boxes of mimeographed brochures, magazine articles and more. Quite honestly, I'm still not sure I've ever seen everything that Don had rat-holed at his place, but I had plenty to begin working on. Don and Doug talked it over and allowed me to bring all this material back to my home in Bluff and for the first year I just spent my time organizing all the information and scanning photos and files. And what I found was that there was so much more to Kenny Ross's life other than his river boating career. His life's endeavors and accomplishments ballooned into a number of occupational directions. The "old man" I met in 1969 was so much more than the owner of a little river company in Bluff. The more I dug into the boxes, the more interesting he became and now I really felt compelled to share his story.

During this time I also began researching the internet, libraries, museums, historical societies, etc and contacting individuals who were still alive who had known Kenny or his wife, Mildred. I also researched various sources for information about the San Juan River, Glen Canyon, Cataract Canyon and the greater Four Corners area that pertained to the geology, geography, ancient history of man up to modern man, political history of southwestern rivers, hydrology, sedimentation results from damming rivers, invasive riparian plants, and on and on and realized that I was now researching material for at least two books and maybe a third. I needed to stop accumulating all this information and make myself focus on one topic at a time – so the Kenny Story surfaced as the obvious one to write first. If I live long enough I'll get around to the geologic and geographic details I have uncovered about the San Juan River and vicinity although some of that information is included in this narrative.

A few comments about how the book is organized and written. It's pretty simple. The book is a fairly complete biography of Kenny Ross – from birth to death and the narrative follows his life's endeavors in chronological order with commentary added here and there for historical clarification. Kenny had so many notes and letters, a significant portion of the book is actually written by him; there are a lot of expanded quotes written by Kenny or those who were replying to him. Several expanded quotes are direct replies I received in e-mails which I felt pertinent and left in the respondents' own words. However, I have employed *silent correction* for minor misspelling or punctuation of original materials without comment when possible.

I suppose my narrative provides merely a guide to the reader, sprinkled with my own thoughts. Due to this format there are numerous endnotes and references which are numbered sequentially in superscripts that are then referenced in each chapter. And, because I'm a geologist and old boatman, I just couldn't stay away from mentioning such incredible geologic landforms exhibited throughout the region or using boating terminology, so APPENDICES have been added that includes:

1) APPENDIX I:

   Table 1 lists the length of the San Juan River from headwaters to confluence with Colorado River and from confluence downstream in Glen Canyon to Lees Ferry with key side canyons and geographic points of interest noted.

   Table 2 lists the length of Colorado River from Green River confluence to Lees Ferry with key side canyons and geographic points of interest noted.

Table 3 lists the length of Colorado River from the confluence with the Dolores River to the Green River confluence with key side canyons and geographic points of interest noted.

Table 4 lists the length of Green River from the town of Green River to Colorado River confluence with key side canyons and geographic points of interest noted.

2) APPENDIX II: Stratigraphic Column of Geologic Formation Names and ages

3) APPENDIX III: Geologic Time Scale of North America

4) APPENDIX IV: Glossary for those readers unfamiliar with both geologic and boating terms. Key words are written in **boldface** when first introduced to clue the reader to check the Glossary for definitions if unfamiliar with the words.

All measurements are *American* (i.e., inches, feet, miles, etc.) with occasional reference to metric system.

∞ ∞ ∞

So sit back and relax. Read about the canyons that Kenny hiked and explored, the rivers he grew to know so intimately, and the stories he shared with others. You might even be able to fill in some gaps about early explorations of the magical Four Corners country and Kenny's remarkable life that you hadn't ever thought about - until now.

~ 1 ~
BEGINNINGS: 1908 to 1933

"In hindsight, I never really was smart enough to pick Kenny's brain for those old memories and he didn't bring that stuff up much. Just as my children don't ask me much about some of the crazy stuff I've done and don't bring them up unless asked. They'll probably be just as frustrated trying to remember my lies, but with far less documentation." – Doug Ross

INTRODUCTION

The early life of Kenneth Irving Ross, or "Kenny" as he was called by most, was similar in many ways to my own father's. Both began their lives in the hardscrabble family farm country lifestyle in the river valleys of the Midwest. Kenny was born in 1908 near the banks of the Missouri River and my father was born in 1909 near the banks of the Mississippi River. Both were young men when the Great Depression hit in 1929 which caused significant changes to whatever their life choices were at the time. I know my father's story and only care to add that he was forced to do many things other than what he had hoped, just to stay alive, throughout much of the remainder of his life. He mentioned many times that he was too young to fight in World War I and too old for World War II. Plus, he was a farmer and by providing food during World War II to the American efforts then that helped too. In the case of Kenny, he was drafted after he had signed on at Mesa Verde National Park and Superintendent Jesse Nussbaum pulled some strings so that Kenny was only in the Army for three days before being deferred. Kenny also benefited from two of FDR's work programs that were initiated in the early part of the Depression, but were failing by 1940. Sad to say that it took a war between the United States and Japan and Germany in 1941 for a jobs program that ultimately pulled the country out of the abyss. Regardless of the many national programs of the Great Depression, following the end of World War II both men were left to fend for their own.

Kenny grew up under those harsh economic conditions and thankfully was a 'self-starter' who worked his way through farming, ranching and various odd jobs until he found a part of the country he wanted to live in and an occupation that rapidly translated into a profession. However, he had to alter his life's plans due to post-war circumstances and fortunately became an innovator in yet another profession where he could combine two occupational loves he had developed – educating those who shared his love of the greater Four Corners areas archaeological treasures and the unmatched geological wonders by providing a new means in which to experience it while taking passengers and traveling down rivers. In so doing, a new form of educational adventure trips was born.

Although he kept detailed records from 1934 throughout most of the remainder of his life, the first twenty-six years are poorly documented and mostly represented by one or two word comments on copies of job applications. Of course, he passed along some of his early experiences to his wife, Mildred, and his two boys, Don and Doug. Like many of us who had simple rural youth and adolescent periods in our lives and hard working parents who weren't famous, we are left with the handed down stories from our parents and if lucky, some photographs or letters. We never thought to really ask for details about certain periods of our parents lives as they grew up, or if we did, it was too late after they had passed away, taking all those memories with them to the great unknown. Such was the case for both Kenny and Mildred (Kenny died in 1990 and Mildred in 1993). Thankfully, Don and Doug were left with their own memories and stories plus a substantial amount of files, records, photographs and movie film to help fill in some gaps about a man, his wife and children and their experiences. Plus, I was fortunate enough to meet Kenny in 1969 and do a few river trips with him. In hindsight, I have followed many of his paths without realizing it until now. Yet, we are still left wanting more details.

When I began this project in 2015, one of Kenny's many protégés was still very much alive. Here was an 83 year old man, William R. "Bill" Dickinson, who at age sixteen entered Kenny's world in 1948. Bill was thrilled when he learned that I wanted to write about Kenny's life and achievements. He openly admitted that Kenny was his early life mentor as his parents had split in a nasty divorce in the summer of 1947, "and for a couple of years thereafter Kenny was a surrogate summer father of sorts to me, teaching me valuable life lessons from his playbook (keep your wits about you and use your own head, tackle anything but plan carefully)." [1] Bill continued,

> Will think about what stories I could tell about the olden days but hardly know where to begin or end. Will focus on tales that illuminate Kenny's style rather than my own life. I may be one of the few still kicking who watched him work his way from Mesa Verde and Ansel Hall through Explorers Camp to Wild Rivers. And not to forget the searches he made for mantle rocks in the Mule's Ear diatreme for the guys at Columbia Univ.
>
> You have a big job ahead of you, my friend! Ciao. WRD [2]

I was so hoping to be able to quiz Bill about Kenny, and he did provide me quite a bit of detail before his shockingly sudden death on July 21, 2015.[3] Kenny didn't have any formal college education in archaeology, geology or the natural sciences. But, he was truly a self-taught man who was fortunate to befriend a number of professional men and women who were at the top of their fields of knowledge when he met them. In the case of Bill Dickinson, "Big Bill," the boy became a world renowned geologist, inspired at a young age by Kenny. Conversely, Kenny absorbed a wealth of information he either read, or heard as he watched his mentors. He became a prolific communicator in his own rights. Via lectures, or as a field guide or the typewriter, he passed along his knowledge of the archaeology, geology, natural history and human experiences in the greater Four Corners region. None of his writings were ever formally published, per se. In fact, three separate fires at his field office in Bluff destroyed files and a huge collection of photographs. Yet, a plethora of carbon copies and mimeographed syllabi and a host of photos and both hand-written and typed originals and his replies, stored in his Mancos home survived and provide the core source for much of what follows.

THE EARLY YEARS 1908 – 1927

The Great Flood of 1927 provided the first record of eighteen year old Kenny Ross rowing a boat. He was part of search and rescue teams looking for survivors along the Mississippi River during the flood.[4] Kenny grew up in Kansas City, Missouri and had been working in a drug store the previous three years as a fountain clerk, where he surely saw the flooded confluence of the Missouri and Kansas Rivers and was keenly aware of regional flooding from newspaper and radio news accounts. Kenny often told a story of his first experience on a river was in 1927 when he volunteered to help rescue people and livestock from the flood. He said the Mississippi River was five miles wide and wider still in places. He and a partner were provided a boat and some oars and told to go rescue folks, but the first thing they found was a house cat on the roof of a submerged house! [5]

Thus, began Kenny's endeavors as a boatman navigating turbulent river water and the beginning of his remarkable career.[6]

MIDWEST ORIGIN

On August 20, 1908[7], Kenneth Irving Ross saw daylight and took his first breath of air in Auburn, Nebraska. Auburn was a small farm town located near the Little Nemaha River in the southeastern corner of Nebraska. His father, Charlie [Charley] Carpenter Ross and mother, Erma V. Gladys Morlan, were married as young teens. Nothing more was known about Charley and Erma as to how they met or how that corner of Nebraska played into the family history. Kenny never mentioned Auburn, Nebraska to either of his sons. Auburn, the county seat of Nemaha County, was established in 1882 and situated about ten miles due west of the Missouri River which also defined the eastern border of the State of Nebraska. Family lore about Kenny's father mentioned that he had some degree of Native American heritage, but that rumor has never been verified. The Iowa Sac and Fox Reservation was just thirty-five miles southeast of Auburn located at the confluence of several rivers including the Big Nemaha with the Missouri River, so there might be some validity to the Native American connection. Pictures of Kenny as a young man certainly suggest a possible Indian heritage.[8]

Figure 1.1 Charley Carpenter Ross, age 17 at front chair working in a Kansas City Barber Shop in 1911. (K. Ross collection)

For whatever reason, the Ross family moved to Kansas City, Missouri soon after Kenny was born. His two sisters, Gail and Wanda were born in Kansas City. Don has a family photo of Grandpa Charley at age seventeen working at the Charley Douglas Barber Shop in Kansas City (Figure 1.1). Kenny attended grammar school in Kansas City from September, 1913 to June, 1920 completing seventh grade. He attended North East High School in Kansas City from September, 1920 to June, 1924 and completed eleventh grade (Figure 1.2). From July, 1924 to March, 1928 he was employed at the R.P. Stauffer Pharmacy in Kansas City where he worked at the soda fountain and as a "drug clerk." It was during this period of employment that he took off some time to search for survivors of the Great Flood on the Mississippi River. By 1928 his father and mother, Charley and Erma were divorced.

Don and Doug both said that Charley moved west in the 1920s, which may have led to his divorcing Erma in 1928. It has long been conjectured in family lore that Charley's move may also have been prompted by the disability or death of his father who had a dryland ranch near Cahone, Colorado. Kenny's grandfather was born in the late 1860s or early 1870s, which placed him in his sixties when he passed away. Throughout the 1920s Charley had traveled back and forth from the Midwest to southwestern Colorado to help his father run the ranch and "cowboyed" for other ranchers and his father.

The Ross ranch was located on homesteaded land west of Cahone, Colorado, and consisted of a parcel of dryland covered in pinon, juniper and sagebrush that had been homesteaded under the Enlarged Homestead Act of 1909 (an amendment to the Homestead Act of 1856).[9] Charley's father built a small cabin and attempted to farm the uplands and also had some livestock. Journalist, Ian "Sandy" Thompson interviewed Kenny Ross in 1982 and wrote an unpublished biography of him. Kenny said he was five or six years old the first time he visited the Cahone ranch in the summer of 1914. Thompson stated that Kenny said the country was covered with stands of purple sage dotted with groves of pinon and juniper. Scattered across the mesas and around the heads of canyons were countless and probably undisturbed Ancient Puebloan Indian ruin mounds as well, all littered with exquisite pottery sherds and projectile points (Figure 1.3).

Figure 1.2 Kenny Ross, June, 1924 High School graduation. (K. Ross collection)

Thompson continued:

> That formative immersion in the actual environment of a departed civilization is what later diverted Ross upon the path of observer, guide and interpreter rather than that of specialist/researcher. The country was too intricate, too beloved, from that child's point of view for an older Ross in his later years ever to achieve total scientific detachment from it.[10]

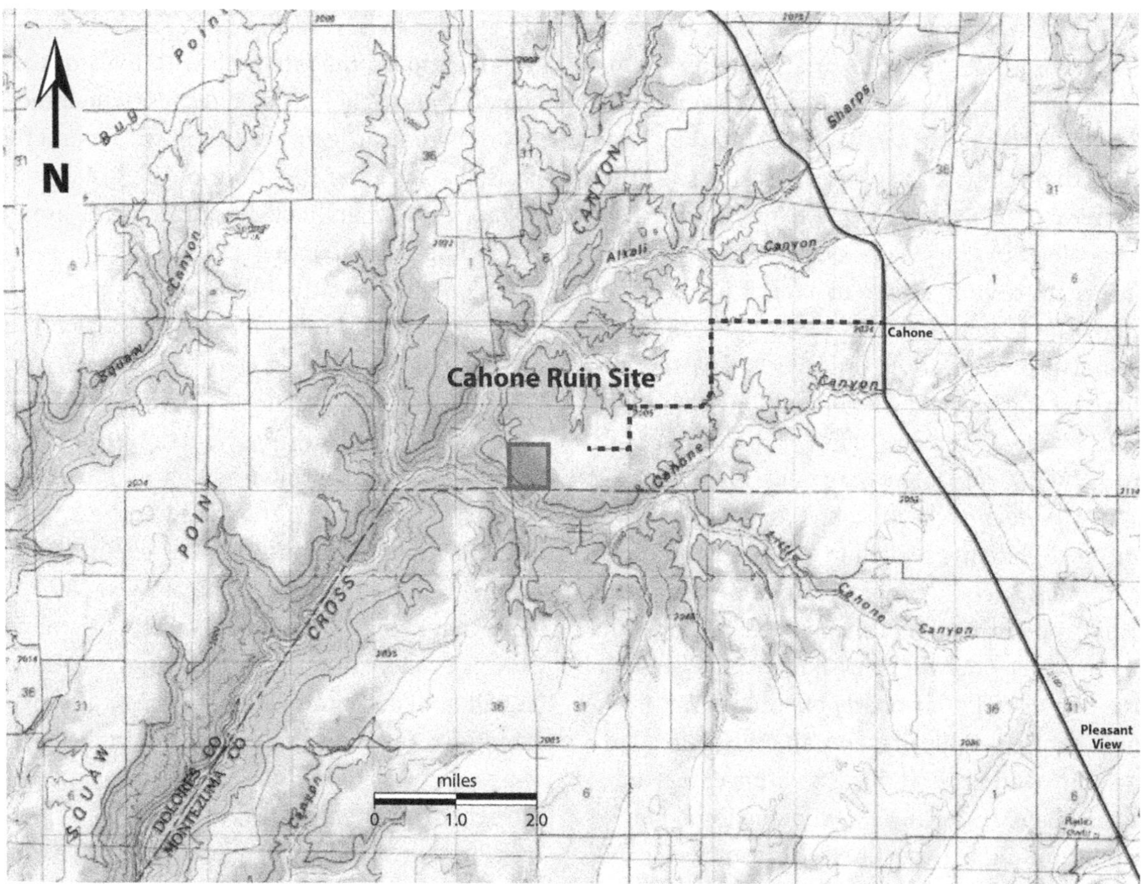

Figure 1.3 Map showing location of Ross family property that contained the Cahone ruins. (Modified from *Esri Arc/GIS* USGS topographic map)

ADVENTURER TO COWBOY 1928 - 1934

Following his Mississippi River rescuing adventure, Kenny moved to Lincoln, Nebraska, possibly to be close to his mother Erma who had returned to Nebraska following her divorce with Charley. From March, 1928 to December, 1930 Kenny was employed by Walter Scott at the Owl Pharmacy in Lincoln and was laid off due to "personnel reduction" [i.e., The Great Depression hit]. Kenny then moved to Palm Beach, Florida in December, 1930 and went to work as a studio assistant for a photographer - C.P. Dietsch and stayed until May, 1931 when he returned to Lincoln. During this brief period in Florida, Kenny no doubt developed his interest in photography and also learned some dark room techniques he would use the rest of his life. But Kenny also developed an adventurous side as well. According to Doug Ross:

> This would fit with Kenny's tale of traveling on a sailboat to Cuba with a couple of buddies and sailing back into a tropical storm and ending up off the coast of Nicaragua. Kenny joked to me one time that he and his pals ended up in the middle of yet another U.S intervention mess in Nicaragua after the storm and got captured by the Marines. I think the Marines hauled the punks out of the water and put them on a boat to Miami. There was a bunch of US Marine activity down there at that time.[11]

It has remained uncertain just when Kenny made it to the Yucatan Peninsula, but it may have been part of that Cuba trip, or after he returned to Lincoln for another dead-end job. Kenny mentioned a trip with archaeologist Earl Morris to Chichén Itzá, a classic large Mayan site in the northern Yucatan Peninsula.[12] Kenny's interest in archaeology in Florida and possibly Mexico was confirmed to some degree in a letter he received dated June 8, 1949 from Dr. Hendrik P. Zuidema, Geology professor at the University of Michigan where he stated that he would not be able to join the Explorers Camp due to "my appointment as party chief at some new Early Man diggings at the headwaters of the St. Johns River, in Florida..." [13] Kenny replied in a letter dated June 9, 1949 in which he congratulated Prof. Zuidema for his appointment and then added, "I know the area in which you will be working rather well, but have not visited it for nearly twenty years" [14] which confirmed his presence in Florida in 1930.

Kenny said his first "brush with a career in archaeology" began in 1931 when he joined an expedition to the Arctic Circle to do an archaeological reconnaissance of the Yukon River. The team led by Bayne Beauchamp flew to White Horse where they built their own boats for the journey down the river. Kenny further stated "My memories of that trip are a haze of mosquitoes; our do-it-yourself scows leaked the whole time. We found a few sites but nothing of real significance. That was left for others, later." [15]

Following his Cuba-Marine rescue experience, and possible disconnect with the photographer in Palm Beach, Kenny returned to Lincoln, Nebraska in May 1931 to be near his mother and tried his hand at being self-employed as a soda fountain concessionaire and manager. By July 1932 he again got the itch to do something more adventuresome and sold his fledgling business and moved west to Cahone, Colorado to help his father, Charley, on the family ranch. That was definitely not his first time out west to Four Corners Country. Although Kenny had visited the ranch as early as 1914 with his father the move in 1932 was the first record of Kenny actually having moved there to help with livestock feeding and general ranch duties, which included working on cattle drives in the spring and fall. It was also a sign of the times of the Great Depression where jobs evaporated and simply surviving became more relevant.

Most importantly to this story – an unexcavated Anasazi Puebloan site was present on the Ross ranch near the point where two canyons merged – Cahone Canyon and Cross Canyon (see Fig. 1.3). Kenny mentioned that he showed up several times as he was growing up and cited working on the ranch in the 1930s when he had to fill out his work experience while applying for a permanent job at Mesa Verde National Park. He no doubt walked all around the ancient Native American ruins on the Cahone ranch land and probably did some exploring along the canyon rims thereby seeing that there was a significant amount of artifacts and wall structures that were perfect for future exploration. He first referred to the site as the "Cahone Ruins" and later came up with a more exotic name "Cibola City Ruins" possibly being inspired in his reading about the early Spanish explorers and incorporating the mystical 'city of gold' name into his personal lexicon. Kenny certainly knew of the unexcavated site and kept it under his hat until 1946 when Ansel Hall was looking for "educational" activities for the boys in the newly formed Explorers Camp. Even though the land had been sold to a local rancher by 1946, Kenny brought Cibola City Ruins to the attention of Ansel Hall, who then contacted the current owner of the property.

The year – "1932" was when Kenny first mentioned going out to Cahone, Colorado to work on the ranch for an extended period of time, run cattle to Disappointment Valley, etc and mentioned doing that cow-punchin' work again in 1934. Bill Dickinson related:

It is intriguing that his dad owned a ranch near Cahone (perhaps began his interest in archaeology, as there are ruins on every mesa top around there). The one thing I can contribute about his pre-RBMV, pre-MV years is that I heard him speak a time or two about cowboying in the Disappointment Creek country. Presume now that such was on behalf of his dad and/or other cattlemen of the Dove Creek-Cortez axis who may well have driven stock to Disappointment Creek for summer range (but no knowledge of what trail they might have taken to drive stock through the intervening rough country). Modern Hiway CO 141 from near Dove Creek north to cross the Dolores at or near Slick Rock (an easy crossing), thence up some easy gulches to Disappointment Valley seems the obvious answer (before the days of modern cattle trucks, a trail drive like that would have been a piece of cake, one that even I could manage myself with a little help from friends!). If he did spend a decade or so largely tending stock, RBMV & MV may well have offered an attractive out from that dead-end lifestyle (geology was my own pathway out of raising horses).[16]

Bill Dickinson also explained in the same email:

When I was involved in Explorer's Camp, Kenny always engaged a wrangler named Dave Sanchez to pack the crew into the north side of the La Plata's for a week or so (son Cliff Sanchez more my age was along to help, and may still be alive and kicking). If there is any way you can run down Cliff (I have no idea how), he might know more through his father about Kenny's cowboy days (always had the feeling Dave and Kenny had known each other for quite some time). Ciao. WRD [17]

KENNY'S COWBOY DAYS

Enter David Lavender, (born February 4, 1910; died April 26, 2003) who was a contemporary of Kenny's and shared a similar youthful history of being reluctant cowboys. Their friendship most likely began between David and Kenny when they were cowboying at the same time, during the period from 1931 to 1934. At that time Kenny and Charley drove cows up past Marie Ogden's Home of Truth and Al Scorup's Dugout Ranch into Indian Creek and Salt Creek and into Disappointment Valley. Those experiences set Kenny up with knowledge that he used later when conducting Explorers Camp trips into the Dark Canyon Plateau and Beef Basin Country. Kenny Ross and his father herded cattle from Cahone to Disappointment Valley and into high pastures on the southwest side of the Abajo Mountains. Kenny most likely hooked up with Scorup riders where he learned about Beef Basin to Dry Basin and the upper reaches of Dark Canyon and Woodenshoe Canyon as well as Elk Ridge to Mexican Hat. He may have even met Buck Lee. He would have certainly heard of him and/or seen some of his leather work.[18]

In later years, Kenny spoke of David Lavender often.[19] Several Wild Rivers crew remembered David going on river trips around 1988 to 1991 and entertained guests and crew with his many stories. Tamara Desrosiers, a Wild Rivers guide, recalled a trip she did with David Lavender in 1989:

I distinctly remember the one David Lavender trip in 1989. It was my first summer at WRx, and I was daily king (queen). Everyone wanted to be on the trip because we had all just read One Man's West. It was not sponsored by an organization. Charlie [DeLorme] advertised the trip on his own, but nobody signed up for it. Instead, a family who had no idea who David Lavender was got booked on it. They had teenaged sons and no interest really whatsoever. There were other people on the trip, but nobody I can remember except for Doris Valle. It was a real pleasure to get to hang out with her and get to know her a bit.

Since Rebecca and I were of lowest rank, we each got to do only half of the trip, which was an upper AND lower canyon trip. Rebecca got to do the lower canyon, as I had to return to do dailies. Lavender was charming. He had a much younger wife who commented to the guides about all our drinking and smoking, saying that she was surprised, given our outdoor, healthy lifestyle, haha. We camped at the mouth of Lime Creek, a hot, dreadful place, and that was the night I remember David finally getting to tell stories in the evening.

I was on the shuttle to pick them up at Clay Hills, and David sat in the front seat of the van on the way home. When I pointed out that we could see Lone Cone, he was absolutely thrilled, and thanked me profusely for pointing it out. That view tied in the geography of where we were and his history and was a nice finale to what was probably a somewhat tedious trip, given the group mostly had no idea of who he was. That's my 2 cents. Tamara.[20]

Tom Rice wrote: "I did one trip with David Lavender and almost knocked him out of my boat when I nicked a rock. I was listening to him tell a story and imagining the places he wrote about and didn't see it coming! He held on." [21]

David Lavender was born and raised on a cattle ranch twenty miles north of Telluride and worked in hard rock mines (Camp Bird Mine near Ouray, Colorado) and as a cowboy in his early years. He was not an academic, but differed from Kenny in that he went on to study law and liberal arts at Princeton University. After graduating in 1931 he briefly attended Stanford Law School before Depression Era economics forced his return to western Colorado to help his stepfather run his cattle ranch. After his stepfather died in 1934, he continued living on the ranch until it was repossessed by the bank in 1935. Based on Kenny's employment records, the most probable period that Kenny and David ran into each other on horseback punching cows was from 1932 to 1934.

David was an American West historian and writer on the same level of succinct accuracy as his contemporary writers, Bernard DeVoto and Wallace Stegner. Much of his writing was influenced by his first-hand practical knowledge and the historical realities and locations depicted in his books—in the mines, on the trails, in the mountains, and on the rivers. Lavender was a two-time nominee for the Pulitzer Prize and perhaps his most famous book, *One Man's West*, was published in 1943 where he wanted to record a way of life he had experienced and felt that it was slowly fading away.[22]

Lavender mentioned that most of the riders were scarcely old enough to vote; and that would certainly fit Kenny as a young adolescent during summers when he was still in school and as a twenty-five year old young man in 1934 looking for any kind of work during the worst of the Depression years. Although there was no definitive documentation that David and Kenny herded cows together, several observations made by them regarding some of the areas more colorful characters along the trail indicated that they both knew these trails intimately. Any rancher herding cattle to high ground pastures out of Dry Valley (that by the 1930s had been completely overgrazed) passed through Photograph Gap by Marie Ogden's Home of Truth and Al Scorup's Dugout Ranch at Indian Creek on their way to the Woodenshoe area and possibly down to the San Juan River passing by the Lee brother's ranch or all the way down White Canyon to the Colorado River near Hite. In the 1930s these few spots were the only sign of humanity in thousands of square miles.[23]

Thus, it appeared that Kenny spent some time in the saddle herding cows anywhere from 1920, when he was twelve years old, up to and including 1934 (age twenty-five) when he finally nailed down a job with the CCC in southwest Colorado and pursued his interest in archaeology and natural science. Kenny didn't particularly take to the cowboy life, but during this period, he was introduced to the back country of south-eastern Utah and it was through this exposure that allowed him to propose and lead the first truly exploratory expeditions for the Explorers Camp from 1946 to 1951. He may not have been a cowboy in either Lavender's bunch, or Scorup's, but the cowboy fraternity was small and he knew who to hire as packers for the 1946 Dark Canyon trek and where to rendezvous. Kenny also knew who to contact to be Head Wrangler to lead the greenhorn boys that rode horses and managed the pack horses in the mountains for Ansel Hall's Explorers Camp.

THE PARKING ATTENDANT

At best, Kenny was a 'seasonal hire' as a reluctant cowboy and when the cowboy experience had worn thin in 1933 he made a trip to California to visit his mother and picked up a job, briefly. His mother had moved from Lincoln to Los Angeles, California and in March 1933 Kenny found work at *Jack Hazard Auto* in Los Angeles as an auto parking attendant at some hot-shot Hollywood business. Doug Ross recalled that Kenny told a story about delivering some sort of package to Marlene Dietrich and some other movie stars, but his funniest story was a tale that Kenny shared when he was parking cars and also doing delivery services for some of the Hollywood bunch:

> He told a funny story one time about dashing around in a car park, moving vehicles around like crazy, in/out, and ran over and jumped into some guy's car to take it quick-like-a-bunny to the back of the lot next to a big office building. Problem was that the guy had been working on the car and had detached the front seat, then just set it back in the car to drive it downtown. Anyway Kenny said he jumped in the car, floored it, had the seat tip over with him and then hit the side of the building, flat on his back with his feet in the air. Hit the building with a horrendous thump...and emptied the building of people because everyone inside thought it was another LA earthquake.[24]

Needless to say, his California visit and short career in parking cars for celebrities came to a crashing end, and Kenny worked his way back to Cahone later that summer of 1933 looking for something to do other than punch cows. Kenny and his friend, Dallas Fullerton, met in a café in Cortez and Kenny bemoaned the lack of work as they sat drinking coffee to which Dallas replied to check out the CCC at Mesa Verde. Unbeknownst to Kenny, the Civilian Conservation Corp (CCC) public works project was signed into law by President Franklin D. Roosevelt on March 31, 1933. So he went to Mesa Verde to apply for work and ran into another friend, Meredith Guillet who later became a co-worker in constructing several dioramas for the park museum (more about that in Chapter Three). However, he wasn't hired immediately by the CCC. It wasn't until October, 1934 that Kenny landed a job at Mesa Verde National Park, but he filed his work experience at the CCC office in Dolores, Colorado and became what was called an "LEM" or a "Local Experienced Man," and of good character as opposed to a regional vagabond.[25]

Aerial view of Merrick & East Mitten Butte (Thorn Mayes, 1933 photo #549; K. Ross collection)

2
THE RAINBOW BRIDGE-MONUMENT VALLEY EXPEDITIONS: 1933 to 1938

BACKGROUND: END OF THE FRONTIER

On May 17, 1884, President Chester A. Arthur signed two executive orders that made all of the land in southeastern Utah between the San Juan River and the Arizona territory boundary, as well as lands south of that border part of the Navajo reservation. But the "land of death" as it was called by many Anglos, that lay north of the expanded reservation included what today encompasses San Juan County, Utah. Anglos also referred to the triangular tract of land as "the Dark Corner." [1]

The Eleventh United States Census was taken beginning June 2, 1890, where the data was tabulated by machine for the first time.[2] The 1890 census announced that the frontier region of the United States no longer existed and that the Census Bureau would no longer track the westward migration of the U.S. population. Up to and including the 1880 census, the country had been considered an unsettled western frontier. By 1890, isolated bodies of settlement had broken into the unsettled area to the extent that there was hardly a frontier line. Unfortunately, most of the 1890 census materials were destroyed in a 1921 fire, but this didn't slow historian Frederick Jackson Turner in developing his "Frontier Thesis" in 1893.[3]

Frederick Jackson Turner (November 14, 1861 – March 14, 1932) was an American historian in the early 20th century, based at the University of Wisconsin until 1910, and then at Harvard. He trained many PhDs who came to occupy prominent places in the history profession. He promoted interdisciplinary and quantitative methods, often with a focus on the Midwest. He is best known for his essay "The Significance of the Frontier in American History," [4] whose ideas formed the Frontier Thesis. He argued that the western frontier shaped American democracy and the American character from the colonial era until 1890. He was also known for his theories of geographical sectionalism. Ever since Turner's "thesis" historians and academics have argued strenuously over his work; all agree that the Frontier Thesis has had an enormous impact on historical scholarship and the American mind.

In 1880, Colorado had been a state for only four years, and Utah, Arizona and New Mexico were all territories each with its own problems. Most local folks called the Four Corners region the "Dark Corner." Army doctor Bernard J. Byrne, stationed at Fort Lewis, Colorado [Hesperus] said,

> A man makes his own laws there. There ain't no pertection 'cept what a man makes himself....Down in the Dark Corner, if a man kills another man he just steps over to Utah. If he steals a horse in Arizona he slides across to New Mexico.[5]

Suffice to say that the Four Corners region was sparsely settled by non-Native American communities and Native American Reservation boundaries were in flux; the exquisitely preserved cliff dwellings at Mesa Verde had only been recorded as having been *officially* discovered in 1888 and the first Anglos of record had visited Rainbow Bridge in 1909. Herbert Gregory was the first college-educated geologist to traverse and publish some of his findings in several papers from 1911 to 1916. And most important to the Rainbow Bridge–Monument Valley Expeditions of 1933 to 1938, Charles Leopold Bernheimer reached Rainbow Bridge in 1920 after visiting cliff dwellings at Betatakin and Keet Seel and published articles in nationally distributed magazines from 1920 to 1923 [6] (Figure 2.1).

Navajos and Paiutes were thrown together by oppressive movements by the U.S. Army chasing Navajos westward into Paiute country. To the Indians, the entire area from the Little Colorado River, a hundred miles north to the San Juan River, was considered Paiute land and the Navajo people were the wrong tribe with whom to be making treaties. Navajo and Paiute had a century's long understanding regarding food gathering throughout the area and farmed the few places with adequate water. The main concentration of Paiute communities was on the mesas around Navajo Mountain and in the canyons on each side of the San Juan River. These communities remained unknown to Europeans until gold prospectors arrived in the 1880s. However, for most of this time, Navajo people were not in the area as they respected or honored Paiute boundaries.[7]

Jacob Hamblin in 1860 had problems with Navajos and one of the Mormon settlers was killed and hostilities lasted another nine years when Hamblin and John Wesley Powell negotiated a peace treaty with the Navajo on the east side of the Colorado River and Mormons were granted safe passage along the course of the Little Colorado River southward into central Arizona.

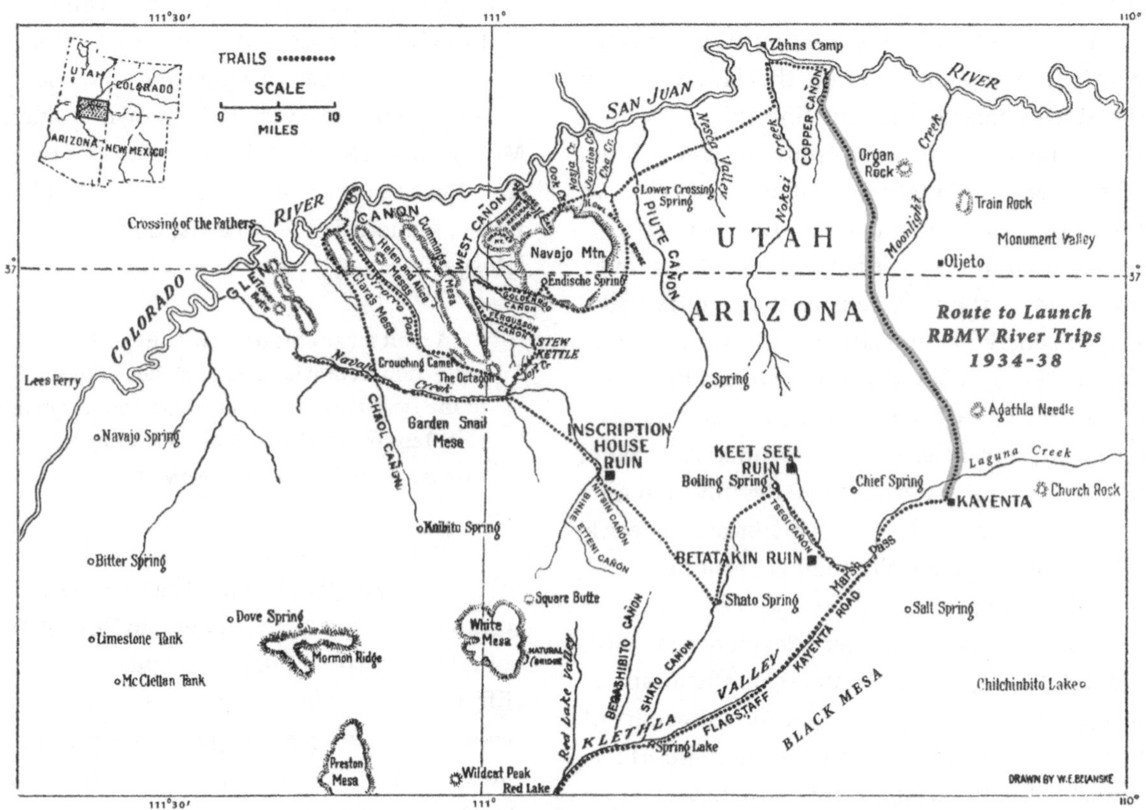

Figure 2.1 Map of Charles Bernheimer's routes to Rainbow Bridge and around Navajo Mountain, 1921; highlighted trail from Kayenta to Copper Canyon was main route for San Juan River launches 1934–38. (Place names and spellings from original map from Bernheimer, 1924; original map has been modified)

The Bureau of Indian Affairs (BIA) was instructed by Laura Work, superintendent of the Paiute Indian boarding school in Panguitch, Utah, to investigate the conditions of the Kaibab and San Juan Bands in 1905 and recommended that reservations be set up. Two reservations were established west of Fredonia, Arizona, for the Kaibab Paiute, and the "Paiute Strip" in southeastern Utah, for the San Juan Paiute. The latter included all the land south of the San Juan River to the Utah/Arizona border and east to about the 110th Meridian. It included Navajo Mountain and the as yet "undiscovered" Rainbow Bridge. Excluded were several valid mining claims along the river and a couple of patented (private) properties.

The Paiute never received a federal agency of their own. Instead, like the Navajo and Hopi, they were placed under the jurisdiction of the Western Navajo Agency in Tuba City. No land near Tuba city was designated for the use of the Paiute that still lived there.[8]

In 1921, Leroy A. Wilson of the Paradise Oil and Refining Company requested permits from the BIA to drill for oil along the San Juan River. He was told that the only way he could get a permit would be if the land was returned to the public domain. What followed is typical of what often happened to Indian land claims across the west:

> The BIA was at the time under the jurisdiction of the Secretary of Interior Albert Fall. Fall was later sentenced to prison for his unethical practices in what became known as the Teapot Dome scandal, in which he pursued a policy of opening public lands to wholesale exploitation by oil and mineral companies by providing them with unauthorized and improperly awarded leases. Under Secretary Fall's instructions, the BIA officials reported falsely that the San Juan Paiute were not using their reservation. In July 1922, the Paiute Strip was returned to the public domain.[9]

The Federal government was pressured to immediately add the Paiute Strip to the Navajo Reservation by BIA officials, members of the newly formed Navajo Tribal Council, and individual Navajos from south of the strip. They stated the "Indians" had used the land from time immemorial and that it should be returned to reservation status. They did not say that it was Paiute land, but in 1933 the Paiute Strip was again made part of the Navajo Reservation.

The small San Juan communities remained isolated from mainstream American society. Until the 1960's, few San Juan Paiute people had any formal education. Government programs to teach English and non-Indian social practices did not reach the Paiute. Nevertheless, the Paiute had been in close contact with their Navajo and Hopi neighbors; however neither group had attempted to alter the San Juan Paiute's traditional ways.[10]

Several other reconnaissance-type geologic surveys had been taken and the Colorado and San Juan Rivers had been surveyed for possible dam sites, but by 1933 little was still known about that part of the United States, now simply referred to as "San Juan Country" by the survey groups. And to complicate land ownership, the United States government had seriously considered making some of this entire expanse of canyon country into a national park and simply ignored the fact that indigenous people called this land their own homeland.

THE RAINBOW BRIDGE-MONUMENT VALLEY EXPEDITIONS: 1933 to 1938

A series of Rainbow Bridge – Monument Valley (RBMV) Expeditions were carried out between 1933 and 1938 during the depths of the Great Depression. The most famous one is possibly the initial 1933 expedition where a photographic collection was compiled by several photographers documenting the following sites and their inhabitants: Bat Woman Pueblo, Betatakin, Black Mesa, Bryce Canyon, Dunn's

Trading Post, Garden of Gods, Glen Canyon, Keet Seel, Kit Seel Canyon, Kayenta, Lily Canyon, Long Canyon, Marsh Pass, Monument Valley, Navajo Mountain, Poncho House, Rainbow Bridge, Red House, Red Lake, Sagi (Tsegi) Canyon, Skeleton Mesa, San Juan River, Twin Caves Ruin, Water Grand Canyon, Zion, etc. It also included images of members of the expedition and Navajo people.[11]

The goal of the expeditions was to research this little-known area of northern Arizona and southern Utah which was commonly referred to as "Navajo Country" or "San Juan Country" so that the National Park Service could determine whether to establish a national park in the region from southeast Utah to Northern Arizona.[12] The person chosen to organize and lead this expedition was the National Park Service's Chief Forester and Senior Naturalist, Ansel Hall.

ANSEL FRANKLIN HALL

Ansel Hall (May 6, 1894 – March 28, 1962) was born in Oakland, California.[13] His father was a clerk in a shop in San Francisco that sold crockery and his mother was a homemaker; Ansel was eleven years old when much of San Francisco burned to the ground as a result of the 1906 earthquake. During high school he worked for concessionaires in Yosemite and learned back country skills. He graduated with honors from the University of California in 1917 with a degree in Forestry one year after the National Park Service became a new Federal bureau. His first government job was as a ranger at Sequoia National Park. World War I was ongoing and he enlisted in the U.S. Army and served as a Second Lieutenant with the U.S. Expeditionary Forces in France.

Upon returning in 1919 to ranger duties at Yosemite National Park, he spearheaded development of the interpretation of Park sites and was eventually named the park's first official park naturalist, serving from 1920-1923. He helped raise private funds to build the Yosemite Museum of Natural History and it was during this stint at Yosemite when he met and became friends with the famous photographer - Ansel Adams. He met June Alexander in 1924 when he was thirty years old and they were married in France. She was from a family of means that may have been a source of "private" funds in his later endeavors. The couple raised six children.

Hall organized the Educational Division of the Park Service in 1925. He was promoted to Chief Forester and Senior Naturalist in 1930. He was one of the early active members and presidents of the American Association of Museums.

According to a National Park Service newsletter, Ansel Hall probably contributed more than any other individual to the formation and early growth of the interpretive work of the National Park Service (NPS).[14]

Ansel Hall was reportedly an enthusiastic visionary with exceptional management skills and always on the go. He made plans and was able to implement them rapidly when resources became available. Ansel's son, Roger Hall, stated that in his opinion, his father's superlative skill was in compiling the resources (people, funding, places, and opportunities) to complete a project.

For instance, the idea of the Rainbow Bridge-Monument Valley Expedition was the result, as Roger Hall recalled, of a meeting of Ansel Hall with John Wetherill at the Wetherill Trading Post in Kayenta, Arizona around October of 1932.[15] After they had seen the Navajo National Monument (of which Mr. Wetherill was custodian and guide), Mr. Wetherill pointed out to Mr. Hall the need for an expedition into Monument Valley.

Wetherill was already recognized as the legendary pioneer and cowboy archaeological explorer. Ansel Hall had also previously stated that Monument Valley and the adjacent region of colorful and spectacular desert and canyon country be set aside as a national park. However, inaccessibility, remoteness, and the lack of definite information regarding the topographic, scenic and archaeological features of the region made it nearly impossible for the Federal government to reach a knowledgeable decision as to which parts of this vast bare-rock, canyon wilderness actually merited national park status.[16]

Hall apparently had given little consideration that several Native American tribes called this country their homeland who didn't particularly want further white man interference.

Nevertheless, with complete disregard for the Native Americans who inhabited the land, and from his office on the University of California Campus in Berkeley he began to organize the privately funded Rainbow Bridge-Monument Valley Expeditions of 1933-1938 to explore, research, and record data about this fascinating region of the Southwest.

He proposed that a scientific exploration of the area was necessary and proceeded to draw together a leadership team of four groups of academics from the east and west coasts elite universities to provide detailing for topographic mapping, geology, geography, ethnology, archaeology, botany and zoology for this little known area of the central Colorado Plateau; some 6,000 mi² of southern Utah and northern Arizona that included Monument Valley, Navajo Mountain, Tsegi Canyon, Black Mesa, Glen Canyon and the Kaiparowits Plateau.

JOHN WETHERILL

Hall mentioned earlier explorers such as William H. Jackson, Jesse Walter Fewkes, Byron Cummings, Herbert E. Gregory, Alfred Vincent Kidder, Samuel J. Guernsey, Charles A. Bernheimer, Earl Morris, Hugh Miser, Harold S. Gladwin, and others had already done scientific field work in various parts of the region and that John Wetherill had established a proven route into Rainbow Bridge on the north side of Navajo Mountain.[17] The Wetherill family had a major involvement in the expeditions as they were primarily traders and wanted to promote tourism in the region. Secondarily, they were interested in promoting scientific research in the area with special interest in the archaeological investigations of the numerous cliff dwelling sites they had discovered. Rainbow Bridge was officially "discovered" by non-Native Americans in 1909.

John Wetherill's wife, Louisa, heard of the huge arch from a Navajo man. She told what she learned to archaeologist Byron Cummings of the University of Utah. Meanwhile, William B. Douglass (from the U.S. General Land Office) had also learned of the natural bridge from a Ute guide by the name of Jim Mike. Cummings & Douglass joined forces with John Wetherill as guide and they first saw the bridge on August 14, 1909. According to Harvey Leake, Arthur R. Townsend and his sister Eleanor were the first tourists to visit Rainbow Bridge in September 1909.[18] In 1908 Townsend had visited Mesa Verde, Hovenweep, and Natural Bridges. Douglass reported the discovery to President William Howard Taft who created Rainbow Bridge National Monument on May 30, 1910.

> The 1909 Rainbow Bridge discovery expedition went from Oljato down Copper Canyon to the mouth, across the mouth of Nokai Canyon, and up onto Piute Mesa on what one Navajo man called the Hacked Out Trail. From there he headed to the Lower Crossing of Piute Canyon and on to Navajo Mountain. John occasionally used that route after that, but more commonly took his clients through Tsegi Canyon and on to the Upper Crossing of Piute Canyon. The Zahn brothers took the first vehicle down Copper Canyon to their mining claim in 1915. There is an Arizona Highways article on that. There is a story that the RBMV party had great difficulty getting their vehicles down there, and it was due to the skill of Ben Wetherill that they succeeded.[19]

John Wetherill was appointed the Government Custodian of the new monument for $1.00/month and was guide to other "prominent and literate visitors" including geologist Joseph Pogue (1911), former President Theodore Roosevelt (1913), novelist Zane Grey (1915), Douglass (1916), Cummings (1910), and Yale geologist Dr. Herbert E. Gregory (1916, 1917). John Wetherill shared his incredible knowledge of the area and helped in providing personnel (Navajos mostly) as well as pack animals and even served as cook on the first of the several river trips down the San Juan River.[20] He also served as associate field director for several seasons. His son, Benjamin, contributed to the archaeological portion of the expeditions and his nephew, Milton, helped as a packer for several summers.

HOT ROD ARCHAEOLOGISTS

It was the height of the Great Depression and privately-sourced money was scarce. Ansel persisted and was successful in securing funds to last through 1938. Originally intending to take only ten experienced men from UC-Berkeley for a preliminary exploration of the area in 1933, the project mushroomed into an almost unmanageable number of seventy-five men from major universities around the country.

A caravan left from each coast, one from The Explorers Club in New York City, the other from UC-Berkeley. They converged on a predetermined date in the remote settlement of Kayenta, Arizona. The expedition archive consists of maps, photographs and negatives, 16 mm movie film, site cards, original field notes and diaries, catalog ledgers, ceramic tabulation strips, cassette tapes, published and unpublished reports on the progress of ethnographic, archaeological, and botanical research, funding and organizational documentation, analyses, and correspondence.[21] The collection also includes primary materials relating to the 1983 exhibition "*Honoring the Dead: Anasazi Ceramics from the Rainbow Bridge-Monument Valley Expedition,*" at the Museum of Cultural History in Flagstaff, Arizona.[22]

The quantity of supplies, food and equipment for up to seventy-five men in the field per summer was daunting, but Ansel was well-connected and found a substantial amount of the expeditions needs without cost. For example, the *Henry Ford Motor Company* agreed to provide twelve brand new trucks and station wagons[23] (Figure 2.2). Besides, it was a great way to promote the Ford brand of automobiles. In return for their use, Ford featured the expedition in its company magazine and in 1936 sent a cinematographer and writer to make a promotional film about the RBMV expeditions showing the Ford vehicles operating in the rugged desert terrain.

Art Nelson was a young volunteer college student from Moscow, Idaho who participated in the 1936 expeditions and kept a journal of his experiences that season. He transcribed entries from his field notebook "verbatim" in a letter to Andy Christenson dated January 24, 1986. His recollection of auto and truck maintenance was particularly noteworthy:

> I had a lot of experience in auto and truck repair, having been a student foreman in the auto mechanic shop of the high school which I attended, and having driven model T fords in the woods during summers. As a result I found myself involved in a lot of truck maintenance problems on the expedition. The so-called "roads" that we travelled were roads in name only. The road across Monument valley was just 2 tracks in the sand, as were most of the roads on the reservation. These alternated with crossings of bare rock, some of which were very rough, and accounted for most of the damages to springs and shock absorbers. The twisting and wrenching which the vehicles went through broke some gas lines. Patches of loose sand caused difficult driving conditions. If you knew the road you could hit them hard and sort of bulldoze through, but if you didn't, and were afraid of the rocks, you often bogged down and had to shovel out. I learned the hard way to carry a shovel at all times after having to shovel out with my hands. The New Ford V8 Ton and a-half trucks had dual rear

wheels. On at least one occasion we had to take off the outer pair of tires because the truck couldn't pull both through the sand. Sand got everywhere in the motors and great care had to be taken in adding and changing oil. Sand was also very hard on the brakes and caused quick wear and necessitated frequent adjustment.

The country was also hard on shoes and boots and some members had only shreds of shoes and boots left at the end of the season. This was particularly true on the second river trip.[24]

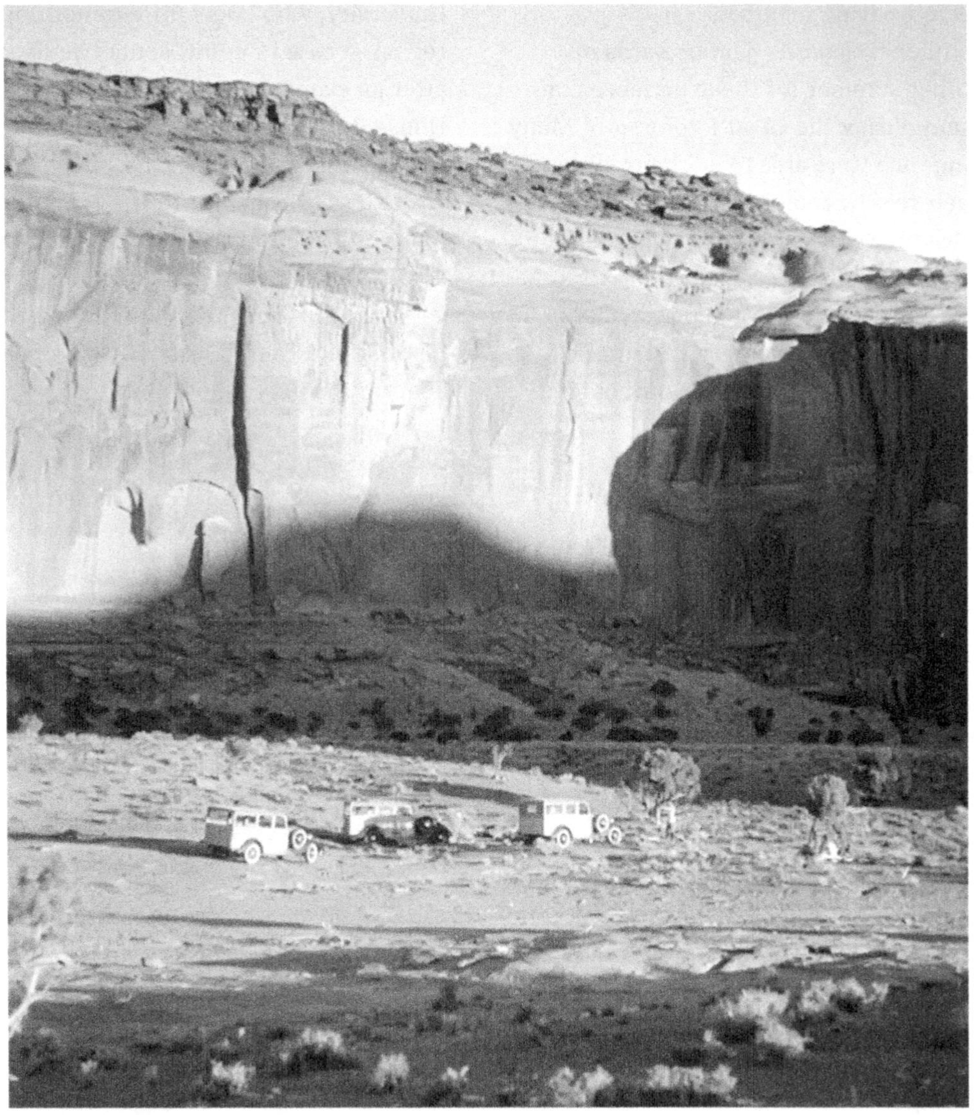

Figure 2.2 The Ford Motor Co. donated 1932 Model 18 Station Wagons to the 1933 RBMV expeditions seen here in Monument Valley. Each cost about $800 & seated eight. Vehicles were powered by newly designed flathead V-8 with a 221-cu inch, 65 HP engine. (K. Ross Collection)

Support staff came from at least thirty various colleges and universities, as well as several museums and high schools from across the U.S. Young males between the ages of sixteen and forty-five (like Kenny Ross and Norman Nevills) were recruited although undergraduate college students made up the bulk of the crew members. Posters, flyers, published announcements, and recommendations from existing members were used to recruit paying members.

Most student *volunteers* paid upwards of $300-400/per summer for the experience....a princely sum during the Great Depression! Many other young men were able to work for all, or part, of their fees by cooking, working with pack animals, driving vehicles [rowing boats as Kenny Ross did], or writing stories about their experiences for their hometown newspapers. Of course, several local Navajos served as pack animal 'cowboys' and as guides to unrecorded archaeological sites as well as some paleontological finds.[25]

From the inception of the project, Hall selected an advisory board[26] of prominent scholars including Harold S. Colton, founder and director of the Museum of Northern Arizona; Herbert E. Gregory, a U.S. Geological Survey geologist and director of the Bishop Museum who had explored some of the Navajo Country and published several Professional Papers based on his reconnaissance investigations several decades earlier; A.L. Kroeber, a distinguished UC-Berkeley anthropologist; and Jesse L. Nusbaum director of the Laboratory of Anthropology in Santa Fe, New Mexico. Hall also invited a mixture of university professors who recruited promising, young scientists to participate, along with men established in their fields to direct day-to-day field operations.

Hall also had other goals that aligned with his close association with the *Boy Scouts of America* where, in addition to the serious scientific objectives, the expedition was to provide young men with an opportunity to experience the outdoors and to learn from nature.

Since Hall was unable to spend much time in the field (an excuse frequently repeated in future years' endeavors), he delegated the day-to-day operations of the project to the hands of others – and mistakes were made. The field director for the first several seasons was Charles D.N. Winning, a professor of Humanities at New York University, who knew little to nothing about the region. A case in point: some twenty-two years after an event occurred circa 1933 at Poncho House Ruin (the largest known ruin in the State of Utah) river historian Otis "Dock" Marston wrote Jesse Nusbaum wanting to know some more information regarding "two claimed discovery items" he had questions about. The verbatim typescript of a hand-written reply to his first question to Jesse Nusbaum dated February 7, 1955 follows:

> Dear Dock:
>
> Ref your letter of Feb. 2 concerning this need of more data on the two claimed discovery items.
>
> 1: Poncho House Ruin by Ansel Halls Monument Valley-Rainbow Bridge Expeditions.
>
> When Ansel's' Hot Rod Expeditions party of youths departed from their field camp base at Kayenta, the leader for the larger group that left by Monument Valley, and thence on to Grand Junction before heading east – to NY where the leader lived & left the travel equipment – visited Poncho House enroute, & were so ill informed, or uncontrolled, that on arrival at Grand Junction, Colo they reported ~~to~~ probably to Robert Walkers' *Grand Junction Sentinel* that they had discovered the largest cliff dwelling ever known, telling all about it to the press representatives, including its generalized location. Whether they talked to *Sentinel* representatives or to Assoc. Press representatives, they identified themselves as members of this expedition, stated their interest in and exploration for archaeological sites in the least known section of the Navajo Reservation – and this story went out nationwide

thru the AP. Wire service under a Grand Junct. date line.

The other section of the expedition left for the West Coast via Flagstaff - & they also gave enuf info out to start an AP. wire release from Flagstaff on the same date as I recall – but this one did not mention *[end page 1; Missing 1st line at top of page 2]* ....did.

I was then Director of the Laboratory of Anthro at Santa Fe, & noted both releases, and was so distressed by the news in the Grand Jct. AP release about their finding of a cliff ruin far larger than Cliff Palace in Mesa Verde – world's largest – that I prepared a letter at once to A.V. Kidder, Chairman of L. of Anthro ___ - and a letter to C. Dr. Colton of Mus. of No. Ariz. telling them their "Hot Rods" Explorers of Ansels had prob. without question visited Poncho House and not knowing the history of W.H. Jackson's visit in 1875 as I recall when he photographed it and described it, - both firsts as I recall – they claimed it as an original discovery. Also I believe I prepared a related press release – citing Jackson's visit and photography & description of the site – I think you will find these pictures & his description in Kidder & Guernsey's Peabody Mus. of Harvard report on their Archeo. Explorations in N.E. Arizona about 1915-16.

Guernsey excavated there for a short while & reports on this research therein, I give these data at once – off the cuff – as it may be weeks or longer before I can locate the related clippings or copies of letters etc.

Anyway Colton reported that he was so upset by the AP Grand Jct. release that he at once sent **Lynn Hargreave** [sic] of his archeo. staff by car with a gallon of paint and a brush, to Poncho House, to paint its name *[end page 2]* so that no one would ever claim to have discovered Poncho House again. I flew over it with Norm Nevills shortly before his tragic death, but it was blowing and dusty & I was not sure that the painted name was still visible then. Ansel alibied out of blame saying "those kids shouldn't have gone there in the first place, etc." [27]

Notwithstanding the kerfuffle at Poncho House, where a well-known archaeological ruin had first been documented by W.H. Jackson in 1875 and later excavated and named by Kidder & Guernsey in 1915, it remains unknown as to just how much "unsupervised" pot hunting "archaeology" was done elsewhere by over-eager student volunteers and clueless professors during the RBMV days. Florence Lister correctly summarized the unsupervised archaeologist in her book "Prehistory in Peril" (1997):

> The years between the two world wars represented the adolescence of Southwestern archaeology. As in human pubescence, the era was characterized by exuberance, turmoil, and lack of self-discipline. Collecting frenzy, casual or no documentation, personality clashes, and a headlong rush to unfounded conclusions were its growing pains.
>
> It was in the early period of Southwestern archaeology that a few men with means but no formal, applicable training embarked on prehistorical research and subsidized publication of their personal ideas. These were also the glory days of pot-hunting, when others without academic credentials – but with strong backs, a sense of curiosity, and sometimes the prospect of turning a profit – tackled ancient ruins with shovels and trowels all across the ....Colorado Plateau.
>
> Because professional archaeologists actively working in the Southwest were still relatively few, both the dilettante-patron and the amateur digger often proved valuable allies in unraveling the past.
>
> It was not just cowboys, traders, and adventure seekers who continued digging in out-of-the-way places to add to private holdings; some federal employees and scientists of varied backgrounds did their share of vacuuming up artifacts. Moreover, respected institutions of learning bought collections without verification of sources or subsidized diggers to unearth specimens that often later were stowed away in museum vaults, never to be seen by the public or analyzed by students. All had voracious appetites for tatters of the past. It was as if a young, drifting society such as embraced the West instinctively needed roots, even those that were neither genetically nor culturally relevant.[28]

LYNDON L. HARGRAVE

However, Lyndon Hargrave, the first field director of the RBMV expeditions and Curator of Archaeology of the Museum of Northern Arizona, did put into practice the new ideas of surface collection as a survey tool, establishing a ceramic sequence, and the concept of open-site excavation.[29] His systematic excavations and meticulous recording of sites and natural resources were important new components to this expedition. Scientific research was on-going in the areas of archaeology, zoology, geology, botany, biology, and the new sciences of dendrochronology, ethnography, and ethnobotany.

Field work was conducted from small auxiliary camps; some based in very isolated areas accessible only by pack train and supplied from the base camp located first in Kayenta at John Wetherill's Trading Post and later at the head of Marsh Pass (see Figures 2.3 & 2.4).

Mapping was a strong focus throughout the six seasons and since only some small-scale government maps had been made, engineers were given the task of creating detailed topographic maps of the greater area, of the major sites, and of major geological features, including Rainbow Bridge itself.

Hall wanted results published for all on-going work. He established an RBMV newsletter where preliminary reports appeared, but lacked circulation to the general public.

Groups were assigned to pre-defined areas of the site and each day explorations were conducted by a group of volunteers, led by an experienced archaeologist. Each man carried a number of blank "site cards" which were completed when evidence of pot sherds, lithic chips from making projectile points, masonry remains, or charcoal concentrations were discovered. Photographs were taken and the site was sketched. At the end of each day's work the cards and pot sherd and projectile points collected were taken back to the camp and the cards were typed in duplicate. The RBMV archives include these site cards, as well as the photographs and sketches.

Many participants later pursued careers that were inspired by their work with RBMV or at the very least they returned repeatedly to the area. The film footage, photographs, and memoirs are a tribute to the well-rounded experience, both professionally and personally, for the approximately 300 men who passed through the expedition. Photographers, pilots, artists of note, well-known archaeologists and scientists traveled to the southwest to work with the expedition as word spread of the work being done in this remote scenic wonderland.

Existing photographs and memoirs of participants indicate that the local Navajo became an integral part of the daily routine and success of the expedition. In addition to acting as guides, they were camp cooks, provided meat and other basic food items to the isolated auxiliary camps, and were packers. Photographs also show Navajo men and their families with the RBMV participants in leisure time playing games, trading, and relaxing with the young men on the expedition. Several participants embarked on some of the first ethnographic studies, including one study, which yielded around five hundred photographs of Navajo daily life.

The archaeological crew headed up by Lyndon L. Hargrave from the Museum of Northern Arizona from 1933-34 attained the greatest success particularly in defining pottery types. His principal assistants were Ben Wetherill, Alonzo W. Pond, H. Clayborne Lockett, John E. Rinaldo, Edward T. Hall, Jr., Watson Smith, George Brainerd, Ralph Beals, Charles Amsden, John W. Bennett, Scotty McNeish, John T. Hack and Omer Stewart. Years later, in 1945, Ralph Beals, George Brainerd, and Watson Smith published the only monograph from these efforts that focused entirely on the archaeological work. In addition, some valuable information pertaining to sediments containing pollen types were tied to the Anasazi culture by Ernst Anteus of the Carnegie Institute and John T. Hack of Harvard University. But possibly, the most important work was done by Angus Woodbury (University of Utah) and Henry N. Russell (Harvard) who published a monograph "Birds of the Navajo Country." [30]

THORN L. MAYES

Although archaeological work was of primary concern, field work in topographic mapping was complimented by aerial reconnaissance photography. The fieldwork in topographic mapping was carried on under the direction of Thorn L. Mayes, engineer, of Oakland, California. Mayes had already spent several summer vacations in the Monument Valley country mapping with a Brunton pocket transit and odometer and was considered by Hall to be well qualified for this particular assignment of directing the engineering fieldwork of the Expedition. One of his field assistants, Norman Nevills of Goodridge, Utah, had worked with Thorn Mayes during his previous reconnaissance mapping in 1930–32.[31]

Figure 2.3 aerial view W-NW of Kayenta Trading Post & Wetherill ranch (tree-lined property across road near curve in road); Warren Trading Post (large building across road); buildings right of Warren Trading Post near wash are the Presbyterian Church and parsonage. Small building across road & slightly left of Warren's was the school for non-Indians; "that building still stands" (H. Leake). (1933 Thorn Mayes aerial photo #626; K. Ross collection)

Aerial reconnaissance was considered necessary for three reasons: 1) to aid in orientation of engineering parties, 2) to enable other leaders for mapping their specific sciences, and 3) to provide photos for reference and for accuracy to complete detailed maps.

F. Linden Naylor of Berkeley, California was chosen as pilot. Flying his own aircraft, a Stearman biplane, powered by a Wright 250-horsepower motor, from California, he was accompanied by Robert A. Kissack, cinematographer, and also a pilot. During the aerial reconnaissance in the Monument Valley-Navajo Mountain regions Messrs. Thorn L. Mayes and Robert A. Kissack served as observers and photographers but observers changed, including John Wetherill several times. A heavy reliance was placed on the geological work by H.E. Gregory, 1916.

Since there were no landing fields closer than Winslow, Arizona, approximately 175 miles to the south, it was necessary to construct one to serve as the air base for the Expedition. All members of the engineering and geological field parties worked for several days leveling and dragging a moderately small field at the abandoned oil camp at Goodridge, some two miles from Mexican Hat. When the plane arrived (flown by Naylor) this was found to be an unfavorable location due to uncertain air currents set up by the adjacent canyon of the San Juan. An emergency landing was therefore made on a flat near Kayenta.[32]

The final air landing strip was constructed about three-quarters of a mile southeast of Kayenta and was named "Naylor Field" in honor of the pilot.

Figure 2.4 aerial view to southwest with Laguna Creek flowing to left (northeast) from Tsegi & Marsh Pass; steep-dipping flat-irons along Organ Rock Monocline; Klethla Valley and Shonto Plateau in distance; Kayenta out of view. (1933 Thorn Mayes aerial photo #622; K. Ross collection)

Ansel Hall outdid himself in convincing the U.S. Army Corps to loan the expedition a state-of-the-art mapping camera. The camera was a "Type K-10 mapping camera" or more precisely a 5"x 7" *Fairchild Aerial Camera* with a Zeiss-Tessar Lens (F4.5; focal length 12"). The film was *Eastman Superspeed Panchromatic*. Exposures varied greatly and it was not possible to keep a photographic record on account of lack of time between exposures. An aero 2 filter was used in approximately one-half the exposures. Before making an exposure the plane's engine was cut back (RPM reduced) and the plane was put into a glide to reduce vibration. [33]

By August, 1937 flights were from a Stinson five passenger cabin monoplane equipped with 320 HP Wright engine with a cruising speed of 140 MPH.[34] Flight #1: Pilot – Andrews; Observer – Winning; Photographer – Beckwith; August 8, 1937. Flights #2 through #6 flown up to August 13, 1937 had the same pilot and photographer.[35] Flying Altitudes ranged from 7,000 to 10,000 ft and averaged 8,000 ft. Therefore, with average ground elevations of 5,000 to 6,000 ft, then most aerial photos were less than 3,000 ft above ground elevation.

Accomplishments from the aerial photographic efforts included general orientation for field party leaders. Approximately twenty-five oblique aerial photos at two-mile intervals were taken along the entire length of Comb Ridge as well as approximately 175 oblique photos of Monument Valley to Navajo Mountain region were made (Figure 2.5). About twenty-five aerial photos of the entrenched meanders of the San Juan from Lime Ridge anticline to Goosenecks were taken as well as some 3,000 ft of motion pictures taken of the region.[36]

Figure 2.5 aerial view looking north at Navajo Mountain (Naatsis'áán: "Earth Head" or "Pollen Mountain"); highest elevation 10,348 ft. (1933 Thorn Mayes aerial photo #610; K. Ross collection)

RESULTS

The RBMV expeditions of 1933-1938 were somewhat pretentiously self-promoted to be the largest self-supporting, multi-disciplinary expeditions ever conducted in North America. But the "field seasons" were actually quite short in duration and always during the late summer months – the worst time of year to try and get things done in a timely manner in the hot arid southwest desert country. Plus, much of the time was spent just getting to Kayenta, or once there, to get to the areas of interests. Roads consisted of sandy ruts or tracks over bare rock with little to no signage and not conducive to automobile travel. Regardless of these logistical problems, RBMV achieved much of its primary goal of recording the natural and cultural resources of the area, and produced over forty technical publications, even though most were nothing more than mimeographed field notes and poorly circulated to academia or the general public.[37]

Although Ansel Hall was strongly interested in using the outdoors for education, he proved to be more of an office idea man and schmoozer for money and let good people like Lyn Hargrave, Watson Smith, Angus Woodbury, and Ralph Beals run the day-to-day operations. Many of the "experts" who came out for a week or two were just looking for a holiday.[38]

Collectively, the effort from the RBMV expeditions was nothing more than a first stab in documenting the cultural history of the Glen Canyon region. Far more comprehensive work was done in the 1950s and 1960s when the Colorado River Storage Project (CRSP) passed Congress in 1956 that gave a green light for the Bureau of Reclamation to begin the construction of Glen Canyon Dam. Contracts between the National Park Service, the Museum of Northern Arizona and the University of Utah led to salvage studies of the archaeology, biology, geology, paleontology, recent and ancient history of the whole area that began to be inundated by Powell reservoir in 1963.[39]

However, the larger national park never did come to fruition as the Navajo Tribe nixed that idea in July 1934. Only the Navajo National Monument remained, established in 1909, to preserve the large and well-known sites of Betatakin, Keet Seel, and Inscription House plus the Rainbow Bridge National Monument established in 1910 (Figure 2.6). The National Park Service realized that Indian reservation boundaries and treaties would have to be scrapped if they proceeded and there just wasn't enough desire by the National Park Service to create another problem with Native Americans.

Most of the archaeological collections were archived at the Museum of Man in San Diego, UCLA Fowler Museum, and the Museum of Northern Arizona. These collections have been used to increase the knowledge of the Ancient Puebloans in the region.

The collection of aerial photographs don't appear to be archived in any single repository, as some are at the Huntington Museum, while others are at the Center for Southwest Studies at Fort Lewis College in Durango, Colorado, and a surprising number of aerial prints and negatives were part of the Kenny Ross private collection. The entire collection of several hundred aerial photographs only had reference numbers and maybe one- or two-word captions.

CHARLES LEOPOLD BERNHEIMER

Of those who came before Ansel Hall, perhaps Charles L. Bernheimer (July 18, 1864 – July 1, 1944) is most noteworthy, even though he openly admitted to being "the tenderfoot from Manhattan."[40] He became a multi-millionaire by working his way up from office boy in 1881 in his family's dry goods business to eventually reaching the top, serving as company president from 1907 to 1928, after which he served as chairman of the board. His first trips visiting the southwest U.S. from 1915-1918 were self-financed tourist trips into the little-known territory of the Four Corners region (accessed from Albuquerque, Santa Fe, Gallup or Flagstaff).

His first horse pack trip was in 1919 from Blanding to White Canyon led by Zeke Johnson. By 1920 Wetherill led him on a trip to pueblo sites at Tsegi Canyon ruins, detouring along the way to visit cliff dwellings of Betatakin and Keet Seel, a climb to the top of Navajo Mountain and his first visit to Rainbow Bridge – *Nonnezoshe*, on May 22, 1920 when he was fifty-five years old. It took five and a half days by horseback and pack-train to reach the sandstone arch and he was first to write an article in *Natural History Magazine* (1920) and *National Geographic Magazine* (1923) and his own book, *Rainbow Bridge* (1924).[41] Bernheimer was utterly unqualified to lead a cultural, educational, scientific mapping or geological "expedition." However, he did help add to archaeological knowledge in that he hired, at his own expense, Earl Morris, from the American Museum of Natural History who participated in five of Bernheimer's expeditions. It was through Morris's archaeological expertise that a number of significant sites were identified and important artifacts collected.

Figure 2.6 Rainbow Bridge (*Nonnezoshe*) 1947; Explorers Camp members hiked from Rainbow Bridge lodge (twenty-six mile round trip); the two teenage boys on top provide scale. (K. Ross collection)

Bernheimer's subsequent expeditions were basically glorified "sight-seeing trips" (John Wetherill's words) in 1921 and 1922 in search of a new route to Rainbow Bridge from the south and west side of Navajo Mountain. In his book he accounts for the 1921 expedition that started and ended in Kayenta; seventeen days in attempting to make a loop around Navajo Mountain by first heading west-northwest thence east to Rainbow Bridge, but not being able to continue eastward then forced to backtrack and go around the south side of Navajo Mountain and then continuing east to Copper Canyon and returning southward to Kayenta.[42] This one map proved indispensable to the RBMV leaders accessing routes to Rainbow Bridge and particularly for those needing to know the shortest and best route to access the San Juan River downstream of Paiute Farms to launch boats (see Figure 2.1; highlighted route from Kayenta to Copper Canyon).

Over the next several years, Bernheimer's book and magazine articles inspired a number of Rainbow Bridge authors. Bernheimer visited the southwest and Four Corners region for a month at a time each year from 1915 to 1930, but the Great Depression reduced his wealth considerably. An interesting and somewhat surprising entry of his name by Beals, et al (1945) as a member of the 1936 RBMV expedition would have placed him at age seventy-two and his role in that inter-disciplinary project remains unknown.

He undoubtedly provided back country information but his vast fortune had slipped away such that he would have been an unlikely underwriter of this expedition in any significant way. It remains curious as to why he was mentioned, but Beals and Hall were name-droppers and Bernheimer had certainly put the area on the map through his populous publications.

Bernheimer, however, was not the firstcomer non-Native American to Rainbow Bridge and the many tributary canyons.[43] Calvin Jackson led twenty-two prospectors along the San Juan River in 1869, reaching the area from the east via Ft. Defiance and Ft. Wingate.[44] Then, in the 1890s; during the *Bluff gold excitement* some 1200 prospectors rushed the region in search of gold.[45]

KENNY ROSS AND RBMV RIVER TRIPS

In Kenny's records of his job applications he only mentioned what he considered *real* work, like his stint in California parking cars, or working at a pharmacy until he finally signed on with the CCC at Mesa Verde in October, 1934. He apparently didn't think that working a few weeks here or there rowing boats down the San Juan River or ranching and chasing cows was worthy in applying for his dream of gaining *full-time* employment at Mesa Verde. Thus, there are no specific details as to how, exactly, Kenny came to realize his "fork-in-the-road" life-changing experience. However it was certainly a matter of record that a big scientific expedition was in the making for exploring "Navajo Country." [46] Posters and flyers were nailed up in Post Offices and Court Houses in the remote Four Corners towns and villages, and announcements were published in local newspapers looking for young men to be recruited as field assistants for a project called the "Rainbow Bridge-Monument Valley Expeditions" (RBMV).[47]

In all likelihood, Kenny saw one of these notices in a Post Office or on a telephone pole and applied for work. There is no definitive documentation as to exactly when, where or how Kenny met Ansel Hall, the director of the RBMV expeditions. But, he kept applying for CCC employment at Mesa Verde between the years 1933 and 1934 at the prodding of his friends Dallas Fullerton and Meredith Guillet. Because of that process he had already been declared a "Local Experienced Man" (LEM) and finally was hired later by Mesa Verde National Park as a temporary worker in October, 1934.

Having been so in touch and involved with the National Park Service, Ansel Hall very likely contacted the Mesa Verde National Park Superintendent, Jesse Nusbaum and/or Paul Franke, for any young men of good character for field support. He possibly contacted the local CCC administrators looking for a few good young men who would have already been vetted through the CCC job application process ("LEMs") and showed some interest in scientific field work.

Although his name wasn't listed in the first official RBMV report by Ansel Hall (1934), Andy Christenson, a researcher from Arizona who has been accumulating materials on the RBMV expeditions over the past thirty years discovered documentation that the following members were on the first RBMV 1933 San Juan River trip: "Robert Kissack was leader; John Wetherill was his assistant; Norm Nevills, *Ken Ross*, Boynton Kaiser, and John Edgemond were on the trip" [48] [Emphasis mine]. In a letter from Lloyd W. Lowrey to Andy Christensen dated December 8, 1988 Lowrey explained that he had signed on as a geologist:

> The last night of the expedition's season, Bob Kissack asked me to go on the exploratory first river trip as official photographer. I accepted and didn't leave for California the next morning as planned. Hosteen John Wetherill and his son Ben went with our group as honored guests. Hosteen John was not our designated cook as your paper states. We all participated in food preparation and K.P. [49]

Kenny recounted over the years to all that would listen that he wound up working as a crew member on the first river boat trip down the San Juan River in late summer of 1933. It was there that he met Norman Nevills who was also hired as a crew member. He mentioned that John Wetherill helped with the cooking on this trip as well (Figure 2.7). He said he was certainly a rookie and had a lot to learn and made a lot of mistakes, but stepping into one of the foldboats just seemed natural too. He said he soon learned how to *read* the river current and waves and to not try and memorize, but rather let the river tell him what it was doing.[50]

In the first report by Ansel Hall in 1934 (General Report Rainbow Bridge-Monument Valley Expedition of 1933, p.11) he says: "A third means of transportation was tried out experimentally during the last month of the 1933 field season." [51] The Western Group engaged in exploration in the Monument Valley-Navajo Mountain region from June 12 to August 1; the Eastern Group arrived in Kayenta on July 3 and were individually assigned to duty with the scientific field parties that had arrived earlier from the West; members of the Eastern Group continued field work until August 2. Lowrey's letter to Christenson noted above stated that the river trip didn't occur until *after* the field season was over; so the river segment had to launch after August 2, 1933. Hall continued:

> Desert exploration by boat sounds anomalous but was found to be quite practicable in its limited field. The passage through the canyons of the San Juan River and through the Glen Canyon of the Colorado was made by means of a fleet of seven small boats for the purpose of reporting on the advisability of conducting more intensive investigations in archaeology, geology, and the other fields of science in the future *[See Figures 2.8 and 2.9]*. The preliminary report indicates that further work in these canyons and their tributaries promises to yield important scientific results.[52]

Kenny certainly knew where the San Juan River was based on his travels from Mancos to southern California in the spring of 1933 and his cowboy contacts, "After all, he was faced with a dead-end job ranching out of Cahone on his dad's ranch and he wasn't cut out to be a cowboy as his interests certainly were mostly directed toward archaeology." [53] Besides, Kenny was a self-starter type and I can only imagine him confidently raising his hand when asked if he had any river boating experience *[Most river guides that*

I know have admitted that when we all started boating, we may have stretched the truth a little just to get a chance to go boating]. So – one way or another, Kenny made his way to Mexican Hat in late summer of 1933 and ended up working his first trip alongside Norman Nevills who was a listed participant. The initial RBMV-sponsored river trip in the Wilson fold flat boats launched from Mexican Hat and got off the river at Lees Ferry – a distance of approximately 193 river miles (Figure 2.10; Appendix I, Table 1).

Figure 2.7 John Wetherill preparing food at river camp on the lower San Juan River, RBMV first river trip, 1933; Wingate Sandstone in background. (Photo taken by Lloyd W. Lowrey; Ross collection)

Figure 2.8 Foldboats on the 1933 RBMV river trip, boats and crew at top of Thirteen Foot Rapid; lower San Juan River. (Photo taken by Lloyd W. Lowrey; K. Ross collection)

THE 1934 RBMV SAN JUAN RIVER TRIPS

As for the 1934 San Juan River trips, it appears there has been conflicting information regarding when the river trips actually occurred. Ralph Beals mentioned that *no* river trips were run in 1934 due to low water. That was certainly the case for late June through early July where the river gage at Mexican Hat indicated virtually zero measurable water[54] (Figure 2.11). However, Beals wasn't even present for the expeditions until 1935 and was never directly involved in any of the river trips, so his source of information may have been wrong.[55] In checking the river gage history for the gage near Bluff (at Mexican Hat) the water year 1934 was truly a super low water year with several weeks with basically no water in the river; yet flash floods were also recorded in late July of up to 1,000 cfs and averaged 400–500 cfs for most of August and peaked in late August at nearly 5,000 cfs, so it's possible that the typical late summer monsoons flashed enough water to be able to launch some trips (Figure 2.11).

A.L. Christenson (1987) mentioned a total of *eleven* river trips were run, but following the 1933 maiden voyage he later adjusted the number to only *three* trips in total based on the following lines of reasoning: [56]

1934 – No record of any river trips;

1935 – John Rinaldo wrote a brief report on the archaeological reconnaissance, but nothing about river trips; but

1936 – at least two river trips were run from Copper Canyon to Lees Ferry; on the second trip, Bayne Beauchamp was chief, Lloyd Lowrey was navigator; Torrey Lyons, Art Nelson, and Fred Coe were on that trip. Christenson has the journals written by Coe and Nelson and fifteen photos taken by Lyons on the second trip of 1936.[57]

Figure 2.9 Foldboats on the 1933 RBMV river trip at bottom of Thirteen Foot Rapid, lower San Juan River. The rapid was the biggest and most difficult rapid to run on the river; formed at mouth of Cha Canyon as debris flow with some rather large boulders. (Photo taken by Lloyd W. Lowrey; K. Ross collection)

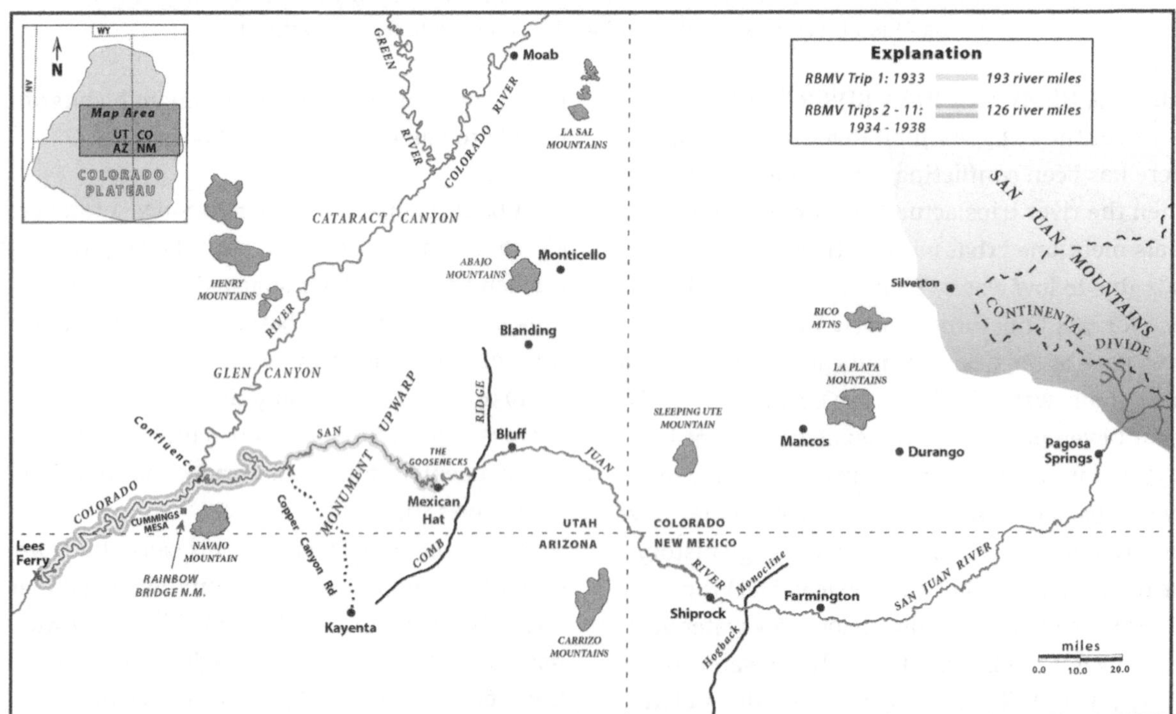

Figure 2.10 Map of the Colorado, Green and San Juan rivers in central Colorado Plateau. The San Juan River from Mexican Hat to the confluence with the Colorado River and lower Glen Canyon to Lees Ferry segments are highlighted for initial river runs in 1933 and subsequent trips from 1934 to 1938. (GMS/TB original map).

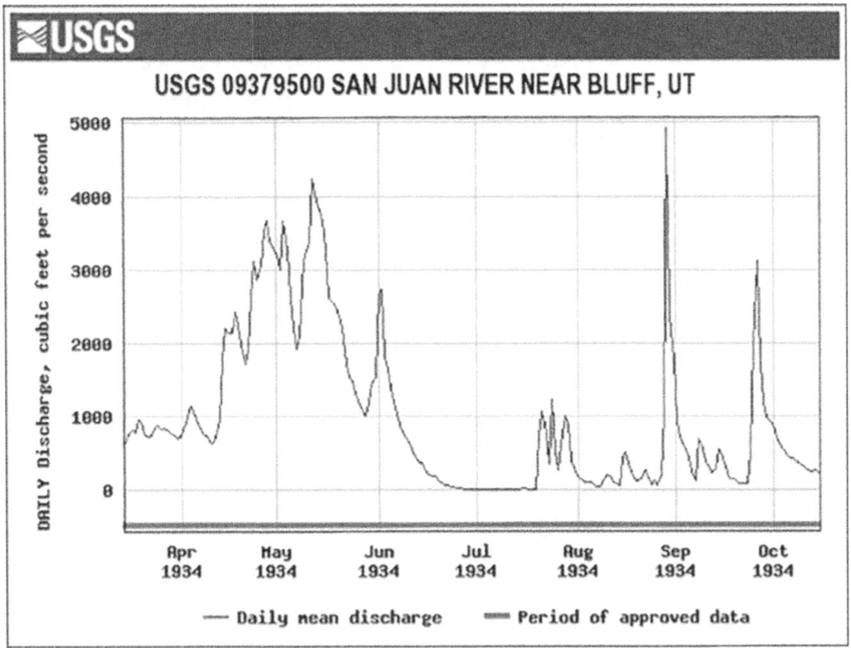

Figure 2.11 Graph shows gaged flow on San Juan River from mid-March to mid-October, 1934. Gage located at Mexican Hat but referred to as "gage near Bluff" which is the last gage above confluence 113.3 river miles downstream; see river miles in Appendix I: Table 1. (USGS Water Data)

In addition; Beauchamp issued two news reports during the 1936 trip that Ansel Hall mimeographed and distributed to the RBMV mailing list and probably the press.

Nevills did not mention going on any 1934 RBMV trips, but Kenny Ross did! In fact, Kenny mentioned having done three (3) river trips for RBMV in fold-flat boats in two years. "Many boat parties have descended the San Juan. During the early 1930s the Rainbow Bridge-Monument Valley Expeditions (forerunner of Explorers Camp) made three descents in boats for scientific investigations." [58] Kenny accurately described the narrow road cut the vehicles traversed down Copper Canyon and how they dragged boats and equipment a long distance down to the river across dry sand bars. They had to push and pull the fold-flat boats across ankle-deep water and sand bars on the two trips launched from Copper Canyon in 1934. Unfortunately, all of the RBMV expedition's river notes and photos (if they ever existed) were lost. However, the difficulties in getting trucks down through Copper Canyon are documented by Torrey Lyons photos in 1936 (Figure 2.12). So there's basically no solid documentation (other than Kenny's word) of how many trips were launched in 1934 and who the participants were. Andy Christenson said, "Grace Hoover was on the expedition in June, July and early August of 1934. She doesn't mention any boat or river trips in her journal. I have the reminiscences of another 1934 member who mentions no river trip. I will keep an eye open for any mention of such a thing." [59] But in Lloyd Lowrey's letter to Andy Christensen he further stated that "In 1934 and all subsequent trips down the San Juan and Glen Canyon I was director except in 1935 when I was in Alaska." [60] So, it appears there were river trips in 1934, even if not supported by Grace Hoover's journal.

If Kenny actually participated in two separate river trips from Copper Canyon in summer of 1934 as he claimed, then he went the distance to Lees Ferry and either **ran the rapids** or **lined** or **portaged** the three big rapids through the lower canyon (Piute, Syncline and Thirteen Foot; see Figure 2.13) before reaching the confluence with the Colorado River and then floated the placid Glen Canyon *two more times before Norman Nevills did*. The group would have more than likely stopped at Forbidding Canyon and hiked the four and a half miles to see Rainbow Bridge. Norm's next trip past Copper Canyon was March, 1936 when he took Ernest "Husky" Hunt and two colleagues from Stanford University on a cost-sharing *(non-commercial)* trip to see Rainbow Bridge.[61]

Figure 2.12 Photographers document vehicle descending roadcut in Copper Canyon in 1936 to launch another RBMV river trip. Front end grille suggests that the station wagon was a 1936 vintage Ford. (Torrey Lyons photos courtesy of A. Christenson & Navajo National Monument)

The Beals, et al 1945 report was entirely about archaeology as stated:

> Since this report does not concern itself with the geological, biological, or botanical phases of the Expedition, we will here mention more fully only the detailed organization of the archaeological parties.[62]

There was little mention of the value from river access in 1933-1934 field seasons, and a short note implying river boat access in 1935:

> A fourth exploratory survey was made by an expedition which navigated the San Juan and Colorado rivers from Moonlight Creek to Lee's Ferry, under direction of Bayne Beauchamp, Walter Buss, and Lloyd C. Lowrey.[63]

However Beals further states:

> In the six summers that the Expedition was in the field *no less than eleven passages* were made by boat through the canyons of the San Juan and the Glenn Canyon of the Colorado. This voyage of some 200 miles *usually* occupied from two to four weeks from the time the party embarked at Mexican Hat *or at the mouth of Copper Canyon* until they arrived at Lee's Ferry, the next accessible point. The trips were made in ten- and fifteen-foot boats built by the Wilson Fold-Flat Company of Los Angeles. This light folding craft proved to be exceptionally seaworthy and tough. [Emphasis mine].[64]

In a letter from Dock Marston to Kenny dated February 22, 1953 he mentioned that he was compiling "the history of the navigation of the River" and had talked to Ansel Hall who told Marston, "Ansel tells me that you are looking for the film of the 1933 San Juan run as well as the journal of the party. I hope you find them." [65] Kenny replied to Dock Marston dated March 3, 1953:

> The journal of the 1933 SJ&C trip, RBMV, will turn up in the course of my spare-time search of the general RBMV files. Am trying to do this systematically but perhaps ought to start at the wrong end---where it will probably be anyway. The movie of that trip could be anywhere. Am afraid Ansel has unconsciously "hidden" it among his private mementos---but he thinks not.[66]

To further exacerbate the problem Lloyd Lowrey's last comment to Andy Christenson adds:

> Incidentally, one reason I made so many river trips was that I was preparing a rather extensive paper on the archaeology of the San Juan and Glen Canyon. *My parents' home burned and unfortunately my labors were lost.* Now, many or perhaps most of the sites discovered are submerged under Lake Powell [Emphasis mine].[67]

So only personal documentation from Kenny where he said that he was on *three* RBMV river trips in 1933 and 1934 exists, and the *official documentation* was lost, or never happened. It's noteworthy that RBMV member, George Brainerd, who joined the expedition in 1935 and according to Christenson, was only interested in archaeology, had taken much of the official documentation home with him to Berkeley. There is no way possible to know precisely what files he had because *they were all consumed in a fire in George Brainerd's garage and there is no mention of personnel participating in river trips in 1934.*

Christenson didn't believe that Brainerd had river files because he (Brainerd) was an archaeologist. But I suggested that Brainerd had volunteered his garage as a place to store files, all files related to RBMV expedition efforts and could have just as likely included the files from the 1934 river trips (including some of Lowrey's notes). After all, if Brainerd volunteered space as a repository, why wouldn't he store *all* the files?

I'm a geologist and have lots of documents and maps and files in my home office, but not everything here is just geology related materials. Had a fire wiped me out, would this same argument apply to me that I had only geological files? I think not; I know this is not the case for me, so why not George Brainerd's fire? Since he was a late-comer to the RBMV efforts, who's to say what actually burned up?

Kenny Ross also had a fire at his boat shop (actually a big surplus military tent) in 1959 in Bluff, where all his files and over *ten thousand* 35 mm color slides were destroyed. And another one in 1976 that destroyed more files. Kenny never made an inventory of all the files that may have been incinerated. Ultimately, it's up to the reader to decide whose story to believe regarding the 1934 San Juan River season.

It is known that Norm Nevills kept one fold-flat boat that was damaged in 1933 and he repaired it. He is pictured rowing it in Gypsum Rapid at Mexican Hat and he reportedly used it as a model for which he built his first cataract boats.[68] However, Kenny ended up with a number of these fold-flat boats in his garage, or in a neighbor's barn in Mancos, Colorado well into the 1970s when he finally disposed of them. It seems unlikely that he would have held onto a bunch of old river equipment if he didn't have some personal connections and memories. Plus, there is no documentation whether Kenny found the reports and movie film[69] mentioned in the Dock Marston letters discussed above.

Figure 2.13 RBMV 1936 San Juan River trip; lining foldboats down Piute Rapid. (Torrey Lyons photos courtesy of A. Christenson & Navajo National Monument)

NORMAN NEVILLS AND RBMV INVOLVEMENT

When the RBMV efforts began, Norm Nevills was hired to assist engineer Thorn L. Mayes in topographic mapping[70] since Norm had been his field assistant for the previous two or three years. Although Norm Nevills was reported as a field assistant to the Mapping Group in 1933, there was no mention in Ansel Hall's report of who else was on the boats for the first river trip in August. Norm's job as field assistant with Thorn Mayes got him to be a 'cook's helper' on the first river run in August 1933. The only other river boat picture shows members of the "reconnaissance party" reporting "need for thorough biological fieldwork along river courses." [71]

There is nothing in the RBMV reports about accessing cliff dwellings or geology. The first trip was a reconnaissance of the river canyon below Mexican Hat. The massive sheer-walled lime-stone canyon winding through the Goosenecks provided little shelter for cliff-dwellers and virtually no irrigable floodplains. Plus, little to no time was allowed to explore the archaeological wonderland of Grand Gulch by the time they reached its mouth. USGS Historical Water Data from Gage 09379500 (Figure 2.14) indicated that early August gaged discharge was slightly more than 3,000 cfs but was on a precipitous decline such that by the end of the month gaged discharge was less than 100 cfs. If the first river trip launched after August 2 as Lowrey stated[72] then the flow could have been less than 500 cfs across an open, braided channel network below Clay Hills that would have resulted in having to wade and push boats, and that was precisely what occurred according to Kenny's recollection. The long slog across the braided sand and mud flats at Paiute Farms down to Copper Canyon definitely dictated that all future river trips would not repeat that section and would, instead, launch from Copper Canyon to explore the lower sandstone canyons down to the confluence with the Colorado River in Glen Canyon and thence down to Lees Ferry.

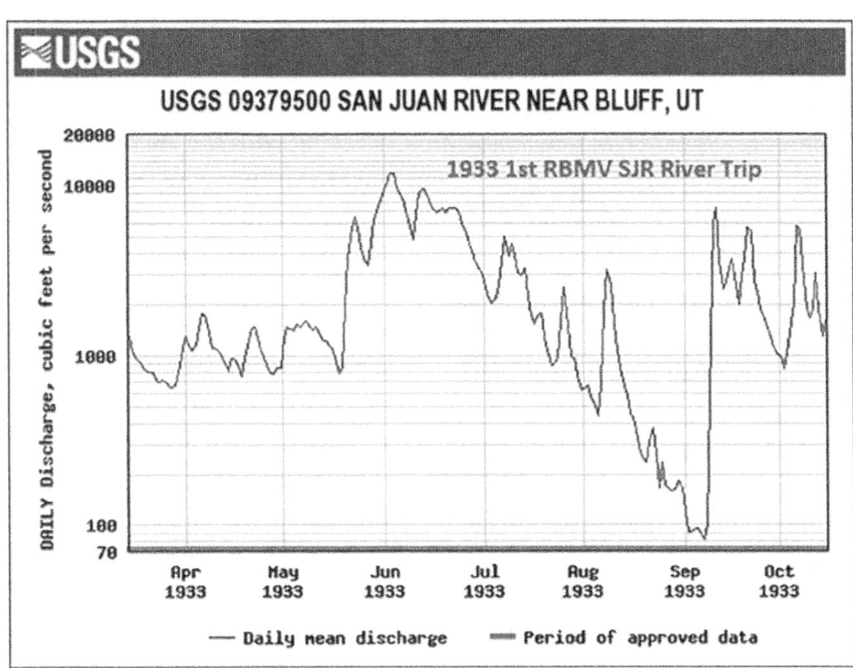

Figure 2.14 USGS Graph from Mexican Hat gage for 1933; First San Juan River trip with RBMV foldboats in August; note precipitous drop in water level throughout the month. (USGS Water Data)

Norman "Norm" Nevills was born in 1908 and grew up in Chico, California, graduating high school in 1925 and traveled to Utah for several summers apparently helping his father (William Eugene "Billy" Nevills) drill wells exploring for oil in the "San Juan oil field" in and around the Mexican Hat vicinity. Norm returned to California where he attended Stockton's College on the Pacific briefly (ostensibly enrolled as a geology major, but was far more interested in drama classes) and dropped out of college during the second semester.

In 1927 Billy had convinced his wife Moe and Norm to come to Utah and work the oil field.[73] Billy had now produced enough crude oil that he built a *topping plant* (a rudimentary refinery) and could pull off kerosene and gasoline to sell, but wells watered out or died by 1930.[74] Norm was quite the salesman who "was not above manipulating the facts" [75] and exaggerated oil production and refining capabilities! The Mexican Hat oil field had been far too over-promoted by all sorts of folks, like Adelbert L. Raplee among many others.[76]

Billy's financial backer had decided to stop funding anymore drilling, so Norm helped Billy build the Mexican Hat Lodge that formally opened in 1933 with his eyes now on tourism and possibly providing room and board for some RBMV folks. Norman had also become more interested in Monument Valley and began "creatively mapping" the area (suggesting more artistically than geologically).[77]

As noted above a Stearman biplane was used for the first several years for aerial reconnaissance and photography and piloted by F. Linden Naylor. Flights were mainly of Comb Ridge from Kayenta to Blanding and the canyons of the San Juan River, Monument Valley, Rainbow Plateau and Rainbow Bridge, and Navajo Mountain. There is no question that Norm and his father had some influence and possibly a California connection in convincing Ansel Hall in 1932 to build an air strip near Goodridge [Mexican Hat] which was also in near proximity to the San Juan oil field and the refined fuel from Billy's topping plant. That was precisely the same air strip that Norm took over for his own use after Naylor condemned it. Unfortunately, Norm did not heed pilot Linden Naylor's concerns of its "unfavorable location due to uncertain air currents set up by the adjacent canyon of the San Juan." [78] The combination of *unfavorable conditions* with rumored engine trouble very likely contributed to the airplane crash that killed Norm and his wife in September 1949.[79]

THE HONEYMOON TRIP

Most river folks who have heard stories of the San Juan River, or have written about them as it pertains to Norman Nevills invariably mention "the honeymoon trip" [80] of Norm and his new bride, Doris. But like many handed-down river stories they tend to get embellished somewhat as the years pass. Truth and folklore tend to get mixed together. Such was the case here, where much of the story has been handed down by Norm's mother Moe and much later, by his daughter Joan.

Norm Nevills certainly did not continue working with the survey team in 1934 as he had met his future wife Doris Drown the previous summer and they ended up getting married on October 18, 1933. Gaylord Staveley married Joan Nevills, Norm and Doris's oldest daughter, and explained the preparations for the river trip in detail, albeit from those handed-down oral accounts. But suffice to say Norm and Doris reportedly did a *honeymoon* float trip some time during December, 1933 with friend Jack Frost tagging along. The plan was to run the river "which was running a bit less than 600 cfs" down to Copper Canyon, and the story goes that they only made it from Mexican Hat to Honaker Trail in December. The trip was aborted at that point due to low water conditions and a poorly built, leaky boat made of scrap lumber. They pulled the boat up onto shore and then proceeded to hike out Honaker Trail and returned to Mexican Hat Lodge (Figure 2.15).

Not to be discouraged, over the winter Norm exchanged letters with Jack Frost about trying this again, but this time they would both take their wives along. Norm and Jack built a new boat and the trip was launched on March 9, 1934 at the Mexican Hat bridge.[81]

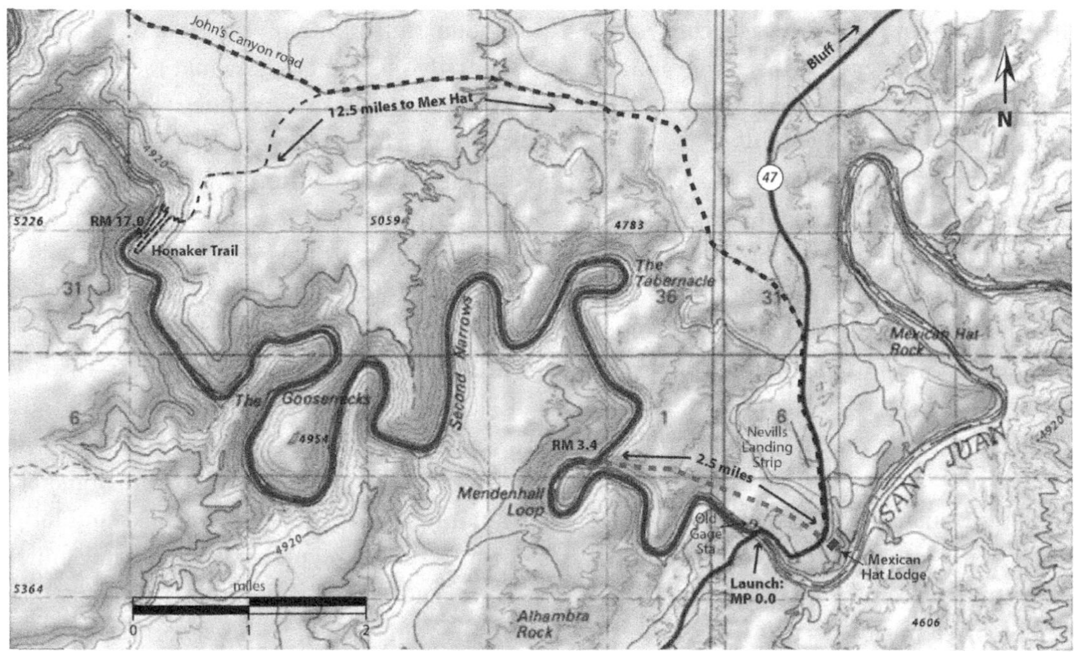

Figure 2.15 Map with road and trails highlighted as of 1933-34; Route 47 was not paved; Johns Canyon road was a two-track trail to access non-producing oil well drilling sites; river gage at this time was below the bridge; river mile distance from Mexican Hat Bridge to downstream side of Mendenhall Loop and Honaker Trail is darkened; overland hiking routes with distances from bottom of canyon at Honaker Trail (thin dashes) vs bottom of Mendenhall Loop (heavy dashes); elevation in feet. (Modified from *Esri Arc/GIS* USGS topographic map)

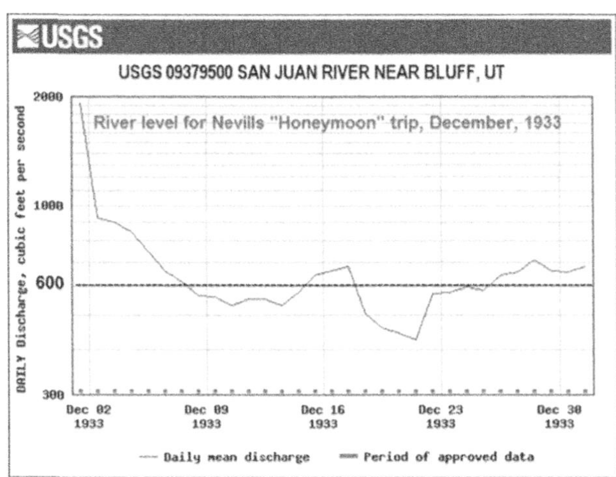

Figure 2.16 USGS Graph from Mexican Hat gage for December, 1933 shows water levels throughout the month dropped from 1000 cfs to ~420 cfs and averaged ~600 cfs. (USGS Water Data)

A TALL TALE WITH TOO MANY LEAKS

That the trip was aborted and restarted the following spring isn't disputed here; however an alternative and more logical interpretation is herein presented, since there seems to be some 'leaks' in the story. Norm had been down the river in August, 1933, so he should have known what to expect as far as rapids were concerned (at least down to Copper Canyon), and the fact that the canyon got very steep and deep quickly after leaving Mexican Hat.

Add to that observation that it was December with minimum hours of daylight and the fact that he would have seen a common recurrence of how ice jams were an annual event that happened right out his front door at Gypsum Rapids and might be a problem at the bigger rapids downstream.

USGS Historical Water Data for year 1933 from Gage 09379500 (Figure 2.16) records discharge rates ranging from 1,000 to 420 cfs for most of December and averaged 600 cfs for the month of December, so moderately low flow conditions are correctly reported in the story.

But did they really take the boat all the way to Honaker Trail? And again, as river historian Roy Webb said, Norm *was not above manipulating the facts* when it came to exaggerated oil production and refining capabilities! So maybe there's been a bit of embellishment about this occurrence as well.

Norm and Jack were not dummies, and when they saw they had a very leaky boat where "the cracks between the boards were caulked by pounding strips of worn-out shirts and under-wear into them....they frequently scraped over rocks, which raked out enough of the underwear caulking that the cracks began leaking badly, putting the boat in danger of foundering." [82] Assuming they launched from the old landing just upstream of the bridge, then it is almost exactly seventeen river miles to the main landing near the foot of the Honaker Trail and not the twenty-one miles reported by Staveley (Figure 2.15).[83]

Honaker Trail is below (downstream) the Goosenecks stretch which, at 600 cfs or less, is slow-going and there would certainly be a number of shallow riffles and lots of rocks to dodge. Depending on the time of day they actually pushed off, it would take most of the daytime hours to make the seventeen miles, particularly if they were re-stuffing underwear, bailing etc. Maximum daylight in December at this latitude decreases to less than nine hours-thirty minutes by winter solstice.[84]

Honaker Trail is located in the deepest part of the San Juan River canyon with a 1,235 ft difference in elevation from rim to river.[85] Getting there in December with winter sun angle would place the boaters in cold shadows almost the entire way. The actual *trail* at Honaker landing is a series of switchbacks and long traverses adding up to two and a half miles just to make it to the rim. Although the trail was built in the mid-1890s, it was seldom used until much later.

There were no wells drilled near the Honaker Trail rim in prior years during the oil boom, so there wasn't any discernable road to the trailhead. Beginning in the early 1950s, geologists began to hike the trail so they could describe the strata that are exposed in the canyon. But the trail really didn't get much foot traffic until an ever-increasing number of river runners began hiking to the rim for a view in the late 1960s and has continued to be a well-traversed trail today.

However, in 1933 the trail would have been barely recognizable from river level. Furthermore, the roadway along the base of Cedar Mesa contoured its way around Johns Canyon enroute to Slickhorn Gulch, and was nothing more than a two-track path located a mile and a half away from the canyon rim (Figure 2.15).[86]

Many modern era boaters have missed this landing as they have wound around through the Goosenecks stretch.[87] In other words, it's not particularly well-marked, especially in 1933 when it was only Norms second time down this stretch of the river. Then after having hiked the two and a half miles to just get out of the canyon it's another ten mile hike overland to make it back to the Nevills lodge, and that's if one followed the two-track roadway; any 'shortcuts' would demand crossing side canyon escarpments cut several hundred feet down into the rim rock and in the dark of night (Figure 2.15).

Now, consider this alternative. If you were in a boat leaking like a sieve, and the fibrous fabric "caulking" (probably cotton or wool) was soaked, your boat was on the verge of sinking, and it was cold and getting dark early, it wouldn't take long to see that the smart thing would be to abort the trip.

It is my supposition that Norm and the other two landed their boat about three and a half river miles downstream from their launch point on the downstream side of Mendenhall Loop. They would have already encountered a few riffles and plenty of rocks to dodge by then and the downstream side of Mendenhall Loop has a good riverbank beach to land a boat and drag it onto and tie off for the winter.

At this point the canyon is just 485 ft deep and the hike to the rim is only a half mile long. Then it's another two miles back to the lodge following a well-used roadway that had been used first by gold prospectors and was still being used by oil company personnel as they continued drilling around the immediate area (Figure 2.15). So let's review:

River miles: to Mendenhall landing: 3.4
To Honaker Trail: 17.0
Elevation difference: at Mendenhall: 485 ft
At Honaker: 1,235 ft
Land miles back home: from Mendenhall: 2.5
From Bottom of Honaker: 12.5

Put this all together and it is my conclusion that Moe's often told story of the romantic trip out of the canyon had been somewhat stretched by either she or Norm or possibly Joan. And think about the following season when the Frost's hiked down with all their personal gear and possibly some caulking for the abandoned boat. Did they go down a steep trail two-and-a-half mile long or one that was one-half mile long? I think this story is one of the many Nevills *yarns* spun by Norm and his followers that just don't hold up to serious scrutiny.

SUMMARY

Even though the American southwest had been proclaimed "settled" by 1890 by urban elitists the truth was that very little was known about the vast "San Juan Country" both geographically and culturally. These misconceptions remain enigmatic to non-Native Americans well into the 21st century. The efforts by the RBMV expeditions only reinforced these attitudes. The incredible scenery of the region was finally made available to the masses through various forms of photography and movies, but the expansiveness could only be realized in person. Adventure seekers vicariously achieved their thrills by reading stories or watching motion pictures of new dare devils like Norman Nevills who immediately latched onto his role as entertainer.

From around 1930 to October, 1934 Kenny Ross was a lost soul floundering around in the midst of the Great Depression trying to find something to sink his teeth into and make a buck. Work was scarce to non-existent. Kenny bounced between working in Florida or California and traveled from Cuba to the Yukon and from Kansas City to Cahone, Colorado. He filled in some of that time on the Cahone ranch with his father, Charley, riding herd on cattle drives a couple months each year; working as a boatman on hit and miss river trips for little to no pay with RBMV in 1933-34; and he also made trips to California to visit his mother, even taking a few odd jobs while visiting - like parking cars. Finally on October 10, 1934 in Dolores, Colorado, Kenny's life took a major turn when he signed on with the CCC at Mesa Verde National Park. The next time he would boat the San Juan River below Mexican Hat and Glen Canyon on the Colorado River and revisit Rainbow Bridge would be sixteen years later.

View from north-facing escarpment of Mesa Verde near abandoned "Knife Edge" roadway on right side in shadow; Lone Cone and San Miguel Mountains in distance (G.M. Stevenson photo)

3
MESA VERDE NATIONAL PARK

BACKGROUND

From a geologist's perspective, the area called *Mesa Verde* was misnamed, as true mesas are generally flat-lying. Because Mesa Verde slants to the south and was actually a rather small segment of the south-dipping strata that defined the northern geomorphic boundary of the San Juan basin, the proper geological term should have been *cuesta*, not mesa (Figure 3.1). A cuesta has an asymmetric planar ridge with a gentle slope on one side and a steep slope on the other. In the case of Mesa Verde National Park, the light-colored tan massive sandstone layers known as the Point Lookout and Cliff House Sandstones formed caprock beds that overlie soft dark gray layers of the Mancos Shale and the two capping sandstone layers were separated by the equally dark gray Menefee Shale (Figure 3.2). The result has created a long and relatively gentle south-sloping backslope, or dip slope. The north-facing front slope has eroded the northern face forming a steep 1,300 ft escarpment. The average elevation of the north-face is 8,100 ft and the base of the escarpment averages 6,800 ft.

The park is actually made up of several smaller cuestas dissected by several steep-walled canyons that were cut by south-flowing streams into the larger cuesta and formed as tributary canyons to the west-flowing Mancos River. The elevation at the mouths of the numerous tributaries averaged 5,800 ft or some 2,300 ft lower than the north facing escarpment. The south facing dip slope contributed to the formation of the many alcoves that were cut into the massive sandstone beds that have preserved the area's cliff dwellings (Figure 3.3).

In 1873, gold prospector John Moss led photographer William Henry Jackson through Mancos Canyon, at the base of Mesa Verde.[1] Jackson photographed several small cliff dwellings and geologist William H. Holmes retraced Jackson's route in 1875. Both Jackson and Holmes reports were included in the 1877 report of the Hayden Survey.[2] Then a journalist from New York, Virginia McClurg visited Mesa Verde in 1882 and again in 1885 and in her quest to find cliff dwellings and associated artifacts, she and her party reportedly discovered Echo Cliff House, Three Tier House and Balcony House ruins. Virginia McClurg was diligent in her efforts between 1887 and 1906 to inform the United States and European communities of the importance of protecting the historical material and dwellings in Mesa Verde. Her efforts included enlisting support through the Federation of Women's Clubs, writing and having published poems in popular magazines, giving speeches domestically and internationally, and forming the *Colorado Cliff Dwellers Association.*[3] The Colorado Cliff Dwellers' purpose was to protect the resources of Colorado cliff dwellings, reclaiming as much of the original artifacts as possible and sharing information about the people who dwelt there. A fellow activist for protection of Mesa Verde and prehistoric archaeological sites included Lucy Peabody, who, located in Washington, D.C., met with members of Congress to further the cause.[4]

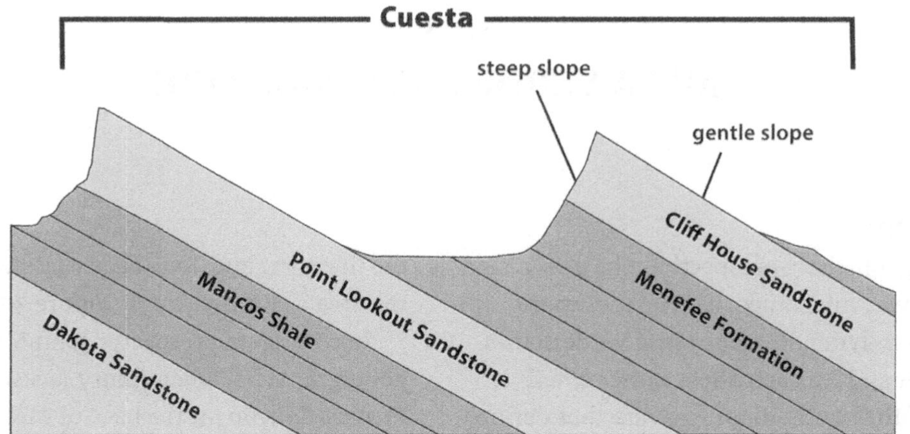

Figure 3.1 Diagrammatic cross-section of the Mesa Verde "cuesta." (GMS/TB original diagram)

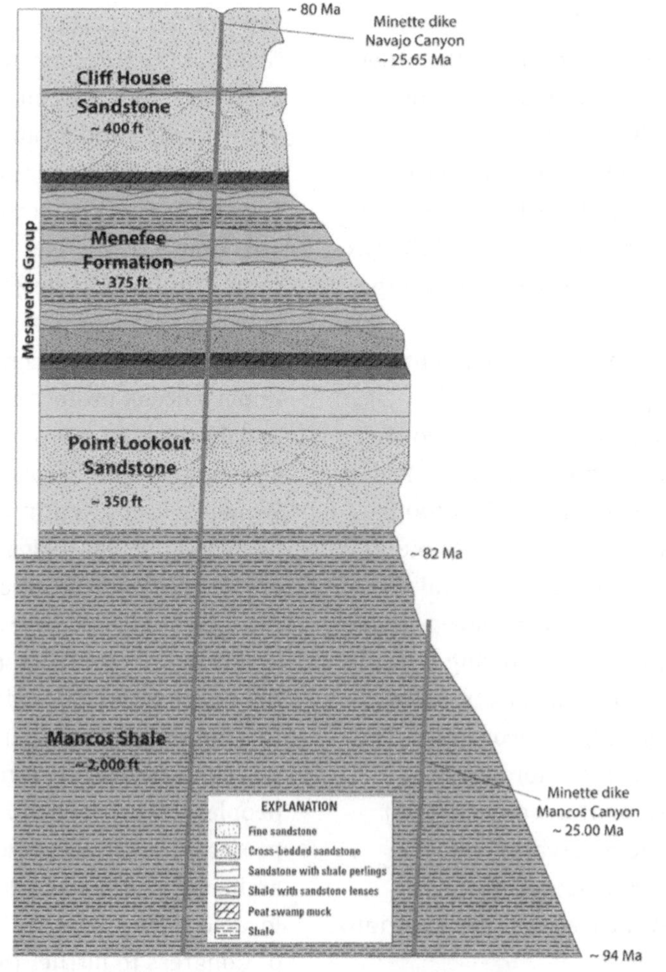

Figure 3.2 Stratigraphic column of rocks exposed in Mesa Verde National Park. (Modified from Carrara, 2012; ages given for intrusive igneous minette dikes from Cobban et al, 2006)

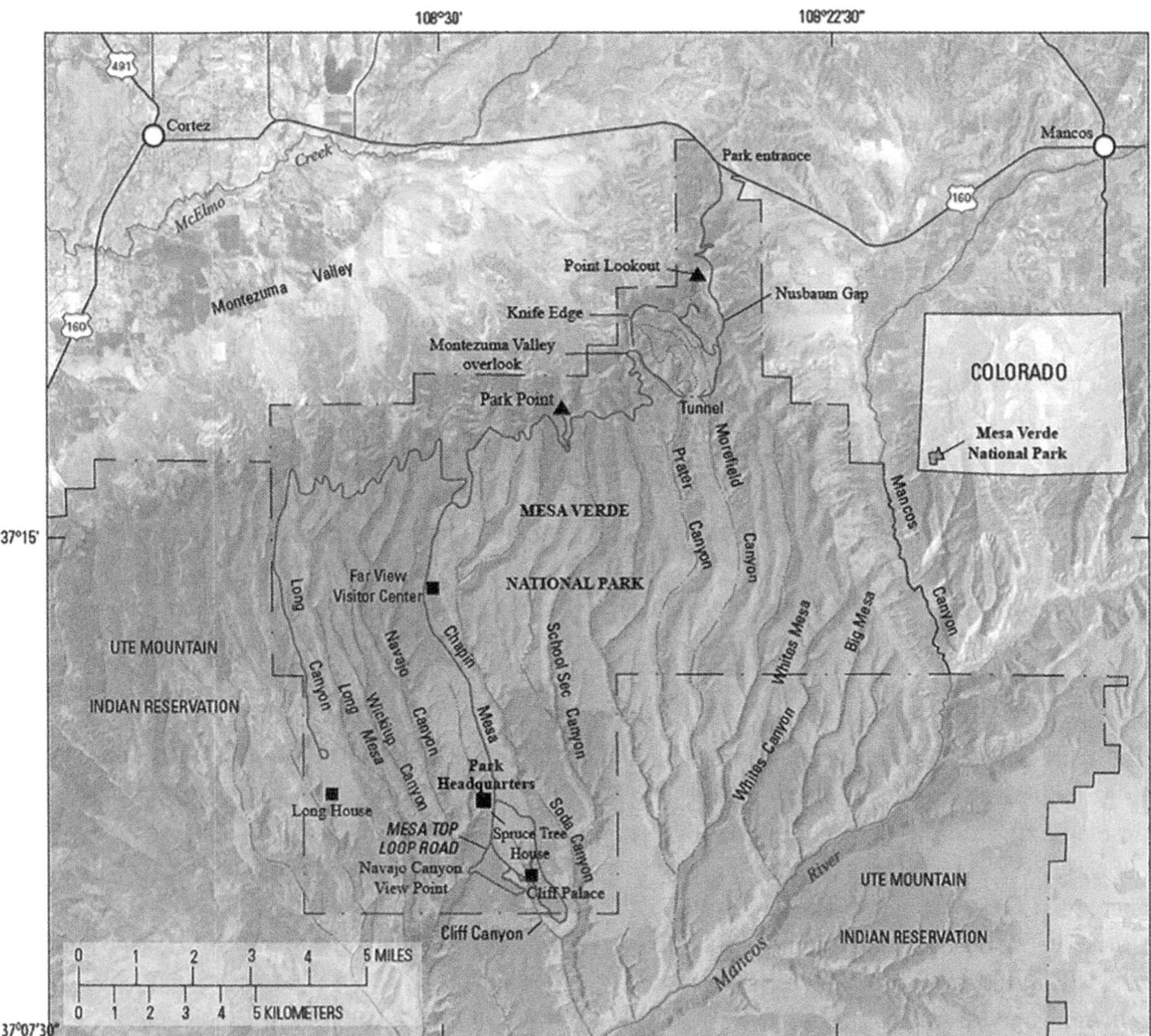

Figure 3.3 Location map of Mesa Verde National Park in southwestern Colorado. (Satellite imagery from National Agriculture Imagery Program accessed in 2011; from Carrara, 2012, p.2)

However, cowboys Richard Wetherill and Charlie Mason are most frequently cited to have discovered and named Cliff Palace ruins on December 18, 1888 and have been chronicled as the official Anglo discoverers of Mesa Verde cliff ruins.[5] The Wetherill family operated from their Alamo Ranch located on the southwest side of Mancos, Colorado. They had befriended members of the Ute tribe and gained their approval to bring their cattle to graze in the lower grasslands near the base of Mesa Verde. The Utes spoke of many great cliff dwellings in the canyons of Mesa Verde but they considered them sacred and taboo. The Wetherill family and friends explored the ruins and gathered artifacts and kept most of their collection although they sold some to the *Historical Society of Colorado.*

Among the people who stayed at the Wetherill ranch and explored the cliff dwellings was author Frederick H. Chapin, who visited the region during 1889 and 1890. He described the landscape and ruins in an 1890 article and later in an 1892 book, *The Land of the Cliff-Dwellers*, which he illustrated with hand-drawn maps and personal photographs.[6] Alice Eastwood, who later became a well-known botanist, visited Mesa Verde in 1889, and joined Al and Richard Wetherill on subsequent trips over the next two years.[7] While the two men roped their way into the massive cliff dwellings she was busy collecting botanical specimens on the vast mesa tops. She got to know the Wetherill family and stayed at the Alamo Ranch in Mancos where, in 1891, she met the wealthy and locally infamous Swedish pothunter/archaeologist Gustav Nordenskiöld. He removed a lot of artifacts and sent them to Sweden, where they eventually went to the National Museum of Finland. Nordenskiöld published, in 1893, *The Cliff Dwellers of the Mesa Verde*.[8] When he shipped the collection that he made of Mesa Verde artifacts, the event incensed Virginia McClurg and her followers about the need to protect Mesa Verde land and its resources.

The Wetherills also took advantage of their findings by presenting their collections at the Columbian Exposition in Chicago in 1893. By the end of the 19th century, it was clear to famed archaeologist, Jesse Walter Fewkes (1850-1930) that Mesa Verde needed protection from "curio seekers" who came and collected artifacts to sell to museums and interested parties.[9]

By 1906, Congress passed the Antiquities Act and on June 29 Mesa Verde was proclaimed a national park by President Theodore Roosevelt, [10] but by no means were all of the prehistoric ruins included in its boundaries. Many were located on lands in the adjoining Ute Reservation and the Utes refused to give them up. However, Congress, in the Act establishing the park, placed under the supervision of the Secretary of the Interior all prehistoric ruins on Indian lands within five miles of the park's border. In addition to the huge number of ruins and artifacts, the park contained archaeological pictographs, petroglyphs and other signs of inhabitation dating from the Archaic Period through Pueblo III occupation. "The Mesa Verde development is among the finest and most appropriate in the National Park system" remarked conservationist Fredrick Law Olmstead, Jr. when he visited Mesa Verde in 1945.[11] Cliff Palace, a consolidation of one to two hundred rooms into a sprawling, apartment-style complex, left little doubt as to the Anasazi culture during their occupation in the Four Corners.

The park boundaries have changed over time as more lands were added following various treaties with the Ute Mountain Reservation. As it now stands, the park covers approximately 52,500 acres with well over 4,300 documented sites (particularly following the Chapin Mesa fire in 1996 where hundreds of Basketmaker sites were discovered) including some 600 cliff dwellings. It is one of the largest archaeological preserves in the United States (Figure 3.3).

JESSE LOGAN NUSBAUM (1887-1975)

In 1907, a survey of the ruins on the Ute Reservation was undertaken. Associated with archaeologists A. V. Kidder and S. G. Morley, Dr. Edgar L. Hewett hired a young school teacher who was also a trained archaeologist as part of this first expedition. He was Jesse L. Nusbaum, or Jess—as he was known to friends and associates.[12] The experience of that year was the start of a long association Jess had with Mesa Verde. In 1910, he undertook the restoration and stabilization of Balcony House, one of the notable ruins still on Ute lands. Nusbaum noted that Balcony House was in a difficult position for such work. It was high up on the cliff, sheer below, sheer above. And it was in terrible shape; visitors were crawling all over walls, breaking them down. It was tottering and would have been gone before long. The work performed at Balcony House can properly be considered a pioneering and successful effort even though ruins stabilization was in its infancy. From 1908 to 1922, Fewkes and Nusbaum led additional efforts to stabilize Spruce Tree House, Cliff Palace and Sun Temple ruins.[13]

Word of the large number of cliff dwellings spread quickly, drawing visitors to Mancos to engage guides to the ruins. Durango initially profited as the transportation hub for the new national attraction. Prior to 1890, visitors would arrive in Durango on the train and endure a wagon trip to Mancos. When the Rio Grande Southern was completed in 1890, the train connection between Durango and Mancos reduced the travel time.[14]

In 1918-19 the first Superintendent of the National Park Service, Steven Mather, was a rich Californian that made his money in borax and wanted an archaeologist to "clean up" Mesa Verde. Mather had visited the park late in the fall of the previous year, and was greatly distressed by the evidences of mismanagement that he observed. Nusbaum was recommended to the Service by the Smithsonian Institution and on May 21, 1921 Jesse Nusbaum became Superintendent of Mesa Verde National Park.[15]

One of Nusbaum's first initiatives was to have the operation headquarters moved up to Mesa Verde from Mancos which upset employees because they were a close knit group (nepotism to the max) and had been handling all park operations out of Mancos. The move also aroused the wrath of Senator Lawrence Phipps of Colorado Springs, Colorado, who made several efforts to have him removed, but Presidents Harding and Coolidge and Secretary Hubert Work all refused to fire Jess.[16]

The Secretary of the Interior pulled Nusbaum from Mesa Verde in 1931 for a job in Santa Fe as head of the Lab of Anthropology that would preside over all archaeological work that was being done in the Four Corner states from 1931 to 1937. Nusbaum did return to Mesa Verde on an interim basis from 1936 to 1939; and for a third time during World War II during the military furlough of Superintendent John S. McLaughlin.[17]

When Jess began as Superintendent he found that the park had been excessively overgrazed. There was no grass under the trees at all, and everything was browsed as far up as the cattle could reach. An early Nusbaum decision was to reduce grazing by twenty percent a year, thereby terminating it in five years. Though the permittees were not happy about it, he made the decision stick.

The result was an almost miraculous recovery of the mesa vegetation.[18] It was also on Jess's initiative that arrangements were made for the restoration of the wild Merriam turkey—which the cliff-dwellers domesticated, and the bighorn sheep, which had lived on the mesa as recently as the 1880s.

Throughout his long career Jess was a stalwart watch-dog constantly on the alert for any kind of damaging activities to these prehistoric ruins or pot-hunting on public lands. Don Ross said: "Jesse L. Nusbaum left the biggest footprint at Mesa Verde!" [19]

KENNY ROSS: THE MESA VERDE YEARS 1934 to 1946

Even with improved roads, getting from Mancos (elevation 7,030 ft) to the main visitor's center at Mesa Verde National Park took more than an hours' drive – on pavement; and that's if it was a clear day! The roadway from Mancos to the parks headquarters in the 1930s could become a life threatening experience, particularly the first ascent up from the Point Lookout turn-off along a stretch called the "Knife's Edge." [20] Simply put, driving on the highways and byways of the Southwest took "pioneering" spunk.[21]

Because of this problem of commuting and other concerns, beginning in 1921, the park employees living quarters were moved to the main headquarters near Spruce Tree House, much to the disgruntlement of some who preferred living in Mancos. Today's route only takes a few minutes to visit the new visitor's center near the entrance to the park. But the route to the ruin sites and park headquarters is still quite slow and has been closed several times in the last few years due to landslides.

For Kenny, getting hired on by the Civilian Conservation Corps (CCC) in October, 1934 meant some stability in his life even though the pay was low.[22] He said the base pay was $1.00 per day and that the saying "another day, another dollar" was coined by those who worked in the CCC. However, the U.S. Civil Service Commission was an early prototype of modern day governmental bureaucracies, and the "Application for Federal Employment" was annoyingly tedious and repetitious. The CCC and the National Park Service required each worker to fill out new applications for work on as little as three to six month intervals, even if they were deemed good workers, and such was the case for Kenny. By January 4, 1944 Kenny had filled out his 26th job application. [23]

Fortunately, Kenny held onto copies of his applications which have proven to be useful when reconstructing his work history during his employment by the Federal government. By sheer luck, Kenny's first job as a CCC worker was to be assigned duty at Mesa Verde National Park. In his own words from a recorded and transcribed interview in 1986:

> So, it's in the middle of the Depression and I didn't have much to do. I had come back out to the ranch from Southern California and had done a little museum work there by the Coliseum. And so Paul Franke was the park naturalist at the time, who later became superintendent of Grand Teton and also Bryce and Zion. But there was no real title of "park naturalist" at the time, so there wasn't money to pay for one. So he was the assistant park naturalist and for many years they had the title of assistant park naturalist, but I don't even know whether they have someone that's called a park naturalist now or not. Anyhow, I was introduced to Paul Franke. I didn't go up there looking for a job, but through Ann Bauer, who was native here (in Mancos), did a lot of archaeology in Chaco Canyon and Ann got to talking and told him she thought I could be made available; that I would be willing to go to work as a L.E.M., that stands for "local experienced man.
>
> You lived at the CCC camp and actually most of the enrollment and all that sort of thing were through the CCC process, but you got paid a few dollars more than the CCC boys, so I went up in '34 just in time for the big fire, and we didn't get started until after the fire was put out.[24]

On February 15, 1935 Kenny received a letter of commendation from Robert Fechner, Director of the Emergency Conservation Work stating:

> You have, no doubt, received commendations from the War Department for your splendid work in rendering life-saving service of merit to fellow enrollees on the night of January 7, 1935. In addition to the praise already uttered, I take this occasion to compliment you for the prompt and unselfish services rendered. Your foresight in preparing for such a service by taking and completing the standard course in First Aid is commendable.[25]

There was no indication as to exactly what service Kenny provided that night, but it may have been in helping to save lives from the forest fire that was still burning. The letter certainly indicated that Kenny was no slacker when action was needed. Then, on July 28, 1935 Kenny received his official "Certificate of Discharge from Civilian Conservation Corps" [26] from Camp No. 1843, NP-5-C, Dolores, Colorado stating that he was being honorably discharged as a CCC Ranger "to accept employment" at Mesa Verde National Park and signed by "Merton K. Leadbetter, 1st Lt. 20th Inf-Res." of the CCC (Figures 3.4 & 3.5). The certificate lists that Kenny was "5 feet- 9 inches in height, had a ruddy complexion," weighed 152 pounds and had black hair and brown eyes.[27]

Early in Kenny's career at Mesa Verde, the Rural Electrification Administration (REA) brought electricity into southwestern Colorado and Mesa Verde National Park. Kenny recalled what that meant:

> That was an experience in the late thirties and early forties to see the lights go on all over the country. Driving back and forth it was very striking. It happened over a period of many months, first a light way out by Pleasant View, then another blinked on somewhere else. It was interesting, you realized something was going on, the country was moving out of the real pioneering life into the modern world. [28]

MUSEUM DIORAMAS

Kenny's first duties as a new enrollee were maintenance, guiding and public contact as well as work on museum dioramas. As early as 1915 the park had a museum of sorts, with poorly displayed exhibits in a small log cabin. Jess Nusbaum had enlisted the interest of Mrs. Stella Leviston of San Francisco in providing funds for a start on the museum. John D. Rockefeller, Jr., a visitor in 1924, supplied the money needed to complete it. But the addition of these types of exhibits (dioramas) was just being introduced into museums. Nusbaum brought in Paul Franke in 1931 to be in charge of the museum and educational activities and it was Franke who saw Kenny's interest in building the displays.[29]

Dioramas originated in 1823 as a type of picture-viewing device where the Frenchman Louis Jacques Mandé Daguerre (1787–1851) was considered the inventor.[30] In addition, Daguerre was a decorator, manufacturer of mirrors, painter of panoramas, and designer and painter of theatrical stage illusions. Daguerre would later co-invent the *daguerreotype*, the first widely used method of photography like that used by W.H. Jackson and Charles Goodman. Both Jackson and Goodman were the earliest photographers to document the incredible scenery, archaeology and pioneers in the Four Corners region.[31]

The dioramas at Mesa Verde were three-dimensional miniature models of cliff dwellings or surface sites designed to depict small-scale replicas of Puebloan scenes complete with miniature Puebloan men, women and children going about their daily duties. The entire scene was built to scale (1/2 inch = 1 foot).The dioramas also included pots, ollas, baskets, etc complete with miniature fires that burned in fire pits. The dioramas were enclosed in glass showcases at the Chapin Mesa Archaeology Museum at the Park Headquarters and have remained a popular exhibit to this day.

Kenny Ross built several dioramas; completing Stephouse Cave with the help of Meredith Guillet and White Dog Cave in 1935 (Figures 3.6 to 3.11). Spruce Tree House was completed in May, 1938 (Figures 3.12 to 3.15). Construction of White Dog Cave was begun by Lyle Bennett but completed by Kenny and Meredith. The actual White Dog Cave was located on the flank of Comb Ridge near Kayenta, Arizona and has some inscriptions from "folks who list themselves as Mesa Verde and may be Kidder and Guernsey, or more likely folks there that were gathering information for the diorama."[32]

The other dioramas were depictions of archaeological sites within Mesa Verde National Park. Alfred Lee Rowell (shown in the Mesa Verde historical photo from Mesa Verde website) worked through the WPA program and was an artist who painted all the backdrops for the dioramas. According to Don Ross "Alfred made the molds for all the little bitty wee people that Kenny painstakingly painted. Furthermore, Kenny made all the miniature ceramics and baskets with equal meticulous care." [33]

The museum was under renovation construction during the time they were making the dioramas and Jess Nusbaum kept a watchful eye on the contactors and would have them tear out sections if not done to his specifications.

During this construction period, the work area for the dioramas was in the old museum where Kenny, Meredith Guillet and Paul Franke set up shop in the basement, or "the cellar" [34] as they called it. Kenny said the cellar was cold in the winter months during construction, so the first thing they did was to make a pot of coffee and sit around and brainstorm about what type of miniature people or artifacts to create that day. After the main building was completed there was a furnace that heated the basement somewhat. They also cordoned off a temporary work space about twelve feet square in one of the rooms in the exhibit area (Figure 3.8; now the bookstore) as their woodshop. That was where the Stephouse Cave Diorama was built. The renovation construction of the museum was finished in 1936, so they moved the operation down to the basement where they completed the Spruce Tree House Diorama in 1938 and Far View Diorama in 1939.[35]

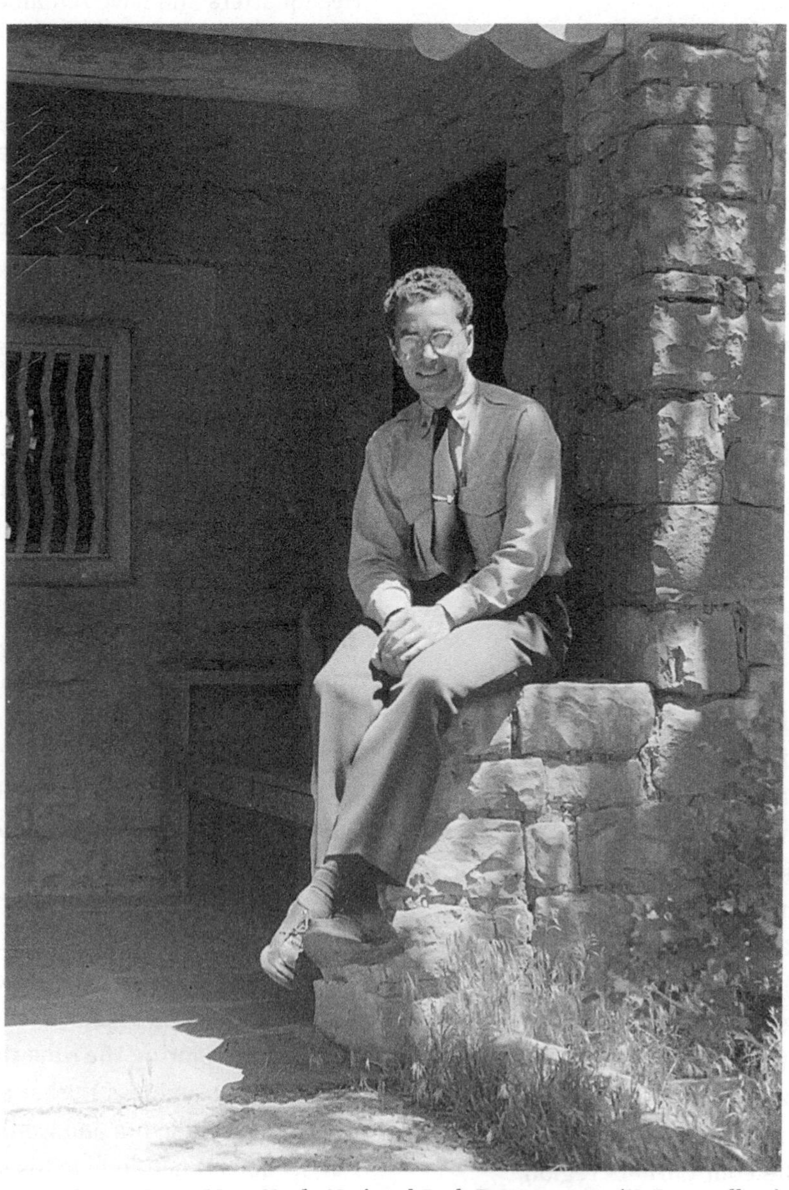

Figure 3.4 Kenny Ross, Mesa Verde National Park Ranger 1944. (K. Ross collection)

Figure 3.5 Mesa Verde National Park Rangers 1935; first row: Kenny Ross on far right, Betty Yelm in center, Paul R. Franke on far left; second row: Park Superintendent Jesse Nusbaum on far right behind Kenny, Don Watson, and Chief Ranger Chester Markley in front of tree. (K. Ross collection)

Figure 3.6 Stephouse Cave diorama began with a drawing by Kenny Ross and Meredith Guillet in 1934. (K. Ross collection)

Figure 3.7 Stephouse Cave preliminary model, winter 1934-35; from L to R: Meredith Guillet, Paul Franke and Kenny Ross. (K. Ross collection)

Figure 3.8 Kenny Ross (L) and Merideth Guillet (R) frame Stephouse Cave diorama in winter 1934-35. (K. Ross collection)

Figure 3.9 Progress on Stephouse Cave diorama, January 1935; Kenny Ross and Meredith Guillet on left. (K. Ross collection)

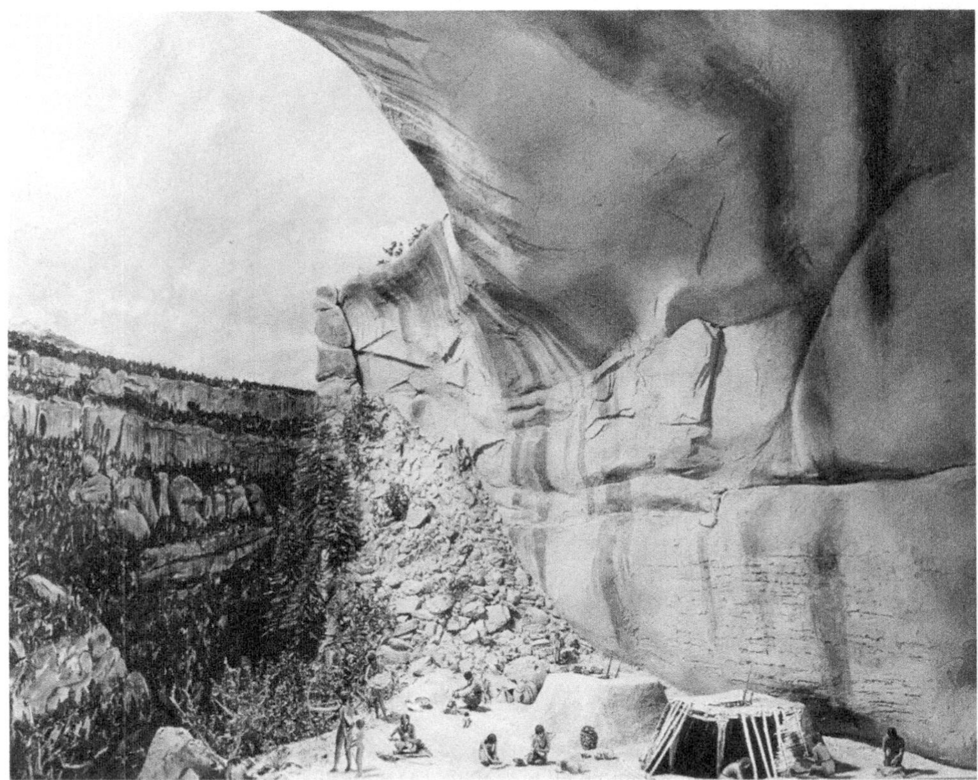

Figure 3.10 Temporary installation of Stephouse Cave diorama, 1935. (K. Ross collection, photo by C.A. Markley)

Figure 3.11 close-up view of White Dog Cave diorama, 1935. (K. Ross collection)

Figure 3.12 Spruce Tree House diorama completed May 1938; (A) underlies close-up of figurine in Figure 3.13; (B) underlies close-up of figurine in Figure 3.14. (K. Ross collection)

Figure 3.13 Close-up of wax figurine made by A.L. Rowell and painted by Kenny Ross; Spruce Tree House diorama. (K. Ross collection)

Figure 3.14 Close-up of miniature figurine and pots from Spruce Tree House diorama made by Rowell & Ross. (K. Ross collection)

Figure 3.15 Close-up of miniature pottery (classic design of a Mesa Verde kiva jar) from Spruce Tree House diorama made and painted by Kenny Ross, 1938. (K. Ross collection)

It was Kenny's ingenious idea to make the miniature camp fires appear to be burning. He used an incandescent light bulb to pass light through a bent piece of glass rod down underneath the diorama where he pasted a variety of colored cellophane strips and then sprinkled cake sparkles (glitter) on the camp fire coals. The result was a sparkling campfire. But the crawl space to reach the light bulbs was incredibly tight and the heat generated by the incandescent light bulbs created a real fire danger. So after several years of dazzling visitors with an apparent miniature camp fire, the incandescent bulb was abandoned.[36]

KENNY ROSS: MVNPS PARK RANGER

On May 18, 1936 Kenny received a letter from the United States Department of the Interior, Office of the Secretary stating,

> You have been appointed by the Secretary of the Interior, upon the recommendation of the Director of the National Park Service, subject to taking the oath of office, a Park Ranger, Grade 7, in the Mesa Verde National Park, at a salary of $1680 per annum, effective on the date of entrance on duty.[37]

The letter was signed by Guy N. Numbers, Acting Chief; Division of Appointments.[38] Kenny's renewed job applications showed that he did more than build dioramas. To provide service to visitors as well as to prevent damage to the ruins, Nusbaum had enlisted some of the park's labor force to serve as guides on occasions when there were many visitors. Their service was preceded by an intensive course in Mesa Verde archaeology and Kenny took to learning about the regions archaeology like "a duck takes to water."[39] The only ruin that visitors were allowed to enter without an escort was Spruce Tree

House, which lay adjacent to the watchful eye of headquarters employees.

Kenny's work history at Mesa Verde National Park was a combination of being a seasonal hire as a Park Ranger and/or park naturalist during a period still suffering from the Great Depression and then followed by World War II. The frequent applications also note that he was alternatively either directly hired by the USNPS, the CCC or the WPA from October, 1934 to December, 1945 and even had two separate periods where he wasn't rehired and was on his own for a period of time.

The following dates of employment and job duties through his resignation on January 16, 1946 were taken from the numerous job applications Kenny kept in his files. The other pieces of his life were taken from a number of letters and memories of his two sons, Don and Doug, and some hand-written notes of remembrance written by Mildred many years later.[40]

When he first started in October, 1934 his salary was $360 per annum, then increased to $1680/annum when he reached Park Ranger status in 1935, then back to $360 as a CCC employee from September, 1935 to June, 1936, then back to NPS Park Ranger at $1680/annum from June, 1936 to September, 1936. Kenny was not "gainfully employed" again until March, 1937 but worked on "Ethnic studies on Navajo Reservation," including ceremonies, medical practices, and weaving as well as research aid in Mesa Verde museum. Kenny received a letter of commendation from Acting Superintendent of Mesa Verde N.P., Paul R. Franke thanking him for doing all sorts of work for the park and a "happy birthday" wish as it was the 4th Anniversary of the CCC program.[41]

A letter from William Newbold, a friend of Kenny's from the early 1930s confirmed when Kenny was in California, as Newbold stated that bad weather and snow at Mesa Verde had forced him to rearrange his trip to southern Arizona. He also mentioned that the school buildings that were being built "when you were here in Pasadena, California are finally finished." [42]

Newbold very likely was a co-worker as a parking attendant. He also mentioned that he was pursuing a college degree in Geology with a minor in Archaeology. Kenny's job applications also show that he named his mother - Erma V. Gladys Morlen from Lincoln, Nebraska, as his beneficiary, although she was now living in California and had remarried.[43]

Then from March, 1937 to May, 1937 Kenny was in Durango working under the WPA with Editha Berry, the local supervisor for education and recreation, for $720/annum acting as "Jr. Recreational director" providing "Indian lectures to grade and high school students and Boy's Club organization." He is complimented by letter for his services as a "Junior Technician NP-6-C" by Earnest Hunter, District Educational Advisor.[44]

Editha sent a letter to Kenny on March 8, 1937 asking if he could come to Durango to lecture to school children and adults on "Indian relics." [45] Under the supervision of Mrs. Helen Sloan Daniels, a Durango socialite, the National Youth Administration (NYA) consisted of boys who spent summer months "unearthing some valuable relics in Falls Creek." [46] One specimen (a mummy of a female human that was later called "Ester") was going to the Peabody Institute for further examination to determine its authenticity and age.

Helen Daniels tried to keep Kenny in the loop through "recreational lectures" during the off-season and hoped he would be re-assigned to MVNPS. Kenny wrote to Helen Daniels thanking her for some archaeological publications she had given him and mentioned that he had added the copies to the Mesa Verde library. He also mentioned that Don Watson and Miss Betty Yelm, the museum technicians and librarians, were sending along their thanks as well.[47]

MILDRED SKINNER

Kenny first met the love of his life, Mildred Skinner, in Durango when he was giving an archaeology slide lecture. She had been invited to lunch at Helen's and Kenny was also Helen's guest and they got acquainted there. Then she and Helen went to Mesa Verde soon after for another lecture and "Kenny was surprised to see us." [48] It certainly appeared that Helen saw herself as a match-maker between Kenny and Mildred. At the time, Mildred was living in Mancos teaching third grade in the old school and also taught music to all grades. Mildred recalled staying at a room and board in 1937 to the end of the year with an [unidentified person] who accompanied her in taking a horse and surrey to Mesa Verde and had to camp out and come home the next day. She moved to the Mancos Hotel in January 1938 where "other gals were there" and they would all go to "Saturday night dances in the old places on S. Main, then to ___ [?]" [49] She also mentioned that Kenny came down from Mesa Verde to the dances. A budding romance was in the making.

She worked two summers for Café D&RG-32 [at the old Mancos Hotel] and met Ansel in 1939. She got to know Kenny better as he was still working with the CCC on construction of the dioramas. "One day I was in [the] museum and K. [Kenny] took me back to see how the frame for Dioramas was done. Remember heavy beams & frame for back panel." [50] Mildred also wrote that she was fed up teaching and doing the music in Mancos and in September she ended up swapping teaching jobs with an unspecified teacher at Mesa Verde. Regardless of how the swap worked, she wound up teaching at Mesa Verde School from 1939 to 1942. Both Don and Doug suggested it was part of a scheme on Kenny's part to get Mildred to move up to Mesa Verde National Park.[51]

Mildred Skinner and Kenneth Ross were married in Aztec, New Mexico February 10, 1940, but Mildred was hardly a newcomer to the Four Corners. The Skinner family had moved from Kirksville, Missouri to Montrose, Colorado when Mildred was a little girl; she graduated high school in Montrose and attended Western State College in Gunnison, Colorado gaining a Teaching Degree. She married Henry Ziegler in 1928 and had one son, Charles, born on July 4, 1929. Her husband (Ziegler) was killed in an auto crash in Illinois in 1932. She taught school at Ridgeway, then at Red Mesa, then Florida River School east of Durango. At some period during the 1930s, Mildred's parents moved to Durango and bought a house on Third Ave. and she moved in with them as she had young Charles to consider his well-being. It was during that time that she befriended Helen Sloan Daniels. Mildred had just moved to Mancos in 1937 following another teaching job when she met Kenny.[52]

From May, 1937 to October, 1939 Kenny was employed by a combination of the USNPS and the CCC at Mesa Verde with his salary ranging from $840 to $1200/annum with duties listed as "Junior assistant to technician" with duties that included: educational guide, lecturer, maintaining exhibits, and archaeological and ethnological research.[53]

Mildred was born in 1906 in Kirksville, Missouri to Calvin Darius Skinner and Grace Fleming Skinner. Mildred had one older sister named Gladys. Her small hometown of Kirksville located in the northeastern corner of Missouri was somewhat famous for a Civil War battle. The town got its name from Jesse Kirk, the first postmaster who shared a turkey and whiskey dinner with surveyors working in the area in 1841 on a forty-acre site that became incorporated in 1857. The Civil War battle of Kirksville August 6-9, 1862 was fought and nearly two hundred men were killed; the Union army won the battle.[54]

Mildred remained a single parent until she met Kenny. Charles went to elementary school in Mancos and when Mildred moved to Mesa Verde, so did young Charles. Mildred recalled the first Christmas she and Kenny shared after they were married (Figure 3.16). They had invited her parents to come up to their home at Mesa Verde, but on Christmas Eve a snowstorm blew in with wind blowing snowdrifts across the mesa. Her folks called and said the road was closed but would be open soon.

> We told them to go back home & we would come on over to Dgo [Durango]. I had gotten turkey, pie etc. ready to cook. Packed up & took off [and] got to Far View, Road icy – did a 360, K & I drove back to C camp, at lunch, & learned that Highway Dept. was going to plow road open. We could follow. New rotary snow blower – glad to try it out.[55]

But they never made it off the mesa and returned to C camp and "ate brunch, Kenny & Me." [56]

Figure 3.16 Mildred and Kenny Ross, Christmas, 1941. (K. Ross collection)

AIRPLANES AND INDIANS

A story handed down from Kenny to his boys Don and Doug was insightful as to how Park Service employees found ways to enjoy their days off. Apparently, Kenny contacted his old friend Dallas Fullerton who lived in Montrose and was a pilot and had his own airplane. This was also about the time Kenny became interested in learning to fly, although he never acquired enough hours to pilot his own plane. One way or the other, Kenny and two other park employees decided to fly with Dallas on a sight-seeing trip over to Monument Valley and the plane ran low on fuel as it was bucking a westerly wind the whole way and they were forced to find an emergency landing.

Most pilots of that era were what would these days be considered *bush pilots* and could land a plane just about anywhere they could find a flat piece of ground. But that is where the story became garbled through the decades as Doug Ross reminisced (Figures 3.17 to 3.20):

> As I remember my Dad's story, he and Dallas Fullerton, a friend from the area, used to take Dallas' old Stearman (I think it was) airplane up and cruise around the Four Corners, and on this journey flew to the San Juan [river] and over Monument Valley. Dallas spent his career as a crop duster, and was fairly famous around the area, flying out of Montrose-Delta area. The plane landed near Gouldings Trading Post where they knew they could get some gas. They weren't out of fuel, but didn't have enough to get back to anywhere. They put the plane down near a road, pushed it off to the flats and wandered over the countryside to Gouldings where they acquired gas, and probably hitched a ride back and when they got there, the place was crawling with curious and amazed locals who had seen airplanes but never been up close to one. Dad took a bunch of photos, or Dallas did...I was never sure who took the photos, but I'd guess Kenny because he was pretty much into photo workings at that time. They did a little tour for the dazzled and curious folks, let em climb into the plane by turns and so forth, and then flew off into the setting sun. Funny part of Kenny's story was that when they set the plane down, there wasn't a soul in sight and when they got back there were folks all over the place. I kind of think that this was before the Gouldings air strip was built... so there probably wasn't a strip there, or not in the present location. Can't think of any other reason they put the plane there if there was a strip at Gouldings, but I definitely remember Kenny said they had a trek to get gas. [57]

Great story I thought, but when I saw the photos the geologist in me recognized that it wasn't anywhere near Gouldings – the strata in the background was wrong. I sent copies of the photos to Bill Dickinson and he concurred that the background where that event took place looked more like thin-bedded strata more typical in the Chinle or Moenkopi section and not the massive sandstone as exposed in and around Gouldings (the De Chelly Sandstone; see Appendix II: Stratigraphic Column). Bill suggested,

> The only place I can think of anywhere near Gouldings (if that is where they got gas) that they could land on a road, push off onto a nearby flat, and then get a photo of a Chinle cliff is that little footstool mesa of Tyende Mesa from which Owl Rock rises just southwest of Agathla Peak (see Cooley et al 1957 USGS PP 521-A, Plate 1, Sheet 3). If they landed west of rather than south of Agathla (closer to Gouldings though still a long trek off), they could have gotten a photo (looking southward to the west of Owl Rock) that would not have Wingate or Navajo in the background. The whitish ledges near the top of the cliff would be Owl Rock Member and the rest Petrified Forest Member. For the life of me I cannot exactly match the combination of clifflets and talus cones shown in the photo on Google Earth but am not sure how closely you can match stuff like that on Google imagery anyway. Run down there some day in your spare time and see if you can duplicate their panorama? [58]

So I did. On Saturday, June 20, 2015 Don Ross accompanied me and we drove over to Monument Valley to attempt to relocate the photos of the 1938 plane emergency landing. I think we got within a hundred yards or so of the plane in the old photos. I also took a number of photos and sent some key ones to Bill along with my conclusions about the emergency landing: the Airplane was not a Stearman, but a Stinson SM 7 or SM-8 Junior (SM-2 only had 110 horse power [HP]; SM-7 had 165 HP and SM-8 had 225 HP). Dallas Fullerton, the pilot, lived in Montrose and the fact that he had three adult passengers suggested that he had a bigger engine than 110 HP to get airborne. When crop dusting or just flying out of anywhere on the Colorado Plateau with average elevation of 5,500 ft above sea level, and runways and bush pilot air strips weren't very long – added HP was necessary.[59]

The plane landed almost due west of present day U.S. Highway 163 at roughly mile post (MP) 401, at or very near a home site with a pickup truck on the south side. The gasoline was most probably provided by the old Wetherill Trading Post in Kayenta rather than Gouldings Trading Post. And Bill's geology was spot-on correct, i.e., Owl Rock Member and Petrified Forest Member of Chinle Formation. For lack of a name, I proclaimed that we should call this small mesa the *Owl Rock Mesita* (Bill liked my name "mesita") and the cliff to far south in the photos are slopes of Segeke Butte.

The aerial photo taken by Thorn Mayes in 1933 is a view of Agathla Peak and Owl Rock (Figure 3.21); note the salt flats in lower right corner of photo which is just about where the 1938 MVNPS sightseeing group made their emergency landing. Also note the faint trace of a trail crossing the flats – that would later become Route 47 and then later, when paved, it became U.S. Highway 163. The airplane could not have landed east of the present day highway, as Tyende Mesa definitely would have been in view with massive Wingate Sandstone and would have shown up in the 1938 photos.

Doug Ross commented further:

> I met him [Dallas Fullerton] once or twice after he was getting close to retiring and he and his wife were living in Telluride. I was there for the summer of '66 and Dad had told me I ought to look Dallas up, even though he hadn't seen him in many years. [He] said I should just go over to his house and introduce myself. So I did. Knocked on a door and this older gentleman came to the door, looked at me and said "Come on in..." I hadn't had a chance to tell him who I was, but here he almost yanks me in the door, tells me to have a seat, excuses himself to another room and left me there, wondering "What the hell....?" In a couple of minutes this old guy comes back with a large album of some sort, sits down and starts leafing through it, and exclaims "I knew it....(or something like that)!
>
> He turns this album around and there's a picture of two young guys standing beside an airplane. Then Dallas said, "You think I don't know who you are? Ha!" It's a photo of Kenny and Dallas standing beside an aircraft when they looked to be in their early 30's maybe. The scary part was the image of Kenny. My god, I thought I was looking at myself! I had never realized just how much I looked like Kenny (at least at certain times of my life) until I saw that photo. So Dallas and I had this great afternoon yapping away about his good old days and flying with Kenny, yada-yada. Turns out Dallas had had 12 (count 'em, twelve, XII !!) airplane wrecks in his career of dumping chemicals on food crops. They do fly low and slow. He walked away from them all, mostly unscathed. His wife told me that she had pretty much convinced him to give it up, but he was still flying when I met him. He was an amazing guy.
>
> Dallas called Don a few years back, had a long conversation after he figured out for sure he was talking to Kenny's kid. I may be wrong, but I think Don may have driven to Montrose to visit him, but I'm not sure of that. Dallas and the old man flew together quite a bit during that time, and interestingly enough, did not auger a plane into the ground.[60]

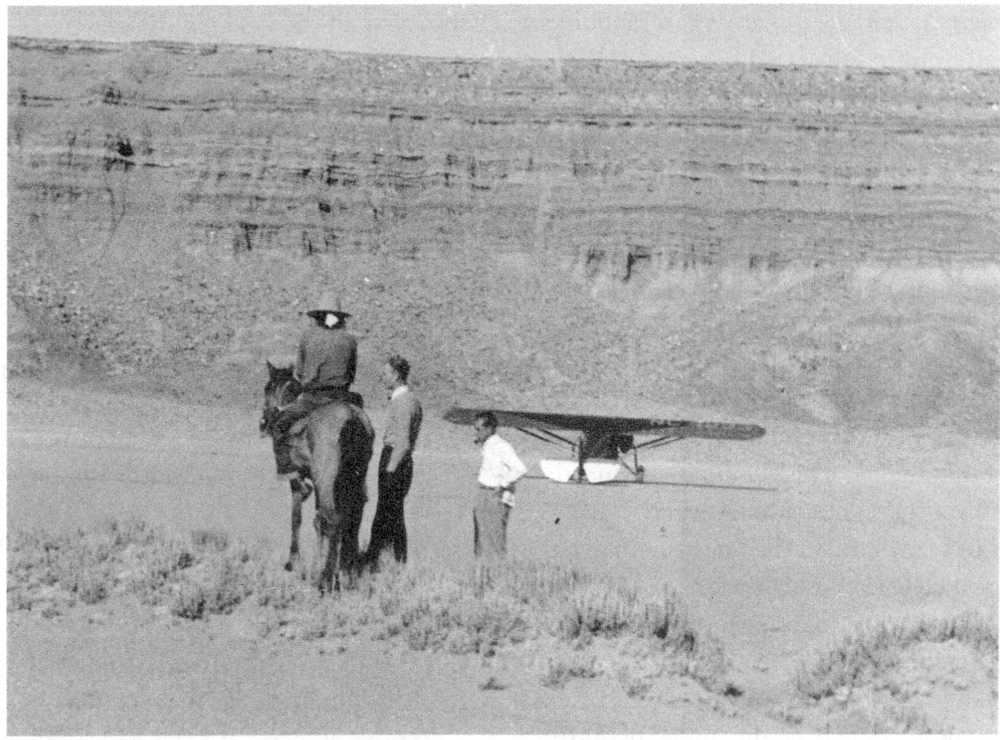

Figure 3.17 Mesa Verde National Park Ranger, Ted Casey, explained the situation of emergency landing to Navajo man on horse, 1938. (K. Ross collection)

Figure 3.18 the airplane attracted lots of locals; note that the Navajo Dine' sit in shade of airplane wing while Bilagáana stand in sun. (K. Ross collection)

Figure 3.19 Kenny Ross (kneeling) explains aircraft to onlookers. (K. Ross collection)

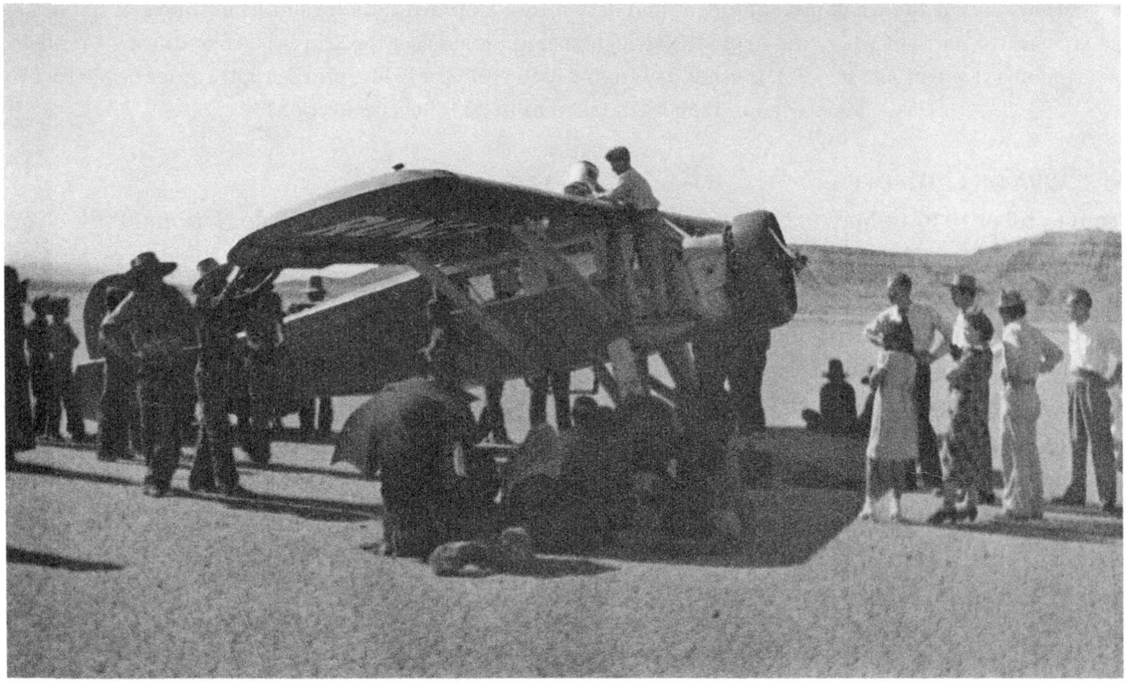

Figure 3.20 Pilot Dallas Fullerton refuels the Stinson airplane as curious Navajo folks watch. (K. Ross collection)

Figure 3.21 aerial view to northeast of Monument Valley; Agathla Peak is the prominent dark monolith in center view and Owl Rock is the small promontory at mid-left sitting atop Owl Rock mesita. The white salt flat in lower right view is just north of where the 1938 MVNPS sightseeing rangers set the Stinson airplane down as shown in previous photos (Figures 3.17 to 3.20). Present day Highway 163 MP 401 is just off the right corner of photo. (Thorn Mayes photograph #534 taken in 1933; K. Ross collection)

MVNPS, WPA OR LAID-OFF

From October 1939 to May 1940 Kenny worked at Mesa Verde National Park under the WPA at a salary of $820/annum with work duties including senior research worker doing general research in history and natural sciences and constructing classic pueblo diorama exhibits. Then in May 1940 he was back as a USNPS employee at Mesa Verde as a Park Ranger-naturalist and also worked as a guide and did contact work, lectures, research, etc., but by October 1940 he was once again "not gainfully employed at Mesa Verde." [61] During this period he focused more on ethnic studies in New Mexican pueblos and made photographic records of Pueblo pottery being made and provided free lectures to schools on ancient life in Mesa Verde National Park. From March 1940 to May 1941 he filled in as an emergency telephone switchboard operator when he was once again hired back by the NPS at Mesa Verde as a Ranger-Naturalist at $1260/annum through October 1941 when he was laid off again and was on his own again until May 1942. During this period he traveled to Los Angeles, California (visiting his mother and his sister, Gail) and scheduled some lectures at area schools but "most are cancelled due to war conditions." [62]

Letters were written between Kenny and Mildred. He also studied southern California museum methods and made a few hundred dollars. Mildred wrote, "K spent the winter of

'41-'42 in L.A. (parked cars) Chuck, Charley [Kenny's father] & I drove out to LA for Xmas. Military check at Cal. Border. Come home in a blizzard." [63] Mildred and Kenny formally adopted Chuck in 1942 when he was thirteen years old. He attended Mancos public schools until his junior year in high school when he attended the Wasatch Academy in Mt. Pleasant, Utah. That was the same boarding school that Joan Nevills and Roger Hall attended. Don Ross said it must have been a school that park employees sent their kids. Chuck entered college at the University of Colorado in Boulder in 1946.[64]

In May 1942 Kenny was rehired by the NPS at Mesa Verde at a pay raise of $1800/annum as Park Ranger-Naturalist. He was also designated as the "Acting Assistant Park Naturalist" and head of museum interpretive staff since Don Watson had been drafted by the U.S. Army and Kenny was appointed to take his place. Kenny's job involved general direction and supervision of the park's interpretive program, including museum exhibits and operations, training temporary ranger-naturalists, guided ruins trips, evening campfire lectures, research, and related reports, correspondence, etc." [65] Several other park employees were drafted that left Mesa Verde short of rangers and maintenance workers. Mildred said they "moved out of 'Futility area' and stayed a short time in old cabin, 'original Park *his squatters*'." [66] [Emphasis mine; an obvious insider play on words] She also noted that they "moved to the big stone house overlooking HQ parking lot [Figure 3.22]. Lived there til Sept 1945." [67] Mildred and Kenny's first child, Donald Kenneth Ross was born March 01, 1944 "a special gift to Mesa Verde." [68]

Figure 3.22 Ross family home 1944-45; stone house living quarters near Chapin Mesa HQ. (G.M. Stevenson photo)

CAMPFIRE TALKS

One of Kenny's favorite stories he told his boys and Mildred regarded campfire talks promoted by Jess Nusbaum. Jess was credited for having park rangers give fireside lectures to visitors in the evenings. Due to the war going on, park rangers were down to a minimum, so Jess had volunteered to give an evening campfire lecture.

Locals and visitors who knew anything about Mesa Verde knew that a talk by Superintendent Jesse Nusbaum was one to not miss, so that particular evening a bunch of folks had gathered at the fire ring near Headquarters and it was time for the talk, but Jess was nowhere to be found. Kenny said he was there and finally noticed Jess way off in the back near some trees motioning him to come over. When Kenny got there, Jess showed him his burned pant leg that went half-way up to the knee. Apparently, Jess had thrown a smoldering cigarette butt into a trash can and the paper caught fire and when Jess tried to stomp the fire out his wool pant leg caught fire.

Now, Jess was a stickler for all Rangers to dress in proper ranger uniforms at *all times* when dealing with the public, and here he was looking less than presentable. Of course, Kenny was cracking up laughing, but then Jess, who was nearly a foot taller than Kenny wanted to trade pants with Kenny so he could go out and give his talk. So that's what they did – they traded pants. Jess had to have worn them as low on his hip as possible without looking like a country bumpkin, but he went ahead and gave his talk and when it was over he and Kenny traded back into their own pants. Kenny loved to tell that story on Jess and always got a big laugh from those who listened.[69]

In the January 1944 job application for "Assistant Park Naturalist," Kenny's present position was then "Acting Park Naturalist" with an annual salary of $2600. His duties and responsibilities included "General supervision of interpretive program at Mesa Verde National Park, including museum exhibits and operations, training temporary ranger-naturalists, guided trips, evening campfire program, lectures, research, and related reports, correspondence, etc." [70] He also listed his abilities in the use of motion picture and still projectors, dark room equipment and still cameras.

By 1944 he also had a rather impressive list of references, including: Jesse Nusbaum, Superintendent of Mesa Verde N.P.; Lt. Don C. Watson, U.S. Army Engineer; Paul R. Franke, Superintendent of Grand Teton N.P.; Carl E. Lehnert, Assistant Superintendent at Mesa Verde N.P.; and R.D. Moorhead, Assistant to the Attorney General of Texas.[71]

LOS ALAMOS SCIENTISTS

Kenny and Mildred also got to know some very special people during the war years at the park – the scientists from Los Alamos, New Mexico who were developing the bomb that would end World War II, and specifically got to know Enrico Fermi (1901-1954) the Italian physicist who has been credited to have created the world's first nuclear reactor.

Fermi and his Jewish wife, Laura, had escaped from Italy in 1938 and emigrated to the U.S. where Enrico served under J. Robert Oppenheimer on the Manhattan Project. He received numerous awards in recognition of his achievements in nuclear physics including the Nobel Prize for Physics in 1938. Fermi was noted for his attention to detail, but at the same time simplicity itself. He was known to always manage to find the simplest and most direct approach, with the minimum of complication.

The following note was Mildred's written account of what she recalled from those days, when the Los Alamos men would come to Mesa Verde just to get away from the highly stressful work – the top secret work that would forever change the face of modern mankind:

During World War Two, in 1944 the security at Mesa Verde was increased, to protect both the visitors and park personnel. Because of this and because of its remoteness from "civilization", the Park Service and Federal military dep't arranged for the lab or other employees at Los Alamos Laboratory in New Mexico to visit Mesa Verde on days off. Park employees were aware that something very secret (and important) was going on at the Lab.

The Lab workers usually spent two or three days, security helped isolate them from other Park visitors by taking them to the ruins and scenic spots in rather private tours. We all were warned not to ask the Lab people any questions about Los Alamos.

In August 1944, Jesse Nusbaum, Park Superintendent, was driving at night back from a trip to Park Service Region 3 in Santa Fe. In the early morning as he neared the Colo state line, he was startled by a blinding light to the south and strong earth-shaking & noise of the area he was in. When he reached home a short time later, his description of the explosion was graphic, to say the least! [72]

Enrico Fermi, director of the work at Sandia, came up for an occasional "break", He spent a lot of time in the Museum, and so he & Kenny got to be friends. Enrico was very aware of the (archaeology of the southwest). Whenever he could break away from the Museum Ken took Enrico out to many of the untouched sites of ancient occupation, and to some scenic spots - heads of the canyons, tree-covered areas, and wherever.

Every evening Ken told of the places they went to, what they talked about, so I had a pretty good picture of the visitor. Because of regulations, Ken couldn't bring Enrico to our house. (Security?) I may have met him at the museum - I don't recall.

Winter passed by, the Park was again open in 1945. Fewer Los Alamos guests came; it appeared. In August, however, they did increase a bit.

How well I remember the second week, and that fateful day, Aug. 7! Mid-afternoon Ken called me with news on the radio announced the drop of the A-Bomb on Japan's Hiroshima and Nagasaki. When Ken came home, he was not his usual self. Later he told me why.

Enrico had been at Mesa Verde a few days. When the news broke, Ken found the man standing alone, gazing across the open wildland across from the Museum. He said he knew what was about to happen, & got away from Los Alamos, where the A-Bomb was developed.

I will never forget his comment. (I may not be 100% accurate) Enrico turned to Ken and said,

"Dropping (or making) the Atomic Bomb is the biggest mistake the US ever made!" [73] [Emphasis mine]

∞ ∞ ∞

"We do not believe any group of men adequate enough or wise enough to operate without scrutiny or without criticism. We know that the only way to avoid error is to detect it, that the only way to detect it is to be free to inquire. We know that in secrecy error undetected will flourish and subvert."

J Robert Oppenheimer

∞ ∞ ∞

END OF WORLD WAR II

When World War II officially came to an end and Japan and Germany had both surrendered, Kenny was notified by letter dated December 27, 1945 that he had thirty days' notice that his current position at Mesa Verde as "Acting Park Naturalist, at $3,200 per annum" was coming to an end. Since he had been hired to replace Donald C. Watson who was returning to work from his military furlough, Kenny had to give up his position as "Acting Park Naturalist." [74]

Kenny had been offered a job at Big Bend National Park in Texas, but neither he nor Mildred wanted to move away from the Four Corners and Mancos specifically. Besides, Mildred was pregnant with Doug. Mildred said "K. had been transferred to Rio Grande-Jefas, 60 miles to nearest town. I was pregnant with Doug & it was too risky to chance it." [75] So on January 15, 1946 Kenny wrote a short letter in reply stating he had "decided to enter private business in Cortez, Colorado. My last day of active duty will be

January 16, 1946." [76] And with that twenty-four hour notice of resignation Kenneth Irving Ross was a 100% civilian, never to go back to work for another governmental agency (Figure 3.23).

But Kenny Ross didn't lose track of the many professional acquaintances he had made in the archaeological world and continued to follow the work by his close friends Earl & Anne Morris who were working sites near Durango to La Plata River to Aztec National Monument. Other archaeological friends included: Paul S. Martin at Lowry, Ernest Antevs at Mesa Verde, the Gladwyns & Deric O'Bryan [Jesse Nusbaum's stepson] at Gila Pueblo, Neil Judd, Jean Pinckley [Don Ross's godmother; Don Watson was his godfather], Al Lancaster at Alkali Ridge [good friends, he and wife Alice Lancaster lived near Pleasant View], and many others.

He, Mildred and young Donald traveled to California and Charles [Chuck] stayed with Mildred's folks in Durango.[77] They returned to Mancos after several months visit and Mildred gave birth to their second son, Douglas Evan Ross on June 16, 1946. Doug recalled being told that, "Right after I was born the family lived for the first couple of months of my life in the stone mansion in Mancos which the Hall family owned but weren't living in at the time. Like I said, Dad and Ansel were pretty tight as much as poor people can be buds with the more affluent. By 1948 the Ross family moved into the old house my mom's folks owned there in Mancos (Calvin Skinner's House; 535 Grand Ave.) and that was the original 'Headquarters' for all of the stuff to follow." [78] That was the home for all the Ross's and where Kenny & Mildred lived to their dying days.

Figure 3.23 Ranger Kenny Ross (on wall) talking to visitors at Mesa Verde National Park. (K. Ross collection)

ROSS PHOTO STUDIOS

Kenny tried to make a go out of his new photographic studio in Cortez, but he wasn't making much money. On April 29, 1946 in a letter sent on Explorers Camp letterhead to "Mr. Kenneth Ross, Ross Studios" in Cortez, Colorado, Ansel Hall wrote a rather curious note, "I planned to get over to see you [Kenny] before shoving off to Denver. I am *extremely eager* to hear about *the outcome of your negotiations*, as I want to make an announcement of our plans pretty soon to the boys who are going to take part in the work." [Emphasis mine] He then asked for Kenny to call his secretary, Muriel Friend, in Mancos with his decision and she would forward to him and that he would be back in Mancos on the 5th of May.[79]

On May 7, 1946 Kenny received a long friendly and newsy letter from his mentor and friend, Jess Nusbaum. The letter was cordial, and apologetic in having not gotten back sooner. "So here are my greetings to Mildred and you, and the children, and hoping all has been going well for you." [80] Jess then asked about how the photo business was progressing. Kenny had opened "Ross Photographic Studios" in Cortez, but the family home was still in Mancos which required Kenny to drive back and forth every day on roads not quite up to today's standards. And his studio was upstairs on the second floor and Jess made mention of that fact and that Kenny would have a much better chance of making a go of his new business if it were at street level. Jess then mentioned how crowded Santa Fe had become after the war was over and how prices had skyrocketed for a space to live. He also made comment of "what a mob of people there will be in Mesa Verde this year." [81]

Nusbaum provided the following noteworthy thoughts regarding Ansel Hall:

> Suppose Ansel is all wound up tight getting ready for the season, with emphasis first on the Boys Camp, and secondly on Mesa Verde Co. I have recently received a copy of his announcement – it appears to be exactly the same announcement that he rushed thru – just a proof he said, at Denver as he returned from Chicago meeting about the turn of the year. Archeology was particularly featured, and exploring ruins and cliff dwellings etc. also excavation. We discussed it that time – with certain apprehension as to its implications to S.W. ruins and resources – and he said it was purely preliminary- subject to change by his new camp manager whenever he arrived, - but I cant note any change. As far as I can see, unless it is rigidly controlled as to archeology, and it was anything "but" last season, it will significantly stimulate, if it doesn't condone, outright pot-hunting. As is his custom, he plans without reference to others, then when it is too late to change arrangements, he confers to get your opinion on what is already fixed and not subject to change.
>
> His excuse to others is that I am so biased, sometimes he includes other university personnel, that he cant even talk to me or us about his planning, etc. Fact of the matter is that he [is] so concerned in having things his way, that he goes ahead secretly, completes the whole plan, and ties it up in ribbons before he even mentions it – for fear that some change will be suggested or recommended. He's a super salesman and I don't mean maybe – and promoting an enterprise and managing it are horses of different color with him. He has yet to promote a self-managing enterprise.
>
> Traffic will snow him under this year – as he hasn't the plant and equipment to handle what may be expected, even if he does get competent help. But he will have no monopoly on this. It will be common over the west. Don [Watson] will catch hell this season, no fooling. As it will be worse than 1941 when the same number of interpretive personnel were working longer hours per week. Then he had additional C.C.C. and relief help to assist – and that's off for 1946. Proportionately, the load in 1946 will probably not exceed that which you and Jean [Pinckley] carried in 1945, with occasional help from others – a responsibility that you carried so commendably, and to the mutual satisfaction of all concerned, visitors and others. As I look back, I don't see how we got by, but we did, and made

> friends in the doing – and that's a record I'm proud of. When Ansel matches the type of service we have rendered, under war time conditions, I'll hire the band at my expense to serenade him.
>
> Do you know who he is planning on for his archeological leader this year – hope its not last years wash-out, or the crusty Colonel [MacNab], - - and what his archeological planning is. His announcement would include anything from a-to-etc., so that holds no meaning to me.[82]

Jess Nusbaum apologized for his rotten typing but passed along kindly thoughts to Kenny and wished him well in his new "photo biz" and invited Kenny and Mildred to come and visit if and when they got a chance to do so. He signed off "All the best to the Rosses from the old man of Mesa Verde." [83] It was obvious that Jesse Nusbaum and Ansel Hall did not see eye-to-eye on much of anything regarding Ansel's use of his concession at Mesa Verde National Park to host a camp for boys. Jesse was very protective of the park resources and did not care for a haphazard approach to archaeological investigations anywhere.

That letter from Jess couldn't have been timelier. Now the inferred urgency in Ansel's letter regarding the *outcome of your negotiations* became clear. It appeared that Ansel Hall wanted a quick reply from Kenny regarding employment from his note of April 29 regarding some degree of involvement in the Explorers Camp. But then Kenny received the letter from his good friend and confidant, Jess Nusbaum, which warned him to watch his step in dealing with Ansel.

Obviously, many undocumented conversations had taken place prior to the April 29 letter and Kenny was now prepared to talk to Ansel and demonstrate his knowledge of how to improve on the camp itinerary. Ansel had big plans, and Kenny knew just the place where this new hands-on work could take place....and that place was on his father's old ranch at Cahone with all the ruins near the west end where the canyons converged! All Kenny needed to do was convince the current owner to sell the parcel of land to Ansel. The wheels were turning in Kenny's mind.

A NEW BEGINNING

By 1937 Ansel Hall saw that participation in RBMV expeditions was waning and funding was drying up, plus he became increasingly frustrated and disenchanted with the politics of a growing federal bureaucracy. Ansel finally had a good reason to resign his federal post as Chief of Interpretive Services for the National Park Service in 1938 when he was ordered to transfer to Washington, D.C. He resigned his post and bought the D&RGW Railroad[84] concession at Mesa Verde National Park and started the Mesa Verde Company. From 1906 to 1929 nine national parks and monuments had been created by the Federal Government that provided venues for concessionaires like Ansel Hall who was the first to establish such services at Mesa Verde National Park.

The RBMV expeditions soon fell apart upon his resignation. However, Hall's involvement with the RBMV from 1933 to 1938 and the interest created for the number of young men who made up the crews indicated to him that the experience had provided a natural history field school and rekindled his youthful memories of reading about boy scouting. It was within that setting of the RBMV experience that the concept of the Explorers Camp for Boys was born.[85]

For two years Ansel shuttled back and forth from Mancos to his California home in Berkeley and finally moved his family (wife June and children; oldest son Knowles, and daughters Merrie and Sylvia). Ansel and June had triplets (Roger, Laurel and Robin) after they moved to the Bauer House in Mancos in 1940 (Figure 3.24). During that time Ansel also went on the lecture circuit and found that there was, in fact, a real need and interest for an outdoor educational program for young men. The apparent interest led Hall to start the Explorers Camp – a summer camp for boys in 1944. By 1946 he had gathered some of his old associates including Dr. Harvey Stork of Carleton College, geologist Henry Zuidema from the University of Michigan (an early participant in the RBMV expeditions), archaeologist Dr. Arthur Woodward of the Southwest Museum, and Larry Reidenour – a forester at Colorado State University. He also attracted two graduate students studying archaeology from the University of Utah.[86]

Ansel and Kenny had gotten to know each other over an eight year period (1938-1946) and possibly earlier if the early RBMV days were included. They had ample opportunity for frequent discussions about all sorts of things related to a youth camp concept after Ansel began the Mesa Verde Company in 1938. When Kenny was temporarily laid off from his seasonal job as a Park Ranger or naturalist and paid by one of the various governmental agencies (NPS, CCC or WPA) he had worked part-time for Ansel's business at Mesa Verde. Kenny had kept a watchful eye on Ansel's start-up operations of his Explorers Camp for Boys in 1944 that based out of Mesa Verde before he resigned from the park service in 1946 and could see that he had several ideas as to how to improve upon what Ansel was trying to accomplish.

Besides, the camp for youth and tourism in general was hardly a unique idea held by Ansel. Others were setting up tourist/adventure camps after the war. In 1949, Bill Groves and his father, Forrest, founded Camp Silver Spruce for boys and girls along the Florida River northeast of Durango. The Groves family operated the camp until 1969 when the business was sold to the Colvig family and the original campground was subdivided into residential lots. The Teelawuket Boys camp and the Rancho Mesa Verde Camp (located near Allison, Colorado) continued operations from the 1920s up into the 1950s.[87]

Figure 3.24 the "historic Bauer House" in Mancos, Colorado where Ansel Hall and family resided from 1940 to the mid-1950s. (G.M. Stevenson photo)

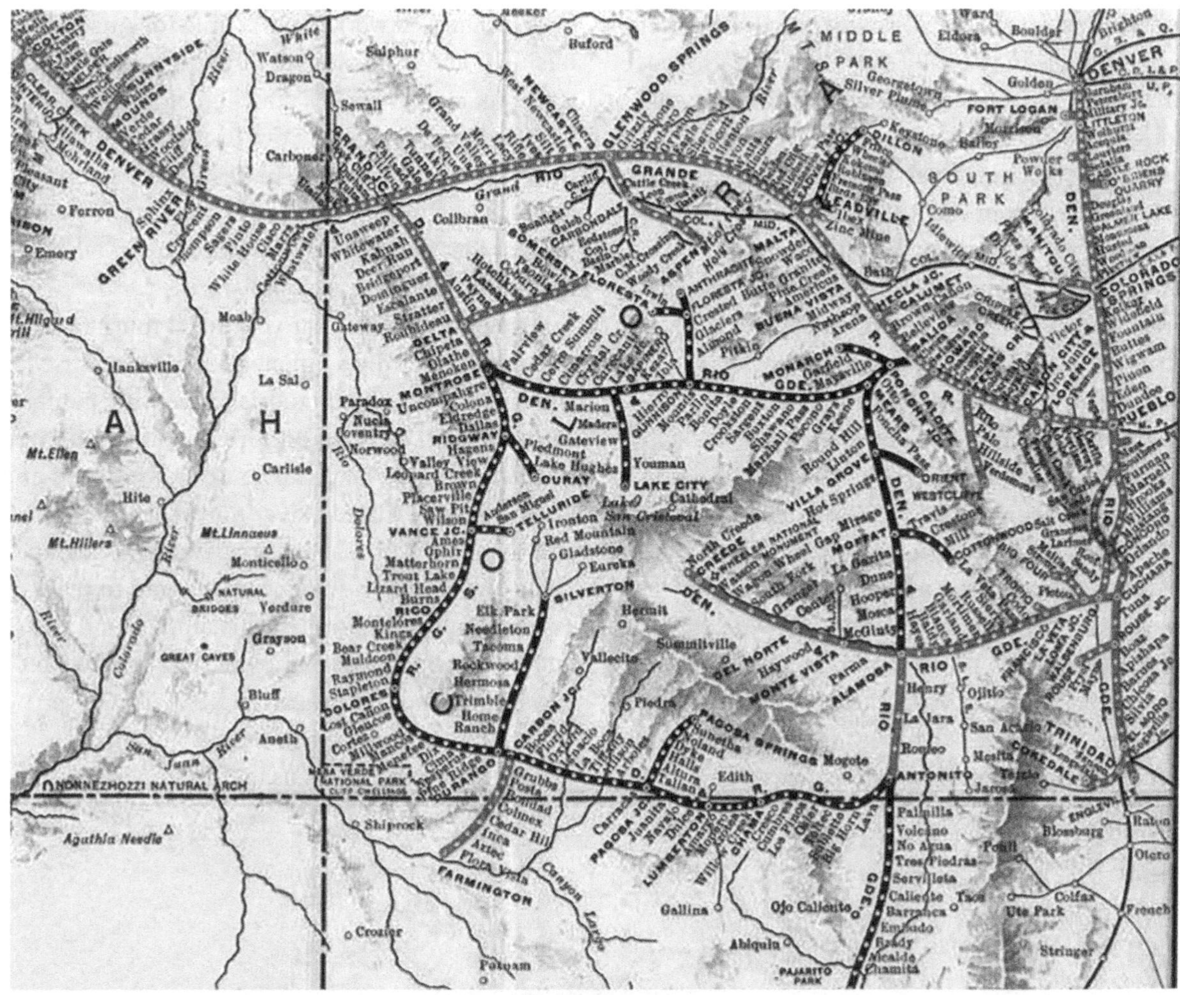

Figure 3.25 a portion of the Map of the Denver & Rio Grande Western Pacific railroad network and rail connecting points at the turn of the 19th Century; the D&RGW Railroad in southwest Colorado and northwest New Mexico was mostly Narrow Gauge (black); Standard Gauge rails (gray). Southeast Utah, northeast Arizona, and to a large degree northwest New Mexico was still best accessed by horse and wagon and even with the advent of the automobile in the 20th Century, all-purpose roads were still decades from being built.

TOURISM DISCOVERS THE FOUR CORNERS

Western politicians had endorsed tourism by traveling on railroads like the Atchison Topeka and Santa Fe Railroad (AT&SF) and the Denver & Rio Grande Western (D&RGW) Railroad that were promoted as the means to access the remote Four Corners region in the late 1800s (Figure 3.25). However, the railroads were supplanted by the invention of the production-line automobile in the early part of the 20th century.[88]

Affordable automobiles were designed for the general public and ownership mushroomed throughout the country such that, by the 1930s, the whole nature of tourism had changed. New roads suitable for autos opened up new territory for tourists. The original route over Wolf Creek Pass that had been constructed and graveled in 1916 was a major hurdle to connect the east slope of Colorado to the west. A new route was completed by the early 1930s. A major north-south route connecting Montrose to Durango and Farmington was built in the 1930s. Auto courts and motor hotels (motels) sprang up along these routes and tourists could now drive to Mesa Verde National Park in their own vehicles. The discovery and promotion of "Indian Ruins" and "Cliff Dwellings" at World fairs and in magazine articles and movie pictures encouraged tourists to come and visit these sites as well as the beautiful mountains in southwest Colorado.[89]

The better part of two decades defined by the Great Depression followed by World War II had slowed tourism to a crawl. Gasoline rationing during the war years along with railroad travel reserved for mostly military purposes had also stymied tourism. But travel by rail and auto was quickly revived after 1945 and a new more mobile society was attracted to the region. A new nostalgia for the old west attracted throngs of tourists to the region, but as historian Duane Smith said "Durango attempted to live off a legend, a legend that never actually existed." [90]

Hesperus Peak viewed from Spruce Hill, 1945 (K. Ross collection)

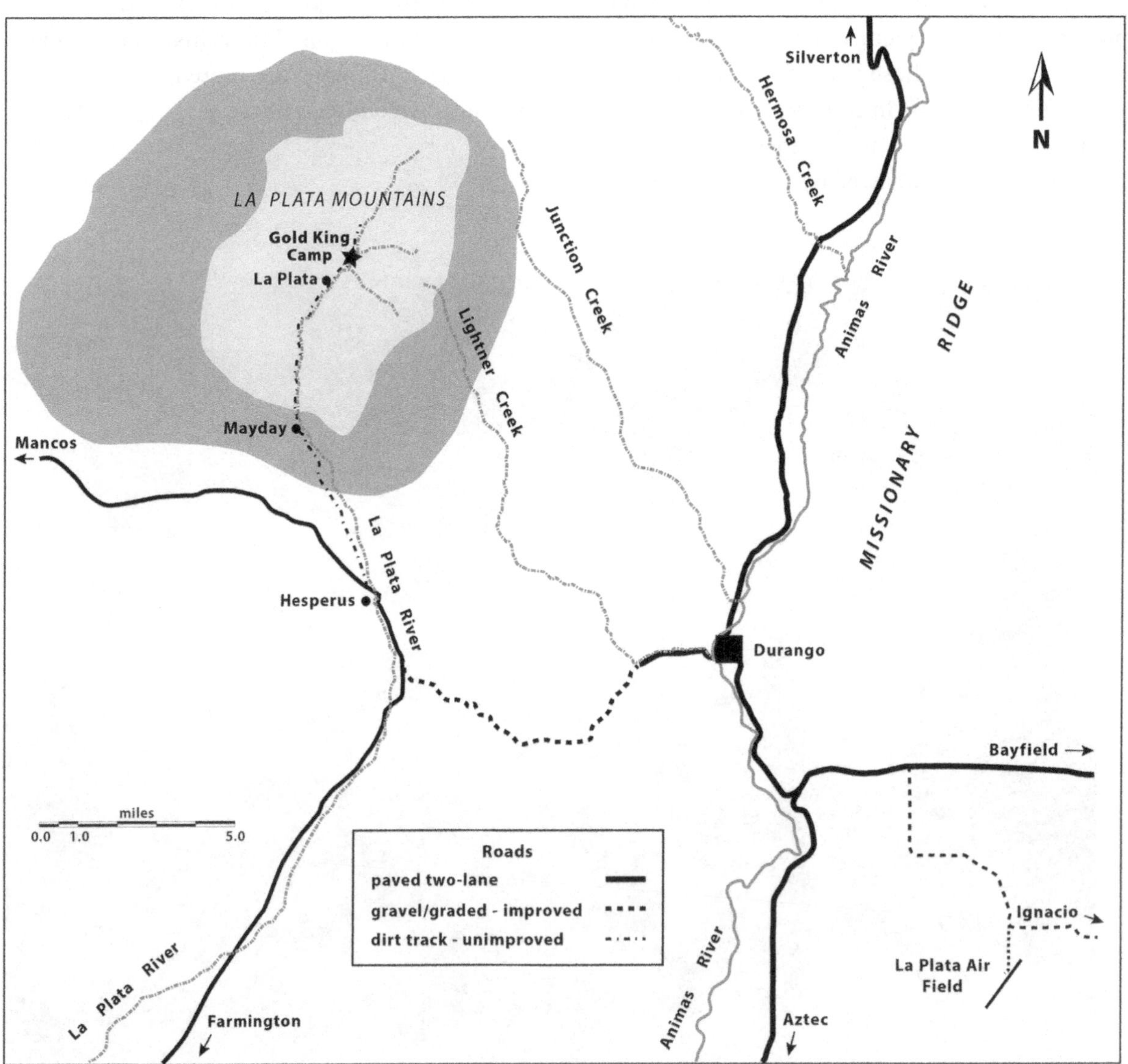

Figure 4.1 Location map of Gold King Camp and roadways as of late 1940s; paved road across Hesperus Hill not completed until early 1960s; prior route west from Durango was by way of Wildcat Canyon road. (GMS/TB original map)

4
EXPLORERS CAMP: 1944 to 1946

START-UP

In 1944 Ansel Hall along with a group of associates started the Explorers Camp for Boys. The associates were listed as "Sponsors in the Advisory Board" [1] in early brochures and were composed almost entirely of highly respected academics associated with universities (many from UC Berkeley) or big city museums and most of them had little to no knowledge of what the Four Corners region offered in regards to archaeology, geology, indigenous Native American cultures and virtually zero awareness of the incredibly rugged terrain and near absence of roads passable by automobiles. They trusted Ansel Hall explicitly with his new concept of establishing a summer camp for boys. Hall had been involved in establishing the Explorer Scouts program in the National Parks when he was at Yosemite National Park and decided to organize a summer camp for boys to participate in outdoor activities that included excavations of archaeological sites in southwestern Colorado.

The boys were all from upper middle-class families ranging from ages twelve to sixteen. World War II was ongoing and having parents send their boys to some isolated camp in the Southwest had multiple motives. Proof that the "Explorers Camp for Boys" wasn't for the general public was stated in his pamphlets: "...for a limited number of teenage boys interested in a program of scientific exploration in the Four Corners wilderness." [2] Ansel initially enlisted Dr. Harvey Stork from Carleton College (Northfield, Minnesota) as Director and Colonel A.J. MacNab, a colorful adventurer and storyteller from Hollywood, California as Camp Manager for the first year. But the scientific exploration program the first two years consisted of nothing more than an *adult-supervised sight-seeing tour* of some known archaeological sites, like Mesa Verde National Park, Canyon de Chelly and Navajo National Monuments as well as some very poorly supervised excavations of an archaeological site on the Hall-Lovett ranch near Mancos, Colorado.

Hall continued to remain the sole proprietor of the Mesa Verde Company, a concession to Mesa Verde National Park and added the Boys Camp as a new venture. He ended up running his first years' program out of some old cabins and a tent camp set up near Spruce Tree Lodge at Mesa Verde National Park much to the chagrin of Park Superintendent Jesse Nusbaum, who was "acting" superintendent during the war years (1941 – 1946). By the end of the first year's program, Jesse Nusbaum was most emphatic that Hall could not continue to run a private enterprise on national park grounds.

EARLY CAMP ACTIVITIES

Following the 1944 season, Ansel scribbled a two page note to Col. MacNab and Dr. Harvey Stork with a list of requests to consider for future camp sites and activities.[3] He noted that the primary objective for that season had been to "facilitate the field work of UC [Berkeley] paleontologist Dr. Sam Wells & Dr. Daugherty." [4] Ansel saw that the landscape of the Four Corners region warranted more than that, and noted that "there seemed to be enough 'virgin' territory in sight to occupy them for a dozen years where they could explore and map all the side canyons as far as the Colorado River." [5] He wanted a full reconnaissance for archaeological sites, and particularly the more spectacular ruins. He proposed biologic, stratigraphic, structural geology, and paleontological surveys. He thought the area would make an ideal "desert outpost" for Explorers Camp and wanted a report from MacNab and Stork about the Four Corners region. Specifically, he wanted a place from which to base the camp operations, but wasn't aware that almost all the land he was thinking about was *public land* and not for sale! He wanted to know who lived in Indian Creek Canyon northwest of Monticello and what the possibilities were of their renting houses and grazing land near Dugout Ranch. He obviously had no idea about Al Scorup and his cattle empire. In that context it would take another year or so before Kenny Ross informed Ansel Hall about the west Elk Ridge country or the presence of an archaeological site (on private land at Cahone) that might be for sale.

GOLD KING CAMP 1945

Over the winter of 1944-45 Ansel purchased the old Gold King Mill site (but not the mine and associated mineral rights) located at the confluence of Tirbircio Creek and the La Plata River (nwse Sec 3-T36N-R11W La Plata Co., CO) at an elevation of 9,400 ft. (Figure 4.1) Ansel may have purchased the Gold King property on his own or with the support of his "group of associates." The property consisted of an abandoned hard rock silver and gold mill and the associated buildings high in the La Plata Mountains above the abandoned mining towns of Parrot City and Mayday. The actual mine was located on the north bank of Lewis Creek at an elevation of 10,500 ft and "a fairly good road and an aerial tramline connects it with the Gold King mill on the La Plata River, less than 2 miles to the southwest." [6] Gold King had been shuttered since 1937 when all the developed ore had been played out and the mine and mill were shut down. Ansel moved his Explorers Camp to this new camp site up La Plata Canyon in time for the 1945 Explorers Camp to open (Figure 4.2 to Figure 4.4).[7]

> It was a great location for accessing the alpine aspects of Explorers Camp, a great spot to put a bunch of kids in surplus 16' x 16' army wall tents on platforms, the perfect spot to give kids a real sense of adventure (isolated, remote). There was absolutely no electricity past Mayday and no running potable water except for the side creeks where daily chores included filling milk cans with water and chopping ice.[8]

Dr. Harvey E. Stork's "Field Director's Report for 1944" [9] provided a lengthy discussion about "FOOD" for boys camp; types of food, perishable problems especially with milk; he came up with the idea for mobilized kitchen boxes for the Big Truck by providing 1) a cabinet designed to have a place for all kitchen gear, service dishes and 2) a provisions cabinet (mostly can goods). Pack trips needed stackable pots, pans etc; plywood collapsible tables to get food off the ground and above sand (Figures 4.5 & 4.6); water barrels lashed to trucks with fool-proof faucets, and a pressure cooker was considered "indispensable."

He also proposed "RECOGNITION" of participation and to set up some sort of reward system; pennants, pins, medals for merit including: horsemanship, camp citizenship (conduct), camping, forestry, plant life, animal life, geology, minerals, surveying, Indian lore, archaeology, etc.[10]

Dr. Stork then provided an outline that detailed the specifics for a structured camp, leadership and activities for the 1945 season. He suggested a ten week period and aimed at registering forty-two boys and having the time divided into four periods: [11]

Figure 4.2 Gold King Mill, La Plata canyon, Colorado; home base for Explorers Camp 1945-1955. (K. Ross collection)

Figure 4.3 abandoned mill buildings at Gold King Mill; base camp for Explorers Camp. (K. Ross collection)

1. One week for "indoctrination" at the Mesa Verde camp with all leaders and members attending. Set aside deluxe cabins for this week; porches for dining space. Conditioning hikes; trips to the fire lookout for instruction about fires and geography of area; lecture tours thru museums; one horse-back trip; steak fry at Soda Tipoff; talks on Nat'l Parks; illustrated talks on various subjects, giving outline of next three periods.
2. Next three weeks. Group A stays at Mesa Verde, Group B to Rancho La Plata & Group C to La Plata City.
3. Next three weeks. Groups rotate.
4. Next three weeks. Groups rotate.

Dr. Stork's summary continued where he suggested how the three programs would work. He envisioned that each camp would have fourteen boys with leaders remaining at the same post for nine weeks. The La Plata City camp needed a leader versed in minerals and geology; Rancho La Plata needed a botanist (and a competent wrangler with horses for all). The Mesa Verde leader should be an archaeologist or anthropologist who was versed in Indian lore who could conduct one week trips to "Indian Country." [12]

THE MESA VERDE PROGRAM

Stork thought that three weeks might be too long since the first week of indoctrination was to be spent there, but a hike to Rock Springs with a truck carrying the boys' duffel by road should be considered and they could camp for several nights there. He thought the trip to Indian Country should be more leisurely and should consume more time than the previous years' (1944) trips.

> Travel in the open truck with boys standing part of the time and with the air stream blowing over them tires the travelers and the trips were too rushed last year. The boys had little energy left and simply could not be interested in scenery such as the Goosenecks, Canyon de Chelly, or Betatakin. Some refused to go down into Canyon de Chelly and most of them did not go down to see the cliff dwellings at Betatakin. They just wanted to stretch out and sleep. A short trip to Lukachukai by the Shiprock plains road and back by the same route would make a better excursion than the one we took. The CCC camp site at Lukachukai affords a good camp site; the kitchen still remains, and several days could be spent there.[13]

Stork thought that the Lukachukai trip should be conducted during the second period. He thought the first period trip to Monument Valley via McElmo Canyon Road and return the same way should last ten days. The third period trip should go to the Gallup ceremonials and should include a visit to Navajo Tribal Headquarters at Window Rock. The cab-over stake-bed Ford Truck was recommended for all these trips.

RANCHO LA PLATA PROGRAM

Dr. Stork suggested that three weeks should be devoted to shorter horse-back trips, that would include camping in Bear Creek Valley, another trip to Golconda and then to Echo Basin and maybe over to Cumberland Basin. Activities would include fishing, swimming in the Reservoir, hiking and "botanizing" in the aspen woods, visiting local saw mills and timber felling. He thought a Lost Canyon day-trip or one to Dolores River Canyon should be included. Overnighter camps along Burro Trail to Sharks Tooth or at the abandoned mines above Hesperus were also recommended. [14]

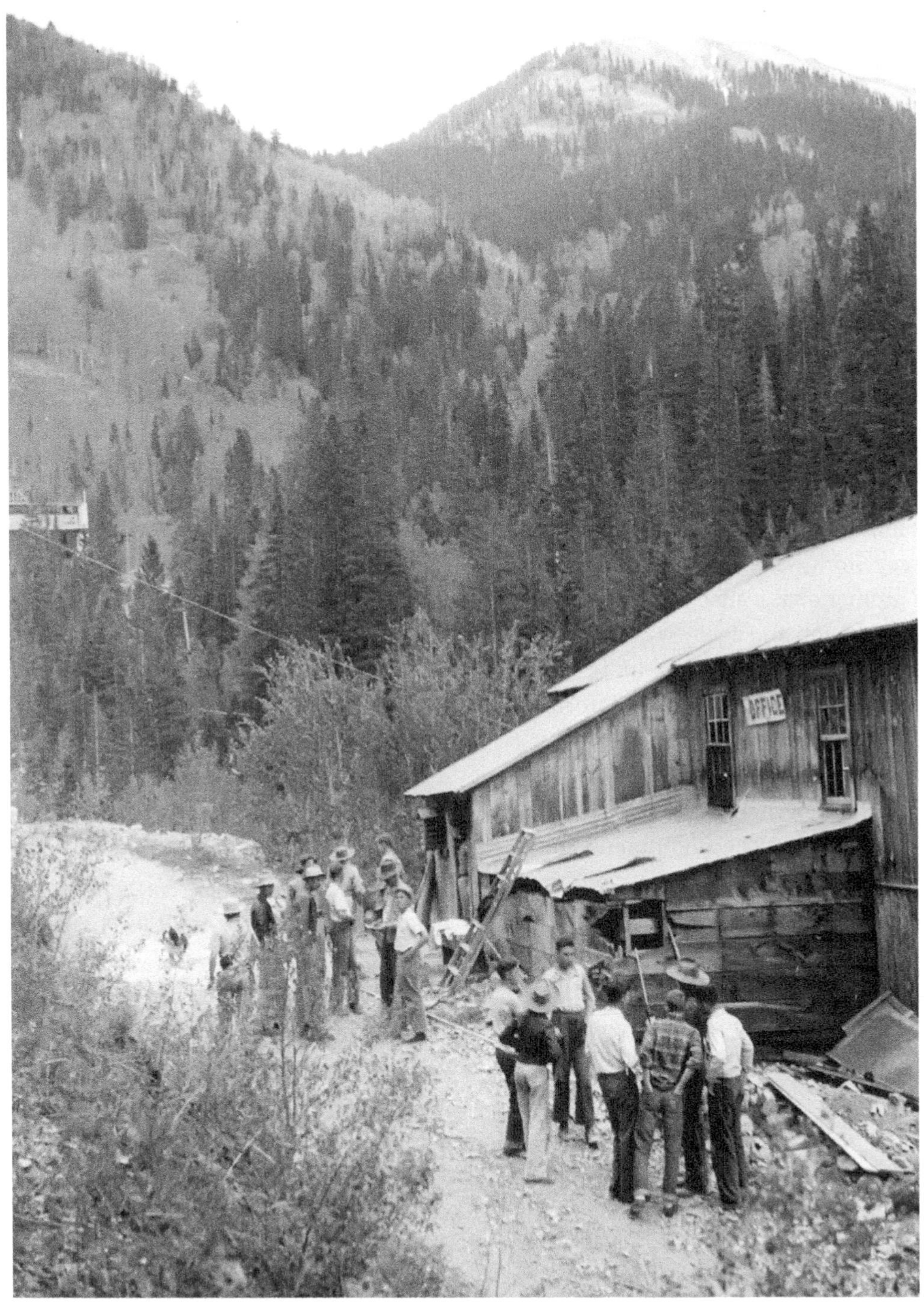

Figure 4.4 mill site building converted to bunkhouse for boys in Explorers Camp. (K. Ross collection)

LA PLATA CITY AREA PROGRAM

Stork thought a geologist and a cook should be stationed at La Plata City for nine weeks. He recommended employee Corbett or some other accomplished prospector. He suggested visiting Parrot City and Bill Little's cabin at Mayday as well as a visit to Mr. Fisherdick's ranch house to see his rock fireplace, furs and mounted trophy heads. A visit to Parrot City cemetery and the Mayday, Iowa, Gold King, Thompsons, and Bessie G. mines were also recommended. "Cumberland & Kennebec Pass, etc affords fine mountain hiking and a lot of fun poking about old mines. Collection of 'pretty rocks,' panning gold, sliding on snowfields, botanizing and collection mammals, all these afford more than enough program material for three weeks." [15]

Based on much of the recommendations made by Dr. Harvey Stork, Ansel Hall had a glossy four-page promotional leaflet printed for the 1945 Explorers Camp and again sent the brochure to a select mailing list of parents with teenage boys. On the first line it read that the information "is not for the general public." [16] He began by referring to himself as "Chief" and proceeded to explain a general itinerary for the upcoming field camp, emphasized physical conditioning and "that you are a normal boy of high school age." [17] It was left to the parents to work out how their boys would get to Durango where they would be picked up to go to Gold King Camp at the beginning of the season. The parents also had to work out their boy's return trip home from Durango at the end of camp. The most popular means were either by bus, train, or by airplane.[18] "You need not be an athlete, but you must be of good health and without organic defects." [19] Ansel went to some length in explaining what clothing and equipment to bring and provided a long list of specific items. He mentioned several books about camping including the *Boy Scouts Handbook.*

However specific dates were neither provided nor specific activities listed.

> ADVENTURE, plays an important part in the life of every explorer-indeed it is perhaps the motivating force that causes him to follow trails leading always to and beyond distant horizons. There will be plenty of adventure this summer-Indians; colorful deserts; treasure hunting, both gold and scientific; high mountains to climb; campfires at timberline; old prehistoric ruins to be excavated; and numerous other experiences. All this is high adventure But I want every one of you to be aware of something else which may seem a little less glamorous but which I consider equally important: I believe that the greatest permanent value that you will realize from your summer at the Explorers' Camp will not be the adventure, not the physical development, not the building up of pioneering skills (although each of these is important), but rather an UNDERSTANDING of the mountains, the desert, the forests, the mesa country, the Indians, the ancient people, Ours is not a "study program" – but if you are alert to your surroundings you will absorb a knowledge of these things by living in the company of leaders who have made field science their life work. [20]

Ansel Hall, Director of Explorers Camp, emphasized "leadership" that would be learned from the men who were picked for their scientific knowledge and their purported rare qualities of inspiring leadership. Adult leaders were to include: Dr. Harvey E. Stork, Botanist from Carleton College, Bayne Beauchamp, geologist and world explorer (and formerly in charge of boat trips for the RBMV seasons of 1933-35), Colonel MacNab (the "crusty" old guy that Nusbaum had mentioned in his letter of 1946 to Kenny), and of course himself, who was Chief Forester of the National Park Service. All were members of the prestigious Explorers Club of New York City. But as per usual, Ansel was nowhere to be found when it came to *direct personal* involvement with the group of boys.

Figure 4.5 Dr. Stork's camp recommendations included this concept of positioning trucks back-to-back to make an ideal mobile field kitchen. (K. Ross collection)

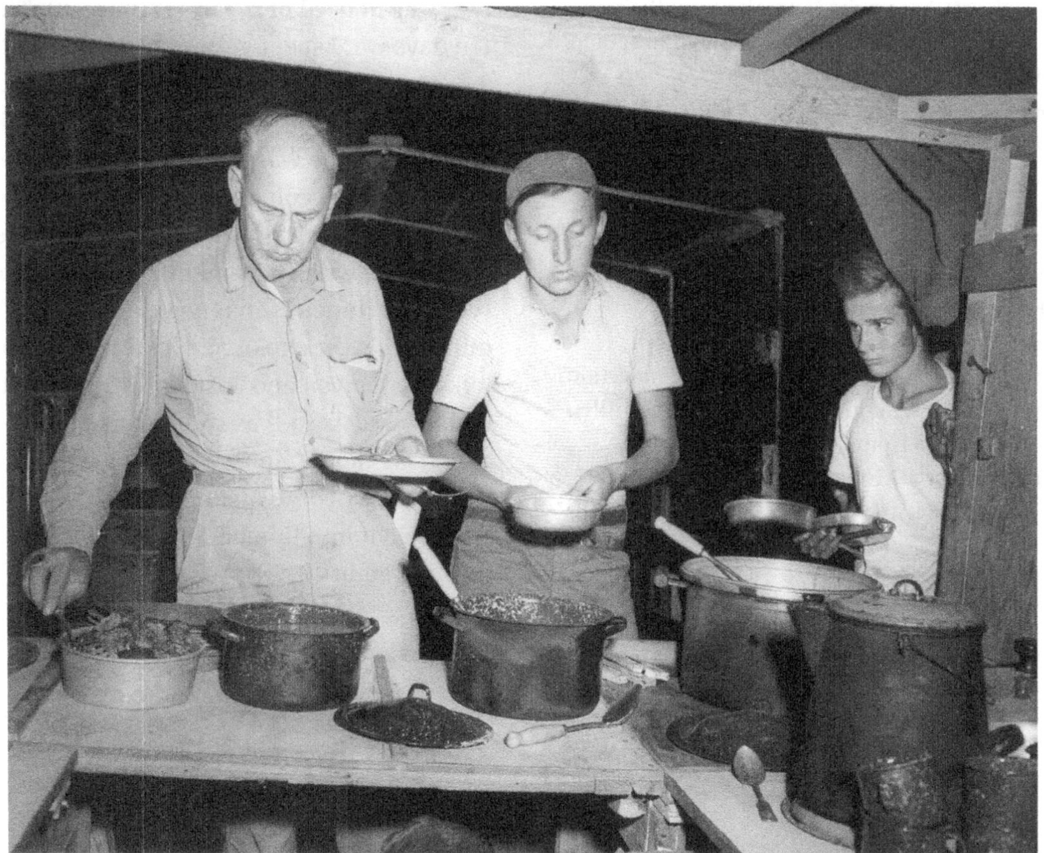

Figure 4.6 Dr. Stork and two boys help themselves to food served from inside the back-to-back truck kitchen complete with tables and cooking pots. (K. Ross collection)

ADVENTURE CAMP OR AUTO-TOURS

The following summary of activities by Camp leader Winslow M. Walker, an archaeologist from Pasadena, California documented the confusing and tortuous 1945 Explorers Camp experience.[21]

1945 CAMP LEADERS

Ansel Hall – Director (The "Chief")
Dr. Harvey E. Stork – Field Director from Carleton College, Northfield, Minnesota
Col. A.J. MacNab – (The "Colonel") from Hollywood, California; story teller, bullshitter extraordinaire
Winslow M. Walker – Archaeologist from Pasadena, California (student of Byron Cummings)
Bill Sanborn – Geologist from Altadena, California (led search for precious metals in old mines; didn't know beans about the country)
George B. Biggs, Sr. – Photographer from Verona, New Jersey (his son was one of the Explorers)
Walter Herz – Photographer from Reno, Nevada (also had a son in Explorers Camp)
Dr. Charles E. Camp – Paleontologist from U of Cal, Berkeley, California; Mesozoic vertebrates; knew nothing about area
Homer Mason – Head of Construction from Northfield, Minnesota (a Harvey Stork connection)
George Allen – Wrangler; and wife "Marge" Allen – one of the cooks from Cortez, Colorado
Laura Washburn – Nurse from Denver, Colorado (as much a cook as a nurse)
Mr. & Mrs. Frank S. Cummings from Oakland, California (parents of a boy in camp; drivers for "Indian Country" treks)
Dr. Sam Wells & Dr. Daugherty, Paleontologists @ U C, Berkeley, California (more vertebrate paleontologists without a clue about the Four Corners geology)

The 1945 Explorers Camp group photo pictured forty youths with five adult camp leaders (Figure 4.7). Winslow Walker arrived at Gold King Camp with Col. MacNab from California on June 19, 1945, and he helped get boys to camp by driving the old station wagon that was in need of repair (Figure 4.8). The next ten days were spent getting boys used to living in a deserted mining camp. They hiked and climbed mountains to 12,500 ft and a supervised rifle shooting-range was shared by some of the boys. Hikes included going into Columbus Basin and hikes to the top of Hesperus Peak. Basic geology was taught with fundamental identification of rocks and minerals in igneous rocks and the old mine digs were explored. Numerous campfire talks were given and basic forestry etiquette was emphasized as well as some basic botany in collecting mountain flowers. Horse pack trips were led by George Allen and local wrangler, Tyler Jekyll into Cumberland Basin (Figure 4.9 through Figure 4.13).

Figure 4.7 the group at Gold King, 1945 of forty Explorers Camp boys; the camp leaders consisted of one woman, Laura Washburn (seated in center) and four men: Winslow Walker (man in hat standing in second row on right), Tyler Jekyll (man with hat, left back row), Harvey Stork (man with hat, far right back row), and Col. A.J. MacNab (seated center next to Laura Washburn). (K. Ross collection)

Figure 4.8 the old Chevy woody wagon in need of repair crossing the desert. (K. Ross collection)

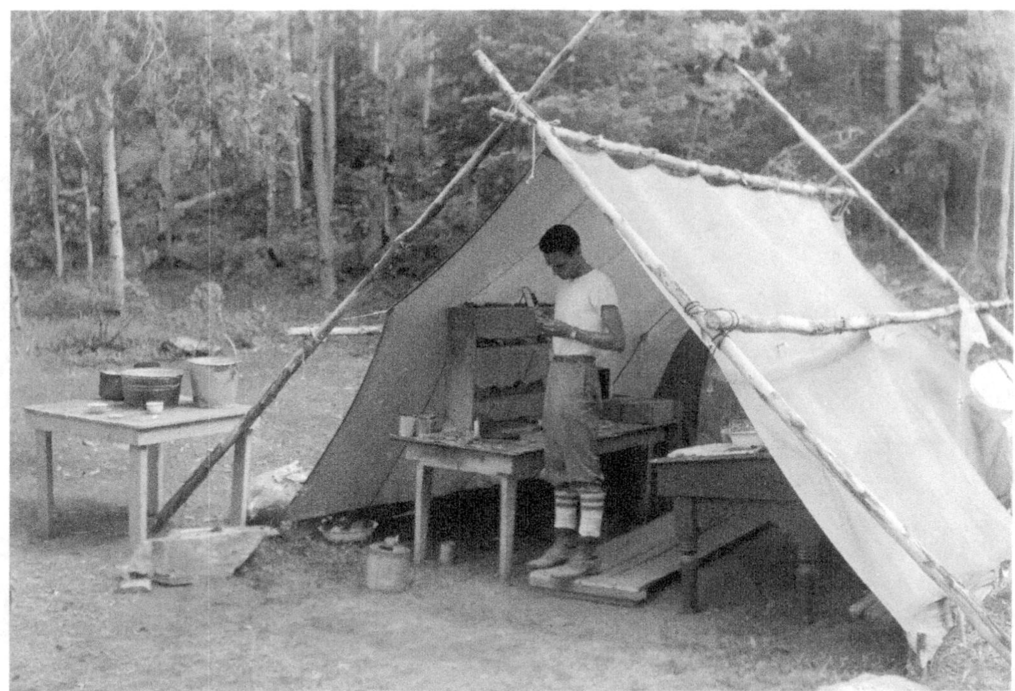

Figure 4.9 an Explorer labeling his specimen collection; the boys learned how to put up tents with aspen poles. (K. Ross collection)

Figure 4.10 prospector in La Plata City shows his mineral collection to boys. (K. Ross collection)

Figure 4.11 always time for some trout fishing. (K. Ross collection)

Figure 4.12 Forest Rangers gave the boys in Explorers Camp plenty of campfire talks and emphasized forest safety and etiquette. (K. Ross collection)

Figure 4.13 saddled up and ready to start another horse pack trip in the mountains. (K. Ross collection)

On Wednesday, July 4 Winslow Walker drove to Mesa Verde for a preliminary orientation before the first group of boys arrived. They met with Supt. Nusbaum and Park Naturalist Ross about the proposed program "which necessitated some changes." [22] On Friday, July 6 Walker brought eleven boys in C group to begin a two week program of hikes and trips to ruins at Mesa Verde.

> Sundays were usually devoted to trips down off the Mesa to some lake or pond where the boys could go swimming. After a picnic lunch they were taken into Mancos to see a movie and returned to the Mesa in time for a late supper. Tuesday, the 17th, we began a four day series of investigations of a large ruin on the Hall-Lovett Ranch. A few artifacts found (stone, bone and shell) but not enough to keep boys interested in the dig; required too much digging work w/pick & shovel. All that most of them wanted to do was to find a few souvenirs to take home. [23]

The final day at Mesa Verde they hiked seventeen miles down to the Mancos River and back to Soda Tipoff; it took nearly eleven hours and he determined it was too strenuous for boys of this age as they were exceedingly tired the next day (Fig. 4.14). The only thing they liked was swimming in the muddy Mancos River! [24]

The second B group consisted of thirteen boys who arrived for the desert trip on Monday, July 23 and Group C shipped off to Gold King. Winslow Walker spent a few days "on top of Mesa" then July 27-30 the A and B parties headed out for "Indian Country" with Dr. Stork as the main trip leader (Figure 4.15). The two groups traveled together to the Navajo Rodeo at Lukachukai in company with leaders Sanborn, Biggs, Mason, Washburn, and Friend, which made a total of forty people in six cars. They drove south and passed by the prominent Shiprock monolith and got to scramble up onto the radiating basaltic dike that extended to the south that crossed the Red Mesa road (Figure 4.16). Then they headed across the Chuska Mountains to Lukachukai, Arizona and arrived in time to watch a Navajo rodeo or *Entah* or "gathering" as it was known to the Navajo. The original Navajo word meant: "Enemy Way ceremony" that was followed by a Squaw Dance. Mr. S.A. Bell, the farm superintendent at Lukachukai, was very cordial and gave them the run of the CCC camp and made the boys welcome. Mr. S.V. Shankland, teacher at the Lukachukai School, was also very helpful with the boys.[25] The most noteworthy observation at the Entah was the near lack of automobiles. Other than the Explorers Camp vehicles nearly all the Indians were still riding in horse drawn wagons or on horseback (Figures 4.17 to 4.21).

After the Entah, the group split and Walker was in charge of his group (Group B). Several cars had more engine problems while they experienced bad roads and heavy rains but they got back to the Mesa Verde camp on schedule. Then, more sight-seeing on the Mesa then back to the ruin on Hall's ranch. On August 6 they established a lab and workshop in the old store building near Spruce Tree Lodge to work on field notes and display specimens they found. On August 7 they went to Durango for the day to see "a one-horse circus and a movie." [26] Walker's group then spent the next two days at the ruin where they found walls in several places:

> Considerable material from a test pit dug down 6 feet of debris in the courtyard without finding the original undisturbed surface. Mapped and plane tabled the site, elevations. Group A returned from desert; Group B seemed more interested in Mesa program than Group C, but no desire for 17 mile hike. Also Group B boys took much more interest in the society of the girls at the Lodge. [27]

Dr. Stork left Group A with Walker and the twelve boys stayed on the Mesa. All was going fine, "but something happened after I [Walker] left which made the boys of this oldest group rather disgruntled and perhaps furnished a reason why so many of them wanted to leave the camp early and return home." [28]

Figure 4.14 view of Mancos River Canyon from Soda Tipoff, Mesa Verde National Park. (K. Ross collection, 1938)

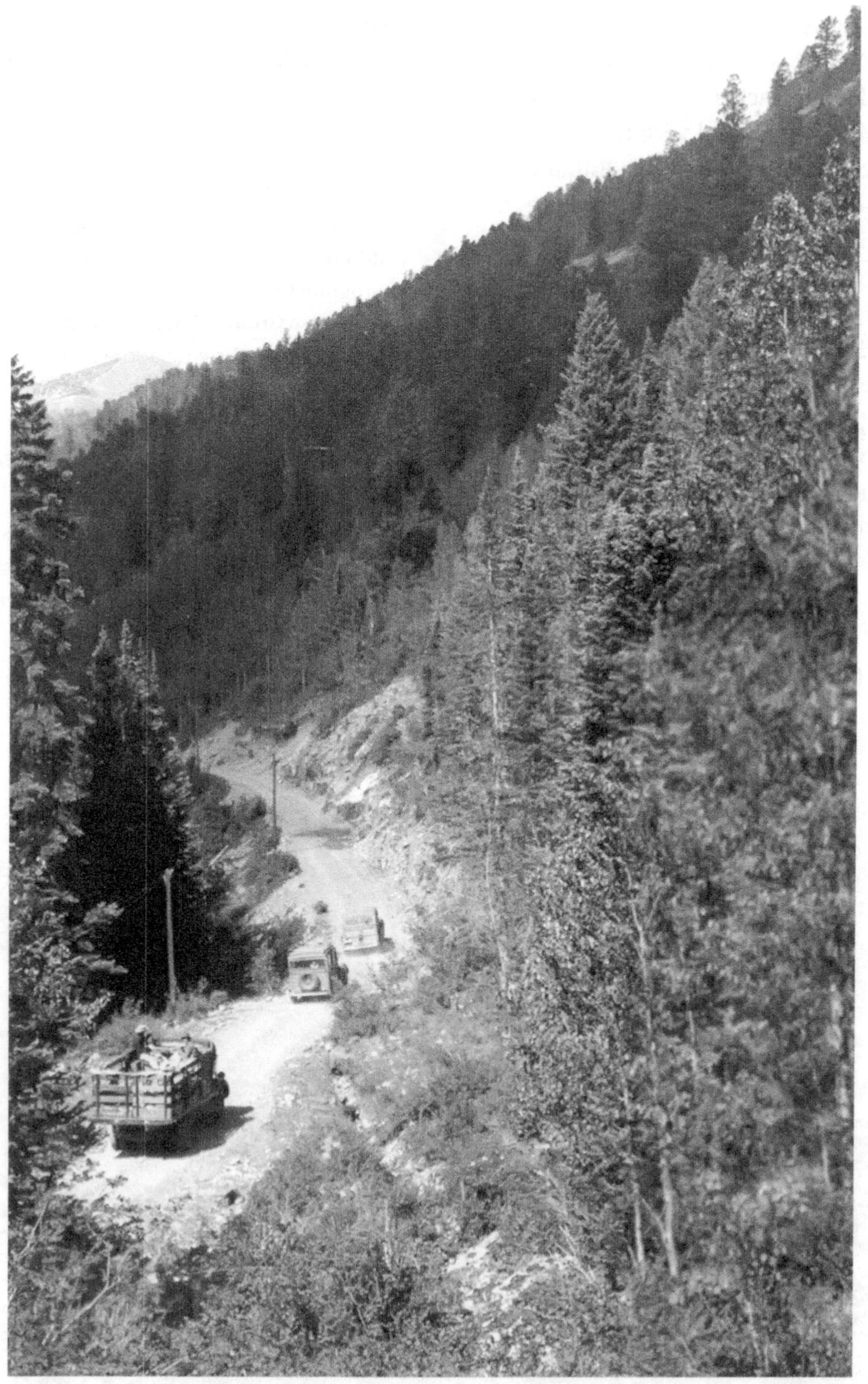

Figure 4.15 Winslow Walker and Dr. Stork's groups left Gold King Camp and headed out for "Indian Country"; the stake-bed Dodge truck (with some of the boys riding in back) is following two Ford woody station wagons (1936 vintage Fords from the RBMV days). (K. Ross collection)

Figure 4.16 Boys in Explorers group scramble up on the south-radiating dike from Shiprock (seen in distance in lower right view). (K. Ross collection)

Figure 4.17 Navajo men and boys near the judges stand watch rodeo events, or "Entah" at Lukachukai, Arizona; note the horse-drawn wagons across the rodeo grounds and the lack of automobiles, 1945. (K. Ross collection)

Figure 4.18 "ready-set-go" the race is on at the Entah in Lukachukai, 1945. (K. Ross collection)

Figure 4.19 along the sidelines at the Lukachukai Entah, 1945. (K. Ross collection)

Figure 4.20 Navajo people at Lukachukai Entah, 1945; people on right are standing in line at various food pavilions; note man in military uniform in mid-view looking back at camera; also note elder Navajo lady sitting on top of truck on blanket wearing traditional clothing but with modern era parasol and sleeping dog under truck. (K. Ross collection)

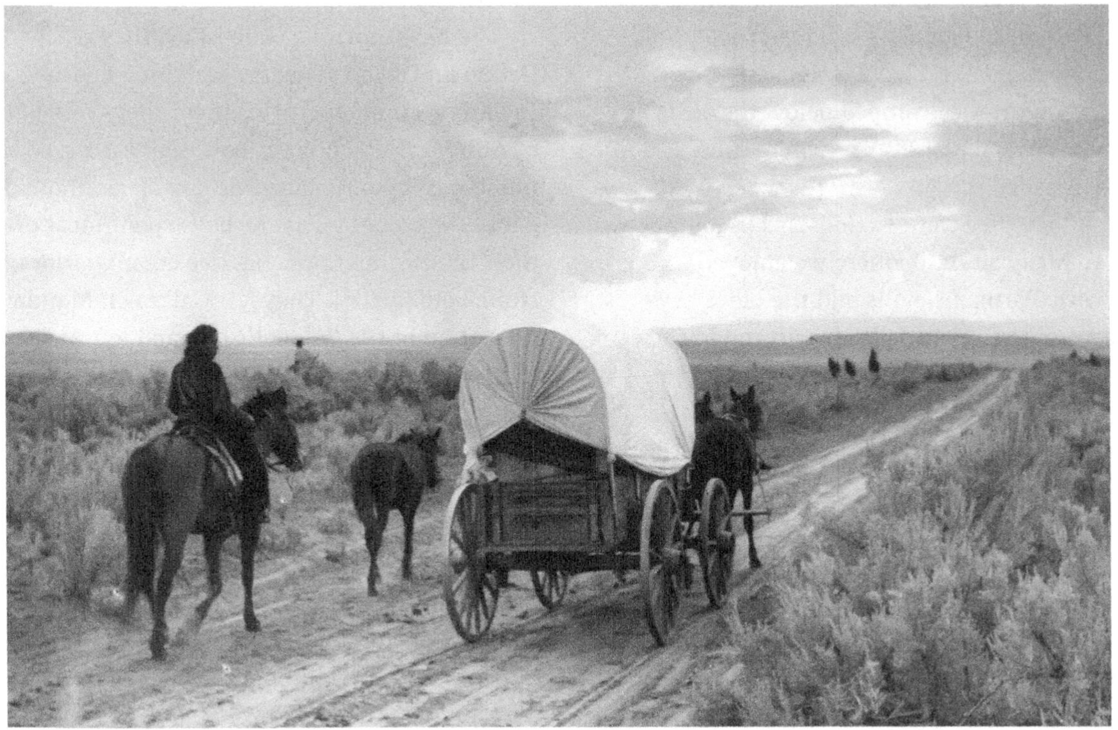

Figure 4.21 the Lukachukai Entah is over and time to head home, 1945. (K. Ross collection)

On Monday, August 13, Walker's group began the third expedition with eight boys of Group C and four from Group B going for the second time. The party was under Walker's leadership with Mr. and Mrs. Frank Cummings, parents of camp participant Dick Cummings, and Ms. Washburn. Mr. Cummings drove the big military surplus troop carrier Dodge truck most of the time and they had a small Ford sedan serving as a scout car until it broke down. The big truck carried most of the boys, gear and all food supplies. The trip lasted ten days and covered *twelve hundred miles* of the Four Corners country!

They went from Cortez to Monticello then turned west toward Indian Creek past Home of Truth and Dugout Ranch and camped and hiked near Bridger Jack Mesa near the confluence of Cottonwood and Indian Creeks (Figures 4.22 to 4.24). Then they back-tracked to Monticello and turned south to Blanding where the pavement ended, then traveled to Natural Bridges National Monument and then back to Blanding *where they heard the momentous news that Japan had surrendered and World War II was over!*

That night, they camped below the cliffs at Bluff on the San Juan River "where there is a fine artesian well." [29]

Next day they went to Goosenecks and then back to Mexican Hat "where we enjoyed a good visit with Norman Nevills and the older boys joined him for a swim in the swift muddy stream. Of course, Norm had to give the boys a slide-show and told of adventures of **shooting the rapids** of the San Juan River." [30] Crossing the San Juan River they drove through Monument Valley, encountering some bad sandy stretches before reaching Harry Gouldings ranch for the night (Figure 4.25). Goulding took part of the group in his station wagon and provided "bunks with mattresses that the movie colony had used when on location there." [31] He also showed slides of Monument Valley. The following morning they continued through Monument Valley on towards Kayenta where they had a complete breakdown of the scout car which had to be towed by the truck for twenty miles. They spent time and money getting the car repaired in Kayenta then proceeded to Marsh Pass. All roads were bad but they made it to Betatakin by nightfall.

The next day the boys had to be prodded to make a short three-mile hike to see Betatakin ruins as they were too tired and protested any hiking. The leaders almost eliminated this part of the plan since a two-hundred-mile-long bone-jarring ride lay in front of them, but they made a quick trip to see Betatakin ruins (Figure 4.26). Then they headed to Shonto and Tuba City, detoured to Moenave and stopped to see dinosaur tracks. They traveled onto Hopi Mesas and headed toward Gallup and stopped for a glimpse of Old Oraibi (this part of the trip they encountered driving sandstorms and rain squalls). Then the car stalled-started-stalled and made it to Jeddito after dark. They had been on the road for twelve hours to cover two hundred-thirty-one miles!

The next morning, August 18, they reached Gallup and spent two days watching another Indian ceremonial. At this point they were joined by Col. MacNab and four boys that increased their number to twenty-one. One day of ceremonial dances was enough as the boys spent most of their time going to movies, ice cream parlors, stores, etc [girls!]. They left Gallup on Monday, August 20 in the Colonel's car, and left Ansel Hall's Ford sedan in a garage for repairs and headed to Canyon de Chelly by way of St. Michaels, Ganado and Chinle. Tuesday was spent going down a six hundred foot "chasm" to visit White House ruin. But the hike up Canyon del Muerto to see the ruins was nixed by the boys who preferred running up and down huge sand dunes or playing in the water puddles in the canyon bottom (Figures 4.27 to 4.28). They returned to Ganado and were joined by the boys of Group A. Now totaling thirty-five people, they all went to the Hopi Snake Dances.

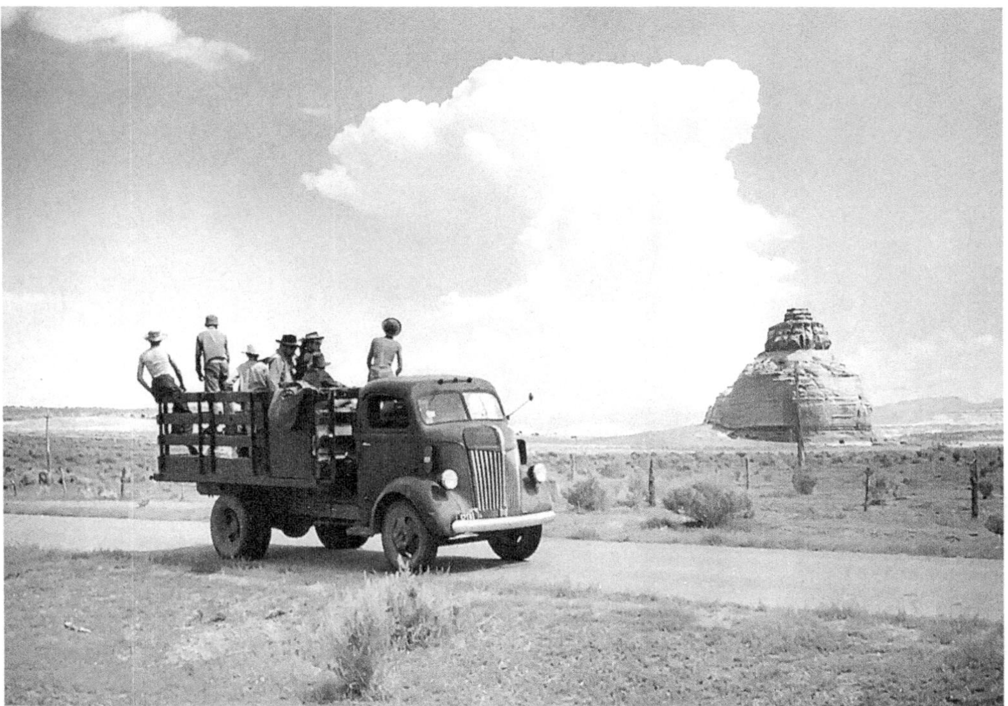

Figure 4.22 "B" group riding in the Dodge stake-bed truck near the "Home of Truth" westbound on road to Indian Creek Canyon; Church Rock in background, 1945. (K. Ross collection)

Figure 4.23 view north from camp in Indian Creek Canyon; "Twin Six Shooter Peaks" in distance, 1945. (K. Ross collection)

Figure 4.24 sleeping bags and shade alongside Indian Creek; time to read and relax, 1945. (K. Ross collection)

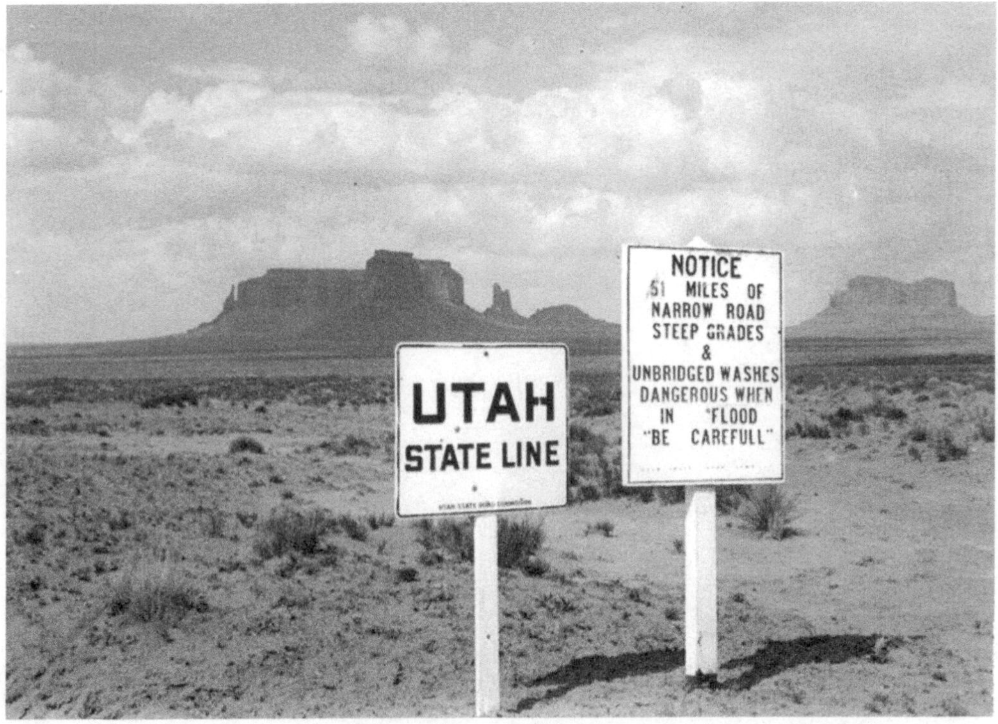

Figure 4.25 view northeast toward Monument Pass from the Utah-Arizona Stateline marker on "Highway 47" (a rough sandy two-track just past signs in lower right – route to Mexican Hat, Utah). (Utah Historical Association photo)

Figure 4.26 the "B" group was forced to make a short hike to see Betatakin ruins, 1945. (K. Ross collection)

Figure 4.27 Explorers on sand dunes at Canyon De Chelly, 1945. (K. Ross collection)

Figure 4.28 Explorers Camp boys decided to have fun running down sand dunes at Canyon De Chelly rather than hike to see more ruins, 1945. (K. Ross collection)

> Wednesday, August 22, was the most memorable day of the trip, the day we saw the weird barbaric Snake Ceremony at Mishongnovi on Second Mesa. Only one of the boys, Henry Hoyt, had seen anything like it before and they were thoroughly awed by the spectacle of men and boys, some of them no older than themselves, carrying live snakes in their mouths, including large venomous looking rattlesnakes, and moving with measured stamp to the shaking of rattles and low chanting through the age old invocation to the gods of Rain. And there was no doubt about its efficacy – we were drenched by a sudden shower while sitting on the roof-tops waiting for the performance to begin! [32]

The Snake Dance marked the climax of camp as MacNab and others left for the west coast. The rest went back to Jeddito to camp for the night. The next morning Mr. and Mrs. Cummings continued with some on the Desert expedition and Walker's group headed back to Mesa Verde. They stopped to pick up the Ford in Gallup on August 23 and nobody wanted to detour to see Chaco Canyon so they proceeded to head home. Nobody wanted to resume digging at the ruin when they got back to Mancos either. They were all worn out. The return to Gold King on Sunday was marked by rain. Walker left on Tuesday, August 28 and offered the following comments:

> He had a good time and he thought most of the boys did too, BUT:
>
> Everyone, counselors and boys alike, would welcome more active participation in person by the Director" [Ansel Hall] The program was too ambitious and strenuous for the younger boys; Gold King Camp needed upgrades as it was a dump; transportation was "manifestly inadequate" too much mechanical problems; poor camp cook facilities; firearms should be restricted; less driving and more doing...like a real exploring trip into little known country like Beef Basin? [33]

Following the honest but negative report of camp activities Winslow M. Walker was not invited to return as a camp counselor for any other Explorers Camps. The whole orderly concept presented by Dr. Stork of rotating the groups so that they could all experience what the other group had done, became completely fouled up. Thus, the first and second years of the Explorers Camp consisted of changing itineraries on the fly. The unauthorized and poorly-supervised archaeological digs conducted in 1944 were apparently continued in 1945 in the Mancos valley, but a significant amount of time was spent driving from point to point across unimproved dirt roads and rutted trails with minimal hikes or anything close to "exploring." There was certainly nothing *archaeological* in these excursions other than some of the group being offered to tour through one of the ruins at Betatakin. But by then the kids were too tired to move. They were exposed to Navajo and Hopi cultures, but simply put; the emphasis was mostly on camping and scenic sight-seeing auto-tours across the expansive Navajo Reservation and into Indian Creek on the northern flank of the Abajo Mountains.

LOOKING FORWARD: THE 1946 EXPLORERS CAMP

In a letter written October 29, 1945, Dr. Harvey Stork first noted that camp needed to be shortened to nine weeks so the boys would have adequate time to get to camp and return home during summer break. The ten week schedule left little personal time for travel, or just goofing off a little in-between the school year. Also, too many boys left early and this needed to end. In fact, there needed to be something to look forward to, rather than the anticlimactic end as it was in 1945. He again suggested some sort of medal awards and banquet or big campfire with really good food to send them off. He also noted that two weeks of orientation (indoctrination) was too long. Leaders, camp managers, cooks, wranglers needed to be set up and ready to go and living quarters needed to be ready and repaired (he provided a number of suggestions regarding roofing, flooring, toilets, etc).[34]

He particularly emphasized making the rifle shooting-range safe, that no pistols should be allowed, and only firearms provided by camp personnel and with strict guidance should be used. He was particularly perturbed with all the bird and animal killing allowed by Hank Setzer in 1945. He emphasized that the scientific leader should be a zoologist with a natural history bent rather than a scientific collector, that the approach should be one of "*emphasizing conservation* of animals rather than that of killing. *This job is for a teacher rather than an investigator*" [35] [Emphasis mine] There was an obvious discord between Stork and Setzer. The rest of his letter was another long list of proposed itineraries and things to do and see.

But by late March, 1946 there was still no indication of any changes to the camp itinerary from that of the previous year as documented with two letters. Porter Sargent, a Boston colleague of Ansel's and an educational adviser to parents and schools, wrote a short note to Ansel reminding him that Colonel Charles A. Lindbergh's son, Jon, might be interested in Ansel's program and that he should be contacted with the programs itinerary for the 1946 field camp.[36] At the suggestion of Sargent, Ansel wrote a self-introductory letter to Lindbergh explaining the Explorers Camp purpose and provided plans for the season that were exactly the same as the 1945 season. Most importantly, the archaeological portion of the season only involved visiting petroglyph sites with Arthur Woodward, touring Mesa Verde National Park ruins and "then will participate in several days of archaeological excavation in a surface ruin here in the Mancos Valley." [37] At the behest of Jess Nusbaum's disgust that Ansel was sponsoring improper "pot-hunting" and that he should cease and desist, Ansel was scurrying to find a site on private property and a scholarly archaeologist to oversee the proposed excavations. Preliminary excavations of the ruins at Cahone and the hike into Dark Canyon were not mentioned in the letter to Lindbergh.[38]

Not surprisingly, Charles Lindbergh or his son did not reply to Ansel in 1946, and Jon Lindbergh was not listed as a camp participant. Jon was only fourteen years old and after the infamous kidnapping and murder of their first born child, Charles and his wife was extremely hesitant to let their children go un-escorted to events. The boys' camp in the wild unknown southwestern U.S. needed further investigation.

1946 EXPLORERS CAMP LEADERS [39]

Ansel Hall – Director (The "Chief") Mancos, Colorado

Dr. Harvey E. Stork – Field Director from Carleton College, Northfield, Minnesota

Arthur Woodward – Archaeologist from Los Angeles Museum, LA, California

S.J. Tobin – Anthropologist – Leader of Cahone ruins "dig" from U of U Salt Lake City, Utah

Richard E. Stultz – Physical Instructor, Ohio Univ – Leader of High-Country Pack Trips; New York, N.Y

Mrs. Richard Stultz – camp mother

Bayne Beauchamp – Camp Manager – Big Shot Explorer friend of Ansel's from Los Angeles, California

Ray Jahn – Assistant Leader from Rolling Hills, California

Bob Melzer – Assistant Leader – Mountaineering from Denver, Colorado

Larry Ridenauer – Assistant Leader – Forestry [camp cook as it turned out] from La Junta, Colorado

Fran Hall – Photographer & Assistant Leader from Carleton College, Northfield, Minnesota

Tyler Jekyll – Wrangler & Assistant Leader from Mancos, Colorado

MEDICAL STAFF [These fellows basically received free vacation excursions and were written up in 'Doctors on the Trail' 1947 by Ansel]; Dr. J.E. Hughes, Shawnee, OK; Dr. Theo A. Kennedy, Legion, TX; Dr. E.M. Loyd, Taloga, OK; Dr. D.B. Williamson, Tivoli, TX and R.E. Forrester, Jr. – PA from Moran, TX.

Thirty-five boys were listed as members of the 1946 Explorers Camp with Ansel's son Roger joining the camp for the first time. Another boy worthy of mentioning was Stuart H. Maule, who would return many times, and later he and his family moved to Mancos from El Monte, California.[40]

DOCTORS ON THE TRAIL

The treks and areas covered by the 1946 Explorers Camp were outlined by Ansel in a publication for the *Clinical Medicine* magazine in May 1947 entitled "Doctors on the Trail," where Ansel Hall explained how professional medical personnel accompanied his Explorer Camp for Boys into Navajoland and the desert canyons of the southwest.[41] The article was inspired by the editor of the magazine who had spent some time at Mesa Verde National Park and had listened to Ansel describe his hobby of the past twenty years – exploration. While at the park they talked of the unique experiment of giving boys of high school age an opportunity to participate in these adventures.

Hall noted that medical staff had always been part of his trips, dating back to his RBMV days and that even though there had never been any major problems the expeditionary group was always prepared for any medical emergency. He was always glad to see a medical professional with "a spirit of adventure," who would be an ideal field companion. Ansel had sent an invitation to members of the medical profession in Texas and Oklahoma in the spring and the balance of his article provided a "thumb nail sketch of their adventures." [42]

In the summer of 1946, the expedition group gathered at Gold King Camp and all the camp's functions that involved the participants and the instructors were photo-documented by professional photographer Fran Hall (no relationship to Ansel;). The thirty-five participants were divided into three groups. Dr.

Theodore A. Kennedy of Legion, Texas arrived in Durango and was met by Dr. Stork, Field Director of the Explorers Camp and was driven to the base camp at Gold King. The boys were just completing their preliminary orientation, practice in camping skills, and physical conditioning. Dr. Kennedy noted, "One of my first impressions was that the chief feature of the Camp was *eating*." He soon was "holding his own" [43] when it came to meals (Figures 4.29 and 4.30).

Figure 4.29 stoking the fire; grilling chicken on open fire at Gold King base camp, 1946. (K. Ross collection)

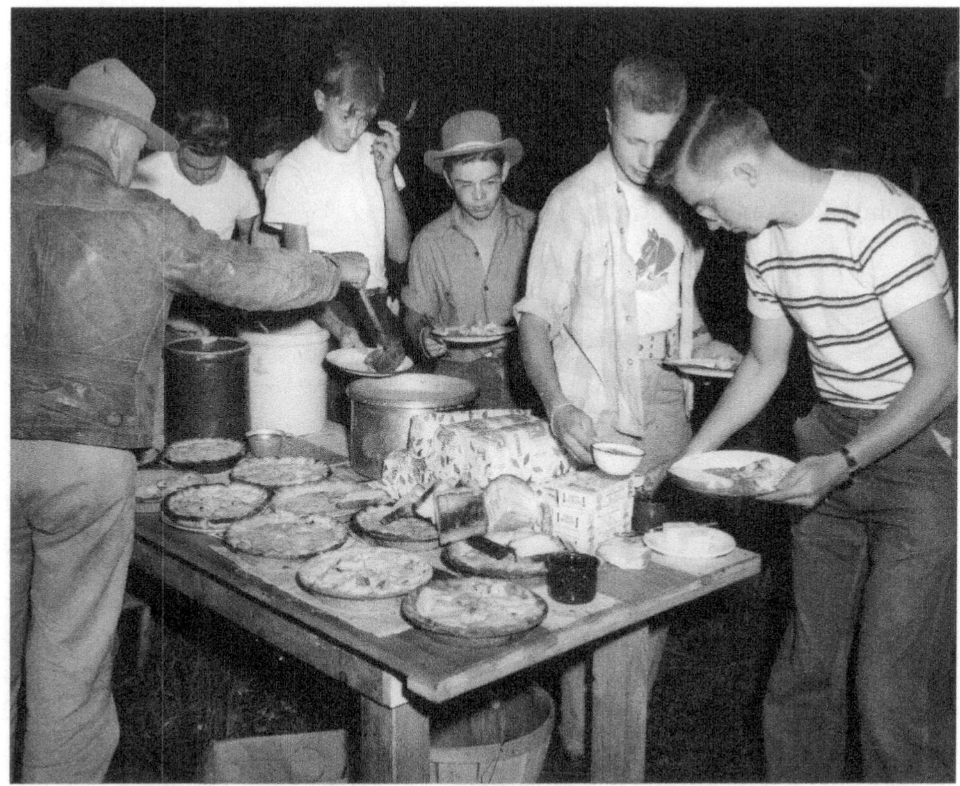

Figure 4.30 serving line at base camp, 1946. (K. Ross collection)

Dr. Kennedy was attached to the mountaineering and forestry group who rode on horseback into the mining district high in the La Plata Mountains and were led by Richard Stultz, a Physical Education instructor at Ohio State College. The pack train of boys, adult supervisors and wranglers worked their way up into Columbus Basin where the boys hunted for minerals and prospected for gold. Kennedy tried his hand at trout fishing. But according to Camp Leader Bob Melzer the high mountain mining fieldwork was practically forgotten due to a lack of knowledge with no real prospector or mineralogist along. Leaders didn't know the subject or where to look and he recommended that Bill Little should be hired as he knew the complete history of all the mines in the area. They had to try panning on their own and no one knew the proper method. He also thought the mountaineering was not conducted as it should. There was no instruction on how to climb, what to wear, how to find a route, rope techniques or how to rappel.

Dr. E.M. Loyd of Taloga, Oklahoma was assigned to the desert exploration archaeological investigations party led by Dr. Arthur Woodward from the Los Angeles Museum that traveled by "jeep, troop transport truck, and motorized field kitchen." [44] Their purpose was to search for petroglyphs and pictographs under the direction of Woodward who was not a "hands-on" archaeologist. His primary interest was the field of historical archaeology. Throughout his career Woodward worked closely with colleagues in the National Parks Service and authored or coauthored numerous Parks Service reports which pertained to California, Mexico and Europe. Thus, Woodward was yet another professional who Ansel had befriended through the park service network, but knew little about the archaeology of the Four Corners area. Therefore, the boys visited the known petroglyph site in Utah near Indian Creek that was accessible by automobile and called "Canopy Rock" by Randall Henderson in his 1946 Desert Magazine article.[45] The name was later changed to *Newspaper Rock* and designated a State Historical Monument in 1962 (Figures 4.31 and 4.32). They visited petroglyph sites near Hopi Mesa and Navajo National Monument as they had in previous years that were also accessed by automobile.[46]

Dr. Loyd mentioned their passing Shiprock enroute to Chaco Canyon where they arrived at the trading post in the afternoon and made camp. He mentioned "an intriguing account of hunting for pictographs in Chaco Canyon – of visiting the spectacular Pueblo Bonito" and discovering "a huge canyon that offers irresistible lure for next summer's fieldwork." [47]

The Monument Valley group explored the ruins in Canyon De Chelly and attended an annual healing ceremony and sing of the Navajos in the Lukachukai Mountains (Figures 4.33 to 4.36). They were accompanied by Dr. J.E. Hughes of Shawnee, Oklahoma who had volunteered to be part of this expedition. Ansel called Hughes the "Dean of our medical staff [who] was that grand old philosopher and adventurer." [48]

Figure 4.31 "canopy rock" as it was called in 1946; later to be named "Newspaper Rock." (K. Ross collection)

Figure 4.32 Dr. Arthur Woodward (second from right) admires the "discovery" of petroglyphs in Indian Creek Canyon, 1946. (K. Ross collection)

Figure 4.33 canyon view above White House ruin, 1946. (K. Ross collection)

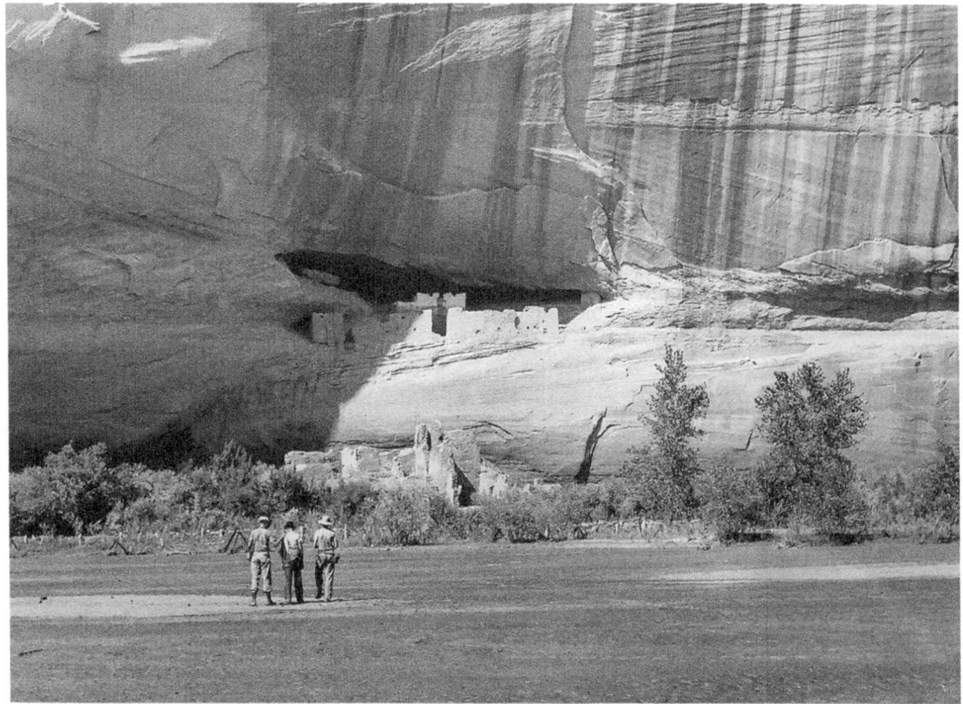

Figure 4.34 White House ruin, Canyon De Chelly, 1946. (K. Ross collection)

Figure 4.35 Canyon del Muerto, 1946. (K. Ross collection)

Figure 4.36 view from Spider Rock, 1946. (K. Ross collection)

EXTREMELY EAGER

In reference to the letter of April 29, 1946 where Ansel Hall was "extremely eager" to hear about the outcome of Kenny's "negotiations," it became clear as to what *negotiations* Ansel was referring (see p.67).[49] It didn't have anything to do with Kenny's possible employment by Ansel, as that was a direct negotiation between him and Kenny. Ansel had already offered Kenny a deal, albeit short, to guide a select handful of boys on a hike into Dark Canyon.

The "outcome of your negotiations" related to something else, and that was the purchase of the land upon which the unexcavated ruins sat at Kenny's father's old place at Cahone. The ruins that Kenny called *Cibola City*! This had to be the situation, as Kenny knew the owner and knew exactly what part of the land parcel to ask about purchasing. In fact, Ansel had already visited the site with Kenny and had a dollar figure in mind for which Kenny had approached the landowner to see if it could be purchased. It was typical in the way Ansel worked; he would get his surrogates to do his bidding for him. It had worked for him for most of his professional life. Ansel was a great *idea guy and organizer* and could find the right people to do the ground work, and then claim the glory and accolades, and as Jess Nusbaum had noted ("He's a super salesman and I don't mean maybe...").[50]

The land in question was covered in sage, pinyon and juniper trees and not particularly suitable agricultural ground. Ancient Indian ruins and artifacts were scattered about, so Kenny negotiated as an agent for Ansel, and convinced the owner to sell the land. Ansel was anxious to close the deal after he returned from Denver in early May because he needed to finalize his brochure listing the upcoming Boys Camp activities. The deal was made just in time. Whether Ansel was aware or not, all public land would soon come under the jurisdiction of the newly formed Bureau of Land Management (BLM)[51] in July 1946 creating new restrictions to his earlier view of exploring and digging up this "virgin" territory.[52]

Kenny and Ansel had discussed adding two new activities to the 1946 camp – a hike into Dark Canyon for a select few, as this was into *terra incognito* and to begin excavation at *Cibola City* ruins at the old Cahone Ross ranch *if* the landowner would sell the piece of land with the ruins to Ansel. The 1946 brochure reflected these late additions: "Veterans of former seasons with the Explorers' Camp are eligible to participate in the exploration of the wild country lying beyond our last year's horizons west of the Blue Mountains in Utah – Beef Basin and Dark Canyon, the last unmapped tributary to the Colorado."[53]

Jesse Nusbaum had not been impressed by the previous year's lack of archaeological guidance of poorly supervised "digs" in whatever excavations that had taken place in the Mancos valley or at the park when he asked Kenny in his letter dated May 7, 1946 "Do you know who he is planning on for his archeological leader this year – hope it's not last year's wash-out, or the crusty Colonel, -- and what his archeological planning is."[54]

The Explorers Camp brochure written by Ansel stated,

> Climax of this program will be several days of archaeological excavation – real "treasure hunting," – under the direction of competent archaeologists who will arrange this practice period so that the boys will obtain practical knowledge of the various techniques used by professional anthropologists in excavating and gathering data about prehistoric peoples. Skeletons, pottery, and the various artifacts collected will probably be deposited in the Mesa Verde Museum for study and interpretation."[55]

The first dig was supervised by archaeologist S.J. Tobin of the University of Utah and overseen by the graduate students at the Cahone ruins.[56] Bob Junior, a wartime medic who was studying to become a medical doctor volunteered to be assigned to the archaeological excavation camp (Figures 4.37 to 4.38). In the "Doctors on the Trail" article, Ansel Hall stated:

> Atop a high unnamed mesa we had located what promised to be a huge, possibly a very spectacular ruin. The first exploratory trenching was to be done under Professor Sam Tobin of the University of Utah and Bob was determined to be in on this "treasure hunt" amid the ruins of that buried city. Here are a few fragments of his report on that exciting experience:
>
> > *"Our group (15 boys from 13 to 17 years of age) drove to Cahone near the extreme southwestern part of Colorado. Here we took off to the westward on side roads which finally ended in virgin pinyon-juniper forest. From here on the boys pitched in and cleared a way through to our proposed campsite a mile or so farther on. We located our camp on the rim of an unnamed mesa jutting over Cahone Canyon. Then we made a preliminary tour of inspection. The ruin itself proved to be tremendous. It stretched in crescent form, about three-fourths of a mile long and with about one-quarter mile between the horns of the crescent. The ruins were almost all fallen, the entire city practically buried except for walls that rose above the surface in places. The ground was actually littered with broken pottery. Mr. Tobin was to start the excavations with a long-time program in mind perhaps 15 or 20 years of intensive investigation. We marked off an area of the smallest mound for this season's preliminary excavations."*
> >
> > *"The boys were allowed to sleep in caves under the rim of the mesa-top shelters which later turned out to have been used for dwellings by the very ancient Basketmaker People. This contact was certainly stimulating to the boys. At night, after supper, we always had a big camp fire on the rocks at the canyon rim when Mr. Tobin would explain to the group about the country, the ruins, and the culture of the long vanished prehistoric Indians. All of this gave a marvelous background to the excavations and things discovered during that day. Thus the boys lived in constant association with archaeology and this tripled their interest in the workings."* [57]

CAHONE RUIN

Originally, the Ross family called these ruins the *Cahone Ruins*, and later *Cibola City Ruins* by Kenny Ross in the Explorers Camp reports he composed and distributed to camp participants from 1947 to 1955. Bill and Merrie (Hall) Winkler asked that the site name be changed to the *Ansel Hall Pueblo*, to honor Ansel Hall, when the site was officially accepted as a national historic place in 1997. After all, Ansel Hall had purchased the land and sponsored excavations by the Explorers Camp participants from 1946 to 1955.

The site was situated on an upland mesa at an elevation of approximately 6,600 ft above sea level just to the east of the intersection of Cross and Cahone canyons that were deeply cut through the Dakota Sandstone into the underlying Morrison Formation (Brushy Basin and Salt Wash Members). Deep dark gray soils (basal Mancos Shale) within which the ruins were located, sat immediately on the Dakota Sandstone caprock (see Figure 1.2 and Appendix II: Stratigraphic Column).

The site was located on land originally homesteaded by Kenny Ross's grandfather following the passage of the Enlarged Homestead Act. The "*Enlarged Homestead Act of 1909*" requirements stated that "a *homesteader* had to be the head of the household or at least twenty-one years old. They had to live on the designated land, build a home, make improvements, and farm it for a minimum of five years. The filing fee was eighteen dollars." [58] As was the case with many homesteaders, Kenny's grandfather never got around to formally following through with these requirements, so the earliest owner of record was Kenny's father, Charles (Charley) Carpenter Ross, who was bequeathed the 320 acre parcel of land from his father upon his death and then it was he who *perfected* the title in his name. A patent from the United States of America was issued to Kenny Ross's father, Charles C. Ross, on May 8, 1936.[59]

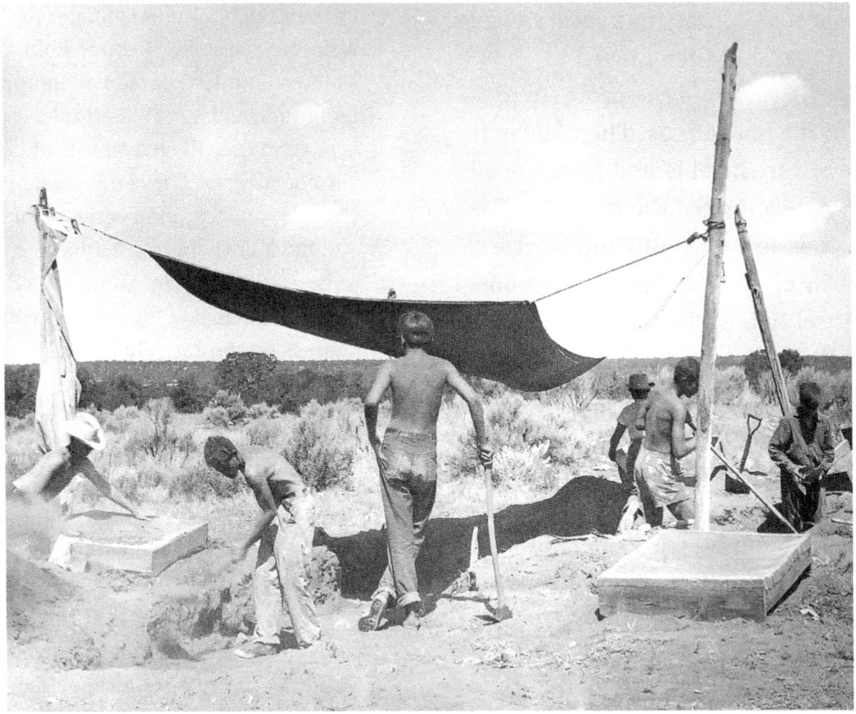

Figure 4.37 Cahone ruin; first supervised excavations by S.J. Tobin, 1946. (K. Ross collection)

Figure 4.38 boys carefully expose human skeleton, Cahone ruin, 1946. (K. Ross collection)

Soon after being issued a legal patent to the land, Charley sold the property to a local rancher, Walter Beyers in 1938 and then moved to California. Walter Beyers sold the property to Edgar Garland in the mid-1940s. Then Edgar Garland transferred to Ansel F. and June A. Hall forty-six acres that contained the ruin site in June, 1946. But it wasn't until Bill and Merrie (Hall) Winkler (Ansel Hall's daughter) re-named the ruin after Ansel Hall in 1997 after the Canyon of the Ancients National Monument was designated.[60] According to Don Ross, a substantial amount of the artifacts were shipped to the Peabody Museum after Ansel hired Alfred Guthe, an archaeologist from Harvard in 1950 to write-up a formal report about the site. The only documented excavations at Ansel Hall ruin occurred between 1946 and 1949, which resulted in a brief descriptive report.[61] Those excavations were initiated by Ansel Hall through the Explorers Camp for Boys. The site had not been systematically mapped other than an unpublished sketch map made by Art Rohn in the 1980s.[62]

Sandy Thompson noted that in those earliest summers of Ross's memory, "the archaeology of the region was focused entirely upon the spectacular cliff dwelling ruins within the recently created Mesa Verde Nation Park. Jesse Fewkes had begun excavations, first with Spruce Tree House (1907-08), followed by Cliff Palace (1909), Sun Temple (1915) and Far View Ruin (1916). It was a time when the era of 'cowboy' archaeology was ending and when generalists of the first order were laying down the foundations of Southwestern archaeology as it is known today." [63]

Kenny's interest in interpretive archaeology was probably not due to his knowing Ansel Hall, as Sandy Thomson surmised, but was from his friend and mentor – Jesse Nusbaum.

> "Cibola City Ruin" is the name given to an ancient Pueblo Indian village which is sometimes also referred to as "Cahone Ruin." It is located in Dolores County Colorado at approximately 108° 51' Longitude and 37° 38' Latitude. Its area is about 20 acres and the village consists of 24 house units of varying size, each accompanied by at least one circular, underground ceremonial room called a kiva and most of them by a refuse heap or midden. The units are grouped into a roughly U-shaped village with the open side toward the west. A large circular depression, tentatively identified as a Great Kiva, occupies a central position within the "U". The village is situated in an open sagebrush glade and is almost completely surrounded by dense pinon and juniper forest. The altitude is a little more than 7,000 feet. [The highest elevation is actually 6676 ft.] Various archaeologists have been associated with the excavations since they were begun in 1946 by Explorers Camp. In the order in which they had charge they are: S.J. Tobin, University of Utah, A.K. Guthe, University of Chicago, George Neuman, Indiana University, and Gordon A. Thomas, University of California. Kenneth Ross, Director of Southwest Explorations and Explorers Camp took personal charge in 1949, 1951 and in subsequent years.
>
> Altogether, nearly 200 members of Explorers Camp have assisted with excavation work. Although the interests and abilities of the young Explorers has always been an important consideration, use of accepted scientific methods, consistent recording, and careful preservation of the physical materials assures scientific integrity.[64]

The brochure written by Kenny continued to explain basic Anasazi periods of Basketmakers vs Puebloans and then places the Cibola City ruins in the general period of occupation from 900 – 1100 A.D. based on a tree-ring date of 1068 A.D. obtained from roof timbers found in kiva C-6 and also based on pottery studies. Kenny continued to detail work that had been done since 1951 and the proposed excavation work planned for the 1955 season (Figure 4.39).

Ansel Hall Pueblo:
A National Historic Place

The Ansel Hall Ruin was entered on the National Register of Historic Places on November 25, 1997. A report was written by William C. Winkler and Bruce Bradley, PhD. wherein the preservation project was sponsored by the *Wilderness Land Trust* through the *Colorado Historical Society*. The property was donated by William & Merrie (Hall) Winkler.[65]

The *Colorado Historical Society*, Office of Archaeology and Historic Preservation described the site as "a loose cluster of individual habitation units surrounding several community structures believed to have been built and occupied between A.D. 1050 and 1150 and is thus considered to be representative of the Pueblo II Period (A.D. 900 – 1150)." [66] With specific reference to archaeological findings at the Ansel Hall site, the community had a great kiva and a number of ruins which may indicate that the pueblo village was at least a moderate-sized community. The Ansel Hall site had about 200 rooms and 36 kivas. A 14.8 acre parcel located in the SW/4 of Sec 18-T39N-R18W, Dolores County, Colorado. More specifically, the ruins are located at Longitude 108º 51' West and Latitude 37º 38' North.[67]

The Cahone pueblo village may have been abandoned by AD 1100, based upon the absence of 12th century white and black pottery. But the more intriguing findings were the nature of artifacts found that indicated: the pueblo residents had connections with the Chaco Canyon center, they traded with other native people, and they had a similar lifestyle with their neighbors. The ruin site presented a unique opportunity to investigate the possibility of *craft specialization at the community level.* Some attention had been paid to the possibility that pottery was being produced by certain communities and exchanged with other communities at various Ancestral Puebloan times. What was interesting about the Cahone Ruin was the large quantity and proportion of debitage that resulted from the manufacture of knives and projectile points. These distinctive byproducts were rare at Ancestral Puebloan sites in the Four Corners region, yet knives and projectile points were found nearly everywhere. There were surfaces of the ground littered with these small stone flakes that came as far away as the southern San Juan Mountains east of Pagosa Springs, the Jemez Mountains in north-central New Mexico and the Chuska Mountains along the New Mexico/Arizona border. Craft specialization at the community level had been generally overlooked although it presented broad implications about the economic organization of the Chacoan System. [68]

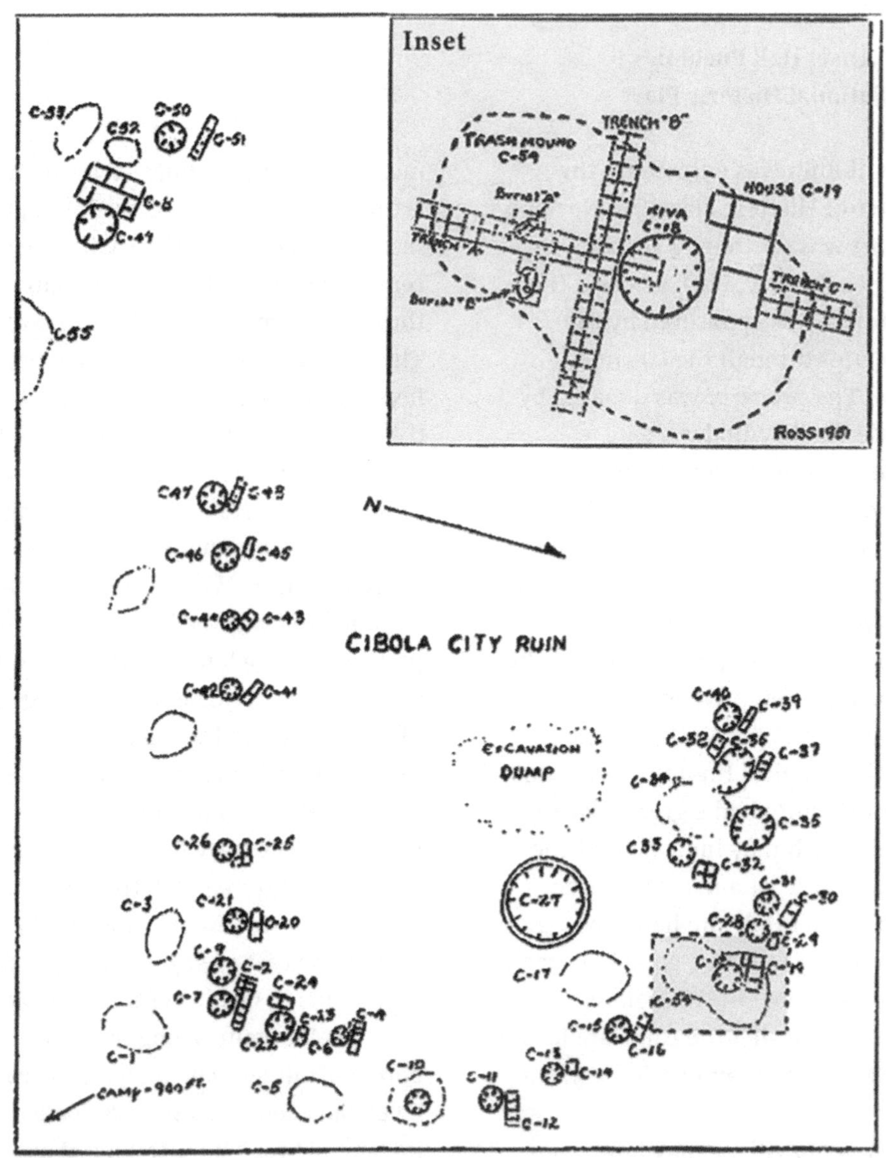

Figure 4.39 Cibola City sketch map made by Kenny Ross showing location of excavations included in his 1951 Southwest Explorers Camp Report, p.6; (no scale provided). (K. Ross collection)

DARK CANYON

In January 1946 Kenny Ross quit his position at Mesa Verde and made an attempt to start his own photography studio in Cortez, but he accepted the job and responsibility of being the trip leader for the Dark Canyon excursion at the end of the boys' camp in August. Kenny had long held an interest in seeing if it were possible to reach the Colorado River by hiking down Dark Canyon. His general knowledge of the area came from his cowboy days punchin' cows from Indian Creek to grasslands on Elk Ridge and talking with some of the Scorup cowboys that knew the canyon narrowed and 'cliffed-out' at least for horses and cattle.

Kenny wanted to add a *real* exploration trip to Ansel's rather tame itinerary and when he suggested the idea to Ansel the concept was accepted with some trepidation but he finally concurred – with some conditions.

Ansel being the consummate promoter saw that if he could find a means to showcase the hike, it would add credibility to the *adventure* aspect he wrote and emphasized in his pamphlets advertising the Explorers Camp for Boys.

Kenny worked out a basic itinerary that included coordinating the big cargo Dodge truck, cowboys with pack animals and he and some boys with backpacks. He also saw the need for a jeep and looked into the cost of such a purchase and discussed the possibility of buying one with Ansel. He had to figure out the food for the drive over and back as well as the food needed to carry in their packs. He also had to figure out where drinking water sources might be to replenish the small canteens they would carry. And he had to figure how long a trip this would be and a general idea of costs.

If he could pull this off, maybe there was a way he could demonstrate to Ansel that he could be the "camp manager" – the much-needed missing link in Ansel's Explorers Camp which at this point was nothing more than a series of wilderness tours – minus the adventure!

He calculated the time to travel from Mancos to a lonely spot on Elk Ridge that was as far as the big truck would go. He knew it would be faster to head south from Monticello to Blanding (where the pavement ended) and then west crossing Cottonwood Creek and following Route 95 roadway along the south slopes of the Abajo Mountains and crossing onto Elk Ridge and turning north onto the forest road near Kigalia Ranger Station and finally arrive at a place called Little Notch on Elk Ridge (Figure 4.40).

He knew the trek would be shortened to a reasonable distance if he could convince Ansel to buy the jeep to shuttle the gear and hikers closer to their 'tip-off' point for the actual hike and to contact a couple of local cowboys to coordinate in bringing a few pack animals and meet the hikers at a pre-determined point with the pack string where the actual hike would begin. He wasn't sure just how far the pack string could go before they would be on their own, but Kenny studied the Elk Ridge regional topographic map and made some phone calls and came up with an eight-day round trip itinerary – four of which would be backpacking on their own to the bottom of Dark Canyon.

Ansel came through with the jeep. In a letter dated June 4, 1946 L.S. Applegate, Sales Manager for *The Ohio Willys Sales Company* wrote Ansel Hall and provided a quote of $1,329.72 for "One (1) Model CJ-2A including freight, conditioning, and draw bar.....including all Federal Taxes applicable.... could be made available for immediate delivery." [69] The Colorado Certificate of Title showed that Ansel Hall became the first registered owner of the Jeep CJ-2A on July 1, 1946.

Ansel saw the need to advertise the "wilderness experience" so he was thrilled that he could sponsor a trip that would splash across the pages. He contacted his reliable friend, Randall Henderson at *Desert Magazine*, to be part of the group to document the small expedition to the mouth of Dark Canyon.

Kenny did a little asking around and found two ranchers, Clarence Rogers and Cardon Jones who ran livestock on Elk Ridge in the summer months. They suggested that they would ride in following Trail Canyon and meet Kenny's group at a corral where the side canyon intersected Dark Canyon. They also discussed where possible springs were along the proposed route that might have potable water (Figure 4.40).

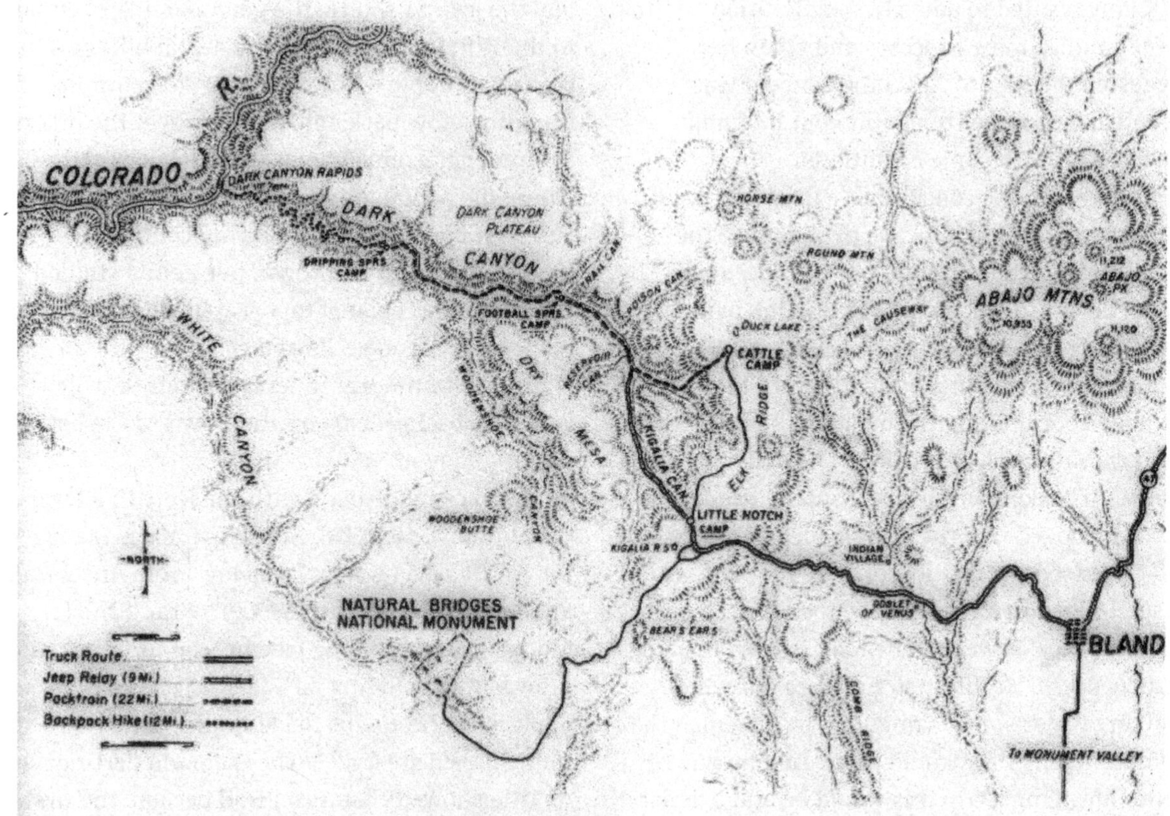

Figure 4.40 Sketch map showing the route for the Explorers Camp Dark Canyon hike in 1946; the hike was highlighted in an article in the Dec, 1946 issue of *The Desert Magazine* entitled "We hiked Dark Canyon" by Randall Henderson. (Sketch map by K. Ross, not to scale)

THE DARK CANYON HIKE

Both the archaeological dig at Cahone and the hike into Dark Canyon became a reality just in time for Ansel to add the little blurbs in his brochure that advertised the various activities planned for the 1946 field camp. He invited Randall Henderson to join him on an expedition *to penetrate deep in the Dark canyon country in quest of Indian ruins* but at the last minute, Ansel backed out due to unexplained reasons. The group consisted of the following participants:

Kenny Ross, Trip Leader
Fran Hall, a mountaineer and photographer (no relation to Ansel)
Randall Henderson, Editor of *Desert Magazine* documented the Explorers exploits[70]
Knowles Hall, oldest son of Ansel's attending the University of California[71]

Explorers Camp boys included:

Roger Hall, age 13, younger son of Ansel's
Ralph Condit, from Greenwich, Connecticut
Clay Doss, of Bloomfield Hills, Illinois
Duncan McEntyre, of Colorado Springs, Colorado
Jack Pickering, of Goshen, Indiana
Paul Shiman, of New York City

Figure 4.41 Kenny Ross (L) tightening knapsack on one of the Dark Canyon hikers, 1946. (K. Ross collection)

When Randall Henderson accompanied the Explorers group into Dark Canyon it was still regarded as a canyon about which little was known with "impassable cliffs" and he was unsure whether it could be followed to its confluence with the Colorado River in Cataract Canyon (Figure 4.41). Canyon names mentioned in his article have been corrected with proper names and mileage distances and elevations verified by re-mapping.[72]

Henderson met Kenny Ross on Thursday, August 15 at Mesa Verde National Park where the expedition was to start. They had the one and a half-ton Dodge truck, a jeep and the ten participants headed out from Mesa Verde to Monticello, then to Blanding where the pavement ended, then west to Elk Ridge past Kigalia Ranger Station to Little Notch where they camped for the night (Figure 4.40).

The next morning (Friday, August 16) equipment was transferred from the truck to the jeep that shuttled the gear nine miles down Kigalia and Peavine Canyons [Henderson map shows it all as Kigalia Canyon] past the intersection with upper Dark Canyon and proceeded another mile to the mouth of Rig Canyon that entered from the southwest where they found a corral. Here they rendezvoused with horse packers Jones and Rogers. The wranglers had shown up with eight pack animals and all the gear was transferred again from the jeep to the horses and mules.

They followed the pack train down canyon a little over five miles to where the packers had made a camp near a spring that the boys named "Football Spring" because a football-shaped balanced rock on a pedestal made quite the landmark [Henderson mistakenly said they traveled eight miles since meeting up with the cowboys]. The spring was just upstream of Warren Canyon that entered from the south and across from Trail Canyon that entered from the north (Figure 4.40).

The next morning (Saturday, August 17) they got underway and intersected the mouth of Woodenshoe Canyon about six miles downstream [Henderson said 5 miles] and noted ruins and crumbling towers below Woodenshoe and mistakenly referred to a "black basalt" stratum dipping at the same fall of the canyon [the presence of a basalt layer is simply wrong; it was most likely a dense dark-gray cherty limestone bed in the upper part of the Honaker Trail Formation] (see Appendix II: Stratigraphic Column), but "this hard rock layer stayed with them all the way to the Colorado." *[NOTE: all marked trails on present-day topographic maps end at the junction of Woodenshoe Canyon].*

The going got tougher and tougher for the pack animals from Woodenshoe on as the canyon narrowed and vertical drops increased in height to where they couldn't go any farther. That was near "Dripping Spring" a distance of six to seven miles beyond the mouth of Woodenshoe Canyon. Based on Henderson's map he showed that the group backpacked the last twelve miles to the mouth of Dark Canyon and the confluence with the Colorado River (Figure 4.40). The packers had to stop when they made it to Black Steer Canyon that entered from the south (not shown on Henderson's map). The distance from Woodenshoe Canyon to the Colorado River was estimated to be approximately nineteen miles (Figure 4.40).

To make the trek to the mouth by backpack and unassisted by pack animals, Kenny Ross made sure the backpacks were reduced to bare essentials.

> We carried food for three days, evenly distributed among the 10 members of the party. There were three 100-foot ropes, camera equipment and first aid kits in addition to food and extra clothing. The elevation at this camp was 5090 feet, and it was warm even at night. Since we would lose another 1000 or 1200 feet before reaching the river, most of the boys carried only a jacket, and no bedding. We could always build a fire to keep warm if necessary, and we wanted to keep our packs under 20 pounds each.[73]

Many years later Roger Hall added a humorous anecdote not reported by Henderson. Although the group had sleeping bags and food and supplies in their heavy canvas backpacks, they expected more substantial food, including steaks, to be air-dropped. Ansel Hall reportedly "directed" this aerial expedition and he flew in a Stinson aircraft over the canyon and dropped supplies and food by parachute, but the parachutes failed and their rations were "splattered all over the rocks and we never got anything." [74]

Henderson mentioned that he didn't know how Dark Canyon got its name and surmised it may have been an early-day explorer who came up from the Colorado River and saw only the end of the gorge (Figure 4.42).[75] Henderson rightly stated that had the route been reversed such that the explorer saw the upper forty miles first he may have called it "Canyon of the Castles" [76] as it carved a twisting course on its way through the Cedar Mesa Sandstone and left pedestals and monoliths similar to that seen in lower Grand Gulch. The lower portion of the canyon dissected massive limestone beds of the Honaker Trail Formation where vertical drops increased from ten or twenty feet to as much as forty feet with deep plunge pools at the bottom, which required the boys to lower their packs by rope. The pools provided refreshing swim breaks for the boys.

They finally came upon a small fresh water trickle of a spring for drinking water and although the canyon walls seemed to wind endlessly, they first heard a faint rumble, but with each turn in the canyon the rumble grew louder and finally the echoing roar of Dark Canyon Rapid – they had made it to the Colorado River. They reached the mouth of Dark Canyon at 6:40 PM and after cooking dinner on a fire of driftwood they slept without bedding on a great sandbar. They had a group picture taken at the mouth of the canyon with all but the photographer lined up on a pile of boulders (Figure 4.43). They proclaimed that they were the first documented Anglos to descend Dark Canyon not considering earlier prospectors and explorers, but it was certainly a feat of accomplishment.

Henderson estimated the distance from where they left the pack train at twelve miles, but based on my re-tracing their route, the distance was closer to fifteen miles. He reported that the [round-trip] hike from the head of Kigalia Canyon to the Colorado River and back was forty-three miles, when it was actually closer to sixty-two miles and had taken four days. He recorded an elevation of 3,650 ft at the river and was within the margin of error depending on river levels. Of course, that's a moot point today, since the mouth has long been covered by silt and muck due to the construction of Glen Canyon Dam and the impoundment of Powell Reservoir in 1962. The group returned safely to Mesa Verde National Park on Thursday, August 22, 1946.

Figure 4.42 deep into Dark Canyon, 1946. (K. Ross collection)

Figure 4.43 the first documented group of "Anglo" boys and men to hike Dark Canyon to its mouth with the Colorado River, 1946; Kenny Ross (3rd from L) and writer Randall Henderson (far R). (K. Ross collection)

THE CAMP FINDS A LEADER

Assistant leader Richard Stultz was asked to write a critique of the 1946 camp season by Ansel Hall. Among the many suggestions he saw the need for two types of leaders. A leader trained in dealing with boys and who provided camp training and he said that last year's [1945] leaders lacked interest and ability. Secondly, since the program contained specialized activities like archaeology, geology, and mineralogy, a staff with these skills needed to be in place. "I think that you will find it practically impossible to find both qualifications in any one man, let alone trying to find a whole staff of such men." [77] Furthermore, Stultz suggested to Ansel:

> Tear yourself away from other obligations and spend more time with your camp. Get to know them individually – and your staff and do some supervising. You must either do this or arrange to turn the entire responsibility (and the necessary authority) over to some one man who will act as director of the whole program. There must be more personal contact between the person who is running the camp and all others concerned, even with the parents of the boys.[78]

Lastly, Stultz suggested that Hall provide the parents of each boy an account of the things that happened that season; a report of the boys activities, his abilities, accomplishments, development, promise, behavior, etc. The parents wanted to know these things. A personal Report for each boy was recommended. He thought that the individual reports to each parent would help bring some enthusiasm to the program such that they would tell their friends and would be the best kind of publicity.

> You must have adequately qualified individuals making such appraisals and writing such letters. They must understand boys and must have an appreciation of psychology and educational methods and techniques as applied to camp situations. You must select such staff members carefully.[79]

Richard Stultz had just described Kenny Ross as a genuine field trip leader and Ansel Hall knew it! The trek into Dark Canyon was a big success and well publicized in *Desert Magazine* which led Hall to offer Kenny Ross a one year contract of $2,000 to be the "Camp Manager" beginning in 1947.[80]

Figure 5.1 Kenny Ross, 1950s. (K. Ross collection)

5
EXPLORERS CAMP: 1947 to 1948

SMOKE 'EM IF YOU GOT 'EM

No one knew exactly when Kenny started smoking cigarettes – maybe as early as his cowboy days, where he learned to twist one up from a bag of Bull Durham with knee bent over the saddle horn, or possibly at Mesa Verde, as Jess Nusbaum and other park employees were big smokers too. Smoking was hard to avoid in the 1930s and 40s – just watch a Humphrey Bogart and Lauren Bacall movie to see what a *trend-setter* smoking had become. The first seen photos of Kenny with cigarette in hand are in many of the Mesa Verde photos and in almost every photo to his dying day. It is hard to find a picture of Kenny without that darn cigarette in hand or mouth (Figure 5.1).

Kenny was a man of medium-build, weighed in at 152 pounds and stood 5 ft-9 inches tall (although he did get persnickety in one of his numerous job applications with the NPS and listed his height as 5 ft-8-3/4 inches tall). His sons and numerous personal witnesses knew that in his later years his favorite brand of cigarettes was either Carleton's or Pall Mall and his favorite beers were either Hamm's or Lucky Lager.

As documented by all his letters from 1934 to the early-1980s Kenny was a prolific communicator by way of the typewriter – an *Underwood* manual version to be specific. Kenny was a competent typist and his communication efforts are duly recorded by the hundreds of documents he saved as onion-skinned carbon copies. He took his new job as "camp manager" quite seriously, and composed individual letters to each and every boy who was ever involved in the Explorers Camp from 1947 forward. Many of his letters are two to three pages long and single spaced with only minor errors or corrections.[1]

RIVER BOATING ERA BEGINS

The first boats to navigate the rivers and rapids on the Colorado Plateau were all made of wood or metal and hard-hulled. They varied over the years in design, but it was the availability of surplus military inflatable water craft that turned river boating into first a sport for the individual and soon a new vehicle to take passengers down the myriad canyons to explore and be over-whelmed by the sheer immensity and beauty one can only glean by looking up at walls of strata thousands of feet thick.

Kenny no doubt got his first "taste" of river boating in those flimsy plywood and canvas fold boats during the early trips for the RBMV expeditions, and his first glimpse of high canyon walls, thrilling rapids and even occasional cliff dwelling and petroglyph panels. But his interest had surely been whetted when he saw Dark Canyon Rapid in August, 1946. He was absolutely aghast at the roar and size of the rapids and began contemplating when he might get the opportunity to try his hand at running this and the other big rapids he had heard about in Cataract Canyon. The river running bug had bitten Kenny.

He read about inflatable crafts being used to go down rivers and discovered that Amos Burg ran the first inflatable boat through Cataract Canyon in 1938. So, to no surprise, over the winter of 1946-47 he typed letters of enquiry to *The Goodyear Rubber Company* as his interest in inflatable military rafts caught his attention. He learned that there was a huge variety of surplus boats and pontoons that ranged from Army Air Force life rafts to Navy and Marine assault crafts to bridge pontoons. They ranged in size from more than 30 ft long to 10 ft long and varied in tube diameters and associated accessories. Most were available through Military Surplus stores that had popped up across the country after the war was over and most of these stores were located near military bases.

The biggest surplus store for the southwest states was near Nellis Air Base in Las Vegas, Nevada known as "Bucks War Surplus Store." [2] Kenny reported his findings to Ansel and they discussed the feasibility of buying a few small life rafts to test and see if these would work on the San Juan River. He suggested to Ansel that they should purchase at least three boats and give it a go. Besides, the life rafts were inexpensive and self-contained.

THAT "SPIRITED LITTLE RIVER"

Kenny was not just interested in river running but he was also interested in the history of the region – both prehistorical and historical accounts. He researched the local libraries for information regarding Spanish Conquistadores to miners to Mormon pioneers. He also made notes – copious numbers of pages of hand-written notes on yellow notebook paper were transcribed into typed texts that he added to or refined as each season of the Explorers Camp progressed.

He already had a pretty good concept and recollection of the Ancient Puebloan culture from all the time spent at Mesa Verde and learned directly from the leaders in the field of southwest archaeology. Now he added river lore to his list and unwittingly became part of it.

By the time Kenny showed interest in the San Juan River a number of USGS professional papers had been published that he may have accessed.[3] He would have known that the San Juan River was the largest tributary to the Colorado River below the confluence of the Green and Grand rivers in Canyonlands (Figure 5.2). He must have had access to early versions of topographic maps of the Four Corners region, yet none were found in Don and Doug's collection of the Kenny Ross files and photos. Perhaps these maps were destroyed, or he only used maps available at libraries. Topographic maps that were available to Kenny in the 1940s and through most of the 1950s lacked details in the canyon country that lay to the west and along the Colorado River through Canyonlands and Glen Canyon. Accurate details of that region weren't added until the 1970 series of maps, and further refined in the "1989 Provisional Series of Topographic Maps" produced by the U.S. Geological Survey Topographic Division.[4] These remain the most recent published maps available to the general public.

Kenny certainly knew that the river's headwaters were along the west-facing side of the San Juan Mountains in southwest Colorado near Wolf Creek Pass and the Tusas Mountains in northernmost New Mexico. And he knew that the snow melt and rains that gathered in the upper drainage basin tributaries provided the bulk of perennial water in the river. His research led him to read about major flash floods in 1884, 1911 and 1927 that had washed away communities, bridges and gaging stations.

He learned that the San Juan was a relatively short river that was about 400 miles long from its headwaters to its mouth with the Colorado River. He knew its course, that it ran south-westerly out of Colorado across the New Mexico state line as it gathered waters from the Navajo, Piedra, Los Piños, La Plata and Mancos tributary rivers and then flattened into a braided sprawling muddy river as it cut northward and crossed back into Colorado near the conterminous point of the Four Corner states and then followed a zig-zagging course through Utah.

He was aware of the deeply carved entrenched meandering course the river had cut across the core of the Monument uplift and finally had cut deeply into the sandstone cliffs north of Navajo Mountain as it entered the Colorado River.

He had experienced a segment of the San Juan River in his RBMV trips in 1933–34, but had not experienced the river above Mexican Hat, Utah. And he knew there were very few towns or villages along its course below Shiprock in which he could launch a boat, or take out without blazing a new trail. Like most folks that are drawn to running boats down rivers, he learned a heck of a lot more by just doing it!

He pondered where to begin his first attempt at running the San Juan River and finally settled upon launching his first trips from Shiprock, New Mexico. He immediately learned that from Shiprock to Chinle Wash, the San Juan River rolled along at a much flatter gradient than in the canyons and he would have to learn how to negotiate an incredible braid of river channels most of the way (Figure 5.3). He also would experience a particular hydrologic phenomenon known as **sand waves** or as he and others named them **sand rollers** (Figure 5.4).

Over the rest of his life running the San Juan, he learned how fickle and unpredictable this river could be. Much of the time, it was just a "spirited little river, hurrying through ragged country." But the canyon stretches were "like an obstacle course."[5] However, it could become a raging torrent when the river suddenly rose, due to desert flash floods or distant mountain rains.

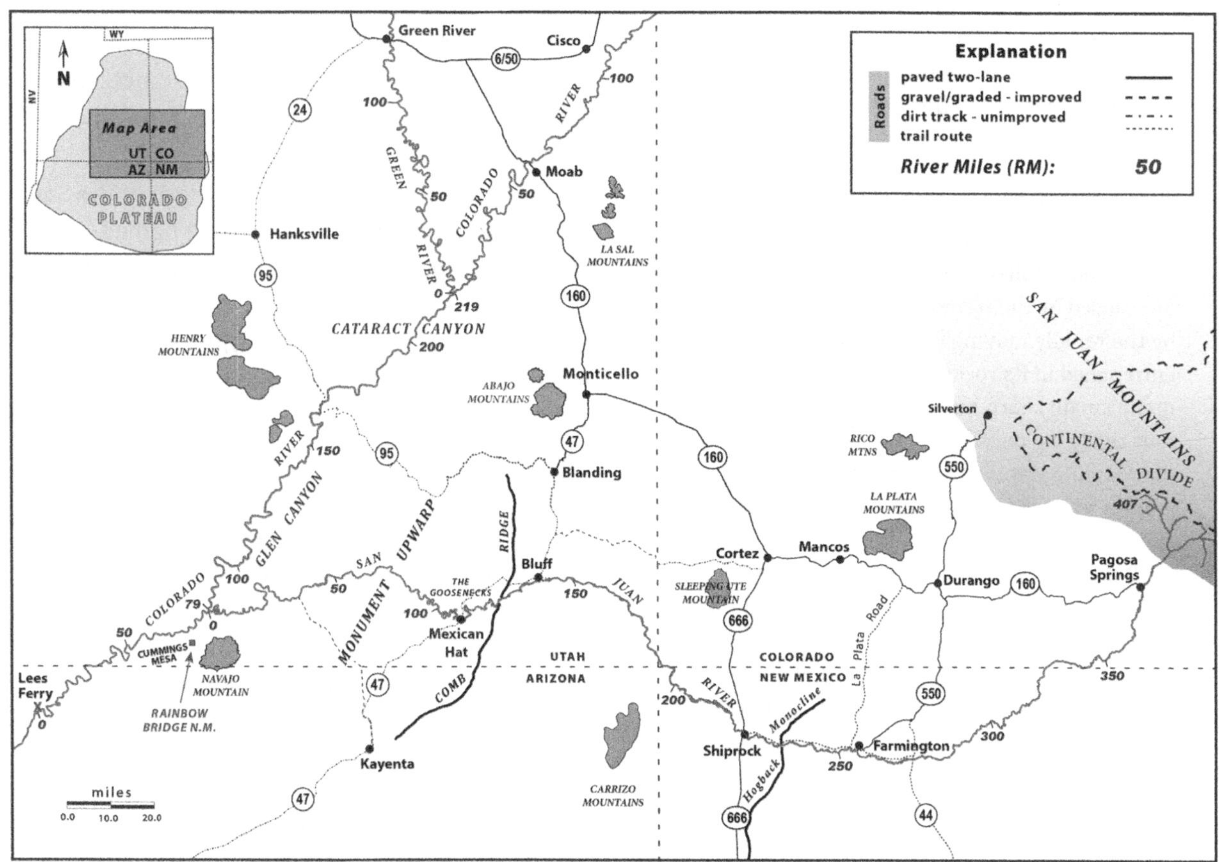

Figure 5.2 Map of Central Colorado Plateau showing surveyed river miles (RM) on Colorado, Green and San Juan rivers and major road network in region as of late 1940s. (GMS/TB original map)

After studying the San Juan River and running it a number of times and finally having completed trips from Bluff to Lees Ferry, Kenny, in his characteristic writing style, condensed his description of the San Juan and Glen Canyon experience into a few poetic paragraphs for his Explorers Camp brochures:

> In its upper reaches the San Juan is a typical mountain stream of tumbling falls and clear, quiet pools. As it gathers the waters of its mountain-born tributaries it becomes a mighty torrent which, crossing northern New Mexico, takes on a reddish hue as it is joined by a dozen or more silt-laden streams that rise and flow from the arid semi-desert. Now, swift and powerful, armed with a hundred thousand tons of abrasive sediments, it slashes and grinds its way across the high plateaus of southern Utah. The speed and power of its current makes it one of the most relentless of major streams where it has gnawed its way downward through thousands of feet of brightly colored, stratified rock representing pages and chapters in the ancient history of the Earth.
>
> One of the most intriguing features of the San Juan is the way its surface tends to break into rolling "sand waves" which, at high and medium stages of water, turn the river into an almost continuous "roller coaster." It is believed that these are caused by the tremendous burden of silt carried by the rapidly moving water. After becoming entrenched in its rocky gorge the river runs over many small, sharp rapids, and there are three or four really big ones that set up a deafening roar as the foaming water rushes over and between the masses of huge boulders which are their usual cause.
>
> Below the mouth of the San Juan, the Colorado rolls for nearly 80 miles through beautiful Glen Canyon, to Lee's Ferry, Arizona. In this stretch it seems quieter, more dignified, and of entirely different character than the smaller San Juan. Where the tributary canyon is narrow, vertical walled, and of sharply angular forms, Glen Canyon is spacious and its even higher walls are gracefully rounded and sculptured into weird, fairyland temples, towers, and domes. Although slower, the current sweeps along with a power and grandeur that puts the San Juan into its proper place – the lusty, brawling child of a regal parent.
>
> For all that the two rivers run a long and turbulent course through a great part of America's largest and least explored wilderness, passage by boat through its scenic canyons can hardly be called original exploration. It has been done before. Nevertheless, such a voyage remains one of the finest adventures left in an over-civilized age. It is an exhilarating roadway; the only access into a seldom visited land of color, silence and mystery. To travel it is to explore in a very special way. It is to leave behind the familiar world of men, convention, political cacophony and strife and to seek wisdom and peace in things not of men but of elemental Earth, majestic, ever-lasting, ever changing; ever heedless of the human creatures it has spawned.
>
> (Kenny Ross, Introduction to the SJ&C River Expeditions, 1951 Southwest Explorations Report)

Throughout the remainder of the book, references to river mileages and distances are included in Appendix I: Tables 1 to 4 for River Mileages.

Table 1 lists the cumulative length of the San Juan River by river mile (RM) with named tributaries and geographic places identified along its course measured below its headwaters in the San Juan Mountains to its confluence with the Colorado River. Key river mileages with named tributaries and geographic places are also identified on the Colorado River through lower Glen Canyon from the confluence with the San Juan River downstream to Lees Ferry. Because original river surveys conducted in the 1920s measured distances *upstream* from Lees Ferry and from major confluences upstream, the table also indicates river mileages from above, or below these zero points. For example, Bluff City is 261.8 miles below the headwaters, 144.8 miles above the confluence, and 223.8 miles above Lees Ferry (see Appendix I: Table 1 for River Mileages).

Figure 5.3 aerial view looking upstream at braided stream network which occurs in low-gradient stretches of the San Juan River between Shiprock, NM and Chinle Wash. The runnable channels can be misleading to an unwary boater; even as water level rises, the choice of which channel to take can still lead to trouble. (G.M. Stevenson)

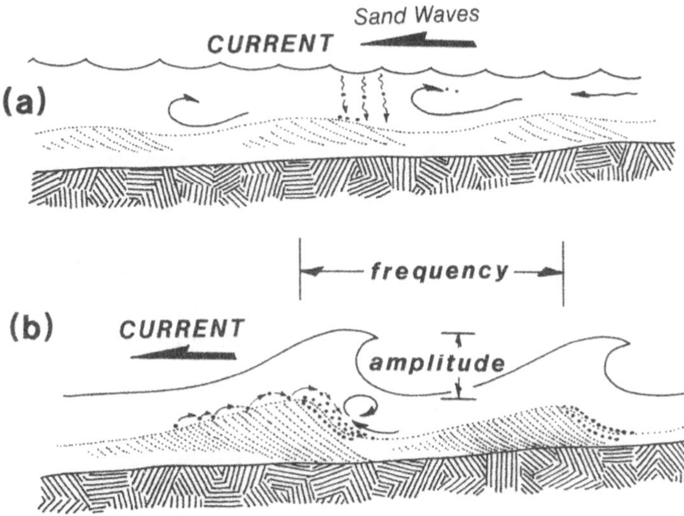

Figure 5.4 diagram of sand waves and how they form; they are the products of a perfect combination of stream bed gradient, suspended clay, silt, sand particles (load), and water velocity. Sand waves normally develop on stretches of the river where the gradient flattens, thus allowing the coarser particles (sand) to settle out of suspension. See Appendix IV: Glossary of river terms for details. (Modified from G.M. Stevenson, 1986)

Figure 5.5 wave trains of sand waves in San Juan River at Bluff, Utah May 01, 1947; river flowing from right to left. (USGS aerial photo)

Table 2 lists the cumulative length of the Colorado River with named tributaries and key geographic places identified from the confluence with the Green River through Cataract Canyon and through the entire length of Glen Canyon to Lees Ferry. Distances were measured *upstream* from Lees Ferry and from the confluence of the Green River and Colorado River.

Table 3 lists the length of the Colorado River with named tributaries and key geographic places identified from the Green River confluence upstream past Moab to the confluence with the Dolores River.

For completeness, Table 4 lists the length of the Green River from its confluence with the Colorado River to the town of Green River, Utah again noting interval distances to named tributaries and key geographic place names.

River miles (RM) for the San Juan River are also referenced based on distances provided in present day river guide books where distances are cited in *descending* order from below Sand Island or the U.S. Highway 191 Bridge. The sides, or river banks, of any section of rivers that are discussed are always based as if the reader was looking downstream: River Left (RL) or River Right (RR).

1947 EXPLORERS CAMP

In 1946 Ansel's friend Porter Sargent had suggested that Charles A. Lindbergh might be interested in sending his oldest son, Jon, to southwest Colorado to be part of the Explorers Camp. Ansel had sent a self-introductory letter to the famous Colonel in the spring of 1946, but had not received a reply. Among the many tasks asked of Kenny in his new position as Camp Manager, he sent letters out to a list of boys that Ansel had given him, including Jon Lindbergh.

Camp costs had been set at $475.00 per participant, not including transportation to and from Durango, where the boys were met and taken to Gold King Camp. The 1947 Explorers Camp boasted a membership of fifty-two boys from across the U.S.A.

The Charles Lindbergh family lived in an upscale community of Scotts Cove, Connecticut. "Lucky Lindy" as he had become to be known to the public, received the Medal of Honor from the U.S. Army Air Corps for his record setting flight in 1927 when he solo-piloted the "Spirit of St. Louis" non-stop from Long Island, New York to Le Bourget Field in Paris, France in a record-setting time of thirty-three hours and thirty minutes. The trans-Atlantic flight made Lindbergh an instant celebrity. He married Ann Morrow, daughter of Dwight Morrow who was a partner at J.P. Morgan & Co. on May 27, 1929. Their first born, Charles, Jr., was kidnapped and murdered in March, 1932. The murder led Congress to pass the so-called "Lindbergh Law" in June which made kidnapping a federal offense. They had five more children and both parents were quite sensitive about protecting the privacy and security of their children. It was a rather normal response following the horrible situation that had happened following the kidnapping and murder of their infant son.

Charles A. Lindbergh's fame and notoriety of the kidnapping forced him and his family to become intensely private and suspicious of a prying unrelenting press. By late 1935, they became particularly concerned for the safety of their second son, Jon Morrow Lindbergh (born August 16, 1932), and for several years lived secretly in exile in Europe. By 1939 they returned to live in the United States along with their third son, Land Morrow Lindbergh (born 1937), and following World War II settled into a wealthy and secure seaside estate at Scotts Cove on the "Gold Coast" in Darien, Connecticut.[6]

So it was quite the accomplishment, at least in Ansel's mind, to have such a famous person contact him for his son to join the Explorers Camp. A letter dated March 5, 1947 from Colonel Lindbergh's secretary, Barbara Mansfield, enquired "about dates, charges, activities and so forth" and mentioned that Jon was nearly fifteen years old and had considerable experience camping the previous two summers. "Colonel Lindbergh feels that Jon is now at an age when he would find the kind of camp experience you offer most interesting." [7]

A series of letters were exchanged between Kenny and Ansel with Lindbergh's secretary where camp accommodations and itineraries were forwarded. In a letter sent by Kenny dated May 31, 1947, he made reference to a newsletter that was sent to all the 1947 Explorers with the special comment, "You will note that Jon's name was omitted from the list of 1947 Explorers. This was done on the assumption that Colonel Lindbergh would prefer not to have his son's name listed." [8] Barbara Mansfield's return letter thanked Kenny very much for his thoughtful consideration in leaving Jon's name off the list of campers.[9]

Besides Jon Lindbergh, several other boys of note included the return of Roger Hall for his second season, Julius Kahn, whose family remained in touch with the Ross family for many years, Mike Maule (Stuart's brother) and Jack Oakes from Mancos.[10]

FIRST SAN JUAN RIVER TRIP WITH INFLATABLE MILITARY CRAFTS

Besides the correspondence with all the boys and parents of the upcoming Explorers Camp, Kenny's discussions with Ansel regarding the purchase of several inflatable rafts had come to fruition as Ansel had purchased three Army Air Corps life rafts. Don Ross described the boats:

> They were yellow and light weight – definitely weighed less than 200 pounds and maybe closer to 150 pounds. They were ten to eleven feet long with 10-12 inch diameter tubes; had thwarts fore and aft with flap seat in back; each boat came with four paddles maybe five feet long, a patch kit, inflatable life jackets [pull a string like Roger Hall did], or inflate by mouth and they also contained C-rations. All these boats came with small first aid kits including pocket knives that my brother and I cherished.[11]

In the May 1947 Explorers Camp Newsletter, Ansel Hall described an exciting preseason adventure – "a voyage by pneumatic life raft down through the canyons of the San Juan River." [12] The trial run down the San Juan River was planned with just Ansel and a few others to see if it might be feasible for a new "adventure" to add to the camps repertoire. On noon Saturday, May 3, 1947 Ansel, Kenny, Roger Hall and his friend Jimmie Carpenter plus four others left Mancos in the new army carry-all which had been acquired as a scout car for the desert expeditions. Jim Cook drove the old-faithful Dodge troop truck that carried the load of rafts and equipment. The two vehicles headed west down the McElmo Canyon road and crossed the "half mile sand trap of Yellow Jacket Wash successfully and rode dry shod across Montezuma Wash" (Figure 5.6).[13]

They arrived in Bluff around dusk and found a lovely camp on the bank of the San Juan River. After all the gear was unloaded Ansel and Jim Cook then drove the two vehicles to Mexican Hat where they left the truck and returned near midnight to an active "bull session" in progress by the campfire.[14]

They got up the next morning and had a hearty breakfast of "flapjacks, bacon and eggs, and good strong camp coffee" and then proceeded to inflate the "new air corps life rafts" and were underway by 7:00 AM. Ansel continued with a lengthy description of the scenery and overstated the number of cliff dwellings that were visible from the river, but he did mention the countless number of petroglyphs at Butler Wash.[15]

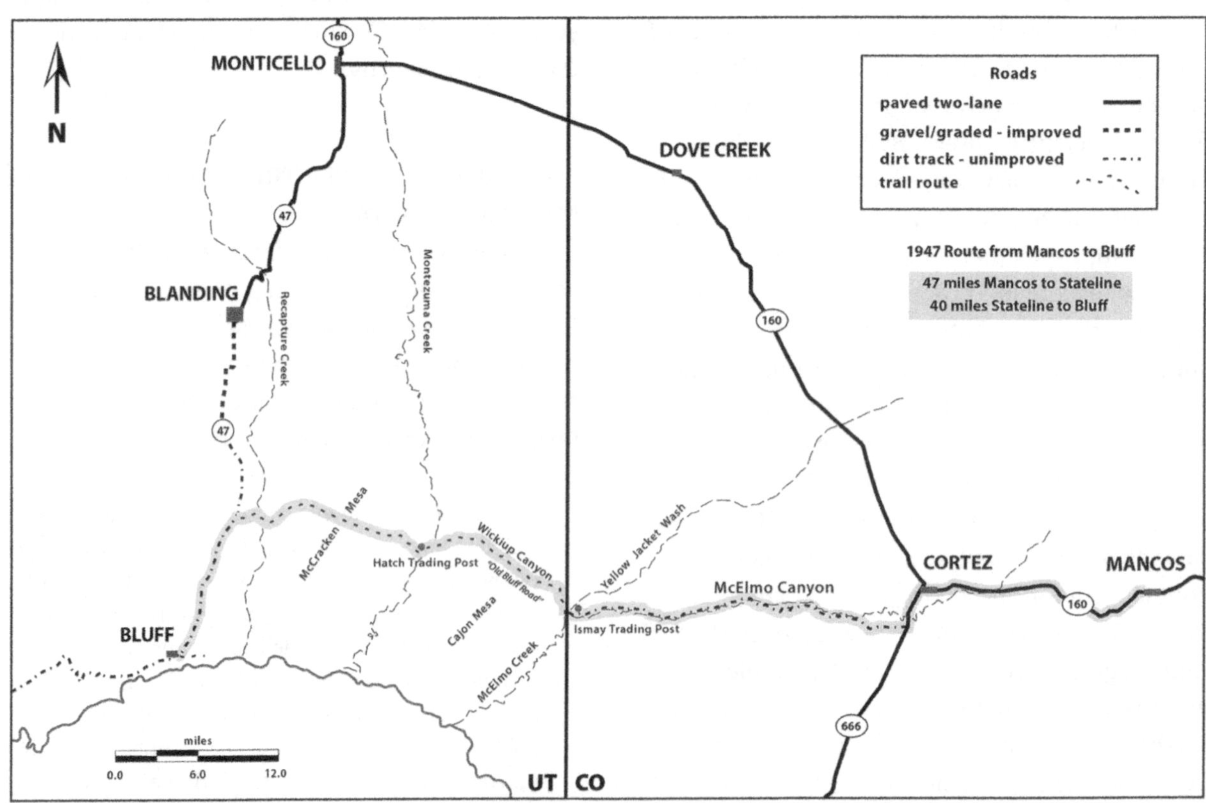

Figure 5.6 Map showing route from Mancos to Bluff in 1947 via McElmo Canyon and sandy bogs along "Old Bluff Road" through Wickiup Canyon and rocky trail to Route 47 – an approximate 87 mile long drive. (GMS/TB original map).

By noon they had made their way to "an old abandoned trading post" and hiked over to "extensive ruins left by Pueblo people" [16] and noted numerous Basketmaker sites. He mistakenly described the "basalt and sandstone cliffs" [17] that towered higher and higher above them. He mentioned "shooting rapids large enough to give us a real thrill and occasionally somewhat of a wetting." [18] He was impressed by the rafts buoyancy and that they maneuvered "very adroitly (after you learn how!)." [19]

Ansel concluded that the "Final results of our experimental expedition was to verify the fact that we are superbly equipped for the extra adventure which we hope may be enjoyed by every member of our 1947 Explorers' Camp – a two- or three-day voyage on the San Juan." [20] Ansel thought all they needed to do was to figure how to *squeeze* the river trips into the itinerary. Little did he know that the river trip segment would become the most compelling part of each camp season in the future.

LCRs: DURABLE & INEXPENSIVE

Kenny had mixed feelings about his first river trip with Ansel and the others from Bluff to Mexican Hat in three Air Corp life rafts. He liked the fact that the inflatable rafts were easy to maneuver but he didn't like them as they were a bit too flimsy, too small for passengers and camp gear and only navigable by paddles. Kenny kept these life rafts through the mid-1950s and Doug Ross recalled that these boats ended up as popular *swimming pools* for him and his neighborhood friends in Mancos. Kenny had already begun searching for more durable boats as a letter from *The Goodyear Tire and Rubber Company* dated May 7 was waiting for him when he returned from this maiden voyage.[21]

Kenny settled on the LCR-S type of military water craft (soon referred to as "7-mans" by river runners).[22] He convinced Ansel to purchase four of these sturdier boats for future trips with boys in the Explorers Camp and not try to use the flimsy Air Corp rafts, but the LCRs didn't arrive until fall 1948 (Figures 5.7). They also had to purchase at least four paddles per boat ranging from four to five feet in length. In addition, Kenny bought a number of small black water-proof knapsacks, water-proof delousing bags and metal ammunition cans with rubber seals in lids for water-proofing. These came in two basic sizes; one small can that held 50 caliber bullets and a larger can that held 20 caliber bullets. The ammo cans would be used to pack food and supplies. He bought life vests and flotation belts, water-proof tarps and rope – all available from military surplus stores. By 1947 there was a military surplus store in Farmington, New Mexico but the boats were in Las Vegas, Nevada at "Bucks" or in Salt Lake City, Utah. And most importantly, he bought several five-gallon sealable milk cans from the local farm co-op store that could be used for fresh drinking water.

THE 1947 FIELD STAFF

Ansel F. Hall, Director, Mancos, CO

Dr. Harvey E. Stork, Field Director; Carleton College, Northfield, Minnesota (only available for part of field season)

Kenneth I. Ross, Camp Manager, Mancos, CO (coordinating equipment, supplies, commissary, transportation, etc)

Earl Mattes, Assistant Camp Manager, Bayfield, CO

Ted Guthe, Archaeologist, Chicago, Illinois

Dr. George Ruhle, Park Naturalist for Crater Lake National Park (for high mtn experience)

Richard F. Van Valkenburgh, Leader for desert expeditions (author of articles on Navajo and prehistoric peoples of the SW in Desert Magazine)

Tyler Jekyll, Horse Wrangler, Mancos, CO

In previous camps the boys were divided into several smaller groups that would take two to three week long excursions hiking in the mountains, exploring the ruins and petroglyphs and scenery in Navajoland, etc and then rotate. Now more options had become available including two to three day river trips down the San Juan River and a *real* archaeological excavation at Cahone ruins. Ansel came up with the concept of naming groups after Indian tribes and assigned adult leaders. His other innovation was in appointing "adventure-cooks" where each was assigned to their own group of the four expeditions.[23]

PLANS FOR 1947 SEASON

In his May 1947 newsletter, Ansel referred to a sixteen page announcement with changes. The first period desert expedition: same as before, plus "we may emulate Escalante by starting expedition from Santa Fe as he did in 1776" [24] and working northward as Escalante did. If needed the jeep and troop transport rig would be replaced with pack and saddle horses. Ansel had conferred with the Director of the State Historical Museum in New Mexico as well as State historians from Colorado and Utah. All were quite interested in this project where their plan was to erect markers at all the recorded camp sites along Escalante's route.[25]

Figure 5.7 LCR-S; Landing Craft, Rubber-Small: a military assault rubber craft that held seven men; it weighed 210 pounds; length: 12 ft-5 inches; Beam: 5 ft-11 inches: tube diameter: 12 inches; two thwarts. LCRs had several compartments, one of which held bullet plugs that were tapered dowels of varying diameters. LCR-L; Landing Craft, Rubber-Large (not shown): a military assault rubber craft that held ten men; weighed 395 pounds; length: 16 ft; beam: 8 ft; tube diameter: 14 inches; three thwarts; the first 10-man LCR-L was purchased by Explorers Camp in 1951; the boys named it "The Monster" since it was so much bigger and heavier than the LCR-S.
(photo courtesy of H. Hoops)

The second and third Desert Expeditions had been modified to follow Richard Van Valkenburgh into:

> two very remote canyons lying about 150 miles southeast of Mesa Verde which are not penetrated by road or trail, but which can be reached from the San Juan River. At the present time we are developing a plan to descend the river by life raft, tying up at the mouth of these canyons for our detailed explorations which we hope may disclose the 'colored pictures' described to Doctor Van Valkenburgh by some of his Navajo friends.[26]

Retracing the route of Escalante didn't happen until the next year (1948). The only canyons accessible by boat from the San Juan River and not by vehicle would have to have been either Chinle Wash or lower Grand Gulch, and both are less than 150 miles *southwest* of Mesa Verde, not "southeast." Both had plenty of Ancient Puebloan ruins and petroglyphs, but there was no documentation that either of these canyons were explored by the Explorers Camp for Boys in 1947 and led by Richard Van Valkenburgh. In fact, there was no record of Van Valkenburgh ever showing up for that season's activities. However, the planned high mountain expeditions were conducted as in previous years.

HEROIC ACTS

In a key letter to Colonel Charles A. Lindbergh dated July 23, 1947, Kenny updated Jon's father as to what was going on at the camp. Rain and snow had forced some alterations for the first part of the camp (the orientation, camp skills, physical conditioning, etc at Gold King) but the Desert Expedition got off to a late start on June 29 of which Jon was a member.

Two new leaders were added to the staff at the last minute: Bob Holmes of Illinois Wesleyan and Bob Russell of Princeton Seminary. They traveled a large part of the Four Corners country "with visits to Aztec Ruins, Chaco Canyon National Monument, Gallup, Canyon De Chelly National Monument, Betatakin Ruin, and the long hike from Rainbow Lodge in Arizona down to Rainbow Bridge (see Figure 2.6) and back which was undoubtedly one of the highlights of the entire expedition (Figure 5.8)." [27]

Kenny explained that Jon had "made himself somewhat of a hero by 'topping out' first and returning two miles down the trail with canteens of water and coca colas for the rest of the party." [28] The hike from Rainbow Lodge to Rainbow Bridge crossed open rocky terrain with little to no shade, with no water available for resupply from springs along the way and it was a twenty-six mile round trip. And it was July, the hottest part of the summer! The elevation changed from 6,400 ft at the lodge to about 2,800 ft below the natural bridge, or a difference of 3,600 ft over rough open terrain (Figure 5.9). The hike was led by Bob Holmes who also complimented Jon for his common sense, energy and ability to grasp a situation in a very mature fashion.

Kenny continued to heap accolades on Jon as a member of the Explorers Camp and that he had adjusted himself perfectly to the other fellows and vice versa and that Jon had been largely responsible for the high morale of his group. "I have had frequent long conversations with Jon as we shared a boat on our recent trip down the San Juan River from Bluff, Utah to Mexican Hat. I find him a good companion and an excellent paddler. We handled the supply boat which led the way and in spite of his much smaller size I had to tax myself to pull with him." [29]

Figure 5.8 aerial view to west of trail to Rainbow Lodge (circled) on south side of Navajo Mountain with dissected canyons of Cummings Mesa in background; the thirteen mile long trail from the lodge to Rainbow Bridge was established by John Wetherill and others on the 1922 Bernheimer expedition. (Thorn Mayes photo #608; K. Ross collection)

Figure 5.9 Rainbow Lodge Trading Post; the trading post was started by the Richardson's; it's located near Endische Spring (see Bernheimer map, Figure 2.1); Barry Goldwater once had an interest in it. (S. Aitchison photo Sept, 2010)

Kenny also led a group back down Dark Canyon by way of Woodenshoe Canyon and Jon Lindbergh was part of that group. He ran up and down along the big rapid at the mouth of Dark Canyon anxiously scouting it in hopes of running it by boat the following year during camp season.[30]

Jon's group (the Zuni's) set out on July 17 for a two-day visit to Mesa Verde and then on to the archaeological camp at Cahone, Colorado where he worked under the guidance of Mr. Ted Guthe excavating the large Pueblo Indian ruin where investigations had begun the previous year. Kenny visited the Cahone site on Friday, August 1 and took the boys on a two-day trip to Arches National Monument for the opportunity to take color and black and white photos.

On Saturday, August 2 the boys returned to Gold King base camp from which they set out on an entirely new adventure. On Friday, September 5 a letter from Charles Lindbergh to Kenny stated that Jon had returned home "in excellent condition and is enthusiastic about the camp. He appears to have had a grand summer with you." [31] A camp relationship report was sent to Colonel Lindbergh with comments from the camp leaders who all gave Jon high marks and Ansel claimed that Jon was certainly the outstanding camper of the 1947 season and was invited back for the 1948 season.[32]

SUMMARY

There were several San Juan River trips led by Kenny Ross in 1947 that went from Bluff to Mexican Hat in the Air Corp life rafts. And the group names had changed during the camp season, as "Zuni" (Jon's group) was not listed in Ansel's earlier letters. There was absolutely no mention of Richard Van Valkenburgh accessing the canyons that supposedly lay 150 miles southeast (?) *or* southwest of Mesa Verde and that were accessible from the San Juan River. Kenny recognized that the twenty-six mile round-trip hike in the hot desert sun to Rainbow Bridge could be shortened considerably to less than a nine mile round-trip hike from the river if he could convince Ansel of his new plan. The idea of traveling by boat down the San Juan River from Bluff past the confluence with the Colorado River and down the serene sandstone corridor of Glen Canyon to Lees Ferry was spinning in Kenny's mind as to what logistical planning would be needed to pull this off. However, the plan for a Cataract Canyon trip was cancelled. Ansel thought it was too hazardous for the average camp participant, plus Kenny knew that the Air Corps life rafts were just too flimsy a boat to test the rapids in Cataract Canyon.

FALL 1947 TO SPRING 1948

In September Ansel received a letter from an old RBMV colleague. Henry "Hank" Zuidema was Geology Professor at the University of Michigan, Ann Arbor, Michigan and his primary interests were in paleoentomology and vertebrate paleontology of Cenozoic fossils in the Ruby Basin in Montana. He was on the RBMV expedition in 1936 [33] and was also aware of potentially well-preserved, intact reptilian fossils in the Triassic age Moenkopi and Chinle formations in the Four Corners region (see Appendix II: Stratigraphic column). He mentioned that the science magazine *The Earth Science Digest (a magazine devoted to the advancement of the geological sciences)* was on its last legs and he had decided to take over publishing duties and move the headquarters to Michigan. He also noted that "the village of Bayfield, Colorado" had staked off a lot near the highway and offered the parcel of land to the magazine for free and even has a sign saying "future home of the Earth Science Digest!" He invited Ansel Hall to be on the "editorial board" and to place his name on the mast-head along with four other geologists. He felt that Ansel's name and association with Mesa Verde would help give it some credibility.[34] Ansel replied by letter and said he was flattered by the offer, but that it would be a mistake because he didn't have any academic credentials in the field of archaeology. He cited that his professional academic background was in biology and forestry. Ansel then *recommended Kenny Ross to join the editorial board* and noted that Kenny had served as Assistant Park Naturalist at Mesa Verde and "is one of the keenest field men in his profession...." [35] He further noted that Kenny had taken over the permanent position of "field director for our Explorers Camp" and that this connection might provide a credible connection to the Earth Science Digest. Ansel had already asked Kenny and he was amenable to the offer.[36]

Then in April 1948, Ansel asked Dr. Henry Zuidema what happened to the Earth Science Digest adding Kenny to its editorial board? Apparently, Kenny was never offered the position since he didn't actually have official degrees in any scientific field. In other words, Kenny was snubbed as a non-scholar; a common problem with academia not recognizing hands-on achievements. Ansel invited Henry to come out and be a "guest scientist" at the Explorers Camp that summer and said he was "shoving off tomorrow on a hit and run trip to the Pacific Coast" and would be back in Colorado by the first of May.[37] Zuidema replied that he had committed to a geology (paleontology) field season in Montana and would not be able to make it to the Explorers Camp and asked about next year (1949).[38]

Kenny was surprised when he received a hand-written letter personally addressed to him from Jon Lindbergh dated January 21, 1948 in which Jon mentioned the storms that had occurred in the northeast that winter, some considerable detail about his fishing experiences and closed by stating that he was looking forward to coming out for camp that summer. A clear friendship between the two was apparent.[39] Plus, the 1948 Explorers Camp brought another young man that would truly become a life-long friend of Kenny's; William R. Dickinson, or 'Big Bill' as he was soon known to most acquaintances. Bill was living in the Santa Barbara, California area on a small ranch raising horses. He mentioned that he had "canoed white water rivers in West Virginia at sub-15 yrs old while living in Tennessee." [40] His mother and father had separated the year before, and his mother was anxious to see Bill accept going off to a boy's camp for the summer.

Little did anyone know at the time, but Bill and Jon became the closest of friends and following their Explorers Camp days they attended Stanford University together. By the end of the 1948 camp season, Kenny would have developed two strong mentor-protégé relationships.

THE MOTORSHIP GILA MONSTER

In January 1948 Kenny and Ansel made a trip to southern California where they spent two weeks buying equipment for the camp and the Mesa Verde Company. They bought four hundred pounds of "prime dates" to supplant raisins for knapsack trips. While in Santa Ana Stuart Maule found a DUKW [41] (Figure 5.10) at Bascom Rush's military surplus business and they test drove it and ended up purchasing it for "slightly less than one-fourth its original cost of approximately $9000." [42] Kenny described his experience to Jon Lindbergh:

> A big (31 foot) Army amphibious 'Duck' parked--or docked- at the curb in front of a used car dealers place and, never having seen one close up before, we stopped and looked it over. It was brand new-only 300 miles on it-and the price was rediculously low so-yep, you guessed it-we bought the durn thing for use on the roving expeditions. It has lots of road clearance, lots of space in the bilges and holds-fore and aft-to stow supplies and equipment and the cockpit (13x8 feet) is plenty big

enough to comfortably seat the 20 fellows who will be along on any one trip.

When I spoke of road clearance I meant both that it has it and it does it. While trying it out I drove right up the main business street of Santa Ana and had no traffic problem at all. Drivers of other vehicles took one startled look and--dodged. What sort of psychosis it will produce in the Navajo Indians and their horses remain to be seen. A 31 foot motor-ship cruising though Monument Valley may be a bit startling. Seriously though, it handles as easily as an ordinary truck, provided you carefully calculate the overhang of the bow, and--I Think--it will prove a very practical piece of equipment for our land cruises. It's now being painted blue and gold with white decks and an awning is being made for it that will make it look quite ship-shape. Its name is to be the "Motorship Gila Monster." [43]

In late March the whole Ross family (Kenny, Mildred, Don and Doug) drove in Ansel's old Ford sedan to California. The car broke down near Gallup, but following repairs and with no further problems they arrived in California at Kenny's sisters' place. The next day Kenny picked up the brand new Army amphibious "Duck" (now painted blue and yellow) and left the old Ford sedan at the dealership. The DUKW was then formally boarded by the Ross family and the *"Motorship Gila Monster"* would forever remain its name. Although Doug Ross was only two-years old at the time, he recalled family photographs at the beach at San Luis Obispo in April, 1948, even though the city of Santa Ana was south of Los Angeles and questioned why they were there. Why did they go that far north of Los Angeles? Bill Dickinson provided the answer:

> I met Kenny in the winter of 1948 when he was prospecting for Explorers Campers with his DUKW in California. Signed on as a camper in 1948 and counsellor in 1949. If memory serves, ran the San Juan from Shiprock to Bluff the first year and then from Bluff to Lees Ferry the second year (came back just for the latter run in 1950 and 1951, again if memory serves). So ran Piute Falls and the Thirteen Footer with him three times (eat your heart out).[44]

Figure 5.10 The DUKW purchased in California looked like this one (file photo; the newspaper article photo of the actual one purchased is too poor a quality to be shown here).

The four members of the Ross family drove the DUKW back to Mancos following Route 66 out of California to Gallup where they turned north and returned safe and sound back in Mancos, Colorado. Don Ross recalled that many eyes were turned as they cruised eastward out of Los Angeles. Doug and Don both confirmed that it didn't go very fast [45 mph tops]. Ansel may have traded the Ford in on some buses as Bill Winkler and his wife, Merrie [Hall] Winkler told me that the two of them drove one of the buses back to Mancos in 1948 following the same route that Kenny did. It's possible that Ansel and Stuart Maule drove the other two buses.

Bill Winkler said that when the DUKW had arrived back in Colorado, Roger Hall and a friend took it out on a lake for a test run. Bill watched from shore and noticed it had listed strongly to one side and motioned the boys in. When they drained the water-logged amphibious craft they noticed that three of the four drain plugs were missing! Bill made the necessary repairs to plug the drain holes and they never had another problem, but he laughed when he told the story as they came mighty close to sinking the *Motorship Gila Monster* before it was officially used.[45]

THE 1948 CAMP STAFF AND EXPLORERS

The camp staff for the 1948 Explorers Camp included: Kenny Ross, Camp Director and Dr. George K. Neumann, Archaeologist from the University of Indiana. Guest scientists who served for one or more exploration periods included: Mr. Art Nielhoff from the University of Indiana, Mr. Norman L. Thomas, Geologist from Corpus Christi, Texas, and Dr. Sterling Maxfield, Physician from Muskegon, Michigan. David Sanchez was the head wrangler and riding instructor from Marvel, Colorado and John Chattalier served as assistant wrangler, from Verona, New Jersey. C.G. Koob served as an alternate leader from Dubuque, Iowa. Mr. Gordon Thomas and Mr. William S. Fulton served as camp cooks. And Mr. Fred Gipson, a feature writer and author was a guest of the high mountain expedition from July 19 through July 23. Nineteen boys had signed up as camp explorers. Following the week of general orientation and conditioning at Gold King base camp that included hiking, climbing, shooting rifles, etc the boys were divided into two groups.[46]

RETRACING ESCALANTE'S ROUTE IN THE DUKW

Kenny already had a trip planned for his Explorers' group for June 26, 1948 for a three-day river trip from Shiprock to Mexican Hat and then to travel via the Motorship Gila Monster from Shiprock to Santa Fe, New Mexico and retrace northward the 1776 trail of Father Escalante. Meanwhile, Dr. Neumann led the other group to Mesa Verde National Park for orientation and then proceeded to the Cahone Ruin to begin the season's archaeological excavations.[47]

Kenny's party left in the *Motorship Gila Monster* with the Jeep towing their kitchen trailer and they traveled to Shiprock, New Mexico where after storing their motor vehicles the group began the trip down the San Juan River in rubber assault craft and Airforce life rafts. The group reportedly traveled 150 miles downriver to Mexican Hat, Utah which they reached at midday on June 30.[48] In a letter to Mrs. Margaret Dickinson, Kenny explained the river trip.

> Tomorrow morning Bill's group, under my leadership, will leave Gold King base camp and start out on our first expedition. We will begin with a three-day, 150- mile trip down the Middle San Juan River in air forces life rafts and landing craft from Shiprock, New Mexico to Mexican Hat, Utah. From there we will go directly to Santa Fe, New Mexico where we will trek northward in an attempt to retrace the trail of the Spanish pioneer, Father

> Escalante. Our expedition will return to Gold King on the evening of July 11.[49]

Upon their return to Shiprock Kenny's group loaded up and traveled via the *Motorship Gila Monster* from Shiprock to Santa Fe where they were to travel northward attempting to retrace the trail of Father Escalante in 1776 as Ansel had planned to do in the previous year's camp. They still planned to erect markers at all the recorded camp sites along Escalante's route. The other group continued with the archaeological excavations at Cahone ruin. In early August, Field Director, Kenny Ross sent a report to the boy's parents that caught them up on what had transpired so far in that year's camp. An excerpt from Kenny's newsletter follows:

> Many miles have passed under the wheels of the "Gila Monster" and our other vehicles since Camp opened. On June 26, the Explorers were divided into two groups, one under the leadership of Dr. George Neumann, Professor of Anthropology at the University of Indiana and the other under my supervision. Dr. Neumann's group went to the site of our archaeological excavations west of Cahone Colorado, and they spent the time continuing the work of excavating an ancient Pueblo Indian village. This archaeological group consisted of Edward Milligan, Carl Lindeman, Clifford Boram, Walter Coffey, Dennis De Shazo, Andrew Pruitt, and Gregory Anderson.
>
> All of the fellows took active part in the renewed excavations and have indicated to me that they returned to Gold King base camp with the feeling they had accomplished something of real value.
>
> Life at Cahone is simple and rugged, with tents provided as sleeping quarters, although most of the boys prefer to sleep out under the stars or in the prehistoric caves which lie just under the camp site. No attempt was made to regulate them in their preference concerning sleeping quarters. The climate at the "dig" is moderate, with warm, even hot days, but cool, comfortable nights. The area is one in which, in the past, I have spent some of my most interesting days walking the Mesa Tops examining prehistoric ruins and enjoying the subtle aromas of the pinon, juniper and wild sage which combine to make the Southwestern air a never-to-be-forgotten experience.
>
> The second party, under my directions, set out June 25 to begin the initial work of retracing the trail traveled by the Spanish Missionary Father Silvestre Escalante ln 1776. The members of this group were: James Beck, Nick Ferris, Frank Harris, Michael Wolff, Hiller Zobel, John Lucas, Bruce Henderson, Bill Dickinson, Neal Thomas, Malcolm Whyte, Jim Jacobs, Jon Lindbergh, and Timothy Gaskin.
>
> We were somewhat lax in getting directly to our objective, Father Escalante's starting point at Santa Fe, and enjoyed a truant four-day cruise down the San Juan River from Shiprock, New Mexico, past that famous point where the four states meet with a common corner, to Mexican Hat which lies just north of Monument Valley in Utah. After stowing away our boats we returned to Shiprock and the "Gila Monster", our Army amphibian, and traveled directly to Santa Fe, New Mexico, where we arrived just in time to take part in the 4th of July celebrations in that oldest capital city in the United States.
>
> After leaving Santa Fe, we attempted to cover as much as possible of the lower end of Father Escalante's trail, stopping overnight at the Pueblo village of Santa Clara on the banks of the Rio Grande River. ALL of the fellows had a splendid opportunity to see the everyday life of our modern Pueblo Indians who are descendants of ancient people, some of whom we call the cliff dwellers. We also stopped briefly at the ruins of the old, adobe mission of Santa Clara de Abiquiu which was established by the Spanish Fathers in the early 17th Century. At one point in northern New Mexico we found a sizable portion of the Escalante Trail now covered by the waters backed up by El Vado Dam and, fortunately with our 31-ft amphibian it was possible for us to approximately retrace this. Everybody had a wonderful time giving the "Monster" its first bath that was sponsored by Explorers' Camp. Of course, we had many onlookers as well as a few guest passengers for this adventure.
>
> Traveling northward and westward from El Vado, some confusion in the diary and maps left by Father Escalante, and, it must be confessed, a bit of stupidity on our part, caused us to become "lost"

for almost an entire day. It is perhaps only a coincidence that near the same point Father Escalante also lost his way 172 years ago. We finally rejoined the Escalante trail in the vicinity of Dulce, New Mexico, and from that point continued generally northward to Durango, Colorado, and thence to our Gold King base camp where we met the group from Cahone.

All the Explorers had a wonderful two days at the base camp comparing experiences of the two expeditions, and taking advantage of hot baths, good meals, and lots of rest.

On July 13 and 14 our group was again divided into two parties with most of the fellows who had spent the first period at Cahone accompanying me on a horseback and packing expedition into the isolated Bear Creek Canyon of the La Plata Mountains. Those who had previously been with me on the Escalante trip went to Cahone for the second period. The new Cahone group continued work started by the first party and worked at some very real if not tremendously spectacular archaeological investigations. The high mountain group spent an interesting two and a half weeks collecting plants, searching for minerals, and generally exploring the head of Bear Creek Canyon.

Only two days ago the two groups again came together at base camp in the La Plata Canyon and are now preparing to set off on the last expedition. One group will go to Cahone to finish up the summers excavations started by the two previous groups; the other party will go into Beef Basin, a little-known area of eastern Utah – one that is still represented by a beautifully mysterious blank of non-existent maps. We do not know just what we may find or accomplish in this area as we will be pioneering it from the scientific standpoint. But we expect intriguing geology and much of archaeological interest is represented there. In addition to myself, who will lead the Beef Basin expeditions our guest scientists will include Norman Thomas, a geologist who is with us during his vacation from duties with one of the major oil companies, and Dr. Sterling Maxfield, a physician from Muskegon, Michigan.[50]

You gotta be careful if you don't know where you're going; otherwise you might not get there!
– Yogi Berra

THE BEEF BASIN – GYPSUM CANYON EXPEDITION

The expedition group of fifteen parted ways with the Cahone ruin group on August 3, and reached Devil's Canyon camp ground south of Monticello, Utah in a steady rain and set up tents. The rain continued the next day so plans to camp on Elk Ridge were scrapped and they decided to stay put. The rain slacked by late afternoon and Mr. Thomas showed the boys some geological methods using a Brunton compass.

After a fairly dry night they struck camp and on the morning of August 5 they headed south to Blanding where they purchased additional supplies and refueled at the gas station. They continued west out of Blanding on the Elk Mountain Road (shown as UT Route 95 on 1935, 1940 topographic maps; present-day County Road 268 toward Elk Ridge; Figure 5.11). They had a slow trip negotiating the seven-ton, thirty-one foot long amphibious DUKW over this twisting knife-edge roadway that crossed Big Canyon, Brushy Basin Wash and across intervening ridges, then across Cottonwood Wash and upward until they reached the top of "the Elk." [51] They turned right (north) and followed an intersecting Forest Service road across Little Notch and Babylon Pasture and "crept across Big Notch where Cottonwood Wash and Dark Canyon meet with opposing heads. At one point we had to back the MONSTER several times to negotiate a curve" [52] The going got tougher as they proceeded and the road dwindled into a cow path that was impossible to follow with the big rig but they made their way westward toward the canyon rim and "made camp in a small aspen grove nearby a spring" [53] [Crystal Spring on North Long Point] (Figure 5.12). They spent the next three days taking short hikes to familiarize themselves with the terrane. It was time to make the plunge into Beef Basin; only the cook stayed behind at the base camp with the DUKW.

Early on the morning of August 9, with their knapsacks filled with food and clothing for a six-day trek they descended into the unknown Beef Basin canyon country to explore and see if they could find their way to the Colorado River. They made their first night's camp at the junction of Beef Basin and Ruin Canyon after having hiked about ten miles to this point (Figure 5.12).[54] Thomas and Maxfield and two explorers stayed behind to map the geological formations. Kenny and ten remaining explorers descended into Beef Basin Wash with an agreed upon rendezvous at the North Long Point base camp on Elk Ridge on August 14 or 15.

The hikers intended to follow the course of the wash to its junction with Fable Valley and then to attempt a passage through Gypsum Canyon from that point to the Colorado River if possible. As they descended westward about four miles the basin narrowed and became a steep-walled canyon with a stream of clear sweet water. Having traveled an estimated six miles they made camp on a narrow, rocky but level spot alongside the stream (Figure 5.12).

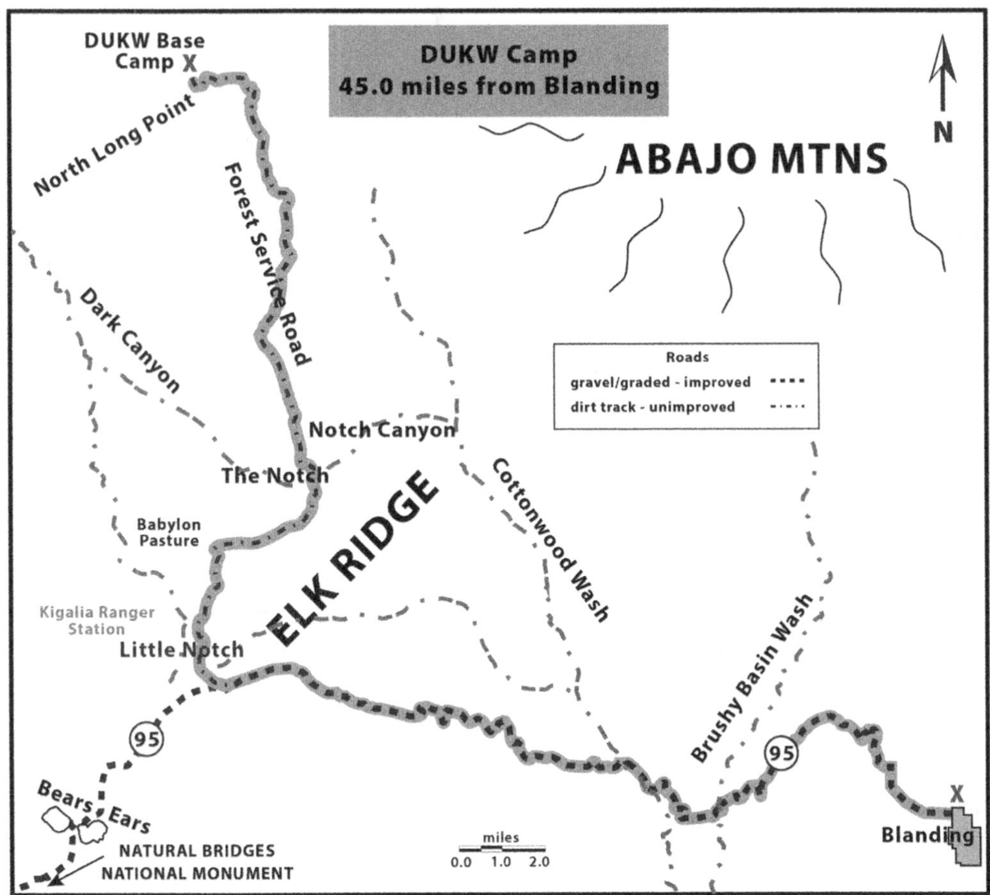

Figure 5.11 Map showing driving route (highlighted) and distance from Blanding to the DUKW Base Camp. Route 95 continued west-southwest from the turn-off onto the Forest Road near Kigalia Ranger Station. Route 95 split the Bears Ears and dropped down off of Elk Ridge to Natural Bridges National Monument. Beyond that point the road turned into a two-track trail over to White Canyon where the Hite Ferry was located. (GMS/TB original map)

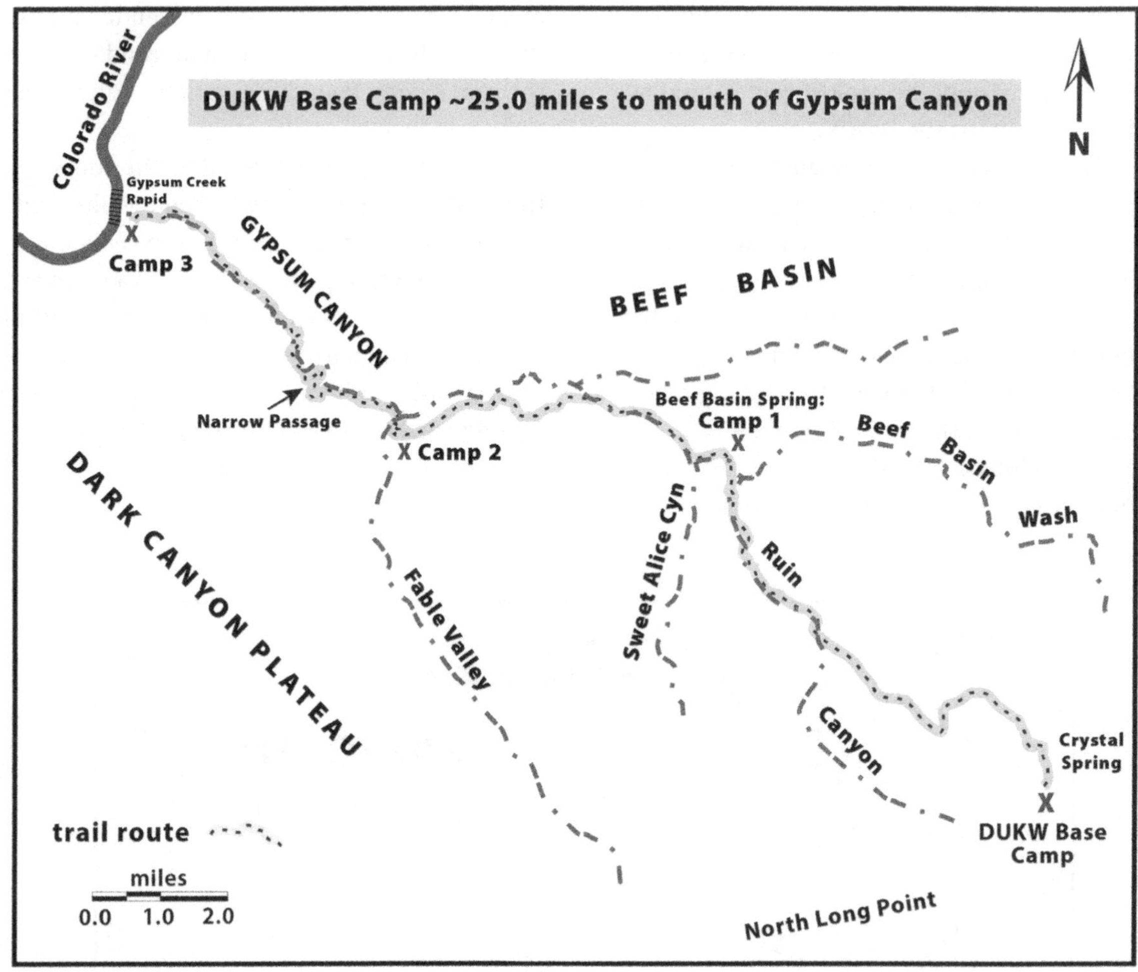

Figure 5.12 Map showing hiking route (highlighted) and first three days camp sites and the narrow passage enroute from the North Long Point base camp down Gypsum Canyon to its mouth at the Colorado River. Their return route past the narrow passage is not shown. (GMS/TB original map)

Early the next morning the party tackled the rocky labyrinth and was soon faced with roping down an 80-ft drop beside a waterfall. They had barely made it to the bottom before the canyon narrowed again and the stream fell into a crevice no more than six feet wide with a series of vertical drops totaling an estimated 800 ft. Just when they thought there was not any way past this tremendous fall and their canyon journey would end here, they found some mountain sheep tracks leading toward the mouth of the canyon and decided to follow and see where the tracks led.

The way took us scrambling for a short distance up the left-hand canyon wall and on to a narrow ledge that appeared to blend into a vertical cliff a short distance beyond. However, when we reached a point where the ledge narrowed along the cliff face we found there was room for human passage around a point of rock. The way then widened and after a little more than half a mile it was possible to descend a long sloping talus to the canyon bed 600 or 800 feet below.[55]

This bed of limestone was nearly at the same elevation as the Colorado River and there was very little grade for the remaining four miles to the confluence. Unfortunately, the stream had completely disappeared except for some occasional pools with nasty gypsum-tainted alkaline water. They reached the Colorado River about four o'clock that afternoon after having hiked about twenty-five miles and descended over 5,000 ft in elevation (Figure 5.12).[56]

There had been a very perceptible trembling of the ground that gradually increased to a roar as they drew closer to the river. Kenny stood in wonder at yet another large rapid he one day hoped to run. Along in the group were Jon Lindbergh and Bill Dickinson. Their dreams would be answered in September, 1949.

> A tremendous rapid in the Colorado is created by rocks thrust across its bed by frequent floods out of Gypsum Canyon. This was responsible for the earth shaking turmoil which we had felt and heard for so great a distance. After cooling ourselves in the shade of a grove of tamarisk trees, whose green color contrasted oddly with the bright red sandstone of the canyon walls, the entire group went for a swim in a quiet pool above the rapids.[57]

The group was unwilling to attempt the treacherous passageway they had skirted on the way down, and spent half of the next day trying different routes to no avail. So they were forced to climb around the big drop and it was every bit as harrowing as had been anticipated. By nightfall they had only traveled five miles, or less. As darkness fell and further travel was too dangerous they camped on a narrow strip of sand scarcely big enough to accommodate all their sleeping bags. They spent another day and a half working their way back to the rim and were glad they had the foresight to have cached some food on the way down. They made it back to the DUKW camp on Elk Ridge about noontime on August 14. The "big" trip of the season was over.

They reached Gold King camp in early afternoon on Tuesday, August 17, in time for the grand camporee the following day. "August 19 was the day of exodus with all the Explorers transported to Durango where they scattered by train, plane and bus to their homes in all parts of the country." [58]

NO CATARACT TRIP IN 1948

Jon wrote to Kenny dated February 7, 1948 that "mother was a little relieved at the cancellation of the Colorado [river] trip, but I think Father was a little disappointed. He said it was a 'conservative' attitude to take and would have agreed to one boat. That is a possibility this year." He later stated that "Father is quite enthusiastic about the Colorado, but he probably won't have time." [59] The cancellation referred to a possible trip following the 1947 Explorers Camp. Now, in 1948, Kenny was again trying to get a group together to go down Cataract Canyon. He wrote to Colonel Lindbergh explaining his plans after the 1948 Explorers Camp season was over:

> Concerning the matter of the projected Colorado River trip which Jon and I are planning for the week or ten days immediately following the close of the camping season on August 19, I am assured by Jon that you have consented to his taking this trip. Also, that you understand that although the river party will be managed conservatively and with safe passage our primary objective, there is still an element of danger involved in the trip. Is this correct?
>
> The trip as planned will be from Moab, Utah, past the mouth of the Green River, through the forty-two miles of Cataract Canyon's rather vicious rapids, and some one hundred miles of the placid Glen Canyon, ending at Lee's Ferry above the Grand Canyon. There is no doubt that much adventure will be involved and that the trip will not be purely a joy ride. Of course, we will have the benefit of the experience of the few who have made this trip before and should be able to plan carefully enough

to avoid the difficulties which befell some of the early parties." [60]

Kenny extended his invitation to the Colonel to join the trip and would appreciate his comments regarding the post-season trip down the Colorado River. Colonel Lindbergh replied July 10, 1948 with his approval for Jon to accompany Kenny on a Cataract Canyon river trip but had reservations "involving extraordinary hazards." Plus, he had a number of questions "since I know, having flown over it, how vicious the Colorado is in spots." He was most concerned that Jon, and Kenny for that matter, had developed sufficient skills to negotiate big rapids and with adequate equipment. "With proper training and experience, the most dangerous projects can be carried on quite safely but without these qualifications, as you know, a great many expeditions have met with disaster in even less hazardous undertakings than that which you and Jon are planning." [61]

No Cataract Canyon trip was pulled off in 1948, and it was probably a good thing. The Air Force life rafts were too flimsy and there was a strong probability that those boats would not have withstood the "vicious" rapids in Cataract Canyon. In a letter from Kenny to Jon he explained that the Cataract Canyon trip was cancelled due in part to finding competent persons to handle a second boat, plus "Chief" Ansel's fear of Jon being endangered but also by Ansel's fear of rapids!

> Despite his [Ansel] telling us last summer that he would never accompany another boat trip on rough water, he is now enthusiastically planning a trip with me down the San Juan starting May 23. We will go from Shiprock to Mex. Hat as the gang did last year, but this trip will be at the period of highest water. The sand-rollers ought to be terrific.
>
> We plan to have several guests---some of the Camp Advisors are being invited. Fred Black, Vice President of Nash-Kelvinator, and a doctor friend of his will be along as will J. B. Herndon, General Manager of the Hilton Hotels.[62]

Ansel was also worried about the Explorers Camp's liability, but Kenny assured him that the trip down Cataract Canyon would be run after the camp was over and there would be no responsibility on the part of the camp or Ansel.

> We will go through Cataract Canyon, at least as far as Hite Crossing, even if it has to be done with one boat. I am glad that your Father would have agreed to only one and am flattered by his confidence. We should have two boats, however, if at all possible.
>
> I, too, am working on boats in my spare time. The two big "bull-nose" boats are inflated on the shop floor and I am getting them ready for the next season's work. Have already repaired the valves and the punctured splash tube and am attaching rings just under the splash tubes onto which we can snap a water-tite cover for the two forward compartments. I also plan to have two rubberized fabric boxes--like panniers--built to fit those compartments, with flexible, sack-like tops that can be tied to keep out even the small amount of water that might get under the cover. Then, no matter how much water we might ship in a rapid, equipment, food, etc., will keep dry. I am enclosing rough sketches of these modifications. If you have suggestions for improvement---shoot 'em to me quick. I believe we will buy a third boat like these before summer.[63]

The "bull-nose" boats were the first of the LCR-S 7-man water crafts that remained part of Kenny's fleet for years to come (Figure 5.13).

TRUE BACKBONE OF EXPLORERS CAMP

As the year turned to 1949, Kenny's duties as Camp Director required more and more responses to enquiries about the Explorers Camp. As originally defined and enacted in 1944 the Explorers Camp had shifted significantly to a much more organized and rigorous field camp for young men after World War II and provided a new awakening of opportunities for everyone. Kenny had moved from observer and confidante of Ansel's in 1944 to Camp Manager and then to Field Director by the end of 1948 and the program reflected Kenny's influence. Gone was the down-talking to teenage boys as if they were juvenile city boys. Kenny was now dealing with them on a one-on-one basis and communicating with them as young thinking human beings and not the offspring of wealthy donors who sent their kids off to some wilderness camp. However, the costs had now risen from $475 to $495 per camp participant.[64]

R. Allan Clapp, Head Master of The Blake School in Minneapolis, Minnesota requested if Kenny would provide him names and addresses of some parents he might contact for references. Kenny obliged and provided information of several parents whose boys had attended the camp, plus a rather modest self-description. Kenny also sent Clapp some magazine articles, newspaper clippings, a camp newsletter and a listing of camp policies.[65] Copies of two letters of which Kenny received provide some insight into what a great leader Kenny was and what the Explorers Camp experience provided the boys who participated. Among those referenced by Kenny was Mr. M.U. Oakes, a merchant who had recently moved his family from California to Mancos where he now ran the largest mercantile business in town. His son, Jack, had been a 1947 Explorer. Kenny also provided Clapp with Stuart Maule's address and his son, Stuart M. Jr., or "Mike" who was a three-year veteran of the camp.[66]

Figure 5.13 Kenny's 1940s "bull-nosed" LCR-S boat shows his much-touted dual stern paddle-mate system of steering and tarping of gear upon which this passenger "rides the waves." (K. Ross collection)

Maynard Oakes replied to Clapp:

My son did attend the camp in 1947 and derived much lasting good from it. He had a fair desire to follow archaeology prior to that time but the fine experience he had under able leadership has made him convinced that it is the profession he wishes to follow. That would not be the case in all instances of course but it does give an idea as to the type of leadership available. I would heartily recommend Kenneth Ross as tops in dealing with boys he understands them and is a real friend to them. He is truly a hardy outdoorsman and a gentleman, an excellent combination. The types of things accomplished at camp are those which bring out the best in the boy. Comradeship of lasting nature, respect for nature in all, its phases an understanding of our Indians, our deserts, our history and our natural resources.

This fact I believe should never be lost sight of, their life is a rugged life filled with many hardships and many marvelous experiences, they sleep on the ground under all types of conditions, spend time under the blistering hot sun, chill when it rains, and don't ever let anyone tell you that it cannot rain on the desert.

One of the finest reports I have ever read is given to the parent of every boy upon the completion of each season. This report points out the good and bad points as they have been observed. They are straight forward reports honestly written telling of the boy's participation, attitude, habits and attitude. If taken right they can be of inestimable benefit and help to the parent who sees the boy under entirely different types of living. To really know a man – go camping with him truly in the rough for a week or more and his real inner self will come out. That is where the leaders have the advantage over the parent.

Again let me say that my son derived a great deal of good from his summers experience and his association with Ken Ross. *Ken is the true backbone of the camp* and as stated before is one who can be wholly relied upon. It gives me a real pleasure to be able to pass on to you my views of this camp and I whole heartedly recommend the venture to any boy who can stand the rugged life.[67] [Emphasis mine]

Jack majored and earned a degree in anthropology at the University of New Mexico.

∞ ∞ ∞

Stuart Maule, Sr. also replied:

Your having asked me for a statement of my impressions of the Explorers' Camp of Colorado, affords me considerable pleasure, largely because it is always pleasurable to be given an opportunity to express enthusiasm for things which one knows to be meritorious.

I consider that I have been most fortunate in having been able to arrange for my son, Stuart [Mike], to participate in the activities of the Explorers' Camp for three consecutive seasons. I say this for the reason that, not only have the experiences gained during that participation been the source of more interest and enjoyment than any others he has had, but their impact upon his mind has caused him to rearrange his life plan so as to direct all of his training, both scholastic and otherwise, into preparation for a career in one or more of the archaeological sciences to which he was first exposed while exploring with the other members of the Camp.

In the order in which they occur, I shall try to answer your questions specifically:

(1) It has been my observation that the Camp leadership has been not only competent, but outstanding. All of the Staff members, without exception, seem to have been chosen with particular regard for their ability to work advantageously with boys in their upper teens, and their familiarity with their respective fields of responsibility in connection with the Camp's activities. Also, each summer there have been present on the Staff three or four scientist leaders of recognized eminence in their chosen professions.

(2) and (3) That both the supervision and the health precautions have been adequate seems to be attested by the fact that although some of the Camp's field activities have been rigorous indeed, no case of injury worth mentioning, or illness other than one case of homesickness, and two or three

minor "tummy aches" has been known to me or Stuart.

(4) Reports on activities of the Camp as a whole and of the individual members, have been sent to the parents, not only after the close of the Camp each year, but upon termination of each of the periods of diversified activity into which the summer has been divided.

(5) It is hardly appropriate, I believe, to say that Stuart has "enjoyed" each of the three seasons. A better word would be "thrilled", or better still, "fired with a lasting interest" which has caused him to try to direct all of his future activities into the study of sciences of which he first was made aware by his contacts with the Staff and his activities with other members of the Explorers' Camp.

I might add, however, that what contact I have had with the boys during and immediately following their exploring activities has led me to believe that possibly the greatest benefit to be derived from the participation in the activities of the Explorers' Camp is that it will make any boy realize that he will gain from an experience only in proportion to his spirit of helpfulness and his cooperation in the endeavor of all participants to make that experience fruitful. I am sure, therefore, that the parents of any boy who is possessed of enthusiasm for venturesome and highly educational experiences in realms far removed from the usual, and who is cooperative and willing to contribute his share of effort, will be truly grateful to you for recommending that their son join the Explorers' Camp.[68]

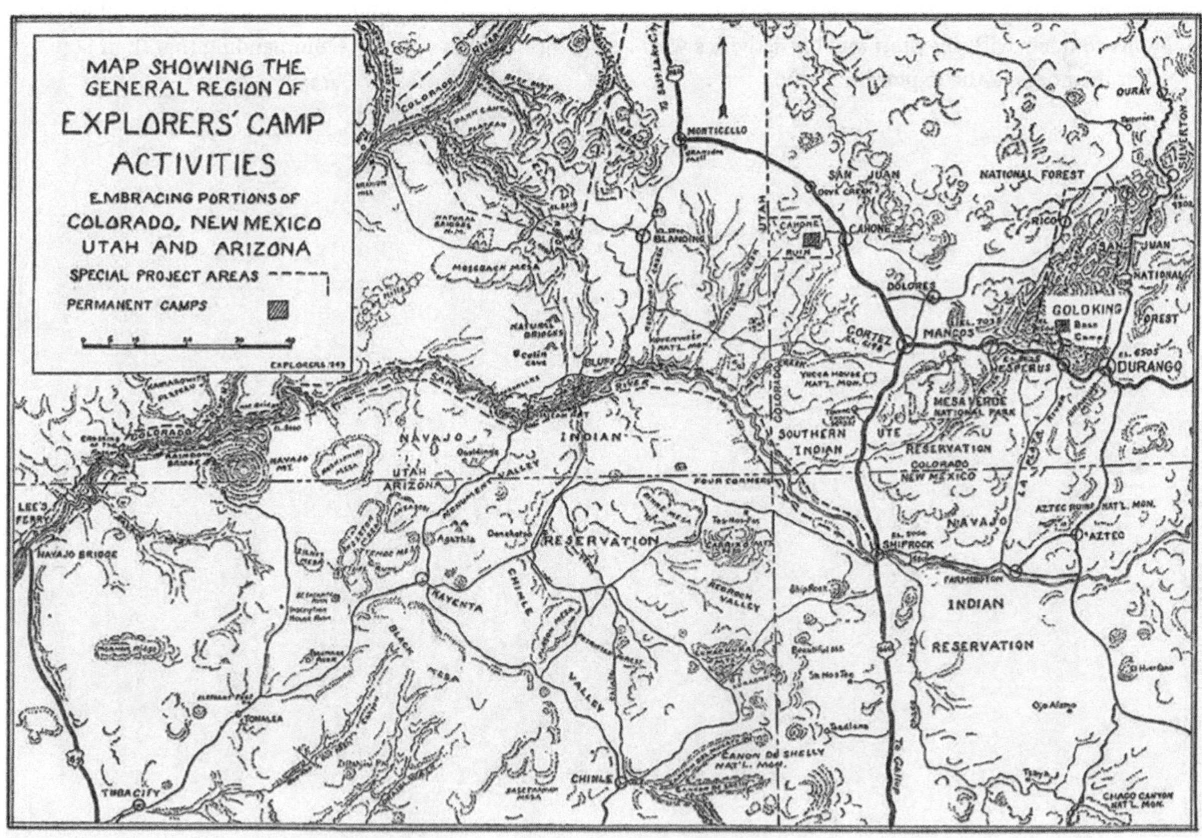

Map showing the region of Explorers Camp activities, 1949 (K. Ross collection)

6
THE BREAKOUT YEAR: 1949

SOUTHWEST EXPLORATIONS FIELD PROGRAM

Not surprisingly, the 1949 brochure and itinerary was professionally printed with a much better index map (drawn by Kenny) from which interested parents and participants could actually follow where the various excursions would take the explorers (see Explorers Camp Activity Map). The Explorers Camp was now subtitled *Southwest Explorations Field Program* and the itinerary was much more precise as to dates and what activities would be accomplished on each segment of the nine to ten week session. The emphasis was more than ever on the group to experience educational adventures. The boys were still divided into smaller working groups, but Kenny had dropped the rather derogatory tribal names for a much simpler system of referral to party groups by letter (A, B, C, etc) and application of what exactly the group would be doing (i.e., River Rats, Grave Hunters, Fossil Hunters, Mountaineers, and Canyoneers).[1]

However, to achieve these lofty goals, of which river trips were now a key component, Kenny needed to document the section from Shiprock to Mexican Hat with more accuracy and in the new sturdier 7-man assault crafts that had arrived over the winter (Figure 6.1). The lower portion from Mexican Hat to Lees Ferry would remain an exploration adventure for the hand-picked participants who would make this journey with him. Kenny would have to rely on his memories from the early RBMV trips as well as quizzing Norman Nevills in Mexican Hat. And the ultimate prize – the post-season river trip down the Colorado River through Cataract Canyon would be reserved for the very best amongst them.

Hank Zuidema replied to Ansel in January with a rather confusing letter where he stated that he would try to be available for field work at the Explorers Camp, and he offered to bring a new light-weight Geiger counter when he saw Ansel. He noted that the Geiger counter cost was $100 and that increased core drilling activity in the Four Corners was occurring under the auspices of the federal government's "**uranium** frenzy"[2] on the Colorado Plateau. He also recommended that they get in touch with Fred Black – a trustee at Cranbrook School for Boys as a possible contact for boys to attend Explorers Camp.[3]

Kenny wrote to Hank Zuidema and thanked him for joining the group who would be exploring "west of the Elk" mentioning it was a "veritable wonderland for the geologist."[4] Hank was also invited to join Kenny on the proposed Cataract Canyon river trip that would go from Moab to Hite and expected to launch sometime around August 26 or 27. The letter confirmed that two LCR-S "7-man" boats were definitely in Mancos and at Kenny's disposal. Kenny also had to "name-drop" to entice Zuidema:

> I would like to make up a party of about six to man two of our heavy Navy-type assault boats. This is a project which, except for the use of equipment, has nothing to do with Explorers' Camp and will be a case of the party members sharing in expenses, which should be very nominal. If it is at all possible for you to take the trip with us you would be a welcome addition to our party which will include young Jon Morrow Lindbergh and possibly his father, Colonel Charles A. Lindbergh.[5]

Kenny mentioned that he had a close view of the larger rapids and that he had been planning the "adventure" for some time and had made all the preparations for a safe passage.[6] Zuidema replied in June that he would not be able to join the Explorers Camp as he now had financial support (from Ford Motor Co. again) to conduct some field work digging for "Early Man" near the headwaters of the St. Johns River, Florida and then would return to Montana for continuing paleontological work where he would be joined by former Explorer, Connie [Conrad] Osborn (from the 1947 Explorers group).[7] Kenny quickly responded with cordial disappointment that Hank couldn't join the Explorers, and mentioned that it had been "nearly twenty years" since he last visited that part of Florida Hank had mentioned. Thus Kenny provided some degree of confirmation about his early years in Palm Beach, Florida in 1930.[8]

Zuidema had connections with Ford Motors probably because he was a geology professor at University of Michigan, Ann Arbor. Ford's headquarters were in nearby Dearborn and the company also published a magazine called the *Ford Times*. Ford's articles typically followed their automobiles into scenic areas and to areas with interesting research in anthropology, archaeology, and geology and had recently published an article about Mesa Verde National Park. Zuidema knew the associate editor of the

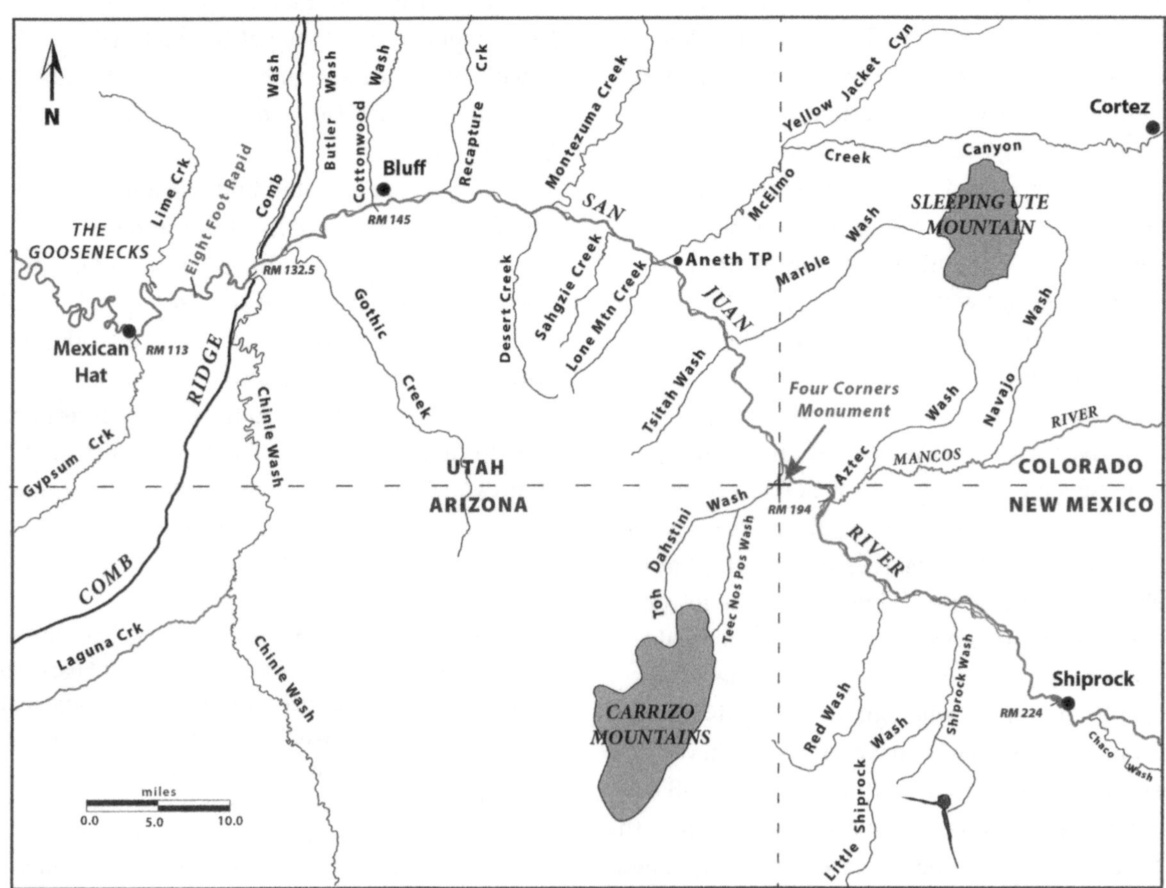

Figure 6.1 map of San Juan River and named major tributaries and geographic points of interest from Shiprock to Mexican Hat (the Fred Black trip of May, 1949); river miles (RM) measured upstream from confluence with Colorado River. (GMS/TB original map)

magazine, Edmund Ware Smith, and suggested that Ansel get in touch with him about all the things that the Explorers Camp was doing. Additionally, Zuidema knew Fred Black, who was a trustee for the Cranbrook Institute of Science (a source for Ansel's boys' camp) and was also the Director of Public Relations for *Nash-Kelvinator Corporation* in Detroit.[9] Nash-Kelvinator was a major manufacturer of pre- and post-war vehicles and appliances.

SHIPROCK TO MEXICAN HAT: MAY, 1949

So, it was no surprise that a "VIP" river trip was offered by Ansel Hall to Fred Black and Kenny did most of the work organizing and preparing for the trip from Shiprock to Mexican Hat in May of 1949 (Figure 6.1). He prepared a packing list of suggested items to bring, and the list was used for many years for other trips (see below). Kenny had spent the winter months working on the three new 7-man assault crafts and the river trip would be the perfect "trial run" before the Explorers Camp began.

Anyone who knew Kenny was soon educated as to the use of the term "raft" as he felt that a raft should be reserved for some form of a floating vessel composed of logs lashed together. Over all his years of boating, he instilled in most of us who worked with him to refer to the inflatable boats as "water craft" or "assault boats," 7-man's, 10-man's, snouts, etc but *never -rafts*! Anyway, the three "rafts" were equipped with paddles painted blue and gold.

Kenny was looking forward to a May run that might catch some high water from spring run-off. He was also anxious to test his new water-proof tarp design that would help keep gear and supplies from getting wet from splashes and waves. Fred Black became the trip's documentarian and kept a humorous journal of the events from meeting at Spruce Tree Lodge at Mesa Verde Monday, May 23 to their return Saturday, May 28.[10] Members of the party were:

Ansel Hall, president and general manager, Mesa Verde Company; Mesa Verde National Park, Colorado
Kenneth I. Ross, field director, Explorers Camp; Box 143, Mancos, Colorado
Jim Cook, former cowboy, member Mancos town council; made aspen wood furniture
Howard O. Welty, lecturer; 6024 Chabot Road, Oakland 18, California
Philip N. McCombs, Manager Allen Clipping Bureau, San Francisco; 1033 Miller Avenue, Berkeley 8, California
Stewart M. Maule, patent attorney; 1825 Peck Road, El Monte, California
L. A. Philipp, vice president, Nash-Kelvinator Corporation; 14250 Plymouth Road, Detroit 32, Michigan
Fred L. Black, Director Public Relations, Nash-Kelvinator Corporation; 14250 Plymouth Road, Detroit 32, Michigan

The three boats were given names and passengers assigned:
Raft #1: "La Canonita" - Kenny Ross, Howard Welty, Stu Maule`
Raft #2: "Perro Caliente" - Ansel Hall, Phil McCombs
Raft #3: "La Cucaracha" - Doc Philipp, Jim Cook, Fred Black

THE PACKING LIST [11]

(Supplies and Equipment to be furnished by Individuals)

A. CLOTHING: All clothing worn on the trip should be old as the river carries much red sediment which permanently dyes light-colored things. White shirts, sox, and underclothing will finish the trip in the pink of condition.

1. Hat or long-billed cap - light colored
2. 2 pair of trousers - jeans or khaki
3. 3 pair of sox - wool best
4. 3 old shirts - light colored
5. Handkerchiefs - and 1 bandana to protect neck
6. At least one change of underwear
7. 1 pair of tennis shoes for wear in boats and a pair of camp slippers
8. 1 sweater or light jacket and 1 warm jacket - rainproof best
9. Gloves - old ones
10. Waterproof bag to hold all above.

B. Bedroll and waterproof bag to fit.
C. Towels and toilet kit.
D. Sunglasses - important
E. 1. Suntan oil-----?
2. Sunburn ointment - not protective - (Ha! You just think you won't need this)
F. CAMERAS - For black and white or color - still or movie
1. Other photo equipment
2. Honest-to-goodness waterproof bags - two or three, for cameras, film, etc.
G. You can't be too careful about getting good waterproof bags and plenty of them.
H. Explorers' Camp will furnish boats, navigator, cuisine, navigating instruments, tents, and good companionship.
I. Navajo Indians will provide human interest.
J. Nature will furnish scenic color and backgrounds, heat and light, music, star-lit nights, cool showers (maybe), gnats, mosquitos, ants, and other wildlife, excitement, discomfort, and other things too numerous to mention.

THE FRED BLACK JOURNAL

Fred was new to the Four Corners area, Navajo culture, and boating down swift-moving rivers such that much of his running narrative ranged from informative to humorous to clueless. In his own way he described braided streams and the danger of "**quicksand**" in the shallows and "sand rollers" in the main current.

> The rule was for one man always to stay in the raft, for if all got out to push, the raft might be caught by the current and dragged away, leaving its passengers stranded--probably in quicksand. We were plagued with quicksand during the entire trip with the exception of the last day. In the deeper channel of the river we frequently encountered sand rollers--a phenomenon characteristic of the San Juan. The best explanation we could get for their formation was that the water, which carries a large percentage of silt and sand, is heavier at the bottom of the deeper channels than at the top, which makes the water flow faster on the surface, and fall over on itself. This creates a series of waves of varying height from trough to crest. We estimated the height of some to be 10 feet. We found it best to ride the rollers with the prow of the raft meeting the waves at an angle of about 45^{0}. If the raft is caught broadside in the rollers, it might be swamped.[12]

He made notice of Navajo hogans, *chaha'ohs* [13] (shade shelters), sheep and goats and that they weren't as alone in a desolate place as he had conjectured. When they landed at their first night's camp site, it seemed that all but Kenny got soaked when they had to jump out of their boats to get them stopped. After the "exciting landing" Fred commented about the desert flora, sandy beach and dinner; plus he was completely aghast at the "trillions of stars in the sky which one never sees in more populated, smoky country."[14] They were up and at it early the next day and some in the group switched boats; Kenny remained in the *La Canonita* and their first stop was at the mouth of Mancos Creek. Here Kenny pointed out a number of ruins, a circular kiva and pottery sherds scattered everywhere and explained that this site was typical of late Puebloan period circa AD 1200, or of *Mesa Verde Classic Period.*[15]

They got underway again and their next stop was on Tuesday, May 24 and Fred Black noted in his journal (Figure 6.2):

> We again embarked and headed for the "Four Corners" where Colorado, Utah, New Mexico and Arizona meet. A one-wire Indian service telephone line crosses the San Juan River from North to South approximately on the North and South line between the four states.
>
> We arrived there at noon, had lunch on the boulder-lined shore in intense heat produced by both sun and rocks. After climbing up the river bank, we hiked over a high hill, through stones and sand, down the hill and across a valley in the most God-forsaken country one can imagine. It was so hot and dry that perspiration didn't gather on one's skin; it was picked up by the arid air before it got to the surface of the skin. Smoking cigarettes was no

satisfaction; they dried out so rapidly they only added to one's discomfort.

Kenny Ross was the only one of the party who had previously been to the Four Corners, but he had not approached it from the point on the river where we landed. The Four Corners marker was about a mile from the river bank at this point. As a consequence, he thought for a while we were lost. At last we located the marker by sighting the remains of the old trading post that 40 years ago stood nearby, but which is now only a burned and charred ruin.

Appropriate pictures were taken of members of the party shaking hands from state of state, including the "State of Confusion." The marker itself, a concrete shaft rising about 26 inches from the ground, was set in 1934. The circular brass plate on its top is divided into quarters indicating each of the four states.

Much of the cacti in the area were in beautiful bloom. Howard Welty and Stu Maule made the best of it with their color film. Then we made the long trek back to the river over a much easier trail." [16]

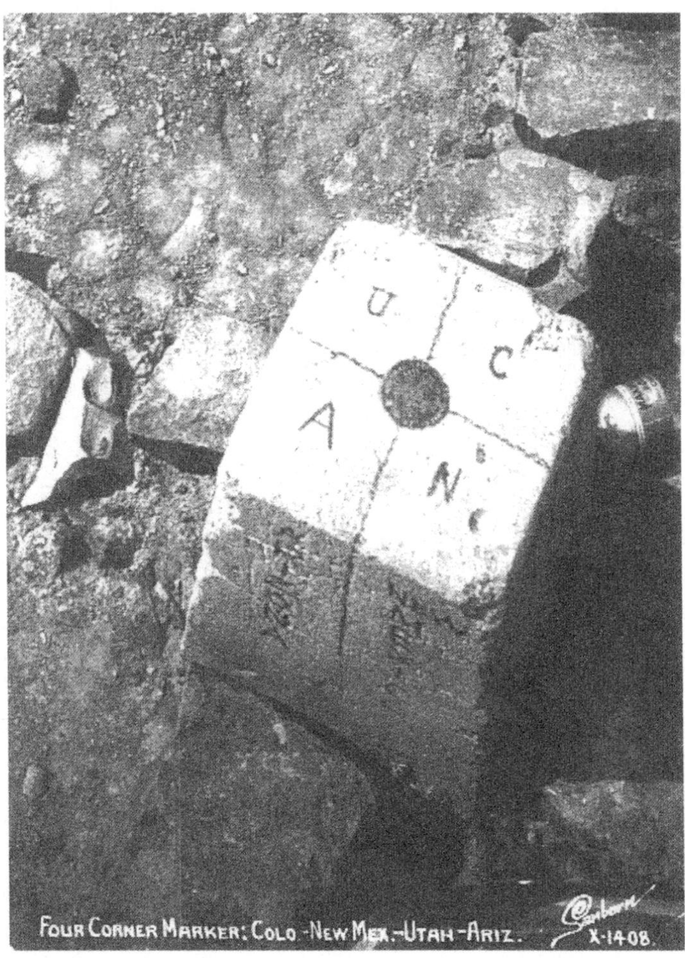

Figure 6.2 a postcard dated January 14, 1908 shows the original stone marker at the Four Corners Monument. (Courtesy: the Florence Daly collection, Dolores, Colorado and the Montezuma County Historical Society)

The river widened and split into numerous channels and all three rafts at some time or another became grounded in shallow water (see Chapter 5; Figure 5.3). They proceeded downriver where they encountered frequent "sand rollers of increasing height" and stopped near Aneth Trading Post (Figure 6.1) so Ansel could go up and phone home to let folks know they were all doing fine, other than getting dehydrated. Unfortunately, Fred didn't transcribe his notes correctly, as his journal entries had gotten out of sequence either due to his delayed transcription, or he simply just got them out of order.[17] For example, he placed Barton's Trading Post upstream of Bluff and River House Ruin above the Butler Petroglyph Panel. Kenny made a keen observation that the channel at Bluff was new and had been diverted south from just the previous year. This would be *Red Dike* as it is locally known to the Bluff residents:

> The U. S. Government last winter at a cost of eighty thousand dollars has diverted the main river channel, which had directly passed the town, and which had been rapidly carrying the bottom farm lands down river.[18]

Phil McCombs elected to stay with the boats while the rest of them trudged through mud and brush in to Bluff (Figures 6.3 and 6.4):

> The population of Bluff, probably about a hundred, is much smaller than it was when Brigham Young instructed some of his followers to settle it, probably 75 to 80 years ago. Today it looks like a ghost town. Most of its oldest houses are large stone affairs with two or three doors, indicating the number of wives its owners could afford.
>
> On the canyon walls above Bluff there is a natural huge rock formation known as the "Navajo Twins" or "The Kissing Rocks."
>
> At the trading post the group tanked up on Pepsi-Cola and orange pop. We completely lost track of how many bottles each of us drank. Also at Bluff we found excellent spring water which came out of a six inch artesian well. Ansel called on Father Liebler, an Episcopal priest, who operates a mission there. The good long-haired father is quite an eccentric character, and has been recently written up in various publications. [19]

Figure 6.3 Bluff City in 1921 that was not appreciably different in 1949. (Original photo by H.D. Miser, 1924, USGS)

Figure 6.4 Navajo Twin Rocks or "kissing rocks" and Sunbonnet Rock in Bluff, Utah; 1960s. (K. Ross collection)

Once they were back in the boats Fred again mentioned that they hit big high sand rollers and a deep channel and finally stopped for their night's camp near the lower Butler Petroglyph panel (Figures 6.5 & 6.6).

The camp site was in a park-like area of about 40 acres filled with trees and a lot of dead wood, and was a permanent home site for the Navajos. Kenny had made camp at this spot the year before with a Boys Explorers Camp party and knew that an excellent spring was located at the edge of the cliffs a half mile away. The fine cold spring water was a welcome treat. Near the camp Kenny found a rare species of columbine which none of the party could identify. He dug up some of the plants and put them in a can to take back to Mesa Verde for identification. [20]

Figure 6.5 View upstream from camp site at Lower Butler Wash petroglyph panel. (G.M. Stevenson photo)

Figure 6.6 the Lower Butler Wash petroglyph panel. (G.M. Stevenson photo)

A quarter mile back in the grove near the cliffs was a Navajo hogan and sweat bath and a sheep corral. In the cliff face some distance from these "modern" Indian structures was a large cave filled with ruins. These were left for exploration until the next morning. The party then started on its exploration of Indian culture. The Navajos, to whom the hogan and sweat bath belonged, apparently had moved on to lusher country with their flocks. A modern padlock secured the hogan door which did not extend to the top. Through this transom we could view the contents of the dwelling. Various equipment and supplies (wool, groceries, harnesses, etc.) had been hung from the ceiling to keep them safe from rodents. On the wall of the hogan was a lithographed calendar open to March, 1949. The circular room was immaculately clean, even to the dirt floor. The little sweat house nearby, half cave and half structure built over it, seemed quite small. Steam is produced by heating stones placed inside the hut and throwing water on them. On the opposite side of the hogan was a typical root cellar.

We went on from here to the cliff dwelling which we found interesting but not unusual [Figure 6.7]. On the way back to the camp, we skirted the shore and stumbled over two canvas tarpaulins which belonged to Jim Cook. He had loaned them to a party of three in April 1948 for a trip down the river. Their boat had been swamped near this point and they had abandoned most of their equipment. Jim knew in general where the accident had happened, but was quite surprised and delighted to recover some of the things he had loaned the ill-fated party.

In the canyon walls farther down and across the river, we could see two large cliff dwelling caves. We embarked on our rafts and made a landing near them [Figure 6.8 Twin alcoves, RL south of River House ruin]. After an arduous climb, we were inside two of the finest, largest symphony shell type caves most of the party had ever seen. One had a perfect proscenium arch about 250 feet wide and 120 feet deep, and at the center of the arch, 100 feet high. It was a little farther back in a side canyon than the smaller cave. The smaller, Kenny Ross said, was undoubtedly a Pueblo III ruin, judging from the stone building construction and pottery sherds. The larger appeared to have been inhabited by much earlier basket-maker Indians. A line of steps cut out of the solid rock by Indians, probably 800 to 1,000 years ago led up to this cave. The floor of the more modern ruin was covered with pottery sherds, but the older contained very few signs of its previous occupants. Neither cave appeared to have been explored below the surface. Two casualties happened as a result of the climb to the cave--Phil McCombs nearly broke a leg, and Fred Black banged one of his so hard it was black and blue for more than a week.

The party re-embarked and soon the canyon became higher and narrower, the water deeper and faster. The sand rollers were more turbulent because one series would dash into others. There wasn't much time to look at the scenery as we were all too busy avoiding being swamped. Kenny said we were near the "8-Foot rapids" which might be dangerous, depending on the water level. When we arrived above the rapids, we all landed at a convenient spot to look them over [Figure 6.9]. We decided to run them one raft at a time. Kenny, of course, being experienced, took the lead raft. It was the understanding that, at the first spot beyond the rapids where he could land, we would again assemble the three rafts. The crews of rafts #2 and #3 scattered the best they could to take pictures and watch the first raft go through. It was rough and exciting, but the trip was made safely. Raft #2 then followed. Ansel, Doc and Fred had wandered far down along the rocky shore of the canyon to observe and shoot pictures, and they took some time to hike back and launch their raft. The rest of the party was worried about the long delay as they couldn't see them from their landing spot. But finally the party was all safety together again and celebrated with lunch.

Then the voyage was resumed. The rafts soon entered the Rapply [Raplee] anticline, famous cliff rock formations which are pictured in most geology texts. The water was unusually high. Kenny said ordinarily rocks now covered with water stood out 10 to 15 feet above the surface. There were spots where the width between canyon walls was as narrow as 100 feet and the walls ran straight up to 1200 to 1500 feet [Figure 6.10]. The water Kenny estimated to be around 50 feet deep. Our speed through the canyon was quite rapid and with the innumerable curves and turbulent water, we were extremely busy paddling most of the time. We entered a stretch of canyon which created an interesting optical illusion. The rock strata gradually slanted upward down river giving the illusion of a terrific fall, and we felt as though we were floating down a steep hill [Figure 6.11].

Figure 6.7 the River House (Snake House) cliff dwelling. (G.M. Stevenson photo)

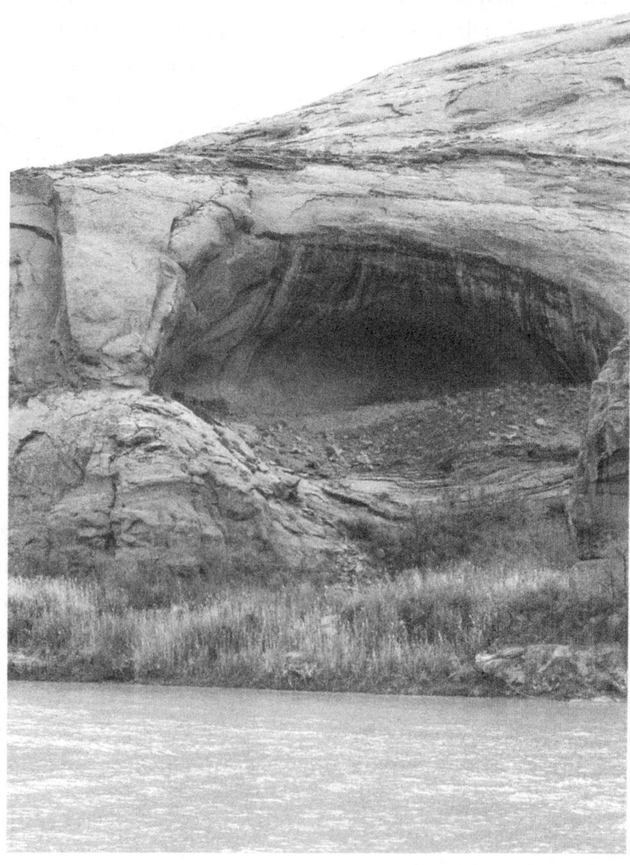

Figure 6.8 one of two north-facing alcoves on RL across from River House ruins. (G.M. Stevenson photo)

Figure 6.9 view downstream at Eight Foot Rapid from talus slope on RL. (See Figure 6.1 map for location; G.M. Stevenson photo)

Figure 6.10 view downstream at "the upper Narrows." (G.M. Stevenson photo)

Figure 6.11 view upstream near Lime Creek looking at Raplee Anticline. (G.M. Stevenson photo)

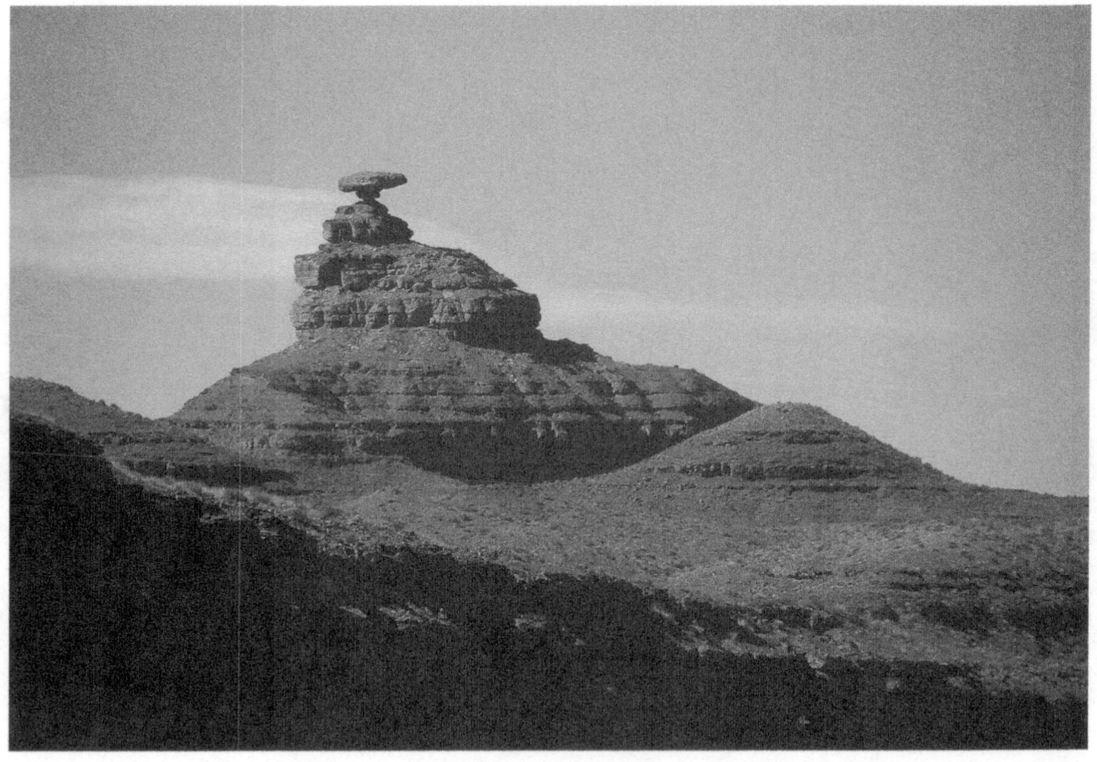

Figure 6.12 Mexican Hat rock viewed from river. (S. Aitchison photo)

Figure 6.13 the most commonly used boat landing and/or launch point upstream of the Mexican Hat Bridge in the 1940s and 50s. (Courtesy: Utah Historical Society)

> Between 3:00 and 4:00 O'clock in the afternoon we ran a second series of rapids [Ledge and Lime Creek]. In the distance we saw the natural high rock tower crowned by a huge cap which resembles a Mexican hat [Figure 6.12]. This was to be the end of our trip. It is from this spectacular natural formation that the small Utah settlement "Mexican Hat" gets its name.
>
> At 4:00 P.M. we landed just above a very swift and rough series of rapids which we were thankful we didn't have to run [Gypsum Rapid]. We camped on a rock ledge high enough above the river to be safe from any sudden rise.[21]

They ended their trip by pulling out above Gypsum Rapids and the more commonly used boat landing located immediately upstream of the Mexican Hat Bridge (Figure 6.13).

> After dinner Norm Nevills, who regularly runs the Colorado canyons with groups [Figure 6.14], and who lives about a mile from Mexican Hat, brought to our camp some of a group of 17 who were starting on a river trip Saturday, May 28. The oldest in this party was a man of 80, the heaviest a man weighing 250 lbs., and the youngest, Nevills' daughter Sandra, who was around 7 years old. Nevills makes the trip in special boats, each boat manned by an experienced river man. Frequent stops are made and no work is required of the passengers. Each pays around $200 for the trip, Mexican Hat to Lee's Ferry, about 196 miles.[22]

The next morning they deflated two boats and left the third inflated that furnished a softer seat upon which to ride in the back of the Dodge troop transport truck that had arrived overnight. Before leaving, they stopped at Norm's Mexican Hat Lodge (Figure 6.15) and then they detoured out to Goosenecks Overlook (Figure 6.16) before returning to Mesa Verde by way of Monticello.[23]

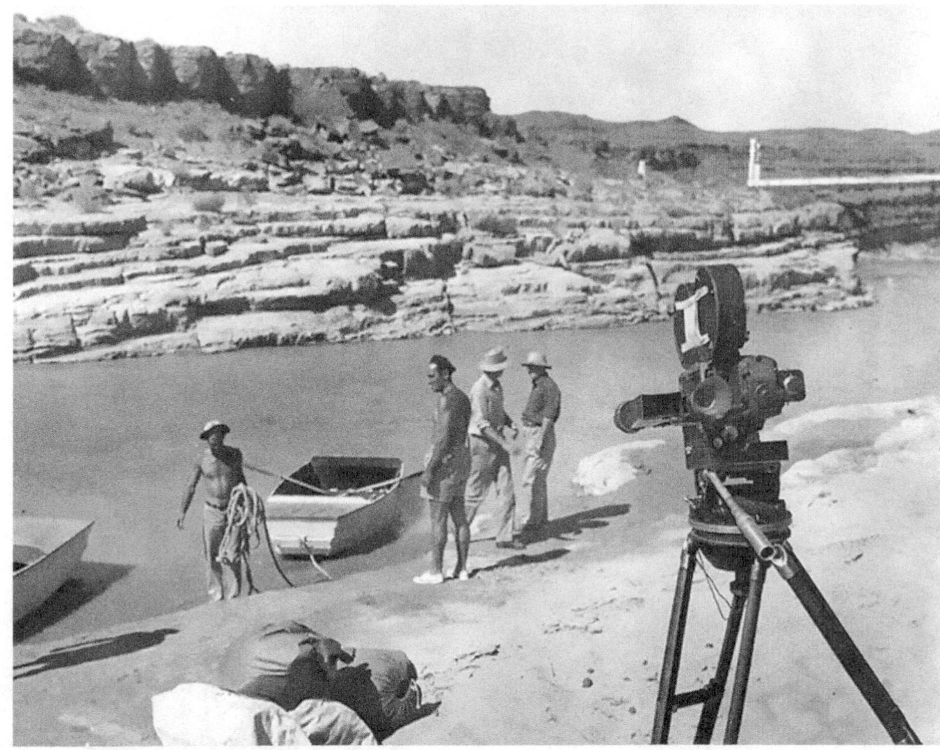

Figure 6.14 Norm Nevills (holding bow line rope on a San Juan punt) and others preparing for trip to leave the next day from Mexican Hat. (Courtesy: Utah Historical Society)

Figure 6.15 the Nevills' "Mexican Hat Lodge" in 1949. (Courtesy: Utah Historical Society)

Figure 6.16 aerial view of the Goosenecks of the San Juan River; river flows left to right. (D.L. Baars photo)

NORMAN NEVILLS - AGAIN

While the Fred Black group had busied themselves setting up their last night's camp above the Mexican Hat bridge and telling stories to the group Nevills brought down, Norm and Kenny sat and discussed running the river and what the rapids were like in the canyon below the bridge and if there had been any major changes or new rapids. Kenny quizzed Norman pretty strongly that evening and the following morning at the lodge. It had been fifteen years since Kenny had seen the stretch through the limestone canyons down to Slickhorn Canyon and past the confluence to Lees Ferry in the fold flat boats used in the RBMV trips. Kenny was planning two trips for the Explorers Camp for the upcoming season and the plan was to launch from Bluff and run all the way to Lees Ferry – some 225 miles downriver and he wanted to make sure of his itinerary. Years later Kenny stated "I knew Norm rather well and liked him a lot and that is about all I would care to say on the matter." [24]

By May 1949 Norm and his *Nevills Expeditions* was perhaps the best known if not famous river running operation in the western U.S. He had been filmed running rapids and had taken many folks down the San Juan as well as Grand Canyon and other rivers.[25] As was the trend in the early years of river boating, carving, etching or painting your name and the names of others in your group on a rock wall or alcove was common practice and most typically at the head of rapids or where some sort of boating incident had occurred. Nevills seemed to have not missed a trip where he listed his groups' names down the San Juan River below Mexican Hat. As documented by the inscriptions listed on several registers beneath an overhanging ledge of massive limestone at the downstream side to the stair-step entrance into Slickhorn Canyon (RR @ RM 74.4; 332.2 miles below headwaters – see Table 1; Appendix I) he had made at least twenty-plus trips by 1946. The slab of limestone overhead protected the list of names Nevills and other river runners had made and constituted an important history of the trips made by Norman Nevills although he ran trips on the San Juan right up to his death in 1949.

The names were later recorded by Greg Crampton but as he said, not all names could be deciphered and there may have been some mistakes in spelling (Figure 6.17). The very first entry for Norm's first trip says "March, 1934" with his newly wed wife, Doris (Drown) Nevills and the two Frost's.[26]

Many additional names were added that Crampton missed, including those by Kenny Ross, Doug Ross and Don Ross but over the winter of 1990-91 the massive overhanging limestone slab collapsed and broke into a rubble pile of angular blocks and buried those many names. However, Doug Ross's name and a few others were saved as they were inscribed on a lower ledge and remain visible.

Figure 6.17 Inscriptions at Slickhorn Gulch with Norm's first trip in March, 1934 and by subsequent individuals who went down San Juan River with Norman Nevills in 1940s. (Historical site 208; Crampton, 1964, Fig.9)

One name of interest buried under the rubble was that of "Jesse L. Nusbaum" who was listed with others that were inscribed July 2, 1941 when he was Park Superintendent at Mesa Verde. Jesse was obviously interested in seeing firsthand what the canyons of the San Juan looked like and was probably most keenly focused on potential alcoves and side canyons that could possibly contain ruins and petroglyphs. Another name of interest was that of "Father Liebler" dated June 17, 1945. Liebler established the Episcopalian Mission east of Bluff and was well respected in the community. He too, showed he had a curious adventurous streak by having traversed the canyon with Norm.

The last known inscription by Nevills was a trip run in June, 1946, and one of his very last trips down the San Juan was the trip that launched the day that Kenny and the Fred Black entourage headed back to Colorado (May 28, 1949). His untimely airplane crash with his wife Doris aboard on September 18, 1949 marked the end of the Nevills era. Thus, it was somewhat fortuitous that he met with Kenny on May 27 and discussed boating down the San Juan River through Glen Canyon and possibly even Cataract Canyon.

Nevills was certainly the pioneer to first run commercial river trips on the San Juan and through Glen Canyon, and by 1949 Nevills had created his own competition.[27] Yet Norm or most of his competitors showed little to no interest in the upper canyon of the San Juan or the flat water stretch above Bluff back towards the Four Corners. This may have been due as much to the problem with roads, or the lack thereof, which added days onto any trips organized out of Mexican Hat. Nevertheless, Nevills demonstrated little interest in the archaeological history that was amassed in the numerous sites and petroglyphs upstream or down, in Grand Gulch.

He appeared to have been most interested in seeing how fast he could make it from Mexican Hat to Slickhorn, a distance of some thirty-nine river miles, or to show-off "facing the danger" of running rapids for the movie cameras.[28] Many of the inscriptions noted the number of days, or hours it took to make the run from Mexican Hat to Slickhorn with the "New Record" of five and one-half hours noted for June 1, 1942 in his favorite boat, the *Hidden Passage*.[29] Of all the trips down the San Juan, Norm was only known to have shown interest in the rapids and didn't seem particularly interested in slowing down to hike Honaker Trail or to examine any geological features or examine fossils (of which there are many) along the way. Norm was a noted camp entertainer and spun many river stories or did stunts for an eager audience of onlookers. "Norm Nevills was a pyromaniac. He liked to go into old mines and find dynamite and blow stuff up. He also liked to make 'fire falls' by bundling up driftwood, setting aflame and rolling the fireball off cliffs; typically at camp."[30]

Norm Nevills may well be remembered as a "first" in many river people's mind, and while he emphasized thrills and his bravado, Kenny Ross emphasized teaching his customers something about the river and how to read the water. Kenny informed his passengers about the river's environs, including the human history from Paleo-Indian to gold and oil prospectors. He pointed out the subtle varieties of flora, birds ranging from small canyon wrens to birds of prey, and animals ranging from lizards and snakes to deer and desert bighorn sheep. Kenny opened people's eyes to the intricacies of the geology, from igneous intrusions to the myriad layers of limestone and sandstone, their depositional history and the fossils that told a story of an ancient world. Norm was an entertainer, the court jester – Kenny was an educator, and both men had their own way of introducing many folks to the new world of river boating. But it was Kenny who emphasized the concept of "educational adventures" by taking passengers on boats through the canyons of the San Juan and Colorado rivers.

FACING YOUR DANGER

This method of running a boat stern-first has frequently been called the *Galloway method*, in honor of Nathaniel (Nathan) Galloway. Norm learned the technique along with Jack Frost by accident. Jack said that both he and Norm were rowing downstream, with their bows pointed downstream in the "Honeymoon trip in 1935" and got spun around backwards by one of the rapids and discovered they had more control of the boat and could see where they were going by "facing the danger" and pull away from obstacles. Norm apparently resisted the method initially, but eventually began trying it.[31]

In replying to Don Hatch's question about some of Norm's rather clunky boat designs, Kenny stated:

> While there are differences in the Nevills and the Galloway designs, to me the really significant feature of both from the standpoint of operation in rapids is the great amount of rake or 'rocker' from the center cross section to either end. While it is true that Norm Nevills developed his San Juan and Cataract Boats many years after Galloway I am not inclined to accept that his designs are independent entirely. I was around quite a bit during this development and know that Norm was very much aware of the Galloway design and had a high regard for it.[32]

Dock Marston, never the fan of Norm Nevills, summarized Norm's boats: "they are good enough if one is too lazy to make them better" [33]

When Kenny began boating down rivers in the inflatable crafts, he preferred having two men sit in the stern with paddles to navigate the LCRs. He later dropped the dual-paddle method and made rowing frames adapted to oars and ran rapids stern-first, or the so-called "Galloway" method. He explained the dual-paddle technique to Don Hatch:

> Personally, I find the 10-man rubber boat a little slower to come about than I do the Cataract or San Juan boats. I also feel that the lack of rake at the stern makes them a little clumsier because I run facing downstream and dislike having to rotate the position of my body 180 degrees upon each shift from quiet to turbulent water. That is one reason that I mostly run 12 footers and handle them from the stern with paddles instead of oars. I first used surplus inflatable craft beginning in 1946--on the San Juan. I do not know if I was the first to attach oarlocks and run them with oars but I was certainly among the first. I first developed the idea of operating the 7-man boats from the stern with paddles in 1947 and have gradually developed this into a highly efficient and very sporting method. Despite any appearance to the contrary, I am entirely devoted to rubber boats, in general preferring them to any design in wood. Oddly, in view of your apparent feeling that the Cat article depreciates the LCRs, a letter from Otis Marston chides me for playing them up as being safer than other types of boats for big river rapids. Such are the differences of opinion. He pointed to last spring's tragedy below Shoshone Dam as an example of the unreliability of inflatable craft. Ha! Not even the Queen Mary could have run that rapid safely under such water conditions as then existed. Imagine anyone trying conditions like that in a 25-ft pontoon with a pair of canoe paddles! I find it next to impossible to understand how even men completely lacking experience with boats and the terrific forces generated in big rapids could be unable to judge between the easy to do and the next to impossible. To me this incident is dramatic proof that there is no such thing as a boat completely safe for the rank beginner. I will grant this much to Marston's view---inflatable rubber boats might give a false feeling of security to both the ignorant and the lacking in judgement and thus tempt him to tackle unsafe conditions. [34]

By 1953 Kenny had eight inflatable boats: the three Air Corp life rafts and four LCR-S and one LCR-L crafts.[35] He continued to justify in some crazy manner his dual-paddle technique to Dock Marston:

I plan to use 5 (or 6) 12-ft Landing boats (I insist they are not rafts) on the Aug-Sept. Cat trip. We have 8 of these, all canvas decked and equipped with waterproof cases, ready for the roughest kind of going. I have found these better--run by my method--than the 10-man, or 15-ft. boats, or the Cataract run. We run entirely with paddles---wielded by two men seated side by side at the stern. Unorthodox? Certainly.

And just as certainly, non-Galloway. But damned practical. With one man commanding and one simply an extra set of muscles and a paddle, these little boats, even with a thousand pound load, are maneuverable as a cricket. If this method has disadvantages they can be offset by careful conning and skill. The big advantage is the ability to DRIVE, forward, right, left, or broadside without preliminary maneuvering (the motor-boat idea). The precision of control is really remarkable, and for working in very close, rocky waters it is superior to the Galloway method. I find that being able to drive forward sometimes means---all other conditions taken into consideration---the difference between a decision to run or to **line** a particular rapid at a particular stage of water. As an example, I have several times ran---not lined---Government Rapid when the water was so low that the only channel was the one slightly to right of center and which is so twisty that a "Nevills boat" could not have maneuvered it without hitting at least three rocks. Also, at near high water last June, my prize protégé boatman, Land Lindbergh and I ran 5 loaded boats thru the entire length of the 13-footer and only had to bail two of them. I'll probably never do that again because it seems unlikely that one would ever be there when the water was just right, twice in a lifetime.

You did not ask for information on my technique (Oh no, not "Developed Technique") and by this time you are probably thinking, "Oh Lord---Another of these river nuts gone loose on the subject of his technique and his boats." I guess that must be the fate of all really enthusiastic river men. As we grow older and gain experience we ought to get over it---but we don't. As THE chronicler of the rivers, I suppose you have grown used to this.

Anyhow, now that I've gone so far I may as well add that I believe that the Galloway style of boat and the "Galloway method" needs a pretty complete re-examination. I've used the latter and developed the usual proficiency at it--but have abandoned it for my own use. It is a good method but, while it has been several times refined, it has never been basically improved---not even by Norm Nevills, who was certainly remarkably proficient in it. I have heard of one fellow---his name slips me---who regularly runs the upper green, who has thrown it overboard completely (or so I understand) and now faces upstream thru everything. It seems that he too feel the need of being able to DRIVE. I sympathize with his reasoning but don't feel that he has much of anything.

Just in case it might possibly further entice you to run Cataract with us----on all my trips we EAT and what we eat is COOKED. I am a bit of a crank on the matter of plenty of good, simple food, properly prepared. Ask Howard Welty about this.

I am planning two pre-camp-season San Juan-Colorado runs this spring. I have not yet set definite dates because several interested people have asked me to hold off. As it looks now, they will be launched at Bluff during the last week in April and the third week in May. Because of Explorers Camp obligations I dare not look upon these pre- season trips in the same way as do Riggs & Wright. My operating policy is one of sound preparation, careful execution, and I expect passengers to consider themselves as crew members---along the lines all my trips with the boys are operated. The fee of 150 bucks is admittedly low but quite okay with me. I am not really trying to cut out those who consider their trips as an important part of making their livelihood.[36]

Bill Dickinson commented many years later about Kenny's dual-paddle methodology:

> Our run through Cataract came at the end of Explorers Camp in August of 1949, using his ridiculous paddle system instead of oars. Our companion was Jon Lindbergh.[37]

As the years passed by, Kenny finally abandoned the dual-paddle technique he was so proud of, and converted all his boats with rowing frames and oars where just one oarsman would sit mid-ship. He realized that two heads were not necessarily better than one – particularly as he couldn't always count on his paddle-mate to react quickly enough in maneuvering the boat through rapids and avoiding obstacles. Long before running rivers as a business he had learned how to handle oars and row a boat (probably on the Mississippi River rescue efforts in 1927).

Kenny also detested the *pin and clip* technique where the oar was fixed to a post, denying the oarsman from rotating, or *feathering* his oar. Kenny had a welder in Blanding make up a bunch of metal rings with a pin that allowed the oar ring to attach to the rowing frame. The rings were then meticulously wrapped with small diameter cordage so the oar wouldn't contact bare metal and allowed the oar to rotate freely inside the ring. By doing so, the oar could be rotated on entrance and exit from the water. From my own personal experience I know that my arms and shoulders didn't hurt nearly as much at the end of a day of rowing when I had adapted from fixed oars to freely rotating oars.

Kenny adapted his rowing technique to the so-called Galloway method where the oarsman faced downstream upon entry into rapids or in avoiding rocks. Most accomplished modern-day boatmen have learned to row both ways out of pure necessity. One learns to face the obstacle and row at an angle to the current (the *ferry angle* as it has become to be known). But on straight stretches, or when the wind howls, we have all learned to turn the boat around and put our back into our strokes. Sometimes, in rather difficult rapids, we may enter the rapid with our backs turned downstream and look over our shoulders and then rotate the boat 180 degrees after avoiding a large rock near the head of the rapid. Some river runners now call this technique of rowing downstream back-first the *Powell method* (in reference to the bow-first rowing method used at the time John Wesley Powell made his famous runs through Grand Canyon).

When the oarsman sat roughly at mid-ship the bow and stern compartments were kept open for passengers, or flooring could be strapped in to allow baggage and gear to be stowed away and tied down. By far, this has become the preferred modern-day method, especially for commercial purposes when transporting paying passengers who may have nary a clue about how to navigate a boat in swift-moving water, avoid obstacles, or safely land the boat. On the San Juan River, particularly when the water was low and sand bars, cobble bars, and rocks required frequent maneuvering, Kenny developed his favorite mantra that he shouted out and instilled in all the novices, *"Run the V's, cut the C's and watch your downstream oar!"* [38]

EXPLORERS CAMP PROGRAM FOR 1949

The summer of 1949 marked the sixth field season of the Explorers Camp for teenage boys. Ansel Hall was still advertised as the General Director, and Kenneth I. Ross was the Camp Field Director.[39] However, almost all the correspondence, brochures, itineraries and activities were now under the control of Kenny and by the time the summer camp rolled around, it was called the "Southwest Exploration Field Program"[40] and precise dates were delineated for the camp activities. The camp was scheduled to last nine weeks from June 21 to August 22. The itinerary indicated that the boys were to convene at Gold King base camp and do some mountaineering the first week before being divided into three "parties" where the main activities would include: a) the first time 225 mile-long river run from Bluff to Lees Ferry to be led by Kenny Ross; b) continued excavations at Cahone on the "Cibola City Ruin" led by Prof. Gordon Thomas of the University of California; and c) fossil collection and touring Navajoland was to be led by geologist Dr. Henry P. Zuidema of the University of Michigan. This last segment was to include the usual stop at Lukachukai to take part in Navajo ceremonies and watch the Navajo rodeo, or Entah. The parties would then rotate so each group of boys could experience each activity and then the final segment d) planned was for the entire group to head to the canyon country west of Monticello and split into two groups: one would explore from the mouth of Indian Creek up to Salt Creek Canyon and the other group would start at the head of Salt Creek Canyon and work their way down canyon where they would meet the group coming up canyon.[41]

However, Mother Nature and a series of cancellations drastically altered the plans and itineraries for that year's Explorers Camp. The winter of 1948-49 was an exceptionally big snow year which caused immediate problems for their orientation period in June; and both Dr. Zuidema (geologist) and Prof. Gordon Thomas (archaeologist) dropped out at the last minute and could not make it to camp. Kenny even tried to entice Dr. A.K. Guthe to return for the archaeology but to no avail; plus, the group of boys was much smaller, numbering only twenty-six. Ansel and Kenny had to make changes "on the fly" and they dropped the trip to Navajoland and Lukachukai since "the show there has deteriorated so much that it is no longer worthwhile considering the amount of trouble we have to go to get there."[42] Bill Dickinson provided a little insight into his youthful years when he reviewed these letters and mentioned that he was quite disappointed in 1949 when he heard about not returning to Lukachukai. "When we went down there the year before I danced all night every night of the squaw dance with a pretty slick Navajo chick name of Jeanie and I was fishing for the future."[43]

Kenny was particularly happy to see Jon Lindbergh and Bill Dickinson's return as they became his main camp assistants, and the post-camp Cataract Canyon river trip with these two was still scheduled, even if it was just the three of them, so all was not lost. Regarding the 1949 Explorers Camp, much of what followed was derived from a lengthy Explorers Camp Newsletter written by Kenny and sent out to parents that described the activities through Thursday, July 28, 1949.[44]

All the boys arrived in Durango according to their schedules and were taken to Gold King base camp where Jon Lindbergh was placed in charge of the younger group of boys and Bill Dickinson was placed in charge of the older ones. The first five days were spent at the Gold King base camp in the La Plata Mountains shoveling snow out of the camp and then "climbing nearby mountain peaks, horseback riding, and working with Marshall Long, an old prospector, who demonstrated the techniques of panning for gold [Figure 6.18]."[45]

"On June 27 [Monday], the group of older boys, led by field director Dave Sanchez, our horse wrangler, made the first reconnaissance of the snow-covered trails leading across the divide from our headquarters in the La Platas to our outpost camp site in Bear Creek canyon."[46] There had been so much snow that the main group of boys traveled by truck to the west side of the mountains and then by horseback and afoot into the Bear Creek camp by a lower trail that was not blocked by snow. Meanwhile, Ansel Hall had learned that there was going to be a dedication of a newly completed reservoir that would provide much needed potable water to Mesa Verde National Park and the greater Mancos community. He made the necessary arrangements and the entire boys group was invited by Mancos residents to join in the 4th of July festivities which included the dedication of Jackson Gulch reservoir, a large irrigation project started by the Bureau of Reclamation before World War II and had been recently finished in late 1948 (Figure 6.19 & 6.20).[47]

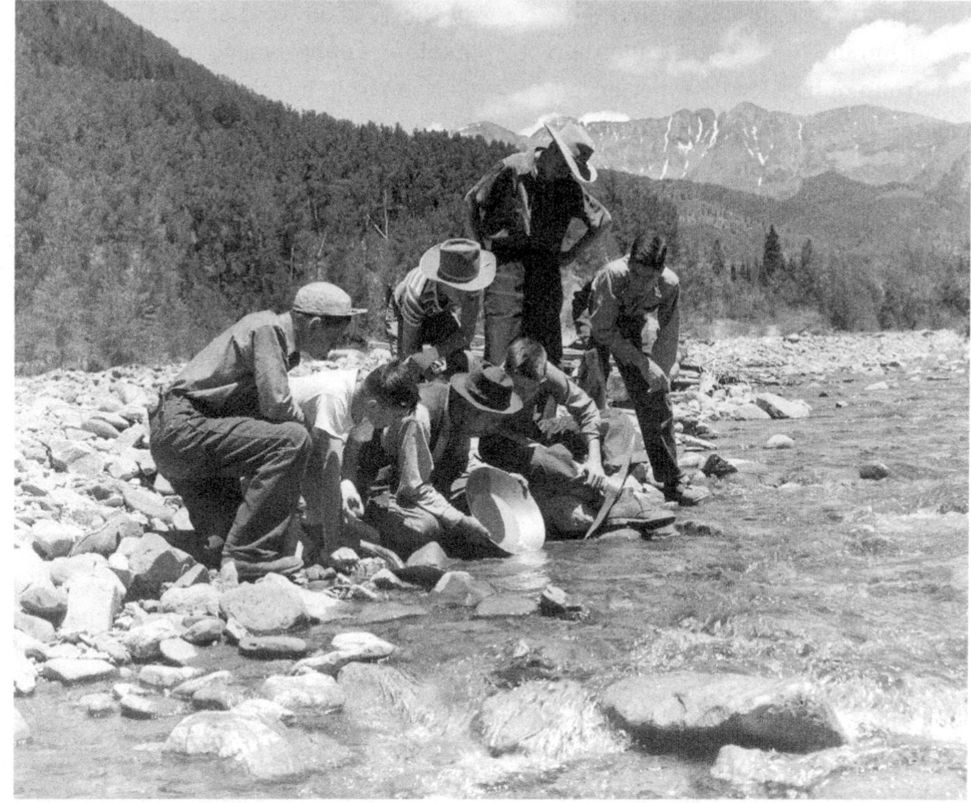

Figure 6.18 Prospector Marshall Long shows the boys how to pan for gold in La Plata Creek. (K. Ross collection)

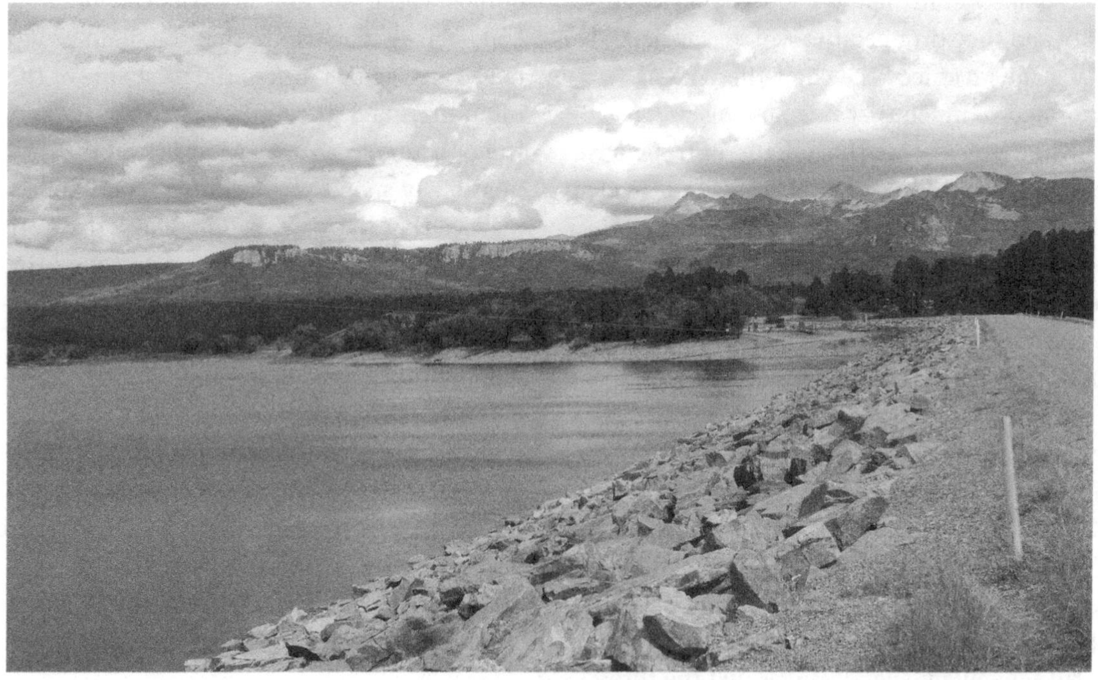

Figure 6.19 view east from dam wall at Jackson Gulch Reservoir; La Plata Mountains in background. (G.M. Stevenson photo)

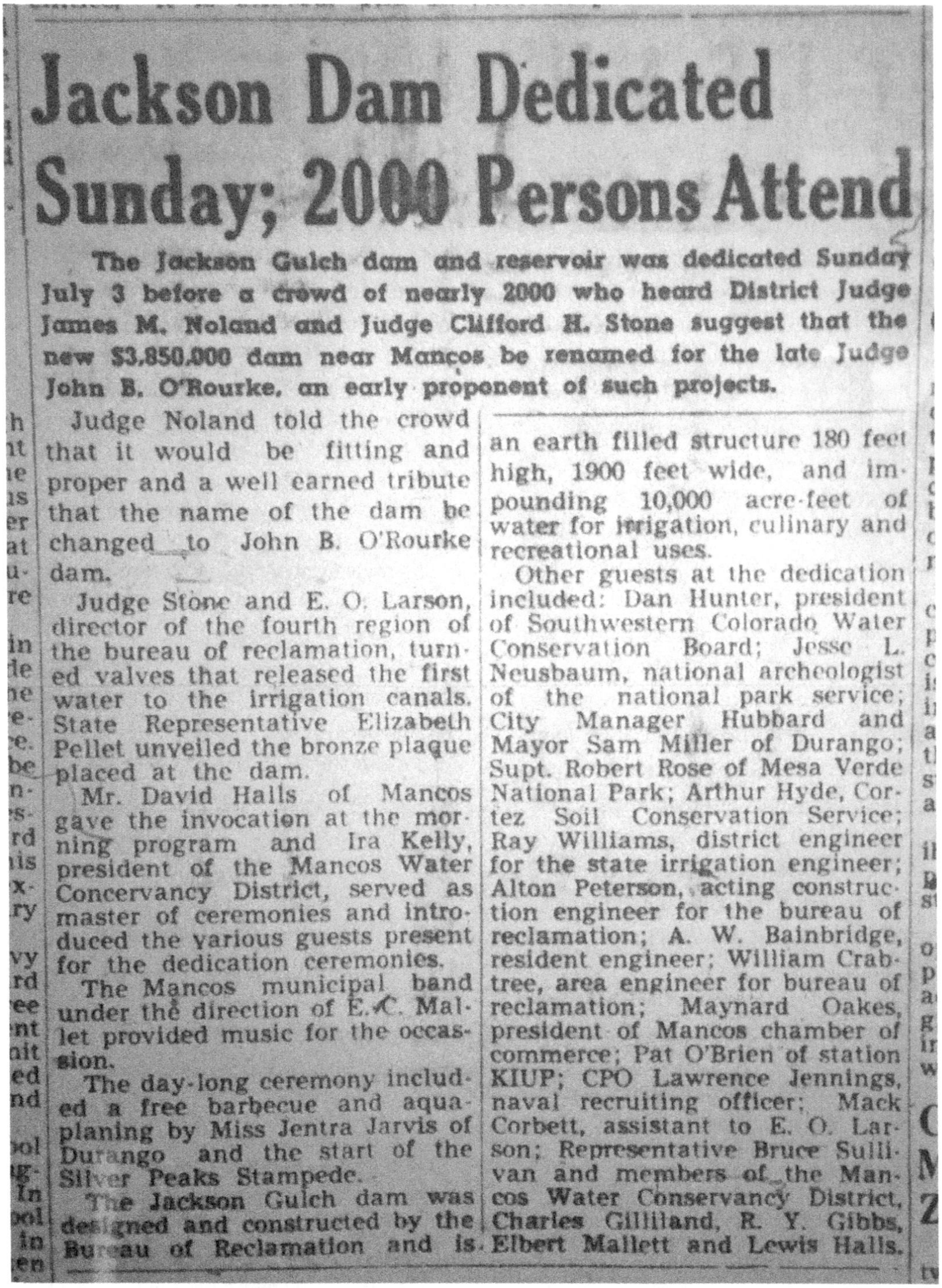

Jackson Dam Dedicated Sunday; 2000 Persons Attend

The Jackson Gulch dam and reservoir was dedicated Sunday July 3 before a crowd of nearly 2000 who heard District Judge James M. Noland and Judge Clifford H. Stone suggest that the new $3,850,000 dam near Mancos be renamed for the late Judge John B. O'Rourke, an early proponent of such projects.

Judge Noland told the crowd that it would be fitting and proper and a well earned tribute that the name of the dam be changed to John B. O'Rourke dam.

Judge Stone and E. O. Larson, director of the fourth region of the bureau of reclamation, turned valves that released the first water to the irrigation canals. State Representative Elizabeth Pellet unveiled the bronze plaque placed at the dam.

Mr. David Halls of Mancos gave the invocation at the morning program and Ira Kelly, president of the Mancos Water Concervancy District, served as master of ceremonies and introduced the various guests present for the dedication ceremonies.

The Mancos municipal band under the direction of E. C. Mallet provided music for the occassion.

The day-long ceremony included a free barbecue and aquaplaning by Miss Jentra Jarvis of Durango and the start of the Silver Peaks Stampede.

The Jackson Gulch dam was designed and constructed by the Bureau of Reclamation and is an earth filled structure 180 feet high, 1900 feet wide, and impounding 10,000 acre-feet of water for irrigation, culinary and recreational uses.

Other guests at the dedication included: Dan Hunter, president of Southwestern Colorado Water Conservation Board; Jesse L. Neusbaum, national archeologist of the national park service; City Manager Hubbard and Mayor Sam Miller of Durango; Supt. Robert Rose of Mesa Verde National Park; Arthur Hyde, Cortez Soil Conservation Service; Ray Williams, district engineer for the state irrigation engineer; Alton Peterson, acting construction engineer for the bureau of reclamation; A. W. Bainbridge, resident engineer; William Crabtree, area engineer for bureau of reclamation; Maynard Oakes, president of Mancos chamber of commerce; Pat O'Brien of station KIUP; CPO Lawrence Jennings, naval recruiting officer; Mack Corbett, assistant to E. O. Larson; Representative Bruce Sullivan and members of the Mancos Water Conservancy District, Charles Gilliland, R. Y. Gibbs, Elbert Mallett and Lewis Halls.

Figure 6.20 Newspaper article about Jackson Gulch Reservoir dedication. (From Montezuma Valley Journal, July 7, 1949, p.1)

The celebration included a big barbeque dinner at the dam site on July 3 and was attended by a couple of thousand people. The Explorers showed off the amphibious DUKW "the duck" by going in and out of the lake for several hours and the honor of plunging the "duck" into the lake for the first time was given to Jesse L. Nusbaum, Chief Archaeologist for the National Park Service and one of the dignitaries present for the big event. All the Explorers had a "turn at the wheel" while cruising.[48] Bill Winkler inherited the DUKW some years later and stripped off the body and added "gin" poles for the powerful winch that was on the truck. He said it served him well for many years.[49]

Unfortunately, due to continuous rain, the gold mining project was cancelled and on July 13 the group headed back to Gold King base camp to prepare for the big San Juan River trip that would take the boys all the way from Bluff through the lower canyons to the confluence with the Colorado River in Glen Canyon to Lees Ferry; a distance of some 225 river miles. But once again, their plans were significantly modified by Ansel Hall. Kenny tried to be upbeat about the altered plans that now had the group launching from Shiprock and only traveling as far as Mexican Hat. River trips to Rainbow Bridge and Glen Canyon would have to wait another year.

> Upon our arrival we found that the whole group had been invited to attend the historic meeting of the Four-State Governors at Four Corners, the picturesque but desolate spot where Utah, Arizona, New Mexico, and Colorado all meet with a common corner. Although, from a standpoint of transportation, this is one of the most remote spots in the United States, joining in the ceremonies fitted our plans perfectly since our river voyage would take us within one-half mile of the "Corners" monument where the ceremonies were to take place.[50]

SAN JUAN RIVER TRIP: July 16-22, 1949 (The Governors Trip)

With food packed and boats loaded on trucks they set off for Shiprock, New Mexico on Saturday, July 16 and made camp. There was an Indian dance in preparation across the river and they all attended, but dancing didn't begin until after midnight so they went back across the river and went to bed. By noon on Sunday the boats were loaded and they took off "on a five-mile current" and, on Monday, July 18 (Figure 6.21):

> Their arrival at Four Corners was exactly timed with the arrival of the Governors and some 1500 other persons who came by plane, auto, afoot, horseback and, of course, by boat. It was terribly hot and since the State of New Mexico was passing out free Pepsi-Cola, all of us indulged in the ice cold beverage far more than was wise. "Chief" Hall met us there. He had arrived earlier by auto as he was to be one of the speakers.[51]

The big event was covered by area newspapers (Figure 6.22): "There will be some 200 cars enroute to the Four Corners Monday morning as the governors of four states meet for the first time at the unique location. The theme of the meeting was to celebrate the opening of the last frontier and scenic possibilities of the area *if a highway is eventually built through the section.*"[52] [Emphasis mine]

Kenny later wrote about this auspicious occasion:

> A few years ago the Governors of the States of Colorado, Utah, New Mexico and Arizona ate a ceremonial meal at a table set amid surroundings as strange and colorful as four such august gentlemen had ever encountered. The place was a barren, rocky flat rising above the San Juan River. The table was centered over a low cement monument which marks the spot where all four of the States meet with a common corner. This was probably the first time in all history that the leaders of four great political units had ever dined together while at the

same time sitting each in his own territory. It happened in the only place such a stunt is possible – at the heart of the Four Corners Country.

Symbolic of the occasion, most of the two hundred-odd people who witnessed the event had reached this lonely place in the Southwestern desert by horseback, afoot, by auto and airplane. The twenty-six young men of Explorers Camp who attended by special invitation came by boat – after a two-day dash down the San Juan River.[53]

At the time of this big event Kenny thought that further description of what occurred at Four Corners was not necessary since pictures and the story would be forthcoming in *Life Magazine* as they had sent Staff photographer Carl Iwasaki to document the event. The local newspapers showed photographs of the four governors standing around a table drinking *Pepsi Colas* at the monument and aerial photos of the crowd, but apparently *Life Magazine* didn't find the event newsworthy (Figures 6.23 & 6.24).[54]

San Juan Boat Trip to Take Youths to Governors Meet

* * *

Air, Land, River Trips to Feature Four-Corners Plan

The Four-Corners will be visited Monday by air, by caravan, and by boat when the governors of Utah, Colorado, Arizona and New Mexico meet to exchange handshakes across the Four-Corners marker.

The boat trip—latest addition to the Four-Corners program—will be made in 10 boats by about 40 youths attending Ansel Hall's Boys' Explorers Camp at the Gold King mine in the La Plata Mountains, Chamber of Commerce Secretary Glenn Skewes said.

The explorers will make the boat trip from Shiprock, N. M., down the San Juan river to a point opposite the Four-Corners. Skewes said it is about a half mile hike from the river to the monument. They will arrive in time for the four-governor ceremony.

Skewes said planes will fly over the Four-Corners for aerial pictures, and the caravan will take the only road, led by Governor Knous of Colorado, J. Bracken Lee of Utah, Thomas J. Mabry of New Mexico and Dan E. Garvey of Arizona in state patrol cars of Colorado and New Mexico.

Hall operates the Mesa Verde lodge and explorers camp. He will make a five-minute talk at the Four-Corners meeting on Monument Valley and other isolated scenic spots of the section which may some day be opened by a direct highway route west.

Hall's daughter is preparing collections of photographs of the area, mounted on unborn calfskin with Indian designs and names of the governors

Figure 6.21 Newspaper article announced Explorers Camp participation in the big event. (From the Cortez Sentinel, July 14, 1949)

Nearly 200 Cars Expected To Join Four Corners Caravan

There will be some 200 cars enroute to the Four Corners Monday morning as the governors of four states meet for the first time at the unique location. Persons from every section of the San Juan basin are invited to attend the meeting which will receive nation-wide publicity.

Among outstanding publications covering the meeting will be Life magazine which will send Staff Photographer Carl Iwasaki to the Four Corners. He is scheduled to arrive in Durango aboard Monarch airlines Sunday.

Persons who live west of Durango and who plan to join the caravan are asked to meet the group at Shiprock. Durango residents and caravan visitors east of that town will form south of Durango on the Aztec road.

The caravan will leave Durango about nine o'clock Monday morning, with plans to arrive in Farmington at 10:50. There will be a ten-minute stop in that New Mexico town.

Persons taking part in the caravan should take their own lunch and an ample supply of drinking water.

Speeches at the Four Corners will be five minutes each by the governors, and a five-minute talk by Ansel Hall of Mesa Verde National park. The theme of the meeting will be the opening of the last frontier and scenic possibilities of the area if a highway is eventually built through the section.

Judge James Noland has been active in arranging the meeting details with Governors Lee Knous of Colorado, Dan E. Garvey of Arizona, J. Bracken Lee of Utah and Thomas J. Mabry of New Mexico. Noland will serve as master of ceremonies for the program.

According to present plans, the caravan is scheduled to arrive at Four Corners about 1:15 and to leave on the return trip about one hour later.

Figure 6.22 Newspaper article announced the four Governors meeting. (From the Cortez Sentinel, July 14, 1949, p.1)

Following the ceremonies – Kenny and the boys returned to the boats and went down stream "a few miles" and set up camp and "after a hearty supper" they went to bed. They got underway the next morning (Tuesday) and stopped about 2:00 PM at the old Trading Post at Aneth, Utah where they had lunch and visited with folks at the Trading Post. A sudden dust and dash of rain storm hit and "tore our boats loose from their moorings, and sent them skittering across the water."[55] There was much confusion but the boats were rescued with little damage done other than one Explorer lost a camera in the water. They floated on downstream and set up camp near Bluff, with the intention of making a run into Bluff the next morning, but "there were a number of members absent from breakfast due to a sudden 'intestinal looseness' which had come upon the party during the night." Kenny mentioned it might have been due to "our orgy at Four Corners."[56]

However, there might have been more to that. Think about this: they had a big barbeque feast at Jackson Gulch Reservoir, followed by the trip to Shiprock and going across the river to Indian dances where fry bread and mutton was more than likely eaten; then the next day they all made a hot hike to the Four Corners event and pounded ice cold *Pepsi's*, followed by another "hearty supper" on the river followed by a stop at the Aneth Trading Post where the boys ate more junk food before making camp near Bluff. The combination was explosive to say the least. Kenny began referring to these intestinal problems as "the San Juan short-step," but in later years he coined the term the *"San Juan quick-step with fluid drive."*[57]

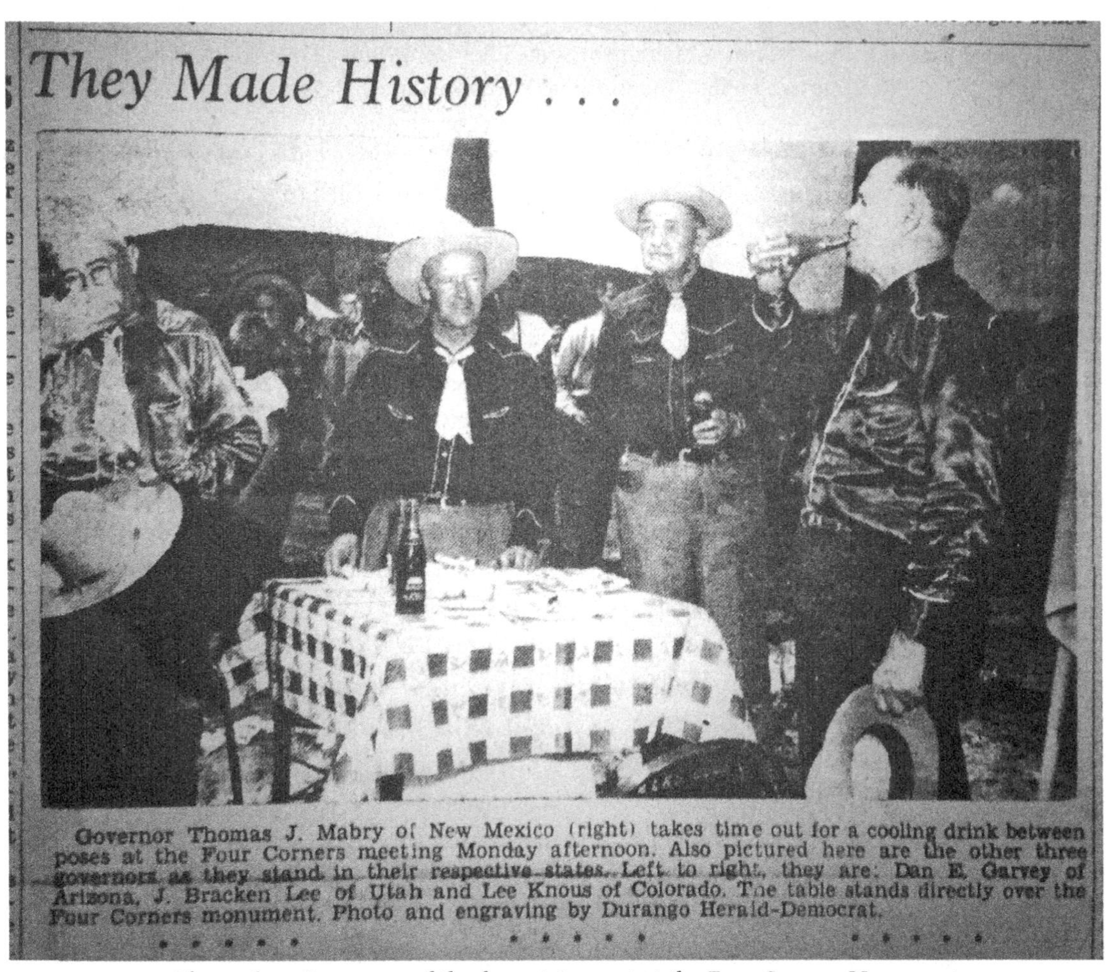

They Made History . . .

Governor Thomas J. Mabry of New Mexico (right) takes time out for a cooling drink between poses at the Four Corners meeting Monday afternoon. Also pictured here are the other three governors as they stand in their respective states. Left to right, they are: Dan E. Garvey of Arizona, J. Bracken Lee of Utah and Lee Knous of Colorado. The table stands directly over the Four Corners monument. Photo and engraving by Durango Herald-Democrat.

Figure 6.23 Governors of the four states met at the Four Corners Monument. (From the Cortez Sentinel, July 21, 1949, p.1)

Figure 6.24 aerial view of the Four Corners Monument; state lines were "limed" by the Four Corners Jeep Club. (June Head photo; Montezuma County Historical Society)

Since everyone had gotten sick and dehydrated from the "scoots" they only traveled about three miles below Bluff before they stopped to "camp for the day and recuperate"[58] [that put them at Sand Island where they laid over on Wednesday, July 20th]. "Thursday morning everyone was fit as a fiddle and raring to complete our journey to Mexican Hat..." and through rapids and fast water and "miles of sporting 'sand rollers'."[59] The last rapid [Gypsum Rapid] surprised the boys described as "a small but extremely rough one just above our final landing at Mexican Hat"[60] immediately above the bridge on Thursday, July 21.

They de-rigged and the trucks showed up and brought yet more food, "a marvelous turkey dinner prepared and sent to us by the chef at Spruce Tree Lodge in Mesa Verde National Park."[61] They camped on the riverbank and the next morning they drove out to Goosenecks overlook and then back to Gold King via Bluff, Blanding, Monticello and through Mancos.

Then they spent "the next two days preparing for our archaeological trip for excavations at Cahone."[62] From Gold King, they traveled to Mesa Verde National Park to enjoy the hospitality of "Chief" Hall at Spruce Tree Lodge where "at this writing" [Thursday, July 28, 1949] they had just finished "the best fried chicken dinner we have ever eaten."[63] They left the next day to set up camp near the Cahone ruin where they were to begin excavation work. Kenny signed off by writing that they were well-fed and tanned and in good spirits. One thing was certain – although the camp activities had been severely modified, Ansel had made up for it through food – these kids had eaten big meals all month!

THE HIKE BEFORE CATARACT TRIP

The whole group worked together for an abbreviated session at Cibola City Ruins under the direction of Kenny Ross and departed for Elk Ridge on Thursday, August 4. The original plan was to split into two groups with one group hiking to the head of Salt Creek Canyon and the other group was to begin their hike at the mouth of Indian Creek Canyon and then the two groups were to meet in the middle. But Kenny was the only adult in the group so the plan was changed and hikes into Salt Creek Canyon would have to wait until the 1951 season.

The group of Explorers ended up hiking into Woodenshoe Canyon and down Dark Canyon to its mouth at the Colorado River. By now, Kenny knew this trek fairly well, having been there twice before – in 1946 and 1947. On this particular trek, Jon Lindbergh wandered up the river bank a mile or so to look over the rapids in anticipation of the upcoming river trip. Kenny recalled that Jon quietly came up behind Dick Griffith and said "Hi there!" and nearly scared him to death. Griffith had no idea any human being was within a hundred miles of him. Imagine his surprise?[64] Kenny's written Explorers Camp notes only state the following when Jon came upon Dick Griffith (Figure 6.25):

> He ran into a lone boatman, Dick Griffith of Fort Collins, Colorado, who, to our knowledge is the only other person to run Cataract this year. Griffith had traveled down the river alone from Greenriver, Utah and seemed grateful for the opportunity to eat supper with us and to sleep near other humans. He told us of his adventures in the rapids above and expressed himself in no uncertain terms concerning the foolishness of anyone who would tackle Cataract without companions. His boat was a 15-foot rubber landing craft, similar to our 12-ft boat and he ran it with oars by the method worked out during the 1890s by Nathan Galloway, of Richfield, Utah.
>
> Following breakfast next morning, Griffith, with Jon Lindbergh as passenger, ran Dark Canyon Rapid, while the Explorers looked on and took pictures. He chose a course near the left shore, where the water is so shallow that there was just enough to grease the rocks so the boat could slide over and around them. Got thru okay but Jon and the other Explorers were a little disgusted because Kenny had always taught them to run a 'clean' boat and that means to avoid bumbling over rocks. However, Griffith knows his business and had good reason to fear the high waves and grinding current of the channel near the far right shore—where most of the river poured thru with demonic power.[65]

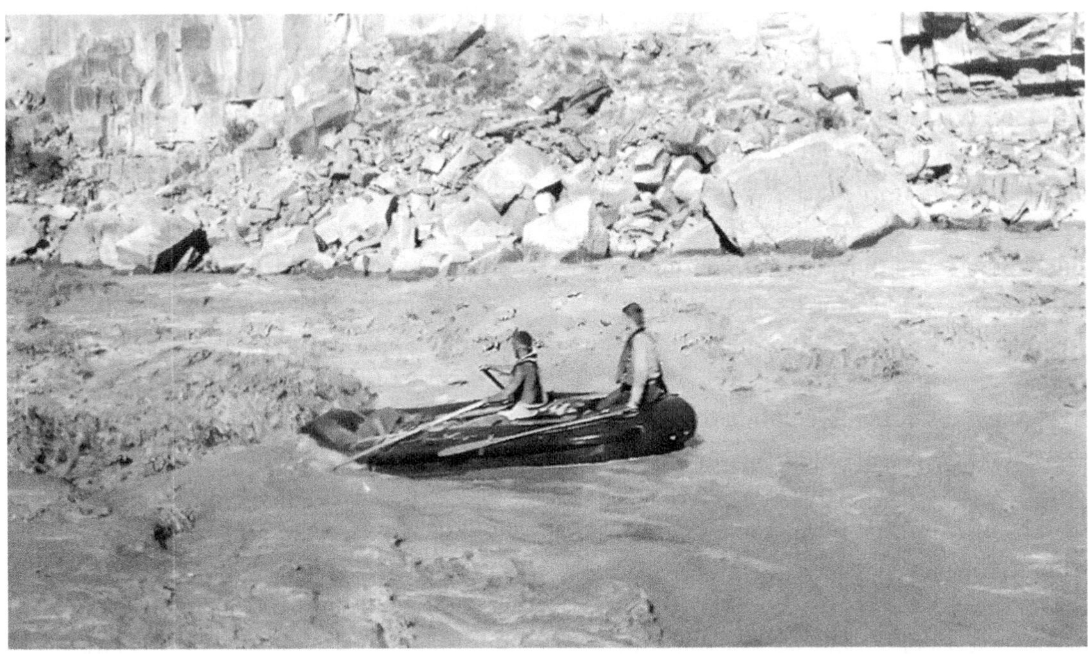

Figure 6.25 Dick Griffith with oars running Dark Canyon Rapid in his 15 ft LCR-L boat with hitchhiker Jon Lindbergh sitting tall in stern, August, 1949. (K. Ross collection)

The Explorers group took a couple of days hiking out of Dark Canyon back to the vehicles and then traveled back to Gold King base camp arriving on Friday, August 19. The boys took a few days to get the camp in order, celebrated with a big campfire and barbeque at that year's camporee and camp was officially over by Tuesday, August 23.

Once again, Hank Zuidema had cancelled earlier that summer in working at the Explorers Camp and in going down Cataract Canyon in August with Kenny, as had Ansel Hall and Charles Lindbergh. Therefore, the scheduled two-boat trip was reduced to just one boat with Kenny, Jon Lindbergh and Bill Dickinson. Kenny had been eying Cataract Canyon for four years now and Jon nearly as long and had at least taken a "thrill ride" down part of Dark Canyon Rapid. These three had been talking about a Cataract trip since the previous year and there was no turning back, even if it was with one boat – the 12-1/2 ft long 7-man LCR. They were fully aware of the remoteness and dangerous rapids. Kenny had studied the canyon and what little was known from written reports and handed down stories. Kenny had made hand-written notes from Frederick S. Dellenbaugh's account from his 1871 trip with John Wesley Powell and Robert Brewster Stanton's count of seventy-five rapids in Cataract Canyon. He read about the 1891 "capsize disaster" in Rapid #15 on the Best Expedition and the Kolb Brothers and the Stone Expeditions run in 1909. He knew that Norm Nevill's group in 1940 had problems in a stretch of particularly big rapids that Bert Loper in 1907 called the "Big Drops."[66] Apparently, Del Reed pinned one of Norm's boats (the *Joan*) in Big Drop #3 in July, 1940 with trip passenger Barry Goldwater on shore taking pictures and in the process of retrieving it, the boat capsized and all the gear got soaked.[67] And Kenny was very aware of the treacherous notoriety of Cataract Canyon which had been referred to as the "Graveyard of the Colorado."[68]

The 1949 Explorers Camp had been exciting and certainly different with all the unscheduled events scattered throughout the summer. The biggest point was that the other camp leaders had bailed for various reasons and the entire season's activities had fallen onto Kenny's shoulders. Kenny had led the San Juan River boat trip, albeit only to Mexican Hat; he served as the archaeologist at the Cahone dig, and he led the hike to Dark Canyon....truly a one man operation! But it was worth it, because now he was about to embark on a trip that had escaped his fancy since 1946 – he was *finally* going to run the rapids of Cataract Canyon!

CATARACT CANYON

The rivers that flow through the canyon country of the Colorado Plateau are typically subdivided into subsections of the numerous canyons cut by each rivers course. Above Cataract Canyon, the Colorado (Grand) River cuts a canyon named Meander Canyon which extends sixty-two miles from *The Portal* west of Moab to the confluence with the Green River.[69] This section has a very low gradient of less than one foot per mile with virtually nothing more than riffles and many sand bars and islands to dodge.[70] The Green River below the town of Green River, Utah is divided into two placid low gradient anastomosing sections (Labyrinth and Stillwater canyons) for a distance of one hundred-twenty two river miles that averaged less than two feet per mile down to the confluence.[71]

Cataract Canyon is that stretch of the Colorado River that extends from the confluence of the Green and Grand (Colorado) Rivers as the river doubles in size and flows generally in a southwesterly course down to Sheep Canyon Rapid in Mille Crag Bend – a distance of slightly less than forty river miles and drops nearly four hundred feet through some of the biggest rapids in North America. Below Mille Crag the Colorado flows westerly through a short seven and a half mile long section called Narrow Canyon down to the mouth of the Dirty Devil River that enters from the north side. Prior to the construction of Glen Canyon Dam and the subsequent inundation of Powell reservoir, from the Dirty Devil to Lees Ferry, a distance of almost one hundred-seventy two river miles the Colorado River flows through the serene low gradient Glen Canyon (Figure 6.26; Appendix I, Table 2).[72]

Present day access to Cataract Canyon by boat requires rowing or motoring down forty-eight river miles if launched from the Potash boat ramp on the Colorado River side, or fifty-three river miles if launched from the boat ramp at Mineral Bottom. But on Kenny's first trip they launched just below the bridge crossing the Colorado River in Moab – a distance of sixty-five miles of flat water before they reached the confluence with the Green River. Then it's still another four miles from the confluence to Rapid #1 (also known as "Brown Betty" Rapid). River elevation at the head of Rapid #1 is 3820 ft and the elevation of the last rapid in Mille Crag Bend (pre-Powell reservoir) at Sheep Canyon is 3460 ft for a total elevation difference of 360 ft over the 35.8 river miles or an average gradient of 10.06 feet per mile (fpm).

But Cataract's gradient has anything but a steady drop of ten feet per mile; it drops in a series of stair-steps with the biggest occurring at Mile-Long Rapids (Rapids #13 - #20) where the river drops forty-nine feet in less than two miles and the biggest drops occur a few miles below the bottom of Mile-Long Rapids at the "Big Drops" (Rapids #21-#22-#23) where the river plunges thirty-two feet in less than one mile! Prior to the inundation of Powell reservoir, the single largest rapid was at Dark Canyon where the river dropped twenty feet across the length of the rapid that was approximately a quarter-mile long. Nearly all the major rapids were due to substantial side canyon flash floods that brought large volumes of boulder-fan debris that caused constriction of the main stem.[73]

On his first trip in 1869, Major John Wesley Powell felt that the sixty-plus rapids over less than forty river miles were of such size and complexity that they deserved a more descriptive name than referring to that section as containing "rapids" and named it *Cataract Canyon*. Cataract Canyon had also gained the name "the Graveyard of the Colorado" due to an unknown number of river runners, trappers and prospectors who entered the canyon only to never be seen or heard from again. Not all these folks necessarily perished in the river however; many were suspected to have hiked out and probably died of thirst, regardless of having climbed out to the west or east rims. This situation still exists today as some of the most rugged and remote country in the conterminous U.S.A. awaits the unwary visitor. Whether traveling overland or by river one must know they are basically on their own and should enter this country prepared for emergencies.

So, just how many rapids or drops exists in this thirty-six mile stretch? What constitutes a rapid being called a rapid in the first place? One man's rapid could be another man's riffle, or even not mentioned. These questions were on all the early boaters' minds and the numbers varied from forty to seventy. The presence of a solitary rapid obviously depended on the volume of water; the lower the river, the higher the number. On Kenny Ross's trip in 1949 they documented sixty-seven rapids between Spanish Bottom to Mille Crag Bend and the detailed river log was one of the first, if not *the first*, to keep a reasonably accurate number of rapids.[74] The river volume on the Ross trip through Cataract was estimated to have been running at approximately 7500 cfs, which, by modern day standards would be a relatively modest water level.[75]

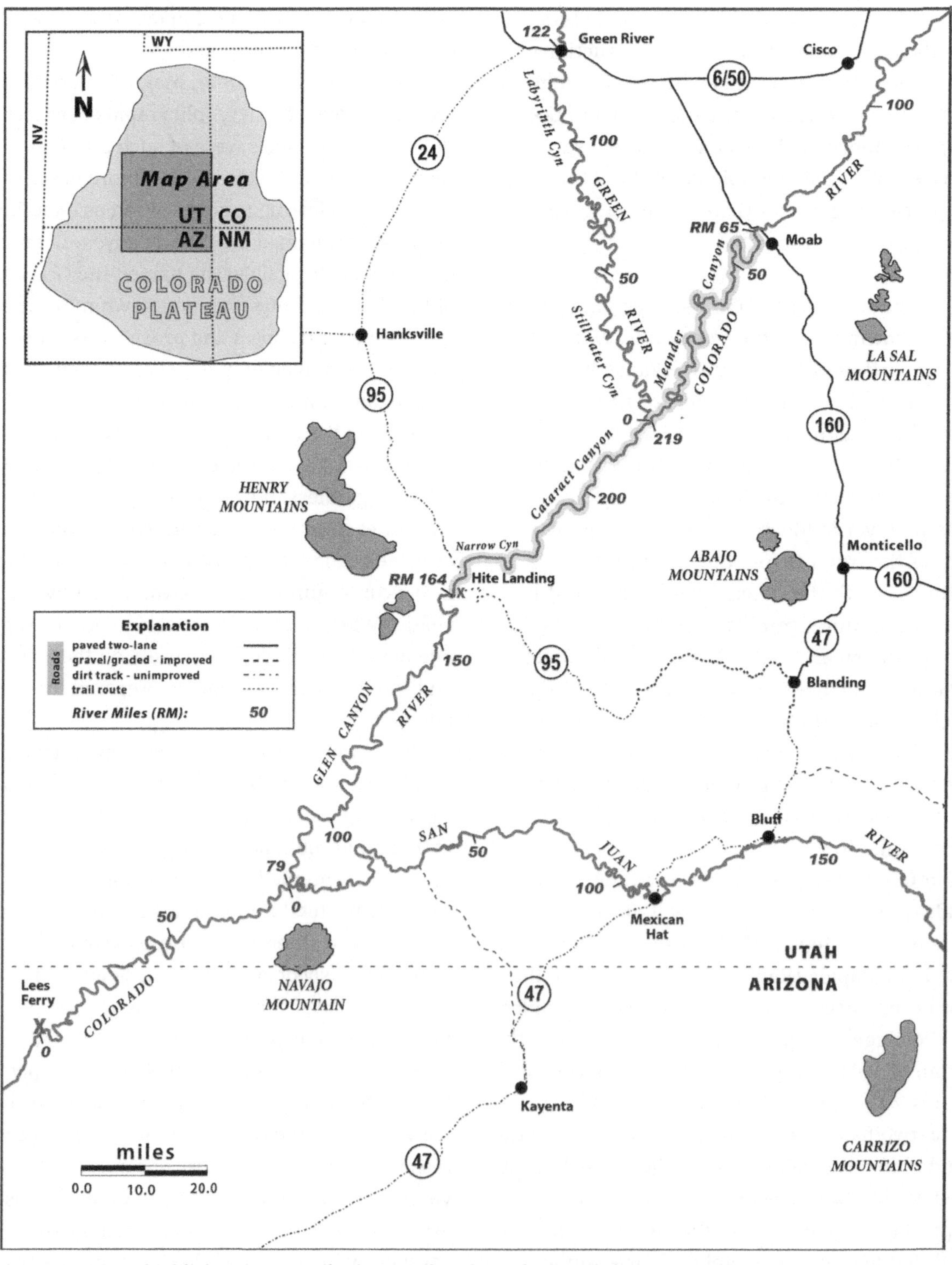

Figure 6.26 Map highlights the 120 mile river section through Meander Canyon, Cataract Canyon and Narrow Canyon from Moab to Hite Landing run by Kenny Ross, Jon Lindbergh and Bill Dickinson in 1949. (GMS/TB original map)

CATARACT CANYON RIVER TRIP LOG
August 23 to September 8, 1949

The log began on the last day of Explorers Camp season, Tuesday, August 23, 1949[76] with a meticulous listing of the details of the boat, gear and weight as follows:

> One boat – Neoprene Land Boat – 7-man – 12 ft – 5 ft. beam – 11 air compartments including air-mattress bottom. Equipped with heavy canvas deck – forward two-thirds. Two forward compartments lined with double nylon tarps for storage – tarps @ 7-11-ft for top waterproofing, under canvas decking. Four spare paddles. Three persons.
>
> Weight of supplies and equipment – including 10 gals water .... 310 lbs at start
> Weight of passengers (combined)....................................... 460 lbs
> Weight of boat empty .... 325 lbs
> Total Weight .... 1,095 lbs
>
> Leader – Kenneth Irving Ross: age 41, 148 lbs; Mancos, Colorado, Director, Explorers Camp
> Jon Morrow Lindbergh: age 17, 137 lbs; Darien, Connecticut, Member, Explorers Camp
> William R. Dickinson: age 18, 175 lbs; Santa Barbara, California, Member, Explorers Camp

From August 23 to August 27 the three cleaned up and shut down Gold King camp for the winter and moved mattresses, beds, surplus canned foods and odds and ends by truck and DUKW to the Mesa Verde Company storage locker. They took the DUKW to Kenny's place in Mancos and removed the battery for storage. By Saturday afternoon Kenny had sorted and packed all the food for the river trip. Jon and Kenny left Mancos in the Dodge Carryall, loaded with the boat and all the supplies, but had a flat tire on the Dodge near Pleasant View. Fortunately, Bill showed up in his car in time to help. They all made it to Monticello, Utah before midnight and camped. The following day they left the boat and supplies at a gas station in Blanding and shuttled both cars to Hite Ferry, by way of the improved gravel road to Natural Bridges National Monument. The road past Natural Bridges was an unimproved rough two-track and it took twelve and a half hours to drive the 175 miles. They left the Dodge at the White Canyon uranium mill and returned to Blanding in Bill's car. They arrived too late to find a restaurant or "tourist court" open and ended up sleeping on the side of the road. Some things just never change in Blanding.

The next morning they loaded up their boat (the *La Cucaracha*) and gear and drove to Moab. They arranged to leave Bill's car with Edith Bish Taylor and unloaded the boat, equipment and food only a quarter mile below the Highway 47 Bridge[77] and proceeded to inflate the boat. By launching from here, they had close to sixty-five river miles of very slow moving water to negotiate before they reached the first rapids in Cataract Canyon. They launched in late afternoon on Monday, August 29 and camped their first night on river right just past the Portal.

They made the long slow float to the head of Rapid #1 by the afternoon of Friday, September 2 (Figure 6.27). The four-day sluggish float was noted by their encountering torrents of mosquitoes any time they attempted landing along the river banks and they decided to camp on sand bars in mid-river (a trick we have all learned who have experienced low water on Cataract trips). They also rigged up a crude sail with a nylon tarp to catch downstream winds, swam, and fished their way down to the confluence where they unloaded the boat and repacked, getting ready for the rapids (Figure 6.28). They ran Rapid #1 and #2 and accurately referenced their location as RM 212. They camped above Rapid #3 (Figure 6.29).

Figure 6.27 Jon Lindbergh (L) and Bill Dickinson (R) on the flat water run down to the confluence, 1949 Cataract Canyon trip. (K. Ross collection)

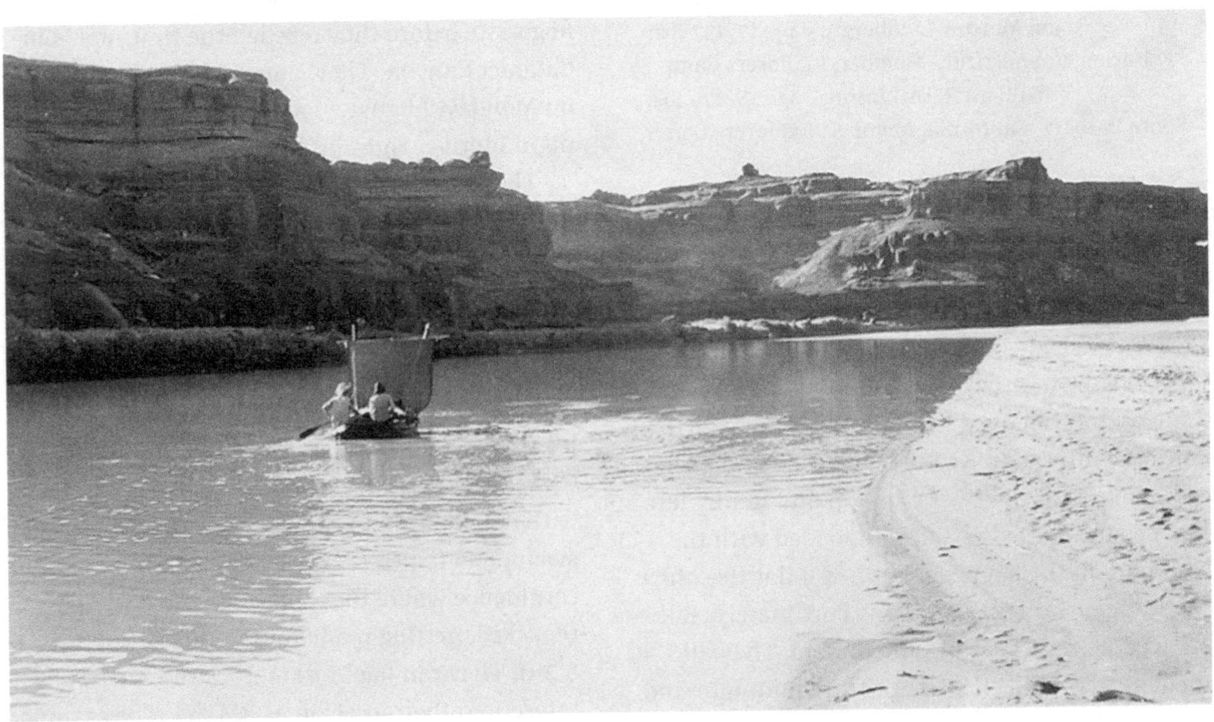

Figure 6.28 improvised sailing down Meander Canyon, 1949. (Bill Dickinson photo)

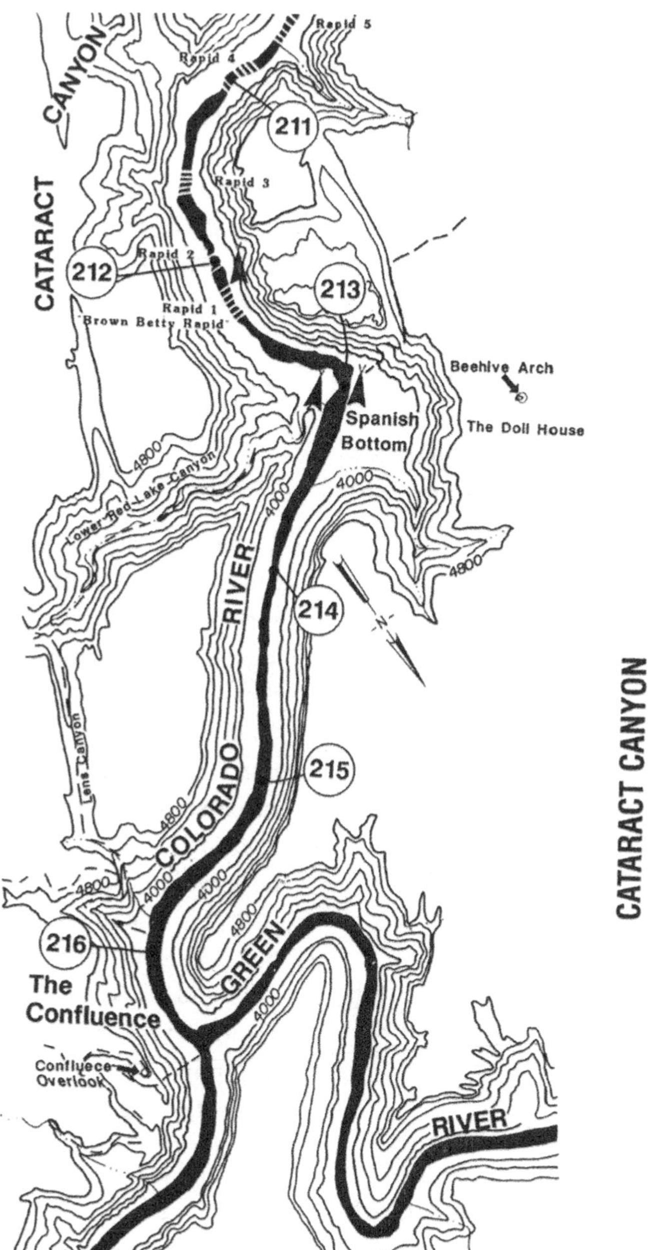

Figure 6.29 Map from Confluence of the Green and Colorado rivers downstream (top of page) to RM 211; note 2.2 mile discrepancy from my measured distance to confluence (218.7) to that shown by Baars (216.5). (From D.L. Baars River Log, 1987)

On Saturday, September 3 they ran Rapids #3 and #4, but stopped to scout or "conn" [78] Rapid #5 with a noted "WOW!"

They *conned* #5 and make mention that the Kolbs and others had described it as bad. A lengthy description followed, as Kenny and Bill were paddlemates and ran the "slick" water tongue between the top rocks just right but got shoved to the left into a big hole which knocked Kenny out of the boat briefly. Both Kenny and Bill lost their paddles but *Kenny lost his hat.* Luckily, they had spare paddles (no hat) and landed on river right to bail the boat and prepare for the next rapids. They conned Rapids #6 and #7 together and had perfect runs. They made note that Rapid #8 was RM 209 "at a point where the river has cut one limb of a sharp anticline, with its axis to the east"[79] and noted they were still in the anticline as they ran #9 and #10. Kenny stayed on shore and photographed Bill and Jon's run through Rapid #10, or the true "Brown Betty" rapid where the boat carrying that name in the Brown-Stanton expedition of 1889 was broken-up and lost.[80]

The large area they were in was formed by the convergence of two side canyon mouths – 'Y' canyon and Cross Canyon and called *Tilted Park* (Figure 6.30). The steep-limbed anticline is caused by an upward bulge or **diapir** of evaporites (mostly anhydrite) named Harrison Dome.[81] Another similar diapiric bulge called Crum Dome is breached by the small canyon entering downstream forming the head of Rapid #12.

Kenny and the boys ran Rapids #11, #12 and #13 and noted that Rapid #14 was RM 205 and they thought that they were at the beginning of what Stanton called *Hell's Half Mile*. Rapid #16 was noted as the "wildest looking we've seen yet (Figure 6.31)." [82] They conned the rapid and Kenny stayed on the left bank and photographed Jon and Bill's run through the rapid. They ran and conned the next series of rapids, with exhilarating runs through #20 and #22 and made camp on the left bank after having run twenty rapids that day by their count and without **lining** a single rapid. They all agreed that day had given each of them sheer adventure and the most thrills of their lives (Figure 6.32). They were most proud of their packing method as their entire gear was perfectly dry.

Sunday, September 4 began a bit later and they all felt stiff from the previous day's hard work. They successfully ran Rapid #23 at RM 203 by their count.

> We thought that this was the most nearly flawless maneuvering we had done yet. In high water one might avoid this rough part of the rapid by passing to the left of an island bar in the river.[83]

Their account provided the necessary comments regarding the island in the middle such that it was possible to correlate to modern logs and numbering systems and deduce that they ran Rapid #20 which has also been called "Ben Hurt" Rapid (Figure 6.33).[84] They ran Rapid #24 (Big Drop 1) and Rapid #25 (Big Drop 2) successfully and their descriptions compare favorably to those of record today, and there was no question that their Rapid #26 was Big Drop 3.

"This was the most fantastic looking rapid we had yet seen." [85] Their mention that the top of the rapid was dammed by a mass of large boulders that create a lake effect was undeniably Big Drop 3. They conned from the left bank and while dashing back and forth several times they found an inscription on a nearby rock:

CAPSIZED No. 3
7-15-40
NEVILLS[86]

They ran the "gut" by entering a narrow chute just left of center then down the left side before the boat spun right and then went through the tail waves.

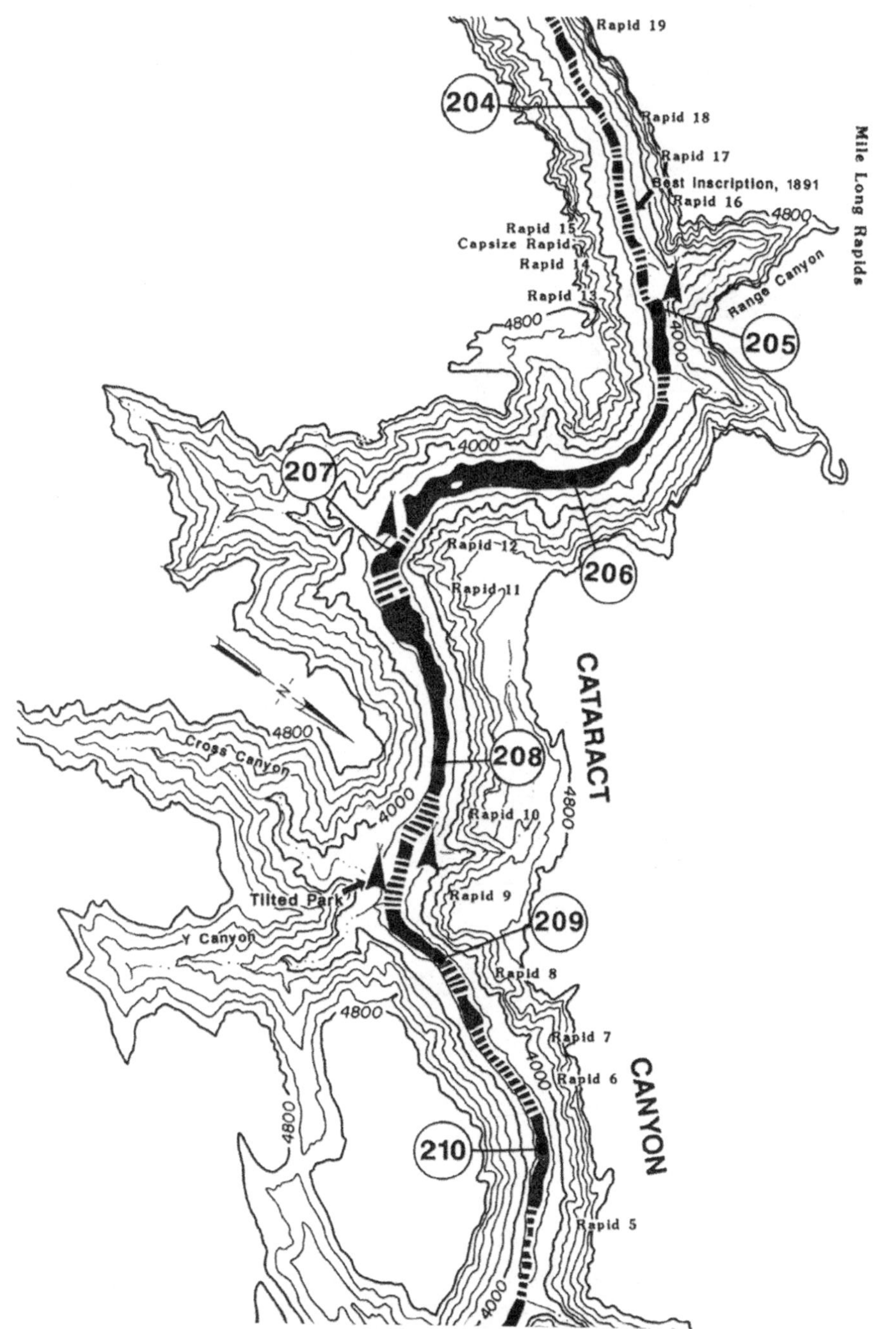

Figure 6.30 Map of Cataract Canyon from RM 211 downstream to RM 203.5 (top of page). (From D.L. Baars River Log, 1987)

Figure 6.31 Jon and Bill conning Rapid #16, Cataract Canyon, 1949. (K. Ross collection)

Figure 6.32 Jon Lindbergh wears the "belt life preserver" Cataract Canyon, 1949. (Bill Dickinson photo)

The Ross Group's descriptions, Rapid Numbers and River Miles from their 1949 journal have been compared to those by Don Baars (1987). My measured distances listed in Appendix I: Table 2, Note #2 vary by two miles with Baars log. However, rapid numbers appears to closely agree with Webb, et al (2004), as follows:

Ross Group, 1949	Baars Log, 1987
Rapid 14 MP 205	Rapid 13 MP 205
Rapid 16 "wildest yet"	Rapid 15 MP 204.7 "Capsize" Best Inscriptions from 1891 Also low wtr inscription "Camp 7, Hell to Pay, No. 1 sunk & down 22 July 1891"
Rapid 20 "worst yet"	Rapid 19 MP 203.6 "The Button"
Rapids 21& 22	Rapid 20 MP 203.1 "Ben Hurt" gravel bar island
Rapid 23/24 MP 203	Rapid 21 MP 202.8 (aka "Big Drop One" or "Upper Big Drop" River drops 30' in a mile; not 75' as JW Powell had estimated
Rapid 25	Rapid 22 MP 202.4 (aka "Big Drop Two" or Middle Big Drop" (aka "Little Niagara" in big water)
Ross Group notes "a lake effect"	MP 202.3 "Lake Cataract" a big backwater monster-eddy; on right bank about 75' above river level is a painted inscription by Kolb Bros in 1911
Rapid 26 "the most fantastic looking rapid yet"	Rapid 23 MP 202.2 (aka "Big Drop Three" or "Lower Big Drop" or "Kolb Rapid" K. Ross attributed as naming it "Satans Gut")
Ross Group found Nevills inscription	CAPSIZED NO. 3 7-15-40 NEVILLS
Rapid 30 "in three parts...."	Rapid 26 MP 201.1 Last Rapid when Baars & Stevenson scouted in August, 1986
Rapid 31 "This is the longest continuous rapid we have run yet"	Rapid 27 MP 200.2 "Imperial Canyon Rapid"
Rapid 40 GYPSUM CANYON "big waves"	MP 196.5 Gypsum Canyon enters on left; drowned by lake
Ross Group ran Rapids 41 - 61 before encountering Rapid 62: DARK CANYON RAPID "The 'bugger' of Cataract Canyon"	MP 182.8 Dark Canyon enters on left; drowned by lake

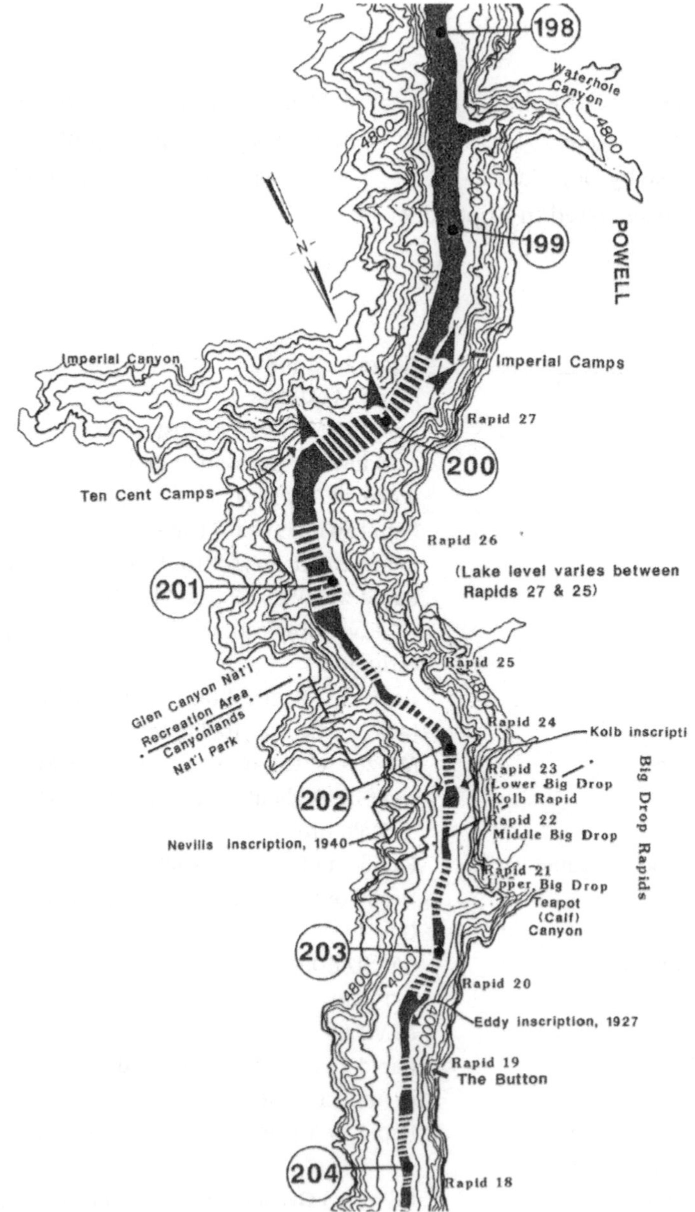

Figure 6.33 Map of Cataract Canyon from RM 204 downstream to RM 198 (top of page). (From D.L. Baars River Log, 1987)

Once they bailed the water out of the boat following their successful run of Big Drop #3 they ran Rapids #27 to #30 with no problems and noted that Rapid #30 was in three parts and the river bent sharply to the right (Figure 6.33). As noted in the comparison above, that would be the last rapid when Powell Reservoir was at full pool of 3700 ft and a camp site on river left named the *Ten Cent Camp* became popular to both river runners and lake boaters which created some heated discussion during full pool years.[87] They stopped somewhere along this stretch for lunch (Figure 6.34). When they got underway again they didn't stop to conn Rapid #31 that they correctly place at RM 200 and noted that "This is the longest continuous rapid we have run yet." [88] This was Imperial Canyon Rapid and has re-surfaced since the reservoir dropped in the early 1990s and reservoir level has never raised high enough to cover it again.

They ran Rapids #32 through Rapid #39 and made camp at the mouth of Gypsum Canyon (RM 196.5) around 5:00 PM:

> This is an old stamping grounds for all three of us. In early August of 1948 we had backpacked down Gypsum, via Beef Basin, with an Explorers Camp expedition, and camped right where we are now. One thing we know for sure and that is it's better not to drink the water from Gypsum Creek. We had plenty of that last year.
>
> We made 7 miles today and ran 17 rapids. We are 20 miles into Cataract Canyon - - with 21 yet to go. Our load was dry again tonight. We are all pretty bushed tonite and will sack in early.[89]

Gypsum Canyon enters from the left and was named by J.F. Steward on Powell's 1871 expedition. This was also the deepest part of Cataract Canyon.[90] The bedded rocks at river level are gypsiferous strata in the Akah Stage of the Paradox Formation and the oldest strata cut by the Colorado River through Cataract Canyon. The Paradox evaporites are overlain by nearly a thousand feet of Honaker Trail gray limestones, then three hundred-sixty feet of red-brown slope-forming section of the Halgaito Shale and then another thousand feet of light-colored massive cliffs of the Cedar Mesa Sandstone (see Appendix II; Stratigraphic Column).

Kenny had lost his hat in Rapid #5 and had gotten way too much sun and was dehydrated. In fact, they were all dehydrated and sun-cooked and they elected to lay-over the next day, September 5, so that all three could recuperate (Figure 6.35). They erected a sunshade with nylon tarps "and spent the day loafing, eating, sleeping, reading, swimming...." Jon walked down the river and "conned a couple of rapids." [91] They got underway early on Tuesday, September 6 and ran Gypsum Rapid (Rapid #40) right down the center noting that this rapid had given them "the best sport so far with waves reaching 10 feet in height." [92]

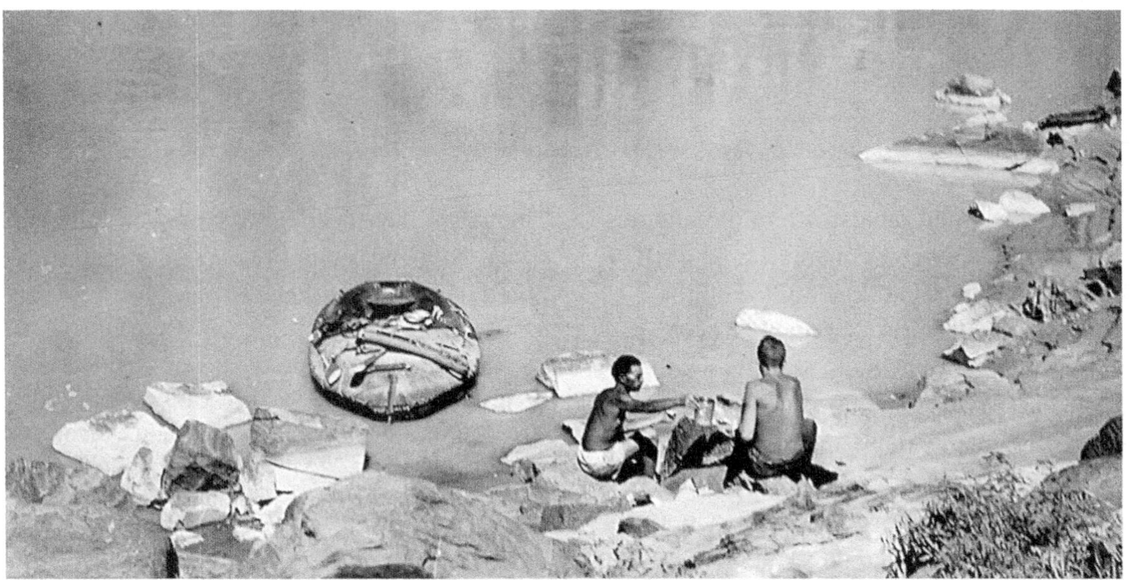

Figure 6.34 Kenny Ross (L) and "Big Bill" (R) make lunch, Cataract Canyon, 1949. (K. Ross collection)

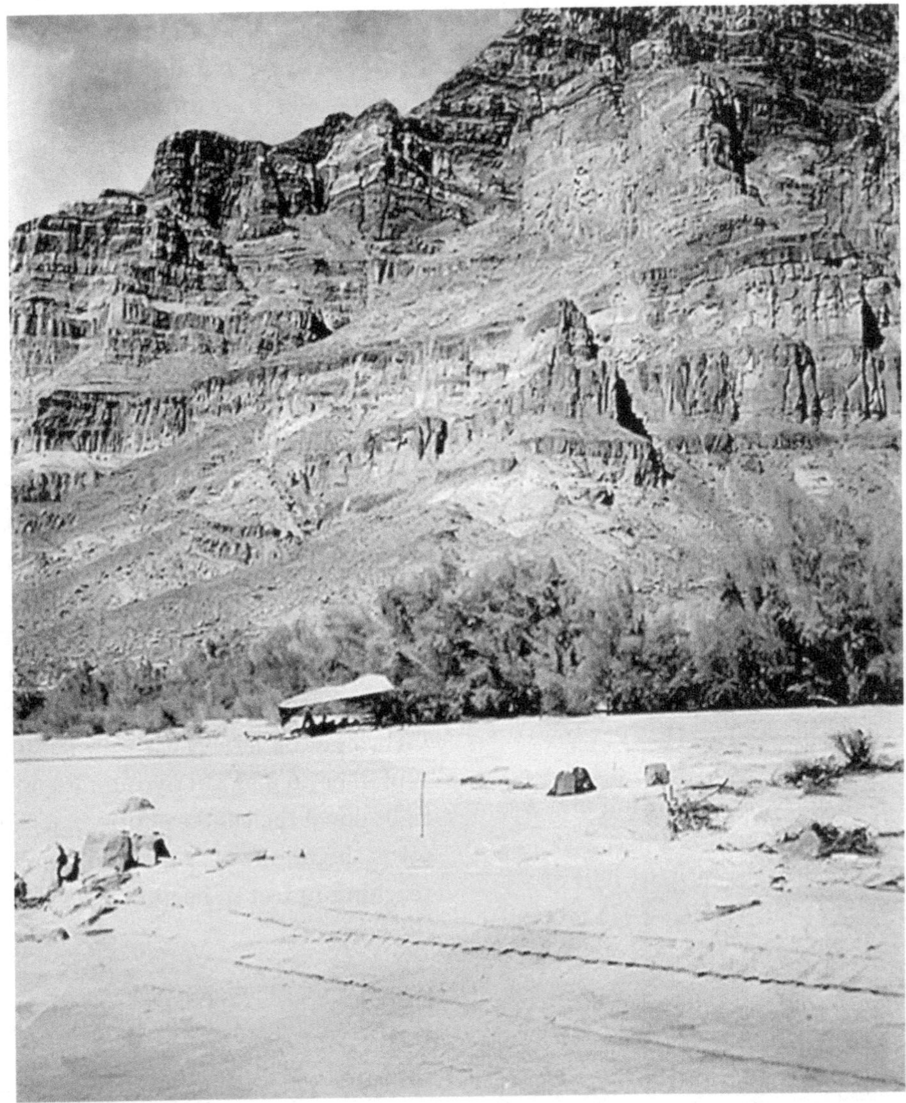

Figure 6.35 shading out on lay-over day at mouth of Gypsum Canyon. (K. Ross collection)

They ran ten small rapids with minimal notes taken down to Clearwater Canyon (Rapid #51). Before they ran the rapid they walked up the narrow canyon and swam in a number of clear water pools similar to those in Dark Canyon. They returned to the boat and noted that the river was very narrow there and bent to the right; they ran the rapid left of center through "fairly high waves all the way through." [93] They noted that Rapid #53 was a rough one as it bent around a left curve and the roughest part was at the top. This *might* have been Bowdie Canyon Rapid at RM 190.5. They ran a number of small rapids and noted when they reached Rapid #59:

> A vicious, rocky descent going around a left bend. Lindy had ridden thru this one with Dick Griffith, of Fort Collins, Colorado, in early August when the water was much higher. It took careful conning and precise handling for a safe run at the present level.[94]

Two more small rapids were run and then they reached Dark Canyon Rapid or Rapid #62 by

Kenny's count with a major tributary canyon that entered from the left. Kenny was finally going to run this "bugger" of Cataract Canyon after first seeing it three years earlier. Because this rapid has remained submerged since being covered in the mid-1960s by the impounded water caused by the construction of Glen Canyon Dam, and because very few modern-day river runners have ever seen this rapid, the full description of their experience is quoted below from the 1949 Cataract Canyon Log:

> This is a real rapid. It is about one-fourth mile long and rips viciously the whole distance. It has speed, rocks, high waves, trickiness, and terrifying power. It is formed by a dam of rock debris - - the "delta" of Dark Canyon, a deep, narrow gorge that spills into the river from the left. This thrusts entirely across the Colorado, whose powerful stream is here narrowed into a space little more than 30 yards wide. The current has cut its deepest channel along the right bank and at the present water level most of the stream rages thru this with furiously compressed power. Near the center of the stream bed, extending from the bottom to more than half way to the top, is an almost submerged island bar studded with protruding rocks. The deep channel runs to the right of this while to the left the water spreads too thinly over the rocks to permit passage of a boat. From the upper point of the bar to the head of the rapid is a complicated arrangement of rocks that makes the task of jockeying for a favorable position in the swift current exceedingly difficult. The crest (the swiftest and highest standing part of the current) is broken up by these into several crests which, as they converge again into one, create high waves. The one crest is again broken by the tip of the island bar into two, the most powerful of which peels to the right into the main channel. Crossing and recrossing these crests had to be carefully calculated in advance because maneuvering here meant going broadside in the waves. The speed and power of each current had to be closely estimated because it would be very important to be on the correct side of the correct crest, at the right time and place. A mistake at any point in the upper fifty yards of the rapid might take us to the left of the bar where tremendous work would be required to get the boat back around into water that would float it. Over-compensating for this would take us too far to the right side of the main current where we would be thrown into the shore and ground to bits on the sharp rocks that line it.
>
> We landed at the head of Dark Canyon rapid a little after five o'clock. It was time to camp for the night but instead of unloading the boat we first walked down the left shore to discover whether we would be forced to run the right channel or if we could possibly bumble over the rocks on the left. We had occasionally speculated about this all the way down to Moab. If there was water enough to permit taking the latter course, we wondered which we would choose to do. Now there was no question. The water was too low to run any but the vicious main channel. The only alternative would be to portage boat and equipment to the foot of the rapid. Also, the question as to whether we would run it this evening or wait until morning was settled. The terrifying, deep-throated roar of the water and the sharper sound of boulders grating along the bottom resolved that. We looked at each other and grinned. Without yelling our throats above the bellowing of the rapid, each knew what was in the minds of the others; "Brotherrrrr, I'd lots rather listen to that thing tonight from the bottom than from its upper end."
>
> Familiar with the rapid from previous visits after "hoofing" it down Dark Canyon, we did not take long to conn it and decide upon a running plan. Then we went back to the boat. Jon was chosen to command the run and took the left paddle while "Big Bill" took the right side where his greater strength might be needed to keep us off the right shore. Kenny sat forward at the center of the boat and, in order to have something to do, grasped the "skirt," or rear flap of the deck canvas and held it up to ward off any water that might come over the bow.
>
> The still water above the rapid made it easy to maneuver to the center of the stream and paddle cautiously down upon a rock and "V" of swift, smooth water that marked the point where we must start over. The "V" was to the left of the rock and we went down its right leg - - gaining speed with every split second - - missing the rock by inches,

exactly according to plan. With this cleared we shot to the right, crossing turbulent crest, then again left - - broadsiding the waves - - passing to the left of another rock and almost skinning it. Then a straight shot down the crest toward the tip of the big bar – thru waves a little lower now but still hitting like sledge hammers. The paddlers were battling constantly now to keep the boat running a little faster than the swift water and Jon's shouted commands could be heard only thinly above the roar of the water. The critical point – the tip of the bar – was coming up fast. Bill pulled a back-stroke and Jon threw one forward, and we slipped off into the grip of the raging main current and the worst of the battle was just beginning. Despite the paddlers fighting with all their strength the current carried the boat higher and higher, almost to the top of the cresting waves, beyond which lay the jagged shoreline. Somehow, by some superhuman burst of energy, the boat was turned to the left, again broadsiding waves, and gradually worked back to safety. The biggest and nastiest looking of the great rocks projecting from the shore lies right at the bottom of the rapid and we missed it only by inches as the boat shot out into the ten-foot high tailwaves. The tailwaves are the "exhaust" of a rapid and it is best to slip out of them quickly as possible but we chose to ride 'em out – shouting at the top of our lungs. Kenny's fingers were sore for hours afterwards from holding the canvas skirt against the force of tons of water that crashed over the bow with each plunge of the boat. Gradually we pulled into a great, left-sweeping back current and landed on a pretty curving beach, right at the foot of the rapid.

The shore of the sandy beach where we are camped is washed by a constant "surf" created by the tailwaves at midstream. This spot has most certainly been used as a camping place by many river voyagers and it is the place where the second Powell expedition had lunch on September 28, 1871, after portaging their boats and equipment around the rapid. It is a real haven and from here, the sound of the rapid is just sweet music to a riverman.

Special Note: A permanent stream flows out of Dark Canyon at this point and the water is drinkable and usually crystal clear. Just above the left bank of this little creek, right at the point where it emerges from the cliff-line, an almost obliterated inscription has been scratched on a flat rock surface. As nearly as we have been able to make it out it is: ?? Turner--???7. A close inspection makes it appear that this was scratched over a still older inscription. Fifty or sixty yards above this a spring of clear, cold water flows out of the cliff near its base. This is completely hidden by a thick screen of redbud trees. A high rock cairn, set in the open in front of the spring was built by the first Explorers Camp expedition that conquered the 43-mile length of Dark Canyon afoot, in August of 1946. Kenny led this one, as well as subsequent expeditions in 1947 and 1949. Jon Lindbergh was on the last two and Bill Dickinson was a member of this year's party. A glass jar within the cairn contains the names of all the members of these expeditions as well as names of at least two river parties.

Wednesday, September 7, 1949:

Up early, packed boat. Took pictures of Dark Canyon Rapid. One series of four overlapping photos show the entire length of the rapid. A single shot was taken from a cliff more than a quarter mile away which shows the entire rapid and surrounding details [Figure 6.36]." [95]

So, they made a successful run through Dark Canyon and camped at the bottom of the rapid where they had camped only a month before (Figure 6.37). The next morning they proceeded downstream and encountered Rapid #67 (Sheep Canyon) which entered from river left at RM 177.0 around noon and passed Mille Crag Bend an hour later. Sheep Canyon rapid defined the termination of Cataract Canyon. Mille Crag (means a thousand crags) formed a sharp, rugged skyline and prompted Powell to give this section the name. The cragginess is due to a series of closely-spaced intersecting faults and joints that cross the river forming the rough landscape.[96] They ran two small rapids in Narrow Canyon before they passed the Dirty Devil that entered from river right and they landed at the Hite Ferry at 6:00 PM (Figures 6.38 & 6.39). They derigged and stayed the night before they drove the Dodge truck the six and a half hours back to Blanding.

Figure 6.36 Dark Canyon Rapid, Cataract Canyon, 1949. (K. Ross collection)

Figure 6.37 camp at bottom of Dark Canyon Rapid, Cataract Canyon, 1949. (K. Ross collection)

The last fifteen miles of slow paddling wasn't discussed in the Ross journal, but Bill Dickinson provided an anecdote when I discussed this trip with him in June, 2015:

> When we got within sight of Hite, some yo-yos had set up a target on a sandbar and were taking target practice by firing rifles upriver (nobody in that direction!). When bullets began plopping into the water near our boat, we began furiously slapping paddles on the water and yelling like banshees. The firing ceased and we floated home (profuse apologies from the riflemen but they really had no reason to suspect that anyone might be upriver from them back in those days). Ciao. WRD[97]

Bill's comments brought about a certain irony to their adventure. They had successfully run one of the most dangerous stretches of rapids in North America, solo, and then narrowly escaped getting shot by unwary rifle sportsmen.

Kenny showed his sincere love and friendship he had developed with Jon Lindbergh in a letter he sent to Col. Charles A. Lindbergh in March, 1950:

> The Cataract Canyon trip which we made after Camp closed was all that we had anticipated. It is probable that we established some sort of record by being the first party to ever run this section, long known as the "graveyard of the Colorado," with paddles. Jon has already regaled you with a first-hand account of our adventures so I will only add that much of the credit for the success of the trip belongs to him. Not many of the hand-full of really top-notch rivermen in the country excels Jon at white-water boating. He is a "natural" boatman. I introduced him to the "rogue" rivers of the Southwest and coached him at running rapids but he has "surpassed the Master." [98]

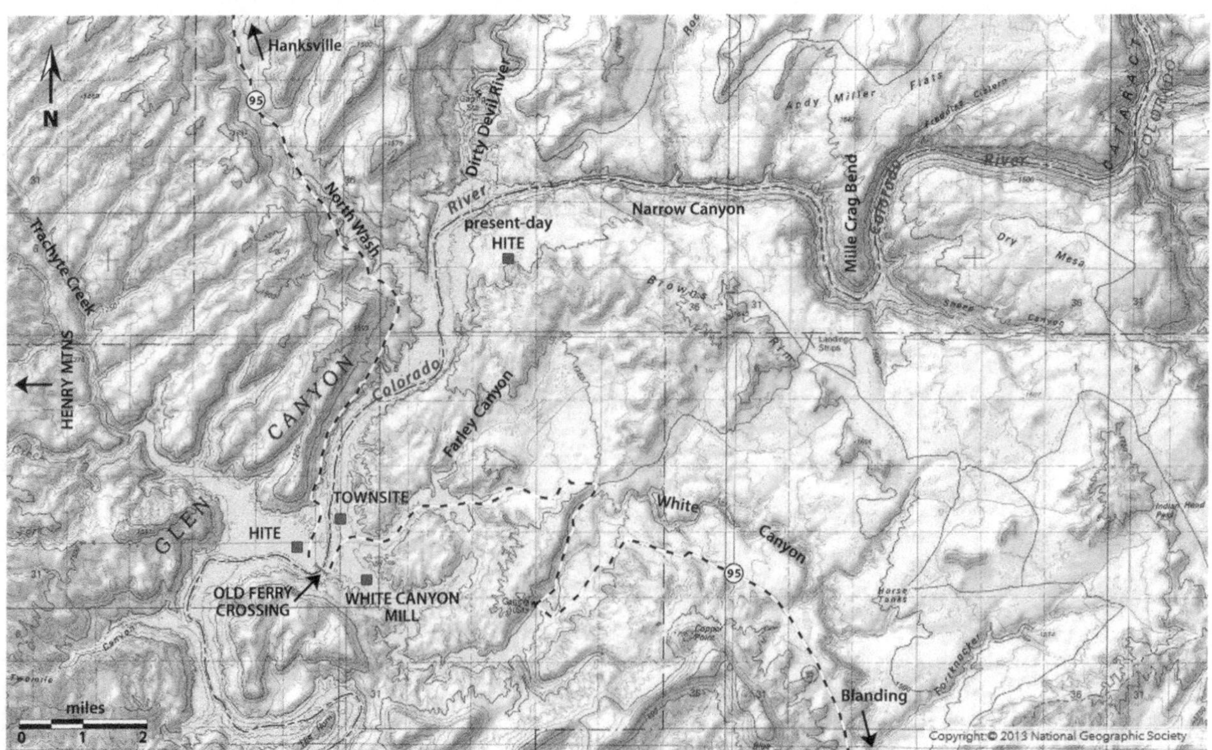

Figure 6.38 White Canyon Townsite and uranium mill located on the south side of the Colorado River at the mouth of White Canyon where the Hite Ferry crossed the river and the narrow road followed "The Big Ledge" up North Wash and northward to Hanksville. (Modified from Esri Arc/GIS USGS topographic base map)

Figure 6.39 Hite Ferry at *Dandy Crossing* circa late 1940s; no crowd was present when Kenny, Jon and Bill landed; just the fellows with rifles "target practicing!" Folks in this photo are waiting on west side of Colorado River. The Hite Bridge wasn't completed until 1966 and the Hite landing was forced to move several miles upstream of this location as Powell reservoir water drowned out the old Hite crossing. (Courtesy: Utah Historical Society photo)

DANDY CROSSING

"The Dandy Crossing of the Colorado" was named by Cass Hite when he staked his gold mining claims in 1883. By the time Kenny, Bill and Jon arrived there the ferry itself was a wooden-decked raft with wooden planking on either end that could be raised or lowered to allow vehicles to drive on and off the decking that set on four inflatable bridge pontoons. It was guided by a steel cable that spanned the 500-foot-wide river crossing. A gasoline motor from the Model 'A' Ford truck provided the power (positioned on left side of ferry; see Figure 6.39). The skipper (1946 –1964) was a weather-beaten fellow named Woody Edgell, and the ferry was operated by the Utah State Department of Highways.[99]

Cass Hite was one of the more colorful characters who roamed the Four Corners region seeking his fortune in the late 19th and early 20th centuries. After prospecting for gold on the San Juan River in 1879 he pursued the lost silver mine of Mitchell and Merrick in Monument Valley and fortunately befriended Chief Hoskininni and spent a few years with the Navajo where he gained the name *Hosteen Pish-la-ki*. *Hosteen* means Mister and *Pish-la-ki* means white metal or silver in Navajo language and he loved that name. Whether Hite grew tired of the Navajo or vice versa, he was shown a good place to cross the Colorado River and where he might find gold. He named the crossing *the Dandy Crossing*. There were sandbars in the river at the crossing that made it a bit easier whether a person was on horseback or driving a horse-drawn wagon crossing the river. He staked a number of mining claims in the vicinity of the crossing and set up his headquarters near the mouth of Trachyte Creek. "Cass started a little store and got a post office and that is when the town of Hite came to be." [100]

It was considered a friendly river crossing. Anyone with a wagon wanting to cross the river in this region of canyon country had to cross at Dandy Crossing. There were river crossings at Lees ferry and another at Moab, over a hundred river miles away in either direction. The railroad bridge was built at Green River in 1883. Dandy Crossing gave Cass the ability to keep tabs on the other people in the country, why they were passing through and whether they had "struck it rich." Cass Hite explored the Colorado River and White Canyon area living the hermit's life to his dying day in 1914 at Tickaboo, Utah at the age of 69.[101]

In 1932 another gold prospector, Arthur (Arth) Chaffin bought all of Hite's holdings and scratched out a living at Cass's old farm. Following World War II the uranium frenzy exploded across the region that brought federal, state and local governmental agencies together to finance improving the road down North Wash and White Canyon to the ferry crossing (Figure 6.38).

The Hite Ferry or "Chaffin Ferry" as some folks called it was put in service September 17, 1946[102] with much fanfare with a crowd of folks from Blanding and Hanksville present as well as the Governor of Utah.[103] By 1949, the White Canyon mill and Townsite was built at the mouth of White Canyon, complete with a post office, store and school, but was short-lived. In 1954 the mill was shut down and dismantled. The impounded waters from Powell reservoir began to drown Glen Canyon in 1963, and the ferry at Dandy Crossing made its last run on June 5, 1964.[104] Arth Chaffin tried to be compensated by the Federal Government for his holdings at Hite, but ultimately he had to settle for far less than what he thought his properties were worth.

∞ ∞ ∞

Kenny Ross's first run through Cataract Canyon in late summer of 1949 would be followed by many more trips, but like so many things in life, the first time was impossible to duplicate! And the team of Kenny, Bill and Jon would never boat together again. Bill began college in 1950, but returned to boat with Kenny a few more times. The following year Jon joined Bill at Stanford University where their friendship continued to blossom. Both Bill and Jon continued to communicate with Kenny via letter writing for a few more years, but the young men were no longer the boys from the Explorers Camp (Figures 6.40 & 6.41).

Although Ansel Hall received most of the accolades for founding the Explorers Camp for Boys, it was Kenny Ross that made it work and flourish. It was Kenny's idea to lead the first Dark Canyon hike in 1946; the first hike into Beef Basin and down Gypsum Canyon to the Colorado River in 1948; expand camp activities to include hikes into Indian Creek-Salt Creek canyons in 1949 and 1951; secured a site for archaeological digs on private land at Cahone and named it "Cibola City" in 1946; encouraged the purchase of the amphibious "Gila Monster" DUWK truck in 1948; encouraged the purchase of durable and inexpensive inflatable LCR boats and added river trips down the San Juan River and Colorado River through Glen Canyon that began in 1947 and started bonus trips for advanced members in Cataract Canyon with the first trip in 1949. The multitude of letters written to the boys and their parents were written by Kenny and Mildred – not Ansel. It was Kenny who arranged all the logistics and determined how groups would rotate. Yes, 1949 was truly Kenny's Breakout year!

Figure 6.40 Jon Lindbergh, 1949. (K. Ross collection)

Figure 6.41 William R. "Big Bill" Dickinson, 1949. (K. Ross collection)

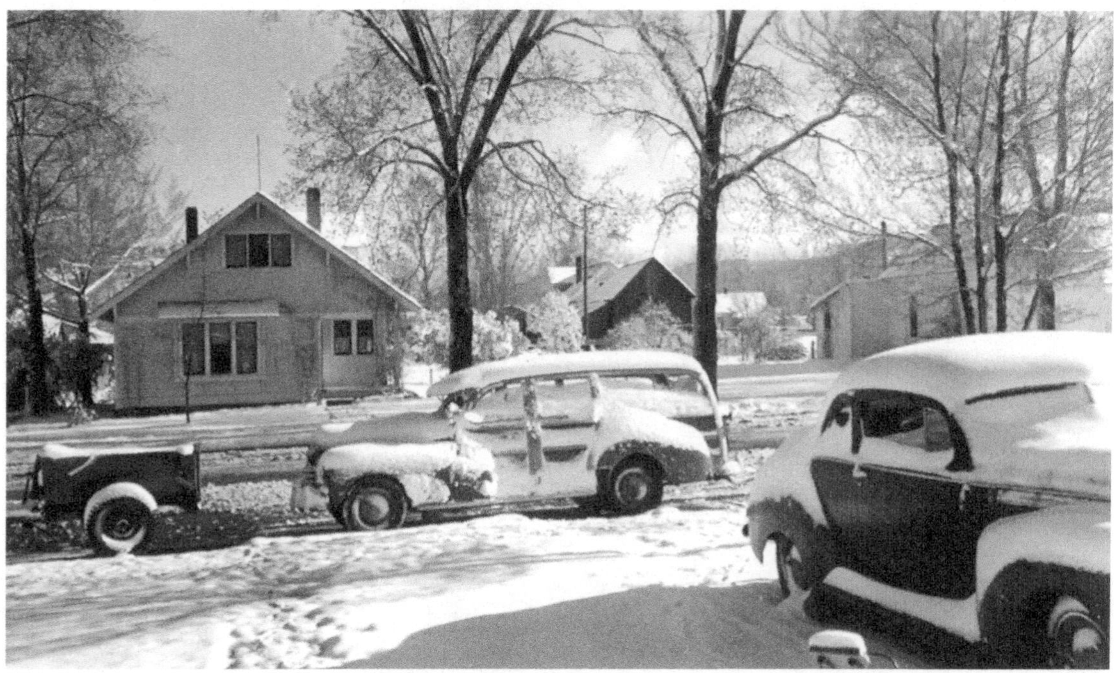

Figure 7.1 snow blankets the 'slightly used' 1948 Chevy "woody" station wagon in front of the Ross family home in Mancos, May 1950. (K. Ross collection)

7

SOUTHWEST EXPLORATIONS: 1950 to 1952

KENNY TAKES CHARGE

By 1950 Kenny had decided to purchase the trucks, the boats and all the equipment from Ansel and began *Southwest Explorations.* From this date forward Kenny began referring to the San Juan River and Glen Canyon of the Colorado River down to Lees Ferry as the *SJ&C trips.* The year began with a lengthy letter from Kenny to Jon where he explained how hectic it had been since their Cataract Canyon river trip and that as of October 15 he had taken over complete charge of Explorers Camp.

> This entailed a tremendous lot of paperwork involving inventories, deeds changing of titles, mortgages, loans and what have you. I had begun to put the pressure on "Chief" as soon as we got back from the Cataract trip and when he finally "gave" things happened so fast and lasted so long that it was after Xmas before I began to get the dazed look out of my eyes and the crick from my neck caused by leaning over so much legal junk. That however was only the beginning of the terrific headache which will be cured only after I am sure of an enrollment big enough to guarantee a gross of $15,660. If it falls much below that I'll be cutting paper dolls in the poorhouse by September.[1]

Kenny mentioned that he was determined to carry on the way he wanted the program to go where no one else could interfere – a strong implication that he was tired of "Chief" Hall's "direction" while he did all the work. He even purchased the little Jeep and the big Dodge troop truck from Ansel and a slightly used 1948 Chevy "Woody" station wagon from a local Chevy Dealership (Figure 7.1).[2] Besides, Ansel was more and more involved with the increased tourism at the park and management of the Mesa Verde Company. Plus, Ansel's track record from the early days as park naturalist to the RBMV expeditions and now Explorers Camp had shown he was first and foremost an organizer, and he had grown weary of the day-to-day grind of actual participation in these type of endeavors after six or seven years. Ansel also saw that Kenny was truly a leader of young men and had that desire and the ability for the thrills and excitement in running rivers and rapids that Ansel just wasn't cut out to do. Kenny also mentioned to Jon a "complete San Juan River trip" for the upcoming year and invited Jon and indirectly, Bill, to come and at least run the river with him. He was hopeful of having thirty boys enroll for camp and mentioned that Jon's younger brother was a possible enrollee. He closed by mentioning that he had received a letter from Randall Henderson (Editor of *Desert Magazine*) who was prodding him [Kenny] to write some sort of camp promotion piece and that the photograph prints of their Cataract Canyon river trip were finally done and each set would cost $52.27.[3]

Following an exchange of letters with Charles Lindbergh regarding his son, Land Lindbergh was given full permission to come out to Explorers Camp with his father's blessings. Kenny had kept the costs at $475 per enrollee as the national economy was experiencing a mild recession and he felt it unwise to raise rates right then.

> Land is fully capable of handling himself in case of weather delays or missed connections in either

direction. There is no need for you to worry about such matters beyond letting us know if he doesn't arrive or you don't hear from him say within twenty-four hours of schedule.

All of our five children diverge from each other greatly in characteristics. You will find this to be true of Land and Jon. Land's relationship and methods of approach are considerably different from those of his brother. Like Jon, Land is capable, dependable, and completely honest. I always have difficulty, however, in realizing that there is an age difference of five years between the two and tend, therefore, to expect of Land much more than I expected of Jon at the same age.

Land is looking forward with great anticipation to his weeks with you this summer. Personally, I feel sure that he will gain as much from the camp as Jon has gained. I know that Jon will miss being with you this year but I am anxious for him to obtain experience abroad and am, therefore, sending him to Europe as soon as he graduates from high school.[4]

FORD TIMES

In early June, just as camp was beginning, Kenny received a letter from Henry Zuidema where he mentioned that he and his wife were planning on attending a "field conference of vertebrate paleontologists" later that month in Santa Fe and that he had arranged transportation for the field trip through *Ford* so the field conference would be written up in the *Ford Times* magazine.

It then occurred to me that this would be a splendid opportunity to do a story in color which I have wanted to do for years--the story of your boys' camp project, and it would appear that if the customary two groups are in the field and could be reached by stock car, I'll try my hand at a color Graphic and do the story. The editor of Ford Times thought it would be a likely one to make the magazine.[5]

Zuidema's letter was also sent to Ansel, the consummate promoter, where he stated:

Kenneth Ross, Field Director for the Explorers Camp, came out of the mountains a few days ago and we were able to get together on plans for your joining the expedition. Both he and I feel that you can get some very spectacular pictures and at least one intriguing human interest adventure story. Kenneth urges me to ask you to adapt your plans so as to meet with him and his field party (15 young men of high school age plus cook, etc.) at Bluff, Utah, on July 5, or July 20. On those dates the Explorers Camp "fleet" of eight 7-man pneumatic assault craft will shove off for the 230-mile, 13-day voyage through the canyons of the San Juan and Glen Canyon of the Colorado. They will shove off from Bluff, Utah, and will be met by trucks 13 days later at Lee's Ferry at the head of the Grand Canyon.

The voyage could be made in half the time but the party will camp in various camps to explore side canyons, including Bridge Canyon and Forbidding Canyon, and the Rainbow-Bridge country. If you cannot spare the time to make the entire trip, you must at least join the party for the first day's voyage from Bluff, Utah, to Mexican Hat. From the latter point it is impossible to leave the river until the party completes the voyage at Lee's Ferry.

I hope that you will be able to adjust your plans so as to join Ross and his young explorers in this very spectacular adventure, which should be especially appealing to anyone with your geological background and ability to dramatically interpret the stories so vividly told in those brilliant canyon walls.[6]

THE NEVILLS MEMORIAL LANDING STRIP

George Hall, Jr. (no relation to Ansel Hall) became somewhat of a fixture with the Explorers Camp, having returned each year from 1949 through 1953. He was from Los Angeles and the camp had been recommended by a family friend – Stuart Maule who had gotten to know Kenny quite well. In 1950, George Jr.'s father was a 'hot shot' interior decorator in LA, was a child movie star, licensed attorney, and now owned and flew a *Beechcraft Bonanza* aircraft and had been written about as having run rapids on the Colorado River. In May, 1950 Papa George wrote Kenny asking to join the San Juan River trip from Mexican Hat to Lees Ferry and wanted to fly in to Mexican Hat. Kenny replied that low water dictated launching from Bluff:

> Your best bet, then, would be to fly directly to Bluff, about twenty (air) miles north of Mex Hat. We will be there the evening of July fifth and launch the boats early next morning. The trip to Lee's Ferry will take 9 or 10 days so you had better figure 12 days from plane to plane.[7]

Papa George quickly replied, asking for more details about the "airport" and accommodations:

> If this would meet with your approval, I would like to know if the airport there is usable and if it would be safe to leave the plane there unattended. I will be flying a nose wheel ship (probably a Bonanza), and the nose wheel limits its rough-field operation. Also is there any place to stay there if I arrive before the expedition? [8]

Figure 7.2 aerial photo clearly shows the "Nevills landing strip" located west of Cottonwood Wash; Bluff City on east side (cultivated farm land on right side and open road west on left side of the wash); note lack of bridge across the wash. (USGS aerial photo, May 20, 1947)

Kenny followed up the questions:

> The landing field at Bluff is a one-way strip into the prevailing wind which is from the S.W. There is no sock but everybody in the town cooks on wood or coal ranges so you should find smoke. The strip was smooth as any dirt runway when I was there a couple of weeks ago. It crosses the dirt roadway about half a mile from town so you can hoof it in if no one comes out after you – as they usually do. I suggest tying down immediately as small but powerful whirlwinds are common there all summer. There is only one place you can stay there and it is at the far end of the town from the strip. I understand the food and beds are good. The river trip will cost you $120.[9]

Gaylord Staveley (2015, p. 127) mentioned that when Norm Nevills negotiated with the county about improving the landing strip in Mexican Hat in 1945, he talked the county road grader operator to blade a flat sandy strip on the west side of Bluff. The grader operator obliged Norm and flattened out a strip so Norm could fly over to Bluff to pick up the mail and fresh milk and bread at the Bluff Store. The Adam's Hotel may have been the place Kenny referred Papa George for overnight accommodations and "good food."[10] The landing strip remained quite visible on USGS aerial photos taken in 1947 over Bluff that today would include part of the rodeo parking area and extended south across the highway onto land east of Faye Belles garage/junkyard (Figure 7.2).

Apparently George Hall, Sr. arrived early for the July, 1950 river trip and took Mildred up for an air tour over to Valley of the Gods and along the river while they were waiting for Kenny and the group to arrive from Gold King camp and that Mildred loved every minute of it! [11]

WITHOUT A HITCH

The two full length river trips from Bluff to Lees Ferry[12] were carried out without a hitch; even though in low water (Figure 7.3). Bill Dickinson confirmed that he did, in fact, join Kenny in 1950 on one of those back-to-back river trips from Bluff to Lees Ferry (Figures 7.4 and 7.5).[13] He mentioned that it was a relatively low water run and recalled having to push boats past Paiute Farms before entering the lower canyon below Copper Canyon. River gaged discharge records for that date indicated that flows in early July were around 2000 cfs but by the end of the month had dropped to 500 cfs (Figures 7.6 through 7.10).[14] The low water run was confirmed in a letter from Kenny to Jon in December where he wrote, "I suppose Bill has told you all about last summer's trip which was made at low water but was still lots of fun and plenty exciting." [15]

Bill also recalled having to portage gear and line boats down Thirteen-Foot Rapid. Bill said that seeing Rainbow Bridge for the first time was truly unforgettable and the hike up Forbidding Canyon was an easy and beautiful walk from the river and concurred that the round trip was no more than nine miles and not the twelve miles stated by other writers.[16] I asked Bill about the two spellings of *Forbidding* vs *Forbidden* and which one he thought was correct. Without hesitation he said that the proper noun was Forbidding Canyon and that western slang of dropping the "g's" had led to Forbidden, which, if spelled properly, should be with an "i" as *Forbiddin'*. Thus, the commonly seen spelling of this canyon in the two popular modes should be reduced to the proper noun: Forbidding Canyon.[17]

The rest of Explorers Camp in 1950 went much like those in the past years with the boys divided into working groups that rotated from Gold King base camp to the river trips to archaeological digs at Cahone and then two major hikes. One hike was their initial reconnaissance trip into Salt Creek Canyon in search of geologic arches, bridges and possibly archaeological sites and the other hike was the familiar hike for Kenny down Woodenshoe Canyon and Dark Canyon (Figures 7.11 to 7.13). Ansel hired Alfred

Guthe, an archaeologist from Harvard to write-up a formal report about the "Cibola City" site and a substantial amount of the artifacts were shipped to the Peabody Museum (Figure 7.14). The lengthy driving tours to Canyon de Chelly, Lukachukai and Navajoland in general had been scrapped – at least for the time being.

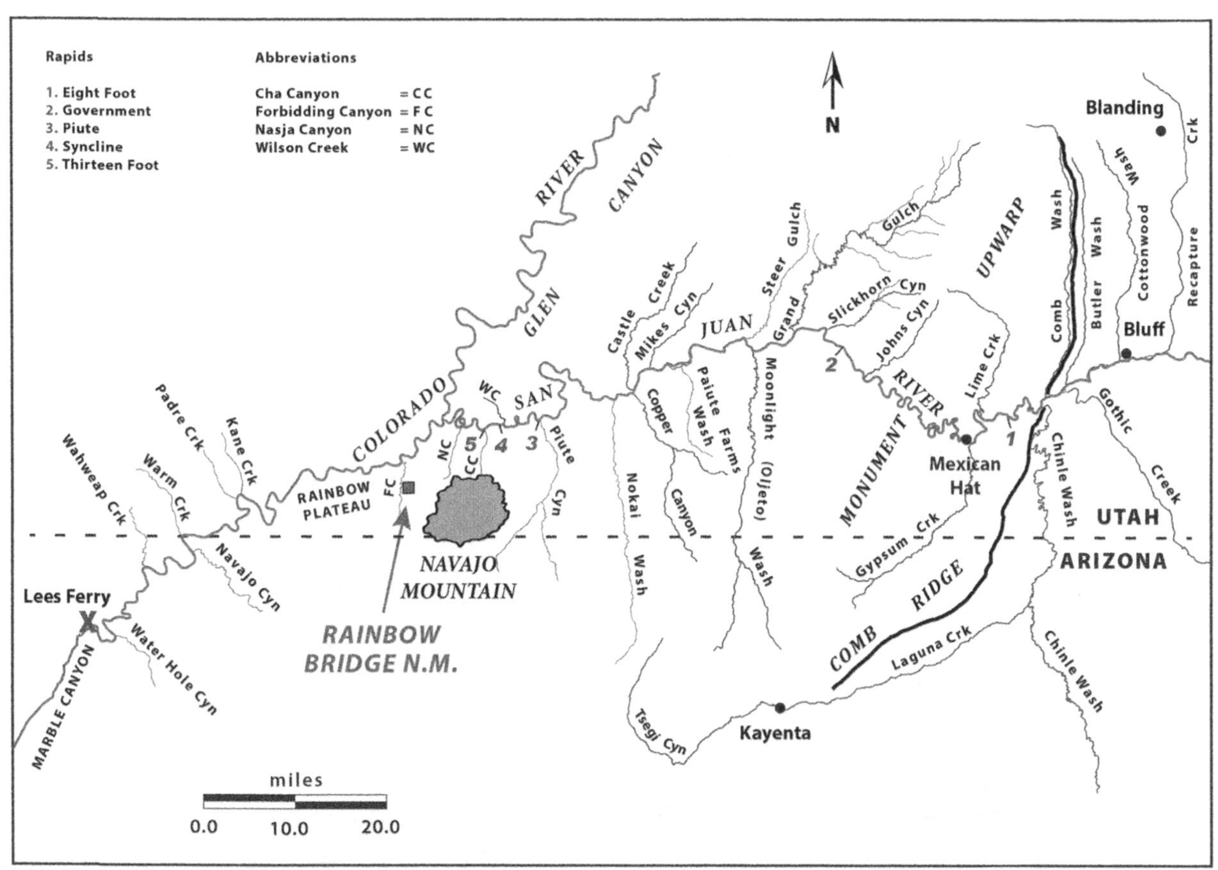

Figure 7.3 Map of San Juan River from Bluff to confluence with Colorado River and southern part of Glen Canyon to Lees Ferry including major tributaries and major rapids; this 225 mile long stretch of rivers became known as the "SJ&C" river trips. River miles measured upstream from Lees Ferry and/or major confluences; see Figure 5.2 & Table 1, Appendix I. (GMS/TB original map)

Figure 7.4 four boys carry one of the boats to shoreline where Kenny is standing; this launch point is 1.5 miles upstream of Bluff across from St. Christopher's Mission (225.2 miles above Lees Ferry). (K. Ross collection)

Figure 7.5 present-day relocation photo; compare sand dune and canyon opposite launch point in previous photo; it is now overgrown with invasive riparian growth; the river distance from this point to Lees Ferry was 225.2 miles; see Table 1, Appendix I. (J. Willian photo)

Figure 7.6 paddle run through Eight Foot Rapid; RM 123.9 above SJ&C confluence, 1950. (K. Ross collection)

Figure 7.7 boys paddling boats near RM 85 in lower San Juan River canyon. (K. Ross collection)

Figure 7.8 view downstream from Ross Canyon RM 88.4 above SJ&C confluence. (K. Ross collection)

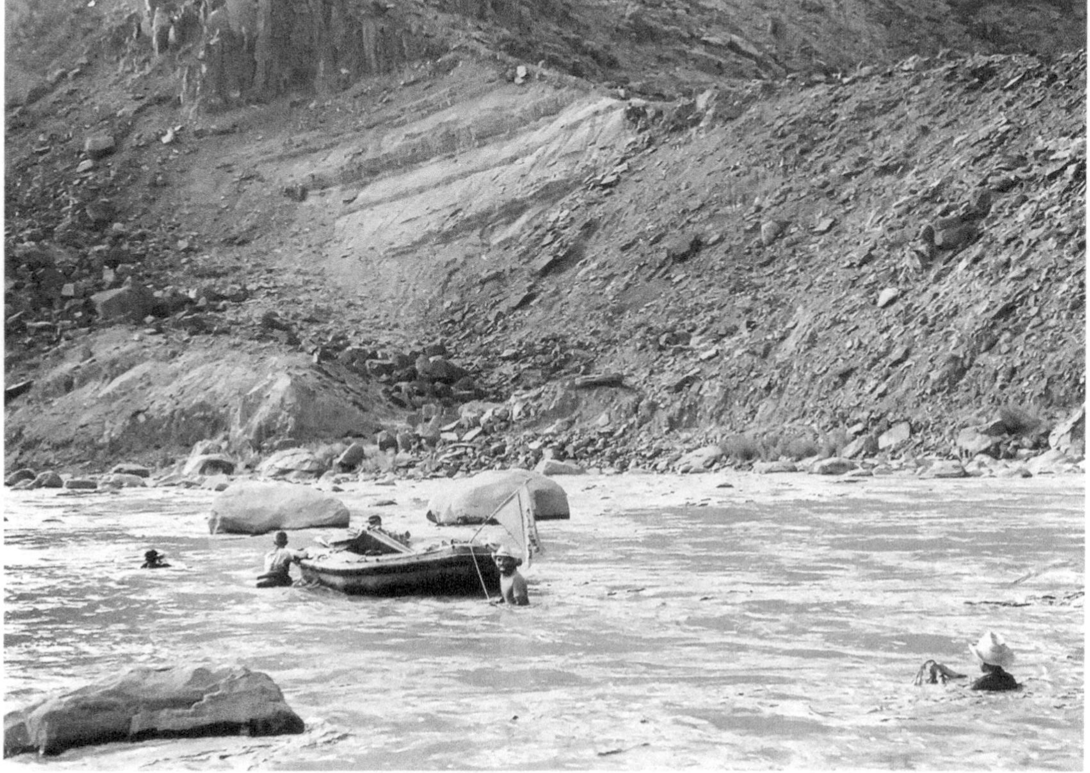

Figure 7.9 lining boats down Thirteen Foot Rapid, RM 11.5 above SJ&C confluence, 1950. (K. Ross collection)

Figure 7.10 boats in Glen Canyon, 1950; the sunlit mid-canyon cliffs eerily forebode the forthcoming drowning by Powell reservoir water. (K. Ross collection)

Figure 7.11 Kissing Rock at the head of Poison Canyon, Dark Canyon hike, 1950. (K. Ross collection)

Figure 7.12 a narrow passage deep into Dark Canyon, 1950. (K. Ross collection)

Figure 7.13 the castles of Dark Canyon, 1950. (K. Ross collection)

Figure 7.14 sorting and labeling samples collected at Cahone ruin site for shipment to the Peabody Museum. (K. Ross collection)

A RAT AND SIXTY MILLION YEARS

As the 1950 Explorers Camp came to an end, Henry Zuidema again explored ways to advertise and promote the boys camp and asked Kenny about the "publicity issue" concerning the Lindbergh boys. Throughout Jon's three years involvement at the camp, he had escaped publicity at Col. Charles A. Lindbergh's request, but Zuidema then wanted to promote Land Lindbergh's involvement. Kenny just couldn't violate the trust that Col. Lindbergh and his wife had in him, and he told Hank to not publicize the Lindbergh connection to the boys' camp.

By the first of the year, 1951, as Kenny returned to the task of replying to the stack of mail accumulated over the fall he was certainly concerned about the well-being of Jon and Bill as the "police action" in Korea had turned into a full-fledged war, even though it was never officially called a "war." [18]

> With all the mess the World has now gotten itself into and the changes in so many lives that have resulted I've been wondering if there has been any effect upon you and Bill Dick. I know that there will be, of course, but am hoping both of you will be able to remain at school for quite a while yet.[19]

The celebrity of Jon Lindbergh never ceased and forced Jon into a peculiar lifestyle while attending Stanford University – he lived off campus in a *tent!* Bill Dickinson in June, 2015 added some insights:

> Jon and I saw a lot of each other up until 1952 when I was off to the USAF and him shortly thereafter into his frogman act [Navy] (followed by marine biology etc). [I] never met either his mother or his father. Although many played off his fame or notoriety or whatever insane sentiment people conveyed upon him as the brother of the brother who was killed, he never really did himself. He just

had an immensely difficult time so much as taking a pee incognito, and he loathed all the unwanted attention he got. I don't think either Land or Scott (whom I knew but not as well) ever drew such inane attention (maybe one was enough, and Jon was the one brother into various brands of derring-do that caught people's attention). Do not know for sure how Jon would react to being contacted by you (or anyone else) about his early life, but my hunch is that he would just say to himself I don't need this, there is nothing in it for me, and I am not going there.

You cannot imagine how crazy people can get about Jon. The only hope he has ever had for privacy is to never mention his father and never let anyone know what he has done or is doing. Living his life is like having a chattering monkey on your shoulder 24/7. When he was in my eating club at Stanford and people would come snooping around about him, we would just say "Charles Lindbergh? Whatever gave you that silly idea?"

Eating clubs at Stanford are somewhat like fraternities but have no living quarters (only dining rooms in a complex housing seven clubs). And (the key attraction for me) they have never had, at any time in their history, any racial membership rules. Of course, most if not all fraternities now have no such rules (and both fraternities and eating clubs may well have women members by now), but in my day it was impossible to be a Jewish fraternity member (not that I am Jewish myself, but have always refused to have any truck with racial or ethnic exclusions of any kind). He had at one time the press value of a Kardashian, and every other yo-yo on the planet seemed to want to cash in on some stupid scoop of some kind. They all got the back of my hand just as soon as I smelled a rat. When Jon set up shop in his tent, it was on a ranch in the foothills just a short drive from Stanford, and he took his meals with all the rest of us at El Toro (the name of our eating club). Not nearly as exotic an existence as one might think (I later had my house and home a little ways farther up the self-same rural road). All this reminds me of a quote I heard somewhere – "A rat and sixty million years produces scientists who study rats." [20]

HENRY ZUIDEMA

Dr. Zuidema had been duly impressed by his San Juan River trip in July. He had finally found time to jump on one of the river trips, and made the full run from Bluff to Lees Ferry. He mentioned that many of his notes got soaked in Gypsum Rapid when he was still using "washable" ink.[21] He wanted to help Kenny promote the adventure and reminded Kenny that it was he, with his Detroit connections, who contacted *Ford Motor Company* who had sponsored the RBMV expeditions in 1933-38 and had made a short black and white documentary movie entitled "Adventure Bound" as their vehicles were driven across the scenic Four Corners country. Zuidema had again contacted Ford and he had suggested to recreate the movie, but this time in color and to include the San Juan River. However, a Ford representative had replied that while interested in the color movie, they would have to postpone any involvement "because of shortages, price troubles and [Korean] war troubles" [22] but brought up the idea of contacting *rubber companies* for color movies as river action sport films were a hot topic.[23] Kenny's reply showed he was a bit distraught in that "Trying to go ahead with planning a program and leadership for it in the face of present world conditions has me a little discouraged at times. One can't have the slightest notion whether those who promise to help can even be here next June." [24]

Kenny didn't address Zuidema's idea of contacting a "rubber company" to promote his business but rather mentioned that for the 1951 program he was going to introduce a special program for boys 10-13 years of age that did *not* include river trips as he thought they needed to be older to risk being on the river. But he definitely wanted to emphasize *explorations* and *adventures*. Plus, Kenny wanted to announce river adventures for adults! This was the first time he began thinking about expanding beyond "boys camp only" excursions. He also wanted to know what Zuidema thought about promoting the

"Duck" (the amphibious DUKW assault craft) being used on expeditions to *Popular Science* or *Popular Mechanics* or other science and mechanics magazines? He wondered if Hank would want pictures of the boys examining a new structure of some kind (an ancient watch tower?) they found that year "in the deepest depths of Dark Canyon's previously unexplored gorge" and could it be used for a "short?" [25]

> Would a story implying that Explorers Camp (would like to use term Southwest Explorations more often) is trying to explore as much as possible of the remote canyons tributary to the San Juan and Colorado rivers before the great dams of the "Colorado River Project" changes the face of the country be any good? Would a story announcing plans for a survey of the fossils of the Moenkopi, led by H.P. Zuidema, be saleable anywhere? Could you use a picture story on our excavation of one of the largest ancient ruins in Colo.? One might play up the rather novel angle that each year's work is being done by a different archaeologist for the purpose of testing the validity of present archaec methods. Etc., etc.[26]

Kenny was clearly fishing for anything to get some publicity and some business. He was also quite aware of what lay ahead with potential damming of river-ways he was trying to promote and explore.[27] He mentioned to Hank that *National Geographic* was just too slow and too difficult to get published. He said they had taken over three years to publish a Nevills trip and a Mesa Verde story was held up from 1941 to 1948. He thought that maybe some friends could get their friends to go on a river trip and "even 4 or 5 hundred bucks will help keep camp going." [28]

Henry Zuidema picked up on Kenny's distress call and sent him a copy of his "tickler" letter he sent to the Vice President in Charge of Promotion at the *Goodyear Tire & Rubber Company* in Akron, Ohio:

> Dear Sir:
>
> As a member of the geology staff of the University of Michigan last summer, I was asked to accompany an exploration party down the canyons of the San Juan and Colorado Rivers, from Bluff, Utah, to Lees Ferry, Arizona.
>
> This 200-mile journey, which included the running of several rapids in the rocky gorges of the two rivers, was made in Goodyear pneumatic rubber boats from war surplus. This was the first trip of its kind. The boats were jammed against rocks, thrown against the canyon walls, dragged over rocky shallows, and subjected to all sorts of abuse in the passage of the rapids, but all five boats came through without damage to the material or injury to the occupants. The trip will be repeated next summer.
>
> The other day I happened to read "The House of Goodyear" in the university library and it occurred to me that the river trip would be of interest to your promotion department or to the agency in charge of your advertising program.
>
> Accompanying the party, which was particularly interested in the reports of uranium deposits in that part of the country, were 15 boys, among them Land Lindbergh, who is 13 years old and the second son of Col. Charles A. Lindbergh, These boys were taken along to introduce them to the methods of scientific exploration and to assist them in choosing life careers.
>
> I am taking the liberty of sending you a set of Leica blowups showing the boats in action, so that you may determine whether they would be of any use to you, and whether you would desire a written account of this unusual use of a Goodyear product.
>
> Several years ago I assisted in the making of a black and white motion picture, "Adventure Bound," for the Ford Motor Company of exploration by truck of this same region. The film met with immediate favor in the schools and universities, has been viewed by several millions of young Americans, and is still popular.
>
> As chairman of a sub-committee of the American Geological Institute, an affiliate of the National Research Council, I have made a survey of audio-visual aids in earth science teaching and there is a need for more good color films dealing with natural resources, etc.

> I believe there would be good institutional promotion in a color film showing the Goodyear boats in action amid the magnificent scenery of the Southwest, and that the film would hold great interest in demonstrating the uses of rubber in war and peacetime. The film would be listed in the various audio-visual lists sent to universities and state departments of education.
>
> If you desire it, a showing of color slides on the boats in action, and of three dimensional color transparencies can be arranged for Goodyear representatives, in Detroit or Akron, as you may see fit.[29]

Kenny received the Goodyear letter but replied to Hank with an urgent observation as the war in Korea intensified:

> This is a history making date for our country. The declaration of a national emergency when, in theory, we are not at war establishes a new and important precedent. It should have been done weeks ago. God only knows what it will do to shatter the plans of Explorers Camp But I guess we can take whatever comes---somehow.[30]

On January 17, 1951 Kenny received a letter from Hank Zuidema that informed him that Goodyear would publish Hank's write-up entitled "Down the River in Rafts" in *The Goodyear News* magazine and it would include two photos of the boats, 1600 words and he would be paid $50 for the story, "which just goes to show how hard times are." [31] Sure enough, in the February-March, 1951 issue of *The Goodyear News*, on page 15 Hank's article appeared under the Heading "Prove Serviceable: Goodyear Rubber Rafts Used On Perilous Canyon Journey." [32] Hank's dramatic writing style exaggerated several things – like forty boys instead of fifteen and, of course, he just had to name-drop and mentioned Land Lindbergh "son of Col. Charles Augustus Lindbergh and Ann Morrow Lindbergh." [33] He mentioned Kenny Ross as Director and leader of the Explorers Camp and his *choice* of using "Goodyear surplus military inflatable craft....because of the safety factor." [34] He wrote that the boats handled the waves and bounced off sharp rocks and "will withstand many seasons of rugged use on the rivers." He generally outlined the course of the trip, but not in sequence. For example he included entering "Forbidden Canyon" and following a trail for four miles to reach Rainbow Bridge before "discovering hidden ruins of cave dwellings" of the first inhabitants of the desert Utah-Arizona country. The two photos included a picture of the five LCR-S seven-man crafts leaving the landing above the bridge at Mexican Hat (Figure 7.15) and the other was a broadside view of one of the boats floating peacefully in the sandstone canyons with the caption, "Goodyear rubber assault boat on peace-time mission." [35]

By April Kenny had only four adults signed up for his May 6 river trip and two enquiries as a result of the Goodyear article. Camp enrollment had picked up. Doc Marquard's *Round-Up Lodge Camp* in Buena Vista had sold and had one hundred-forty boys enrolled but the new owners wouldn't accept boys under age seventeen, so Kenny thought he might get some of those boys. Kenny was also counting on Hank to ram-rod a geology project that summer (Hank had mentioned digging up the hills down by Lukachukai – fossil hunting). Kenny mentioned to Hank that Ansel and June were now "Grandparents; twice in two days; Merrie had a girl & Sylvia a boy. Nothing in the Hall family is ever done by ones." [36]

Hank Zuidema sent a copy of the Goodyear article to their mutual friend, Fred Black at Kelvinator, and a copy of the full magazine to Kenny "so he could identify the article based on the magazine's cover." [37] Hank once again bailed on coming out to do geology work and he suggested Dr. Camp at Berkeley for tips about fossils in the Chuska section. He thought the slow enrollment of boys was probably driven by the "country's instability" (i.e., Korea).[38] In a follow-up letter Hank mentioned two medical doctors from the Detroit area and that one had a twelve-year old boy who "has shown that he can take it in the field" [39] who showed interest in the Explorers Camp program and both adults were quite interested in the river trip(s) and the Cahone archaeological dig, but not the whole camp season. He suggested Kenny send him the river trip dates and costs.[40] Kenny quickly replied that it would be fine for the twelve-year old and the two doctors to join the camp, albeit for an abbreviated camp season and he would reduce the boy's fee to $270 to include the thirty-six days from June 27 to August 1. Kenny figured he would have to charge each doctor $150 for the river trip and they would need to be in Durango June 26 as they would "pull out for Bluff very early the next morning." [41]

Charles 'Dusty" Dustin, a member of the 1949, '50 and '51 Explorers Camp was a local boy from Farmington, NM that became another one of Kenny's flock. His mother had initially contacted Dick Springer of the *Mancos Times Tribune* in 1949 asking about the camp as she was concerned about drinking and smoking. She confided in Kenny that her husband and son-in-law were both alcoholics and that her husband had just recently died. Dusty had grown up in a tough family environment but Kenny helped straighten him out. In 1950 he shuttled cars to Lees Ferry for Kent Frost and a Farmington high school group and in January, 1951 he wrote Kenny asking about pontoon boats to buy. Kenny advised against it as they were too big! *He also mentioned that 7- and 10-man boats were all but gone from surplus stores!* [42] But by 1952 Dusty had his own *second-hand* boat and took Alan Carlsen, an Explorer from the 1950 camp, with him on a private San Juan trip. The military surplus stores had apparently sold all the reusable LCRs.

THE GOODYEAR NEWS, *February-March, 1951* 15

Prove Serviceable

Goodyear Rubber Rafts Used On Perilous Canyon Journey

Travelers familiar with the use of **Goodyear assault boats** by the **Marines at Tarawa and the** dramatic record of **Goodyear rubber** rafts by the **Navy and Air Force in World War II might have glanced** down into the **depths of the canyons of the** Colorado **River last summer and been** surprised to **see the same types of** boats **plunging among the rapids and** rocks (see **photos) deep in the great** chasm.

This expedition was **not a military operation,** however, but **a peacetime use** of rubber **craft by 40 boy explorers** who safely **completed a journey of 200 miles from** Bluff, **Utah, on the San Juan** River, to Lees **Ferry, on the Colorado,** in Arizona.

The trip was **made in 10 days, with** time out **to explore the surrounding** desert country, **the land of the Navajos** and the Hopis, **and to see one of the great scenic features of the Southwest — Rainbow Natural Bridge.**

. . . *Rubber rafts "take off" after overnight stop* . . .

Figure 7.15 newspaper article published by Hank Zuidema promoting Goodyear Rubber boats in THE GOODYEAR NEWS, *February-March*, 1951, p. 15. (K. Ross collection; cover to full article)

CAN'T MAKE IT

Jon Lindbergh wrote to Kenny in April that neither he nor Bill Dickinson would be able to make the San Juan River trip that spring and it "would be much nicer to study rapids on the river than calculus and history in a classroom."[43] He said he went home for Easter and on the return flight flew over the Colorado River from Grand Junction to Lake Mead, noting towns, Cataract Canyon, Dark Canyon, Mille Crag, the San Juan River and "they sure look different from 18,000 feet." [44] He noted some really "vicious country" just east of the junction [confluence of Colorado and Green rivers and probably referencing the Grabens and Needles] and drew a diagram of rectilinear orthogonal fractures. He also noted that one minute of flight equaled one river day and "you sure don't get a feel for the country up here in an airplane." [45] He mentioned he was going to Alaska or South America later that year.[46] Kenny replied that he and Land Lindbergh and some other boys had scaled Babcock, Madden and Spillers peaks the previous year and he had been taking the Mancos high school seniors out climbing local cliffs on weekends.[47] Kenny heard from Bill in late May that Jon was about to leave for Alaska on a 'mountaineering' trip with a party to do some first ascents on some unexplored mountains. In preparation and in typical Jon style "Jon is already the top mountain climber here at school. He scaled a once-climbed pinnacle in Yosemite the way the other guy had done it and then proceeded to climb it three other ways of his own!" [48]

Kenny wrote to Colonel and Mrs. Lindbergh in May about how glad he was that Land was returning for the 1951 season:

> His is a most gregarious, happy- go-lucky and pleasant personality which adds much to the general morale of any group of which he is a member. Land's personality is so different from Jon's that, despite being forewarned by you, I was almost caught off balance by it last year. Both are wonderful youngsters. Jon's appeal to me is his calculated self-sufficiency, reserve; his efficient handling of individual and group situations and his shy seeking for one or two intimates to whom he can pour out his delightfully zany humor. Land is all warmth and color and good-will that make a host of friends without his consciously seeking them." [49]

Regarding Land's return for the 1951 camp, Col. Lindbergh wrote how much he appreciated Kenny's efforts: "The boys [Land & Jon] accounts of their river trips often make me envious. The balance you achieve, in your camp, between organization and freedom, develops initiative and independence in an important and extraordinary way." [50]

THE GREAT RACE

Kenny learned of a white water "race" on the Arkansas River where prize money would be paid to the first three "winners" and had written a "quickie" note to both Jon and Bill wanting to know if they were interested.[51] The race was scheduled to take place just before the opening of that years' Explorers Camp and would fit just right with his itinerary for the summer. Bill replied that he was interested, but Jon would not be able to come.[52] Kenny was stoked! After having successfully tackled all the rapids in Cataract and the big ones in the lower San Juan canyon, he felt confident that he and Bill would blow the socks off these Arkansas River boaters by using their dual paddler technique they had mastered in the 7-man LCR. This overconfidence led Kenny to write Bill more details about the "race" on the Arkansas River from Salida to Cotopaxi (25 miles) through the upper part of Royal Gorge that was scheduled for June 17; 1st prize: $500; 2nd prize: $300;and 3rd prize: $150.[53]

> In anticipation of our entering, I have been doing some figuring and work on the "La Cucaracha", of Cataract Canyon Fame (?). Have worked out a method of stopping most of the slosh of water over the stern and developed a bow which,

when used with the boat cover, will act as a splash board to keep most of the water that could dash over the bow or quarter from flowing back into the rear cockpit. Also, have worked out a quick-release safety belt to keep you from sliding out of the boat. Me too. This thing is a dilly and will not interfere with paddling nor leg action---and it can be released with only the tiniest jerk of a cord.

Oh yes, am also experimenting with a gadget which has the purpose of making the boat go faster in a swift current. Don't know whether it will work or not or, if it will, whether it is desirable from the standpoint of control. Will try it out on the Animas and find out. It is simply a piece of 3/4" plywood, 16x26", hinged to the motor-mount that attaches to the stern. When running in swift, deep water it becomes almost entirely immersed and, theoretically, would add speed by presenting a broad surface to the current which, as you know, tends to run a little faster than these rubber skows. In shallow or rocky places, the hinges allow it to turn up to the rear to prevent its catching on anything. Seems like a bright idea which I will test before the race. What does your "engineering mind" think of it? Meybe not.

With the entire boat covered except for foot room and the stern freeboard raised with a large truck innertube, I believe that if we can stay in, we can put it darn near anywhere except over Niagra Falls. And I believe that our ability to refuse portages will be deciding factor toward winning the race.[54]

Many more letters were exchanged that led up to Kenny and Bill registering to enter the race in the 7-man. Kenny described the river course as he had just returned from a trip to Boulder, Colorado to visit his older son Chuck, who was in the Air Force and about to be shipped off on some top secret mission – as part of a special radar unit.

Stopped at Salida and had a visit with the Secretary of the Chamber of Commerce. Learned that our competition is not likely to be too stiff but there are certain other aspects of the race I am not very happy with. In cutting down the mileage of the race they **seem** to be cutting out the roughest part of the river. I followed the course quite carefully Saturday afternoon and have the feeling that fewer boats will be eliminated in the early part of the race than were eliminated by rough water below Cotopaxi last year (only one boat finished). Here is how I figure the course: from Salida to the entrance to the gorge--about four miles--it is comparatively smooth going, with one short portage made absolutely necessary by a low foot bridge which, at higher water, will shut off any chance of passage. Entering the upper end of the gorge the water will be turbulent but not too rough for a mile; then for 3/4 of a mile will be rougher than a cob--unless higher water smoothes it--and will give most boats trouble. below that there are occasional rapids and a **very** narrow river--even at high water--but not bad enough to bother a really river-worthy boat. Then two bad rapids and a long, two or three mile stretch of valley and easy going for quite a long way. For five or six miles above Cotopaxi (the end) it gets rough again but not too bad, although there could be eliminations here.

The actual course is only about 24 miles long. It will be exciting as hell but I am not sure we will have as much advantage due to really tough going as I originally thot. The extremely narrow bed and twisty course which, in the fastest water, will, end to toss poorly manned boats on the outside bank, into the rocks, may help us. The water is now just below a medium stage and the nature of the bed makes it difficult to judge what it will be like at highest water. On the whole I believe that it will probably be considerably rougher than now.

I already have crash helmets. Buddy Starr found em.

I am going to leave the matter of whether we run the race up to you. I feel that we have more than a fighting chance to cop one of the first three places but no special advantages except experience. So far, the rest of the entrants do not impress me as being specially prepared by experience or, for that matter, equipment. It is possible, of course, that someone we know to be good may enter.

In case we run it, Buddy Starr wants to go along as an extra crew member---to help with portages, etc. I think he will be good help.

Hope to try out on the Animas next Sunday but the run-off seems very slow getting started here and it is still too low today. We are beginning to have hot days tho and maybe a few more of them will do the trick.

The San Juan trips are scheduled for June 27th and July 17th. I have my fingers crossed bout water levels. I believe that they will be higher than last year but wouldn't bet on it.

Other than the entry fee, our expenses will be chiefly food and gasoline for travel. Don't know what the total might be but it will be modest.

In case you would want to stay and take one of the river trips with the gang--I can see no reason why you should not. It will be fun to have you.[55]

Bill wrote back stating that he needed a registration form – pronto – as he had to have his mother sign off as guardian so he could enter the race. And he added that the whole issue of the latest *Arizona Highways* was devoted to southwest ruins, and Bill had seen one of Larabee and Aleson ads in *Desert Magazine* where they were running a trip through Cataract in August for $850 per person! The trip was planned to take twenty days from Green River to Hite.[56] Bill confidently wrote that they should "cut Buddy in" [57] on the winnings and that he had planned on arriving in Mancos in time to help rig the boat for the race. There was absolutely no mention of the outcome of the race in Kenny's files, but Bill Dickinson added the final comment when he reviewed all these letters in June, 2015:

Our Salida foray was a total bust; we stuffed bedrolls or the like longitudinally under the seats in an effort to devise a horseback keel to reduce drag on the bottom of the boat; whether we reduced drag or not is moot but we for sure reduced stability; Kenny and I wound up balancing precariously in the stern like a guy in a log-rolling contest; we never stood a chance against even a semi-skilled kayaker and the guy who won the race was pretty good; we wound up playing the role of a donkey in the Kentucky Derby and if we won any prize money for finishing the race it was trivial.[58] [Emphasis mine]

THE 1951 SOUTHWEST EXPLORATION CAMP

Kenny Ross had endured through the Great Depression by working at Mesa Verde National Park as a seasonal employee, and then came the sacrifices brought on by World War II followed by a sluggish Recession and then the Korean military conflict – but he managed to persevere and build the Explorers Camp for Boys into a functioning educational adventure program that had finally gained some national attention. But in the early 1950s, a different form of "war" was on the minds of parents across the country – it was the onslaught of POLIO! Although major polio epidemics were known to have occurred in the past, the increase in this disease in the United States in the 1940s and 1950s reawakened the fears of parents. The polio epidemic of 1951-1952 was notable because serious outbreaks occurred in all of the forty-eight states, and in the territories of Alaska, Hawaii, and Puerto Rico.[59]

People didn't know how polio was spread, but they did know that most diseases were spread from person to person. When polio came to town, isolation was the name of the game. Events were cancelled; children were confined to their homes. During the hottest days of summer, pools were closed. Schools and camps were shut down and this image loomed large for the Ross family and their two little boys. Movie theatres were closed on order of the health authorities. Drinking fountains were abandoned. Draft inductions were suspended. Isolation that had worked for influenza and plague and a host of other diseases, did not respond to polio. Polio had always seemed cruel in the way that it targeted children. Now it seemed hostile. For every action of the *March of Dimes* that empowered the populace, the disease seemed to gain strength to meet them. In the early 1950s, polio epidemics were rising even faster than the population, and this was the height of the baby boom.

Figure 7.16 Hand-drawn cover to the 1951 Southwest Explorations season. (K. Ross original drawing)

Now the fear of the disease added to the chagrin of Kenny Ross trying to get teenage boys to enroll in the Explorers Camp. Along with brochures that advertised the camp, Kenny sent out insurance information for accidents and specifically for polio. The cost was minimal for each policy ($6.00) but the mere mention had its effect of causing parents to think twice about camps with other children from across the country.[60]

> By then [1952], polio epidemics were second only to the atomic bomb in surveys of what Americans feared most. Bomb and virus alike were terrible agents of destruction that might arrive at any moment to devastate a family, a community, or an entire nation. The disease seemed like an omnipresent threat, and its cure became a national responsibility. Epidemics struck other countries, but never as heavily as here. America was the center of polio, and the place where people knew they must work first, and fastest, to end it. They gave their time and money to help the growing swell of victims and to find a way to stem the rising tide of injury. When the call came, they even volunteered their children, millions of them, to test a new vaccine. The fear that had once driven Americans apart was now the force that pulled them together.[61]

For Kenny Ross, the 1951 season marked the transition from "*Explorers Camp*" to "*Southwest Exploration Camp*" with the new logo on all the promotional material. Kenny went all out in his description of the daily activities that had occurred during the 1951 Explorers Camp in a forty page report entitled "SOUTHWEST EXPLORATIONS: Narrative Report – 1951 Expeditions."[62] The report was mimeographed on colored paper and used as his promotional syllabus for future camps (Figure 7.16). The syllabus had a hand-drawn cover page of *Explorers Arch* in Salt Creek that the boys group had discovered that year, plus hand drawn maps of his expanded site map of the Cibola City archaeological excavation, a detailed map of the San Juan & Colorado Rivers (SJ&C) from Bluff to Lees Ferry, a hand drawn inset diagram that showed, in detail, the preferred course to run through Eight Foot Rapid, a detailed map of the west Elk Ridge country and specific locations of camps and the Explorers Arch discovered in Salt Creek, and a regional map of the greater Four Corners area that he had made in 1949 and continued to refine (see Map beginning of Chapter Six). Most of the day to day descriptions of activities were taken from the boys' journals and transcribed in their own words. Kenny added minor clarifications but he also added a substantial amount of historical information he had garnered in his research that ranged from the current knowledge of the Ancient Puebloan culture, the Spanish explorations, mining and prospector history, and geography and geologic setting in each area they ventured.

The Explorers Camp convened June 21, 1951 at Gold King base camp in the La Plata Mountains for its eighth consecutive season; members of the field staff and explorers were: [63]

FIELD STAFF

Kenneth I. Ross: Leader and Camp Director; Mancos, CO

Harold W. Lambert: Physician, M.D.; Berkeley, CA (river trip only)

William R. Dickinson: Assistant Leader; Santa Barbara, CA (river trip only)

William Procter: Junior Leader; Pelham, NY

Stuart H. "Mike" Maule: Cook; El Monte, CA and Mancos, CO

THIRD YEAR EXPLORERS

George Hall, Jr.; Los Angeles, CA
Charles Dustin; Farmington, NM

SECOND YEAR EXPLORERS

Alfred Hoyt and Edward Hoyt (twin brothers): Santa Fe, NM
Land Lindbergh: Darien, CT

FIRST YEAR EXPLORERS

Bruce Buck; Littleton, CO
James Huie; Haines City, FL
Michael Herz; Excelsior, MN
Rawson Harmon
Richard Laing; Wichita, KS
John Lambert; Berkeley, CA
Thomas Vaughan; Bronxville, NY
David Wendt; Williston Park, NY
Howard Lambert; Berkeley, CA (river trip only)
Christopher Bronson; Greenwich, CT

Three boys, Thomas Vaughn, Jimmie Huie and Rawson Harmon who had been in Doc Marquard's *Round-up Lodge* camp had signed on with the Explorers Camp. The "adult" river trip in May was cancelled because only four adults had shown interest; plus Hank Zuidema had backed out again. The list of boys showed a meager attendance compared to earlier years where thirty to forty-five boys were enrolled. Only thirteen full-season enrollees and two part-timers made up the total number of Explorers for 1951 and reflected the nation's nervous tensions as the war in Korea intensified and the fear of polio had reached its zenith. There was also no academically-credentialed archaeologist, forester or geologist; Kenny fulfilled these rolls as he had done in 1949. Of course, with the smaller group size, there was no need for rotation of activities, so the one group stayed together throughout the summer camp and went together from one activity to the next.

Following the six day period of orientation at Gold King base camp the group left for the river trip down the San Juan River. The written narrative for the river trip log was a compilation of notes primarily taken by three boys who were on the trip as well as Kenny's overview commentary. The day-to-day notes consisted of young boys' exuberant rambling style of writing about what they saw and experienced. USGS historical water gage records indicated that 1951 was not an exceptional run-off year having peaked at 9,000 cfs in early June. For the dates of the river trip the river level fell quickly. They launched on a decent flow of 5,500 cfs, but by the time they reached Paiute Farms and the big rapids below Copper Canyon it had dropped under 800 cfs.[64] The following day-by-day narrative written by the boys in their journal has been shortened and edited for brevity.

SAN JUAN RIVER TRIP

June 26: At Gold King base camp; the group loaded equipment and supplies into the Dodge truck and then split up into passenger groups in the jeep and station wagon and drove to Mancos where they rolled up the boats and stuffed them into big canvas sacks. The boats consisted of four 7-man boats that measured 12 ft by 5 ft and weighed 325 pounds and one 10-man boat that measured 15 ft by 7 ft and weighed 400 pounds (and called *the Monster*). They camped in the public park in Mancos.

June 27: The group was ready to head for Bluff by 9:00 AM and Mildred Ross with the two young sons, Don and Doug, plus a young Mancos man [surname: Amrine] went with the group so they could drive the jeep and station wagon back to Bluff; the Dodge truck stayed in Mancos (Figure 7.17). The boats were loaded onto a trailer towed by the jeep nicknamed "Esther." They traveled by way of Monticello and Blanding to reach Bluff – a distance of 127 miles. Mention is made that they were not in the town of Bluff and were close to some Navajo hogans (see Figure 7.4).[65] They unloaded all the boats and gear and puffed up the boats and got them in the river, and then they had supper and went back to Bluff for a swim at the "swimmin' hole" behind cemetery hill. They commented about the artesian wells and good drinking water and filled up several five- and ten-gallon milk cans of drinking water at the well at Twin Rocks on their return to the boats.

June 28: After the boats were packed and readied for the trip, Kenny and "Big Bill" conducted a safety meeting and instructed the boys how to wear their "life-belts" that fastened around the waist and had to be worn at all times when on the boats. The belts were inflated by blowing up by mouth. Kenny said "You are supposed to get so used to the belts that it feels like your pants are off if you don't have one on."[66] The boys were shown how to handle the paddles and how the two-paddle system worked with the paddlers sitting in the stern. Each boat had a "Captain" that had been on river trips before; they were: George Hall, Land Lindbergh, Eddie Hoyt, Charles "Dusty" Dustin, and Alfie Hoyt. Three boys were distributed on three 7-man boats, and four on the lightest loaded 7-man. The "Monster" carried five.

Kenny rode in the lead boat and "Big Bill" rode in the last boat. Doc Lambert and Mike Maule rode in the middle boats. The boys learned how to paddle and dodge sandbars and experienced floating through sand waves with amplitudes up to three to four feet. They ate lunch at Butler Wash and visited the petroglyph panel and made mention of the Barton Trading Post as they floated by. They stopped at Comb Wash long enough for Kenny to explain the folded strata before them and referred to the fold as the Raplee Anticline (actually the Lime Creek anticline; there was no mention of the Mule Ear diatreme). They made it down river to the top of Eight Foot Rapid and made camp.

Figure 7.17 Don, Mildred and Doug at the river launch site above Bluff, June 1951. (K. Ross collection)

June 29: Following breakfast they all walked down to the foot of the rapid and learned how to "conn a rapid" with Kenny and Bill pointing out rocks to avoid hitting and the preferred run through the rapid (Figure 7.18). Kenny and Bill took turns helping the crews run their boats through. They ran to the *left* of the large top-rock where most present-day runs enter the rapid to the *right* side into a narrow chute. They made non-consequential runs through the remaining rapids down to Mexican Hat where it was noted "All there is at Mexican Hat is a bridge across the river and an Indian Trading Post."[67] While Kenny and Bill topped off the drinking water cans, the boys got their last chance to buy candy and soda pop before floating through the Goosenecks (Figure 7.19). They ended up camping at the foot of Honaker Trail. The boys wrote that they traveled twenty-seven miles that day and the river dropped 125 ft.

June 30: "We ran three small rapids today and one 'Big, black, hairy one' as Kenny says. It is called Government Rapid."[68] The river log noted that it was a much more complicated rapid than Eight Foot, which required a long time of "conning" before the boats went through by going right of center but not the far right "ledge run."[69] They reached Slickhorn Gulch where it was noted "This is the best camp we have had yet. The beach is high and wide and there is plenty of firewood."[70] Kenny said they only made twelve miles that day and the river dropped 180 ft.

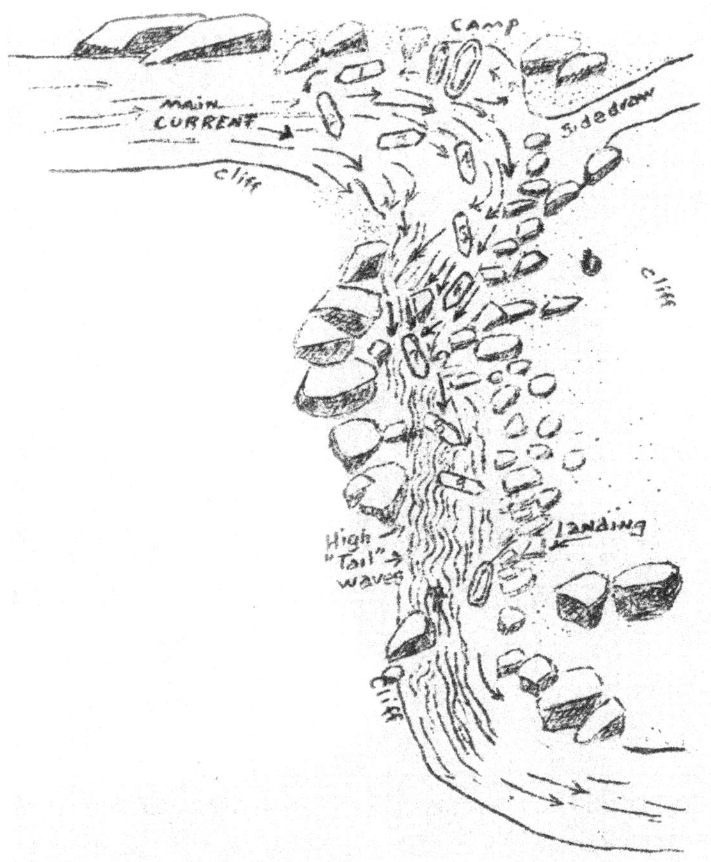

Figure 7.18 sketch map of Eight Foot Rapid and suggested maneuvers to make in negotiating the rapid and obstacles to avoid at varying river level and preferred landing point. (K. Ross original drawing)

July 1: They got a late start and floated down to Grand Gulch thinking there might be some water spilling over the cliff, but it was dry. They ran through the "large room-size boulder course" that Kenny named "Boxcar."[71] They stopped and ate lunch at the mouth of Moonlight Creek which was noted as "a very big place like half a bowl. The cliffs are high all around and the water from the creek, when it has any, pours over thru a notch in the wall."[72] The river was quiet and Kenny let the boys swim without their life-belts. They ended up camping on river right at the inside elbow turn to the straight-away to Clay Hills (RM 60.2). "From this camp, which is as good as Slickhorn Gulch, you can look straight down the river and see the left bend at Clay Crossing."[73] They traveled fourteen and a half miles that day and the river dropped 105 ft.

July 2: The boys noted that day they experienced "The Death March Thru Paiute Farms."[74] The tug of pushing and pulling the boats upwards of nine miles through feet to inches-deep water took nearly three hours for the group, but had taken up to a full day for others. The exhausted group camped across from the mouth of Nokai Canyon on river right. They made seventeen miles that day and the river dropped only 90 ft.

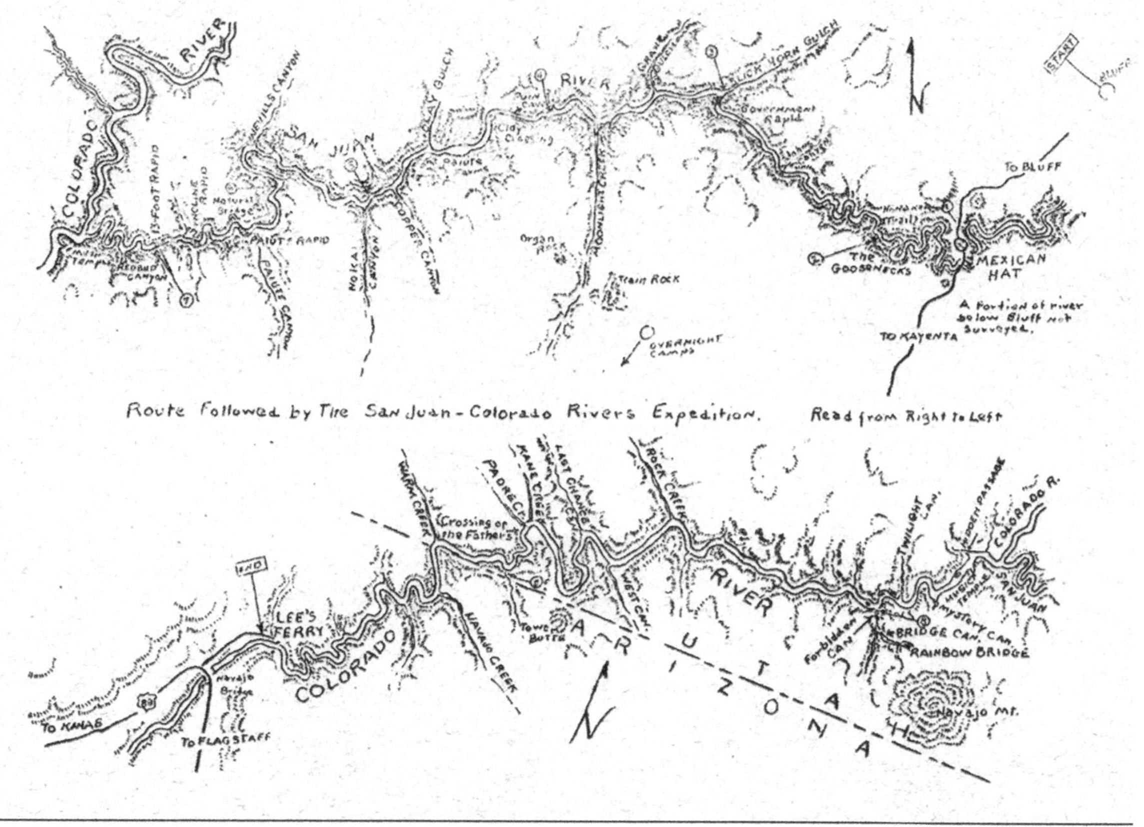

Figure 7.19 Sketch map showing San Juan River from Mexican Hat to confluence with the Colorado River and thence downstream through Glen Canyon to Lees Ferry. (K. Ross original drawing)

The Paiute Farms bog is geologically controlled by the presence of soft shales in the Permian age Organ Rock Shale and Triassic Moenkopi and Chinle formations that are at river level in the synclinal axis of the Nokai Syncline between the west plunge of the Cedar Mesa limb of the Monument Uplift and the rising east limb of No Mans Mesa Anticline. Due to the easily eroded nature of these shales, the canyon walls have eroded away and the river gradient has flattened such that the river has briefly returned to a complex braided network of numerous channels like that seen in the river section from Shiprock to Comb Wash. Once past the Paiute Farms braided bog, the river has regained a steeper gradient. A main channel has cut into the Wingate Ss near Copper Canyon.

July 3: Their camp was not shaded from morning sunlight so it was a hot pack to get back on the river. They stopped at the abandoned Spencer gold mining camp in Zahn Bay where rusting gold dredge equipment was strewn about. The river was mellow that day and they stopped at Alcove Canyon at a fresh water spring and filled their water cans. According to Kenny they traveled eighteen miles and the river dropped another 105 ft. They camped near the mouth of Neskahi Wash.[75]

July 4: They ran the "Big Three" rapids in the lower San Juan: Piute Rapid, Syncline Rapid and Thirteen Foot Rapid (the biggest rapids on the San Juan River prior to inundation by Powell Reservoir water in the 1960s) and camped at the lower end of Cha Canyon, the mouth of which forms Thirteen Foot Rapid (Figure 7.20). The water was so low they couldn't take the main channel on the right side so they took a rocky left run and "rumbled" the boats safely to the bottom. No mention was made of Syncline Rapid (due to low water) other than a few small rapids run before they had reached the head of Thirteen Foot Rapid. The water level was so low (probably <600 cfs) that following "conning," Kenny deemed it unrunnable. The normal right channel run was barricaded by large boulders, so they carried all the gear to the bottom of the rapid and lined the empty boats part way down the left side until they picked up sufficient water from the main channel. Then Ken and Bill paddled the first three boats on down to the bottom. Alfie and Eddie Hoyt ran the fourth boat and hung up on some big rocks, but got free and then ran the last boat through, still hitting the same rocks, but did not get stuck as before. They were tired from the day of portaging and running rapids and although fire crackers were shot off, most of the boys "sacked out" early. According to Kenny they traveled eighteen miles and the river dropped another 105 ft.

July 5: They got an early start and reached "Redbud Canyon" by 9:00 AM where they filled up water cans and then bathed in the clean water.[76] They reached the confluence with the Colorado River and noted the dramatic color change from red-brown San Juan water to green Colorado water. The Navajo Sandstone was now at river level and a few more miles down they stopped to make camp at a large sand beach that separated the canyon cliffs from the river near the mouth of Forbidding Canyon. The river was too low to pull their boats up into the cliffs bordering the mouth of the side canyon. After the boats were secured, Dr. Lambert and some of the boys left on the hike to Rainbow Bridge to spend the night. The others planned to go up the next day. The boys' journal notes that power boats that had come upstream and also camped there had left trash. They noted that the Explorers lived by the motto, "where we go *we leave no trace*."[77] According to Kenny they boated twenty-four miles that day.

July 6: The day was spent hiking up to Rainbow Bridge. The boys noted that somebody had carved a sign on a rock saying it was six miles to Rainbow Bridge. This was possibly etched by Norm Nevills, as all his accounts (and those who have written about Norm) say it is six miles to this geologic wonder. USGS topographic maps show it was little more than four miles. The hike was in a beautiful shaded cool canyon with plenty of pools of "good water" along the way. First impressions seemed to be consistent – witnesses were in awe of its grandeur and size. A registry was there and they added their names, noting that there weren't very many names recorded. They also noted that they had not seen any other groups there and hadn't seen anyone other than their own group since leaving Mexican Hat. They also noted seeing Explorers names that had come down from the trail from Rainbow Lodge in 1947 (where Jon Lindbergh had made a name for himself helping out others).

July 7: The group was up early and moved on down the river, they lunched at Rock Creek and reached Padre Creek in mid-afternoon. Some boys went exploring the creek in search for steps cut by the Escalante party in 1776. They camped there and noted that it was the same camp as the 1950 Explorers group.

July 8: The Explorers group arrived at the boat landing just below historic Lees Ferry shortly after 2:00 PM. The boats were cleaned and rolled and gear was ready to load when Mrs. Ross and her two little boys arrived about two hours later with the vehicles. They ate an early supper at the river then drove four miles over the rough road to Marble Canyon Lodge and Trading Post where they made camp.

Figure 7.20 aerial view to southwest of Navajo Mountain; Cha Canyon enters San Juan River in mid-view with outwash forming the largest rapid on the San Juan River – Thirteen Foot Rapid. (From G. Crampton, 1964)

July 9: The long drive home began early and they crossed Navajo Bridge and followed the paved highway southward to Moenkopi Wash and then turned northeastward onto State Road 47, "A very, very rough road" and they lunched at Tuba City. They reached Marsh Pass at 4:30 PM in a high wind and camped there. They ended up killing a rattlesnake and skinned and cooked it. Although small, everyone had a piece to eat and exclaimed it to be delicious. Don Ross remembered eating some snake meat.

July 10: The next day consisted of driving along "bad road conditions" with several stops for photographs in Monument Valley. They arrived in Mexican Hat in the early afternoon and after a brief stop they continued on to Bluff "the road is terrible from being pounded to pieces by heavy uranium trucks." They decided to camp at the Bluff swimmin' hole "for a last swim in good water." They had completed a grand circular tour.

GOLD KING BASE CAMP

July 11: Home Again. They returned to Gold King and ate kitchen cooked food at tables and slept in beds.

July 12: Personal Day of Leisure: [Bill Dickinson left camp and returned to California and resumed his school work at Stanford University.]

July 13: Cumberland Basin and the Bessie G. Gold Mine: the group jeeped and hiked in to a high trail that connected Cumberland Mountain to Snowstorm Peak. From there the trail continued to the Bessie G., the principal gold mine in the La Plata Mining District. The mine had been operated almost continuously since 1887. Tunnels, chutes, and stopes followed the ore veins, sometimes very rich in gold. Bert Thompson was the mine representative and the miners knew they were coming and fitted them all with carbide lamps and took them 400 ft to the back of the tunnel. They saw how charges of dynamite were shot and then how ore was washed, graded and sacked for transport by mule-pack down the mountain.

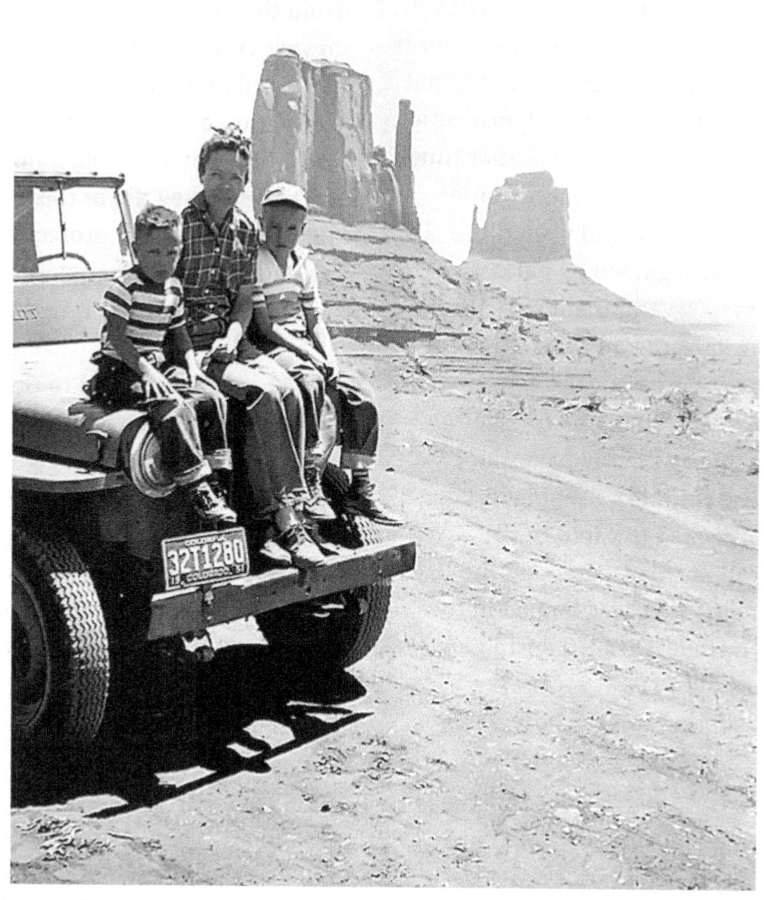

Figure 7.21 Doug, Mildred and Don in Monument Valley July 10, 1951; on trip home after picking up Kenny and the boys at Lees Ferry two days earlier. (K. Ross collection)

July 14: storms postponed any climbs that day; instead, the boys readied the equipment for the archaeological trip.

July 15: Boren Basin and Burwell Peak: Bright sunny weather; the group hiked to the lower end of a cirque basin then climbed the left shoulder of Burwell Peak to timberline. Oxygen deprivation above 12,000 ft was felt and proper slow hiking got them to the top of Burwell for an incredible view of the entire Four Corners points of interests. This ended the mountain segment.

"CIBOLA CITY RUINS"

The summer of 1951 marked the sixth consecutive season at Cibola City ruins. Kenny's brochure repeated much of the basics and went to considerable detail in his descriptions of Ancient Puebloan periods of occupation and identification of cultural aspects that were known at that time. On July 16 – 18 the group visited Mesa Verde National Park for orientation and visited the museum. They were also guided by Park Rangers/naturalists to several main sites. On July 19 they departed Mesa Verde and arrived at the Cahone dig to set up base camp that consisted of three 16 ft x 16 ft canvas tents; one for the kitchen/mess hall, one as the field laboratory (Figure 7.22) and the third for sleeping although most of the boys preferred to camp in the alcoves under the rim of Cahone Mesa amongst the ancient ruins. Potable water was hauled in two 250 gallon tanks on trailers from a spring located about three miles away.

Under Kenny's supervision the boys were divided into three teams and shown how to layout the lines for trenching. Once laid out they started work by carefully digging trenches (Figure 7.23) and were shown the painstaking art of digging, screening, and close observation and detailed note-taking as artifacts were unearthed. Digging tools consisted of small trowels, whisk brooms and brushes; shovels were only used to lift loosened earth to the screens (Figure 7.24). The boys found several burial sites and documented the skeletal remains, pottery, projectile points and other artifacts and carefully labeled and bagged the collection after drawing their findings and documenting photographically. The boys took turns surveying, digging and recording.

On Saturday, July 28 the group took a break from the excavation work and set out in the jeeps to visit Hovenweep National Monument (Figure 7.25) and on Sunday they showed their excavation efforts to visiting ranchers in the area. On Monday and Tuesday, July 30-31 they spent the time as they did at the end of every seasonal dig by covering and protecting the excavation area and cleaning up before breaking camp and heading back to Gold King base camp.

The group returned to Gold King and began preparation for the Salt Creek Canyon trip, but the group worked so diligently that they all agreed to delay the departure for a day or two so they could attend the colorful "Spanish Trails Fiesta" in Durango on August 4 and 5. The annual event consisted of a huge parade of cowboys and Indians, street dancing and "a bang-up rodeo" and girls. They were all glad to have taken part.

Figure 7.22 Explorers dig new trenches at Cahone ruins, 1951. (K. Ross collection)

Figure 7.23 digging trenches at Cahone ruin, 1951. (K. Ross collection)

Figure 7.24 carefully exposing a dog skeleton at Cahone ruin, 1951. (K. Ross collection)

Figure 7.25 the road to Hovenweep National Monument. (K. Ross collection)

THE SALT CREEK CANYON EXPEDITION

The exploration of Salt Creek Canyon (August 6 – 18) was the most significant segment of the 1951 *Southwest Exploration Camp* efforts in that access was largely unknown and Kenny made sure the boys were prepared for extended hiking and backpacking. The Salt Creek country had been by-passed by earlier explorers. The Macomb Survey in 1859 with geologist John Newberry got within six miles of the confluence of the Green and Colorado rivers before turning back completely baffled by the geologic maze of intricate canyons. The area was described from a distance as a land of "standing rocks" in a report by F.S. Dellenbaugh on the second Powell expedition of 1871-72. Other than cowboys working for the Scorup Cattle Company, it was unlikely that anyone had spent much time exploring this remote section of standing rocks. In 1946 while Professor Arthur Woodward was leading the Explorers Camp survey of petroglyphs at Newspaper Rock and vicinity in Indian Creek, they were told by the Scorup cowboys of "big ruins over in Salt Crick and lots of picture writing; even more than here." [78] That same year Kenny had led the first documented group of Anglo boys and men down the full length of Dark Canyon to its confluence with the Colorado River and heard stories from their packers about the wonders of Salt Creek.

Kenny had returned four times since then to explore other canyons that drain the west Elk Ridge country and the previous year, in 1950, while he led one group down Woodenshoe and Dark Canyons, the other group had attempted to access Salt Creek Canyon from above. After eight days of trying to get below the canyon rims and benches they failed to find a safe way to access the canyon. They noted the weird erosional architecture of the lower country enough so that Kenny had changed his plans to accessing Salt Creek from below.

Kenny erroneously stated in his report that Salt Creek was a tributary to Indian Creek but it is not. Salt Creek enters the Colorado River several miles downstream from the mouth of Indian Creek (Figure 7.26). He also mistakenly noted that there was a "middle fork" when in fact the upper half of Salt Creek consists of just east and west forks. Of course, in such a dissected terrain, there are numerous unnamed short tributaries which might have confused this initial entry into the Salt Creek drainage where Kenny and his group planned to explore the East Fork of Salt Creek.

Geologically, most of the Salt Creek drainage consists of numerous intricately incised box-work erosional features through the Cedar Mesa Sandstone of middle Permian age (see Appendix II; stratigraphic column). The added colorful curiosity is the "banding" of interfingering redbeds of the Organ Rock Shale with the white cross-bedded sandstone of the Cedar Mesa (Figure 7.27). In the 1950s there wasn't a formal name for this complex topography and was referred to as pinnacles or mushroom rocks but later the name officially became the Needles District of Canyonlands National Park.[79]

August 6: The Explorers loaded up the Dodge truck, two jeeps (one pulling a heavily loaded trailer) and headed west (Figure 7.28). They camped on the west side of Monticello, took in a movie and hit the sack.

August 7: Kenny had spoken with a local Monticello man who advised him to enter Salt Creek by way of following the Dugout Ranch road and to head west after crossing Indian Creek where the whole caravan could enter the Salt Creek basin by crossing a broad sandy floodplain. They should then follow a cowboy jeep trail and then abandon the truck when the going got too tough and continue the rest of the way with the jeeps.

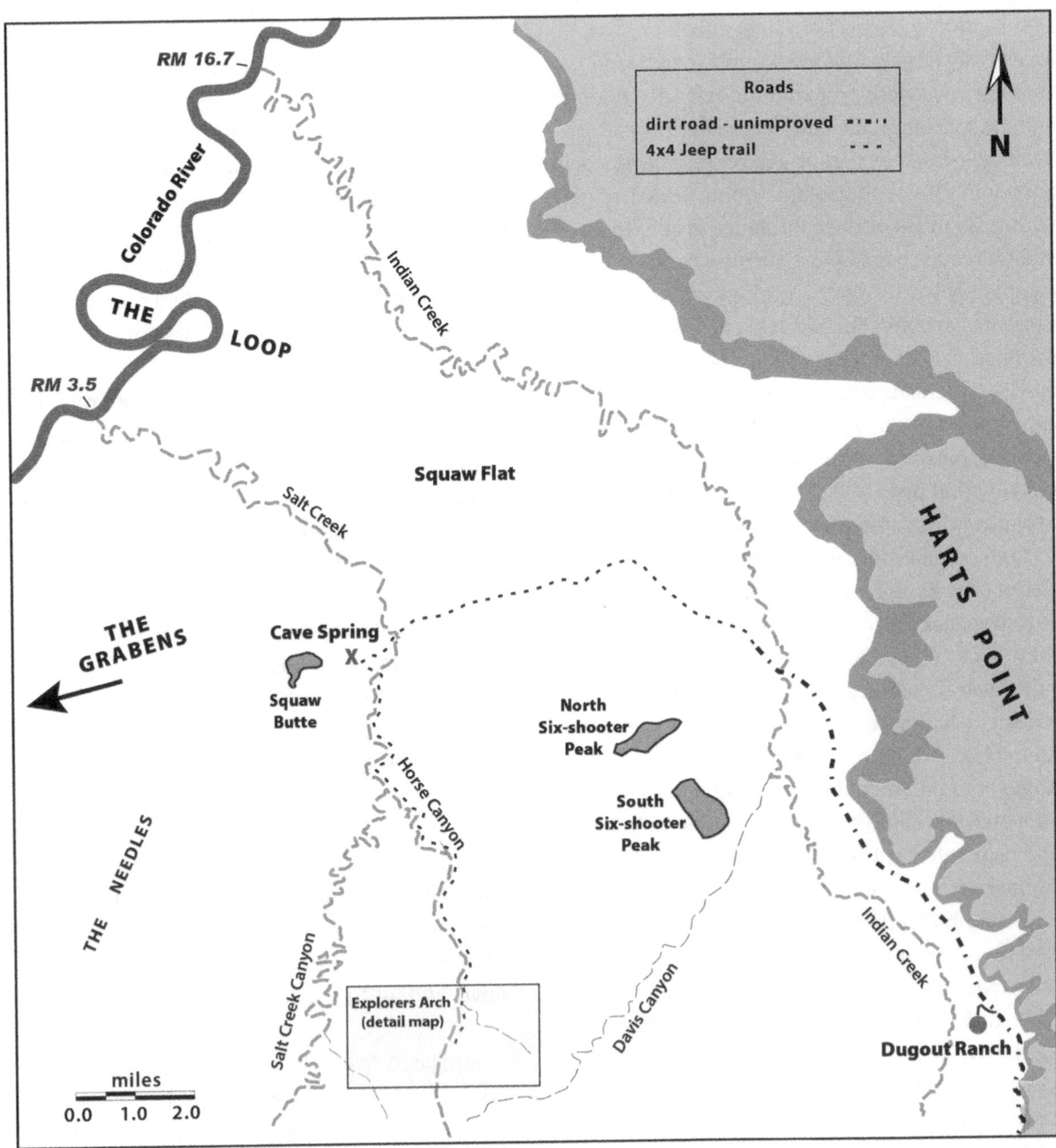

Figure 7.26 Base map highlights the course of lower Indian Creek and Salt Creek to show they are separate drainages that enter the Colorado River above the confluence with the Green River. Map also shows route taken by 1951 Explorers group past Dugout Ranch on an increasingly poor road (trail), past sand traps in Squaw Flat and mistakenly went down Horse Canyon rather than Salt Creek Canyon; inset map of Figure 7.31 shows details at "Alamo Park" where they discovered and named "Explorers Arch." (GMS/TB original map)

Figure 7.27 "Land of Confusion" is what Kent Frost called it; the banded layers of Cedar Mesa Sandstone and intricate box-work drainage could confuse the most experienced hiker of his day. (G.M. Stevenson photo)

Pavement ended fifteen miles north of Monticello at the turn off to Dugout Ranch and Indian Creek. They followed a dirt road past Marie Ogden's Home of Truth, into Indian Creek Canyon and after twenty-two miles came to Dugout Ranch (Figure 7.26). After talking to the ranch foreman who said he'd been to Cave Springs the day before they followed his tracks only a few more miles to the entrance of the lower Salt Creek drainage. The jeeps were driven up to Cave Spring after which point they were on their own. The country opened up when they left Dugout Ranch where sheer walls cut through the Glen Canyon Group gave way to the open red landscape of the less resistant Chinle and Moenkopi formations before cutting into the white sandstone spires in the upper Cedar Mesa Ss (see Appendix II: Stratigraphic column). The area was not called the Needles yet and was called the "pinnacles."

Kenny again stated erroneously that when they passed by Six-Shooter Buttes that it marked the mouth of Salt Creek, but that location actually marked where Indian Creek veers northward (Figure 7.26). He said they crawled through deep sand above the south bank of Indian Creek. They continued westward following splayed unnamed outwash plains but eventually crossed into Salt Creek after pushing and working hard to get the truck and jeeps across the broad sand wash to Cave Spring where they made camp (Fig 7.26). The camp was in an alcove and they noted signs of occupation that extended back to Ancient Puebloans up to recent cowboys. There was good potable water at Cave Springs.

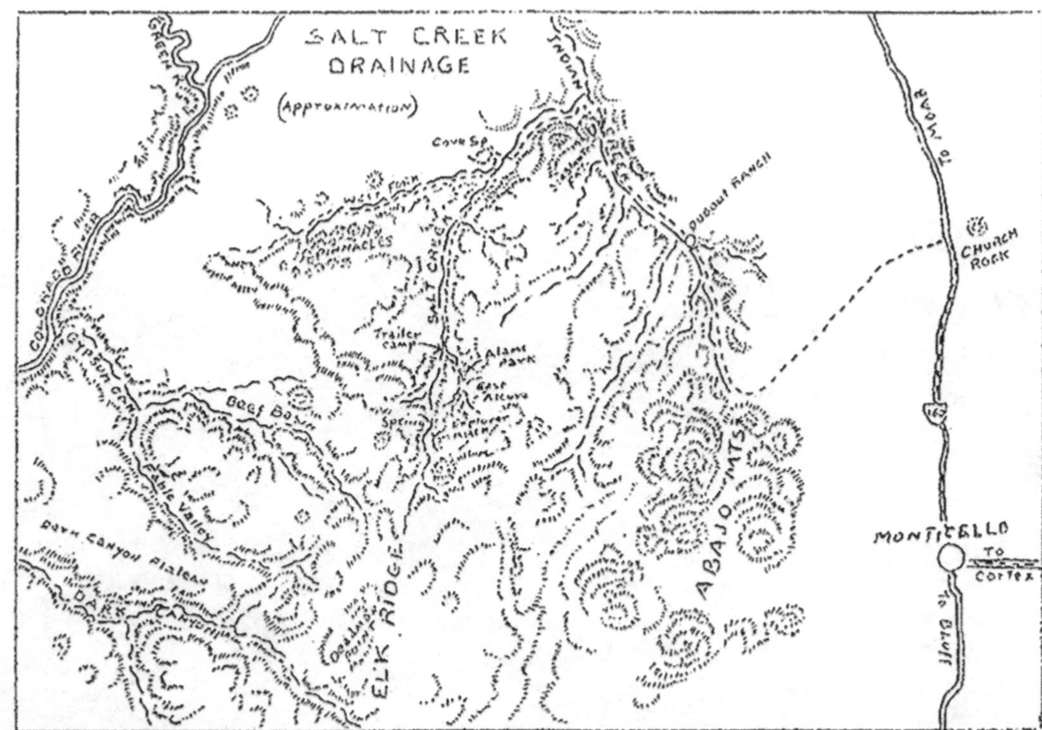

Figure 7.28 Sketch map Kenny made in 1951 following the first exploratory trip to Salt Creek Country; not having any topographic maps and only following local cowboys' directions and his own nose he assumed he went down the east fork of Salt Creek where they discovered "Explorers Arch." Compare his map and notations to those shown in Figure 7.26 and discussed below. (K. Ross original hand drawn map)

<u>August 8:</u> they repacked the two jeeps; this was as far as the big Dodge truck was going to make it. They turned south following jeep tracks, almost getting stuck in quicksand and reached an unnamed spring. Kenny thought they were at the junction of the East Fork and what Kenny called "Middle Fork" of Salt Creek, but they were actually at the confluence of Salt Creek and Horse Creek.[80] They continued following the eastern drainage (Horse Creek) thinking they were in the East Fork of Salt Creek Canyon (Figure 7.26). They proceeded several more miles and dropped the trailer when the twisting canyon narrowed so much it was unwise to negotiate the tight turns pulling a trailer. [This reduction to just two jeeps was possibly in the SESW Sec 4-T31S-R20E]. They continued through twisting narrow canyons glad they had left the trailer. Kenny described a bizarre land of mushroom-like rocks fifty feet or more in height; a fretwork of deep canyon gorges spreading fan-like "their thin, broadly banded red and white walls rising in heights eight or nine hundred feet. The walls were knife-thin and serrated at their tops; carved into spires of a thousand goblin forms." [81] Someone remarked it looked like an enormous honeycomb and it did (Figure 7.30). They passed through narrow passages it almost seemed impossible for the little jeeps to squeeze through but at last they reached a spot with cottonwood trees and "a trickle of clear water emerging from the stream bed and flowed a short distance before sinking again into the sand." [82] This was the most attractive spot they had found; it was a cool, green refuge and they deemed that it would make a perfect campsite from which to proceed on foot and to explore the high-walled chambers of the surrounding canyon maze. As it was getting late in the day they decided to return to the trailer for camp and to reorganize for the upcoming hikes.

Figure 7.29 stuck in sand enroute to camp at Cave Springs, August 7, 1951. (K. Ross collection)

August 9: They returned the next morning to the spot they found the day before and named it "Alamo Park" [estimated location: NWSE Sec 21-T30S-R20E; elevation ~5350 ft]. Everyone pitched in setting up camp (Figure 7.31). While the kitchen area was set up, others dug a well into the wet sand near the little stream and set up a shower system by hanging a can with holes punched in it from a bough of a tree and a platform of flat stones were arranged under it; a garbage pit was dug near the kitchen area and a camp latrine set up behind a brush screen. Sleeping areas were claimed and within minutes a loud *"chini-ahgo-heh!"* [83] brought all hands dashing to the kitchen for lunch.

> Thru-out our stay in this canyon wilderness all of us retained something of the excitement and thrill we felt upon first entering it. Familiarity never quite banished awe of its looming immensity. It was a magic place of other-worldly aspect; a land of disturbing contrasts of color and form that only artful Nature could blend and harmonize and make soothing. Shocking red and white and green were fused; sharp angles and soft roundness reconciled, by the living play of hot sunlight and cool shadow. It excited and urged and enticed with a promise of hidden secrets. It gave us little time to remember the world outside and had it not been for the presence of the jeeps we might even have forgotten that such a world existed.[84]

They proceeded to hike south of the camp and within a half-mile they discovered "Explorers Arch."[85] Present-day topographic maps refer to the feature as "Castle Arch" and it became known as such in 1954 when photographed from below by Bates Wilson (Figure 7.32).

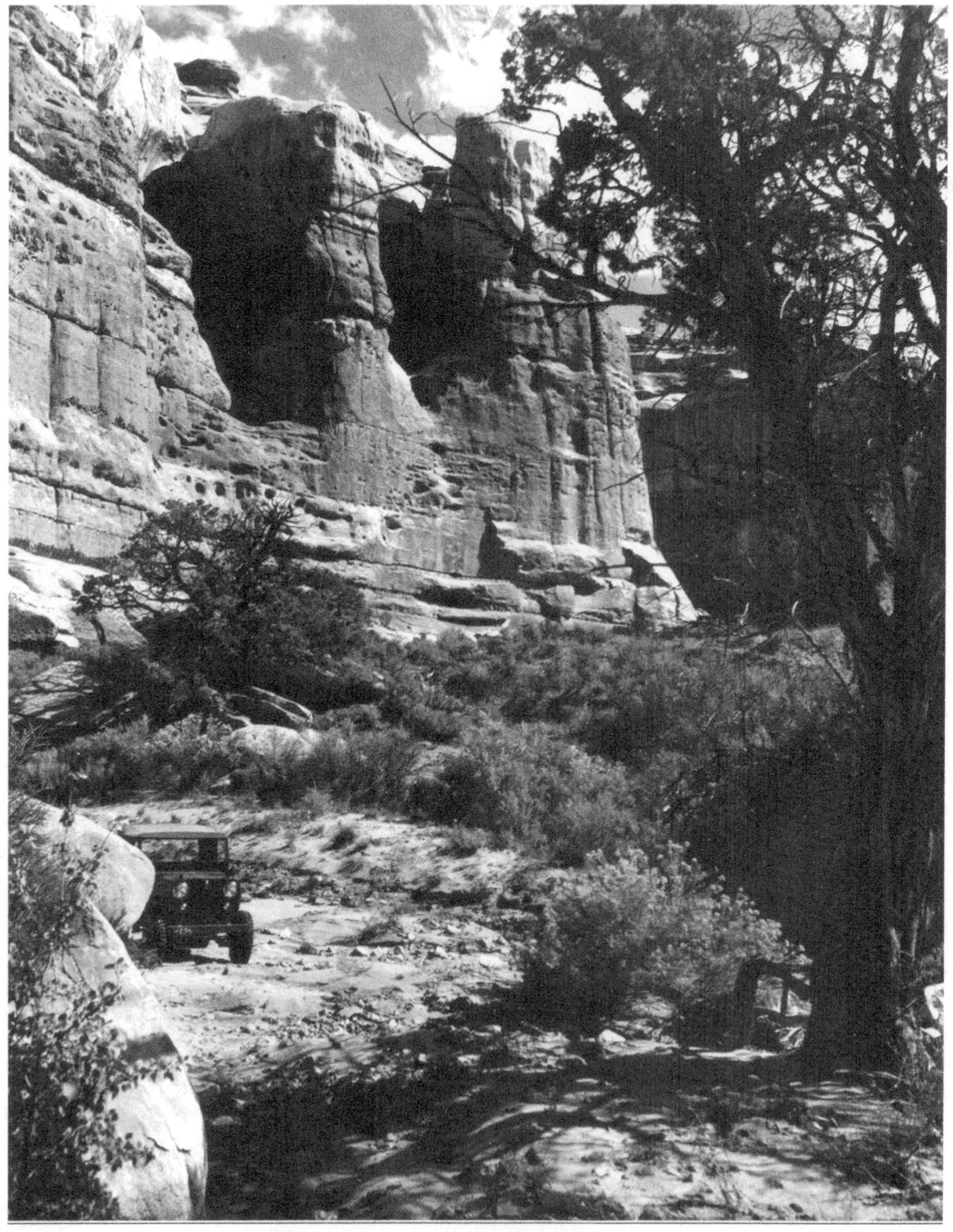

Figure 7.30 a jeep in Horse Canyon near Castle Arch, 1954. (Bates Wilson, CNPS archive photo)

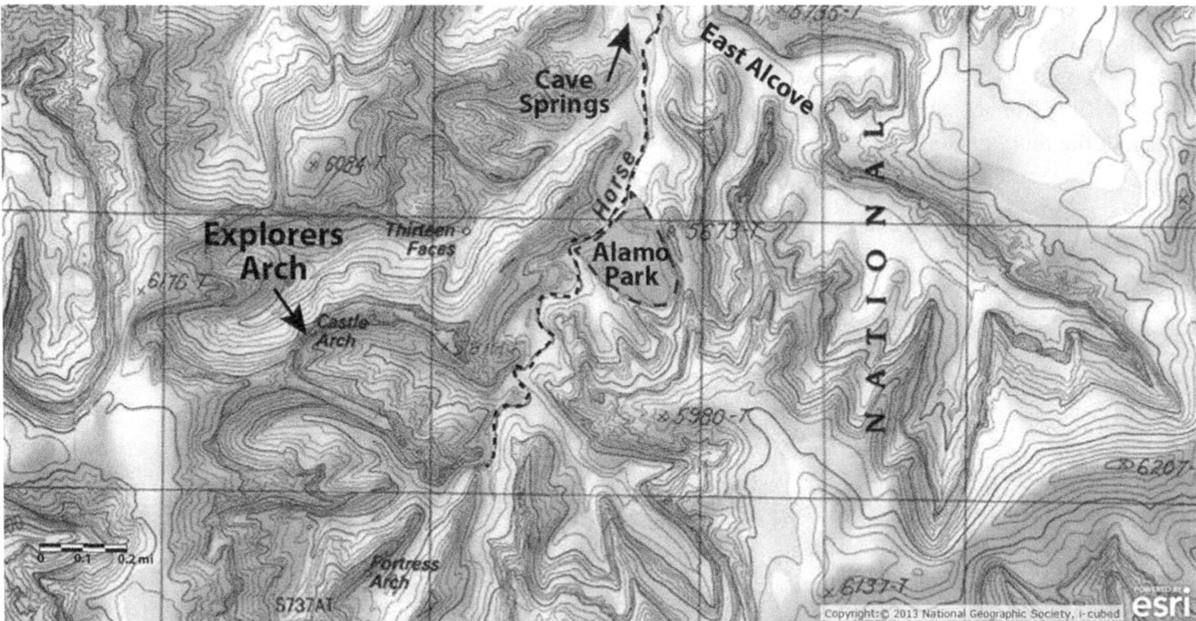

Figure 7.31 Map shows location of "Alamo Park" and the short distance to "Explorers Arch" (Castle Arch); see inset box on Salt Creek Area Map (Figure 7.26) for specific location. (Modified from *Esri Arc/GIS* USGS topographic map)

The newly discovered "Explorers Arch" was described as being seen from a point a half mile above "Alamo Park." It was curiosity that took them beyond a ten foot-wide notch in the right wall [west side] of the canyon (Figure 7.33). They estimated its height from the floor to the underside of the span at eighty to ninety feet and the length exceeded one hundred feet. The thickness at the center of the span was no more than five feet and its width was about seven or eight feet. Its position in the top of a wall that separated two canyon alcoves made it one of the more spectacular arches they discovered. In mentioning this arch, Kenny described several others including one with a double arch with one horizontal span and one vertical span they called "the two-holer" which may be *Fortress Arch* or *Thirteen Faces*. A third arch or window was the largest of the major arches but was too far away to reach on this expedition [*Angel Arch?*]. It appeared more like a large tunnel when viewed through binoculars and located in a thick wall separating the East Fork from the Middle [main] Fork drainages.

They spent four days (August 10-13) exploring the East Fork (or Horse Canyon) and numerous ruins and wall structures, one of which they named "Skylight Cave" [86] and about twenty-five by sixty feet long. It was floored by juniper bark and corn husks and two "digging sticks" of a type common in the Ancient Southwest along with a two-piece wooden shovel found in a foot wide trough between flat slabs of sandstone at the front of the floor. They removed these "souvenirs" and later turned them over to the museum at Mesa Verde National Park. They realized they were never going to see it all and decided to spend the next day climbing up on Salt Creek Mesa to get the big picture of where they were (Figure 7.34).

> August 14 was spent climbing out to the level of the broad, high mesa lying between the head of the East Fork and Elk Mountain, for a bird's-eye view of

the area in which we had been working. Viewed from this elevation, the canyons below appear more than ever like a cyclopean architecture, roofless and falling to ruin. From here we could see Explorer Arch, Tunnel Arch, and a few more that had not been visible from below. Alamo Park lay like a green gem at the foot of Submarine Rock and East Alcove, thru which we had found a steep exit to this point, stretched its wide, half-mile length below our feet. After making a rough, sketch map of the adjacent area and projecting lines to distant points of interest, we descended – to break up our field camp in Alamo Park which had given us more pleasure than any other camp of the summer.[87]

Figure 7.32 Castle Arch as seen by Bates Wilson with Bill and W.G. Carroll, 1954. (CNPS archive photo)

Figure 7.33 "There, high atop the far wall of a long alcove, a magnificent white stone arch soared against the blue sky. Carved by the elements in the topmost layer of white sandstone, it rises from the left out of an underlying band of bright red; sweeps sharply upward into a long, threadlike span and descends in a graceful curve to join the white cliff on the right." (K. Ross, August 9, 1951; K. Ross collection)

Figure 7.34 the Explorers hiked to "Cedar Mesa" on August 14, 1951 to get a better view of the incredible country where they had been hiking. (K. Ross collection)

The "broad, high mesa lying between the head of the East Fork and Elk Mountain" was probably Cedar Mesa [elevation ~6900 ft; Sec 10-T32S-R20E] and about four miles (as the crow flies) south of Alamo Park. They made it back to the junction of "East and West (Middle) Forks" (junction of Salt Creek and Horse Canyon) by darkness where they had left the trailer. The next two days they planned to scout the Middle and West Forks to see what might be expected for the next seasons Explorers Camp. On the morning of August 16 they returned to "Trailer Camp" where they hooked up the trailer and moved down to Cave Springs where the Dodge truck had been left and they spent the afternoon preparing for their return to Gold King base camp.

On the 17th everyone boarded the jeeps and headed west to get as close as possible to the 1,000 ft tall spires called "the Pinnacles" and hiked around looking "at the most stupendous sight we had yet encountered."[88] They returned to Cave Spring and got the truck and headed back to Colorado, camping again outside Monticello. They made it back to Gold King Camp on August 18 and began preparations for each to head in their own direction to their homes. Explorers Camp for 1951 was over and Kenny packed up and returned to his home in Mancos, Colorado.[89]

BEHIND THE SCENES: 1952

Newsletters and general correspondence dropped off in 1952, but were sufficient enough to indicate that the winter of 1951-52 was above normal snowpack. In a letter Kenny sent to Jon Lindbergh dated January 27, 1952, Kenny asked about Jon's Alaska mountaineering trip and then expanded on his impression of the Salt Creek area and the Pinnacles and said it was beyond description and that Jon would just have to see it for himself someday. He mentioned finding and naming Explorers Arch and the plan to return to Salt Creek later that season (1952):

> A topographic map, the Elk Ridge quadrangle, purports to show the upper part of Salt but we found that some cartographer (?) must have just sat on a high butte and tried to draw in what he "saw". We found that part of the map to be complete bunk. Those natural bridges and arches we used to hear about are really there, only more so---scores of 'em. One we named Explorer Arch ranks with Rainbow Bridge, Landscape Arch and Delicate Arch to become one of the four finest examples of nature's engineering yet discovered. Another, we called the "Two Holer" is very odd--and a beauty too.[90]

Kenny then went into considerable detail about the winter snowpack:

> We are going to have what may be the finest, highest water ever on the San Juan and Colorado next Summer. We've never had such a deep sno-pac in the mountains as right now, and winter is just getting started.
>
> I suppose you have been reading or hearing about our heavy snows out here. They've made national headlines and justly so. More fun and more people killed---literally. Unless you live in the high mountain country it's hard to realize how completely isolated one can become when the jaws of the mountain passes snap shut with drifts and slides. We have been completely shut off from the east most of the winter. Almost as soon as the passes are opened up they snap shut again. Just thinking about a trip to Denver is adventure. Any way you plan to go there is at least two passes to cross and you have to figure on getting caught for a few hours on one of them--at the very best. At worst--well, there are still a few bodies under the slides in the bottom of Wolf Creek and Monarch. Guess they'll be okay there till the spring thaws.[91]

Kenny asked Jon if he would be interested in coming and helping out with a river trip or two "like Big Bill has for the past two summers." Kenny was aware of Jon's living in a tent at Stanford and he offered to ship him some river tarps to cover his tent as California was experiencing a wet winter too. He added a comment about Jon's brother – Land:

> Incidentally, that brother of yours is a first rate explorer. He has had the rather difficult job of living up to the Lindbergh tradition in camp but never once has he let it down. He is just about the happiest natured guy I have ever known; a real morale builder. I am glad it will be possible for him to be here next summer.[92]

Kenny said he had gotten fat that winter and now weighed 160 pounds. "Ain't that something?" A letter from Kenny to Land in December, 1951 also mentioned high snow pack and plans for his annual ski trip to Gold King with local boy scouts and not being able to get a car past Bill Littles place [Mayday] and then ski up to Thompson's cabin and spend a day or two and ski up to Cumberland Basin.

Kenny's letter to Colonel and Mrs. Charles A. Lindbergh dated December 28, 1951 included Land's Camp Report for 1951 which named Land as one of the two outstanding Explorers of the 1951 season; the other boy was George Hall, Jr. from Los Angeles [no relationship to Ansel Hall]. Kenny again mentioned the big snowy winter and how the last two years "drouth" [drought] had been broken, then:

> Should either or both of you ever find yourselves in this area I hope you will take the trouble to look us up. We can always find room for guests at Gold King base camp and would be most happy to entertain you. I still have hopes that, someday, Colonel Lindbergh may be able to join us for one of the expeditions and the invitation to him to accompany one of our river trips, or any of the other projects, will always remain open.[93]

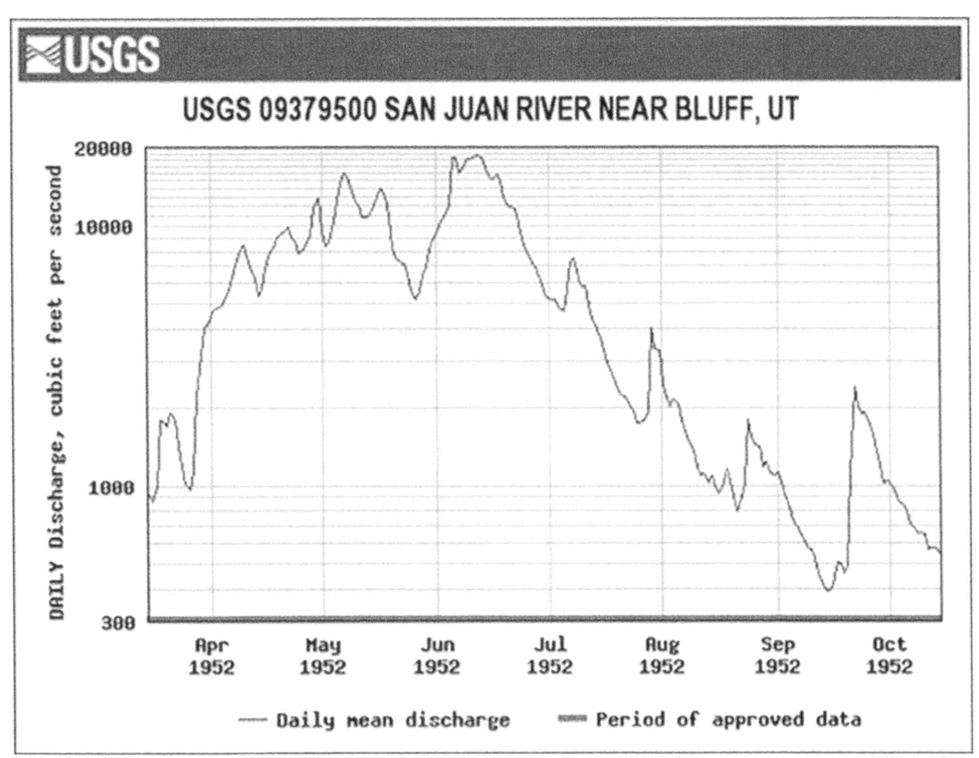

Figure 7.35 Graph shows gaged flow on San Juan River from mid-March to mid-October, 1952. Gage located at Mexican Hat but referred to as "gage near Bluff" which is the last gage above confluence 113.3 river miles downstream; see river miles in Appendix I: Table 1. (USGS Water Data)

Kenny wrote to Land Lindbergh, and enclosed the 1952 itinerary which included the San Juan and Colorado River trips (SJ&C), Cahone "Cibola City Ruins" excavations and a return to Salt Creek country to explore more canyons.[94] The winter of 1951-52 was exceptional and provided high water for most of the year and excellent boating conditions. The historic gage measurements at "the gage near Bluff" at Mexican Hat reached 8,000 cfs by early April; 10,000 cfs by May 1 and dropped back to 8,000 cfs by June 1; then it peaked at nearly 20,000 cfs in the first two weeks of June, then gradually dropped to 1,000 cfs by early August. The usual late summer monsoonal flash floods kicked the river up to 4,000 cfs and then dropped to 500 cfs in early September before an early fall flash flood kicked it up again to 5,000 cfs (Figure 7.35).[95]

Kenny finally broke away from just focusing on Explorers Camp as he and Buddy Starr and others made two runs of the Animas River from Durango to Aztec in the spring. He also took a mix of eight adults from southern California, Nebraska, Iowa and Michigan on a SJ&C trip from May 23 to May 31, 1952 as noted on his food pack list for an eight-day trip.[96]

He stated in a letter to a parent of a prospective new Explorer for that year, Bill Dumont, who had shown an interest in geology, that "The river trip just completed was a marvelous one; plenty of water, plenty of thrills and an especially congenial group of adults." [97] Kenny also mentioned that he had received a letter from a man who had three sons in Explorers Camp [the Hoyts] and the father had summed up what many parents thought of Kenny and the Explorers Camp experience regarding science:

> Science seems to be an important part of any over-all picture of Explorers Camp but I would not say that it is the principal goal. Rather, the scientific achievements are products of a summer of wonderful fun and adventure. Boys with a special interest in the sciences, or who develop such interest, as two of mine did, at camp have unparalleled opportunity to learn basic methods of field research. To me, however, the most important benefits accruing to all the boys come from the practical leadership training each receives and the self-confidence and self-sufficiency they acquire as responsible members of a successful, exploring team.[98]

Kenny received an interesting enquiry from Mrs. John Glover in May. She and her husband John had four children and their fifteen year old boy was interested in Explorers Camp and she requested more information and some references. They lived in Denver and the boy's name was David. In a hand-written letter from David he said he was most interested in fishing and high mountain streams. He had talked to Bruce Buck (a former Explorer) and wanted the names of boys that Buck had mentioned. He said "I am very anxious to learn more about camping as I want to be able to learn how to pack and camp out." [99] Kenny replied and explained fishing opportunities in mountain streams and on the river trips. He said there were seventeen boys currently signed up, including Land Lindbergh, Tommy Vaughn, George Hall and the Hoyt twins who were returning. He also mentioned Dave Scott and Pete Griffith from the 1950 Explorers Camp. David became close friends with Land, Bill Stitt and Bob Loudermilk and returned for the 1953 Explorers Camp.

Kenny invited David and his father, John and older brother, Jack on the end-of-camp Cataract Canyon river trip planned for 1953, but all this changed after the camp mutiny (see 1953 Camp). David didn't come back to camp after 1953, but he followed in his father's footsteps and became a lawyer in 1964. He married Anne Irene McGill and the couple had two sons, J.J. and Neil, and a daughter, Stephanie. In February, 2017 President Donald J. Trump nominated Neil Gorsuch to be the next Justice of the U.S. Supreme Court and he was immediately labeled a big-time *anti-environmentalist conservative* from Colorado who had grown up in Denver. It now seems more than ironic that all young David was interested in was trout fishing and hiking in the mountains and he got this opportunity at Kenny's camp in 1952-53.

Dr. Harold Lambert, M.D. served as camp physician in 1951, but wrote in May, 1952 that he would not be able to make it out that summer. Doc followed up with several letters where he asked that *if* he could break away could he and his wife stay with the Franklins.[100] Mildred replied and mentioned high water and that Charles "Dusty" Dustin had boated from Bluff to Mexican Hat in five hours! She then added:

> The boys recovered from measles in jig time, once they broke out. Did Kenny tell you that Donnie had a birthday party and was beautifully "measly" the following morning? Fortunately, all the kids present had had the measles except Doug! So that is one Childhood disease I can write off – my boys never get anything when everybody else has it.[101]

THE 1952 SOUTHWEST EXPLORATIONS CAMP

The ninth consecutive camp season began as they had in the past on the third week of June, at Gold King base camp in the La Plata Mountains. Even with all the letter writing and enquiries there were only fifteen boys listed as members at a cost of $475/person. Kenny was reeling under the back-to-back years of low-enrollment that resulted in a continual financial pinch as he began having second thoughts as to how long he could keep the camp afloat. Due to the small group size Kenny was relegated to being "chief cook and bottle washer." No other professionals could join as assistants, so he ran the whole program himself – again!

Perhaps the lack of documentation regarding any specific details about the excursions taken in 1952 was due to Kenny having to be responsible for everything else. But there was no question that the regimentation of the program followed the now tried and true formula of first conducting a week or so of orientation and mountaineering at Gold King base camp before heading to Bluff to launch the 225 mile-long SJ&C eight-day river trip. And with an excellent runoff from the previous winter's snowpack there was no question that a river trip was in order (Figures 7.36 and 7.37). The river was still running high, probably in the teens (i.e., 13,000 - 16,000 cfs) with big sand waves along most of the flatter stretches.

This particular trip was well remembered because that was the *first year that eight year old Don Ross went on a full-run river trip with his father from Bluff to Lees Ferry!* (Figure 7.38) [102] Don recalled that on this high water trip Kenny and Land Lindbergh ran all five boats through the Thirteen Foot Rapid without having to portage gear. That was a first for Kenny and he was thrilled to have successfully run the rapid fully loaded without a spill.

The return trip home was another testament as to how rugged the roadways were at that time. As per usual, the group was met by at least one truck and Mildred drove the jeep pickup with young Doug in tow. The normal plan had been to make it from Lees Ferry to Marsh Pass west of Kayenta for the first night's camp and then on to Bluff and maybe even Mancos on day two of the return shuttle. But 1952 was a wet year, and sure enough they encountered a big rain storm complete with lightning strikes near the vehicles as they made their worse leg of the return trip from Kayenta to Mexican Hat. That section was always a tough run, rain or shine, dust and sand traps, or rutted mud bogs and always lots of just plain old rocky roads. As they proceeded through the storm they saw they weren't going to get any farther than Mexican Hat, and arrived there in a pouring rain with fifteen boys in the group, as well as the Ross family and truck driver.

Figure 7.36 Explorers group at mouth of Oljeto Wash, 1952; the large flat-face tabular boulder behind the group has been completely covered by impounded San Juan River silt and mud following Powell reservoir construction in 1963. (K. Ross collection)

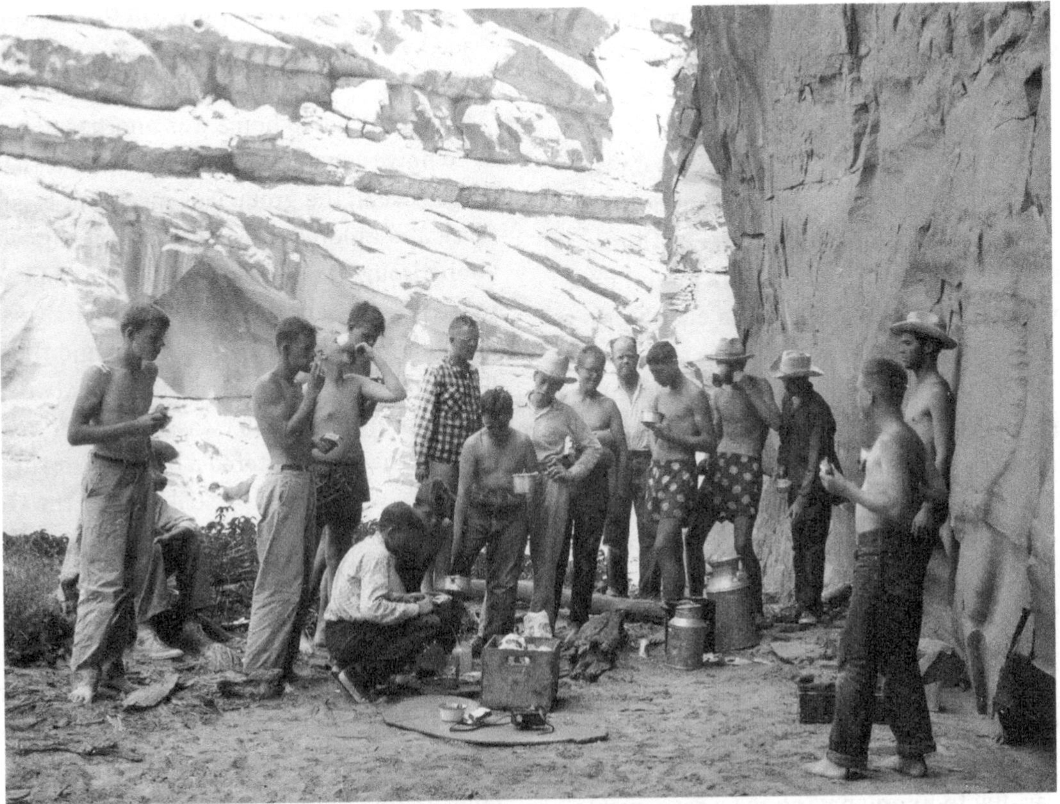

Figure 7.37 Explorers group stopped for lunch in the shade at the mouth of Oljeto Creek, 1952; Don Ross kneeling in front in long sleeved shirt. (K. Ross collection)

They knocked on the door at Moe Nevill's Mexican Hat Lodge and she greeted the soaked river rats with open arms. She not only fed the motley crew, but made room on the floor of the lodge for everyone to throw down a sleeping bag and get some rest. Moe was definitely Norman's proud mother as when Kenny bragged about having run all five boats down the Thirteen Foot Rapid fully loaded and no mishaps she wistfully replied "well, Norman would have *never* done that!"[103] The next morning, they thanked her after a warm breakfast and headed for Bluff. Such were the days then that your best made plans and itinerary were at the mercy of the elements and the not so perfect road network that were marked as highways. These were still dirt-track trails at best. But, they all got back to Gold King safe and sound and Don and Doug returned to Mancos with their mother.

The boys in camp spent several days cleaning and storing river gear, resting up and writing letters to home before the group proceeded to Cahone for another round of excavations at Cibola City. The group then returned to Salt Creek Canyon for another crack at exploring the box work of side canyons. Following that adventure they returned to Gold King camp and packed up for their trips back home. Since no Cataract trip had materialized over the year, Kenny wrapped things up at the base camp and closed it for the winter and returned to Mancos wondering what the next year would bring.[104]

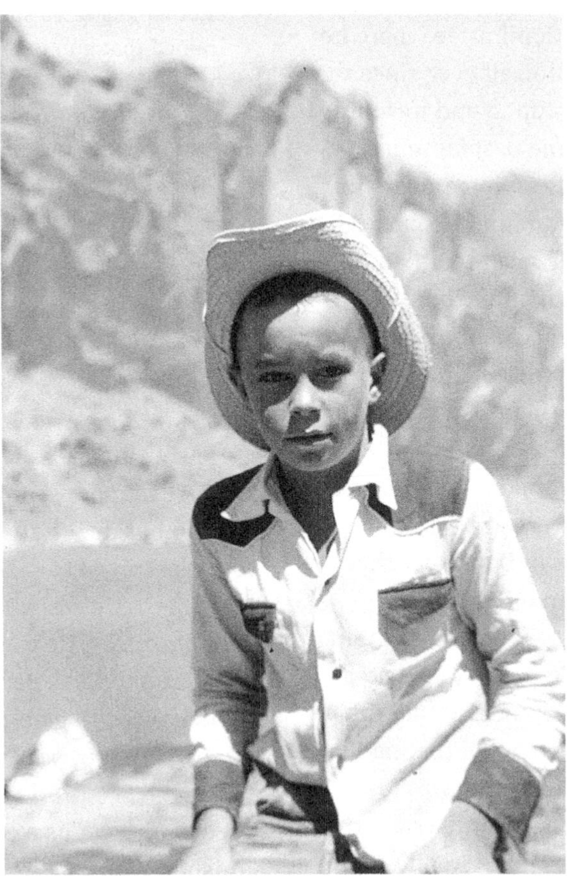

Figure 7.38 first full length SJ&C river run for eight year old Don Ross, 1952. (K. Ross collection)

WINTER 1952: STAYIN' ALIVE

In a lengthy November 16, 1952 letter from Kenny to Jon Lindbergh Kenny tried to console Jon's "recent flurry of publicity..." [regarding a *LIFE Magazine* article] as journalists continued to write about every move he made, and he told Jon that he couldn't escape his family fame forever, particularly when doing adventurous things that drew publicity and that "fame" may not be so bad and he should embrace it. Kenny said he had always tried to avoid unwanted publicity for him and his brother. Kenny then went to excessive length of praising Land's enthusiasm, overall abilities and "happy-go-lucky" personality. Kenny also mentioned how delighted he was to hear about Jon's interest in marine biology and knew he would be quite successful in following his dreams. Kenny then asked for the privilege of offering Jon's name for active membership to the Explorers Club Membership Committee where he said that Jon had "proven" himself ever since the 1947 Dark Canyon expedition up to and including his marine expedition from the past summer. Kenny thought that Explorers Club membership would be of real future value to him. He closed by inviting Jon to visit sometime and to join him on a planned Cataract Canyon trip after the 1953 camp season was over. He asked about Bill Dickinson and where he was since he hadn't heard from him. He told Jon that Mike Maule was in the Army and that his father, Stuart, had purchased a farm in Mancos and had agreed to be the camp manager for the 1953 camp season.[105]

Kenny wrote Doc Lambert in December that he had just returned from a month of volunteering his services to the Forest Service in their efforts to control Spruce Beetle (*dendroconus englemanni*) in northwest Colorado. He said the Salt Creek pictures were ruined by oil that had leaked out in his ammo can and "this was just not my year for pictures as most of my river stuff was wrecked by one of the boys." [106] Kenny also mentioned that he ran a hunting camp for a few hunters and all did well. Kenny shot his two deer by sun-up on the first morning and all the hunters "did not go home empty handed." [107] He made out alright financially too; "made good wages for myself." [108] But in a note to Bill Stitt, Kenny went full bore in his explanation of his hunt:

> That big old 30-06 felt like a stick of dry ice in my cold little paws. Just as it was light enough to shoot I topped a brushy hill and just across a shallow canyon (about 280 yards) saw six deer jumping for the brush. I ups and, "blam," gave a buck a spinal injection of lead; a second snap shot got a doe in the foreleg but she got away. Believe me, I really hurried to get over to that buck. My hands were so cold I could think of nothing better than to get them inside his warm belly. It worked too. By the time he was cleaned out and my hands were nice and comfy, two bucks came across the hill and stood right where I had first shot from. "Blam," another shattered spine – it's uncanny the way I've trained that gun to hit the spine – and by the time I got that one opened up the sun was up and I didn't have to stick my feet in him. That afternoon I got a doe to fill my cousin's license and the next morning another for my uncle – yep, both shot in the spine; it saves meat and lead; boy it's final. A Texas boy about sixteen wounded a bear just a couple of miles above Mancos. The bear charged him and tore him to pieces. It was sure a tough deal. The others hunting with him shot that bear 13 times before they killed him.[109]

He continued his letter writing to Doc Lambert that his son, Howard, Jr. had done well in camp but due to the small group sizes he would be forced to raise rates for the 1953 season. The costs were eating him up, plus he needed more enrollees. He was going to increase the fee from $495 to $525 per person. Kenny then asked if Doc wanted to go on the 1953 Cat trip. "'Tis now snowing 'popcorn' flakes. After long and almost too beautiful fall weather real winter descended upon us a couple weeks ago and has punished with the longest continuous cold spell on record – day after day of near-zero temperatures." [110] Kenny said there was three feet of snow on the ground and ended: "That September river trip did not pan out and I've just about given that gang up for good. They now want to plan one for the end of April." [111]

Doc Lambert replied Dec 29, 1952 and enclosed a check for $495 for young Howard for the next year (1953); then he mentioned that *he might get drafted in the Army* as the Korean War was going full tilt and he hoped he would be deferred due to his age. Doc wanted to know if a friend (Dan Wagner) of Howard's could come on the 1953 SJ&C river trip. Doc also said he really enjoyed Kenny's friendship ("I have so much enjoyed the last two summers with you – the companionship has been the finest and apparently we got along extremely well." [112]) Kenny replied in a January 8, 1953 letter that it was OK for Howard's pal to do a SJ&C trip for $105.

Kenny also said that Doc Zuidema would be leading the Salt Creek Canyon trip in 1953 and thought that he was a great guy who had moved to Wayne University:

> He is a great guy, formerly Editor of the Detroit News, he "assigned" himself to cover the Rainbow Bridge-Monument Valley Expedition of 1933 and became so interested in geology that he went back to school and took his PhD in that science. He has specialized in fossils, particularly insects but is originator and most persistent plugger for the term "Earth Science" to cover all aspects of geological endeavor, founder of Earth Science Institute and the Magazine "Earth Science," of which I was once Associate Editor in archaeology. Was camp geology leader in 1950 but disappointed us in 51 and 52 because of making Earth Science educational films. Says nothing can keep him away in 53. Has more vim, vigor, enthusiasm and poosh than almost any man I know.[113]

PLANS FOR 1953

By the end of 1952 Kenny had written Hank Zuidema that it had been "another touch and go year for the camp" but they had cleared enough to reduce the indebtedness [to Ansel Hall] by $2500, but ready cash was scarce. He had to cut out the "Adventures" program for the younger boys ten to thirteen years of age as it took "something special to handle the many details of a traveling camp beyond just camp experience." However, he had convinced Stuart Maule to be Camp Manager for the 1953 camp season and they had discussed a junior boys program that would be conducted mostly from Gold King base camp. He envisioned an enrollment of ten boys' age ten to twelve and to find a general science teacher to lead the group. "My idea would be to give the kids a lot of work in the mountains, with trips to Mesa Verde, Cahone Ruin, Lukachukai and Silverton for spice." [114] He thought a six week program at $300 per boy should work and wondered what Hank thought about his idea and if Hank had any geology teachers to recommend. And once again, Kenny asked if Hank could "look in on us this year" or better yet, be a science leader or Staff Advisor for the senior program.

Hank quickly replied and agreed to have his name added as a Staff Advisor on geology and he still had hopes to someday explore for "primitive mammal" bones in the Lukachukai Mountains. He said he was sending along a list of geology books that might be of interest to young boys and suggested that Kenny mimeograph the list and send along with camp information to "some of the parents you know who want their kids to know something about the earth." He continued:

> As you know, geology has all but disappeared from the lower grades, and the secondary schools, and only recently, through such groups as the Earth Science Institute, has the need for more in this line been stressed. Now the country finds itself short of earth scientists--and the government will pay any kid who has 30 hours of credit in geology a starting salary of $3,200. Top for government geologists is nearly $9,000, and they are crying for more. So there is a vocational angle, too, as well as cultural.[115]

Goodridge Bridge circa 1920s (Courtesy: Utah Historical Society)

Goodridge Bridge, 1952: note warning signs; gross load limit was 7.5 tons (Courtesy: Utah Historical Society)

8

TURNING POINT

URANIUM FRENZY

Hank mentioned the need for geologists as "uranium frenzy" was at its height at this time. He had located a Geiger counter and sold it to the Explorers Camp for $100 only a few years earlier and "looking for uranium" had been added to the camp's program in minerals identification and learning how to pan for gold. For the first time in American history, the U.S. government's Atomic Energy Commission (AEC) offered a guaranteed price for uranium ore. The Colorado Plateau was known to contain this valuable strategic mineral and a down on his luck, unemployed geologist from Texas, *Charlie Steen*, had recently located the largest deposit of high-grade uranium ore in the U.S. at Lisbon Valley in San Juan County, Utah. The story had just broken August 30, 1952 in the *Denver Post* newspaper about his *"Mi Vida Mine."* [1]

Everybody in the area knew about Charlie Steen, and when Bill Dickinson asked about him, Kenny replied:

> This guy, Charlie Steen, of Moab is quite a case. Yup, I guess you might call him a millionaire, even tho he might find it hard to rake up 10,000 cash. He certainly stumbled onto the real stuff and is now in the process of consolidating claims, getting rid of partners, etc. He is a funny little guy with brains and a rapidly growing noggin. Seems to be a rancorous rooster who gets a big kick out of putting others in their place by saying "what's your price on the whole goddam business, I'll buy you out." And doing it too. I understand he has his bankers on needles and pins all the time. He is set upon convincing the world that he has "The biggest goddam mountain of U-ranium in the world". It frustrates others to think he is right and he knows it. He is going great guns and, because of what he has underground, he will probably continue. Smart as the devil--literally. Has been kicked around a lot and there are plenty who fear to see such a dog have his day, and with good reason.[2]

Closer to Kenny's operations north of Mexican Hat, the Mokee Dugway[3] was cut down the south face of Cedar Mesa (a 1400 ft vertical escarpment) in the mid-1950s and was originally known as "Isabel Hill" (named after the Isabel Construction Co.) and locally pronounced *IZ-Bel* Hill.[4] The dugway was cut so that uranium ore could be transported by truck and trailer from the Happy Jack mine and smaller mines in White Canyon west of Natural Bridges down off of Cedar Mesa to the nearest mill located at Halchita, across the San Juan River south of Mexican Hat. The old White Canyon Uranium mill had ceased operations in 1952 due to some contract disputes with the AEC. Besides, rumors continued that the Glen Canyon dam was going to be built and the village that had grown down at the mill site would be inundated, thus the need to transport the ore down off Cedar Mesa.

The Happy Jack mine was purchased in 1946 by a road contractor from Monticello, Joe Cooper and his partner and father-in-law Fletcher Bronson. They paid $500 to buy the copper claim, but when they started to work the ore, they found that it was contaminated with **vanadium** and **uranium**! The copper was so low-grade they tried to sell the mine, but then the AEC announced its uranium buying program. Cooper and Bronson put the mine into production for uranium and the Happy Jack mine earned them $25 million.[5]

The primary reason a new steel bridge at the Mexican Hat crossing was built in 1953 was because the old suspension bridge couldn't handle the weight (see chapter divider photos). On June 5, 1953, Bill Weidman, driving a truck hauling a thirteen-ton compressor was north-bound and the heavily loaded truck lost its brakes as it dropped down the steep grade of the Halgaito anticline. The driver knew that the old suspension bridge had a warning sign of a seven-ton limit. Anyway, as the story goes, when the truck reached the center, the bridge gave way and truck and driver dropped fifty feet through the suspension bridge. The driver jumped out and although badly shaken lived to tell the story.[6] Doug Ross swore that there was a weird rounded rock below Pontiac Wash (the first side canyon on RL below the bridge that had an old 50s vintage Pontiac car pushed over the cliff and into the wash) that he thought might have been the compressor, but if it was there it has been eroded and washed away.

Anyway, when the truck dropped through the old bridge it helped highlight the long standing need for a sturdier structure to bear the ten to twelve trucks that crossed daily with their loads of uranium ore. The state repaired the cable bridge temporarily, but within a year and with the financial assistance from the AEC, to the tune of $180,000, a new steel and concrete bridge spanned the river.[7] The new steel arched bridge spanned 190 ft over the San Juan River and was not common to other Utah bridges (Figure 8.1). Based on its rarity, it was considered significant as one of relatively few bridges of this type and was designated a "Utah Historic Bridge" in 1954 even though it didn't meet "historical" criterion.[8] But as historian Allan Kent stated, "roads in San Juan County were built because of the need for natural resource development." [9]

The old suspension bridge that was adjacent to the new steel bridge finally collapsed in the winter of 1975. It collapsed under its own weight one night and there were bridge cables and timbers with big iron spikes in the river for many months [I know, because in 1976, I had to row my boat through a mile long obstacle course immediately downstream where the old bridge stood].

In an article that Hank Zuidema published in the 1952 *Earth Science Digest* where he emphasized the deplorable lack of earth sciences in the secondary schools and added a promotional over-view of the value of Kenny's "outdoor labor-atory" he stated that "Geiger counters will be carried along, as the route leads through an area where deposits of uranium are being worked and where additional deposits are being sought." [10]

Hank also replied to Kenny's question regarding funding through *Jim Handy Co.* for "action movies on running the river:"

> The ambitious plan I had to produce some really good geological-commercial films didn't get needed support, when the top guy in the Handy outfit found he could get more cash faster with such accounts as Chevrolet and Frigidaire, and when I found myself writing scripts around ice boxes and storage batteries, and doing gags for Dinah Shore, who is not very appetizing at close sight! I considered what we were put on earth for and went back to the rocks. But we did pave the way with some pretty good stuff, the story of iron ore from earth to chassis.[11]

Kenny immediately replied in January, 1953 and said he had been busy in the dark room[12] making a batch of two hundred-forty "8 x 10s," and asked if Hank "manages to come out" could he possibly bring a 16 mm movie camera as "George Pierrot, of World Adventure Series, wrote recently that he would use a camp movie on the explorations if we can add some close-up action to the really good stuff we already have. George would use it on his weekly television show. 'Twould be a wonderful publicity break if we can just add those shots." [13]

Figure 8.1 Mexican Hat "Historical" steel arch Bridge dedicated 1954 (Courtesy: UDOT photo)

In February, Kenny sent a letter to Hank in which he said it had been a long time since they had a boy from the Detroit area, but the previous year he had a "fine lad from East Lansing by the name of Frank K. Thorp. His father is Frank Thorp, Jr., Professor (Research), Animal Pathology, Michigan State College." He provided an address and mentioned two boys from the upper Midwest who had been at camp the past two years: Frank Haynes and Michael Hers.[14]

UPSETTING MAGAZINE ARTICLES

In the early 1950s telegrams were still reserved for fast important messaging, and expensive when compared to a six-cent air mail stamp for a letter. So Kenny was somewhat taken aback when he received a *heated fifty-plus word* telegram on February 9 from Bill Dickinson that said he "emphatically had nothing to do with Sunday supplement article on Jon in *This Week Magazine* mentioning you." [15] A hand-written letter soon followed on February 11 where Bill spelled out the reason he was so distraught:

> Here's the deal on the article on Jon in "This Week." Last winter Carol Barnes wanted to write a character sketch of Jon for an English course or some damn thing. He sent her over to talk to me about the river because I had my pictures with me. She was in the Alpine Club [at Stanford University] and got to know Jon awhile and then, since she seemed interested, just plain rivers. Later she asked if she could read our notes and I innocently let her.
>
> Well, the result of the character sketch was the article. I know Jon is mad as hell because he started into the whole thing in friendly good faith. The article is, however, much better than I ever thought she could write. The part about the river is understandably garbled since it all came from the

brief interview a year ago, with the exception of one passage which is damn near a direct quote of our notes which annoys me no end. Neither Jon or I, so far as I know, ever saw the article until it hit print. As long as she was going to pull a stunt like that, I wish she had let us check the article for accuracy. Oh well, at any rate we are evidently record-holders for the trip thru Cataract – she has us running 67 rapids in one day! And – oh, yes – how is the boy scout five coming along, "camper"?

Hope you aren't too griped about the erratic part about the river. I was mad at her quoting me and the notes at first, neither of which did she have any authorization for. But now I sort of chuckle at the whole thing. I don't see why they don't tell Jon about these articles they write so he could correct the wild inaccuracies that crop up. He got a copy of "Life" issue the day before it hit the newsstands.[16]

Bill was in the Air Force stationed at Forbes AFB in Topeka, Kansas and didn't like it. He had been in San Antonio for a while and was about to leave for a month's stay in Puerto Rico before returning to Forbes. He said that overall he had a good deal as he was a "cartographic officer" and left his mailing address and "Incidentally, where's Charley and how is your wife and the little ones." [17]

Of course all this news led Kenny to reply immediately:

Believe me, Lieutenant, that wire of yours sent me looping the loop. Interpreted it that someone had been pirating my files. As you know, after protecting the Lindbergh clan from embarrassment lo these seven years, any publicity involving this end of the line and over which I have no control, starts the old blood boiling. Having not yet seen or even heard of the article on our Jon--and willing to imagine the worst, I nearly flew off in all directions at once.

Ruthanne Cox, a cute little blonde who was on last spring's pre-season trip down the S-J&C, sent me a copy of the article from Covina, Calif. about two days **after** your gram. Boy was I relieved. I agree that it isn't too bad except for the snide trickery. Am in perfect agreement with the Lindbergh's that any private person, not a criminal, should have the right to control what is said about him in the press. You know the gal and I don't but mister, I'd like to have a certain would-be jennet of a journalist by the neck---if she has one.

Better still---I would like to turn her loose in a boat to run 67 Cataract rapids in one day---without a paddle. That'd larn her.

Just to keep the record straight; I have to this date received exactly 17 copies of last weeks This Week. Wot'll I do with 'em; send 'em to mom an pop Lindbergh for their scrap book? Oooooo, what I just said! [18]

Kenny invited Bill to come out for a river trip if he could get a couple weeks off. He also said that it looked like they would have quite a crowd of boys that year, and it was about time! He mentioned some of the boys that were scheduled to return and that this year would be Land Lindbergh's fourth season – a record. Kenny said he was glad the Air Force wouldn't be a career decision for Bill as it "doesn't quite fit my idea of the thing for you to do." He also asked about a rumor he had heard that Bill had married "and well on the way to becoming the father of triplets or something equally repulsive." Although light-hearted and somewhat sarcastic in tone, Kenny was obviously bothered by the Carol Barnes article when he uncharacteristically signed off as "Another Camper." [19]

Bill Dickinson replied with another hand-written letter in which he said he was glad to hear that "Charley got out of this rat race" [military duty] and "had gotten things squared away." He said he would be getting out of the Air Force in 1954 and planned to return to school and get his Master's Degree on the GI Bill, but would have to put in two years of ROTC. Bill then threw a zinger when he said "he's not married yet" but it wouldn't be long and to please not say anything about this to the "fellow campers" or it would be all over the damn country. He said his fiancé was a "great gal and you will like her when you see her." Bill then turned to explaining his Puerto Rico assignment and how he would not be able to make any river trips until 1954 or '55 but he was raring to tackle Cataract Canyon again and closed his letter by saying, "Oh yeah – if you take Carol Barnes along, you can make it a one day trip. Hallelujah! Ignorance is bliss and all that...." [20]

Kenny turned his attention to ask Bill's permission to use the 1949 Cataract Canyon notes for an article to be published in the "Denver Pest" and said he had received Jon's telegraphed permission to do so. However, Kenny wasn't going to write it. He planned to turn over the writing responsibility to "Doc" Zuidema and reminded Bill that Zuidema was the geologist who was on the first river trip they were on in 1950. He continued:

> Doc is a geologist but before that was Editor of the Detroit News and still does a lot of free-lance writing, and is plenty slick. Also, he is very understanding and sympathetic concerning the "Lindbergh viewpoint" and would not permit anything he handled to become a "Lindbergh story". He has done several articles (short) on camp since Land has been here but has never built him up more than the others. Once casually mentioned that he is the son of the "lone eagle", and thats all.
>
> Jon's permission is predicated upon my volunteered promise that the Cat story would be simply one of **three** fellows who had the adventure and that nothing sensational from his viewpoint would be permitted. Nevertheless, he realizes that his being one of the three names will have considerable effect upon whether or not it is published. Poor guy!
>
> Now, I want your permission, if you will grant it. That way things will be square all-round. Better still, I wish you would put down some of the thots on what you got from it, your previous water experience, how much you think the general explorer training you and Jon had at camp helped with the success of the trip and your enjoyment of it. If you go this far you might also put down what you think of me as the ogre back of training the fellows in out of doors work, safety, techniques, etc. You know damn well I'm not "fishin". In fact, if you would rather I didn't see what you write just send it direct to H. P. Zuidema, 130 Lawrence, Avenue, Detroit 2, Mich. This sort of info and anything else you can think of will help him do a better job of presenting the story in case he will take it on.
>
> I guess I never did give you my "expanded version" of the Cat log. Meant to. Soon after you sent me my typewritten copy I sat down and translated its somewhat telegraphic style into a little fuller explanation of each point. Now, with this story possibility coming up, I am recopying and adding several paragraphs in reference to previous Ex Camp river training---the things you, Jon and I have discussed about the "Galloway technic" versus the paddle technic we have developed (incidentally, the latter will probably be the subject of much discussion in Marston's forthcoming book on the rivers and rivermen of the West); how we felt and what we did at #26 and at Dark Canyon, etc., etc.. When I've done the worst I can to the log I'll send a copy to you.
>
> I might just as well tell you that Marston is entirely favorable to the paddle technic we have developed. He plans to go along the post-season Cat trip just so he can learn it. I believe that he will conclude we really have something. In fact he has already told me that we probably have the best thing ever to come out in river technics. Nice to know, isn't it? Altho I had started working on this before you came into it, I am glad to say that I feel you and Jon have both contributed many of the tricks that make it more useful. Old Marston's viewpoints may not be acceptable to everyone but he **is** the only one who has cared a damn about studying all the technics and comparing them. He may be a self-appointed chronicler of the rivers but his ideas will have importance---at least for a few years to come. He is a fussy and opinionated old devil and will probably make a nuisance of himself on the Cat venture but I must admit that he knows infinitely more about the rivers than anyone else and I expect to learn a lot from him---particularly from the historical angle. We have developed a most interesting correspondence on that already. Brotherrrr, did we ever miss a flock of inscriptions near various Cat rapids. Probably turned our backs on them to take a piss.

Among other things, he tells me that Lon G. Turner (probably inscription at Dark) took boat loads of freight from Green River (Utah) to Hite, several times in 1907--- ALONE! What a man!

I understand that the topo job on Dark will start in June. It also appears that USGS will act favorably on such names as Tinaja Canyon, Thousand Springs, Canyon del Agua Verde--or Lime Creek, Mummy alcove, etc..

Yer gonna hafta hurry if you want to write the paper on the Gypsum salt block. Everybody's gettin' inta the act! There's gonna be a lot of dead geologists.[21]

The last thought in Kenny's letter related to Bill Dickinson's interest in the geology of Gypsum Creek and Dark Canyon – areas he had hiked in his Explorers Camp days and how he was going to "kill" any geologist that beat him to it. However, the area did get the attention of the USGS topographers and provisional maps were upgraded. In addition, my mentor, Donald L. Baars and several other geologists from *Shell Oil Co.* in the late 1950s beat Bill Dickinson to Dark Canyon, Cross Canyon, Gypsum Canyon, Red Lake Canyon, Spanish Bottom, Elephant Canyon, and Young's Canyon by mapping, describing and sampling detailed measured sections. These detailed stratigraphic studies included identifying key microfossils, particularly foraminifera known as *fusulinids*, that helped refine the precise ages of the Permian and Pennsylvanian stratigraphy.

The article written by Carol Barnes for *This Week Magazine* didn't just hit Kenny's eyes, but he was informed in a whimsical way by none other than Hank Zuidema when he wrote:

Well, Well,--my champ hits the big time!

I hope you liked the mention in This Week, but I would have given anything to have had them put in "Explorers Camp, Mancos." My impression, and I don't know the inside story, was that the little gal writer "conned" Jon into talking. I think she went a little overboard on relating too many eccentricities, let us say, on the part of the boy, because I assume he is just a normal collegian who wants to live his own life.[22]

Geology was on Hank Zuidema's mind as well, as stated earlier where he lamented about "the deplorable lack of earth sciences in the secondary schools."

I have had another brainstorm that may work to the advantage of your operation. As you know, I have been drumming up interest in geology and natural resources in this area for years and have been slowly "infiltrating" these ideas into the minds of the dunderheads who are called university administrators.

For some years, the Wayne geology department has been struggling to get some summer camp facilities. I think a cooperative plan with your Gold King operation could be worked out--good graduate students would do geological work in areas around the camp and perhaps the University would finance their board and housing. It would publicize the camp and give you your choice of senior counselors. Anthropologists and biologists also could be interested. When the thing has gelled a bit in my mind, I'll outline the ideas for you for criticism and comment.[23]

"Doc" Zuidema closed by saying that Fred Black would help in securing funding for his "brainstorm" and he relished the thought of spending the summer in the Four Corners where he could focus on some paleontological collections and "the chance to do some real constructive work in the rocks." [24]

But the continued publicity of Jon Lindbergh, including an article in *LIFE Magazine* was what was on Kenny's mind. He was angry with journalists who continued to hound the young man. In an earlier letter from Kenny to Jon Lindbergh[25] Kenny had mentioned Jon's "recent flurry of publicity..." as journalists continued to write about every move he made. Now, in the letter to Hank he explained this latest big splashy article in *LIFE Magazine* and he really let Hank know his (and Jon's) true feelings:

Poor Jon. His first inkling of the Life article of last Fall came as he walked down the street and saw his own face shrieking at him from a news stand. Was most upset. This Week caught him equally unaware, as it did everyone involved except the author. A slicker, more deceitful, more unethical stunt has never been pulled by even the yellowest of the Yellers. Despite her statement that the article was prepared with Jon's knowledge and consent, it most certainly was not---and there is hell to pay. The material (factual, that is) and the photos were all obtained under false pretense. The "little gal" was a classmate of Jon's alright. She was a journalism major and on the pretext of needing adventure material for a class assignment story, pumped Jon for info on the Alaskan trip of the summer of 51--swearing -- or so I understand-- that it would never be released to the public. The pics were obtained from one of Jon's companions on that trip but he says he gave no permission for their use and I understand is about to sue. She got the log of our Cataract Canyon trip from Bill Dickinson-- whom you have met. He did not let her keep the log but only to jot down ideas from it. The result of that was a very garbled MESS and gives Jon credit for working out the particular rapids running technique I have been developing for the past seven years-- and which I taught to Lindbergh and Dickinson. Both are practically in tears over that. One touch of humor saves nothing because it was the result of not knowing what she was talking about. She quotes Jon directly as saying---- "We ran sixty-seven rapids that day." I know Jon did not even discuss the Cat trip with her. She got the misinfo from the log and 67 is the total number of rapids in all of Cat and took us four days to run. Poor gal apparently did not even know that Cataract Canyon is a part of the Colorado. Jon says----"Wish I had that jennet [a female donkey] of a would-be journalist by the neck---or, better still---you could put her in a boat without a paddle and send her thru 67 rapids in one day."

So you see, your journalistic intuition that the author "conned" Jon into talking was absolutely correct. Also, you are dead right about the kid being--or trying to be-- just a "normal collegian". You are pretty good mister!

Now----as a result of all the above, I have at last asked and received permission from Dickinson and Lindbergh to publish the log, or a story based on the log of our Cataract Canyon trip. This was a post-season trip these two boys and I planned and carried out in 1949---and it is pretty thrilling. As you may know, Cataract Canyon is that portion of the river that was long ago nicknamed the "Graveyard of the Colorado". The log was mostly kept by Dickinson and I am presently trying to expand its telegraphic style into something complete enough to base a story upon. In fact this is almost finished. As yet there is no story, and while I would like to be able to write it myself, I will be unable to do so at no presently foreseeable time. If I turned the log (expanded version) over to you would you be willing to do something with it--say an interview with me type of thing? Or, what would you suggest? There are plenty of good black and white pics (50 or so) and it is possible that this is Sat. Eve. Pest [Saturday Evening Post] material. It will have to be handled carefully from the Lindbergh angle. Jon telegraphed me a few days ago---"Go ahead with a Cataract article will write soon." This was in reply to my letter assuring him that I would guarantee that any story based upon the log would not be a "Lindbergh story" but would only give him a rightful credit with the other two of us for an adventure that is newsworthy. Neither title or headline would mention the Lindbergh name without full mention of the other two. His letter, a day or so later, presents suggestions which pretty well show his point of view. For one---"I think that any story should be prefaced by a brief but pointed exposition of the kind of exploring training you give the boys on the expeditions and that it be made clear that the Cat adventure is not the dangerous sort of thing that you would permit any of the Explorers to experience until they were perfectly trained." Readers should understand that this was a special affair that you made possible for Bill and me only because we knew how to work with you almost perfectly. Another---"In spite of our all sharing the planning and cost, you were the leader and should get the credit for making it a safe trip. I think it should be written up in such a way that the camp and you get recognition for giving the boys good training. If anyone gets played up more than the other it should be you." "I would hate it (and you too) if this got out of hand. I like to think that something I have a part in gets credit and me for my part in it but this crap of playing up just LINDBERGH is going to ruin everything. If that bull shit don't stop it will take all the pleasure I get out of doing the kind of things you and I like to do."

Thems his sentiments and I agree with them and believe that you do too. Anyhow, if you want to do the story and try to keep things under control the material is all yours. What say? Say it airmail quick, willya? Jon will be 21 next Aug. 16.

Another thing. This is the first time Jon has ever given specific permission to publish anything he has had a part in. He indicates that he is absolutely against Life or This Week getting anything. I don't entirely agree---but---.

I realize that it may be a little foolish of me to want to see things his way but I do--because I feel pretty much the same anyway. I don't have to get his permission but I like it that way. I've protected him for a long time and I guess I want to keep on.

Enough of that for now. Your idea re a cooperative plan between the University and us at Gold King sounds great. When it jells I'll be all ears. I am sure it could be worked out from our end. It seems to me to have endless possibilities.

Have you noticed lately that I have been building up the term SOUTHWEST EXPLORATIONS and keeping Explorers Camp subordinate to it? This idea has come slowly and is due to my discovering that the boys all like to use the name of the program instead of the camp when telling their friends about their summer experiences. You can see why, I'm sure. Need to keep the word camp, however, to attract attention of parents looking for that sort of thing.

Charles (ours) is now out of the Air Force--but a little too late to feel that he wanted to go back to CU full time this year. So he took an apartment in Boulder, a job with a big paper house in Denver (at what seems to me a fabulous salary) and is taking nite classes at the University in preparation for starting (next Sept) his graduate work in journalism. Commuting between Boulder and the big city, a full-time job, and night classes-- plus an insistence on a full social life, is a bit thick. Just got back from a week with him and am fully ready to slow down again to my pace. Oh to be young and speeding on life's hiway---instead of skidding.

Hasta la vista,

KIR [26]

THE DOCK MARSTON LETTERS (Part I)

Throughout this entire foray regarding the Lindbergh con-job and exploitation by *LIFE* and Carol Barnes, Kenny was contacted by river historian, Otis "Dock" Marston who was compiling the history of navigating the rivers of the west. His introduction was to "San Juanner Ken" where he immediately told Kenny,

> You are too modest in your estimate of fees for dude runs of Cat. The Wright-Rigg outfit has a full booking for their Cat run in June and the price is $600 per passenger.[27]

Marston then said that he had asked Ansel to ask Kenny for the film from the 1933 RBMV San Juan run as well as the journal of the party.[28] Dock also asked about the various San Juan trips Kenny had made; how many; when was the first; did he have dates? He said he understood that Kenny used 7-man neoprene rafts and wanted to know what other equipment he had used. Dock self-invited himself [by asking Ansel] about going on a Cat trip with Kenny that season "as there are a number of points I would like to check. Do you know the location of Corona Arch? Have you checked the various inscriptions in Cat Canyon?" He closed by saying "If I go, I'll try not to be a headache." [29]

Not to be outdone or intimidated, Kenny replied to Dock Marston as "Dear Siltstrainer" and then proceeded to say he would be pleased to have him as a "guest" on his Cat trip even though he hadn't been "invited", or on "any of my other modest little river junkets."[30] Kenny mentioned that he had met Marston in Dolores when he (Marston) had given a river lecture there and then flattered Marston when he said he thought Dock knew infinitely more about the rivers than Kenny did and he would like to learn more.

Kenny then proceeded to answer some of Marston's questions and requests and went into considerable detail about his rather arcane dual stern-paddler technique he was so proud of (at the time):

> I will put aside what meager material I have on my river trips but, except for a good log of one Cataract trip and one SJ&C run, there will not be very much. Beginning with the spring of 1947, I have made 19 San Juan trips, four of them starting at Shiprock and all the rest at Bluff; Two Cat runs--Aug. 29 to Sept. 8, 1949, Aug. 27 to Sept 7, 1951[31]; two hi-water Animas trips, Durango to Aztec, May, 1951; two Arkansas River runs, from Salida to Canyon City--thru Royal Gorge--June 1951. Besides 7 & 10-man neoprene landing boats, I have used 2-man Fold-Boat Kayaks (on occasion) but don't think much of them except for "thrills". Frankly, I like to think of myself as a practical riverman rather than as a sportsman.
>
> The journal of the 1933 SJ&C trip, RBMV, will turn up in the course of my spare-time search of the general RBMV files. Am trying to do this systematically but perhaps ought to start at the wrong end---where it will probably be anyway. The movie of that trip could be anywhere. Am afraid Ansel has unconsciously "hidden" it among his private mementos---but he thinks not.
>
> I plan to use 5 (or 6) 12-ft Landing boats (I insist they are not rafts) on the Aug-Sept. Cat trip. We have 8 of these, all canvas decked and equipped with waterproof cases, ready for the roughest kind of going. I have found these better--run by my method--than the 10-man, or 15-ft. boats, or the Cataract run. We run entirely with paddles---wielded by two men seated side by side at the stern. UNorthodox? Certainly.
>
> And just as certainly, non-Galloway. But damned practical. With one man commanding and one simply an extra set of muscles and a paddle, these little boats, even with a thousand pound load, are maneuverable as a cricket. If this method has disadvantages they can be offset by careful conning and skill. The big advantage is the ability to DRIVE, forward, right, left, or broadside without preliminary maneuvering (the motor-boat idea). The precision of control is really remarkable, and for working in very close, rocky waters it is superior to the Galloway method. I find that being able to drive forward sometimes means---all other conditions taken into consideration---the difference between a decision to run or to line a particular rapid at a particular stage of water. As an example, I have several times ran---not lined---Government Rapid when the water was so low that the only channel was the one slightly to right of center and which is so twisty that a "Nevills boat" could not have maneuvered it without hitting at least three rocks. Also, at near high water last June, my prize protégé boatman, Land Lindbergh and I ran 5 loaded boats thru the entire length of the 13-footer and only had to bail two of them. I'll probably never do that again because it seems unlikely that one would ever be there when the water was just right, twice in a lifetime.
>
> You did not ask for information on my technique (Oh no, not "Developed Technique") and by this time you are probably thinking, "Oh Lord---Another of these river nuts gone loose on the subject of his technique and his boats." I guess that must be the fate of all really enthusiastic rivermen. As we grow older and gain experience we ought to get over it---but we don't. As THE chronicler of the rivers, I suppose you have grown used to this.
>
> Anyhow, now that I've gone so far I may as well add that I believe that the Galloway style of boat and the "Galloway method" needs a pretty complete re-examination. I've used the latter and developed the usual proficiency at it--but have abandoned it for my own use. It is a good method but, while it has been several times refined, it has never been basically improved---not even by Norm Nevills, who was certainly remarkably proficient in it. I have heard of one fellow---his name slips me---who regularly runs the upper green, who has thrown it overboard completely (or so I understand) and now faces upstream thru everything. It seems that he too feel the need of being able to DRIVE. I sympathize with his reasoning but don't feel that he has much of anything.
>
> Just in case it might possibly further entice you to run Cataract with us--- on all my trips we EAT and what we eat is COOKED. I am a bit of a crank on the matter of plenty of good, simple food, properly prepared. Ask Howard Welty about this.
>
> Am planning two pre-camp-season San Juan-Colorado runs this spring. Have not yet set definite dates because several interested people have asked me to hold off. As it looks now, they will be launched at Bluff during the last week in April and

> the third week in May. Because of Explorers Camp obligations I dare not look upon these pre- season trips in the same way as do Riggs & Wright. My operating policy is one of sound preparation, careful execution, and I expect passengers to consider themselves as crew members---along the lines All my trips with the boys are operated. The fee of 150 bucks is admittedly low but quite okay with me. I am not really trying to cut out those who consider their trips as an important part of making their livelihood.[32]

Marston replied to "San Juanner Kenny" where he stated he would try to make the Cat trip, but a pending photo-op trip with Disney was in the works. He then described where Corona Arch was [so why did he ask?] and all the inscription locations he was aware of in Cataract Canyon including those by Lon G. Turner (1907), the first Steamer (1892 or 1893), the 1891 Best inscription at the top of Mile-long, and the Kolb names painted on the wall above Rapid #26 (first noted by Marston in 1945). He then went into the history of Flavell running bow first in Grand Canyon in 1896, then Galloway and Richmond following through a few months later using the Galloway technique and that Stone claimed to have run stern-first before Galloway. He said that the Swain-Bus Hatch parties' row rapids bow-first but face the stern and that Bus Hatch was now using rubber on the Yampa but their trips may be using the name of Frazier-Eddy.

He said that Moulty Fulmer built a double-ended boat that he had been using on the San Juan and the upper Green and had seen him run it in Desolation-Gray and "it is way ahead of anything I have handled." [33]

> I put in a lot of miles in Nevills queer craft and do not think they have outstanding merit. They are good enough if one is too lazy to make them better. I have caught hell from Jim Rigg because I criticized this equipment. I don't think anything is perfect and I think we still have a lot to learn about river technics.
>
> I agree that Nevills did not make any particular improvement in the Galloway technic. I can't find evidence that he improved it at all. Some parts of what he chose to call the Nevills Technic I would not accept and he gave me up as a cranky old fool that had to be left alone to go his way.
>
> The Wright-Rigg outfit has me on the blacklist for not going 100% for what they have adopted from Nevills. They have changed virtually nothing.[34]

Marston wrote again in July in which he said he regretfully wouldn't be able to make the Cataract Canyon trip due to the Disney commitment. He asked that Kenny pay particular attention to locate some springs between Dark Canyon and the Dirty Devil as they had not been spotted on a map.[35]

THE 1953 SOUTHWEST EXPLORATIONS SEASON

The *1953 10th Annual Southwest Exploration* promotional leaflet announced the nine weeklong camps planned from June 21 to August 22 would include: (two back-to-back) 225 mile river expedition boat trips through the canyons and rapids of the San Juan and Colorado rivers (SJ&C) from Bluff to Lees Ferry; continued archaeological investigations of a large, ancient Pueblo Indian village near Cahone, Colorado; mountaineering and forestry in the San Juan Mountains plus a four-day saddle pack trip; Indian Ceremonials in late July where everyone would go to Lukachukai, Arizona to join the Navajo in celebration of their annual "Entah" with feasting, summer healing ceremonies and dances, and an all-Indian rodeo; and finally the Canyon Exploration segment where the Explorers were to divide into two parties to hike and explore "the mysterious canyon gorges" of Dark Canyon and Salt Creek Canyon.

Staff members included: Ken Ross, Camp Director; Stuart Maule, Camp Manager; Henry Zuidema, Geologist from Wayne Univ; Ansel Hall, General Advisor; Bill Fulton, camp cook; Alfred

Hoyt, 1950-51 and Land Morrow Lindbergh 1950-52 Junior leaders. Cost: $525.00 [36]

The 1953 camp season was one of the busiest for Kenny, particularly following the previous two lean years plus the expansive letter writing hubbub about Jon Lindbergh. Kenny's records indicate he had thirty-two boys listed as members at a cost of $525/person. But Kenny was ready and had a reasonably full staff, minus only a bona fide archaeologist for the excavations at the Cahone ruins. Of the thirty-two boys enrolled for Explorers Camp, thirteen were returning for their second, third or even fourth seasons. Kenny called the returning boys "Viejo's" and the new boys "Nuevo's." In addition to the formal announcement brochure, Kenny wrote an informal newsletter directed toward those who were returning to camp:

> We have driven up and down that steep, one-way road over Comb Ridge for the last time. The tortuous road up the stream bed of Snake Canyon is a thing of the past. Now a wide, new road connects Blanding and Monument Valley and we can skim from Bluff to Mexican Hat, Utah in minutes instead of hours. Butler Wash is bridged and the new Bridge across the San Juan at the Hat is high, high above the old one. In a way it's nice. I guess its progress – but darn it, I do hate to see civilization messing up that country.[37]

Although there was normal snowpack in the central Colorado Mountains, the snowpack in the San Juan Mountains was well below normal. The Historical USGS Discharge graph for the San Juan River (Gage 09379500 near Bluff, UT) [38] showed that the San Juan River never exceeded 9,000 cfs for the year, and it had dropped precipitously below 1,000 cfs in late June with some minor late summer spikes due to monsoons before bottoming out at less than 200 cfs in late September. Kenny prepared the readers for low water:

> Lots less snow on the San Juan watershed than last spring, so there will be no "cushy" river trips this year. Instead, every rapid will be a battle and we will be straining eyes and seventh senses to find those just-right channels that will get us thru without "barring up." You can bet that the "Death March Thru Paiute Farms" will be no joke. Then there will be Government Rapid, Paiute Rapid, the 13-footer, and a dozen more --- all showing their teeth and fighting back. We've whipped them before at low water so I reckon we can do it again. With a good road to Mex Hat I am almost tempted to start the trip there. However, the section of river between Bluff and the Hat makes a wonderful "shakedown" stretch for new boatmen. I would kinda hate to miss any of the rapids in it--- especially the 8-footer and "Gyp" in low water.[39]

Kenny explained how the canyoneering segment would work out that season by dividing the group into two groups; the younger less experienced group would hike into Salt Creek Canyon and the older, more experienced group would tackle Dark Canyon by entering from the north off of the Dark Canyon Plateau. That approach had yet to be attempted and by doing so they would have covered all three approaches to entering Dark Canyon. Kenny led the group and mentioned it had been three years since he had been down Dark Canyon. He also mentioned that he had jeeped into Salt [Creek] Canyon[40] country the previous September to reconnoiter and see if there was a way to reach the Colorado River through the Pinnacles section. He found the country interesting from the Pinnacles west to Chesler Park and into the "Grabens" area via Devil's Lane "rift valley." Geologically, the Grabens area consists of an arcuate series of fault-bounded strike valleys formed by the dissolution and collapse of the underlying Paradox salt section, and isn't strictly a "rift" (Figure 8.2). He *thought* a jeep could make it to the river but it would be "very, very rough going." [41]

Kenny also mentioned that another Cataract Canyon river trip was planned after the regular camp season since there was a normal snowpack in the central Colorado Mountains that should provide adequate water levels. Besides, there had been lots of interest given by eleven "Viejo's" and their fathers. If some "Nuevo's" proved themselves as capable boatmen on the earlier San Juan River trips he would consider including them too. Kenny, at forty-four years old thought he was getting "fat," and stated that his weight was now 163 pounds and his waist size was 33-1/2 inches." [42]

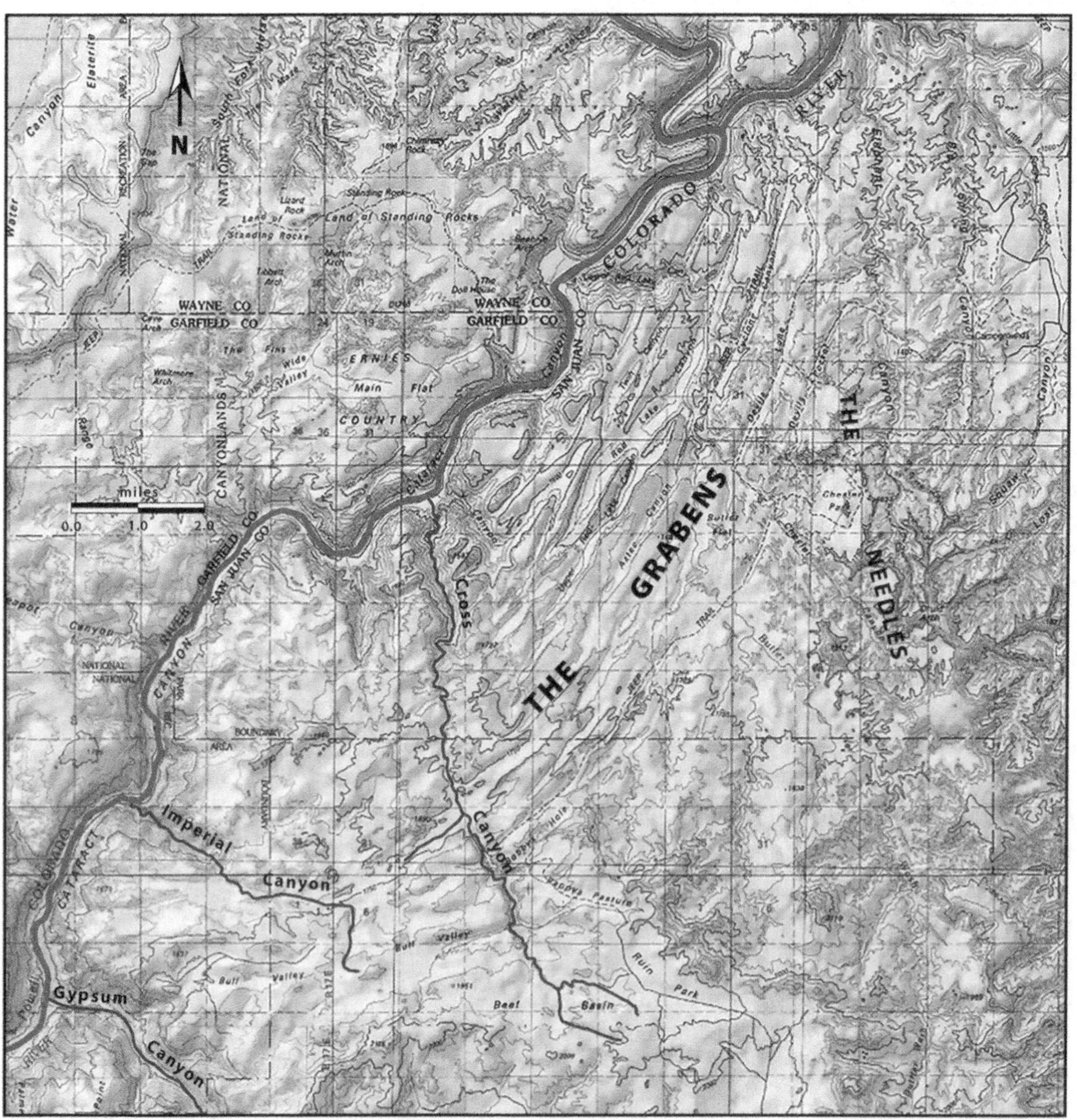

Figure 8.2 Map of the "Grabens" area west of Salt Creek Country and northeast of Beef Basin and Gypsum Canyon where Kenny wanted to explore in 1953 but never made the trip. (Modified from *ESRI Arc/GIS* USGS topographic map)

SAN JUAN RIVER

During the past few years, Kenny had been running at least one pre-season SJ&C river trip for adults. However, in 1953 he had decided against it until suddenly he was contacted by a number of interested parties. He mentioned to Hank Zuidema in April,

> Talk about a goofy situation. I had not planned to run a pre-season San Juan-Colorado river trip this spring--so, when I do not send out literature to people previously interested, I get long-distance calls from all over the Nation, practically demanding that I make good on last year's promises to set one up. I'm stuck in spite of all else that must be done. The trip launches at Bluff, May 19 and goes all the way thru to Lee's Ferry. There will be ten passengers. Incidentally, four of them, H. R. Thies, Manager, Chemical Div. Goodyear Rubber Co. his son and daughter, and Clayton Lewis, Lewis (Ford) Motor Co., Marshall, Texas, first contacted me as a result of your article in the Goodyear trade magazine. Delayed action, eh? [43]

The trip he mentioned consisted of five from the Thies group, including Herman Thies wife, Pat, plus their son and daughter and Clayton Lewis. There was no indication just who the other five folks were in the river group. Kenny ended up providing three LCR 7-man boats to accommodate the Thies passengers, plus all the gear and food. In a series of letters from Herman Thies to Kenny and Mildred it appeared that the trip had some serious boat problems that culminated at the camp at Forbidding Canyon. Thies was most complimentary to Kenny and thanked him for "a wonderful time and most interesting trip" and stated that they marveled in Kenny's steady demeanor when working "under trying conditions and take the good with the bad." Thies also mentioned his wife, Pat, and they all had a "nice trip down the river on the power boat" and stopped about two hours and went to "the Cross of the Fathers" and "we got down to Lee's Ferry about four o'clock Thursday, got to a telephone about eight o'clock that night and made arrangements with Oscar Thomas of Thomas Air Service to pick us up Friday morning." [44] Thomas had a single-engine Beech Bonanza aircraft but due to the size of his family and all their gear they were forced to leave sleeping bags and duffel bags at Art Green's Cliff Dweller Lodge which would be forwarded to them.[45] Thies letter continued that they picked up some Indian rugs at Art's place and made it into Farmington by about 10:30 Friday morning. Then they rented a "U-Drive-It" to Mancos and were driven by Mildred to Durango for the night. He and his wife, Pat, got home (Kent, Ohio) at 6:00 o'clock Monday. "We had a great time. We were sorry you had as much trouble as you did, but we know those things will happen. I am doing some checking on boat repair material and will write you again shortly concerning that." [46]

In follow-up letters Thies said he was sending a repair kit and a roll of vinyl film (patching material) along with recommended repair directions ("heat sealable at 350^{0} – 375^{0} F, it will be impossible to tear"). He mentioned that he had gotten the movie film back from the trip and in reference to Clayton Lewis, who he called the "producer," that a high quality movie was in the making.[47] A later letter said they had "thirty-two of my boys out for dinner"[48] and they all watched an hour and a half of movies of the whole trip. "The shots of you are really marvelous. All in all, I think the production will stack up with any Hollywood travel stories." [49]

Mildred finally replied to the slug of letters in mid-July and said that "Kenny was busy as could be and their first week at camp had been a nightmare with plumbing problems, boys missing airplanes, lost baggage, two new cooks to train on how to feed thirty-six starved boys, and so on." [50] One of the positive highlights had been Jon Lindbergh's visit. He stopped in at Gold King during the first week of the season and helped to get the mountaineering program underway before he had to leave and return to his Navy training on the west coast.[51] Mildred continued to tell Herman Thies what trouble they had finding someone who could repair the boats [plural!], and she thanked him for the rubber patch film:

> You will be interested in knowing that the first river trip for the boys was pretty tough. The San Juan is practically dry--well, barely damp, the boys say--and they were two days late getting into Lee's Ferry--did a fifty-six mile paddling job the last day in order to get in. The rapids were more work than fun, they had some bad winds, though not as bad as those you experienced, and they barred up at the point where the San Juan and Colorado join. *This is the first time in all our years of river-running that we have had to call off the second river trip for the boys.* Some of them were quite disappointed, of course, but after talking it over, they decided it was not worth the effort involved. The ironic thing about the first trip was that after all their work, they were held up for eighteen hours at Carrizo Wash [Redrock Creek] ten miles west of Shiprock while a wall of water rolled by. Heavy rains had fallen too late to do our party any good.[52] [Emphasis mine]

Mildred also mentioned that two cartons containing personal effects and rugs had arrived in good order and thanked him (Figure 8.3):

> I do want to thank you again for the gift for the little boys which you tucked in my pocket just as you were leaving. It is very generous and thoughtful of you, and the little boys asked me to give you their special thanks. They are saving it at the moment for something very special-- just what; they haven't made up their minds.[53]

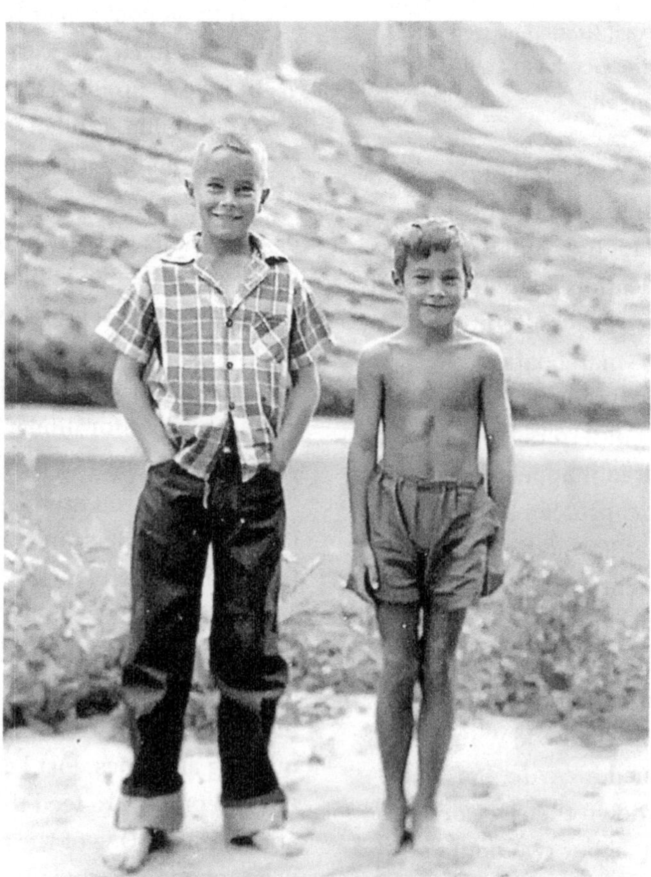

Figure 8.3 Don and Doug, summer of 1953; they got a little gift from Herman Thies following all the troubles Kenny had with his boats. (K. Ross collection)

Figure 8.4 boys paddling one of the Air Force life rafts through Glen Canyon, 1953; this photo accompanied the *Rocky Mountain News* article about the three boys from Denver. (K. Ross collection)

THE MUTINY OF '53!

At least the river trip for half of the boys in camp got some positive press coverage as a newspaper headline read: "Denver Trio on River Adventure Down San Juan, Colorado Canons" a short article in the *Rocky Mountain News* with a photo of three boys from Denver with the following caption "David Gorsuch, 15; Bob Lowdermilk, 16; Bruce Buck, 13 - all part of Southwest Explorers Camp for 1953 enjoying their last days on the river trip through Glen Canyon" (Figure 8.4).[54]

In a series of letters exchanged in February, 1954 between Kenny and one of the boys who was a camper in the 1953 Southwest Explorations group the reason(s) that the camp was cut short became painfully clear.[55] When the second river trip was cancelled there were a lot of disappointed young fellows. Hank Zuidema, the geologist (paleontologist) from Wayne State College in Michigan was one of the camp leaders and he had always talked about digging for Mesozoic vertebrate fossils in the Lukachukai area. The annual "Entah" was in full swing, so the entire group of boys – all thirty-two of them went to Lukachukai for the rodeo and Indian dances.

But here was where some of the boys (five to be exact) went into a hogan one night, unannounced, and after poking around one of the boys stole a jar containing turquoise gemstones. Kenny thought he knew what had happened at the Lukachukai hogan before they ever left there, but did not realize that a fair amount of turquoise had also been stolen. *"The Indian who came into camp at breakfast time the day we pulled out was the owner of the hogan and he had read tracks right into camp."* [56] Kenny told the Navajo man that he didn't know for sure who was responsible, but Kenny promised to get to the bottom of it. The man said he understood curious kids and didn't want to make a big fuss about the matter. They agreed they just wanted to be sure the culprits knew it was wrong and that *"their actions could cause very bad feelings between the Indians and groups like ours."* [57] [Emphasis mine]

The Explorers group packed up and headed north with plans to do some archaeological work at the Cahone ruin site before breaking into two groups to hike either Dark Canyon or Salt Creek Canyon. At some point at the Cahone camp several of the "junior" leaders decided to hold court and took matters into their own hands to discipline the boys who had trespassed into the hogan at Lukachukai.

Kenny wrote that *"the tip-off"* came when he started asking one of the perpetrators about his puffed lip. He soon *thought* he had the whole story including the names of those responsible and the much worse story from *"the Kangaroo Court that took the law into its own hands to punish them."* [58] But Kenny still didn't know about the stolen turquoise; he only knew about the break-in! At this point Kenny felt that the leaders of the "Kangaroo Court" had committed the unforgiveable and dishonorable crime of taking the law into their own hands. Kenny rightly thought the camp leader [himself] was responsible for disciplining the break-in artists. He also felt that the *self-appointed Court members* were due punishment for having taken matters into their own hands. When Kenny confronted two of the boys that presided in the Kangaroo Court they *scoffed* at him and said there was nothing he could do about it and their group thought they could run the whole camp. Kenny chewed them out, gave them a piece of his mind and retired to his tent. [Emphasis mine]

Then the self-appointed leaders decided to cook up a scheme to force Kenny out of control of the camp, thinking it was their only way they could stay on for the rest of camp season. They concocted a story that Kenny had made homosexual advances toward one or more of the boys. This damning accusation hurt Kenny to the bone as he knew that he had done nothing wrong. He decided then and there that the entire remainder of the camp season would be cancelled – immediately! And it was! They returned to Gold King base camp and by early August all the boys were unceremoniously sent home. Letters to parents were written explaining some of the reasons for the aborted season and the cancellation of the much anticipated father-son post-season Cataract Canyon trip. Kenny explained the situation in rather vague terms in a letter to Bill Dickinson:

> Some were very disgruntled, which led to considerable difficulty and incident piled on incident piled on deviltry made things most distasteful toward the last. That's the reason there were so few on the Cat trip. I sent a lot home early. I have never been so dismayed as at the final attempt of a rabid clique to force me into their way of thinking and doing. The plotting, lying and conniving of this group to run the outfit to their liking was sickening. But that's the story that must be told at another time.[59]

In a letter from Mildred to the Thorp family she simply said that the camp had been terminated and that "entails canceling the trips to Dark and Salt Creek." [60]

THE 1953 CATARACT CANYON RIVER TRIP

Fortunately for Kenny, a Cataract Canyon trip *did* happen in August, 1953[61] but with far fewer participants than advertised over the previous year, with only nine people and in three boats instead of the projected eighteen participants as noted in the pre-season narrative. The details of that trip were explained in letters between Kenny and Bill Dickinson in January, 1954 and became significant in that the number of rapids had remained inconsistent within the river running community. During the following years the rapid numbering was fine-tuned to where most present-day river runners use the naming and numbering system worked out from 1949 to 1956.[62]

In addition to Kenny as trip leader, the 1953 Cataract Canyon river trip crew consisted of: the two Hoyt twins, Eddie and Alfie who turned in excellent performances as boatmen; Bill Fulton, who really fouled up a couple of times and he couldn't swim a lick either; Doc Lambert who acted as the camp's part-time doctor the previous two summers ('51, '52) and was on the only Explorers Camp SJ&C trip of '53; the two Lambert sons, John and Howard who "managed to get tossed out in one or another of the rapids;" and Frank Thorp (Explorers camp of 1952) and his father, Frank Thorp, Jr. [a Professor at Michigan State University] who was not a capable boatman. Kenny explained the trip and rapids in detail to Bill Dickinson:

> We had more water than in '49 -- about the same as Griffith had in August of that year [estimated flow of 10 to 12,000 cfs]. As we guessed then, some rapids that gave us no trouble at all on that trip were hellers, and visy-versy. Altogether we counted five rapids not recognized on that first trip; three of them between #13 and #14. Had no trouble with #5 but it **was** wooly. Ran #16 with all three boats--right tight up to the big left-hand rock in the sharp bend and did not catch the back-lashing wave you and Jon made good use of to keep off the center rock in the bend. The lower end was wild, wild, wild! Three perfect runs here, Ed Hoyt and I running two of them, Alfie and Fulton the other one.
>
> We hit exactly the same schedule as in '49 and camped in the same places.
>
> Do you recall #23? We camped just above it. It has a big bar separating the right (main) channel from the left. Remember? Well, next to #26, it scared some of the gang worse than all the rest of this trip. Fulton looked at it for about ten seconds, then went back to the boats and stayed there with gritted teeth until we finished conning half an hour later. As he had not conned, he ran with me in the first boat and swore that the only water in the boat at the end of the perfect run was his sole responsibility. For some reason it did not scare me, perhaps because I was anxious to do it as you and Jon ran it in '49 while I stayed on the bar for pictures. Never have I experienced such killing power and high waves. WOW! All three runs were perfect, with Eddie and Alfie running the other two boats.
>
> #18 is where we dumped Doc Lambert. If you recall, it has a single big, sudden drop, with a center rock splitting the current and smaller rocks barring the right side for a safe run. First two boats went according to plan--on the left; Fulton, with Doc as paddlemate in the last boat, got "lost" above the rocks and at the last moment tried to run right of the big center one. Boom! They hooked it and dropped into the hole below. Boat sucked down but all stayed put. Started to clear edge of hole and was nearly out when they stopped paddling (goddammem). Natch! The whirler gave another big gulp, carrying the stern down about three feet--with the bow standing at about 80 degrees. When they came up---no Doc. Fortunately, they were at the edge of the hole and he must have been pushed away from the hole it, as he came up about 200 ft downstream. Seemed like he was under for hours but it was only 50 seconds by the sweep hand on my watch. The rest of us were as wet with sweat as he was with river. Yer dern tootin' it scared him, but that didn't stop him from running the next rapid.
>
> #20 and 22 were okay but we conned em good and ran em just right.
>
> #26-----well you know all about #26. With **three** boats to get down safely I developed a psychosis (or maybe it was left over from '49). This time there was no slow, easy approach to the narrow top of the channel. With more water, the currents were all mixed up there and it really looked tough to even get in it. Much to the aggravation of all, I took two hours to con it. And Bill F. pulled his

disappearing act again. Said if he looked at it any longer he would be sick to his stomach. He might as well have stayed because he was anyway--at the bottom of the run. You see, I took him as paddlemate on the first boat, with A. Hoyt bellybustin' the bow. We came down on the top slowly as possible. Just as I got the nose set between the two top rocks the stern, which was cocked a little to the right, grabbed a stray current and slammed around the rock on the right. We hung for a second, fighting to get bow on again, and then we went over the rock, plop into the hole below. Everyone, including me grabbed the safety line as the stern took a five foot dive and the bow made like a flag pole in an earthquake. Alfie was the flag. We came out like a cork out of a pop-gun and bowed into the main drag again, filled to the gunnels and managed to slop thru. You know me pal. I had to either get mad or get scared, so I got mad. So mad that I hotfooted it toward the top and the next boat where Eddie was waiting. Most of the gang were sitting on the big rock where Nevills inscription is where they had been taking still and movies of the whole sorry affair. I paused long enough to snap, "Anybody want a ride thru on the next one?" and everyone started crawling behind rocks. As I started on I heard Doc complaining, "He's already scared me (dirty) and now he wants to roll me around in it."

Ed and I took the next thru perfectly--this time I cocked the stern to the left a little--and Alfie and I took the last. Both were dandy runs and thrilling as only #26 **can** be.

Between 26 and Gypsum Canyon Numbers 30, 31, and 35 were all rough. Arrived #40 (Gypsum Canyon) in late afternoon and rooted down there until the morning of the second day after.

Gyp Canyon was r-r-r-r-rough, but, if you stayed in the center after entering, it was entirely clear of rocks. First boat and all others just bowed on the big rollers all the way thru the whole long way. Some excitement as the second boat hit the first big, slanting roller at the top. It was handled by E. Hoyt and John Lambert. Eddie, commanding, ran a little too close to the center of this wave which rolls off a big, buried rock to right of channel. Top of wave (estimated 12' high) rolled over boat and swept John into the rapid. He went **all** the way thru and after the first brief submersion, treaded water, holding the paddle above his head with both hands. I had already run thru and was standing on the bank about midway. His head never went under the second time although the top of every one of the thirteen big waves slapped his face. I believe it was the biggest thrill I've ever known. I certainly don't want it repeated--ever. I should add that Eddie repeated the performance of Bordie Stevenson the time you deserted him in the 8-footer on the S.J. He was half way thru before he knew he was going it alone. The passenger bellying down up front didn't know anything was wrong till the last tailwave was cleared. Ed said he yelled for help all thru the last half but the rapid's roar was too much for him. He just kept her bow on and did a perfect job. The hell of it was that all of us on shore were too excited to keep taking pictures. Doc was making movies but stopped when he saw John go out.

#59--Where Jon first met Griffith--was a dilly, one of the worst in all "Cat". Had big waves, too many rocks, and worst of all, had a terrific swirl at the bottom that caused every boat to suck back up into the lower tailwaves. It caught me in the lead boat, causing me to run the tail twice. Alfie was sucked back up four times before he managed to fight clear.

Dark Canyon was bad but we ran it a-la Griffith. By the time we fought thru 59 we were damn glad to do it that way. Take my word that running it the way we did in '49 would have been just plain suicide in our stage of water. Does all this revive the old lust for the river and its excitement? [63]

Prior to his leaving for the Cataract Canyon trip, on July 30, 1953 Kenny finally paid off the 1948 Chevy "woody" Station Wagon he had paid $1890 for in 1950 and recorded it in the name of Mildred S. Ross; the vehicle had been a necessary purchase indeed.[64] Kenny sold it in 1961 for $25!

Following the Cataract Canyon trip he also took the opportunity to be alone and to clear his mind of the embarrassing Lukachukai incident and the nasty false accusations he had thwarted from the boys in camp that summer. Kenny wrote another considerably detailed letter to Bill where he explained that he took a week-long jeep trek in September to the West Elk country –along a tortuous route from Long Point across Dark Canyon Plateau, Beef Basin then down some "notches" that connected to Chesler Park over to Devil's Lane, the Pinnacles into Salt Creek Canyon and down into Indian Creek, then south to Dugout Ranch and up Cottonwood Canyon and back to Long Point. He also made a loop down Woodenshoe Canyon, alone and much of this by just using his wits as there were no mapped jeep tracks; he blazed his own trail and loved every minute of it even though he had to "sweat" his jeep through some rough stretches.[65]

Kenny didn't learn about the stolen turquoise and all the names of those involved in the Mutiny of '53 until the following springtime. The toxic false accusations of his misconduct very likely added fire in his eyes about the 1953 boys' camp. And it was most probable that the incident spelled the beginning of the end of the Southwest Explorations Camp for boys. One thing was certain. There never was another group of boys sponsored by Kenny Ross to return to Lukachukai. His attention switched more and more toward conducting adult river trips, and in the spring and fall when the San Juan River and Cataract Canyon were at their best. He would still offer summer camps for boys for a few more years, but he saw that if he were to ever make any real money, it would have to expand beyond the nine summer weeks for a boy's camp that he had dedicated his time and energy to for the past eight years.

Wedding Day: December 26, 1953 (L to R) Don, Father Hammond, Bitsy, Grace, Chuck, Kenny, Mildred and Doug (K. Ross collection)

Grace and Charles (Chuck) Ross, December 26, 1953 (K. Ross collection)

9

THE END OF SOUTHWEST EXPLORATIONS: 1954 to 1956

WEDDINGS AND ADIOS

The year, 1954, began with some happy family news. Mildred's son, and Kenny's adopted son, Charles got married – twice! [1] The initial announcement came on the same day that Bill Dickinson had informed Kenny and Mildred that he had just gotten married to Peggy two weeks earlier. Kenny said that Charles arrived at the doorstep dragging his "bride-to-be," Grace Lockerbie, and announced that they didn't have time for an elaborate wedding so they had come home to be married by a Justice of the Peace. They were married October 2, 1953 in Farmington, New Mexico.[2] Kenny took them back to Boulder and then they had a "formal" church wedding on the day after Christmas in Mancos. He mentioned that Grace was a North Carolinian and that they all had acquired her southern accent.

The Ross family almost moved to an eight-acre farm just on the outskirts of Mancos, but "the deal on the farm went bluey at the last moment." [3] A deal with Stuart Maule regarding moving to the farm got nixed when his son came home from the Army "and a long and beautiful friendship now seemed a bit tarnished." [4] They thought the deal was so sure that they had begun packing for the short move, but they had to unpack when the deal fell through. Don said that the Ross family really wanted it and Kenny was devastated. Don was planning on having a horse and the farm had a big barn where all the RBMV fold boats were already stored. The Maule's ended up selling the farm to someone else. One can only wonder if the deal had gone through, would Kenny have ever moved the boat camp to Bluff? After all, the barn would have made a superior boat shop compared to the early tent camps in Bluff (see Chapter Ten).

Kenny also made note that Buddy Starr had quit school at the University of Colorado and had joined the Air Force and had started flying the past summer and was nearly ready for his pilot's license. He also mentioned that Dick Millard (camp member of '49-50) was in Japan and a dozen or so old Explorers were also stationed in Japan and had formed a little club and noted that they all said that it was Kenny who made it possible in helping them become accomplished young men.[5]

> The Elk and west of the Elk country is lousy with cartographers, geologists and kindred hangers-on. I don't know exactly what they are all doing and neither do they. It is a muddled mess for sure. The AEC has mobile camps all over the place and the USGS outfits have settled with a little more dignity in White Canyon, on Deer Flat (just west of Woodenshoe Butte), and on Long Point. That country over there is fuller of wonders than it used to be; you ought to see some of the places new jeep roads go. It's marvelous.[6]

Kenny mentioned that it looked like the Glen Canyon Dam would definitely get built and that when the impounded water rose to the projected full pool elevation that the Thirteen Foot Rapid on the San Juan River and Dark Canyon Rapid in Cataract Canyon would be lost.

> Woe, Woe! Imagine going clear up to Rainbow Bridge by boat! It's a definite possibility. The age of

motors will really come on the old Colorado. Now, get mad and stomp and cuss. Nature was grand. And with that parting shot I will leave thee to thine own devices for a while.[7]

And with that letter to Bill, it would be twenty-two years before he and Bill would ever see each other again. They kept in touch by occasional letters and phone calls, but it was 1976 when they finally met face-to-face again. I asked Bill in 2015 about this sudden end to their regular lines of communication, and about how or whether to make an attempt to get in touch with Jon Lindbergh for my book. Bill replied:

> No doubt Kenny himself awakened some latent interest in geology in my brain but I was an engineering major for three years at Stanford until I took a course called "Geology for Engineers" taught by Aaron Waters. That is what set me off. Then I had a host of mentors on the Stanford faculty, chief among them Bob Compton who passed away early this month. Jon and I saw a lot of each other up until 1952 when I was off to the USAF and him shortly thereafter into his frogman act (followed by marine biology etc).
>
> Doubt I have seen him now in over 50 years, and really no idea how to contact either him or either of his brothers. Never met either his mother or his father. Although many played off his fame or notoriety or whatever insane sentiment people conveyed upon him as the brother of the brother who was killed, he never really did himself. He just had an immensely difficult time so much as taking a pee incognito, and he loathed all the unwanted attention he got. I don't think either Land or Scott (whom I knew but not as well) ever drew such inane attention (maybe one was enough, and Jon was the one brother into various brands of derring-do that caught people's attention). Do not know for sure how Jon would react to being contacted by you (or anyone else) about his early life, but my hunch is that he would just say to himself I don't need this, there is nothing in it for me, and I am not going there.
>
> You cannot imagine how crazy people can get about Jon. The only hope he has ever had for privacy is to never mention his father and never let anyone know what he has done or is doing. Living his life is like having a chattering monkey on your shoulder 24/7. When he was in my eating club at Stanford and people would come snooping around about him, we would just say "Charles Lindbergh? Whatever gave you that silly idea?" He had at one time the press value of a Kardashian, and every other yo-yo on the planet seemed to want to cash in on some stupid scoop of some kind. They all got the back of my hand just as soon as I smelled a rat.[8]

DOC LAMBERT

In January Kenny asked Doc if he could borrow movie film as he was giving lots of off-season talks in Durango. Doc replied that he, indeed, had film: two reels of the 1951 San Juan River trip, one of the 1952 Salt Creek Canyon jeep trip, two of 1953 San Juan River trips and a big reel of the 1953 Cataract Canyon trip. Their discussion was also serious about the inevitable construction of Glen Canyon Dam. Doc Lambert had also given talks in the Berkeley area about "rapids and Canyonlands." [9] In a February letter Kenny complained that the weather was too warm (60s–70s) and only 30% of normal snow pack, but noted that the upper Colorado River and Green River headwaters had normal snow packs. Kenny was looking forward to a Cat trip and wanted to begin in Green River, Utah and take two weeks. Don Ross said he had mumps in late February-early March and Doug followed shortly thereafter with his "ownself's mumpiness" calling it a "special gift from his big brother." [10]

Lambert appeared interested in doing a family trip in late summer of '54.[11] Kenny mentioned that he was running two SJ&C trips in May while he had good water but expected the San Juan to be dry by summer. He said he would need to charge $150/person for the Cat trip instead of cost-sharing as before. For unexplained reasons the Lamberts and Kenny didn't manage to pull off the Green River to Hite Cataract trip. John Lambert enlisted in the Army.

AMERICAN WHITE WATER ASSOCIATION

In early April Kenny wrote to David Stacey who was one of the organizers of the *American White Water Association* – a group of kayak enthusiasts from Denver that were using this new product "fiber-glass." Kenny wrote that he had received the deposit check from David's father, retired Army General Wayne Stacey, for a May SJ&C river trip. Kenny advised Stacey that their kayaks would move faster than his LCRs and emphasized their staying together. Kenny wanted to know more details about their boats and what the carrying capacity they might have. He also noted that by mid-May there should be enough water, but he would still like to see more snow.[12]

On April 26, Kenny replied to General Wayne Stacey who had asked about having their car's shuttled to Lees Ferry and Kenny also wanted to know the total number of participants so he could plan the trip. He said he had cancelled an earlier May trip so a launch from Bluff on Monday May 17 was possible. He added that barring any strong winds or low water they should arrive at Lees Ferry by the evening of May 25 or no later than evening of 26th (eight-day trips were planned). Kenny planned to leave Mancos the morning of the 16th and lead the group over to the Bluff launch site. He assured the General that the cars would be stored in a safe place in Mancos and would be driven to Lees Ferry on the 25th; the drivers would return with Kenny in the truck to Mancos. "Mrs. Ross will probably be one of the drivers." [13] Kenny also mentioned that he didn't know Harry and Mike Goulding very well, but they struck him as a very wonderful couple; he just usually didn't have time to stop in at the Gouldings Lodge. Kenny again assured them that the river should have an adequate amount of water to run, but not as high as normal [whatever 'normal' is?]. "And we may anticipate that the rapids will be showing

Figure 9.1 Mrs. Wayne Stacey ("Joanie") in first fiberglass kayak to make a full SJ&C run May 17-26, 1954; shown here in Glen Canyon. (K. Ross collection)

their 'teeth' and will give us many a thrill." [14] Based on historical gage records from the Gage near Bluff (at Mexican Hat) the maximum discharge recorded was approximately 8,000 cfs in late May.[15] The group put together by David Stacey was wonderful and Kenny mentioned this trip many years later as one of his best with good people. This trip also marked the *first full length trip from Bluff to Lees Ferry with kayaks –* particularly the "modern" *fiber-glass variety and was corroborated two years later by Dock Marston* (Figure 9.1).[16]

1954 SOUTHWEST EXPLORATIONS CAMP

Only eleven boys were recorded as members in the 1954 Southwest Explorations program. Several boys were referred by previous camp leaders like geologists Norman Thomas and Hank Zuidema which helped Kenny's conscience that he had successfully weathered the rumor mill from the previous year's mutinous debacle. Kenny also noted that he traded the red jeep for a '51 FWD Jeep pickup on June 4, 1954. Frank Thorp enjoyed the camp so much that he returned to work at the camp the next two summers. Due to the small group size there was no need to rotate – so they did everything together including much mountaineering activity followed by the SJ&C river trip from Bluff to Lees Ferry. *But this time, eight-year old Doug Ross was permitted to go on his first river trip.*[17] Kenny apparently felt that the youngest age he allowed on his trips was the same age of Don Ross on his first trip in 1952. The trip went without any significant mishaps and Doug said it was on that trip that he added his name to the lower ledge at the mouth of Slickhorn Gulch.

Beans and Weenies: Somewhere along the line of running his river trips Kenny developed a knack to break-up the normal humdrum of scheduled lunch stops. No one knows when he began the special treat of stopping for lunch and instead of canned foods, he would build a small fire on the river bank from driftwood and while the fire got going, he'd cut off the needed branches of river willows, whittle the leaves off and make a pointed end. Then he'd break out some weenies (hotdogs) and some buns and possibly some ketchup, mustard and pickles and the boys would get to roast their weenies to whatever degree of burnt they wished and slide em onto a hotdog bun! Kenny also brought the necessary number of canned pork & beans along (Van Camps were his favorite) and the cans would get passed around. It was up to the boys to either break out their mess kits, or just use a fork and eat some beans right out of the can. Kenny repeated this type of lunch two or three times on longer trips and maybe only once on shorter trips or when there were large groups. This custom of stopping, making a fire and roasting weenies was passed along to me and my generation of those whoever boated with Kenny. As time marched on, he even broke out the paper plates on occasion, but eating beans out of the can seemed to taste better.

Hot Tea at Camp: Another favorite of Kenny's was to make a pot of hot tea for everyone to share when he landed for camp in the evenings. It could be the hottest day of the year, but Kenny would hit the beach with the kitchen box and while the rest of the crew unloaded their gear for camp, he would hurry and make a small camp fire, pour some water in the big coffee pot and bring it to a boil. Then he'd add some good old Lipton's tea and yell out to everyone that the tea was ready. He encouraged everyone to have at least a cup. He said the hot tea helped bring your body temperature down and help settle your innards for the evening meal.

I asked Doug if Mildred ever went on any river trips and he said, "Yes! She boated from Bluff to Mexican Hat, but was not a fan; on the other hand she was disappointed that she never saw Rainbow Bridge up close and personal." [18] Another interesting comment came from Kenny in a letter to Hank Zuidema where Kenny mentioned that Mildred ran for office of Mayor of Mancos in April, 1952 and lost by two votes and tried again in 1954.[20] There was never any more mention of her political endeavors, and suffice to say, she did not win the mayoral race in 1954 either.

The "dig" at Cahone ruin was a big hit that camp season as the excavation was completed on a ceremonial kiva (Kiva C-18) and preliminary work was started on another structure. One of the boys, Pete Goodwin, from Millbrook, New York was so enthusiastic that everyone thought he would major in archaeology in college, but he ended up as an early developer of solar energy systems and landed in Santa Fe.[19] The group also returned to Salt Creek Canyon and explored for more ruins, arches and hiked in the Pinnacles section of the Needles District.

AMERICAN CANOE ASSOCIATION: *ORGANIZED* "PRIVATE" BOATERS UNITE!

Larry Zuk with *American Canoe Association* wrote a letter to Kenny in May, 1954 thanking him for some information Kenny had sent to him. He had shared it with members and they felt they "definitely could not afford it. So we will not be joining you this time." [21] Zuk confided to Kenny that these folks would see that their expenses would be close to his "generous offer." Zuk appreciated the information about the river and canoes, but then he confessed that he and his group were not "experts" but they were not novices either and that Kenny wouldn't be taking "raw beginners." He mentioned that he was president of the club they called the *Colorado White Water Association* and asked if Kenny had ever heard of them. Zuk mentioned that they had a rubber raft, if needed and a group in fold-boats from Los Alamos. Zuk added that he ran a French slalom canoe decked over with removable canvas plus some of the others ran regular kayaks. He said he was committed to going with his gang, but maybe they would call upon Kenny the next year in May. He noted that Kenny had a reputation as a good camp cook among other things and was already well known. He also asked if Kenny ran Cataract or Grand Canyon.[22]

In a letter from Larry Zuk to Kenny in April, 1955 he said that Dave Stacey had "highly recommended" Kenny's San Juan trip as he [Stacey] was with Kenny in his "glass" boat last year (1954). Now Zuk, his wife and friends were planning a May trip. In a very condescending way, Zuk said "Some of the individuals in this party have been hesitant about *taking a guide* and want to go through without one. Although all of this party is experienced white water men I have always found it more fun to *take a guide* and would like to convince them of it" [23] [Emphasis mine]. He resumed by asking Kenny if he could take a party through from May 15-21 or the following week. They would have their own canoes and then he *told* Kenny he would "only need to take one rubber raft and supplies, and how much would you charge for a party of five or six?" [24] He also asked about transportation back to their cars or could Kenny have them shuttled to Lees Ferry? If Kenny couldn't do it, then did Kenny have someone else to recommend?" And he asked for a quick reply! [25] Kenny replied and said it sounded interesting but their safety and comfort would be greatly increased by having a *real* guide and cargo boat along – no doubt about it! Kenny was noticeably upset with the demands and he fired back and didn't mince words regarding canoes on the San Juan and clueless "experts" like Zuk and his "gang." Zuk and ACA never took Kenny up on his offer, as he probably figured out they were just pumping him for information. But he didn't hold back after receiving these letters from such a presumptuous ass:

> You mention that you plan to make the trip in canoes. It can be done. It has been done. Also, the only attempt by a canoe party to descend the San Juan unattended by a heavier, more stable boat to

carry supplies ended in failure and almost incredible hardship for the members, who were all highly experienced "whitewater experts".

What I know about canoes (other than a moonlit cruise on a pond) comes second hand--mostly from canoe experts who have accompanied me on one of my trips, sans canoes. The consensus of opinion is that empty canoes could run all but four of the San Juan rapids below Mexican Hat but that canoes carrying a load of supplies could not run any but the most minor rapids. Even kayak parties portage. As I understand it, trouble has always come in certain stretches between rapids or in the "tailwaves" beyond the foot of a rapid. These latter are the "exhaust" of a rapid and on the San Juan and Colorado can reach remarkable heights, again depending upon water level. There are two or three stretches of the San Juan where, altho no rapids (as I call 'em) exists the descent of the river bed is great enough that high, powerful waves cover almost the entire surface of the river for distances up to 3/4 of a mile. These would be tough on loaded canoes. The San Juan is famous for its Sandwaves. I believe that most of these could be run in empty canoes and that doing so would be really great sport.

Perhaps I could have skipped most of the above by simply saying; my own experience at whitewater work covers some ten thousand miles--mostly in heavy boats--and in my opinion the chances that loaded canoes could descend the San Juan without serious loss or damage to equipment and supplies are absolutely nil, period. I believe that Dave Stacey would agree. I have come to judging rivers by "weight". The San Juan carries a large volume of water in a narrow bed with considerable deescent. It is a "heavy" river, quite different from "lightweights" like the upper Green, the Yampa, and the Arkansas. The difference in weight is POWER and this power is added to every aspect of the river; in the rapids, the waves, the current in even the smooth stretches. Even in large, stable boats, both rigid and rubber, I have had plenty of thrills, tense moments and close calls on the San Juan. It is never a "milk run".

So much for general information which you did not ask for. Here is what I can do, provided your party can come to an agreement within the next few days. I can take one of my 12-foot LCRs to carry food and a minimum of personal equipment, an assistant, furnish everything except bedrolls, stand the cost of hiring drivers for two cars from Mex Hat to Lee's Ferry for the cost for a party of six would be $550; for five, $525. This is figuring everything right down to the nickel and includes less than half the return I usually expect for such a trip. I would expect your party to help with all camping chores except cooking, altho help with the latter is always appreciated. I am considered an expert camp cook and the meals on my trips are better than people seem to expect for an extended camping trip away from any source of supply; certainly far superior to what you could possibly provide from the amount and type of supplies possible to carry in canoes.

I would want to reserve the right to bring along an extra passenger at my regular rate if such should wish to come. There would be room in my boat for an "extra". At present several persons are trying to arrange their time so that they can take either my trip scheduled for May 15 or May 29. The latter trip is mostly filled. The regular May 15 trip went blooey because of conflicting vacation dates to those who negotiating for passage. Also, as you can see, I could only be free to accompany your party on the fifteenth.

As to the amount of time required for your trip. I believe it can be done in 7 days provided that we could get started very early the morning of the fifteenth, spend long days on the water and take the minimum time for the walk up to Rainbow Bridge. I would not care to guarantee that it could, however. If water levels are favorable and we do not have too much upriver wind (if it blows its always upriver) we can go skitin' right along. Usually we do the trip in a comfortable 8 days.

Dave may have told you that I am touchy on one point; the matter of all the boats keeping together. This is highly important to safety and smooth running, as well as an overall saving of time. I will work on no other basis. It is only fair to add that my LCR will be slower than canoes and at times may seem to slow up the party but, in the end, the total time for the trip will be little if any more than if only canoes are involved. The total time for an extended trip like this (barring adverse water and weather conditions) depends more upon the people of a party than upon the type of craft. Unless, of course, one wants to turn the trip into a seven-day race.

> I checked with the only other persons with the experience and equipment to take you down the San Juan, by long-distance telephone this morning. They are not available during the period you suggest because of another commitment. Anyway, they expressed indifference to the idea of taking the responsibility for a canoe party. I wanted their opinion on the proper charge for a proposition like yours and found it too outrageous to even quote.
>
> The proper charge for drivers from Mex Hat to Lee's Ferry is $50, plus fuel and meals. Considering the difficulty of getting anyone to drive that lonely, isolated country, the fact that it takes three days of a man's time coming and going, and the cost of his own return transportation, that is dirt cheap. I included two drivers for your cars in the charge I quoted for your trip--but not gas and oil. You pay for that.
>
> One more unasked for suggestion. If the time available to your party is so tight that more than 7 days would work a hardship, do not even consider the trip even without a guide. I am very serious about this.[26]

1955 TRAGEDIES

The year began on a sad note. Kenny wrote to Doc Lambert that Mildred's father (Mr. Skinner) had died in Illinois after having returned from Florida. Kenny and Mildred had just returned from the funeral in Beverly, Kansas where Mildred's father wanted to be buried and they had begun to settle his estate, etc. Kenny had been sick most of the winter; first with flu, then pneumonia, pleurisy, rheumatism and arthritis. He also discovered he was allergic to penicillin. He had been loading up on vitamin B-12 shots twice weekly. "He felt like shit!" [27] The year was also tough on the small community of Mancos. Two young men lost their lives in separate airplane crashes only months apart. Earlier, in 1954, Hilary Sprenger was reported as "missing" when an airplane he was in went down somewhere in Alaska. It was some period of time before the wreckage was found with no survivors. When that happened and in the months that followed, Hilary's mother, Louise, had become somewhat perturbed by another young Mancos lad who was making the spotlight in town as the local flyboy who had gotten his wings as an Air Force pilot and was the talk of the town. His name was Raymond H. "Buddy" Starr and he was just another one of Kenny's boys in many ways. He was several years older than Don and Doug and had been a big help to Kenny with the pre-camp river trips and had become a capable and trusted boatman. In the spring of 1955, Kenny had written him a long letter with plenty of "fatherly advice" regarding several things; a) Buddy's apparent casual response to Hilary Sprenger's death and how Louise had reacted and, b) Buddy's discomfort around his rather overweight and odd-couple parents and how he had expressed his hesitancy and embarrassment for their coming to Greenville, Mississippi for his graduation from Air Force Cadet school. Kenny told him to embrace his mother's pinning his wings on him and that he should invite Louise Sprenger to come as well. Kenny congratulated him for having applied for Basic Flight Instructor and that he must have a lot of jet hours logged, but then Kenny returned to comments about Buddy's parents:

> I know exactly how you feel about your folks coming down there next month---at least I think I do and I feel bad about it because maybe I am at least a little bit responsible. You are a sensitive cuss in some ways (in lots of ways) and you are building up some ideas---good ones---that don't exactly go with a small town and good ordinary people. The ideas are good alright but they still have a lot of rough edges on 'em. You've indicated to me often enough that you (at least sometimes) consider your family a Cross which you bear and that you are unique in this. Well, they are not, and you are not, period.
>
> When your ma and pa get down there, as I hope and pray they will, you better be damn glad to see 'em and to show it. They are what you've got, but, more important, they are what you are. You can't substitute them and, even if you could, you couldn't

possibly beat them. You better be damn proud of them---show them everything and introduce them to everyone, and do it with a great big beautiful blond smile. You will gain so much more in the eyes of everyone and in your own eyes, than if you try to half hide them, that there in nothing in the world more important to do. If you keep that good head of yours working straight you should be able to see that your parents are the biggest asset you have.[28]

Kenny had also asked Buddy about his upcoming wedding plans in May and commented that being twenty-four years old was "just about right for weddings" citing that marriage lasts longer "after a fella's experience and brains catch up with his glands." [29] Within weeks of sending the letter the town of Mancos learned that Buddy Starr had crashed to his death! He had a trainee handle the plane's controls and somehow it had spun out of control and crashed to earth. Don and Doug recalled that the whole town turned out for the funeral, including his fiancée! Kenny was devastated.

Doug Ross recalled a fun moment after Buddy was in the Air Force. One late afternoon there was a knock at the Ross's front door and when it was opened there stood Buddy in full Air Force flight suit with parachute in a backpack and helmet in hand. Buddy said "Howdy, just dropped in to say hello!" [30] He was sorely missed by all.

In honor of Buddy, Kenny started calling a favorite camp on the San Juan River about three miles above Clay Hills landing "Starr Bar." The small cobble and sand beach was on river right (RR) in the right-angle elbow bend as the river straightened out almost due west toward Clay Hills with the massive Red House Cliffs looming in the background. "The straightest stretch on the whole San Juan River" Kenny said.[31]

The small bar was finally covered by silt as Powell reservoir inundated all the low bars and beaches along this stretch of the river in the late 1970s, but some of us recall camping there – including me on one occasion. The cobbles are beautifully preserved as one of the first photographs in Eliot Porter's famous photo album book *"The Place No One Knew."* Unfortunately the caption was misspelled.[32]

SOUTHWEST EXPLORATIONS CAMP of '55

Enrollment in Southwest Explorations continued to dwindle as there were only seven boys of record that participated in that year's camp.[33] One of the boys was another referral from Norman Thomas who told Kenny he was then working as a petroleum geologist for Pure Oil. Another boy, Ted Rynearson was the son of Doc Edward Rynearson who was a leader for some of the very first Explorers Camps. Peter "Pete" Presnell was a Hollywood kid and son of a Hollywood director and brother to actor Harvey Presnell. Frank Thorp returned to help and was much needed as the Gold King camp had been seriously vandalized over the winter. There had been some minor intrusions in the past but Kenny noted that "uncontrollable vandalism" was forcing him to reconsider Gold King and to possibly consider abandoning the mountain base camp. Although small in number, all the usual segments of camp were achieved. Because the group size was so small, young Don Ross (Figure 9.2) got to invite his next door neighbor, Conrad Wagner to join him on his second-ever SJ&C trip and they both learned to paddle a boat! They both took part in the dig at Cibola City ruins.[34]

Kenny continued to hear from some of his old ex-Explorers like David Scott (1950). Kenny replied in April that Land Lindbergh spent the past summer in Mexico and had stopped by for a two-day visit. "Jon and his lovely wife" had stopped by for three days in June enroute to Stanford from Connecticut and he was now a marine biologist and Lt. J.G. in the Navy. Another ex-Explorer, Max Friedlander got out of the Marine Corp and was going on a scientific trip to Africa, and Bill Dickinson was in the Air Force in

Florida. Kenny wrote to David Scott's parents about Don, Doug and their son David:

> Our boys keep right on growing, and, we hope, improving. Don is now nearly the age that Dave was when we saw him last and, I believe, about the same size. He is looking forward to spending most of the coming summer at camp but also has so many interest that I wonder if he can. Doug is active as a cricket but grows so that we will have to find some other equally active but larger critter to compare him to. Both are in everything that goes on here, particularly all the outdoor activities. Principal indoor activity right now is stamp collecting.[35]

Archaeologist, Polly Schaafsma, one of the premier rock-art specialists in the Southwest and a frequent scholar on Wild Rivers Expeditions archaeological trips from the period 1990-2010 told me when I asked her if she knew Kenny or Ansel Hall:

> Me and Curt [her husband] worked for Ansel in the summers of 1955 and 1956. I (we) owe a great deal to Ansel as his decision to hire us as teenagers to work in the Mesa Verde concession he ran, effected the course of our lives; pure chance of course. But we only learned about Ansel's archaeological past over the years. At the time we worked for him we knew nothing about anything. Only something about a Rainbow Bridge expedition -- sounded interesting-- and Amy Andrews, his pilot on the project, who was in 1955-56 Curt's bell hop boss and worked at the front desk. Kenny Ross was around too because he advised Curt NOT to hike into the Ute Rez because people had disappeared down there. That inspired Curt to do it anyway, and he barely made it back because he was stalked by a Ute on horseback with a rifle! Not knowing any of this, I went down there too with a ranger.[36]

Figure 9.2 Eleven year old Don Ross paddles boat in Glen Canyon, 1955. (K. Ross collection)

So Kenny was reinvigorated with some new faces and some old friends in 1955. He ran May and June SJ&C trips on 4,000 to 6,000 cfs (Figures 9.2 – 9.8), and in a letter to Larry Zuk, Kenny said that he ended up with pneumonia following the May trip. It could just as well have been a melancholy reaction to the cold reality of Buddy Starr's startling death. Regarding the boy's river trip down the San Juan and Colorado rivers that summer:

> Water levels were only fair last year; certainly nothing spectacular. The Ex. Camp trip I made (June 27 to July 10) was a very good one however. Government Rapid, Paiute Falls and the 13-footer were all pretty tricky and we had to run the boats thru the latter empty---as is usual. Paiute Farms, with its wide spread of shallow channels, was our only "ordeal" but, at that, we made thru in only about 3 hours. There is not "usual" time for this. I have done it in as little as 49 minutes and taken as long as 5½ hours. The boys in camp have come to call this 5-mile stretch "The Death March".[37]

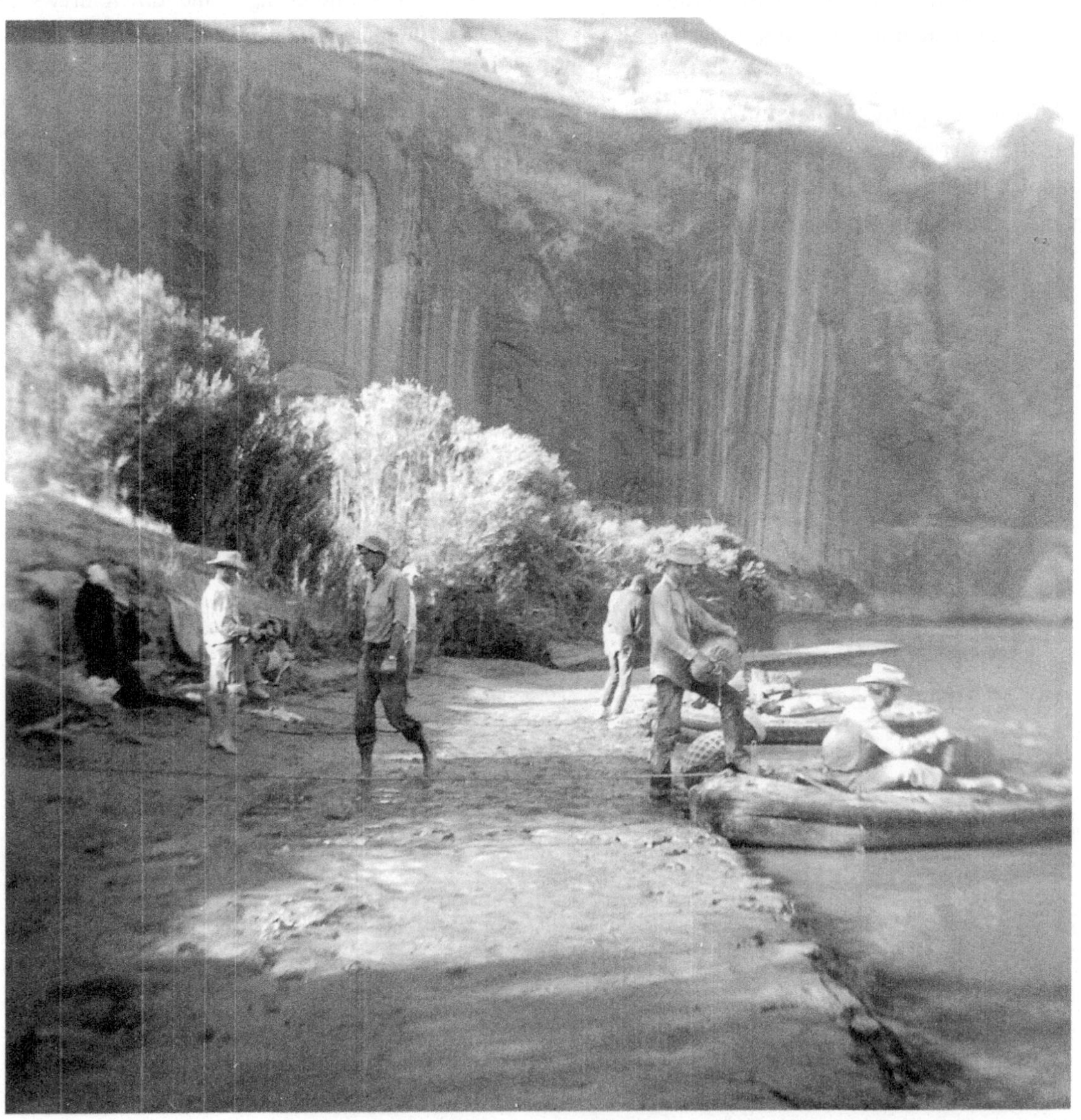

Figure 9.3 camp on RL in Glen Canyon; stripped cliff of Navajo Sandstone in background, 1955. (K. Ross collection)

Figure 9.4 boats at Mexican Hat landing, 1955; note "new" bridge. (K. Ross collection)

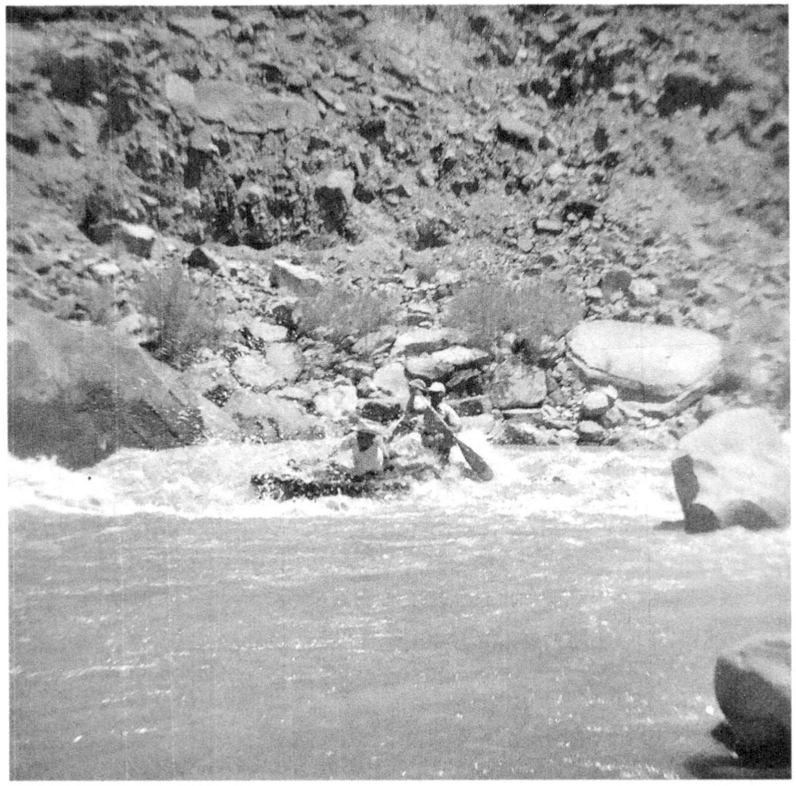

Figure 9.5 Kenny Ross (white cap) with paddle in hand enters Thirteen Foot Rapid, 1955. (K. Ross collection)

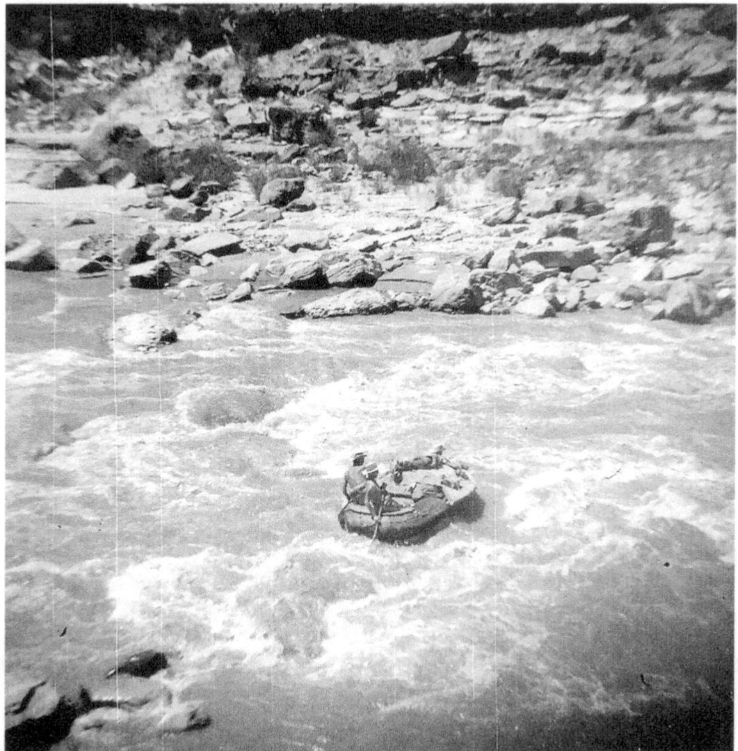

Figure 9.6 Frank Thorp paddles second boat in Thirteen Foot Rapid, 1955. (K. Ross collection)

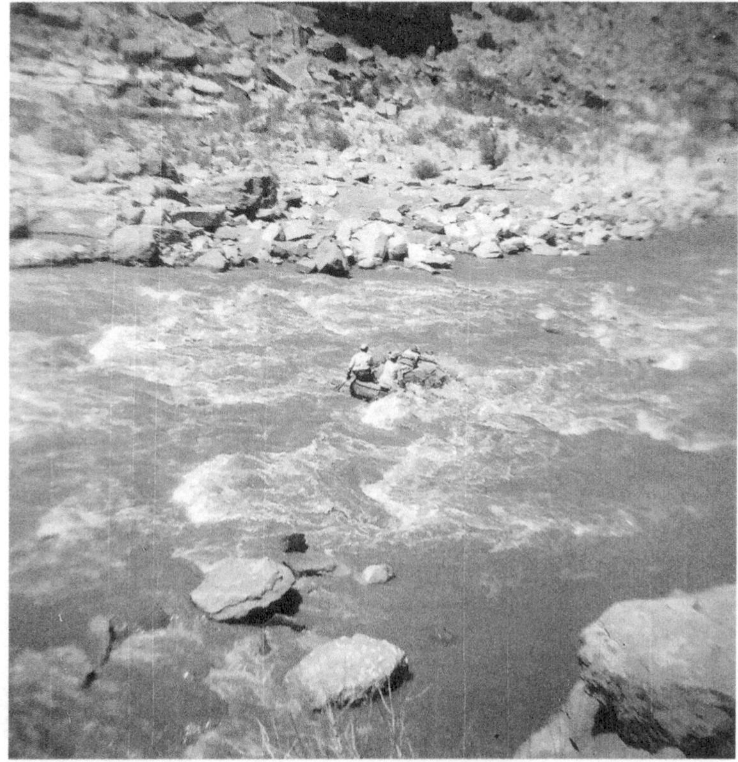

Figure 9.7 Kenny Ross paddles on left side in lower Thirteen Foot Rapid. (K. Ross collection)

In a January, 1956 letter Larry Zuk said that, in fact, they had run the SJ&C trip from May 16-22, 1955 at 4,000 cfs as gaged at Mexican Hat. He and his wife ran the French Slalom canoe and Harry Shade and Dr. Wes Reynolds ran a six-man rubber boat, plus six folks from Los Alamos were in three kayaks (Mr. & Mrs. Bob Douglas, Mr. & Mrs. Jim Fretwell and a fellow named Duff and a Colonel Mac – somebody). They all stayed together until Thirteen Foot "Falls" and then his group split and ran ahead of the Los Alamos group who had more time to spend in Glen Canyon. He said they were on the water seven days and that on the last day they ran from Catfish Canyon to Lees Ferry in eight hours with a head wind. They ran everything except Thirteen Foot Rapid (because they didn't want to jeopardize their boats for the Arkansas race). Overall, he said the trip was magnificent in scenery and the water was fine and *they had a lot healthier respect for the Old San Juan when they came out than when they went in.*[38] [emphasis mine]

Now Zuk's friends were interested in Cataract Canyon and "taking a guide" and he wanted to know if Kenny would be available before his May 15 SJ&C trip? A price quote was requested but he said they would run their own boats. Zuk again just basically wanted a camp nanny.[39] The last Kenny heard about ACA was a letter he sent in reply to the January, 1956 enquiry by Zuk. Kenny said nothing had panned out yet for his proposed May SJ&C trip so that time slot was currently available. He said the only Cat trip scheduled was following the closing of camp around August 24. He would be tied up in July with boys' canyoneering. Kenny cautioned Zuk about high-water runs through Cataract and said he [Kenny] ran it in June in high water and, "while I made it without serious mishap (no upsets) and would do it again with sufficient reason; I just plain didn't like it and am not going out of my way to find another excuse to do so." [40] Kenny invited Zuk to join him on the August trip and then mentioned that he needed to launch from Moab, or at best, at the MGM oil well about eighteen river miles downriver which still meant forty miles of very slow water before reaching the rapids. For that reason, Kenny said he liked to pack a 5-HP "kicker" just for this, even though it was a nuisance.[41]

Kenny answered Zuk's earlier question about Cataract or Grand Canyon trips:

> I do take Cataract Canyon trips, and in my opinion "The Cat" tops everything else the Colorado has to offer in the way of a short trip. In fact, except for the super-sized "standing" waves at the foot of some of the biggest rapids, Cat equals anything found in Marble or Grand Canyons. My problem in trying to organize trips thru the latter is the time involved and the fact that it is just expensive enough that it is difficult to get a big enough group together to make it worthwhile. The problem of re-supplying and cargo capacity is not an easy one either. However, I have been doing some close figuring and believe that, if i could by-pass the problems and expenses of getting the group together, I could take a group of 20 thru from Lee's Ferry to Lake Mead for less than $200 per person. This would truly be a "share the cost" deal and would not allow for the usual high "salary" for leadership and assistance with the cargo boats. It would be a "share all the work" deal too. I guess you know that three weeks is about the minimum time required to go thru Marble and Grand. One of these days I am going to bust loose with an offer to make the trip at a cost I will probably be sorry for. In the meantime I am willing to listen to any reasonable proposition made by an organized group.[42]

PORTABLE ICE CHESTS – NOT YET!

And by the end of the year, a new invention made itself available to the outdoorsmen of the day. A little known fact: the first portable ice chest was invented by Richard C. Laramy of Joliet, Illinois on February 24, 1951. It was finally patented on December 22, 1953 and the *Coleman Company* took Laramy's design and galvanized

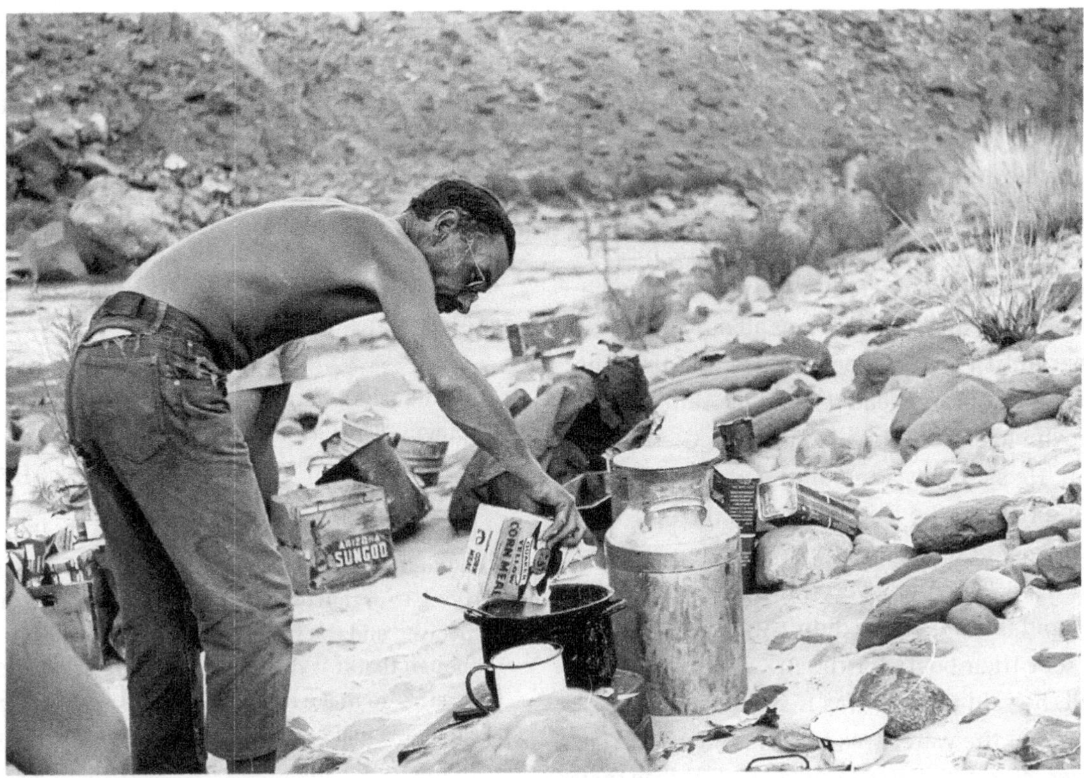

Figure 9.8 Kenny prepares dinner at camp below Thirteen Foot Rapid; he prided himself in his camp cooking and serving "hot meals" although most of the ingredients were either canned or boxed. The metal milk can held drinking water; most cooking water was right out of the river; it would be several more years before ice chests and fresh vegetables, etc were introduced to WRX camp menus. (K. Ross collection)

versions were first on the market in 1954. But it took another four years before Kenny owned his first one! [43] The development of the portable ice chest would gradually be added to private and commercial river trips and radically changed river cuisine from canned goods to fresh foods (Figure 9.8). Several river companies that I'm familiar with, pride themselves more with their multi-course, white table cloth cuisine than they do on their boating skills or interpretive knowledge of the area. Some, including this writer, think that it has led to making food too important and has taken away the whole concept of "roughing it" and learning how to enjoy living in the great outdoors or to learn about the natural surroundings including the geology, archaeology and history of the river corridor one is experiencing.

ONE MORE CAT TRIP - 1955

After the 1954 plans for a Cataract Canyon trip had fallen through, Doc Lambert and his son, Howard, decided they really wanted to do another Cat trip as did the Thorp family. Doc wanted to bring a young doctor friend too, named Dick Hardenbrook, but the trip notes did not include that name. Unfortunately John Lambert (Explorers camp of 1951) couldn't break away from the Army for that long a period. Kenny had written Frank Thorp in March and said there was a new road down Indian Creek clear to the river and his plan would be to start the trip there, thus avoiding the long, tedious run down from Moab and avoid all the mosquitos too. Indian Creek enters the Colorado River seventeen miles *above* the confluence with the Green River.[44] But there never has been a road built to the Colorado River along that drainage, so it's unclear what rumor-mill had influenced his thinking. Kenny provided details about the 1955 Cataract Canyon trip in his 1956 Southwest Explorations newsletter:

> The trip went off without a hitch – but not without a flip. We launched 18 miles below Moab, Utah the morning of Aug. 27 and, after an exciting but leisurely run, landed at Hite Ferry Sept. 4. Besides myself the party members were – Dr. Harold Lambert and his son, Howard, of Berkeley, California; Dr. and Mrs. Frank Thorp, Jr. and daughter and son Marjory and Frank K.; Alfred and Edward Hoyt, Santa Fe, N.M. All were members of other Southwest Exploration river expeditions and all but Mrs. Thorp and Marjory had been with me on a previous "Cat" Canyon trip. Pete Goodwin, of Ipswich, Mass., drove the party and equipment to the launching place then took the truck back around to Hite where he left it for the party. Doc. Lambert and Howie flipped the "Jon" near the top of Gypsum Canyon Rapid – the second boat to be flipped in all our years of river running. Legitimately confused by a "washboard" obscuring the entrance into the runnable channel, they fell into a "sousehole" and emerged in a slightly up-side-down condition. However, they, the boat, and contents rode out the long, long rapid and tailwaves with no loss or damage to anything except egos.[45]

Following the river trip they all returned to Mancos and the Thorp family left with plans to climb Long's Peak on their way home to Michigan where Dr. Thorp was Research Professor at Michigan State University. When they reached Denver Prof. Thorp became quite ill and *died* the next day on September 9, 1955 with a sudden and acute case of *bulbar polio*! [46] Kenny notified everyone that had been on the trip about their being exposed to the deadly virus. He mentioned to Dave and Joanie Stacey that "My nice little doc shot 11 cc of gamma globulin into each, ahem, hip. My Gawd! I couldn't sit down for days and that is a literal fact."[47] On the 1953 trip Dr. Thorp had been considered to not be a strong paddler and on that trip he had complained of leg and back pain but no one thought it to be serious. Perhaps these were early signs of polio? In any event, the death of a good friend from polio was a wake-up call that it was still a serious disease. The Thorp's continued to remain good friends with the Ross family and stopped by in Mancos several times in later years.[48]

THE DOCK MARSTON LETTERS (Part II)

One last "key" point about this Cataract Canyon trip should be pointed out. Marjory Thorp was more than likely the passenger in Kenny's boat when they ran the Big Drops and when they ran Rapid #26 (Kenny's count) she yelled that it was like running through Satan's gut! Kenny thought the name was apropos and began calling it Satan's Gut to avoid the use of numbers. In a flurry of letters exchanged between Dock Marston and Kenny in 1956 Dock said "A short time back, I had the pleasure of seeing your run of Cat via the movies of Dr. Lambert." [49] He proceeded to write about the confusion of duplicate names of rapids in different canyons and that the use of "Falls" should not be used as they are all "Rapids." Kenny replied and said that he agreed and also mentioned that he liked the name Vulcans Rapid instead of Lava Falls in Grand Canyon. He said that the Frank Wright group had started calling Rapid #26 in Cataract Canyon "Little Lava Falls" and that he had even referred to it as "Nevills Rapid" where one of Norm's boats, the *Joan*, had spilled in 1940. But Kenny really liked the name "Satan's Gut" that had been suggested by one of his passengers.[50] Dock Marston replied and said he didn't like the use of the Nevills name as it was now in use in Grand Canyon and to use "Little Lava Falls" was extra stupid since there wasn't any lava near it. Marston then said he liked the name Kenny had come up with and suggested that the apostrophe be dropped.

The usage gained popularity to this day and now Rapid #26 is also known as "SATANS GUT" Rapid.[51] Unfortunately, several authors of books about river running have either misstated who named the rapid, or when it was named, or the number of rapids.[52] Just to be clear, the rapid in Cataract Canyon called SATANS GUT, got its name on a Kenny Ross river trip on approximately August 30, 1955! And for further clarification in regards to just how many rapids are in Cataract Canyon Kenny wrote the following to Dock Marston:

> My Rapid #26 or SATANS GUT in Cataract is the one pictured opposite page 144 in Kolb's book (bottom) but according to the USGS map it is not part of the 75-ft drop in 3/4 mile as it is captioned. That this was #24 in Nevills reconning [reconnoitering] is not surprising to me because it would have been about #30 for the Kolbs. Their #22 appears to be my #18. It just ain't possible to number those rapids so that everybody comes out right. For example, my #10 simply does not exist at a moderately high stage of water. For the life of me I couldn't tell you the exact number of rapids in Cataract but it is somewhere between 66 and 74, depending on the water stage and how you want to call 'em.[53]

Dock also agreed with Kenny and other pioneering river runners that "rapids" should be rated on some sort of sliding numbering scale depending on flow.

> In line with your comment about the inadequacy of the name RAPID, it might be pertinent to bring up the suggestion that is now circulating that rapids be rated according to a number scale with a 10 as the top for rough going. The rating would need to be subject to the flow. This idea has created a good deal of interest and several have expressed ideas of method.[54]

Finally, when Marston had agreed with Kenny that the "glass kayak" run on Kenny's 1954 SJ&C trip had probably been the first to do so, he added that he had been suggesting a river boat museum be built.

> I have been suggesting here and there that there should be a boat museum built – possibly at Art Greene's – it would be a roof and it might be necessary to set some wire around a little. Some of the RB-MV boats should be in it. The old tub at Mexican Hat used by Nevills in 1936 should be there. It would be a good place for Art Greene's windmill – etc.[55]

Kenny had already sent Marston four pictures from the 1933 RBMV expedition when he sent the photo of the fiber glass kayak. He further stated he still had the plywood boats used by RBMV expeditions and they had not been used since 1935, "but seem in fairly good shape." He continued, "I just hate to throw them away even though I have no use for them. I guess you know that these trips are said to have inspired the Nevills trips – but certainly not his boats." [56]

THE END OF SOUTHWEST EXPLORATIONS: 1956

Besides Kenny's correspondence with Dock Marston he was once again trying to get a group of boys together for Southwest Explorations Explorers camp and was not getting much positive feedback. Even with all the letter writing, the usual mass mailing of mimeographed brochures, the movie films, the articles published in river running magazines, the referrals from friends and families from earlier Explorers Camp days, the responses were next to nil. Of course, he replied to the usual letters wanting input about the San Juan River, or Cataract Canyon, but most were just fishing for free advice which Kenny gave back freely. One such series of letters was with a young college student, Peter Thune, from Williams College in Williamstown, Massachusetts. He had canoed some eastern rivers and had read one of Kenny's brochures about the trips he offered and wanted to know all sorts of things about canoeing the bigger rapids out west. Kenny patiently replied, but his letters were becoming a bit terser regarding novices wanting all the free information but declining, ultimately, to commit to paying for a commercial trip, or even partial payment as a support boat. Plus there was always the questions about how to get vehicles shuttled to and fro, costs, but little action. And Kenny still owed Ansel Hall a significant amount of money for all the equipment he had purchased and refinanced several times already. Kenny was nearing bankruptcy and a mere *six* boys had signed up for camp that summer, yet his love of the rivers kept him busy typing letters.

He received a letter in January from Dave Stacey at *American White Water* congratulating him on his short article about the San Juan River trips and asked if Kenny could expand his informal notes about Cataract Canyon into a full-blown six page article that would include photos for the organizations magazine; by April 15! Plus, Kenny had just received a request from Clyde Jones, Chairman of the AWWA asking if Kenny would be an exhibitor at the National Camping Association Convention that was to be held in Detroit. Kenny's sarcastic reply to Clyde reflected his mood:

> Unfortunately Explorers Camp will not be represented at the NCAC convention in Detroit. *You see we are not really a camp in the conventional sense but rather an organized exploring group carrying on a long-range program of true explorations and investigations in several of the field sciences.*[57] [Emphasis mine]

NO WAY OUT

Now through his communication with Dave Stacey and all the "tire-kicker" letters he kept receiving about *canoeing and boating* Cataract Canyon, Kenny let Stacey know how he felt about this new "sport" and how incompetent boaters, or novices were asking for trouble by going down Cataract before even trying something like his SJ&C trips:

> Would like to indicate that the Cat is for experts only. I did not realize that I might have encouraged too much interest in the Cat run until I began to get so many "odd" inquiries about it. After hearing from you (Feb. 15) I re-read what was in the article and sure 'nough got the impression that either too much or too little had been said about the difficulties in there. I am definitely with you about warming up to the San Juan. Still believe that most people should run the S.J. &C. before tackling Cat. Right now I am plugging the late May-early June run on the San Juan because of the prospects for really wonderful water conditions. With the river rolling sandwaves all the way and with high turbulences thru most of the Goosenecks and between John's Canyon and Moonlight Creek, it ought to satisfy every desire of the sportboat crowd for an interesting run. In fact, at high water, no one should ever disdain the San Juan--- as I am afraid some of the sport boat crowds are beginning to do.
>
> Nevertheless, I would like very much to do the Cat run with a crowd of really good kayak and canoe men. Very early May or late August would be the best time as during high water periods it becomes a holy horror even for large stable boats. If you and Joan would pick a crowd and head it up I would gladly take you thru at the lowest possible figure. Right now I am very much interested in doing a really good guide to Cataract and feel that I need first hand info on sport boats in there to complete the material.
>
> Since I am "coasting" today I might as well sound off a little more about Cataract. I feel sure that if you were to check with Otis Marston he would tell you that few, if any, living men know Cataract any better than I do. Nor am I boasting in saying that no one who has ever lived knows the complex canyon country on each side of it as well---as I have been in and out of Cat some ten times afoot and walked nearly all the areas between the canyon and civilization. Therefore, I believe that I speak with some authority when I say; it is a deadly fact that there is NO WAY OUT OF CAT for anyone

who has not been intimately initiated in the areas on either side. Hardiness and luck might bring one to safety in case he lost his boat and supplies in the canyon but more likely he would die of starvation or exhaustion. You say in your editorial that most people who have died in Cataract starved and that may be close to the mark. I don't know where you got the question concerning that but it could be the truth. The record however does not support it. Rather it indicates that very little is known about what may have happened to the many that went in the upper end and did not show up at Hite Ferry. It is certain that far too many drowned and that the rapids got 'em. And it is known that at least two starved to death and at least one showed up in a demented condition. There have been no known deaths in Cataract for more than a quarter century largely because of improved boats and techniques but I am willing to bet that past tragedies will be repeated many-fold when hordes of sport boat people try to run it--- as now seems inevitable. Let's go on-----

One is safe in saying that Cataract Canyon is more difficult than Lodore, and that many of its rapids are worse than anything in Split Mountain. The first kayaks to ever go, go all the way from Green River, Wyo. to Lake Mead made their only portages in Cat. With few exceptions, all the rapids---there are 72 worth counting---are of such nature that it is best to stop and "conn" them. The greatest continuous declivity is 75 feet in a little less than a mile but there are several individual rapids which drop 10 to 20 feet. In trying to compare the rapids in Cataract with those of the Green one must take into account the relative "weight" of the waters and the fact that Cataract Canyon is almost as narrow, infinitely rockier and the flow is more than doubled. This means more than 60 times the corrasive [abrasive] ability and perhaps five times the carrying capacity. "Velocity is greatest in channels with the smallest areas in proportion to volume of water;" also, "Velocity increases with gradient". Simple and familiar enough quotes but too often overlooked as facts. Anyhow, above the junction with the Green the Green and Colorado are relatively "light." Below the Green the Colorado is "heavy" and below the San Juan "heavier" still.[58]

In the same letter, Kenny told Stacey he had been contacted by a spokesman for a Denver group that had asked about Cataract Canyon and Kenny mentioned the man's name [withheld here]. Kenny said he thought the fellow had over-rated his skills in the letter and asked Dave Stacey what he knew about him and his group.[59]

Stacey replied quickly to Kenny warning him about the Denver group and said that this was the same group that Don Hatch had so much trouble with in Dinosaur because they were all rowdy and drunk all the time. He thought there were some good boatmen in the bunch, but there were lots of flips and spills and Kenny should be "dubious about their ability." He said he heard that "they were requested to never come back to Dinosaur by the head ranger." [60]

On the other hand, Stacey said Larry Zuk was thoroughly competent, sound and sensible and ran good trips.[61] Thus went the correspondence regarding river trip enquiries. Some folks were capable and competent while others were out for good times but had little to no respect of the dangers involved in river running and all the associated logistics. This same degree of disparagement in understanding what river running entails remains much the same today when seasoned river veterans are confronted by clueless novices.

Kenny replied to the Denver party-boy with a lengthy letter where he explained all the pitfalls of running Cataract in high water and suggested either early May or late August; the same to Larry Zuk, but neither party appeared to have taken Kenny's offer to be part of one of his trips. Kenny then turned his attention to completing his article for the AWW magazine and although late, he sent his final manuscript and photos to Dave Stacey on April 4, 1956. In the cover letter Kenny said he had the manuscript finished the previous Friday, but had wanted to proof it one more time before sending it.

> In the meantime, the whole family took an Easter trip to Canyon de Chelly. Gad what a trip! Windy! A WHITE Easter in Arizona! Anyhow we had a nice visit with the old friends the Aubuchon's who is Superintendent there. They are soon to be transferred to Custer Battlefield in Montana and we had put off our visit almost too long. Whitehouse Ruin is gorgeous when mantled in snow.[62]

THE AWW CATARACT CANYON ARTICLE

Kenny's six-page article "Cataract Canyon" was published in the Winter Edition of the *American White Water* magazine and was generally well received with many accolades regarding his literary style and how well it was written and illustrated.[63] However, Don Hatch typed a three-page letter dated December 15, 1956 to Kenny where he listed a number of questions he had pertaining to the AWW article. Don Hatch asked about the origin of the rapid names – *Satans Gut* and *Maelstrom* in Cataract and wanted clarification as he hadn't heard these names used before; giving credence that Kenny had only begun using these names after his 1955 trip:

> I'm curious to know where you got the names "Satan's Gut" and "The Maelstrom" for rapids in Cataract. Our Western River Guides Association members have never heard of these names. Otis Marston, a foremost authority on rivers, has never used, and I doubt heard of the names.[64]

Don Hatch was not aware of the many correspondences regarding these new rapid names that Kenny had explained to Marston in his letter of March 17, 1956 and all the "exchanging of river information and ideas" over the previous several years with Dock. Hatch also had comments regarding rubber vs wooden boats, Galloway vs Nevills boat designs, vertical drops across rapids, number of rapids, numbering of rapids, rowing with oars on fixed frames vs paddles, etc.

Following his explanation of the name, *Satans Gut* to Don Hatch, Kenny added "*The Maelstrom*" to his Rapid #43 at RM 195.5, stating that it was a long curving island rapid which had a long swinging back current sweeping up the right bank. At 8,000 to 11,000 cfs the re-entry into the lower end of rapid was near the top of the tail waves creating a bowl-shaped "maelstrom." He then addressed some of the other questions posed by Don Hatch:

> Actually, I list 67 rapids between mile points 212-1/2 and 176. My original list was made during the course of a trip in 1949 when the river was flowing 7500 cfs and I included every "noticeable declivity which produced definite Rapids which might cause difficulty at any but the highest agitation of the water." Stages of water were described in detail; others were described as "insignificant", "Only a riffle", "lacking hazards from rocks", "no hazards but having good tail waves" etc. During subsequent trips made at different stages of water comments concerning the changed aspects of each have been added. It is interesting to note that all but one of the rapids listed is noticeable as at least a mild agitation at flows up to 13,000 cfs and that some which are listed as "tricky", "vicious", or "extremely rocky and complex", at 7500 ft. are no more than riffles producing 4 inch waves at 15,000 ft. I question the value of any list made at flows above 10,000 cfs which does not include every riffle producing noticeable waves. So far as I am concerned my 67 rapids list does not exaggerate the true number of rapids in Cataract Canyon.
>
> "A 75-foot drop in ¾ mile" is a statement which has been repeated several times in print. It is inaccurate and perhaps I should not have repeated the error but gives the true impression I like it because, regardless of split-hair accuracy, is that this relatively presents some short section of the Colorado of the toughest going anywhere on the river. It of course comprises those rapids between Mile 204 and Mile 205, which Loper called the "Big Drop", Stanton called "Hell's Half Mile", and of which Stone remarked, "It's more than half a mile, perhaps that's the hell of it." It includes your rapid

> at Mile 204-3/4, which I believe must be my Rapid #16; a plenty rough one at any water level. I have taken a fair number of people through Cataract Canyon and, inevitably get howls of disbelief when I show the river survey plan map as proof that this section drops much less than the 75 feet classically attributed to it. One seasoned engineer who has been through there twice with me took what he called "eye-level measurements" in this section and states that he feels sure that the total drop is greater than that shown on the plan and profile maps. Personally I am willing to accept that survey measurements are probably not too far off---even tho I know for sure that surveys made under such difficulties as there are here sometimes contain some inaccuracies.[65]

Kenny closed by saying:

> Thanks again for your letter and comments. You need have no fear that I would take criticism of anything I write in any way other than it is intended. Anything I write is subject to yours and anyone else's criticism. When I am wrong or even partly wrong I'll gladly admit it. If I disagree with the criticism I'll defend my stand with right good spirit. Yours for drier spills.[66]

Don Hatch had also written a letter to Dock Marston dated December 18, 1956 where he critiqued Kenny's AWW article:

> About Ross and his paddles: I doubt that he has ever used a good oar set-up on rubber boats, has he? Personally (and being perhaps too frank) I wouldn't be caught dead with Ellingson's or Ross' paddles on a river with respectable – or should I say, I'd be dead if I used them.[67]

Finally, a late 1956 letter from Dock Marston to Kenny commented on a subject that required explanation. The key comment pertained to Government Rapid on the San Juan River:

> And I also enclose print of the repair work on the government boat which cracked in a rapid above Slickhorn. All you need to do is to identify the spot and we will have the right location for GOVERNMENT RAPID.[68]

If Kenny replied, the letter has not been located, but the following information has been added to clarify Dock's question of 1956: "WHERE IS GOVERNMENT RAPID?"

WHERE IS GOVERNMENT RAPID?

Present day river runners who have been down the San Juan River from Mexican Hat to Clay Hills landing know about Government Rapid; or they think they do. It's the toughest rapid to negotiate, particularly in low water (under 800 cfs). Most modern day river logs show river mileage (RM) 0.0 running *downstream* that begin in the vicinity of the present-day BLM concrete ramp at Sand Island, or the U.S. Highway 191 Bridge crossing a half-mile farther downstream; so right away, there's a half mile or so discrepancy when downstream measurements start from arbitrary points.[69]

The discrepancy immediately created some confusion when referring to points downstream. When the San Juan and Colorado rivers were surveyed in the 1920s, the zero points (0.0 miles) were at confluences and mileages were measured *upstream*. Even though the confluence of the San Juan and Colorado rivers are submerged under Powell reservoir, the zero point is still present and shown on USGS topographic maps and was very much present as a confluence of the two rivers when the Kelley Trimble Survey was conducted on the San Juan River in 1921.[70] These are geologic/geographic data points that will take many centuries to move any appreciable distance; a geologic fact and certainly much less than one-half mile as presently depicted on modern river logs/maps. Refer to Appendix: Table 1: San Juan River to Lees Ferry, for both upstream and downstream measurements mentioned in the following discussion.

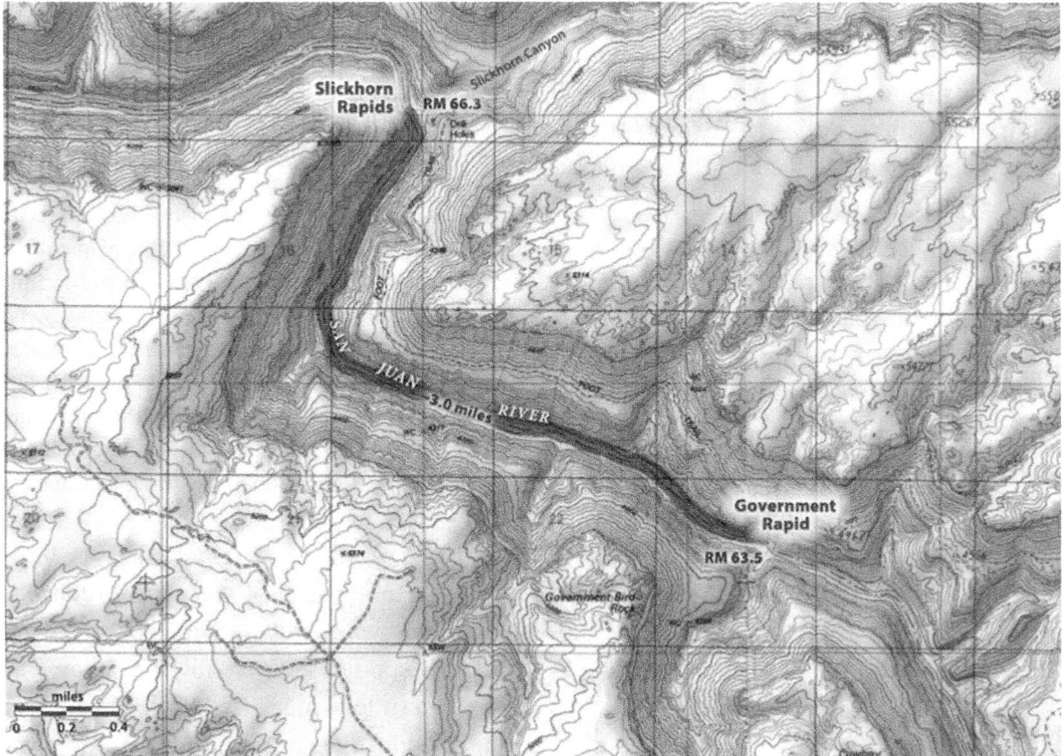

Figure 9.9 the rapid *three miles above Slickhorn Canyon* is what has become to be known as "Government Rapid" but nothing happened here to warrant the name. (Modified from *Esri Arc/GIS* USGS topographic map)

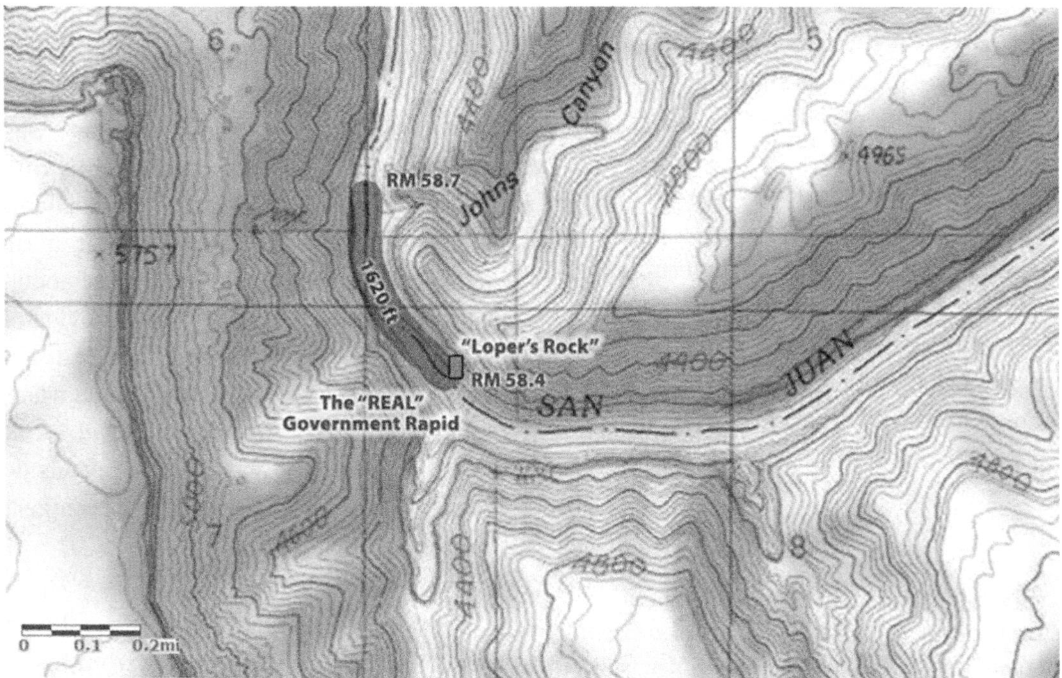

Figure 9.10 the "real Government Rapid" is shown here, about 1620 ft (0.3 mi) above the mouth of Johns Canyon. (Modified from *Esri Arc/GIS* USGS topographic map)

Modern river logs show Government Rapid somewhere near RM 63.5 miles downstream of Sand Island, or the bridge.[71] Hugh Miser, geologist on the Trimble Survey party of 1921, noted that this rapid occurred about three miles upstream of the mouth of Slickhorn Gulch (RM 66.3)[72] which, by my measurement is 77.2 miles above the confluence (Figure 9.9). Gregory Crampton noted many San Juan Canyon Historical Sites in 1964, including Government Rapid: "This is a short sharp rapid at mile 77.6 caused by big sandstone blocks near the right bank." [73] Although sandstone boulders are present, most of the boulders in the rapid are actually comprised of large angular blocks of dense cherty *limestone* containing marine invertebrate mega-fossils. The boulder strewn constriction is due primarily to a boulder fan derived from a small steep canyon on river left (RL); not the "right bank" (RR) as mentioned by Crampton. Plus, dense limestones erode much more slowly than do sandstones. In low water this rapid is quite the technical boulder field to negotiate, but in water levels of 1200 cfs or greater it is a big wavy, bumpy ride that can be run right down the middle as shown in the 1921 photo by Robert N. Allen.[74]

Hugh Miser was still alive in 1963 and he told Greg Crampton on November 5, 1963 that the name came from the rumor that a government boat was wrecked there. Miser was referring to the U. S. Geological Survey party of 1921, of which he was a member that mapped the canyon in cooperation with the Southern California Edison Company of Los Angeles. *"No boats were lost there, he said."* [75]

> The boats of the Trimble expedition were run through most of the rapids. In shooting the worst ones Loper, the boatman, was the only member of the party to stay in the boats; the other men walked along the banks around such rapids. The loaded boats were nosed one at a time through a few rapids by the boatman, who in wading held on to the bow and guided it downstream ahead of him. The equipment was portaged around a rapid 3 miles above the mouth of Slickhorn Gulch, and then the boats were run empty through the rapid. *[Author's note: This is Government Rapid and no mention of any boat damage here]* [76] The loaded boats were run through a small rapid half a mile above the mouth of Johns Canyon, but one of the boats containing two members of the party not only narrowly missed striking the canyon wall but struck a boulder and was burst on one side from bow to stern. The boat was nearly filled with water by the time a landing place was reached. Then the wet equipment was unloaded, and the boat was dragged ashore and repaired." [77]

Therefore, the *government boat* referred to above that was badly damaged occurred about 1620 ft (0.3 miles) above Johns Canyon (RM 58.7 on modern logs measured downstream from the Highway Bridge datum point).[78] In high water at about RM 58.3 it is a small riffle with sand waves, but at low water it is necessary to sneak along a sheer wall on far river right (RR), staying right of an emergent gravel bar, then pull hard left to miss a huge boulder on RR at the bottom (RM 58.4). This was where the 1921 government boat hit "Loper's Rock" [79] (Figure 9.10) and was damaged – and NOT the rapid roughly three miles above Slickhorn Gulch! But the boatman, Bert Loper, who was rowing the boat on that 1921 incident had a slightly different take about how badly damaged the boat was and provided more details that led up to the accident. *He also firmly defined that the accident did not occur at what is popularly known as "Government Rapid."* It is also informative as to how the boatman considered the damage as minor, while the passenger saw the damage as catastrophic!

The following account was originally typed by Bert Loper, apparently working from his original notes. Brad Dimock deciphered and retyped Loper's notes from his diaries. Dimock graciously provided me his entire collection of retyped notes when he learned of my plans to write this book about Kenny Ross and the San Juan River.

> August 5 – I ferried Elwyn across the river the first thing on starting out and it was soon after that a mountain sheep broke back up the river past him it had become rimmed so it had to get back up the river—I had to ferry the main bunch across the river on account of the being rimmed and in crossing we ran into some sand waves and one of the bed rolls was thrown out of the boat but was recovered then we had a rapid to go over and one of the row locks broke and things looked rather serious and in fact we did strike a rock and the boat was split rather bad but we landed and took the boat out and it was soon repaired—it was a rather unwielldly out fit to handle any way for I had two boats with two men in each boat but the accident was not so serious—by the time the boat was fixed it was noon so we had lunch and this was at the mouth of Johns Canyon and at the mouth where the canyon pours over there is about a 60 foot drop so there was a basin of clear water so the boys had a swim in the clear water—In p.m. we continued on our way and had good going but some very swift water—had a very good camp, for the night.

> Aug-6—saw us on our way good and early—I took Trimble, Allen, Hebe in one boat and Elwyn took Miser and Hugh in the other and we drifted down to the head of a rather severe rapid—the river is very narrow and swift—In p.m. we came to where we had to portage the loads but I ran the boats through—Elwyn saw another Mountain sheep. Mr. Miser found a perfect piece of pottery— we reached the mouth of Slick Horn Canyon and made camp and will have to wait for Wesley Oliver with the supplies—In 1894 this was the camp of Bill and John Clark and Al Rogers they placered out a small bar just above the mouth of the Canyon—[80]

Thus, the rapid located approximately three miles above the mouth of Slickhorn Canyon almost certainly was mis-identified, but by whom? My research has not come up with a definitive answer, but I suspect that it was by none other than Norman Nevills who began calling this *rather severe rapid* "Government Rapid" at some point after March, 1935 and the name stuck. He made numerous runs (at least 19) down the river typically launching at Mexican Hat and almost made a race out of it to see how fast he could make it to Slickhorn where he and his groups left their signatures and later catalogued by river historian, Greg Crampton. Norm made little mention of the rapid, or much else along the way, but he ran it enough times and at different flow rates that he saw it was a rapid to pay attention to and most likely gave it the name.[81] No government boats were damaged at this rapid in 1921!

Kenny Ross made his second full run of the SJ&C in his LCRs in 1951 and he described the rapid and their run of all the fully loaded boats through "Government Rapid" as the "big, black, hairy one." [82] But he didn't have any upset or damage. He had seen this section of the river the previous year and then nearly eighteen years prior when on the 1933 RBMV trip where they more than likely lined and portaged the foldboats and every twist and turn in the river was new.[83] But one thing is for sure – *the USGS survey group in 1921 did not give this rapid its name*. Regardless of who named it, all of us who followed – right up to modern day river runners relying on modern day river guide maps, as well as the most recent USGS topographical maps continue to carry this mis-named rapid as Government! Fittingly, the San Juan River cuts across the Paradox Basin. How appropriate to have a most paradoxically named rapid.

THE BOAT CAMP MOVES TO BLUFF

The 1956 Explorers camp for boys, meager as it was, opened on June 22 with the six boys signed up, but the camp was operated out of some run down cabins about five miles northwest of Spruce Mill on the west side of the La Plata Mountains. Ansel Hall had sold the entire Gold King mill site buildings forcing Kenny to relocate.

Kenny had advertised for a camp cook and ended up hiring an Israeli man – "Ike" Haussmann who had been working in Pasadena, California.[84] Due to the low enrollment, Kenny wanted his oldest son, Don, who was now twelve years old, to take part in the whole camp season. Other than the Salt Creek Canyon hike Don participated in all the activities. That included the last excavations at Cibola City ruins near Cahone, Colorado. Don brought along a Mancos friend, Conrad Wagner to participate in the last dig. The site was duly cleaned up after their final excavation, and remained untouched by Kenny Ross or anyone associated with the Explorers Camp or Southwest Explorations.

Don Ross made his third SJ&C river trip from Bluff to Lees Ferry, much to the disappointment and disgust of his younger brother Doug. That was the last year where river runners could take out at Lees Ferry. In fact, the Bureau of Reclamation had sent notices out to known river runners prohibiting river traffic past Wahweap Creek, but Don said they didn't have any problem from the bureaucrats on their trip. Later that fall, Kenny received notice from the Bureau stating a river boat takeout was under consideration at Warm Creek located a few river miles upstream from Wahweap Creek, but overland access was problematic, to say the least.[85]

There was very little additional information other than Don's comments about the 1956 season. There was no indication Kenny took any adult groups down Cataract Canyon post-camp time in late August or early September. Kenny knew things were going to change regarding running the two rivers he loved so much. He did not like the Spruce Mill location as a base camp, plus his primary source of income had shifted almost entirely to river trips, so a move to Bluff with all the boats and equipment seemed to be more appropriate.

The hard, cold reality of a dam at Glen Canyon had been signed into law and the impounded waters of a huge reservoir would adversely affect his trips on the SJ&C and Cataract Canyon; he just didn't know how detrimental it would be, and no one else did either. President Dwight Eisenhower signed the Colorado River Storage Project (CRSP) Act into law in 1956 that authorized four main-stem water-storage units, including Glen Canyon Dam. Construction of Glen Canyon Dam began on September 29, 1956 and the last bucket of concrete was poured on September 13, 1963. The proposed purpose of the dam was for water stored in what would soon be known as "Lake Powell" would allow upper basin states to meet their obligations to lower basin states during drought years as set forth in the Colorado River Compact of 1922 (CRC).[86] Times were definitely changing.

10

WILD RIVERS EXPEDITIONS IS BORN

COW CANYON TRADING POST

Kenny had gotten to know some of the residents, business owners and land owners in Bluff which led him to work out a deal with Rusty Musselman in the fall of 1956. Rusty owned and operated the new *Cow Canyon Trading Post* which he opened in 1955 and was located at the east end of the tiny village near the intersection of Highway 47 and an east-bound county road that led to St. Christopher's Episcopal Mission. The Trading Post also had a detached automobile garage and gas pumps operated by "Duke" Simpson. A breezeway separated the two buildings and Rusty said Kenny could set up some big tents behind the gas station. Thus, over the winter of 1956-57 Kenny bought a 16 ft x 16 ft military surplus pyramid-shaped tent and erected it on the south side of the gas station[1] and moved all his river boats, truck, jeeps and all the gear to his new base camp. This would later be known as *Boat Camp No. 1*.[2] There still wasn't any electricity available and no phone service other than at Twin Rocks Trading Post, so he returned to Mancos where he could resume his letter writing and correspondence.[3] The 1957 notification of trips and camp was still under the header of *Southwest Explorations*, but the colorful mimeographed brochures were replaced by a simple inexpensive two-page typed newsletter that listed river trips and costs.[4] Gone were the lengthy and colorful descriptions of the mountains, the canyons, Spanish Explorers and Anasazi ruins. The newsletter was entirely committed to "River plans for the season of 1957." [5] Kenny advertised three kinds of river trips for 1957.

Figure 10.1 the first day-trips from Bluff to Mexican Hat launched east of Bluff on the riverside of the Curtis Jones farm and across the river from "the Dance Plaza" archaeological site; dailies were run with paddles, but a 3-HP "kicker" outboard motor was included in case winds kicked up. (K. Ross collection)

> Two of these will be on the San Juan River and will operate during the period, April 22 to June 10—the time of best water conditions. The third trip will be through the Cataract Canyon of the Colorado and these will be launched in late August and early September.[6]

He mentioned that a camp for boys of high school age would operate from June 10 to August 25, but that information regarding the Explorers Camp for Boys was *only available by request.* [Emphasis mine] And, for the first time, Kenny advertised one-day river trips that were to be run on Saturdays and Sundays, although he mentioned that he first ran day trips in 1956 "for the purpose of giving San Juan Basin residents and their guests an opportunity to enjoy a sample of white water boating on an especially scenic and interesting section of the San Juan River." [7]

For a short period of time Kenny moved his launch point closer to Bluff, right across the river from an archaeological site known as "the Dance Plaza" (Figure 10.1). But he soon moved three miles farther down river and trips were launched from Sand Island and ended at Mexican Hat. The 1957 newsletter was the first time the "Sand Island" launch point was actually referred to by name. Access was down an unimproved rocky cobble-strewn ledge next to Buck Creek; the road cut that present-day boaters use was not completed until the 1960s. The boat takeout at Mexican Hat was still the fast water landing located immediately upstream of the bridge. If you missed this landing your next opportunity to get your boat off the river was fifty-six river miles downstream at Clay Hills Crossing! Kenny mentioned key points of interest that included Indian "picture writings," ancient cliff dwellings and "sand waves." All trips were still by paddle! The cost for the one-day trips were: Daily: $12.50 per person; if ten or more: $10.00 per person; and a maximum size of eighteen: $8.75 per person.[8]

His "Four-Day San Juan River Expeditions" launched near Bluff and took out at Clay Hills Crossing "where uranium miners have recently built a road to the river from near Natural Bridges National Monument." The cost for this wilderness experience required a minimum of five people: $70/person, but if eight or more: $60.00/person with group size maximum of sixteen.[9]

The Cataract Canyon "Adventure" trip was marketed as an eight-day 120 mile trip launching near Moab (Potash) and taking out at the Hite Ferry at the mouth of White Canyon costing $175.00/person, "with substantial reductions offered for group participation" where Kenny was now covering his costs with a *support boat* for private boaters.[10]

It's unclear how successful the 1957 season was, but Don Ross said that Kenny was using the name *Wild Rivers Expeditions* by the time summer rolled around and Kenny did another late August-early September Cataract Canyon trip. The river business wasn't bringing in enough income for the family so Mildred gave up being a *stay-at-home mom* and went back to teaching fifth grade at Mancos School in 1957-58. She had taught school at Mesa Verde from 1937 to 1942, and was still qualified to teach. Plus, she had been raising two rambunctious boys and keeping them in line had kept her on her toes.

Mildred had a wry sense of humor and knew the boys would be unsettled by seeing her at school so she played a little prank on them. Doug and Don had spent part of the summer in Boulder with their older brother Chuck. They biked and hiked and had a grand time and when they returned home Mildred told Doug that she was going to be teaching sixth grade! Then she turned to Don and said "if not sixth grade, then it would be eighth grade" knowing full well that Don would be entering eighth grade. Both Doug and Don were mortified by the news, but she soon retracted her little joke on the boys and said she was really going to be teaching fifth grade. They were both relieved to know they would avoid this embarrassment of having their mother as their official teacher! [11]

RED DUST ATOMIC MUSHROOMS

Frank Thorp had gone on to medical school at the University of Chicago. He wrote Kenny in January 1957 and stated that he and his mom were still working on the Cataract Canyon notes from the 1955 river trip.

> We all read your article in White Water with great excitement – it's a corker as per usual! Is Georgie White's report about the San Juan being closed to further river trips true? It seems impossible to believe that such a day is actually at hand." [12]

Kenny replied to Frank with a long newsy letter where he said the Ross family sent greetings to Frank and that it had been a busy fall and winter but not much to show for it. He also assured Frank that the San Juan River would still be navigable, but trips would have to take out above Lees Ferry due to the construction of the Glen Canyon Dam:

> This whole section of the State is just beginning to dig out from under one of the biggest snow storms in many years; you have probably been hearing reports of the "plight" of people down here. Its lots of fun to listen to radio network newscasters giving news of all we poor snowed-in people, "on the hour, every hour." Wolf Creek Pass has been closed for a week and just re-opened this morning. They say it will be another week before regular traffic can be resumed – if it does not snow any more. We have only about 3 feet on the ground here in the yard but it is reported that there is 22 feet on the level on Wolf Creek and Cumbres Passes, 45 feet in drifts. The big hazard in the high hills now is snow slides.
>
> The Glen Canyon Dam has everyone in a dither. There has been an official announcement to the affect that boats will not be allowed to pass by construction site but there is a question as to whether any agency has the right to make such a ruling. I'm darned if I know what the score will be. Its tough to make plans for the coming Ex Camp trips. Am planning on taking two or three spring trips from Bluff to the head of Paiute Farms where it is possible to jeep out via Natural Bridges. *[The first take-outs at Clay Hills]* This will be a four day trip at high water – including the day it will take to move passengers and equipment from Paiute Farms back to Blanding and Bluff. There is a slim possibility that it may be possible to continue San Juan-Colorado trips and take the boats and people out at Padre Creek. As you may recall, Jeeps have occasionally been driven down there from Escalante and it appears possible that only a little scraping might make it a practical way for heavier equipment to haul out boats – especially as the dam construction involves making a pretty decent road near the vicinity. If all this seems ambiguous, it fits the situation perfectly. This riverman will not give up without a struggle.
>
> Cortez is suffering – ecstatically – the throes of a big oil boom. Seems that the area on both sides of the San Juan in the vicinity of the mouth of Recapture Creek and on up to Hatch's Trading Post and Hovenweep has been hiding what may turn out to be one of the world's biggest oil pools. Anyhow, all the major and some of the minor oil companies are in it with both feet (ugh!); there are now big producing wells (a dozen or so) and scores of wells in the drilling stage. Pipelines are being constructed but now all oil is being hauled by truck out thru "our" road between Hovenweep and Pleasant View, and up the more treacherous McElmo Canyon road. Company cars, drilling crews, equipment trucks, Service Company crews – the whole panoply of the oil business – has made a traffic shambles of both roads. There has been no money for significant improvement of either and of course they cannot safely handle the 90-mile-an-hour temperaments of hurried executives, drilling supervisors, pressured truck drivers, et al. Twisty McElmo has become a veritable death trap and "our" quiet little, rocky wilderness road is only slightly less dangerous. Wrecks, bad injuries, fatalities, all are almost daily occurrences. The State has assigned a

Highway Patrolman for almost exclusive duty in McElmo and his emergency runs for succor and law are so frequent that he has acquired the name "McElmo" Jack Stone.

The result of all this activity in Cortez, where oil companies, service companies, material suppliers, hangers-on, geophysical companies, camp-followers, jackals – the works – are wrangling for office, yard and living space, is absolutely stupefying. The town doesn't have enough space, houses, water, power, schools – or enough of anything, including doctors, hospitals, bars, and especially policemen and lawyers, to handle the situation. The situation has developed so rapidly that local money, although eagerly offered, you bet, and local effort simply hasn't been adequate to cope with it. Building construction companies have come in from elsewhere and joined in the effort to provide housing and offices. Housing developments are blossoming on every hill around town and the vales are filled with trailer villages. But Main Street still has only curbs and paving in town and the red dust mushrooms in atomic splendor above the Sleeping Ute. Among the silly sidelights concerns the question of a "Daily" newspaper – both Weaklies are eyeing each other like starved coyotes across the carcass of a dead horse; both afraid to jump in, each certain that the other will get there first. Perhaps a big, bad wolf will come in and get the gravy.

Some of it all is spilling over into Mancos, of course, but not too much as yet. We take it calmly except when some trailer family proposes to move into our back yards and hook into our power and water lines as one did recently at our house. We said, "NO, by golly!" Thank God, the drilling here in the Mancos Valley has resulted only in gaseous burps.[13]

Sometime during the winter of 1957-58 Rusty Musselman got the idea of how to make a buck and convinced Kenny to join him and they started the *Monument Valley Stage* with a VW bus that they planned to run from Flagstaff to Monticello and back three times a week. Kenny worked for Rusty over the winter months but the enterprise didn't last long (Figure 10.2).

Figure 10.2 the Monument Valley Stage was a short-time enterprise run by Rusty Musselman and Kenny Ross, 1957-58. (K. Ross collection)

OARS - FINALLY

By the end of 1957 Kenny realized that if he were to continue to take paying passengers down rivers he needed to "bite the bullet" and forgo his dual paddle technique and convert some of his boats to oars with rowing frames.[14] The dual paddle method always required recruiting a paying passenger to be one of the paddle mates, and some folks just never got the hang of it. By converting to oars only one boatman per boat was needed and particularly on day trips where baggage and gear was not needed, he could significantly increase his ratio of boatman to paying passenger. So over the winter he made his first conversion to rowing stands which consisted of a double stack of two by six inch pine wood blocks and had circular metal rings for the oars manufactured by a welder in Blanding. The oar posts were bolted to the wooden blocks and then the blocks were tied to the boat's tubes in a most precarious fashion (Figure 10.3). The wooden blocks proved to be more of a proto-type and were soon replaced by frames constructed from half-inch to three-quarter-inch diameter electrical conduit in 1959. Rusty Musselman had the welding equipment and know-how to do the welding and the oar posts were then welded to the frames. Doug Ross recalled that one of his jobs was to wrap one-quarter inch diameter hemp rope, and re-wrap worn out rope around each oar ring as needed.

Figure 10.3 Kenny at upper Eight Foot landing, 1957 with his first set of proto-type oars; note the oar pins are set into holes drilled in wooden blocks that are tied with rope to the boat. (K. Ross collection)

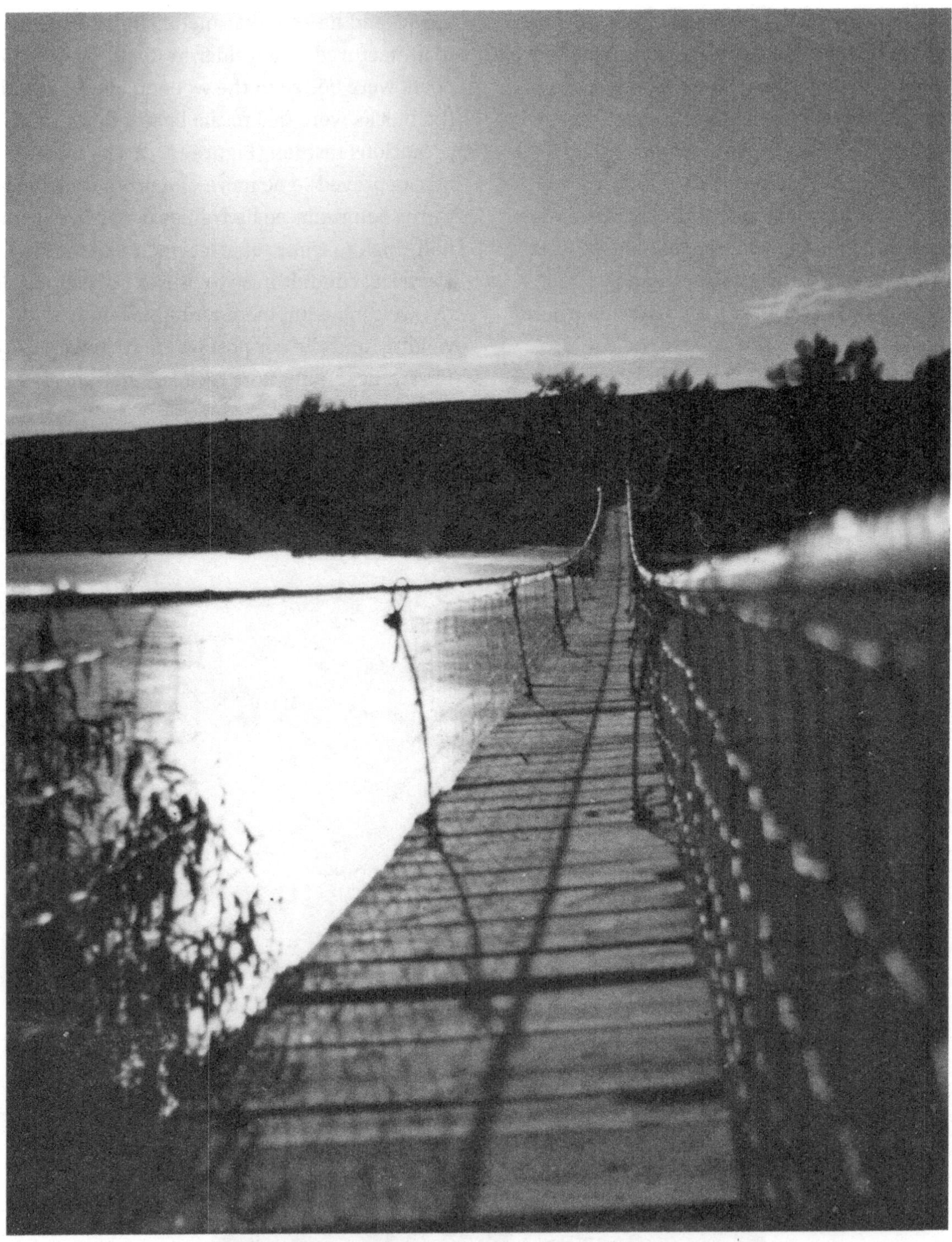

Figure 10.4 looking to the south (the "Navajo side") at the Swingin' Bridge at full moon on August 15, 1975; it was just a footbridge but the only means of crossing the San Juan River safely – upstream or down for decades. (Photo by Bruce Steinhaus; K. Ross collection)

Kenny advertised in local newspapers and committed to San Juan River trips with lots of focus on locals in 1958. Folks from Durango, Cortez, Mancos, Farmington, etc booked some trips from Bluff to Mexican Hat.[15]

Don "graduated" from eighth grade at Mancos Elementary School and joined Kenny for the summer. They moved the big tent to *Boat Camp No. 2* a few hundred yards east of Cow Canyon Wash and north of the Mission Road to the north side of the "Mushroom Rock" as it was called. Kenny bought another big tent and they erected both tents with a breezeway between the two; one tent served as living quarters and the other had river equipment stored inside. The boats sat outside.

Don Ross ran (paddled) his first commercial trip (a daily) on the San Juan that year. The group arrived in a *Continental Trailways* full size Coach Tour bus and somehow made its way down the steep, unimproved rocky trail next to Buck Creek at Sand Island with fifty "seniors" aboard for a day-trip from Bluff to Mexican Hat. Don said that after the bus was off-loaded the driver gunned the engine and charged bucking and banging straight up the hill and was waiting, unscathed, for the group when they reached Mexican Hat that afternoon. He said he had "three old farts telling him how to run his boat" [16] but somehow the trip made it to Mexican Hat successfully and Don was paid ten bucks! The rest of 1958 Kenny plodded along in another low water year.

THE SWINGIN' BRIDGE

One of the new attractions on the river was built in 1958. The "Swingin' Bridge" located about four miles upstream from Bluff, was built in early 1958 by the *R.L. Manning Company*, a Denver based oil-drilling firm.[17] It was a cable suspension bridge with a single center support and a wooden deck walkway (Figure 10.4). It was initially built to facilitate the company's drilling operations on the south side on the San Juan River, and over time the roughly 300-foot-long span became an important link in the transportation network of San Juan County. A good friend, Hanley Begay, recalled walking across the bridge to St. Christopher's Mission many times in his youth. Don Ross said he walked across the bridge to work on a drilling rig one summer in the early 1960s. During my years of boating for Wild Rivers in the 1980s and 1990s we occasionally guided tourists across the bridge to the south side to visit "Sixteen-room ruin" (or "many-room ruins" as some of us called it) located in a large broad alcove near the base of the Bluff Sandstone.[18]

The bridge had survived the "Labor Day flood" of a measured flow of 52,000 cfs at the "Gage near Bluff" (USGS gage located at Mexican Hat) in the fall of 1970.[19] On September 11, 2003, a large summer monsoon storm moved across the Four Corners area and the San Juan River, which averaged about 1,000 cfs at that time of year rose to 23,000 cfs, making it the third highest recorded flow since the completion of Navajo Dam in 1962.[20] The bridge withstood the flash flood but was badly damaged. The bridge was repaired in 2004, but under the strain of the river, the center support began listing downstream thus effectively lowering the cables. The wooden planks on the bridge walkway were either missing or rotted making walking across an adventure for those who dared. By 2005 even moderately high flows of 12,000 cfs threatened its survival. In late spring of 2007, after nearly fifty years, the bridge was deemed a hazard, and Utah State Parks and Recreation River Rangers spent two days removing it.[21]

Oil drilling continued at a brisk pace twenty miles east of Bluff. As the giant Aneth oil field was developed a sturdy bridge strong enough for oil field trucks and drill rigs to cross the San Juan River was required and the "Texaco Rd" bridge was completed in 1959 at the Navajo Chapter

House site of Montezuma Creek located 247.3 miles below the San Juan River's headwaters and 159.3 miles above the SJ&C confluence. Highway 191 Bridge near Sand Island wasn't completed until 1971 – over eighteen miles farther downstream with only the Swingin' Bridge in-between (see Appendix I: Table 1).

EARLY BOAT CAMPS

Boat Camp No. 2: Don and Kenny began restoring *Esther the Jeep* and had it on blocks in the breezeway between the two tents. Don said it was very "comfy quarters." In mid-July, 1959 the propane-powered refrigerator caught fire in the "living quarter's tent." Kenny and Don were able to extinguish it without too much damage to the tent or its contents. They went to Durango and bought a new tent at *Thompson's Saddle Shop* to replace the burned tent.[22] Everything else appeared to be fine and the jeep stayed in the breezeway. After they erected the new tent and moved all their cots and personal effects in, they returned to Mancos.

In August, Rusty called Kenny and said there had been another fire, but this one was BIG! Kenny and Don hurried back to find that the living quarters, along with some ten thousand 35mm slides, and all the contents were destroyed, along with an untold number of documents. Plus, the equipment tent was also completely destroyed along with all the river equipment (e.g., life vests, tarps, cookware, cans etc) and "Esther the Jeep" that was in the breezeway was totally destroyed too. A big loss! [23] Apparently, the propane-powered refrigerator caught fire again. Fortunately, all the boats, paddles and oars were saved. Rusty and some others had dragged them away from the burning tents.

Don and Kenny went down to the river where they cut a bunch of young cottonwoods and built a *chaha'oh* slightly south of the previous tent camp and this location became *Boat Camp No. 3*.

A chaha'oh is a Navajo word meaning "shadow" or "summer shade house" and some Navajo say *chahash'oh.*[24] It is most commonly built by erecting at least four corner posts eight to twelve feet tall of straight sturdy cottonwood or cedar and then longer cottonwood limbs are tied along the back and two sides and across the top. Then the top is covered by interwoven leafy branches until sufficient shade is created. They liked it as it was much cooler than the heavy canvas tents and found it to be "comfy." [25] The chaha'oh continued as the boat camp through 1960.

The 1959 Wild Rivers season saw lots of dailies and four-day over-nighters to Clay Hills, and Don learned more about the finer details of how to row with oars, including how to read the water, learn ferry angles, feathering, landings, etc. This was when the Kenny Ross mantra was born and drummed into every boatman's head:

"Run the "V's", cut the "C's" and watch your downstream oar!" [26]

A Cataract trip was scheduled for late August-early September and they bought new life "horse-collar" preservers[27] and other needed gear for boating and camping. Land Lindbergh had heard about the fire(s) and sent Kenny a big air pump and miscellaneous gear – enough to be able to pull off a Cat trip. Don got to row his own boat, the *No Name* for the first time through Cataract Canyon at age fifteen. Kenny and Doug claimed Don was the youngest "paid" boatman to run all of Cataract Canyon. Mildred had agreed to Don running the trip and missing the first week or two of school on the condition that there would be "no football!" Don agreed and had a great trip and recalled that the trip included Frank Thorp and his sister, Ben Humphrey and his sister, plus about ten other folks. Kenny ran the ten-man LCR-L, but Don's not sure who ran the third LCR-S boat. Thorp & Humphrey brought a two-man foldboat/kayak but they dumped in Rapid #5 and twice in Mile Long. Kenny and Frank agreed that it was too much too soon for the boys and agreed to pack the foldboat away. Other than having to line the boats down Dark Canyon Rapid all ended well with Don going back to school in Mancos.[28]

KANE CREEK LANDING

Doug Ross said he made his first SJ&C trip as a boatman when he was thirteen years old in the summer of '59 and they took out at "Kane Creek." In researching these new spots to take boats off the river after the coffer dam was built and Glen Canyon Dam was under construction, Warm Creek was mentioned early on, but then "Kane Creek" was mentioned by most folks after 1958. Gaylord Staveley (2015, p.148-150) explained that a "bootlegged" bulldozer trail had been scraped twelve miles farther upstream from the Warm Creek landing that had been proposed by the government. The elevation at river level dropped from about 3178 ft at Kane Creek to about 3160 at Warm Creek. The mouth of Warm Creek is some 28.5 river miles above Lees Ferry and the mouth of "Kane Creek" is located another 12.7 river miles above Warm Creek (41.2 river miles above Lees Ferry; see Appendix: Table 1). Both takeout locations were on river right (RR) or the north side of the river and the middle of the Colorado River marked the county boundary between Kane and San Juan Counties (Kane Co. lies to the west or in this spot, north of San Juan County, Utah).

However, "Kane Creek" or "Kane Wash" is only shown as a geographic place name on the 1953 Gunsight Butte USGS topographical map. The wash lies west of Kane Point (later named "Gooseneck Point" in 1958).[29] The mouth of Kane Wash lies at the strong northerly bend in the river that wrapped around Padre Butte. Kane Wash had "right, center and left forks" where the left fork was the route taken across the sand flats to bedrock that became known as the "Kane Creek" take out. Overland distance from river bend to a marked trail on bedrock via the Left Fork entered on the east side of Cookie Jar Butte was about five and a half miles. Another twenty-three miles across a rocky trail led to Highway 89, for a total distance of twenty-eight and a half miles to pavement. To add to the confusion and the comment from Georgie White referred to in the Frank Thorp Christmas card,[30] the Bureau of Reclamation denied that any of these roads even existed in their attempts to discourage river traffic after 1956. They even erected signs on the boat landing at Mexican Hat that stated the river was closed and that downstream travel was not permitted below the Mexican Hat Bridge![31] But someone with the Bureau finally realized they couldn't legally outlaw river traffic, so they accepted the fact that the nearly thirty miles of rocky rough road from Highway 89 at "Glen Canyon City" (or what is today known as Big Water, Utah) to the newly named Kane Creek landing did, in fact, exist. To insure that river boaters did not proceed past that point, in the summer of 1957 they erected a large sign stating that **"all boats must leave the river at Kane Creek Landing one mile ahead on right; violators will be prosecuted!"**[32]

By 1959 the impounded water level had risen such that the greater Padre Bay sand flats were inundated thus omitting the five and a half miles of possibly getting stuck. But there was still some twenty-three miles to drive across bone-jarring rough barren rock before reaching pavement. For three years from 1956 until the Glen Canyon Bridge was completed in February, 1959, river trips were forced to take out at "Kane Creek Landing." To get home Wild Rivers' trucks, equipment and personnel had to travel by highway *west* from Big Water to Kanab, Utah then south to Fredonia, Arizona and then backtrack southeast to Jacob Lake, then east to Marble Canyon where they could cross over Navajo Bridge, a detour of some one hundred thirty-five miles. Then they continued south another fifty-seven miles to the Moenave turn-off onto Highway 47 (still a poorly-maintained graveled road) that took them across Navajoland to Kayenta, Mexican Hat and finally to Bluff. And if they really wanted to get home without more sand washes or rocky rutted roads, their best bet was to drive north to Monticello, then east and south to Cortez and then east again to Mancos.[33]

The highway from Kayenta to Teec Nos Pos, Arizona and north to Cortez, Colorado wasn't opened until the bridge across the San Juan River near Four Corners was completed in 1961.[34] The completion of Glen Canyon Bridge cut the one hundred-thirty-five mile detour towards the North Rim of Grand Canyon out of this rather arduous shuttle, but it still took two full days to make it home after a SJ&C trip. Kenny continued to run river trips down the Colorado River as Powell reservoir filled, and takeouts continued at the "Kane Creek Landing" until the end of the river season in 1963 when river current completely died as the reservoir filled. The lower canyons of the San Juan River and Glen Canyon on the Colorado River were then drowned and lost forever to river enthusiasts.

TEN WHO DARED

In the fall of 1959 Rusty Musselman heard about a Disney movie that was in the works about John Wesley Powell's famous river trips down the Colorado River in 1869 and 1871 that was being filmed along the Colorado River upstream from Moab, with iconic background features in Professor Valley including Fisher Towers, Priest and Nuns, and Castle Rock (Figures 10.5 & 10.6). Almost all close-up shots of the movie cast were taken along a sandy beach near the modest White's Rapid.

Rusty thought there might be a need for some real boatmen with river boating skills, so he and Kenny talked it over and decided to go see what it was all about. The director, William Beaudine, took one look at Kenny and saw that with a little makeup Kenny was the perfect double for the star, John Beal, who was playing the part of John Wesley Powell (Figures 10.7). Kenny's river boating experience couldn't have been more opportune. Rusty ended up doing some roustabout work, but he also substituted for the youngest actor, David Stollery, a "Mouseketeer" in a scene where his character, Andrew Hull, was thrashing oars trying to negotiate a rapid (Figure 10.8).

The production had started as a movie short or docudrama for the weekly TV Disney show "The Wonderful World of Disney" but was soon expanded into a full length movie. Hollywood star actor, Brian Keith, got top billing playing the role of the rebellious William Dunn who supposedly led two brothers, Oramel G. and Seneca Howland to their demise when the three men parted ways with the Powell river party in the lower Grand Canyon at a rapid that became known as *Separation Rapid*. The Howland brothers and Dunn were never seen or heard of again, and for many years were considered to have been killed by Indians, and that was certainly the version adopted for the movie.[35]

If that was the only fact that was wrong in the "docudrama" then one might look past the old misconception, but the movie was so horribly wrong in so many uncountable ways it gained notoriety by movie critics as one of the ten worst movies ever produced by Hollywood! Otis "Dock" Marston was listed as the Technical Assistant, but his input must have been completely dismissed. Even John Wesley Powell's own accounts of his journeys down the Green-Grand-Colorado Rivers in 1869 and 1871-72 are merged and his *embellished* accounts in *The Exploration of the Colorado River of the West and Its Tributaries* must be read with a healthy dose of skepticism.[36]

All real river action scenes of rowing calm water or running rapids (the White Ranch rapid) or camp scenes were filmed in the stretch of the Colorado River from the confluence with the

Dolores River down past Dewey Bridge to the small rocky rapid at White Ranch. A road (now Utah Highway 128 and referred to locally as "the river road") paralleled the river and followed it along the northeast side which made it easy for film crews to maneuver for all the scenes. All river scenes show the river running from right to left, indicating the camps were always on river left (RL).

The scenery in these shots was actually *real* (in Technicolor) and consisted mostly of Mesozoic and Permian red strata that outcropped along the river northeast of Moab. But all of the "close-up action" scenes of the actors are superimposed "studio shots" of them getting splashed and bounced around in rocking boats with movie footage of the Inner Gorge of the real Grand Canyon as backdrop. The Inner Gorge is a narrow, eight-hundred to a thousand-foot-high walled corridor where the rocks consists of Precambrian-age very dark-colored metamorphic schists dissected by diagonal streaks of cream-colored dikes composed of granite. Even to a non-geologist these background rocks couldn't be more strikingly different. And the movie scenes continue to alternate at mind-numbing speed between the narrow inner gorges of Grand Canyon to the open valley near Moab. Only one segment of the movie showed a wooden "Powell boat" actually running a real Grand Canyon rapid, over and over again, but from different camera angles; the majority of the river action took place in the red rock open canyon country northeast of Moab. Kenny loved telling stories about his involvement in this cinematic fiasco (Figures 10.9 through 10.18). Doug Ross commented about the movie:

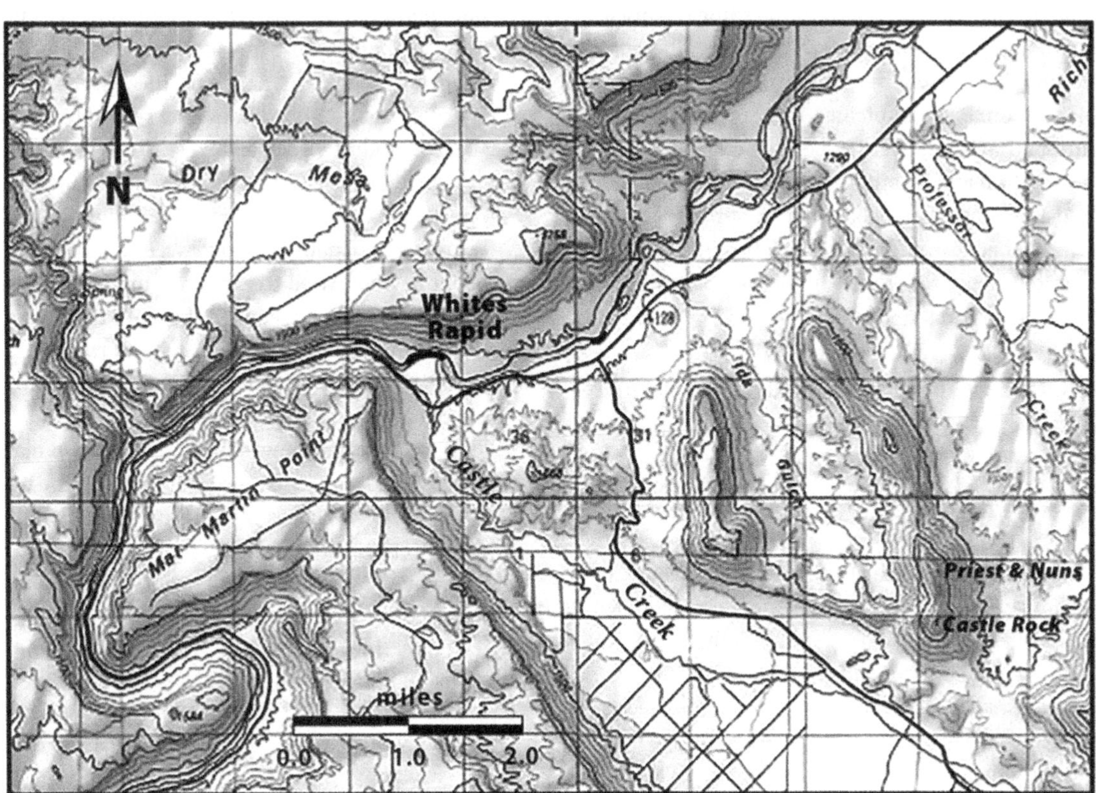

Figure 10.5 Map of Colorado River in Professor Valley with Whites Rapid at the mouth of Castle Creek where most of "Ten Who Dared" was filmed; river flows from upper right to lower left; rapids and riffles denoted in black. (Modified from *Esri Arc/GIS* USGS topographic map)

William Beaudine directed this Disney mess, with John Beal as Powell, Brian Keith as Bill Dunn, and Ben Johnson as George Bradley. One of the Disney Kids, David Stollery, played young Andrew Hull. He was Marty on the old Disney "Spin and Marty" show, from the 50's...a godawful Disney kid show of some kind. Dad really liked the kid, and had some great stories about Brian Keith, et al. The movie was released in 1960, and Kenny worked on it for about seven weeks in the fall months, Oct-Nov, out of Moab. I think the photos are all 1959.

The 'star' John Beal and Kenny were absolute dead ringers for each other with the make-up. Dad had gotten on the scene first, just to run the boat and had no idea he'd end up being the stunt double. There had already been some water scenes shot when Beal showed up, and he had to shave his beard he'd grown so they could match Kenny's. When makeup was done, the resemblance was uncanny. Close enough that Dad showed up in the movie in a couple of accidental close-ups and the directors left the scene in just as it was. Turned out Beal and Dad had been born in the same county a month apart, in Nebraska; pretty funny. There are two photos somewhere of the two "Powell's" for comparison. Dad complained the damn stump dummy that fitted over his hand and arm just wore holes in him and he still had scars to prove it.

If this movie had been made in our modern era, it was so bad it would have gone straight to DVD, never to see the silver screen. Bet it lost money. But the Old Man had a hoot.[37]

In his interview with Kenny in 1986, Herm Hoops asked Kenny about the movie set and about rowing those boats and if he did a lot of takes? Kenny replied:

The one place on the Green, Upper Disaster Falls, where they lost the 'No Name' we pretended to run Disaster Falls and we didn't actually run them. We ran Disaster Falls at the mouth *[the Dolores River]*. We started in quiet water, passed under Dewey Bridge but you know the bridge didn't show and then quit and went on down to White's Ranch, you know and ran the little rapid behind the ranch house; and we were filming the loss of the No Name there and that's a pretty nasty little rapid at times; rocky as all get out. I had been complaining because those boats had motors, only they were hidden underneath the rear deck; you had to lift the lid to get to the motor; we had gone chinchy *[cheap, low budget]*, which Disney people are famous for, and they'd gone chinchy and only each boat had just one motor that would start electrically. And the rest you had to jerk the line to start em and there were two motors on each boat, and so I hollered so much about this business of having to stop, maybe in a dangerous place; and the special effects man didn't like that the propeller wash would sometimes show, when he followed the rear of the boat with a camera.

And so he boarded up where the boat turned up this way in back. Had boards put on there and didn't say a word to me about it. And I was running the boats, at least I was commanding the boats, and so I started down through that rapid with one boat, the Emma Dean, started down through it and the first thing that happened was that both motors cut out; one motor cut out then the other motor cut out. They weren't getting any air, you see. And so, we spoiled that shot. Managed to, the next boat followed me in and we kind of wrecked both boats! Well, we didn't wreck em exactly, but we messed em up. Yeah, messed em up so that the special effects department had to work all night to get things going again! And they were disgruntled about it. And I tried to explain – motors won't run without air; you have to let air get in there before the motors would run.....so that with every toss of every wave, why, the boat would bob and gulp in a big mass of air, which would do you until you hit another one! Well, I was mad....oh I was so mad about that because the next day, why all the boats, see just the two boats that had messed up in the rocks were fixed that night, so we could shoot the next day, and the other two boats, they didn't fix them; they needed to gulp air too, but we finally ran the boats through OK; I just reached down and I only had one arm you know.

Herm asked: "How did you do with one arm?" Kenny replied:

You just had to play it right to the camera; I had a boot on here; I've still got scars from that damn boot.....after all these years! But, just turn the boat toward the camera, you never let the camera catch you broadside; this way....your arm would be too long! So we had trouble with the last two boats and one of them was the No Name, so it didn't matter, the No Name didn't have a motor on it anyhow, so there's just the one, so I just reached down and I got hold of that board that they spliced in there, and jerked! Well, we went through, we got all four boats through, we got three boats through then we went back up to wreck the No Name. And it was all elaborately planned. I had studied it for a couple hours the day before, so we had hidden cable wire, tiny cable underwater. Come down and hook an eye, eye screws in the boat so it would guide the boat right through because, you see, when the No Name was wrecked it went broadside on a rock, which, as you know, is the best way to turn a boat over and mess up a boat. And, so, we set it up and I got in the boat. Oh yeah, the No Name was part of a story that was all fouled up by the writers. But Bo Dean didn't care; he was a slap dash funny kind of director. Why, he was just great! And if something wasn't just right, he'd make it right....on the cutting room floor; so we hooked that all up to the rock and the rock was an artificial one. I kept the rock for years. It looked like the real rock that was being struck.[38]

After the movie action scenes were done, Kenny and Rusty came back home and according to Doug:

> They brought home the fake rock (wreck of the No Name) in the back of the '59 International pickup and parked it in front of the house. Kenny and Rusty got some good reactions out of the Utah weigh station guy at the port of entry at Monticello too. That rock later ended up on the roof of Rusty Musselman's Cow Canyon Trading Post.[39]

Jerry Howell, my Bluff neighbor, said that he remembered the big rock when he was a kid and wondered where it came from and apparently the fake rock remained on top of the trading post for years, but no one who lived in Bluff at that time could find a photograph of it; too bad.

Figure 10.6 cast and crew of the Disney movie "Ten Who Dared" take a break near White's Rapid with iconic Priest & Nuns and Castle Rock in background; red rocks and open desert terrain is not at all similar to topography in the inner gorge in Grand Canyon or upper Green River where true events occurred; the movie was mostly filmed in Professor Valley northeast of Moab along a stretch of the Colorado River that John Wesley Powell never saw. (K. Ross collection)

Figure 10.7 Kenny Ross (L) and actor John Beal (R) in makeup as John Wesley Powell. (K. Ross collection)

Figure 10.8 from L to R: Kenny, David Stollery and Rusty Musselman in front of Kenny's International pickup truck. (K. Ross collection)

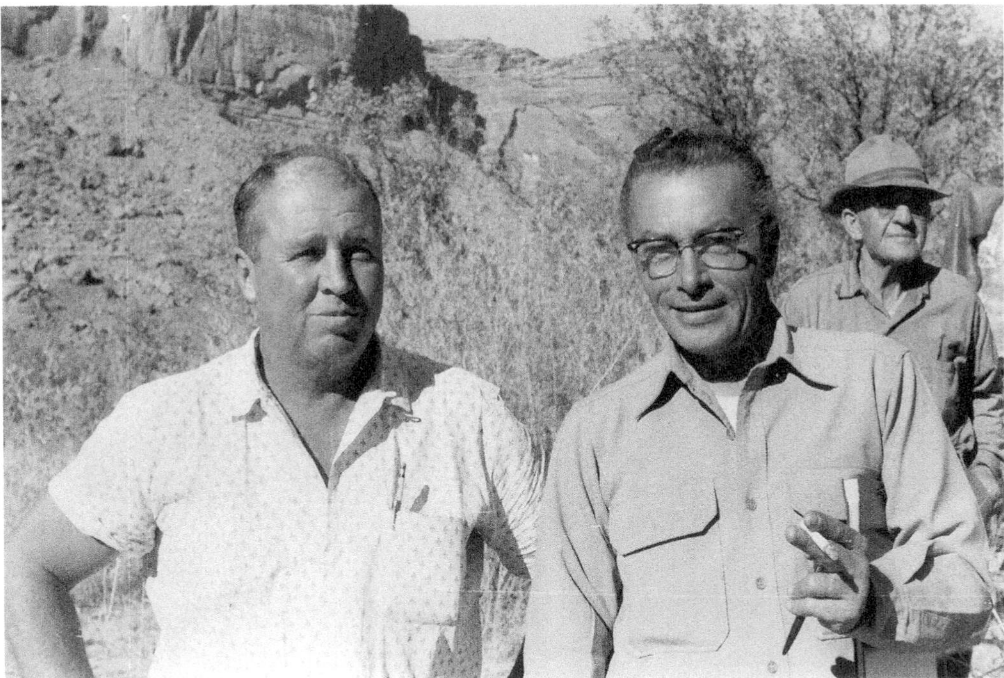

Figure 10.9 Director William Beaudine and Kenny Ross; "a lot of film was left on the cutting room floor." (K. Ross collection)

Figure 10.10 the *Emma Dean* with stern covering the two outboard motors; propellers wash still showed up in the movie when boats were supposedly being rowed. (K. Ross collection)

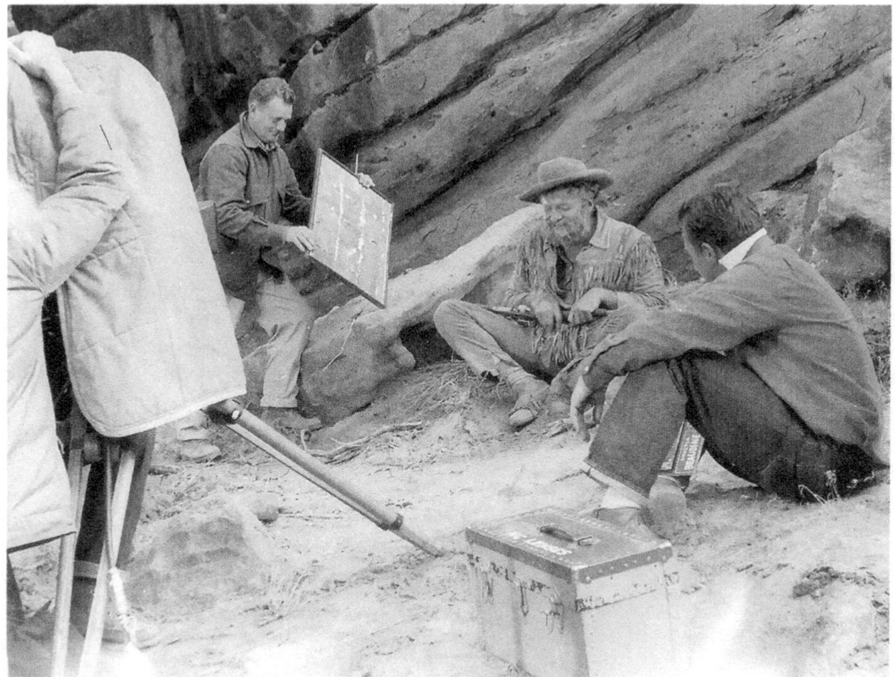

Figure 10.11 Brian Keith (as Bill Dunn) in buckskin garb preparing for the rattlesnake scene. (K. Ross collection)

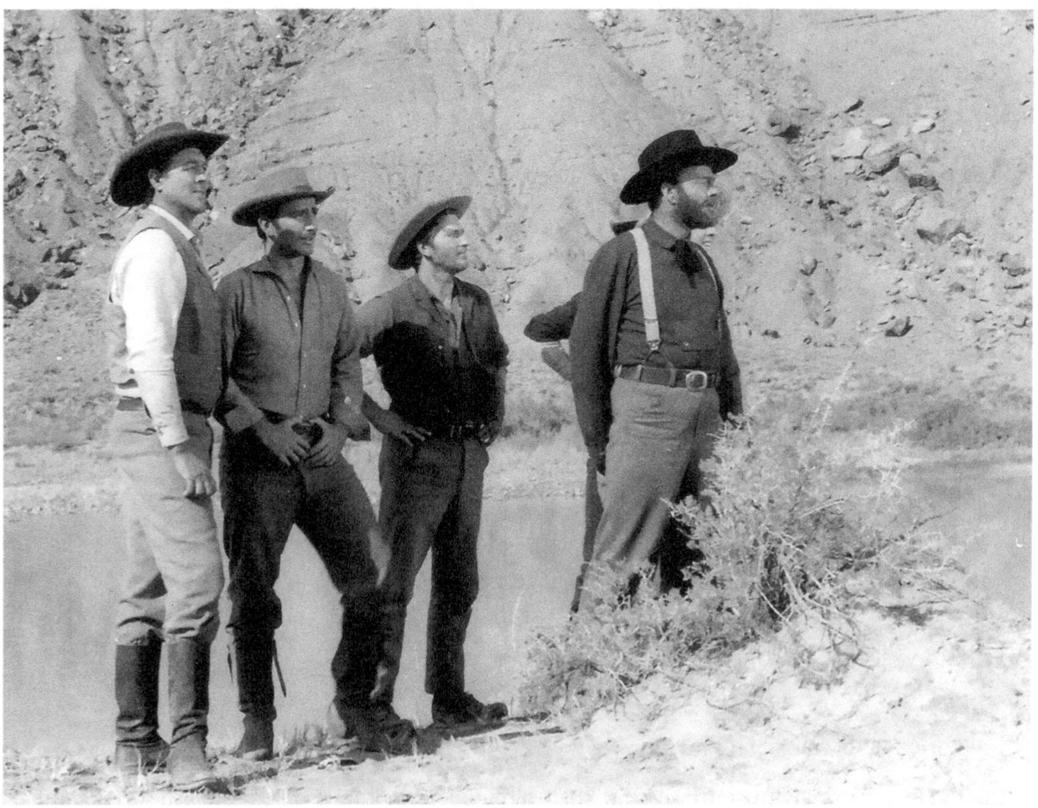

Figure 10.12 (L to R): Actors: Ben Johnson, James Drury, L.Q. Jones and John Beals. (K. Ross collection)

Figure 10.13 film crew waiting on actors to get their lines right. (K. Ross collection)

Figure 10.14 film crew and river boats; note Castle Valley anticline in background. (K. Ross collection)

Figure 10.15 Moab caterers all set up for chow time. (K. Ross collection)

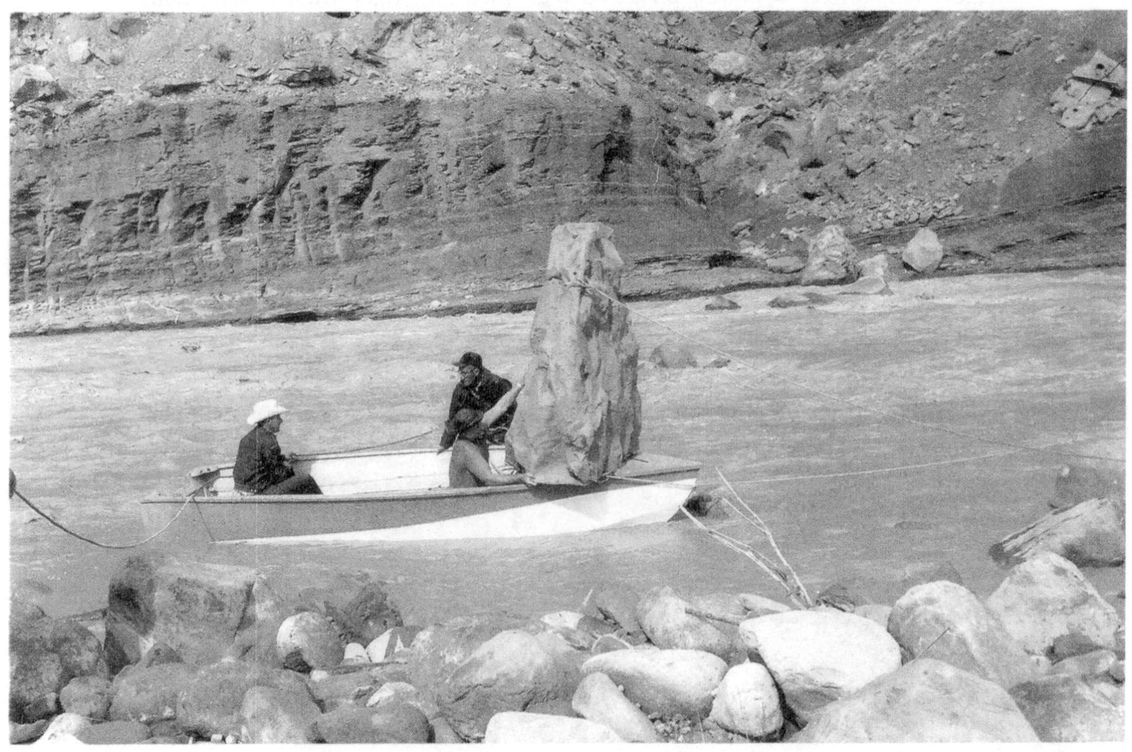

Figure 10.16 fake fiberglass "rock" on board ready to be placed in the river. (K. Ross collection)

Figure 10.17 securing the fiberglass "rock" in mid-current; river flowing right to left. (K. Ross collection)

Figure 10.18 the fake rock is in place and camera crew ready for scene where the *No Name* hits the rock and breaks perfectly in two. Kenny & Rusty took the fiberglass "rock" back to Bluff and placed it on top of Cow Canyon Trading Post where it remained for years to bewilder residents as well as visitors. (K. Ross collection)

∞ ∞ ∞

Lastly, Kenny's father, Charley Carpenter Ross died in 1959 in California, but there was *no* indication that Kenny made any effort to go to his funeral (if there was one), or to make mention of it, which has led me to wonder what level of estrangement there may have been between father and son. Neither Don nor Doug had much to say about their grandfather either. Personally, I think it had everything to do with the quick sale of the Cahone property in the 1930s! After all, Kenny knew about the extensive amount of ruins that substantially increased the value of the land that his father sold for next to nothing. Of course, there may have been any number of unknown extenuating circumstances as to why Kenny seemed to disinherit his father. Conversely, Kenny and family made several trips to California to visit Grandma Erma in the '50s and '60s, who didn't pass away until the early 1970s, but they apparently never looked up Grandpa Charley.[40]

∞ ∞ ∞

Glen Canyon Dam under construction, 1964 (USBR photo; K. Ross collection)

❧ 11 ❧

WILD RIVERS EXPEDITIONS, TOURISM AND SCIENCE

BLUFF BEER JOINTS

Kenny was certainly correct in describing all the hubbub of activity brought into the Four Corners area with the discovery of major oil reserves, but all that activity also brought many of the roads and bridges that were constructed in the early 1960s. During that period roads were widened and paved, while bridges and culverts were built across sandy washes, creeks and rivers. Of course, more people came to the region. Not all the activity was just drill rigs and roughnecks. Bluff residency mushroomed and the west side of Cottonwood Wash began to be developed. For a brief period of time from mid-1950s to mid-1960s Bluff boasted as many as five bars serving beer mostly, but still their presence was a sacrilege for the close-knit Mormon town.

When I asked Winston Hurst what he knew about this period he said that he thought all the stores except Powell's may have sold beer, and that San Juan County historian, Laverne Tate called all of them "beer joints."

> That suggests that the distinction between bars and stores that sold beer may have been a fuzzy one. Johnny Johnson had a bar at one time, not sure where or when. He talks about it in one of the Gary Shumway oral history interviews, but I don't think he gives dates or describes the place. Not sure who had the little wooden one by Linda Sosa's, but I think it was a relative latecomer. I think Twin Rocks was the main bar in the '50s.[1]

I asked Doug Ross if he had anything to add and he provided the following colorful detail and a story or two about Bluff bars:

> There were attempts regularly to open up some sort of beer purveyance during the 50's and 60's. But I'm pretty sure the Huber family arrived before 1960 and the *Silver Dollar* was going by '60, I'm pretty sure, because Don and I used to walk across town for the night social life that generated around the Silver Dollar and the *Kiva Café.* The Kiva Café was located on the west side of the Silver Dollar Bar with a doorway into the café which was run by *Warren Reck* and *Frieda* (an ex-Episcopal nun) and they both cooked. The food was great. *Bill and Gladys Huber* were super strict about kids even poking a nose in the door let alone coming inside the Silver Dollar. But because it was busy all the time and there were lots of construction workers, uranium truck drivers, oil guys' etc coming and going with families in tow, the bar had lots of adjunct social life for the teens. This must have been '59 or '60 for sure, and maybe earlier. My memories are package sales from anybody with a grocery store. The Twin Rocks and Bob Howell maybe had his grocery going by 1960, but definitely by '62 and the K & C probably did, but I can't swear to it, the Jones brothers being of the Faith.
>
> But when the Heyday of Beer and Brawls hit in the early 1960's, on any given weekend the hoof across town led us past the *Twin Rocks Trade* (who had by that time gone to consumption on site) and then down around the corner to the little log shack at Linda Sosa's place (which was notorious for the inter-tribal wars between the locals) and then on to the *Silver Dollar.* The Silver Dollar was far and away the busiest, with a pool table and the huge space. Bill and Gladys would not put up with anybody who got out of line and would boot anybody who caused trouble.
>
> The Huber's were a great family. Bill, Gladys, Lynn (teen, heartthrob of several), Billy (Lil' Bill) and another sister whose name I have forgotten. The bar lasted as the Huber families until about 1970 when *Johnny Lester* took it over I think. Bill Sr. died of cancer in 1970 while I was in the army and I never encountered the family after that. Nice people and pillars of the town. They took care of a

lot of people who were down and out. What a different place Bluff was in those days.

Bill boated with us quite a bit, did a really fun Cat trip with me....'63 maybe? On my 21st birthday in 1967, at 8 O'clock in the AM, Bill pulled up to the boat camp in his Jeep and hollered at me to get in the car...puzzled, I did. Bill didn't say anything except that he needed me to help him with something....huh? Ok. We drove across the wash to the Silver Dollar and pulled up in front. Bill got out and I followed him over to the front door and he unlocked it and we went in. Bill pointed to a bar stool and said "sit!" I did. He was up to something, I knew. He walked around behind the bar, reached into the cooler and grabbed two Lucky Lager beers came back over and sat down beside me and opened the beers and handed me one. "After all these years of fishing and river trips and drinking beer with you, I was damned if I was going to let anybody else buy you your first legal beer! Cheers!"

Gladys was the supreme "bouncer" at 5'-2" and a bit hefty. She would just step in and convince the offender that they needed to leave and could come back tomorrow and if they didn't, then they would be 86'd. Nobody argued with the Jewish mother from NYC. I watched her escort a 300 lb. Ute woman out the door that no male in the place dared to go near. She went by the name *"Big Frances."* She would get thrown out and then go sulk by walking out into the highway and lying down in the middle of the road. Frances was probably 6'-2" and easily 300+, so it was a problem because it stopped traffic, of which there was....So somebody would convey the information that Frances was "at it again" and the bar would empty out to watch the fun.

Picture if you will, a large (did I mention Frances was really big?) woman laying completely limp, having mastered passive resistance, and watching several males of varying degrees of sobriety, sizes and capabilities attempt to lift, drag and cajole this massive flesh Jersey Barrier and move her to the side of the road. Poor Frances...she got dropped, dragged, bruised and cussed at, but she would hold her own. Then everybody went back to the bar while Frances gathered herself for another round. Usually it ended with a second round and lots of cussing and Frances would give up, convinced to fight another day.

Good times and huge entertainment for the assorted urchins hanging out. It got really busy in the later years when the Army showed up to pop off missiles to White Sands from Black Mesa. No beer for the Army in Blanding, so guess where they all ended up? 1969 when you got there was when the Army was quite busy cranking out Honest Johns and Pershing [missiles] to scare sheep all the way across the Rez into New Mexico. That might account for the hoppin' place to which you made reference? [Author's note: 1969 was my first time to visit Bluff and we stopped at the Silver Dollar on the way to Sand Island].

Damned if I can remember the name of the silly little log cabin bar...it would get packed full and then some sort of brawl would break out, the local deputy would have to show up and settle things, sometimes at great risk, because he was outnumbered. One was a total badass (Max King, later became sheriff) and if word got out that Max was coming, it frequently ended the dispute. Ex-marine with a special set of skills, so to speak. Them were the days.... And that's the truth, as much as a boatman can actually find that elusive snake slithering around in his memory.[2]

Winston Hurst added another comment about "Big Frances," her name was *Frances Posey*:

> She once faced down Melvin Adams when he tried to make her move her goats off his cattle range at the foot of White Mesa. She just sat on top of that rocky outcrop on the east side of the highway to the south of the intersection, arms folded and chin out, and ignored his fuss and bluster until he finally said 'Oh shit' and smacked his hat against his pant leg and huffed off in resignation. [3]

GAS STATIONS EVERYWHERE

With all the hustle and bustle activity taking place in the area it was no surprise to see a need for more than one filling station, and within a matter of a few years Bluff boasted as many as eight stations in a community of only a couple hundred permanent residents! It was a surefire way of measuring the needs for a growing transient population of uranium ore truck drivers to oil field workers. And along with the filling stations came garage mechanics and trading posts. Local folks were happy to see some variety of gas choices too, plus someone to fix a flat tire, or work on their vehicles when needed.[4]

For years, the first and only gas pumps were located at the original Twin Rocks Trading Post (located at the present-day corner of 7th East St and Black Locust Ave). Then Connie Conway put in some gas pumps near Cottonwood Wash, but didn't provide any other facilities. That property was soon purchased by Keith and Curtis Jones in the early 1960s and established the K&C Trading Post and gas station which, in turn, was sold to and operated by Vance Nielson sometime in the 1980s.

Rusty Musselman had opened the Cow Canyon Trading Post and gas station in 1955, and sold Mobil gas with the iconic flying Pegasus on the sign and Duke Simpson operated the station. Grat Wilson owned and operated the other Cow Canyon gas station that opened for business in the late 1950s and sold gas under the Sinclair brand name. Not to be outdone, Johnny Lester opened the Enco gas station in the early 1960s adjacent to the Silver Dollar Bar and Faye Belle followed suit when the Dairy Café and Trading post opened on the west side of town around the same time. She hired Art Yerby to build the shop and big garage building next to the café, but they got cross-ways with each other, so Art went to the east side of the wash and started his wrecker service and mechanics shop.

Jack Hale and wife Lupe started the Turquoise Café and gas station right across the street from Gene & Mary Foushee's Recapture Motor Court in the early 1960s and Roy Pearson operated the gas station for years even after Clema Johnson bought the business. In the late 1970s the husband and wife team of Bob and Barbara Boot took over. They had been hauling coal from Helper, Utah to Page, Arizona earlier in the 1970s when a coal strike at Black Mesa Mine had forced the new Page power plant to get coal elsewhere. When the strike was settled, the Boots decided to make a go of it by buying the Turquoise business.

The Painted Horn Trading post on the western outskirts of Bluff was started by Burton Pierce, but he didn't put in gas pumps. Curly Wallace bought the place from Burton in the mid-to-late 1960s and put in pumps and sold gas under the sign of the Chevron. And the Wayside Trading Post was operated by Buck and Lydia Carson beginning around 1970. Buck had been working for Mack and Hack Trucking and wanted to settle down with their two children – Patsy and Ruben. Buck sold gas under the Phillips Petroleum signage and was my favorite spot to stop when I came through Bluff in the 1970s.

And what about today? Most of those named above have passed away or moved on. It's all reverted back to one filling station – the K&C Trading Post and no mechanic on duty; closest town to get a flat fixed or anything else mechanical needing attention is in Blanding, twenty-five miles north.

TURMOIL IN MANCOS SCHOOLS

Such was life in Bluff in 1960. Kenny had put *Boat Camp No. 3* to bed following his "movie star" period and moved back to the Mancos house for the winter. Doug was now in the eighth grade and Don was a sophomore in High school. By springtime there was major turmoil in the Mancos schools as the new school board, in a fit of "vengeance" abruptly fired Don Morgan, the school superintendent and his wife Mrs. Morgan who was Don's English teacher. Kenny had gotten involved and stood up for Don Morgan in defense of his character. But the school board prevailed and dismissed Mr. and Mrs. Morgan. By late April Kenny was disgusted over the situation and went back to Bluff to get the boats and gear ready for another boating season. However, the vindictive school board notified *Mildred that she was also being fired* at the end of the school year presumably because of Kenny's open support for the superintendent. That acutely vindictive news was completely unexpected which left Mildred embarrassed and devastated. She was mainly upset with the school board's ruling and that the kids would not get proper schooling! Upset as she was, Mildred started looking around for work and finally found a job in the County Social Services in Cortez by mid-summer.

Don stayed in Bluff after school was over in Mancos and began running more San Juan trips while his boating skills continued to improve. He struck up friendships with several Bluff kids but he and Bob Musselman became particularly good friends. Bob worked on Kenny throughout the summer trying to convince him that Don should transfer to San Juan High School for his junior and senior years. Kenny discussed the switch to Blanding with Mildred, and although they were hesitant they agreed to Don's request as they were fed up with the entire situation with the Mancos school board. Don enrolled at San Juan High School (SJHS) and finished his junior year there.[5]

GOING, GOING – GONE!

As the construction of the Glen Canyon dam proceeded in 1960, everyone who had been down through these river canyons wanted to see Glen Canyon one more time before it was flooded. Kenny also received more and more enquiries about Glen Canyon trips from newcomers as the cold hard reality was sinking in with the general public.

By the winter of 1961 Kenny's new advertisements promoted trips that launched from Hite as well as his normal SJ&C trips for the last chance to see the lower part or all of Glen Canyon. By the end of the 1962 river season the lower canyon of the San Juan River had begun to show the effects of rising lake water and the drowning of rapids and river current. River enthusiasts who had run Cataract Canyon or the SJ&C trips with Kenny knew their days were limited before the encroaching dead waters of a lake drowned out their beloved rivers and rapids. Few river runners had taken the time or interest in floating the placid stretch of the Colorado River from Hite down to the confluence with the San Juan. So running rapids was not particularly the sales point it had been; instead it was experiencing the beauty and serenity of a canyon that would soon be drowned; it was going away fast and would soon be gone! Forever!

The mandatory takeout at Kane Creek had shorted forty-six miles off the original SJ&C trips to 179 miles rather than the 225 miles. The distance from Hite to Kane Creek was 124 miles. Regardless of which trip any potential participant chose, Wild Rivers Expeditions was as busy as conceivably possible during these early years of the 1960s.

In spring 1960 on a fun family SJ&C trip, Don recalled that he finally got to row his own boat down Thirteen Foot Rapid for the first time. Doug, at age thirteen, had beaten him to it as he had run the rapid the previous year! The river gage near Bluff indicated that 1960 was excellent boating on the San Juan for spring and early summer with the river never dropping below 2,000 cfs from April to early July with much of those months at 5,000 to 9,000 cfs. But late summer monsoons never amounted to much and the river fell precipitously to 100–300 cfs in mid-August through mid-September (Figure 11.1).

Doug, Kenny and Bob Musselman ran an early June SJ&C trip with a group of friends from Durango and got off the river at Kane Creek due to the "damn dam construction." [6] Don launched the group and ran the shuttle to pick them up at Kane Creek. The group started out from Sand Island and stopped at the usual archaeological spots soon after they got underway (Figure 11.2). Dennis Irwin, a well-known Paradox Basin geologist, and his wife Pat were particularly good friends of the Ross family. "Denny" was happily surprised when he met Vito Vanoni, a hydrogeologist with the USGS who had been working on experimental flume studies regarding how sand waves formed. Vito was accompanied by his wife. And rounding out the group was Bill Bogle and a lady friend; Bill was the editor of the Durango Herald newspaper at the time (Figure 11.3). Doug recalled that Vito was absolutely incredulous with all the sand waves and he got to dive in the river with Vito to feel around on the bottom to touch and grab sand samples of antidunes not knowing what Vito was trying to convey to him regarding variable sand grain size, etc and how sand waves formed (see Appendix IV: Glossary). They all had a marvelous time knowing full-well that the beautiful Glen Canyon would soon be inundated by lake water (Figure 11.4).[6]

One of the respondents in 1961 was Frank Thorp who had done several SJ&C trips with Kenny. He and his family had experienced the lower San Juan, the Thirteen Foot Rapid, and Rainbow Bridge and taken out at Lees Ferry or Warm Creek. The Thorps had also done several Cataract Canyon trips from Moab to Hite, but the section from Hite to the confluence remained an unknown to Frank. Kenny knew their days were numbered before all the cool stuff got inundated by Powell reservoir water so he was more than eager when Frank booked a trip to see and explore all of Glen Canyon by launching from Hite and taking out at Kane Creek. Unfortunately, the trip ended up being a single boat trip with just Kenny and Frank Thorp. Frank felt guilty that Kenny wouldn't make any money on the trip with just the two of them. However it gave Kenny more time and flexibility to stop and explore spots he had previously passed by. Both Don and Doug confirmed that Kenny and Frank stopped at all the iconic spots and hiked just about everywhere and every side canyon one could imagine [7] (Figures 11.5 to 11.10).

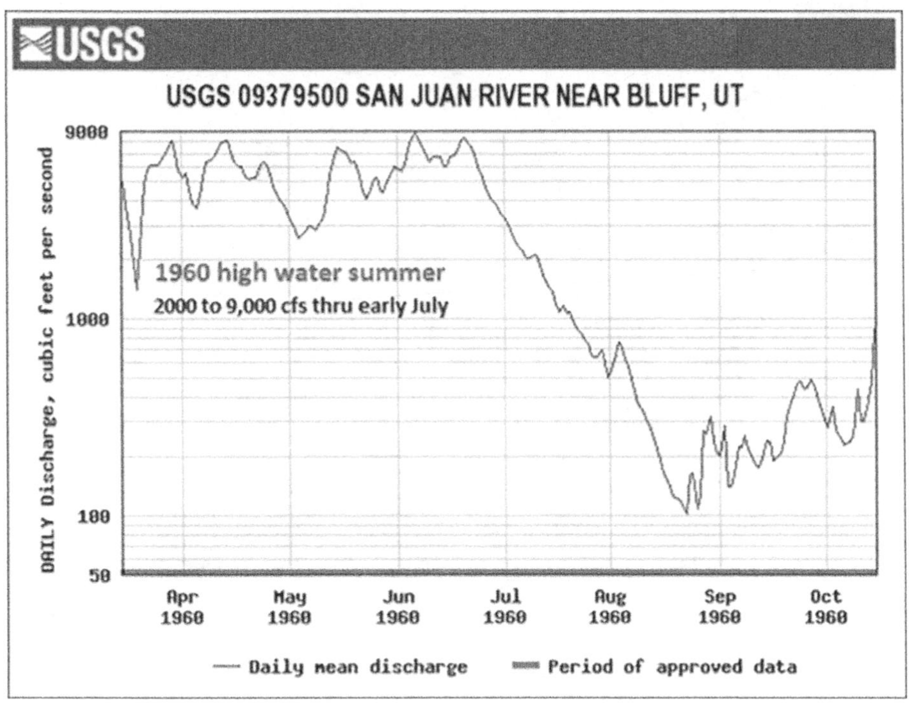

Figure 11.1 San Juan River gaged flow rates for mid-March to mid-October, 1960. (USGS water data)

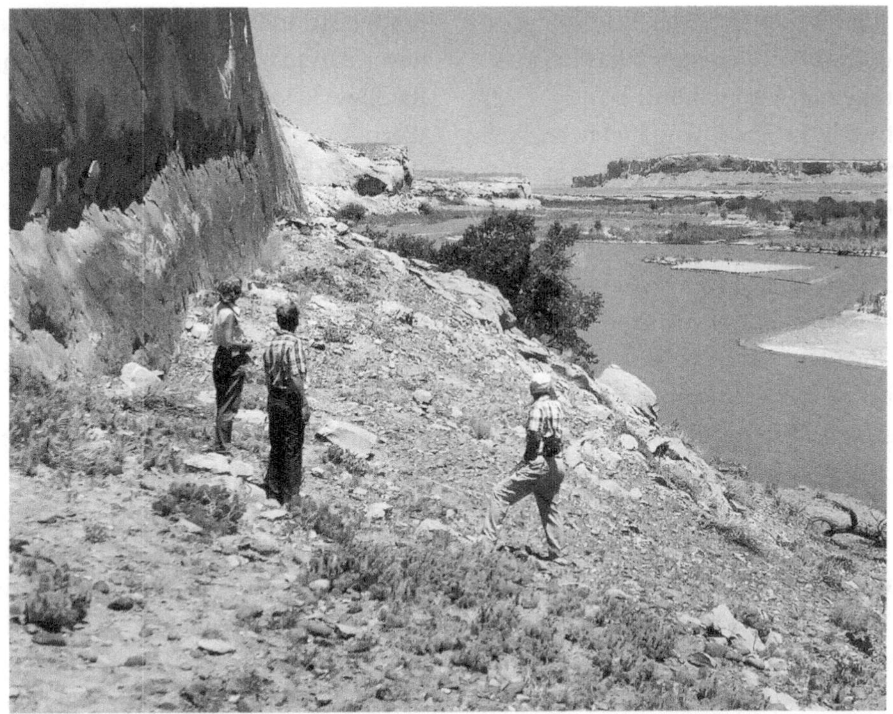

Figure 11.2 Kenny (down slope) at the Butler petroglyph panel pointing upstream; Casa Del Eco Mesa on skyline. (K Ross collection)

Figure 11.3 June, 1960 SJ&C trip: standing, L-R: Mrs. Vanoni, Dennis Irwin, Doug Ross, Bob Musselman, Kenny Ross, Vito Vanoni, Bill Bogle; kneeling, L-R: Bill's friend & Pat Irwin at Kane Creek takeout. (K. Ross collection)

Figure 11.4 floating along in Glen Canyon, June, 1960. (K. Ross collection)

Glen Canyon trips weren't the only trips in 1961. Doug, Don and Kenny kept on doing San Juan trips and Don recalled that the flow made for an "OK season." Historical river gage data for 1961 indicated a peak of 7,000 cfs in June with an early season average of 3,000 cfs before it dropped under 500 cfs by August. And those lower canyon rapids were beginning to lose their energy.

Also, in 1961 the Wild Rivers boat camp was moved slightly east a few tens of feet to *Boat Camp No. 4*. Kenny bought an old thirty-three-foot-long *Spartan* trailer from Bob Howell and he made it their living quarters. He had an electric line strung to their trailer, so they finally had lights, a refrigerator, as well as beds, a cook stove, etc and they felt like they were in "hog heaven!" Kenny, Don and Doug poured a concrete foundation for a future stone house that was never built. They operated out of the trailer and a new chaha'oh was fabricated for the equipment/boat shed. Mildred continued to run back and forth from Mancos to Bluff and brought food for trips and for the camp, but had ceased running shuttle trips at Kane Creek take-outs.[8]

Figure 11.5 Bert Loper's Hermitage at Red Canyon, spring, 1961. (K. Ross collection)

Figure 11.6 view from Colorado River below confluence with San Juan River; snow-capped Navajo Mountain (elevation 10,346 ft) lies ten miles to southeast; spring, 1961. (K. Ross collection)

Figure 11.7 approaching Olympia Bar, an abandoned gold dredge operation (wooden structure on RL on shaded ledge above boat in Glen Canyon), spring, 1961. (K. Ross collection)

Figure 11.8 arch in Glen Canyon, spring, 1961. (K. Ross collection)

Figure 11.9 hike the Rincon; Colorado River below; view north across east- dipping strata of the Waterpocket Fold; Henry Mountains (Mt. Pennell and Mt. Hillers) in background forty-five miles away. (K. Ross collection)

Figure 11.10 arch with rubble in front defines a site of Ancient Puebloan occupation; near Music Temple, Colorado River; spring, 1961. (K. Ross collection)

THE CANYONS NO ONE KNEW

Eliot Porter [9] (the famous photographer) and his son, Stephen, scheduled a regular ten day, SJ&C trip in June to photo-document the San Juan River and lower Glen Canyon before it was completely inundated. Details of that trip are scant, but Doug recalled that Eliot was a bit demanding. He also recalled that he and Stephen, who were close in age didn't get along too well. Kenny and Doug ran a two boat rowing trip and Eliot was so overwhelmed with the lower San Juan River canyons and Glen Canyon that he needed to schedule a follow-up trip so he could photograph all the scenery. The first trip went from Bluff (Sand Island) to the Kane Creek take-out; a distance of 149.0 river miles, but only 37.6 miles in Glen Canyon on the Colorado River (see Appendix I, Table 1). Several photos from that first trip that were taken by Eliot using a hand-held 35 mm camera while riding in Doug's boat are in the photo album book.[10]

The second Eliot Porter trip took place in late August, 1961 and launched from the old Hite Ferry crossing in White Canyon and took out at Kane Creek again, a distance of approximately 124 river miles (see Appendix I, Table 2). Don Ross launched that trip, but wasn't sure who picked them up. Doug continued running San Juan dailies during this time. Kenny Ross and Gene Foushee[11] ran the boats and Eliot brought along friends and family including artist *Georgia O'Keeffe*, and fellow photographer Todd Webb.[12] The details of that trip are described below. Eliot returned almost immediately with Georgia and Todd Webb on a motorized run from Wahweap with Art Greene's *Canyon Tours, Inc.* to Rainbow Bridge, but found that he still needed to return a third time with Kenny to complete the task at hand. All the trips were supported by the Sierra Club.

Kenny's third trip included only himself with Eliot and Georgia. Eliot had not been satisfied with his summer pictures due to any number of factors, including: high sun angles, the hot summers and monsoonal rainy weather, and possibly the distractions of the group in August, or his motor boat trip in early September. By then he had seen enough of the canyons to know what he wanted to focus on. Plus, the low sun angle in late fall provided him the most ideal lighting for scenic photography in the southwest. For whatever the reason, Eliot scheduled a fall trip with Kenny. Art Greene at Wahweap Marina rented Kenny one of the motor boats for that follow-up trip in late October. The threesome took the boat upstream to various spots in Glen Canyon below the San Juan River confluence so that Eliot could finish photographing the canyon and Georgia came better prepared with her art supplies. They camped at Music Temple for three days and crossed the river to Hidden Passage. It was during this third trip that most of Eliot's finest photos were beautifully captured in the photo album book *"The Place No One Knew."* but three river trips were definitely led by Kenny Ross in the summer and fall of 1961. Unfortunately, Kenny wasn't acknowledged by name in the book and only referred to as "a guide." [13]

THE SECOND GLEN CANYON TRIP

Of the three trips led by Kenny Ross, the second was the best documented, thanks to Todd Webb and his photos as well as his journal, all of which has been graciously provided by the *Todd Webb Archives, Portland, Maine USA* (see photos: Figures 11.11 to 11.27, below). But Georgia O'Keeffe didn't bring her paints or any canvas on this trip as she was just going to "take a vacation." Georgia regretted her short-sightedness and ended up making sketches in a small borrowed notebook – Todd Webb's notebook! She also made some sketches on brown paper grocery sacks using campfire charcoal. She had a camera with her and she took some photos. Both a paper sack drawing and two or three photos from Glen Canyon (the only photographs ever exhibited by Georgia O'Keeffe) have been on display along with her masterpiece floral collection in her museum in Santa Fe.[14]

The following information has heavily relied on Todd Webb's journal.[15] Following the first reconnaissance trip Eliot knew he had to see *all* of Glen Canyon, so a trip was planned with Kenny to launch from the old Hite Ferry landing and float the full permitted distance down to Kane Creek.[16] The group consisted of twelve passengers altogether; nine folks comprising the Porter-O'Keeffe party and three others unidentified. Kenny, Gene Foushee and a young swamper rounded out the group to fifteen in total for two 10-man LCR boats with one motor. Kenny had designed a way for the two boats to be lashed together side-by-side and then an eight-foot-long two-by-twelve transom board was bolted across the stern motor-mounts to which a motor could be attached for the long flat water run down Glen Canyon. The tandem boats were rowed, or steered, with a boatman handling one oar on either side of the two boats. The motor was mostly run to negotiate the riffles and occasional small rapids or when upstream winds slowed the float trip.

THE TODD WEBB JOURNAL

Monday, August 21, 1961: Todd Webb left Tesuque, New Mexico with Paul and Tish Frank in his Jaguar sports car at 8:30 AM and had an uneventful drive to Bluff, Utah. They arrived shortly before Georgia, Doris and Marshall Girard and in another hour the party was completed with the arrival of Eliot, Stephen and Kathy. They all stayed at the Reĉapture Motel. Kenny had the boats, food and gear ready to go and they were all given waterproof bags and did some of re-packing before going to bed.

Tuesday, August 22, 1961: The entourage of passengers, boatmen and all the boats and gear left Bluff before noon and rode in the two trucks and station wagon enroute to Hite.[17] Once they arrived, they unloaded the truck; "a herculean task" and got the boats in the water and inflated. Todd Webb wrote:

> We took the long hard road to Hite Ferry. Most of us rode in the back of Ross's truck, picking up a sun and wind burn and enjoying the magnificent if desolate country. Hite is nothing now but a measly little ferry and no population at all. There were some uranium mines nearby but since they were condemned for Powell Lake everyone moved away. We had quite a good stew for dinner and laid out our sleeping bags on a ledge overlooking the muddy river.[18]

Wednesday, August 23, 1961: After an early morning dust storm that "sent sand flying and everyone appeared for the ham and egg breakfast gritting their teeth" the boats were finished getting loaded for what would "be home away from home for the next eight days." Todd continued:

> In less than an hour we ran our first rapids and at a critical point, the prop hit a rock, broke the shear pin and the lashed together boats spun crazily out of control, finally wedging against huge rocks with white water foaming on all sides. Ross reassured everybody and with a new pin in place we muscled the two heavy boats off the rocks. A few minutes later another rapids cost us another shear pin, but without any excitement. Then we started to make the rapids runs under oars and we had no more trouble. Actually, the rapids were mild and I am sure any of them could have been run in a canoe. At noon we stopped on a bar and everyone tried the Colorado for a swim. A bit thick with mud but the day was hot and soon after four we found a fine campsite. The meals have been plain and with the continually blowing sand everything is gritty. We all seem to sleep well.

Thursday, August 24, 1961:

Everyone up at five and after a good breakfast we are on the river before eight o'clock. In five minutes the water pump on the motor gave out and we traveled on oars until we came to a fine spring of running water. Took several hours to repair the motor and while waiting a party passed. We had lunch and were on the river again by one. Made a stop at Warm Spring Canyon and we explored it. Marshall and Chris went swimming and Eliot and I photographed. Another mile downstream we made a fine camp on the upper end of Olympia Bar just under the beautiful tapestry wall. It was a lovely spot. Marshall and I decided to entertain with a beach fire. As we were about to light up – the sky suddenly darkened over the cliff and a minute later there was a deluge, scattering everyone to tend their bedding. An hour later the rain slackened and the poncho clad crew gathered around with all kinds of advice while Marshall tried to kindle his fire. With his last match he got it flickering and with much huffing and puffing there was at last a good blaze. By then the rain stopped and it was nine o'clock – an hour past bedtime and everyone yawningly said goodnight.

Friday, August 25, 1961:

Had a good sleep if a little damp around the edges. In spite of the rain the water in the river had dropped four inches during the night and our two great rubber boats were high and dry at the edge of the mud bank. We had to unload them and then manhandle them to deeper water while the rock hunters plied their trade to the last minute. We had a passing line to get all of our gear out to the boats. It was sort of fun and we were on the river by nine o'clock. [We] stopped soon after to explore an old placer mining camp on the lower end of Olympia Bar and the rock hunters had another picnic. Eliot found the most coveted rock to date last night on upper Olympia Bar. It is a flat, round black beauty that everyone agrees is venerable. Had an easy afternoon, running Bullfrog Rapids and having a hard time finding a campsite. [We] finally made a landing on Gretchen Bar; a tough stony landing place and only a fair place to bed down. All were tired and it was hard to stay awake until moonrise so we could see the total eclipse of the moon. Just before the almost obscured moon rose over the mountain the *Echo satellite* made its deliberate way across the heavens.[19] I just managed to stay awake and see the moon. [Emphasis mine]

Saturday, August 26, 1961:

Up at dawn – a good breakfast – soft boiled eggs, toast, cereal, grapefruit and coffee. Hard loading job on the rocky shore but finally away by 8:30. Made slow time – running a long series of shallow rapids and time and again we were over the sides pushing off sand bars and rocks. Had lunch with the usual fun and good natured bantering. Hot dogs broiled on sticks, cheese and pickles. The afternoon good with several shear pins sacrificed to some piddling rapids. Made Navaho Canyon[20] for a fine camp. Up a narrow canyon there was a clear cold waterfall where all could bathe in turn. It was a real treat after days of bathing in muddy Colorado water. Dinner of macaroni and cheese, a can of spring-cooled beer and a fire to light the bed-making preparations.

Todd's journal is interrupted with his comment dated October 13, 1961 where he noted that Georgia had borrowed his notebook for a sketch pad and he never got it back until she returned it November 9, 1961 (See Figure 11.18 with Georgia using Todd Webb's notebook as sketch pad). The remaining notes were recorded in a separate notebook and some of his comments appear to conflict with observations he made earlier. For example, his entry under the date August 27, 1961 mentions "quite an exciting evening with Echo 1 and the total eclipse of the moon" when it is noted that they saw the *Echo1* satellite and partial eclipse of the moon on August 25th. [See endnote #19] He does write that "the best part of the trip was still to come."

Sunday, August 27, 1961:

Good ride in the morning stopping at Hole-in-the-Rock for a sunbaked lunch. Several good rapids. Stopped at Hidden Passage, a most delightful and spectacular canyon and then at a lesser place called Music Temple where I found and photographed names carved in the rock by members of the 1871 Powell party. Made a fine camp at the mouth of Forbidden [sic] Canyon and all to bed early after what seemed like a good Mexican dinner.

Monday, August 28, 1961:

Up soon after four in bright moonlight so the Rainbow Bridge walkers could make one way in the cool of the day. Walked the first mile or so with them and the canyon did look interesting. Georgia, Tish and I passed up the trip.[21] It is now 11:30 and we have a fine, quiet and restful morning mostly trying to stay in the shade of the willows or the cliff. Even borrowed Kenny's mirror and shaved and I feel cleaner for it. Our rest has been a welcome change and the sun beats down unmercifully on the walkers. About three o'clock the tired travelers began to drift in and in spite of dehydration and sore feet they all felt Rainbow Bridge was worth the effort of twelve weary miles of hard waking.[22] Doris finally came in just before dark and soon after dinner the weather became very threatening and by bed time it was on the verge of rain.

Tuesday, August 29, 1961:

Not much sleep for anyone; blowing sand one minute and light rain the next. A bedraggled looking crew this morning. Started off in the rain – all of us bundled in ponchos and the like. At the first stop there was a general digging for as yet unused sweaters and jackets to keep out the biting cold. Had lunch under an overhanging north-facing wall out of the rain. Built a fire to warm and dry ourselves by. By three o'clock the rain had stopped and a bright blue sky replaced the overcast. Tomorrow will be our last day on the river and we hope for good weather and a fine camp tonight. Everyone seems well and happy in spite of the weather trials and tribulations of last night and today. Soon after lunch we visited Dungeon Canyon and I made some photographs of Georgia that I am anxious to see.

Wednesday, August 30, 1961:

RANK DANK BANK CAMP – or CAMP DREADFUL

Our last day on the river and what a dilly of a beginning. At 3:30 AM the sky suddenly opened up and spilled tons of wet, wet water on our peacefully sleeping party. There were only minutes of warning – thunder and lightning – but so ominous looking that I rolled and packed my sleeping bag. I was just about finished with my packing when the rain came in torrents of the largest drops I have ever seen. I got into my poncho and sat on my pack covering my head with my plastic ground sheet which was very transparent. The lightning flashed – almost in my lap it seemed and I sat there thinking about Tyler Dingee who was killed by a lightning bolt a few weeks ago. I had wet feet and a wet behind but really managed quite well. By 5:30 the rain let up and the wettest, coldest looking crew you can imagine gathered around with all kinds of friendly advice about starting a fire with soaked wood. Finally with the aid of a bit of precious gasoline we managed to get some wood burning and proceeded to have a fine breakfast. This being our last morning of camp we were at liberty to eat all we could. Marshall set a record of eight eggs and God knows how many pieces of cornmeal mush. We were off by eight and even though we ran out of gas and had a limping motor, thanks to the stout rowing of Georgia and Eliot we made landfall at Kane's Creek by noon. And got to Page and slept in bed after drinks and a dinner – and a bath of course.[23] Good, good trip and wonderful company.

Todd Webb closed his typed notes (after finding the original notebook) by saying:

It was a dandy trip and the people could not have been more congenial. Tish, Eliot, Georgia and Marshall were standouts for me. But everyone was just fine. I have made quite a book of prints. Georgia had a party for the survivors and their loved ones at her house. I showed the book and Eliot showed his fine color slides.

Georgia O'Keeffe and Kenny Ross struck up a cordial friendship during the course of their two trips together as Kenny really enjoyed the strong smoky flavor and aroma of the *Lapsang souchong* tea she brought with her. She sent Kenny a tin of *Lapsang souchong* tea several weeks after the last trip was over thanking him for such a wonderful time. Don Ross still has the tin can (Figure 11.24).

Figure 11.11 rigging the two boats alongside the old Hite Ferry at the mouth of White Canyon. (Courtesy: Todd Webb Archives, Portland, Maine USA)

Figure 11.12 Todd Webb at Hite landing; note excavated landing on west bank. (Courtesy: Todd Webb Archives, Portland, Maine USA)

Figure 11.13 fourteen folks on board the double-rigged boats. (Courtesy: Todd Webb Archives, Portland, Maine USA)

Figure 11.14 Georgia gets a helping hand from Stephen; note Kenny in stern with motor and double-rigged transom board. (Courtesy: Todd Webb Archives, Portland, Maine USA)

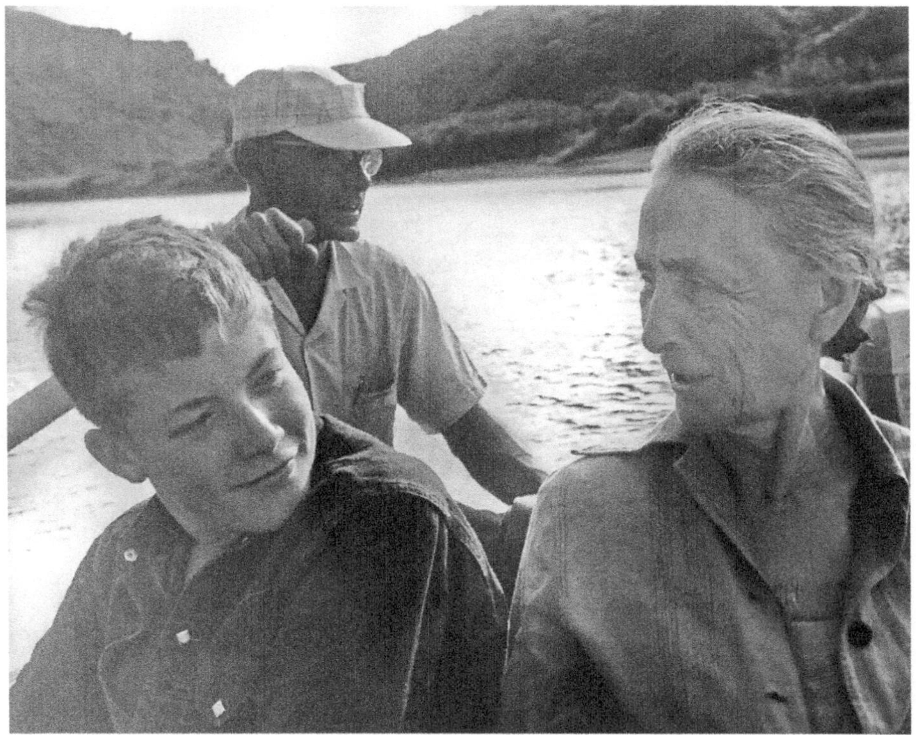

Figure 11.15 "Georgia O'Keeffe, Marshall Girard and Guide Kenny Ross," 1961. (Photo by Todd Webb; courtesy of the Georgia O'Keeffe Museum)

Figure 11.16 Eliot Porter checking out the scenery. (Courtesy: Todd Webb Archives, Portland, Maine USA)

Figure 11.17 sunrises on cliffs across from the mouth of Forbidding Canyon camp. (Courtesy: Todd Webb Archives, Portland, Maine USA)

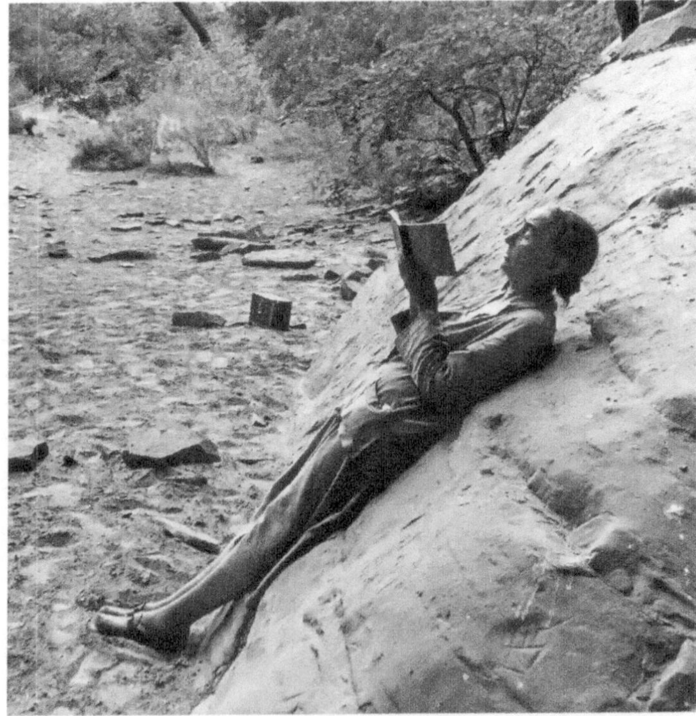

Figure 11.18 "Georgia O'Keeffe sketching in Glen Canyon," 1961. (Photo by Todd Webb; courtesy of the Georgia O'Keeffe Museum)

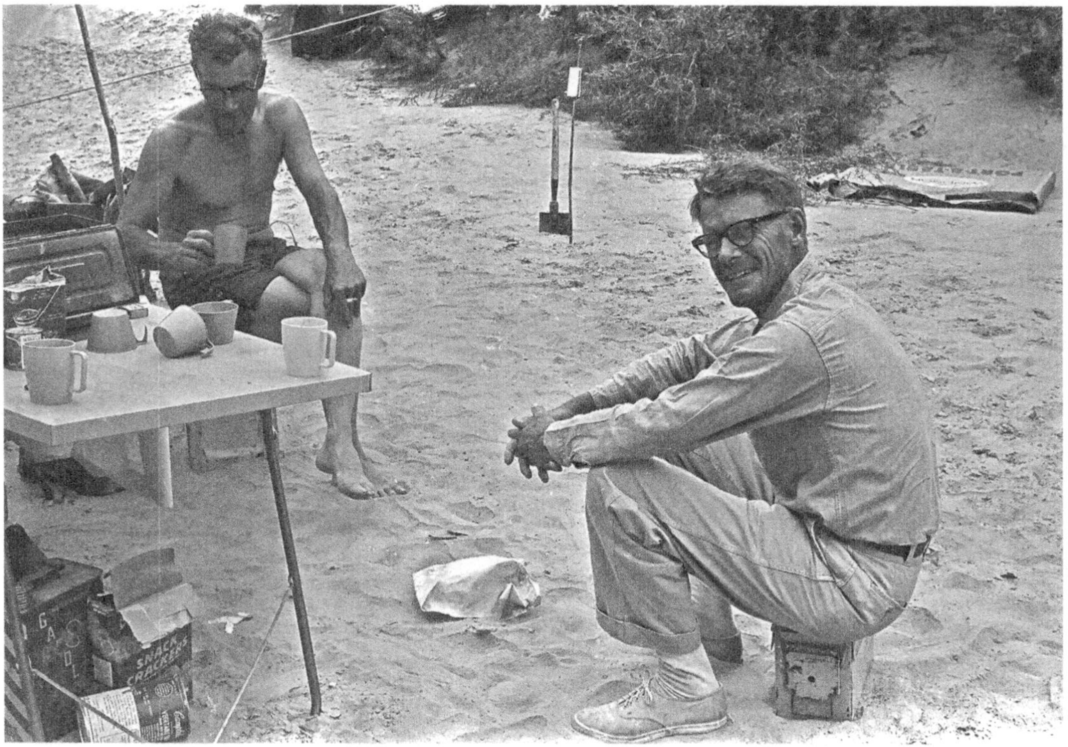

Figure 11.19 Kenny and Eliot at camp. (Courtesy: Todd Webb Archives, Portland, Maine USA)

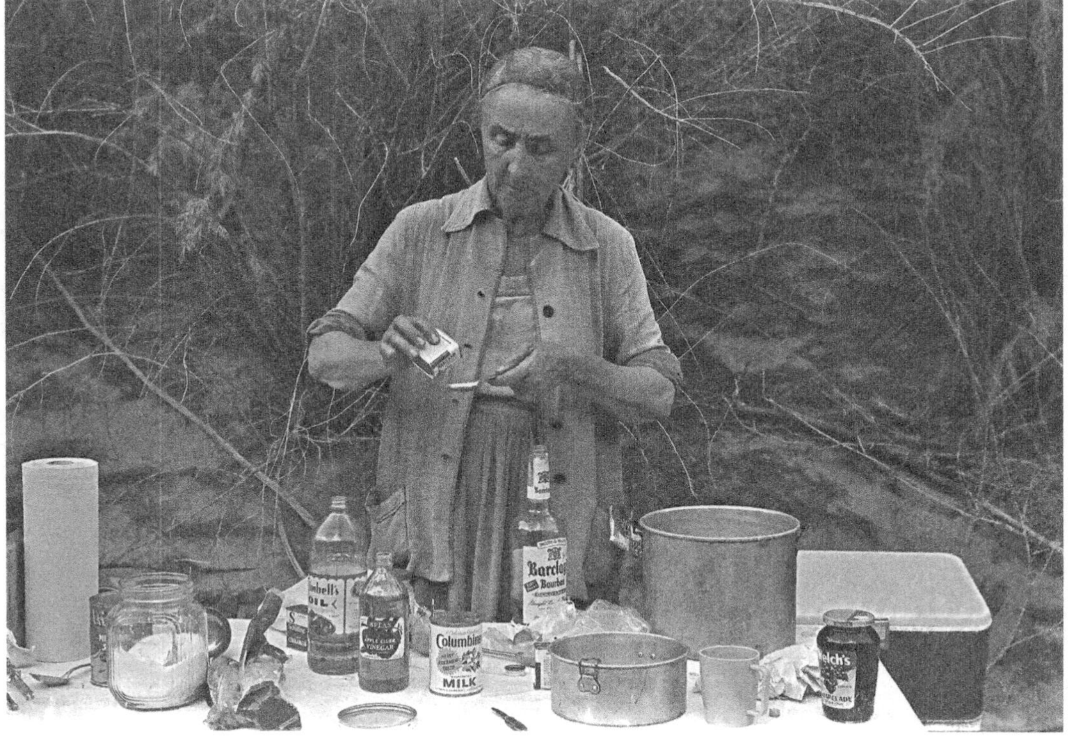

Figure 11.20 Georgia concocting an adult beverage. (Courtesy: Todd Webb Archives, Portland, Maine USA)

Figure 11.21 Kenny and Georgia in the camp kitchen. (Courtesy: Todd Webb Archives, Portland, Maine USA)

Figure 11.22 Georgia near warm springs in Dungeon Canyon. (Courtesy: Todd Webb Archives, Portland, Maine USA)

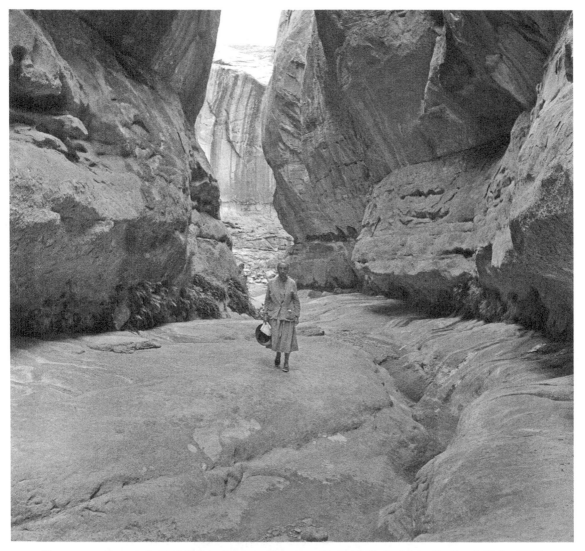

Figure 11.23 Georgia in Forbidding Canyon. (Courtesy: Todd Webb Archives, Portland, Maine USA)

Figure 11.24 the *Lapsang souchong* tea box Georgia O'Keeffe sent Kenny in 1961. (G.M. Stevenson photo)

Figure 11.25 Georgia in motor boat, 1961 Glen Canyon.
(Courtesy: Todd Webb Archives, Portland, Maine USA)

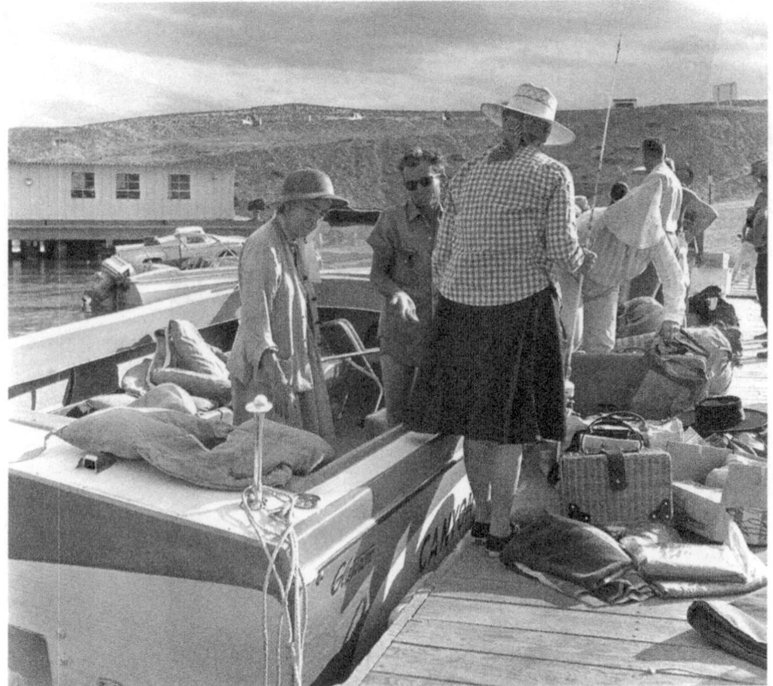

Figure 11.26 Georgia getting off motor boat at Wahweap marina, 1961.
(Courtesy: Todd Webb Archives, Portland, Maine USA)

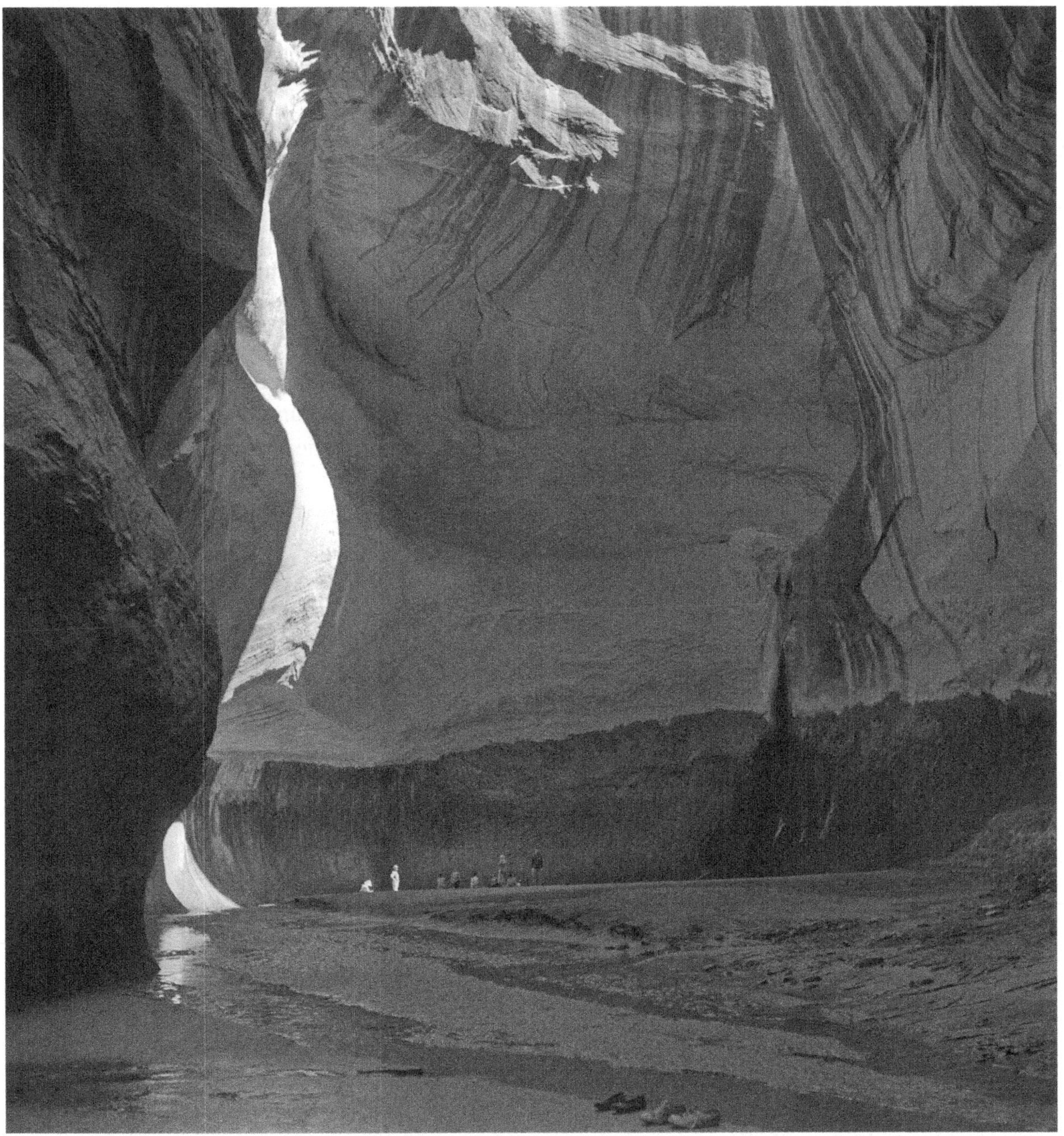

Figure 11.27 the grandeur of Music Temple; people are looking at JW Powell inscriptions from 1871. (Courtesy: Todd Webb Archives, Portland, Maine USA)

ooooo

In the fall Don returned to San Juan High School in Blanding for his senior year and the winter of 1961-1962 was one of the coldest on record. He and Kenny were still living in the drafty trailer, but after their boots froze to the floor overnight they decided to move their living quarters. They rented Don Ripley's small stone house that had a fireplace, across Cottonwood Wash in West Bluff. The winter was so cold that everyone's water lines froze, so Don and Kenny still had to go back and forth to the artesian water well at the base of the Navajo Twins on the east side of town to fill up water jugs.

At some point during spring 1962 Kenny decided to paint some advertisements on the doors to the 1958 International pickup truck. On one side, in his characteristic choice of blue and yellow colors he scrolled "Ride the Wild Rivers" and on the other side he painted "**R**un **R**ivers with **R**oss" where the three R's were extra big and bold. Gaylord Staveley wrote an article in *Western Gateways* magazine in 1969 about Kenny and the photo of Kenny running Eight Foot Rapid is captioned with "Three R's" (Figure 11.28).

Kenny was saddened to hear that Ansel Hall died of a heart attack on March 28, 1962 in Denver where he and his wife, June had moved several years prior. He was 67 years old and would have been 68 on May 6. June never really liked Mancos, preferring San Francisco or Denver metropolitan life over the quaint towns of Mancos or even Durango.[24] Their son, Roger Hall, managed Mesa Verde Company for about six years, then he quit and Bill and Merrie (Hall) Winkler took over managing Mesa Verde Company along with June Hall's input and blessing. Under Bill Winkler's management Mesa Verde Company became a first class NPS concession. Other Hall family members became involved in various capacities as employees over the years, but by the early 1980s most had opted out and Bill decided to sell to ARA Services in 1982-83.

Don graduated high school in May, 1962 but Kenny couldn't attend commencement as he was on a Glen Canyon trip. Mildred made it to the ceremony and brought along a friend from Social Services where she had been working in Cortez. Don went back to Bluff for the rest of the summer and did a number of early summer trips on the San Juan. The river peaked at 10,000 cfs in late April and again in May and averaged 4,000 cfs until July. It then fell precipitously to less than 100 cfs by early September.[25]

In early June Don rowed a *San Juan punt*[26] from Mexican Hat to Clay Hills with Gaylord Staveley and others. Joan Nevills Staveley called in late June and asked Don if he would be interested in rowing the lower half of Grand Canyon for their company. He agreed to the offer and drove to the South Rim and waited for Joan. She finally showed up and Don met the passengers and then they all hiked down the Kaibab Trail to the Bright Angel beach and met up with Gaylord and three other boatmen. They spent the night at Phantom Ranch and Gaylord lined Don out on what to expect regarding the lower canyon big rapids. Don rowed the *Mexican Hat III* wooden boat and had an admirable run. They took out at Temple Bar on the Arizona-side of Mead reservoir – a good end to his first Grand Canyon trip.[27]

The 3 R's of the San Juan

by Gaylord Staveley

Figure 11.28 "Run Rivers with Ross" Kenny Ross running Eight Foot Rapid on San Juan River circa 1960s; photo for *Western Gateways* magazine article by Gaylord Staveley in 1969. (K. Ross collection)

NEW NATIONAL PARKS

Arches National Monument was established April 12, 1929 and in the early 1960s a much bigger National Park was proposed just to the west of Arches. The area was known as Canyonlands and the Arches National Monument Superintendent *Bates Wilson* advocated its creation. He led government officials on jeep tours that featured lengthy talks over campfires and hearty Dutch oven dinners. Secretary of the Interior Stewart Udall joined one of these tours in 1961, and began lobbying for the proposed park. On September 12, 1964, President Lyndon B. Johnson signed Public Law 88-590 that established Canyonlands National Park. Initially it consisted of 257,640 acres, but Congress expanded Canyonlands to its present size of 337,598 acres (1,366 km^2) in 1971 with the addition of the Horseshoe Canyon annex. On November 12, 1971 Arches was re-designated as a National Park that consisted of 76,679 acres (310.3 km^2).[28] The designation of two new national parks in southeastern Utah, along with the near completion of the massive Glen Canyon Dam and the flooding of Glen Canyon to create "Lake Powell," put the slumbering mining town of Moab on the map as a destination town. Tourism took off like a rocket. Over the years Moab has added a myriad of motels and restaurants to accommodate the constant influx of tourists.

In 1972, the Glen Canyon National Recreation Area (GCNRA) was established "to provide for public use and enjoyment and to preserve the area's scientific, historic, and scenic features" [29] even though most of the historic and scenic features were by then submerged by the giant Powell reservoir. The new recreation and conservation area was to be managed by the National Park Service and covered 1,254,429 acres (5,077 km^2) and encompassed the area surrounding Lake Powell and lower Cataract Canyon in Utah and Arizona. The GCNRA was bordered to the west by Capitol Reef National Park (241,904 acres; 979 km^2) and Grand Staircase-Escalante National Monument (1,880,461 acres; 7,610 km^2). Vermillion Cliffs National Monument (293,689 acres; 1,189 km^2) and the northeastern most extent of Grand Canyon National Park provided borders to the southwest and the Navajo Indian Reservation bordered it to the southeast.[30]

Another area to the south of Canyonlands National Park and east of Glen Canyon Recreation Area, known as Cedar Mesa and Elk Ridge, also gained attention as an area worthy of national monument protection. In December, 2016 the area plus much more public lands father east and north was designated Bears Ears National Monument by President Barack Obama, which added an additional 1,350,000 (5,463 km^2) acres to the protected lands status. In December, 2017 President Donald Trump rescinded Obama's presidential order and substantially reduced the size of Bears Ears that has insured years of litigation between environmental groups and the federal government.[31]

Kenny Ross knew this back country "west of the Elk" as well as most adventurers of his day and would have felt that the Federal government was taking away all his freedom to roam. The lower San Juan River was now drowned as was Glen Canyon. Now he wouldn't be able to just load up and go into Salt Creek Canyon, Beef Basin, Woodenshoe or Dark Canyon without applying for permits; same for Cataract Canyon trips. Kenny's remaining freedom to the open wilderness was still intact for a few more years on the San Juan River down to Clay Hills, but that freedom would soon change too.

SOCOTWA

An organization of youths from LDS church wards (Southern Cottonwood Wards) from the Salt Lake City area had been floating Glen Canyon since soon after WWII when surplus military inflatable water crafts (LCRs) became available.[32] SOCOTWA had over a thousand members and owned over thirty LCRs and a few busses. Their heyday was the 1950s and '60s before many river regulations, or basic common sense was in play. And play they did – right up to 1961 when a large party group couldn't negotiate landing the cluster of boats that led to the tragic death of a young man on a trip near the boat ramp at Split Mountain on the Green River. This was soon followed in the same year, in September – flash flood season, when a large group of Scouts were caught clueless by a wall of water in the Zion Canyon Narrows. Four boys drowned. Their bodies were found miles downstream. But then:

> In June, 1963, a large group of Boy Scouts from the Pleasant View Ward in Utah Valley were in the back of the SOCOTWA truck on the 50-Mile Mountain road south of Escalante, Utah, on their way to meet a SOCOTWA river trip at the bottom of the Hole-in-the-Rock trail. There they would trade passengers, the river crews hiking out, while the Scouts hiked in to run the last stretch of Glen Canyon. It was one of the most isolated spots in the entire state. As the truck labored up a steep grade out of Carcass Wash, the engine stalled, and as it began to roll backwards the driver could not stop it. The truck rolled off the road and overturned, spilling all passengers and gear and then rolling over some of them. Four adults and eight scouts

were killed instantly, while twenty-six more were injured, some critically.[33]

No wonder Kenny could never recruit kids for his Explorers Camp from Utah – they were all recruited by SOCOTWA; and the boats too! An interesting footnote to Roy Webb's article was his naming of all the operators in Glen Canyon at the time, except he omitted Kenny Ross and Wild Rivers Expeditions. Other notable outfitters of that era include: Gaylord Staveley, Jack Brennan, Don Harris, Dee Holiday, CK Wyder, Kent Frost, and Ken Sleight.

> There were still some of the old timers from the 1940s around, but others were gone: Norm Nevills and Bert Loper had both died in 1949, Buzz Holmstrom in 1946. Other river rats had started their own companies and "gone commercial," like Bus Hatch, Harry Aleson, and Malcom "Moki-Mac" Ellingson. Hatch stayed up on the Green and Yampa, for the most part; Aleson was too crotchety to ever get much of a following; Moki didn't really have his own company, he went along on trips run by Al Quist and his sons Richard, Clair and Bob. In the Colorado drainage, the San Juan was about the only river to have an active river company running regular commercial trips: Mexican Hat Expeditions, formed by former Nevills boatmen Frank Wright and Jim Rigg, had taken over Nevills boats and customers after Norm and Doris' tragic deaths in a plane crash in September 1949. Glen Canyon was especially wide open, given the fact that you didn't really need whitewater skills to get down it safely. Running Glen Canyon was only restricted by the terrible road (or what passed for a road) from Hanksville through North Wash down to Hite. If you could get there without breaking an axle or leaving your oil pan on a ledge, you were home free, no rangers, no rules, no regulations, almost nothing save for scenery, the river, and the night sky until you got to Lees Ferry, some 180 miles downstream.[34]

Webb continued with his commentary about commercial river outfitters of the day:

> It's also important to point out two other major differences between SOCOTWA and its contemporaries on the river: unlike the other river runners of the day, who were portrayed as, and quite often were, hard-drinking, hard-bitten manly men, SOCOTWA was thoroughly Mormon—not just in the outward trappings of Sunday School and Sacrament meetings during the trip, daily prayers, no smoking or drinking allowed (but plenty of opportunities for romance, which was winked at by the leaders)—but in the detailed organization, the pioneer spirit, and the shared heritage of ancestors who made a home out of a wilderness.[35]

Doug Ross recalled that rather odd-ball name and bunch of folks in Glen Canyon in the 1960s when he was making trips from Bluff to Kane Creek.

> We bailed the SOCOTWA goofballs out several times in Glen. I retrieved one of their boats that were left floating loose at Hidden Passage. Another time we fed a couple of their scouts over at Forbidding camp when they poked into our camp and begged us for something decent to eat...or at least *enough to eat.* Good thing it was Glen Canyon....the Salt Lake council of Boy Scouts would have killed half their troops in anything mildly turbulent.[36]

Even after all these mishaps the SOCOTWA river trips continued. Heck, the group still exists to this day. I may have run into that group in the 1990s when I worked at Wild Rivers. A large group of Boy Scouts and their leaders were about to crawl all over the fragile River House (Snake House) cliff dwelling along the San Juan River when I almost came to fisticuffs with one of the "adults" as I tried to convince them that this sort of behavior was totally and completely out of line and disrespectful of the site. Roy Webb said the heart went out of the organization following the big accidents in the 1960s. I can only add that their brains were also left at home when they went on these poorly supervised joy trips. Perhaps the biggest impact they had was what brought about strict river safety rules and regulations and the increase in required liability insurance.

BIG FCGS GEOLOGY RIVER TRIP

The 1963 Wild Rivers Expeditions season was highlighted by a week of monstrous trips for 140 petroleum geoscientists from June 12-16, 1963. The Four Corners Geological Society (FCGS) sponsored only its fourth field conference, but this was, by far, the first big geological group to go down the river. They were interested in learning more about the overall geology of the Four Corners with a special emphasis on the limestone oil-bearing zones that outcrop so marvelously along the canyon walls of the San Juan River.[37] The river trip was the highlight although it was just an overnighter from Bluff to Mexican Hat where the group camped at Eight Foot Rapid. The "little black guidebook" that was printed for trip participants was one of the most popular guidebooks about the "Shelf Carbonates of the Paradox Basin" and remains so today, even though it has been out of print for decades! [38]

The trip drew such a large number of participants it had to be run as two separate trips back to back with seventy participants and sixteen boatmen and helpers each time.[39] Kenny had to spread the word to Moab and Flagstaff to round up enough boats and boatmen for the river segment of that week-long field trip. They even rented four San Juan "punts" and one Cataract boat (all wooden of course) from Gaylord Staveley and Don Ross ran the Cat boat.

Besides the river trips, the rest of the week's field trips were conducted via motorcade that covered the Four Corners region, but were based out of Bluff. Kenny and several other Bluff residents helped out by volunteering as drivers and helped with the mobilized lunches served during the week. Overland trips included: Farmington, New Mexico to Bluff, Utah via Kayenta, Arizona; Red Mesa, Arizona to Bluff via Aneth oil field; Bluff to Honaker Trail via Goosenecks State Park; Goosenecks to Muley Point via Mokee Dugway; and Bluff to Monticello.[40]

James A. Peterson (Chief Geologist with Shell Oil Company) was the man in charge in setting up the river trip segment of the field conference, but was not particularly versed in field camp etiquette for a hot thirsty and hungry crowd of men, plus he wanted to keep the trips affordable, so he had decided to provide "boxed meals for the 150 participants." [41] Doug Ross recalled that the boxed meals were basically military C-rations and furthermore, Peterson hadn't considered bringing beer or any alcoholic beverages on the trip – a major mistake as most adult group trips always had some sort of libations. Doug said that Kenny had sixteen boatmen to feed each day and provided steaks for supper and asked Peterson to "please make the announcement to the poor bastards staring at them grillin' steaks and that it was *not* the responsibility of Wild Rivers that all the participants were left eating C-rations" while the river men enjoyed grilled steaks and other amenities (i.e., beer).[42]

I am absolutely certain that there was major negative feedback to Peterson about this "oversight," as during my entire river guiding experience, beer, wine and to some degree hard liquor was always available to *all participants* on adult organizations' field trips/river trips – particularly *geological* trips; and plenty of food, canned or fresh. The omission of libations was just another sign that river trips for large groups was in its' infancy!

Trip leaders and/or authors of the many articles in the guidebook were among the "who's who" of the day in geology of the Colorado Plateau, including: Greg Elias, Phil Choquette, John Traut, John Wray, Lloyd Pray, "K" Molenaar, John Parker, Ralph Bass, Seymour Sharps, Allan Loleit, Dennis Irwin, Paul Fitzsimmons, and Paul See. James A. Peterson was responsible for the river log and Sherman A.

Wengerd led the discussion regarding the relatively new subdivisions to the Hermosa Group stratigraphy. Although Donald L. Baars was not the main trip leader he was possibly the most frequent speaker using the "foghorn" describing the detailed **petrology** of the carbonate rocks for the FCGS crowd and he rowed one of the Wild Rivers boats on both days. Kenny had met several Shell Oil Co. geologists who had conducted field work the previous six or seven years as they accessed their geologic focal points by boat and frequented Kenny's boat camp where they asked for logistical assistance of various kinds. Among those who stopped by were Don Baars and James A. Peterson. However, Don Ross hadn't met Don Baars and he was surprised when Baars got up and seemed to "run the show." [43] Don Ross didn't know that Don Baars had been conducting field work all over the Four Corners region by then and had refined various correlations of both Permian and Pennsylvanian age strata in the Colorado Plateau and was already recognized as an upcoming expert in the stratigraphy of the region.

Kenny added in his notes that smaller field trips for the Four Corners Geological Society were also conducted in 1965, 1967, and 1970. Most of the major oil companies that operated in the Southwest during those years regularly used the services of *Wild Rivers Expeditions* to conduct their research scientists down the San Juan River. Numerous academic groups such as the University of New Mexico, University of Montana, Ft. Lewis College and the Naval and Air Force Institutes of Technology that were located in Massachusetts and Ohio also booked river trips with Kenny.[44]

THE OLD MAN & THE BOYS – TOGETHER

After 1963, Kenny stopped running his SJ&C trips (San Juan River past the confluence with the Colorado River through Glen Canyon down to Kane Creek) as the impounded water had risen and the rivers had lost their current velocities which made a long slow row out on dead water too time consuming. From 1964 to the present day, *Wild Rivers Expeditions* trips went no further down the San Juan River than to Clay Hills Crossing. Thus, the year of 1963 denoted the end of an era for the Ross boys and Kenny who had experienced the challenge of Thirteen Foot Rapid and had soaked in the beauty of the majestic side canyons in Glen Canyon.[45]

In late August to early September 1963 Kenny ran his usual "fall" Cataract trip and both Don and Doug rowed boats. While scouting, or "conning" the Big Drops, Virgil Culer, one of the group snapped the only known photograph with Kenny, Don and Doug on the river together (Figures 11.29). Don took the photo of Kenny running "the Gut" and Doug caught Don running the same rapid (Figures 11.30 & 11.31). And Kenny photographed Doug running Dark Canyon (Figure 11.32). Don Ross said the trip was great and Bill Huber was the other boatman. Bill was better known to many locals as the owner and proprietor of the *Silver Dollar Bar* located in west Bluff next to Johnny *Lester's Corner* gas station.

After the construction of the Mokee Dugway in the early 1950s Wild River's trips returned from Clay Hills or Hite, more times than not by way of going down IZ-bell Hill and it was always good to check brakes before descending the steep switchbacks. On this return, Doug was driving the old Dodge stake-bed truck full of gear and when he hit the brakes the pedal went straight to the floor. He said he barely got the truck slowed down by down-shifting and rolled to a stop after turning onto the Muley Point road that enters from the right side just above the dugway "at about 40 mph!" Kenny was following in another vehicle with Bill Huber and after determining that the brake line had busted, Kenny, Bill and Doug went to Bluff and Don spent the night with the broke-down truck and all the gear and boats. The *McFarland and Hollinger Trucking Company* out of Tooele, Utah (or "Mack-and-Hack" as it was known by locals) had been contracted to haul uranium ore from mines over by Fry Canyon down the dugway. Most of the drivers and mechanics lived in Bluff. Boyd Anderson was one of the mechanics who helped keep Kenny's rigs running and the next day he returned with Kenny with all sorts of tools, parts and brake fluid. After replacing the brake line and filling with brake fluid the old Dodge was carefully driven back to Bluff. Just another adventure in traveling the roads in San Juan country! That fall, Don returned to Fort Lewis College and Doug returned to Mancos High School.

Figure 11.29 From L to R: Kenny, Don and Doug conning Big Drop #2, Cataract Canyon, 1963; the only photo of Kenny Ross and his two boys together on the river. (Photo by Virgil Culer; K. Ross collection)

Figure 11.30 Kenny Ross runs Satans Gut, Cataract Canyon, 1963. (K. Ross collection)

Figure 11.31 Don Ross runs Satans Gut, Cataract Canyon, 1963. (K. Ross collection)

Figure 11.32 Doug Ross enters Dark Canyon Rapid, 1963. (K. Ross collection)

Boat Camp No. 5: Kenny decided to move out of the old trailer and chaha'oh that had been set-up on the east side of Cow Canyon and moved into a real building over the winter of 1963-64. The gas station farther up Cow Canyon (an old Sinclair gas station) north of Rusty Musselman's trading post was owned by "Grat" Wilson (Figure 11.33). Grat was a retired tunnel engineer and had made some money and ran the gas station for several years. He owned it and pumped gas for a while but wanted to sell. More importantly, he also owned the forty acres of State land it was setting on. Kenny couldn't afford to buy, but he worked out a rental agreement with Grat for the old gas station and he moved the boat camp there over the winter months. Grat Wilson also had a small *Airstream* trailer on the side he used as living quarters and it went along with the deal.

Kenny used the old cinder block gas station as his boat shop and kept the boats on the outside. Grat was also an excellent welder, and welded up a pipe trailer for Kenny to haul boats. It had regular leaf springs and sat higher off the ground than most conventional flatbed trailers, but it has held up to this very day. Soon after Grat made the trailer (shaped more-or-less like a 10-man boat) the Ross boys started calling it the "Bullet Trailer" and the name stuck. It's still in use, and known as the *bullet trailer* to the current owners of Wild Rivers Expeditions. The old gas station remained the headquarters for Wild Rivers Expeditions until Kenny sold the business to Charlie and Susan DeLorme in 1986 when operations were moved to *Boat Camp No. 6*.

THE HOUSE UNDER THE CLIFF

In 1964, Kenny's older sister Gail called from her home in Wellesley, Massachusetts to tell him her husband had died and left a fair amount of money to her in his will and that she wanted to move to the southwest. Kenny went back east for the funeral and to help Gail move out west. At some point during this upheaval in Gail's life,

Kenny suggested that she invest some of her money by purchasing the forty acres from Grat Wilson and to build her a home on it in Bluff. Plus, she could then rent Kenny the gas station and he wouldn't have to find yet another location for his boat camp. So she did.

At that time there still wasn't a regular grid of electricity for Bluff residents and culinary water was also pretty much left up to the individual homeowner. Gene Foushee had constructed a modest water tank on the south side of Cemetery Hill that could provide water to his motel and a few homes, but the closest potable water to Grat's gas station/boat camp, was still the flowing artesian well across the highway at the base of the Navajo Twins. By some fortuitous act of luck, the U.S. Geological Survey had been in the area and had core-drilled random locations into the Navajo Sandstone aquifer to evaluate the geologic parameters that would provide measured physical properties of the aquifer. They spot-cored a well on the Grat Wilson property almost due east of the gas station/boat camp. The State of Utah's Division of Water Rights data show the well was drilled to a depth of ~300 ft and at the sixty foot drilling depth, six inch steel casing was cemented in with twenty sacks of "neat cement." [46] As of March 03, 1964 the well was gauged to flow at 10 gallons per minute (gpm) and was capped, but accessible for landowner use. Then the USGS drilling crew moved on to other locations in their effort to assess the geologic parameters of the aquifer.

When Gail visited Bluff and was considering buying some land, she just "fell in love" with the location tucked up against the steep sheer canyon wall. So now, the possibility of building a house in Gail's dream spot was possible. Not only was a water-well drilled close by, but there was no problem to extend electric lines northward from the old boat camps (Boat camps 2-4).

> The House in the Rocks was built for Gail in 1964-65. It was built for Gail by the Hurst Construction goofs from Blanding, and it was wrong from the get-go. Gail had all sorts of difficulty with the builders and subsequent post-building problems. Don't think it went to court but the Hurst's screwed her royally. Overcharged, didn't make finishing dates, etc. No question of the shoddy building; real crap. As to location, Dad tried to talk her out of it, but she wasn't going to hear it. I just remember that during the building process that there were pains and consternations expressed damn near every week. Kenny was pretty pissed off because he had pointed Gail toward building with the locals....I have vague memories of the well digging...it sure didn't seem like a strat test to me....I always thought that it was supposed to be the well for the house.[47]

Doug graduated from Mancos High School in June and began his freshman year in fall 1964 at Colorado State University in Fort Collins, Colorado. He had been awarded a "merit scholarship" and became absorbed into college life. Doug said he didn't run a single river trip in 1964. By September 1964, Don was back at Fort Lewis College (FLC). After April, 1965 he ran numerous San Juan River trips and Gail's house under the Bluff cliff was finally finished. Joan Staveley called in early June, and wanted Don to run another Grand Canyon river trip with "some special people" that turned out to be Barry Goldwater and his family. They all met at Marble Canyon and they launched five Cataract boats with Gay Staveley, Fred and Maggie Eismann, Ron Smith, Bob Rigg, and Don Ross on low, clear water. The trip was uneventful other than to have taken an *almost* President of the U.S. on a Grand Canyon river trip. Doug said he worked rowing boats for Kenny in 1965, but provided no details. In 1966 Jack Curry of Green and Grand Canyon fame told Don that his first trip on the San Juan was with some friends who used some Styrofoam that floated and they had no idea what they were doing and Kenny and Don rescued four very sunburned folks and ferried them across the San Juan River at "Ford's ford." [48]

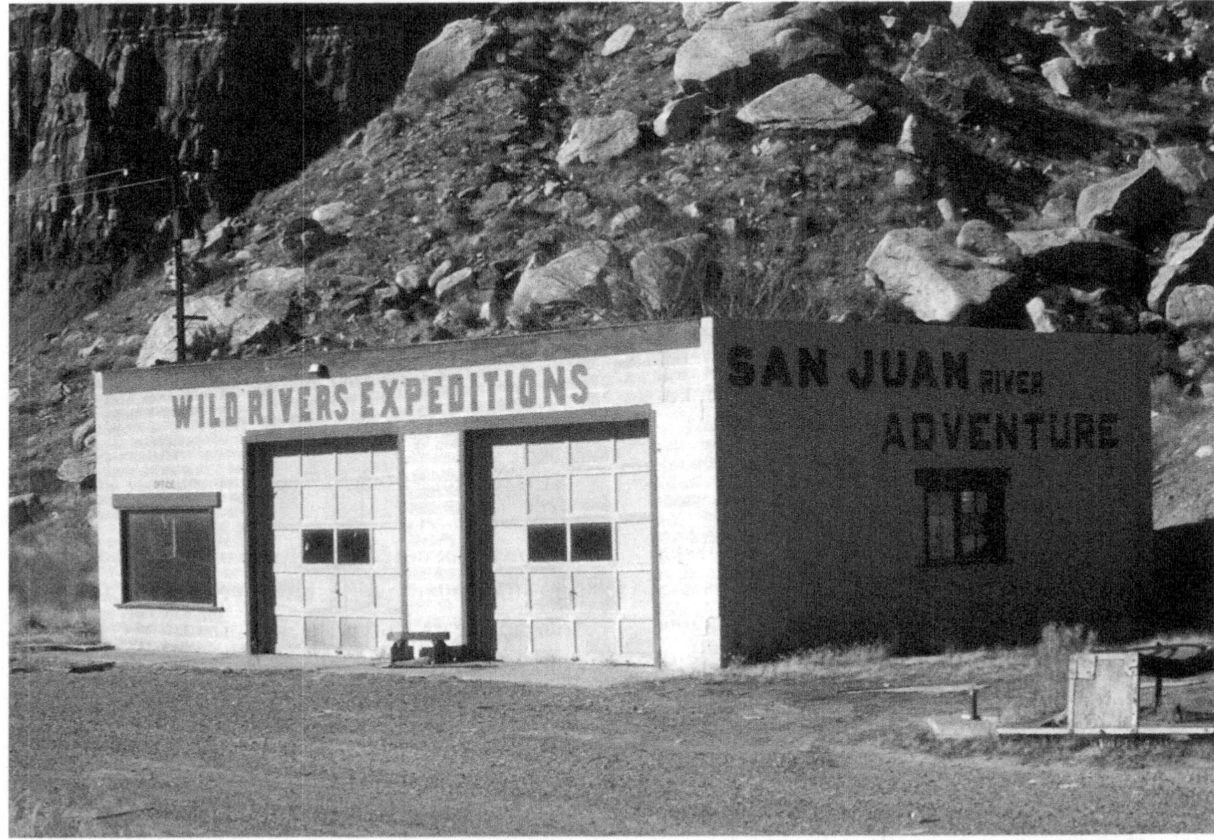

Figure 11.33 Wild Rivers Expeditions "Boat Camp 5" 1964 to 1986. (G.M. Stevenson photo)

LIMESTONE AND OIL

Both academic and economic geologists had been poking around in the canyons of the San Juan River and the greater Four Corners portion of the Colorado Plateau since the early 1900s where they refined their correlations and coordinated formational names of all the Mesozoic and Paleozoic strata.[49] In fact, geologists are still refining these correlations. In the 1950s the first detailed descriptions of mostly the limestone strata was upgraded and further subdivided, as almost all the new oil that had been produced upstream near Aneth and Montezuma Creek was from these very same limestones that crop out in the canyon walls dissected by the San Juan River (Figure 11.34).

Following the early oil discovered at Mexican Hat in 1908, the entire section of strata exposed in these canyons, from rim to river, was called the "Goodridge Formation," and by 1933 recognized to be correlative with the "Hermosa Formation" that crops out north of Durango, Colorado along Hermosa Creek.[50] In 1951, a geologist from the University of New Mexico, Sherman A. Wengerd, further subdivided the section by upgrading Hermosa to "Group" status and named the upper portion of the canyon the "Honaker Trail Formation" as his detailed descriptions had been conducted by describing the strata exposed along the old mining trail built by the Honaker family west of Goosenecks.[51] The lower portion of the canyon strata from Horn Point to river level was found to be correlative to the "Paradox Formation" [52] and was formally designated as such in several geological publications in 1954 and 1958.[53]

Figure 11.34 outcropping porous algal mounds at Eight Foot Rapids have been described and studied by petroleum geologists since the early 1950s; note geologists in lower right corner for scale. (From Grammer, etal 1996)

Meanwhile, more and more oil company geologists were increasingly interested in specific details of the paleoenvironment and depositional setting of the cyclically deposited shallow marine sedimentary strata by revisiting the outcrops near Eight Foot Rapid or the various mounds in the Goosenecks stretch of the San Juan River. And the only sure means to access the oil-bearing porous limestone rocks in the canyons was by boat, and here Kenny Ross opened several new chapters into what he would learn about his beloved river. Kenny began reading everything he could get his hands on to better understand these new concepts in petroleum geology and geophysics.

By 1957, geologists from Shell Oil Co. had performed numerous detailed measured sections and description of some of the porous and permeable strata in the Paradox Formation outcropping at Eight Foot Rapid and the side canyon that entered from the south and gained the informal name of *Wild Horse Canyon*. This rock sequence and the interval below was correlated to the same units that outcrop immediately downstream from Soda Basin to Lime Creek and also throughout the Goosenecks all the way past the bottom of Honaker Trail to Slickhorn Canyon; all of which are layers of the Paradox Formation.[54]

In November, 1957, Shell Oil geologist James A. Peterson recorded nearly fifty-one feet of core that was recovered when cut by a small portable drill rig located on river left (RL) about three river miles above Eight Foot Rapid.[55] Although informative, this core did not intersect the porous type of rock that contained the oil at Aneth. It took another thirty-two years before *Wild River Expeditions* was contacted by the *Kansas Geological Survey* under the leadership of Director, Lee Gerhard and a similar portable drill rig was brought down the river by several boats in August, 1989 (Figure 11.35).

Previously, Don Baars and I had discussed that the optimum spot to drill was on river right (RR) about two hundred yards downstream of the Shell core hole and on the BLM-side of the river. The coring operation recovered forty-four feet of core, of which more than twenty feet consisted of very porous limestone that was saturated with *oil*, exactly like that recovered in Aneth (Figure 11.36). While some folks find this fact disturbing and contrary to their concept of keeping the canyon country clear of oil companies drilling in or near the canyons, it must be pointed out that even though live oil was present in these core, there is virtually zero hydrostatic pressure to force the oil out – at least in any volume beyond the natural seeps that occur throughout the canyons of the San Juan River.

Additional studies of that interval cored and the underlying strata that crops out for approximately sixty miles forms a nearly uninterrupted continuous succession that has been studied by innumerable geologists, both academic and economic. This rare continuously exposed outcrop has become recognized as a world class outcrop exhibiting the geologic nuances of a mixed siliciclastic-carbonate-evaporite succession.[56] All levels of geological research have continued to this day, proving once again that scientific research is open-ended and seldom has reached consensus! [57]

Figure 11.35 portable coring rig set up on RR San Juan River, at RM 126.2, August 1989. (G.M. Stevenson photo)

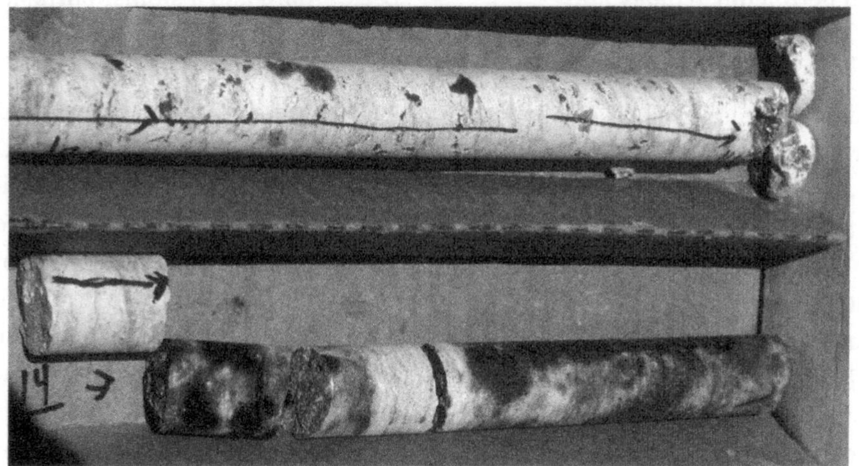

Figure 11.36 two-inch diameter core of porous limestone recovered; black spots are oil. (G.M. Stevenson)

View of the "Mule Ear" (highest point in brown-red sandstone) with dark-gray rubble mass adjacent to it (the Mule Ear diatreme) and the entrance into the upper canyon of the San Juan River as it cuts across the east-dipping strata of the Monument upwarp. View from Lime Ridge. (G.M. Stevenson photo)

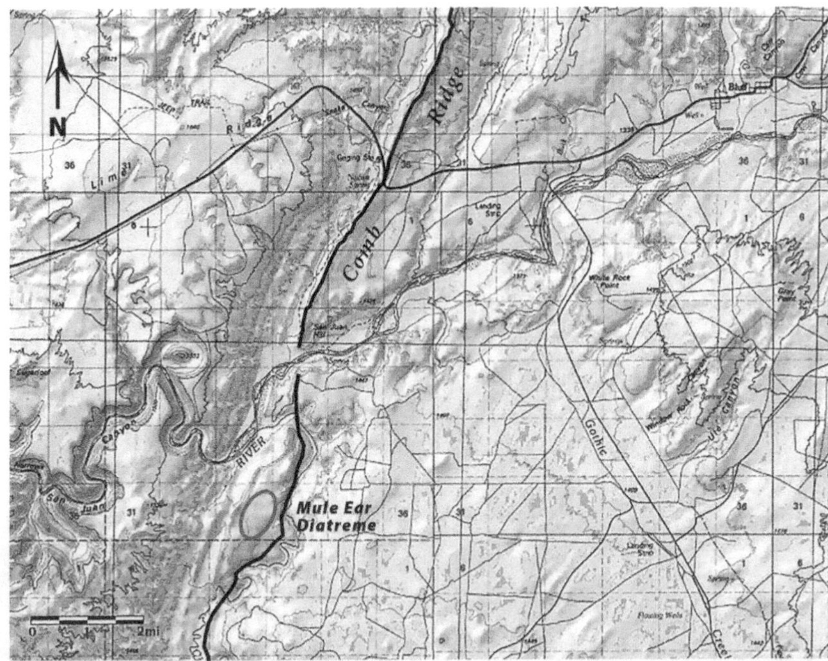

Figure 12.1 Topographic map showing location of Mule Ear diatreme (oval) along eastern boundary of Monument upwarp; black line denotes crest of Comb Ridge. (Modified from *Esri ArcGIS*; USGS topographic map)

Figure 12.2 aerial view looking south along steeply dipping beds that define eastern flank of Monument upwarp; Comb Ridge, Mule Ear diatreme, San Juan River and geologic formations labeled. (G.M. Stevenson photo)

12

PARADIGM SHIFT: NEW CONCEPTS ABOUT THE COLORADO PLATEAU

INTRODUCTION

As much as the incredible stack of sedimentary rocks that were deposited in a multitude of varying conditions and environments over millions of years was spectacularly exposed across the Central Colorado Plateau and lay open to research by geologists studying **sedimentology** and stratigraphy there was another group of geoscientists scurrying about the Four Corners. These researchers were comprised of geologists, physicists, geophysicists and geochemists who were interested in a rather peculiar type of **igneous** rock that had intruded from deep below the earth's surface millions of years after most of the sedimentary strata had been deposited. These were a special form of **volcanic** intrusions known as **diatremes.**

Diatremes commonly contain a rare **meta-igneous** rock called **kimberlite.** And one of the very best outcrops laid bare to research efforts was what became known as the "Mule Ear diatreme" and its access was best made by boat down the San Juan River. It sat only a few miles downstream of Bluff, Utah on the south side, the Navajo side, of the river in a most inaccessible location overland but a man with rubber boats just happened to operate a small river company there. Kenny's awareness of the limestone canyons and how outcrops near Eight Foot Rapid that had piqued the interest of petroleum geologists was soon moved to the back-burner as he witnessed the scientific curiosity in diatremes explode on the scene.

The actual "Mule Ear" is a name given to a distinct promontory landmark that is part of the Comb Ridge monocline that dominates the eastern flank of the Monument upwarp in southeastern Utah (Figures 12.1 and 12.2). Rocks that comprise Comb Ridge consist of a reddish tan-colored sandstone complex collectively known as the Glen Canyon Group (the Navajo-Kayenta-Wingate sandstones of Jurassic age; see Stratigraphic Column: Appendix II). The Mule Ear diatreme lies adjacent to the sandstone promontory at a lower elevation and is first noticed from river level about one-half mile past the mouth of Comb Wash which enters from the north side (RR) (Figure 12.3). At first, the diatreme is obscured at river level by cottonwood trees and brush, but finally comes into full view as the Chinle Wash channel enters the San Juan River from the left bank (near RM 132.5; see Table 1, Appendix I for river miles).

The "diatreme" appears as a non-descript lower relief dark jumble of rock with three distinct promontories (Figure 12.4). The dimensions of this volcanic remnant become more apparent as one draws closer (it is approximately 1800 ft wide and 3300 ft long). When preparing to hike the diatreme, the best spot to land a boat is near a thicket of tamarisks and willows at the rock-strewn top of a small riffle (near RM 131.7) along the left side of the river (RL) (Figure 12.5).

Figure 12.3 Mule Ear diatreme as first seen from river level at RM 133.5, one-half mile downstream from the mouth of Comb Wash. (G.M. Stevenson photo)

Figure 12.4 Mule Ear diatreme in full view near landing spot on river left at RM 131.7; note three distinct promontories defining the top of the diatreme. (G.M. Stevenson photo)

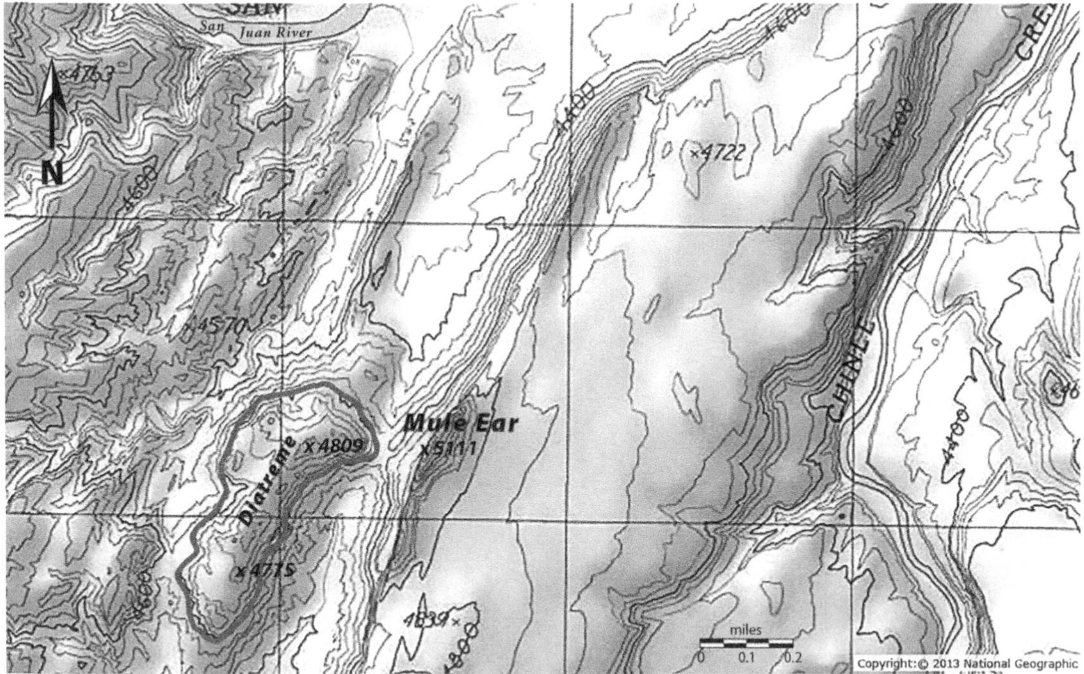

Figure 12.5 Close-up topographic map showing location, elevation and size of Mule Ear diatreme [outlined]. (Modified from *Esri ArcGIS*; USGS topographic map)

The diatreme is located where the southward flowing San Juan River turns abruptly to the west and cuts into the upper deep canyon. Within a quarter mile the relatively wide river corridor changes from tan, red and pink-colored sandstones to a narrow canyon 800 ft deep and dominated by the gray limestone beds of the Honaker Trail Formation (see Figure 12.2 and Chapter Divider photo). To hike the diatreme, one should be prepared to hike approximately four miles round trip, carry plenty of water, and be prepared for full exposure to the sun and wind because there is absolutely no shade or cover. The hike is mostly a rocky scramble as there is no specific trail other than following an unnamed wash (diatreme wash) along the west flank of this feature for the first half mile or so before beginning to ascend the dark ominous pile of bare rock (Figure 12.6). The elevation difference from river bank to the top of the diatreme is about 570 ft (highest pinnacle on the diatreme is 4809 ft elevation; river is approximately 4240 ft elevation; Figure 12.7).

One of the most striking aspect when standing atop this feature is the huge flat vertical face of the Mule Ear escarpment immediately adjacent to the east side where it reaches an elevation of 5111 ft, or roughly 300 ft taller than the top of the diatreme (Figure 12. 5 and Figure 12.8). The total elevation difference of the Mule Ear, from highest tip to the wash below is over 710 ft, of which the upper 400 ft is a shear vertical wall before the angle slopes steeply to base level and strewn with large boulders and talus (Figure 12.9).

Another important observation when standing on top of the Mule Ear diatreme is to notice the relationship of how this explosive intrusion dissected the tilted strata along the eastern flank of the Monument upwarp. The thick sandstone layer (the De Chelly Ss) that seems to come to an abrupt stop when viewed from the river or when hiking up the north face of the diatreme suddenly reappears when viewing south (Figures 12.10 and 12.11). Plus, the view in either direction is breathtaking.

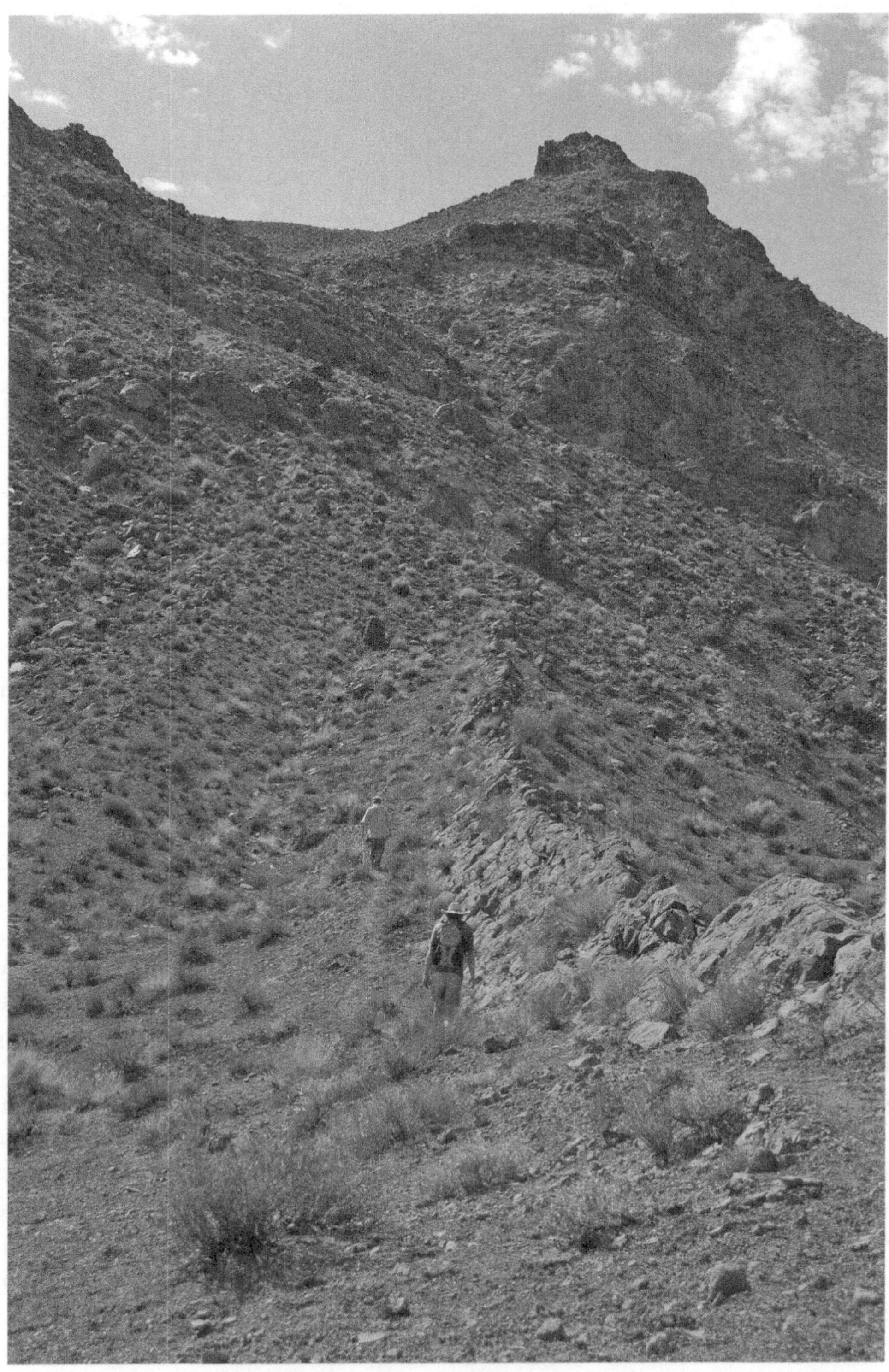

Figure 12.6 hiking the Mule Ear diatreme; the ascent soon turns into a scramble with no defined trail and zero shade. (S. Aitchison photo)

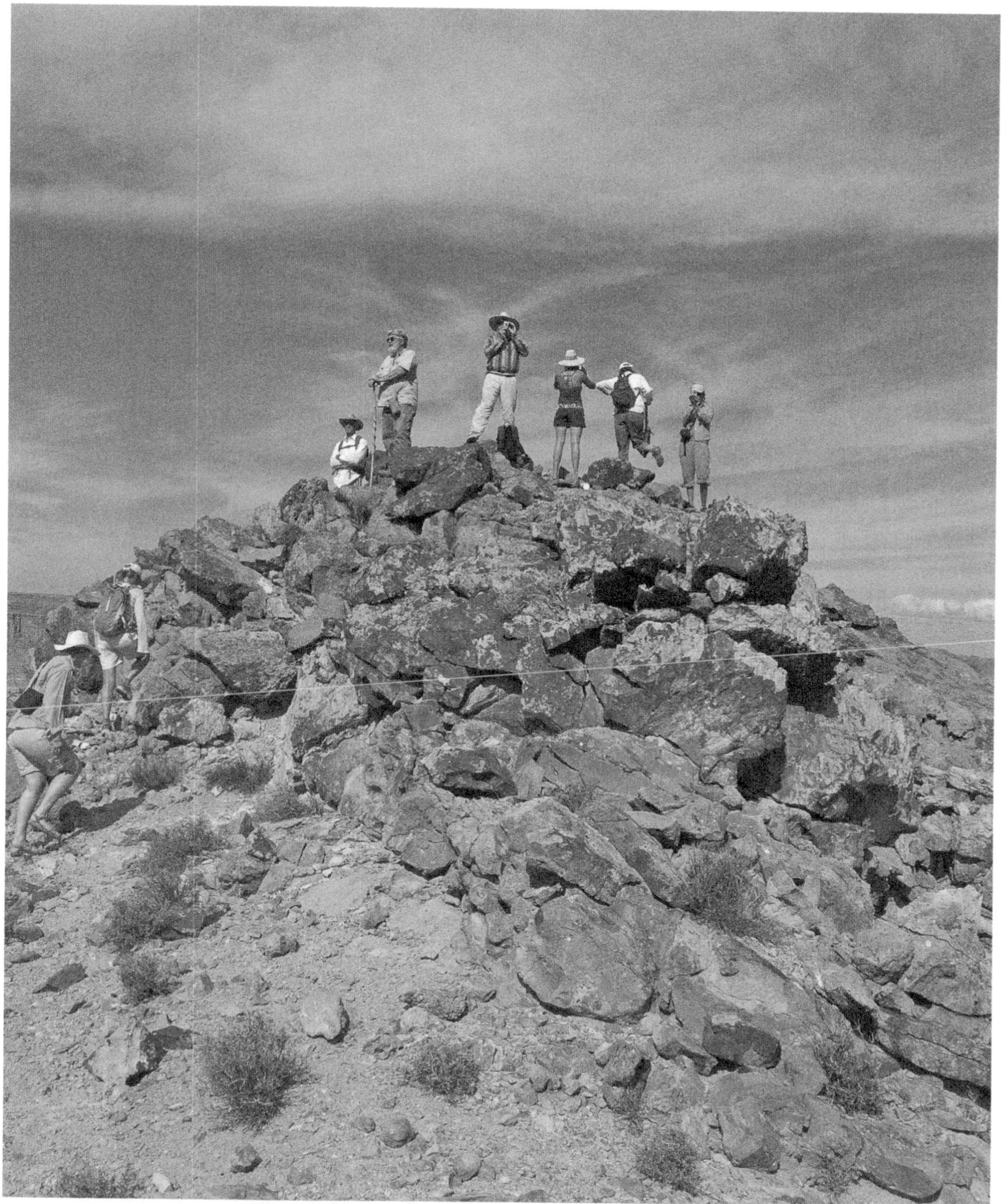

Figure 12.7 top of middle Mule Ear diatreme promontory [elevation: 4809 ft]. (S. Aitchison photo)

Figure 12.8 closer view of "Mule Ear" sandstone wall adjacent to Mule Ear diatreme; the pinnacle with hikers shown in Figure 12.7 is indicated with arrow (upper right). (JR Lancaster photo)

Figure 12.9 the "Mule Ear Wall"- a sheer wall in the Kayenta-Wingate sandstones; the "ear" stands nearly three hundred feet higher than the top of the diatreme (dark rock in bottom right). (JR Lancaster photo)

Figure 12.10 view northward from atop the Mule Ear diatreme; Abajo Mountains in distance; Comb Ridge is well defined in upper right with San Juan River flowing from right to lower left. The strongly dipping Halgaito Shale on left side defines the eastern flank of the Monument Upwarp; the massive sandstone in lower-right. (De Chelly Sandstone) is abruptly truncated by the diatreme intrusion. (G.M. Stevenson photo)

Figure 12.11 view southward from atop the diatreme; note Comb Ridge Monocline in distance skyline and continuation of the tilted De Chelly Sandstone as it wraps southwestward around the Monument Upwarp. (S. Aitchison photo)

SIGNIFICANCE OF THE MULE EAR DIATREME

So what does the Mule Ear diatreme tell us? Why is it considered so important, and how do we know all this? The answers are explained below, but the most simplistic explanation is that the eruption happened fast about 28 million years ago – on a Tuesday, by fluidization and volatile gas expansion following a crack that propagated from the base of the **asthenosphere** to the surface that accelerated the last 30 to 50 miles and substantially exceeded supersonic velocity upon eruption at the surface as it moved in a swirling, turbulent tornadic motion. It contained rocks brought up from the deep **asthenosphere-mantle boundary** some 125 miles below the surface along with **Precambrian meta-sedimentary** and meta-igneous rocks and **Phanerozoic** strata and dropped large blocks of sedimentary strata that were at the surface down the vent from nearly 5,000 ft above (Figure 12.12). The diatreme followed a weakness in the asthenosphere caused by unsteady eddies brought on by the underplating of a subducted oceanic plate from the Pacific about 930 miles (1500 km) to the west; and the subducted plate brought a tell-tale rock associated with oceanic crust known as **eclogite** which among other minerals contains red **garnets**; and **xenoliths** are impregnated in all the wall rock like raisins in a cookie. And it's preserved today near the entrance into the upper canyons of the San Juan River, as that non-descript lower relief dark blob of rock.

THE NAVAJO VOLCANIC FIELD

In reports from the late 19th **Ce**ntury and ongoing into the 21st Century, geologists have sampled, mapped and described these mysterious volcanic spires like Agathla, Alhambra or Ship Rock or the many others that dot the north-eastern portion of Arizona and southernmost part of Utah and became collectively known as the "Navajo Volcanic field" [1] (NVF; Figure 12.13). The Four Corners region has a high concentration of this variety of volcanoes and geoscientists are still trying to understand why they are in a relatively small geographic area. The Navajo volcanic field [2] encompasses nearly a hundred volcanoes and intrusive features of Oligocene to Miocene age (ca. 28-19 Ma; see **Geologic Time Scale**; Appendix III) distributed across the central Colorado Plateau southwest of Gallup, New Mexico, to approximately 150 miles northeast to the Four Corners and Mesa Verde National Park, and then to about 80 miles west-southwest to the Monument upwarp on the Utah-Arizona border (Figure 12.13).[3]

The diatremes first attracted attention as the source of the gem-quality red (**pyrope**) **garnets**, or "Arizona ruby" which the Navajo collected in the Tyende Valley and brought to the trading posts. Geologist D.B. Sterrett visited the Garnet Ridge diatreme east of Kayenta in 1909 and erroneously described the garnet-rich sands and the admixed boulders of **gneiss** and Carboniferous limestone as well as the unusual igneous rocks as "glacial deposits." [4] Likewise, in 1912, Woodruff mistakenly identified the source of this garnet-rich conglomeration of rock types at the Mule Ear diatreme as possible "glacial debris." [5] But, it was argued that if these were truly glacial deposits, then the latitude of glaciers would need to be lowered far to the south and at much lower elevations than what was already proven to be the extent of Pleistocene glaciers.

These enigmatic geologic features prompted H.E. Gregory (1916, 1917) to map the three regions of these so-called "glacial erratics" at Mule Ear, Moses Rock and Garnet Ridge and he correctly identified their origin as part of a **volcanic neck** or **dike**.[6] Miser's (1924) geological map of the San Juan Canyon and adjacent country showed the Mule Ear diatreme as a volcanic neck.[7] Williams (1936) and Hack (1942) studied the petrology of the volcanic rocks and compared their findings to similar features and petrologies in Europe and Africa and correctly identified them as "diatremes." [8]

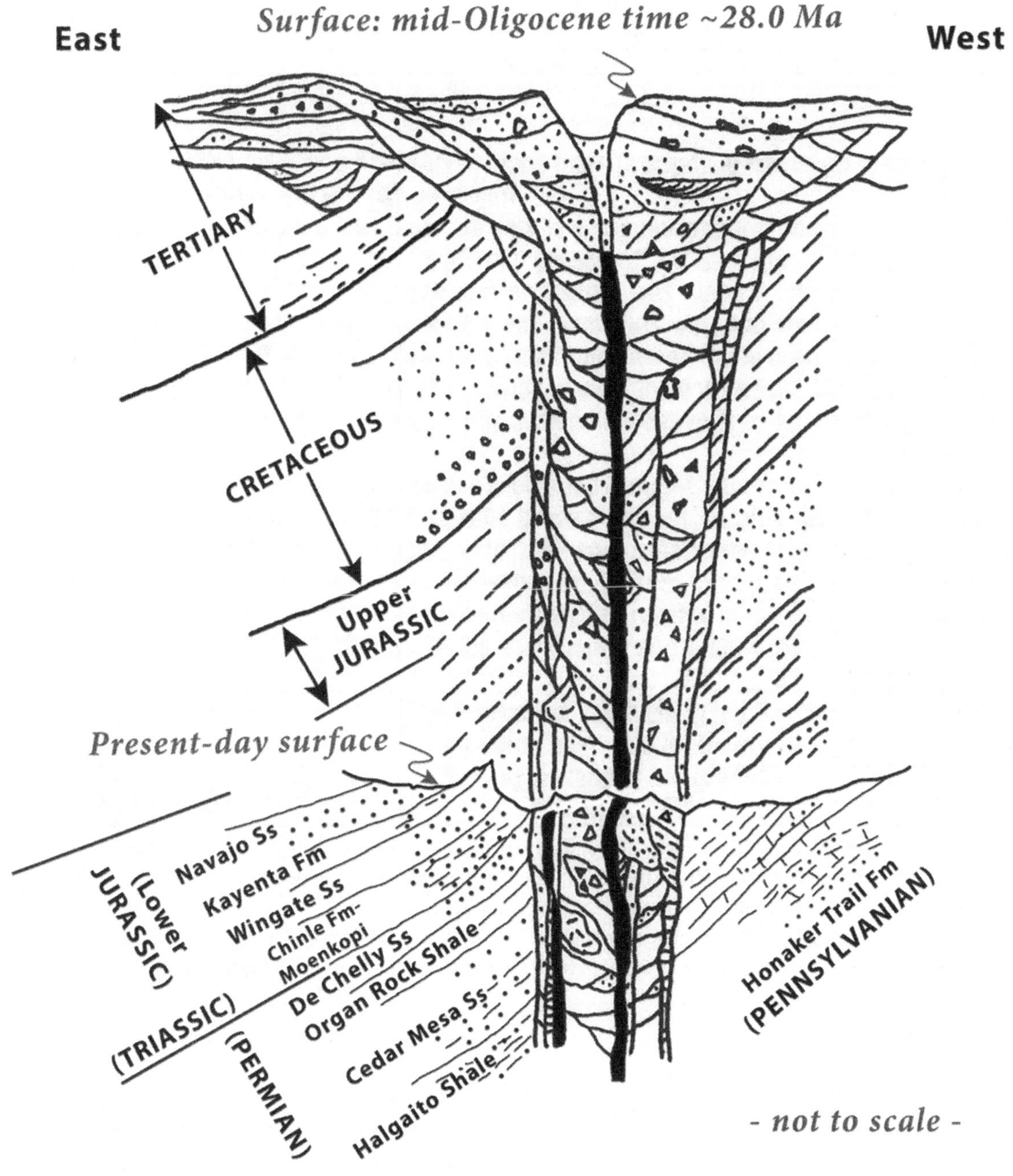

Figure 12.12 Diagrammatic cross-section of Mule Ear diatreme pipe. (Modified from Ellingson, 1973)

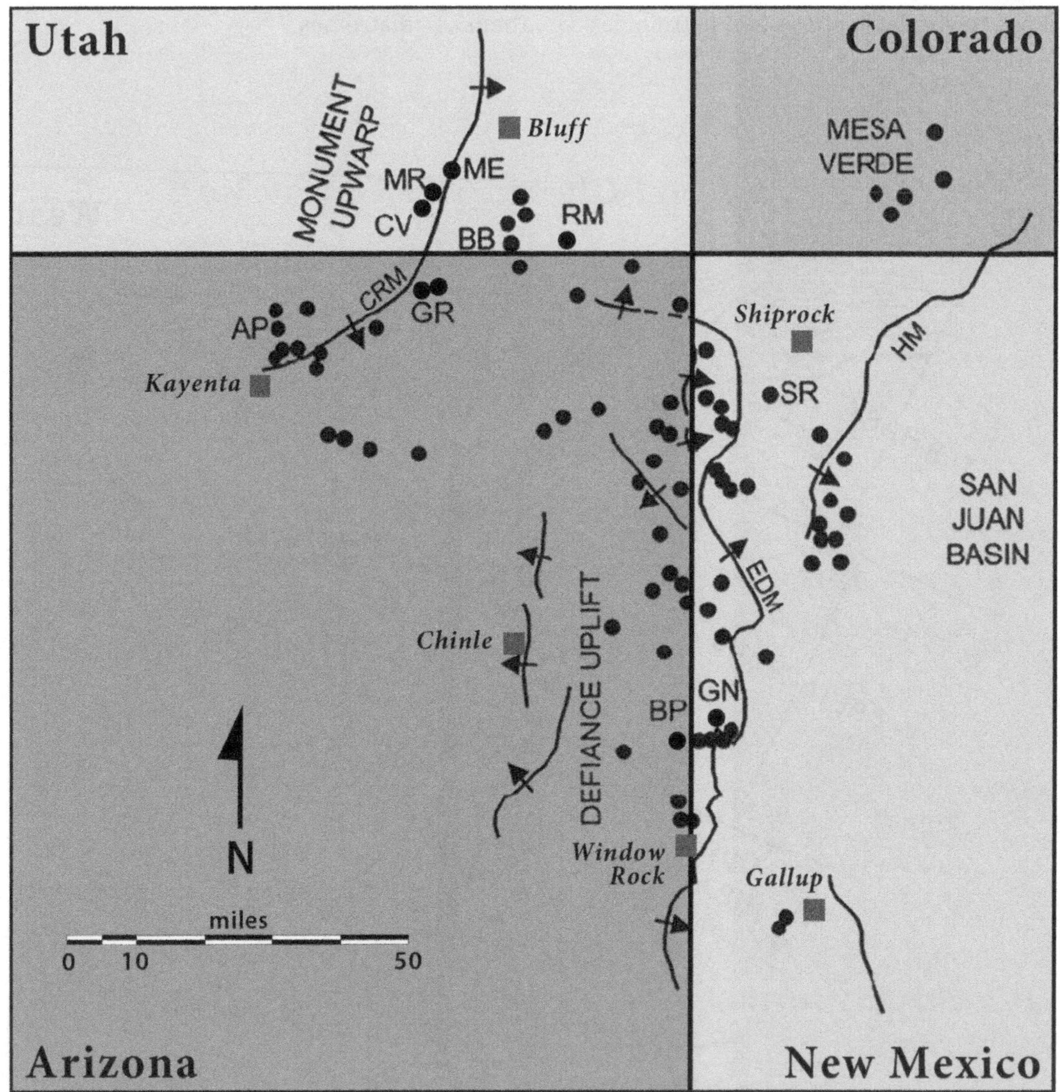

Figure 12.13 Map of the Navajo Volcanic Field (NVF); dark circles indicate "kimberlites" as defined here; see Geologic Glossary, Appendix IV. Monoclines are indicated by black irregular lines. Abbreviations: AP, Agathla Peak; BB, Boundary Butte; BP, Buell Park; CRM, Comb Ridge Monocline; CV, Cane Valley; EDM, East Defiance Monocline; GN, Green Knobs; GR, Garnet Ridge; HM, Hogback Monocline; ME, Mule Ear; MR, Moses Rock; RM, Red Mesa; SR, Ship Rock. Major communities are also shown as squares (modified from McGetchin, et al, 1977; Roden, 1981; Smith, 2000; and Semken, 2003).

WHAT IS A DIATREME?

When **magma** from deep in the earth rises up through a crack in the earth's crust and makes contact with a shallow body of ground water, rapid expansion of heated water vapor and volcanic gases can cause a series of explosions (the actual diatreme). The result is a relatively shallow crater (known as a **maar**) that is filled by a jumbled mix of rocks and called **breccia-filled volcanic vents**. The Navajo Volcanic Field (NVF) eruptive centers are sometimes known as ***maar-***

diatreme volcanoes formed by such a process (Figure 12.14). Diatremes breach the earth's surface and typically produce an irregularly shaped teepee. The *Diné* (Navajo people) call these erosion-sculpted features *tsézhiin 'íí 'áhí* ("black rocks protruding up") and hold a special place along with other landforms in their ethnographic stories and cultural identities.[9] Two of the most prominent exhumed diatremes in the NVF are Ship Rock and Agathla Peaks (Figures 12.15 and 12.16). *Ship Rock* or *Tsé bit'a'í*, "Rock with Wings" stands some 1,583 ft (482.5 m) tall and *Agathla Peak* (Navajo: Aghaałą́, Spanish: *El Capitan*) near Kayenta, Arizona stands 1,436 ft (438 m) above the surrounding terrain. The blasts migrated downward as the aquifer was locally depleted, and left a conical breccia pipe that incorporated magma and wallrock.[10] (Figure 12.14)

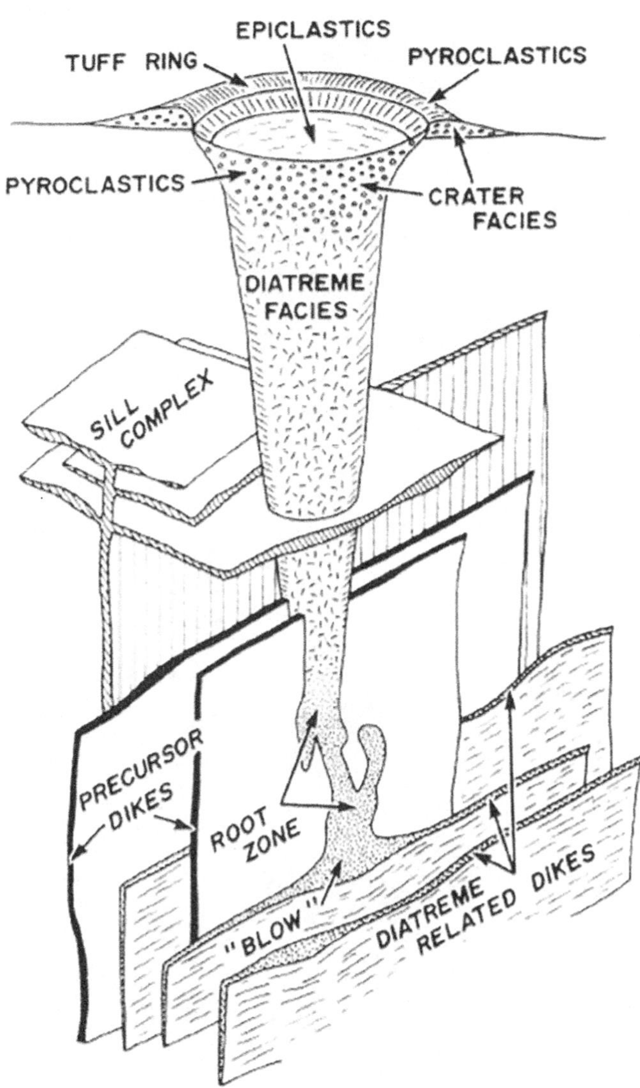

Fig. 12.14 schematic diagram of idealized kimberlite magmatic system, illustrating the relationships between crater, diatreme, and hypabyssal rocks (not to scale); hypabyssal rocks include sills, dikes, root zone and "blowout." See Geologic Glossary: Appendix IV for geologic definitions. (From Orson L. Anderson, Tutorial #1, 1997)

Fig. 12.15 Shiprock (*Tsé bit'a'í*, "Rock with Wings") diatreme "neck" stands some 1,583 ft above the surrounding surface near Four Corners. (G.M. Stevenson photo)

Fig. 12.16 Agathla (Navajo: Aghaałą́, Spanish: *El Capitan*) diatreme "neck" stands 1,436 ft above the surrounding surface near Kayenta, Arizona. (G.M. Stevenson photo)

As mentioned above, these features were initially passed off as volcanic necks or dikes which are the prominent features, or even glacial deposits as described at Garnet Ridge. Then after **uranium** was recognized as a strategic mineral and one of the sources of uranium occurred in volcanic rocks, a renewed interest in these strange intrusions brought a new group of geologists to the area. The one man that really opened the science world to diatremes in the Four Corners region was none other than *Eugene Merle Shoemaker* [11] while working for the U.S. Geological Survey out of Grand Junction, Colorado in the early 1950s (Figure 12.17).

Shoemaker recognized he was looking at atypical volcanic features and went about his field work in describing the various mineralogies, lithologies and various enigmatic characteristics of these explosive features. By his count there are 250 diatremes in the NVF where these diatremes are partly filled with house-sized blocks and sub-angular to rounded boulder fragments with small raisin-sized inclusions in the wall rock, all of which are called xenoliths and part of the earth's crust. The xenoliths range from Proterozoic Precambrian age (ca.1.6 to 1.8 Ga) crystalline rocks of the crustal "basement" to shales and sandstones of Late Cretaceous or younger age (ca. < 80 Ma) (see Geologic Time scale in Appendix III). The vents in the northernmost points on the Navajo Reservation have been so deeply eroded that they show most clearly the initial stages of opening of the diatremes – the *maars*! [12]

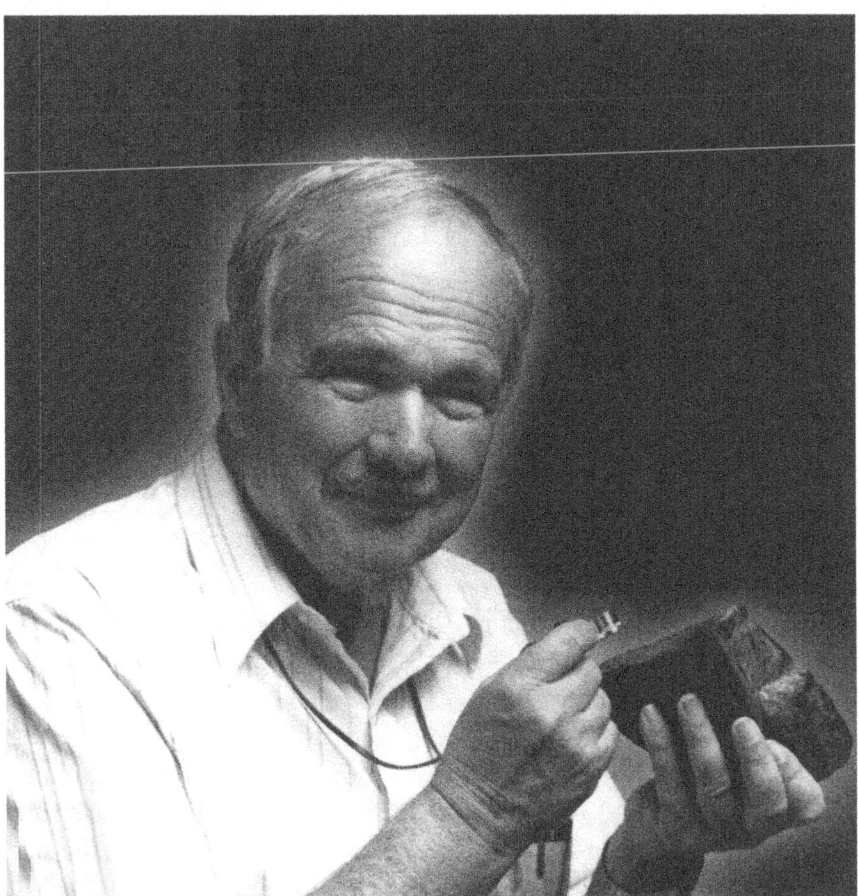

Figure 12.17 Eugene Shoemaker (From GCRG, Boatman's Quarterly, winter 2000, v. 13, no. 1, cover).

The vents included dark-colored igneous rocks consisting chiefly of **biotite** and **orthoclase** (**minettes**), kimberlite (now called **serpentinized ultramafic microbreccia,** or **SUMs**), and a variety of **ultramafic** rocks collectively known as **lamprophyres** that are high in potassium, magnesium, nickel, chromium, and thought to have been derived from the mantle (See Glossary; Appendix IV). And perhaps most importantly, kimberlites found in diatremes in South Africa were known to contain **diamonds**! So why were these diatremes on the Colorado Plateau apparently barren of this precious stone?

THE DIAMOND-GRAPHITE CONUNDRUM

Natural diamonds are only found in kimberlite pipes or drainages away from the pipes. It is also known that diamonds occur under conditions of high temperature and pressure from deep in the earth. But diamond is not the only form of carbon that occurs naturally; **graphite**, the amorphous form of carbon, is plentiful on earth and it is also stable at high temperatures and pressures within the earth. It turns out that there is a stability field for each and they are separated by a thermodynamically-determined phase boundary in pressure-temperature space and has been verified by many measurements since 1955.[13] Diamonds are thermodynamically unstable, even though diamond is the hardest known natural substance. So how can it be that diamonds are brought to the surface from over 125 miles deep in the earth without burning up or altering to graphite as they pass through this phase boundary? Experiments show that the effect of pressure on the rate of graphitization is not very large. Thus, if diamonds are to survive in kimberlite moving up through the earth's surface, they must arrive at a relatively cool temperature and their rate of movement through the diamond metastable region from 90 to 60 miles can't be too rapid [longer than a few months], and if volatiles are included, then the rate of movement would need to be even shorter.

Various models have been proposed but it appears that the origin and eruption of kimberlite magmas, a **diapir** holding partially melted magma rises to about 45 mile depth where the magma crystallizes, and that CO_2-rich gases evolve which initiates crack propagation through the overlying lithosphere. The crack, by necessity would have to move very fast or else the diamond would alter to graphite.

But the kimberlites in the northern NVF expose xenoliths from the upper mantle devoid of diamonds, and there is no magma. Therefore, either the path of the xenolith from its source to surface was too slow through the diamond-graphite boundary to not survive graphitization, or the volatiles released from the magma hastened the rate of graphitization sufficiently that diamonds are vaporized by the time of emplacement of the diatreme. Regardless, there are no diamonds in the NVF; at best, they contained graphite, which has been easily weathered and eroded.

PROJECT MOHOLE

Diatremes had gained importance by 1966 when Congress scrapped funding of the ultra-deep drilling program called "Project Mohole." Project Mohole was an ambitious attempt to drill through the earth's crust into the Mohorovičić (Moh-ho-ro-vee-chich) discontinuity, or more commonly referred to as the Moho boundary between the earth's crust and mantle (Figure 12.18).[14] The Mohorovičić discontinuity was first identified in 1909 by Andrija Mohorovičić, a Croatian seismologist, when he observed the abrupt velocity increase of earthquake P-waves at the boundary. During the cold war, while the Space Race pitted the Soviet Union against the United States to conquer the skies, the two countries were also vying to drill as deep as possible into the earth. The USSR embarked on drilling a hole in 1970 on the Kola Peninsula located east of Finland. The USSR's efforts at the *Kola Institute* as it was called, finally reached a drilling depth of 40,230 ft (12,262 m or 7.62 miles) over a nineteen-year time span before that program was abandoned. It never reached the mantle. Bottomhole temperatures reached 180^0 C (356^0 F) and steel drill pipe could not withstand any higher temperatures without all types of metal fatigue.[15]

Several interesting observations were finally shared with the USA after the collapse of the Soviet Union circa 1990. It had been assumed that the earth's crust increased in density with depth. The hole instead revealed highly-fractured rock that was saturated with water. Until then it was assumed that water could not be found underneath the impermeable layers of rock at these depths. Researchers believe that the extreme temperatures and pressures at this depth caused atoms of oxygen and hydrogen to decouple from surrounding minerals and form into free water. Apparently, it is possible to squeeze water from a stone. Another important finding from the project was the discovery of twenty-four species of microscopic single-cell plankton fossils. The fossils, which are normally encased in limestone or silica, were instead found in organic compounds. Even more surprising was how, despite the extreme temperatures and pressure, the micro-fossils had remained intact for 2.7 billion years.[16] The diameter of Earth is 3,963 miles (6,378 km to the center of the earth), so a little over seven and a half miles drilling depth had barely scratched the surface! [17]

However, in the late 1960s, these natural volcanic necks that contained sections of the earth's crust, and possibly the upper mantle, were estimated to come from as deep as thirty miles or more beneath the Colorado Plateau and were viewed in a new light. The measurements of the physical properties of these xenoliths were to help improve our understanding of the composition of the thick mantle that underlies all the earth's crustal layers; both oceanic and continental crusts (Figure 12.18).

THE MULE EAR DIATREME

In the 1950s there were still questions regarding the temperatures, pressures and just how this type of eruption could occur in the middle of what was considered at the time to be a stable massively uplifted plateau. As Shoemaker proceeded with his field descriptions another scientist began looking at this problem from a mechanistic point of view. *Orson L. Anderson* [18] (Figure 12.19), a mathematician, a pure physicist turned geophysicist at *Lamont-Doherty Laboratory* at Columbia University was approaching the diatreme emplacement from a bottoms-up viewpoint. Why did they blow where they blew? At what rate? How deep was deep? What provided the fuel since there was basically little to no magma associated with many of the diatremes?

Gene Shoemaker had approached the problem of trying to understand diatremes from a mineralogical standpoint while Orson Anderson was more interested in the raw physics of just what allowed these turbulent explosions to occur where they did and to what role plate tectonics played. As Orson worked on these new concepts at Lamont-Doherty, he was gradually drawn toward trying to understand the rate at which these strange mantle-sourced diatremes were emplaced, and his curiosity brought him face to face with Shoemaker. As Orson Anderson and Gene Shoemaker were trying to develop an explanation of what they were looking at, these two scientists met Kenny Ross where the three developed strong friendships that lasted for the rest of their lives.

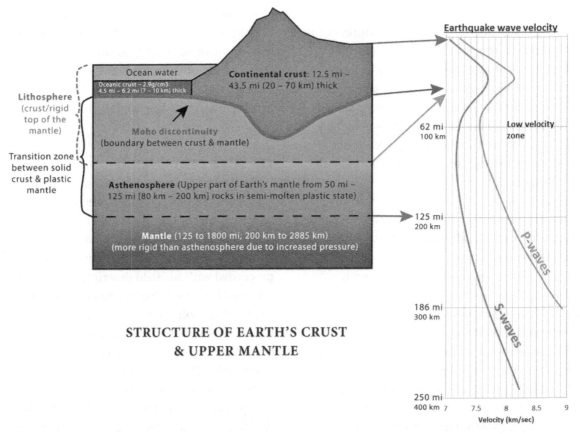

Figure 12.18 Diagram of the structure of Earth's crust and upper mantle; note the "Moho" discontinuity (or zone) that separates the crust from the underlying lithosphere and is defined by a velocity contrast in seismic P and S waves as measured by seismographs. (Modified from Rob Gamesby @ coolgeography.co.uk)

Figure 12.19 Orson L. Anderson (Internet photo from 1960s).

PRELIMINARY SURVEYS IN SOUTHEASTERN UTAH, 1966

The first time Orson Anderson saw the diatremes was when he was introduced to them by Gene Shoemaker during a river boat trip with Kenny Ross in March, 1966. A more thorough field trip took place with more personnel from October 31 to November 4, 1966. The scientific expedition field party was granted permission to explore and sample the diatremes by the Bureau of Indian Affairs from Window Rock, Arizona. The group from Lamont Geological Observatory at Columbia University, New York consisted of the following personnel: Naohiro Soga, Edward Schreiber, Robert Liebermann, Tosimatu Matumoto, Peter Molnar and Orson Anderson. They were accompanied by Eugene and Carolyn Shoemaker, Maurice Brock, Robert Sutton, Harold Krivoy, Martin Lane and Jack Murphy from the USGS Astrogeology Branch in Flagstaff, Arizona. The two boatmen from Bluff were Kenneth Ross, and Gene Foushee.[19]

The week's field work was documented in a report by Robert Liebermann.[20] The whole group arrived at the Mule Ear diatreme each day by boat or by jeeps driven down Comb Wash and then hiked down to the entrance to the canyon at which point those that jeeped and hiked were ferried across the river to the south side. Reconnaissance mapping and sampling the diatreme ensued and was repeated for two days. Then part of the group traveled to Bluff Bench and described the Brushy Basin section of the Morrison Formation up to the mesa caprock- the Cretaceous Dakota Sandstone (see Geologic Stratigraphic Column; Appendix II). Another group went to Garnet Ridge and did reconnaissance work and sampling, while the other group finished up their work at the Mule Ear diatreme. On the last day, November 4, "the entire group traveled to Garnet Ridge and met up with Hank Dee of KSL-TV from Salt Lake City to film a newsreel of the field work for the Air Force and local news media." [21]

Liebermann summarized the transportation methods and said the boat trip took only forty-five minutes while the jeep trip down Comb Wash was incredibly dusty and still required the one and a half-mile hike to the crossing point where they were ferried across the river which was far less feasible than just arriving by boat. He mentioned a third means of accessing the Mule Ear diatreme had been undertaken by Gene Foushee where they came in from the south by jeep and on foot, near Moses Rock, and followed Chinle Wash but it took the better part of two days "with considerable road-building to make the trip." [22] He also mentioned that accommodations were available in Bluff at Foushee's "Recapture Court Motel" at a cost of $4.50 per night for a double bed and that food was available at the "Kiva Café and was excellent all around and that the "Turquoise Café is only recommended on Saturday night for the Mexican special." [23]

Following the 1966 field trips to Garnet Ridge, Moses Rock and the Mule Ear diatreme, Kenny Ross was contracted in early 1967 by Orson Anderson at Lamont-Doherty Geological Labs and appointed "Consultant in Geology in the Four Corners Area" for Lamont Geological Observatory of Columbia University, New York, which was involved in a NASA – Apollo Program in geophysical research.[24] His specific duties were "to collect ultramafic rock specimens from the Earth's upper mantle" [25] on the diatremes of southeast Utah and northeastern Arizona for laboratory analysis, preliminary to the study of moon rocks that were expected to be recovered in the first moon walk planned for 1969. So over the next several years, Kenny was hired to collect rocks from the Mule Ear diatreme, which meant that Don and Doug, along with Kenny worked as *human mules* as they spent many a day roaming over the diatreme gathering the special rocks their eyes had been trained to find: eclogite,

enstatite, **peridotite**, **dunite**, kimberlite and any rocks with xenoliths that caught their eye and then the collection was shipped to Orson's lab [26] (see Glossary: Appendix IV for descriptions of rocks and minerals).

At the encouragement of Gene Shoemaker, Tom McGetchin, a Ph.D. candidate from California Institute of Technology (Caltech) began his field work in 1964 on the compositional relations in minerals from kimberlite and related rocks at the Moses Rock dike and had financial support for his research provided by: a Penrose Grant from the Geological Society of America, the AEC, the USGS Astrogeology Branch in Flagstaff, Arizona, and NASA. He completed his dissertation in 1968 and published his initial findings in 1970 with co-author, Leon Silver at Caltech, who was his principal advisor during his graduate work.[27] McGetchin was by then an associate professor in the geology department (now called the "Department of Earth and Planetary Sciences") at the Massachusetts Institute of Technology, Cambridge, Massachusetts.

Their refined observations[28] of the occurrence of kimberlite in the Moses Rock dike indicated 1) the mineral grains in kimberlite are unlike associated dense rock fragments, 2) kimberlite was emplaced as discrete angular mineral clasts, *not* a silicate melt, 3) electron microprobe of the compositions of certain minerals in the xenoliths suggested derivation over a depth range in the upper mantle of about 125 miles, or much deeper than the 30 miles conjectured in the 1960s), 4) the kimberlite was derived by *physical disaggregation* of mantle minerals, 5) emplacement by a fluidized system consisting of gas and possibly a low density fluid phase consisting mainly of water and particulate solids was postulated, and 6) dense rock fragments are unrelated to kimberlite and are chunks (xenoliths) of the vent wall from the crust and/or upper mantle. He also calculated the accelerated exit velocities that were required to accommodate the explosive intrusions to exceed the speed of sound for Moses Rock and by at least two-fold if not greater for the Mule Ear diatreme as both of which had penetrated rock with variable densities (Fig. 12.20).

WHAT WE KNOW ABOUT DIATREMES IN THE 21ST CENTURY

Much work has been conducted on the Navajo Volcanic Field (NVF) over the past half century since that initial field trip in 1966 with Shoemaker and Anderson. Unfortunately, Gene and Carolyn were involved in a bizarre automobile crash near Alice Springs, Australia in 1997, killing Gene immediately and seriously injuring Carolyn. Orson Anderson contacted Carolyn soon after he learned of Gene's untimely death and wanted to do something in his honor. She said that Gene would want his friends to continue the work he left unfinished, and not take time to grieve. Thus, on short notice Orson organized a "Memorial Kimberlite Excursion" to visit the Mule Ear diatreme in September, 1997. Orson was joined by Priscilla Grew and five other geoscientists for a five-day river trip and I was the trip leader. Priscilla had been one of Orson's graduate students at Columbia and had last visited the Mule Ear in 1970. She had authored and co-authored a number of papers with Orson on this subject and was excellent in conveying the importance of these complex mineralogical names to me. As we passed below the bridge near Sand Island, Orson and two others on my boat were talking in quadratic equations, and the rest of the trip I referred to them all as "mega-thinkers." The other boatman was Doug Ross and a new crew member, Anne Egger, joined in her kayak as a helper. Anne had recently come to Bluff after she received her Bachelor's degree in geology at Yale University and saw this trip as a great opportunity to learn more about diatremes from the "mega-thinkers."

Orson said that our way of honoring Gene was to try to discover the "geophysical mechanism of kimberlite emplacement by satisfying the laws of physics" [29] (e.g., conservation of momentum, mass, and energy). He noted that by then, in 1997, a lot of petrological mechanisms had been proposed to explain the emplacement of igneous pipes (Figure 12.21). Most of the petrological models of kimberlite emplacement have relied on a method of transport called *fluidization* and Orson used the analogy where he compared the toe of a rock avalanche in which there is a tremendous variation in size of the rocks, but the stream of rocks are transported more or less uniformly and very rapidly, as if the rock slide was fluidized. In these fluidization models for diatremes, a stream of compressed gas-rock mixture passes to the surface. This gas-rock mixture increases its pressure during the ascent, because the confining lithospheric pressure becomes smaller. This volatile-rich magma that ascends from the upper mantle along fractures is channeled into potential or pre-existing fractures in the upper crust. As the mix rises, the lithospheric pressure drops, thereby increasing the internal pressure of the magma and accelerating the flow to high speeds.[30]

MOSES ROCK			MULE EAR	
Diameter of pipe	Velocity	DEPTH BELOW SURFACE	Diameter of pipe	Velocity
16 m (52.5 ft)	415 m/s (928 mph)	50 m (164 ft)	282 m (925 ft)	750 m/s (1678 mph)
7 m (23 ft)	182 m/s (407 mph)	400 m (1312 ft)	91 m (299 ft)	464 m/s (1038 mph)
6 m (20 ft)	110 m/s (246 mph)	1 km (0.6 mi)	63 m (207 ft)	318 m/s (711 mph)
3 m (10 ft)	29 m/s (65 mph)	10 km (6.2 mi)	34 m (112 ft)	92 m/s (206 mph)
<3 m (9 ft)	18 m/s (40 mph)	50 km (31 mi)	30 m (99 ft)	58 m/s (130 mph)

KEY

m: meters
km: kilometers
ft: feet
mi: miles
m/s: meters per second
mph: miles per hour

speed of sound:
in air: 343 m/s (768 mph)
in water: 1484 m/s (3,320 mph)
iron: 5120 m/s (11,453 mph)

P wave in Earth travels @ 6-8,000 m/s
(13,422 to 17,895 mph) or
(3.73 to 4.97 miles per second)

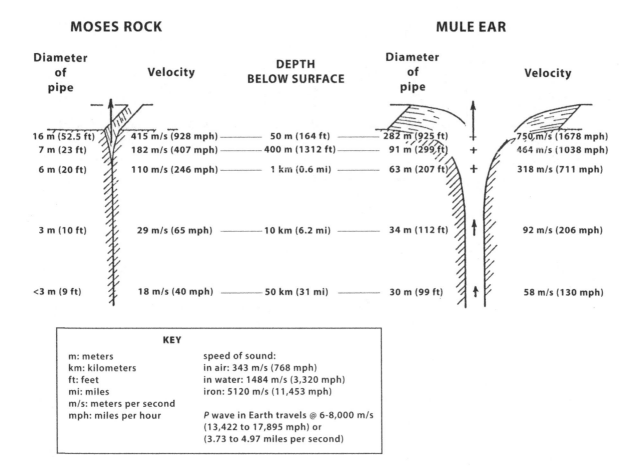

Fig. 12.20 Schematic diagrams illustrating calculated velocities and pipe width for Moses Rock dike and Mule Ear kimberlite eruptions as they tore through the upper crust; note increase in diameter of pipe and incredible eruptive velocities indicate that these events would occur virtually instantaneously as a "blow-out" – even in human measurement of time. (Re-drawn by GMS/TB from T. McGetchin, 1970 thesis *in* O.L. Anderson Tutorial #5, 1997)

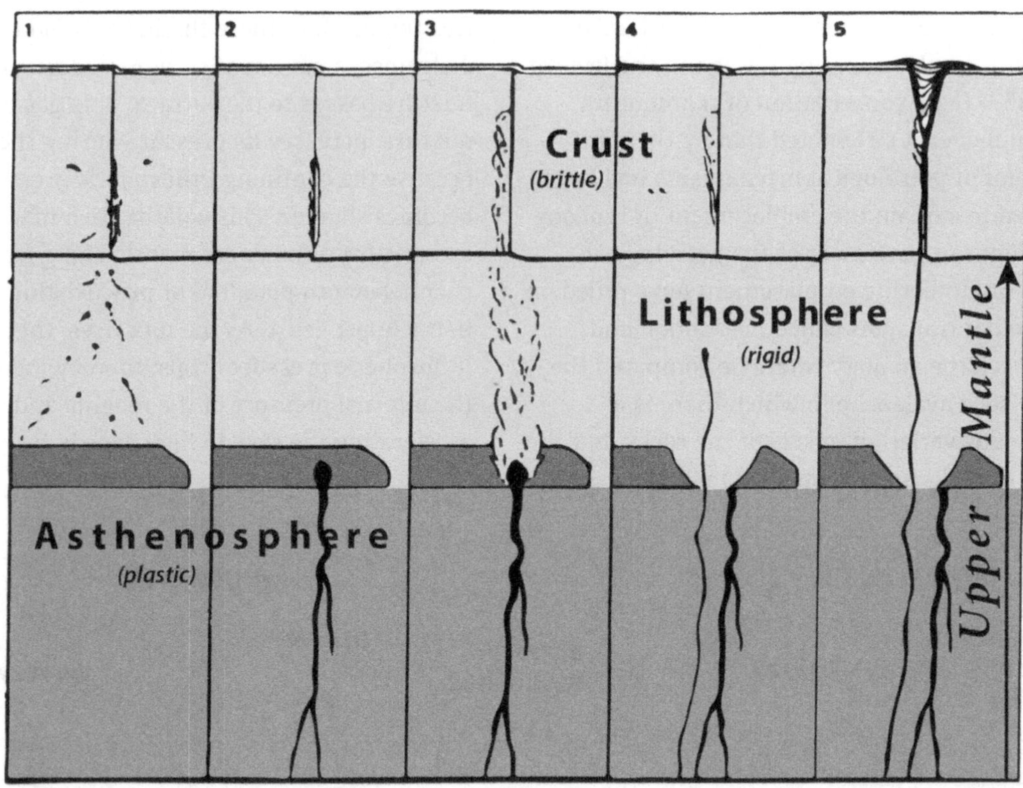

Figure 12.21 Schematic diagram of the *hydrovolcanism model* showing sequentially from L to R (1-5) how a crack might form in the upper mantle and propagate and provide the proper gas-fluid conditions for diatreme eruption; not to scale. (Modified by GMS/TB from J.R. Broadhurst, 1986, p.344)

This mode of emplacement was assumed in the McGetchin model at Moses Rock dike, but there was also the *hydrovolcanism model*. In this model, a crustal crack provided the space for surface water to migrate relatively deeply (or occur by "squeezing the molecular water out of the deeply buried lithosphere" as witnessed in the deep Russian well), where it meets upwelling magma with a subsequent large steam explosion. This explosion would drastically widen and deepen the original crack, which would allow a large quantity of deep-seated magma to rise, gain speed as it neared the surface, and thus form the pipe and fill the diatreme (Figures 12.12, 12.20 & 12.21). Regardless which model is invoked, (*fluidization* or *hydrovolcanism*) a great deal of deep-seated energy would be required to move such mass so far and so fast. Orson concluded from McGetchin's paper in 1970 that the likely candidate for the energy source was CO_2 from deep in the mantle. He was correct in his early observations and this process is now known as **metasomatism**.[31]

Orson Anderson recalled from his field trip in 1966 with Gene Shoemaker that Shoemaker stressed that the large boulders had been rounded by a ball mill action within the diatreme pipe. He conjectured that in order for the ball mill to take place, there had to be turbulence in the gas and solids when the pipe breached the lithosphere, and this turbulence caused the rocks to ricochet off each other and off the wall surface, chipping off smaller fragments. The colliding rock fragments kept changing direction, so that a fragment would leave the opening of the diatreme only after many collisions. In order to get the turbulent flow, the rock fragments would have to be traveling at very high velocity, requiring a large pressure gradient and a large source of vapor or steam. The process would proceed so that a pressure drop would accompany a large temperature drop and the rock fragments would exit at cold temperatures.[32]

Regardless of modes of emplacement, researchers suggested that a conduit, or crack, to the surface had to be established first (see Figure 12.21) and this basic assumption provided a dilemma to Orson and Priscilla Grew, who had earlier addressed this *theory of crack propagation*.[33] They addressed this fundamental problem of how a crack could remain open when under extreme pressure without magma in it that would keep it open. They concluded that a symbiotic relationship had to exist between the crack, magma in the fluid state, and CO_2 in the gas state and that these mechanisms could not be treated separately. They suggested that the interplay of these three states was necessary to explain the explosive ejection of cold rock to the surface. In other words, fracture mechanics and petrology of these deep-seated rocks needed to be addressed.

Orson had spent years at Bell Labs studying "stress corrosion crack propagation" [34] calculating crack velocities in a variety of mediums. In a paper he wrote in 1979, he discussed the requirements of a large crack moving upward from the base of the lithosphere and filled with magma.[35] He postulated that the dynamics of the crack would have to be controlled by the stress field in the lithospheric plate wherein a crack would nucleate under the following conditions: 1) a sufficient accumulation of a fluid at the base of the lithospheric plate; 2) the density of the fluid would be less than that of the plate, and 3) a tensile stress must exist parallel to the surface.[36] In order for the crack front to move upwards, a fluid must be in the tip of the crack. The crack can't move faster than the fluid or else the crack will slow or stop. Also, the crack cannot grow faster than the fluid can flow in the crack's channel, and the fluid flow would be limited by its viscosity and supply.[37] Furthermore, the supply of the fluid was tied to its volatility. A volatile phase in low viscosity fluids may allow the crack to accelerate to high speeds, even to the terminal crack velocity. However, a highly viscous magma would limit the speed of the crack to one meter per second or slower, depending on the properties of the magma and width of the crack.[38]

GEOBAROMETRY

The determination of points of equal temperature by finding the equilibrium conditions of rocks in a particular mineral suite is called geothermometry or geobarometry. In examining the xenoliths, petrologists presumed that the details of composition of a xenolith transported from a certain depth in the earth were characteristic of that depth. Experimental petrology has shown that some compositions are sensitive to temperature (T) while others are more sensitive to pressure (P). By combining these two measurements, a P-T point is derived where both temperature and pressure at depth can be deduced. Through this methodology petrologists agree that ultramafic rocks are thrown up from the upper mantle. Key minerals and rocks representative of the deepest ultramafic rocks in the Mule Ear diatreme are: pyroxene, enstatite, olivine, pyrope garnet, eclogite, peridotite and diopside.[39] (See Glossary, Appendix IV for rock & mineral names)

AGE OF DIATREMES AND KIMBERLITE

A study was conducted by A. Janse in 1984 regarding the world-wide distribution and age of kimberlite pipes and he concluded there was no evidence of periodicity or correlation with major tectonic events.[40] They range in age from Archean (2.0 Ga) to Pleistocene (1.0 Ma) and they are world-wide, and mainly in rigid, thick cratons, where the basement is formed by weakly to moderately deformed rocks of low to medium metamorphic grade. The rigidity is assumed to be necessary to sustain the deep reaching fractures that reach from the surface to the base of the lithosphere. For Colorado Plateau kimberlites, the crust is not as thick as the Canadian Shield and is bordered by the Basin and Range Province which has a very thin crust.[41]

PLATE TECTONICS AND DIATREMES IN THE NVF

For years the Colorado Plateau was considered an anomalous region of uplift in the North American Plate which had been pierced by "kimberlite pipes" containing lawsonite-bearing eclogites. *Lawsonite is an uncommon constituent of eclogite.* **Lawsonite** is known to form in high pressure, low temperature conditions, most commonly found in subduction zones where cold oceanic crust has been subducted down oceanic trenches into the mantle.[42] Eclogites are helpful in elucidating patterns and processes of plate tectonics because many represent oceanic crust that has been subducted to depths greater than 20 miles and then returned to the surface. The initially low temperature of the subducted slab and fluids taken down with it managed to depress isotherms and keep the slab much colder than the surrounding mantle, allowing for these unusual high pressures, low temperature conditions. At the present time the Colorado Plateau is a region of east-west compressional stress between two regions of extension, the Rio Grande rift and the Basin and Range Province. In the 1970s it was thought to be underlain by a convective flow in the asthenosphere and/or a number of mantle plumes. Furthermore, the regional geology was difficult to reconcile with fluid dynamic models of laminar flow in the mantle.[43]

In their 1975 paper, Orson Anderson and Priscilla Grew (Perkins) [44] were aware of newly postulated theories of plate tectonics[45] that suggested the subduction of a sub-plate of the east Pacific oceanic crust beneath the North American continental plate such that a downward moving slab might cause stress variations along the lithospheric boundaries, creating regions of reverse flow and turbulence forming "eddies" near the lithosphere-asthenosphere boundary (Figure 12.22).[46] The postulated eddies of thermal instabilities were on a small scale and not stable in time or space and they proposed the term "*unsteady eddies*" [47] suggesting that their path and intensity would be hard to predict. They concluded that the subducted plate would create changing thermal and pressure gradients in the asthenosphere beneath the southwestern United States and this disruption of laminar flow would form unsteady eddies.[48]

As more work was done by Bill Dickinson[49] among others, by the 1990s the subducted oceanic plate gained the name of the "Farallon Plate" (Figure 12.23) as it exhibited variations in the angle of subduction.[50] The term "shallow-slab subduction" also came into vogue in explaining the plate subducting at shallower angles between 80 Ma to 30 Ma (Paleogene Period). Based on the recognition of offshore magnetic anomaly patterns a convincing argument was presented that stated several hundred miles of oceanic crust were subducted beneath the western continental margin since the Late Cretaceous and could be related to early to mid-Paleogene intraplate magmatism. Among the findings was the recognition of approximately 30 Ma (Oligocene Epoch) low-temperature eclogite xenoliths derived from ultramafic microbreccia diatremes in the NVF on the Colorado Plateau were tied to products of subduction zone metamorphism[51] (see Geologic Time scale, Appendix III).

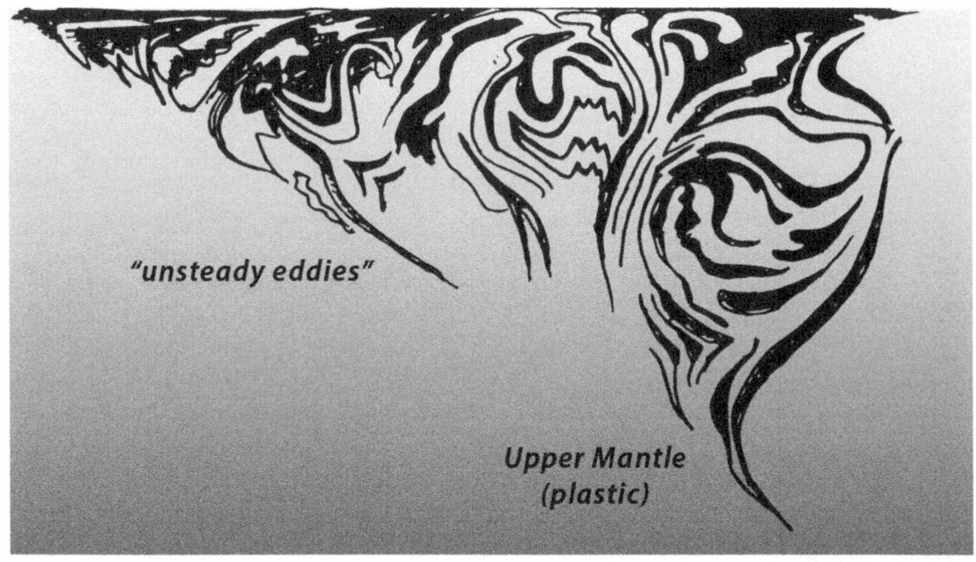

Figure 12.22 Schematic diagram of envisioned *"unsteady eddies"* in the upper mantle/asthenosphere. (Modified from Anderson and Grew, 1975)

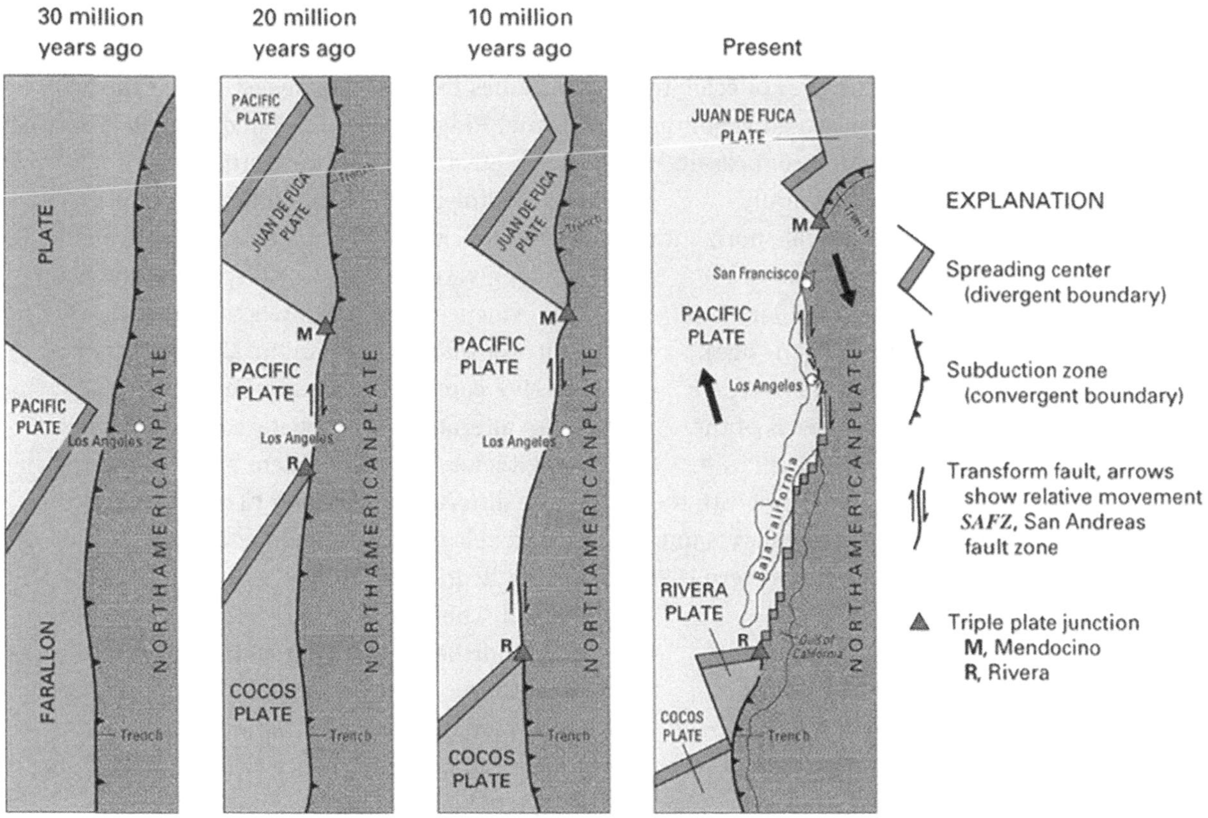

Figure 12.23 Map showing sequential convergence and subduction of the Farallon and Pacific oceanic plates beneath the western North American continental plate. (USGS internet illustration)

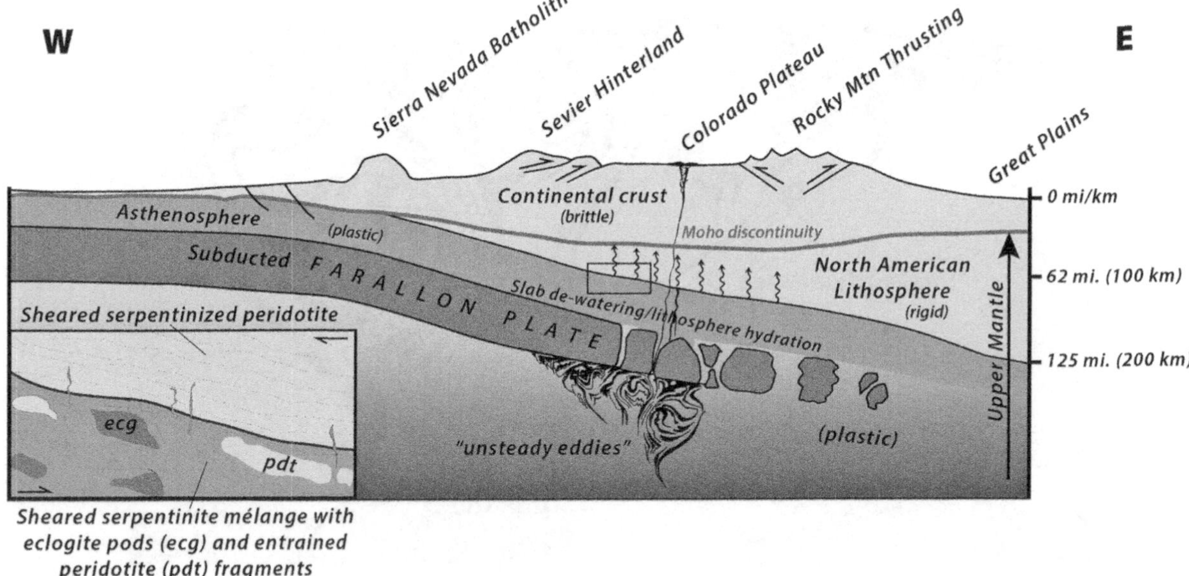

Figure 12.24 Diagrammatic cross-section of the postulated flat-slab subduction of the Farallon oceanic plate; not to scale. See Figure 12.21 hydrovolcanism model for details regarding slab de-watering and crack propagation. (Modified by GMS/TB after concepts forwarded by Behr & Smith, 2013; Dickinson & Snyder, 1978 and many others)

But the metamorphic assemblages of eclogites are incompatible with those associated xenoliths of Precambrian age high temperature rocks and it was reasoned that they were structurally juxtaposed at depth during large scale horizontal translations involving the entire crust of the Colorado Plateau. Based on their similarity to Franciscan eclogites (also of Paleogene age), plate tectonic theory and isotopic researchers interpreted the xenoliths as fragments of the Farallon plate and proof that the oceanic lithosphere had been "underplated" beneath the Colorado Plateau from as far as 930 miles (1500 km) from the plate boundary in the western U.S. (Figure 12.24).[52]

By the late 1990s researchers from New Mexico had examined the Tertiary-aged diatremes of the NVF and concluded that a wide variety of Proterozoic xenoliths had been brought to the surface. In their reconstructions of pressure-temperature histories they found that diatremes from the northwest part of the NVF (Garnet Ridge, Moses Rock and Mule Ear) carried the greatest variety of xenoliths, including metasedimentary rocks, high temperature meta-igneous rocks, "and crustally derived eclogites; showing variable degrees of hydrous alteration and evidence of complex reaction histories." [53] In contrast, diatremes from the southeast part of the NVF contained primarily **mafic** rocks showing fewer alterations and "metasedimentary and eclogitic xenoliths are absent altogether." [54] These differences led them to conclude that Proterozoic tectonism had juxtaposed two distinctly different blocks beneath the Colorado Plateau. Their work confirmed work by others that a northeast-trending boundary existed beneath the Four Corners area separating the older Yavapai Province (1.72 – 1.8 Ga) from the younger Mazatzal Province (<1.7 Ga) [55] (Figure 12.25). In addition to the abundance of metasedimentary xenoliths in the northern province they also noted; evidence for counterclockwise *P-T* paths in the northwest vs clockwise paths to the southeast [Orson & Priscilla's "unsteady eddies"]; extensive retrogression *P-T* reaction values of samples from the northwest versus a complete absence of similar reactions in samples from the southeast [the inverted metamorphic gradient of Helmstaedt and Doig (1975)] and the presence of eclogite xenoliths derived from Proterozoic oceanic crust in the northwest and their complete absence in the southeast [eclogites may be much younger and derived from the subducted Farallon plate, and/or mixed with Proterozoic wallrock].

By 2002, a consortium of geologist and geophysicists called the CD-ROM Working Group (Continental Dynamics of the Rocky Mountains) led by Karl Karlstrom from the University of New Mexico provided very convincing evidence through an integration of seismic reflection, seismic refraction, teleseismic, and geological data into the nature and evolution of the lithosphere of the western United States.[56] This combined process of imagery is called **tomography** and it now shows the upper mantle down to depths greater than 125 miles that contain several dipping velocity anomalies that project up to overlying Proterozoic boundaries. Throughout much of the southern Rocky Mountains (including the Colorado Plateau) seismic refraction data have delineated a 6-10 mile thick mafic lower crustal layer. The base of this layer (the Moho boundary) varies from 25 to 35 miles in depth. Continued efforts by the CD-ROM group as well as others, such as Hawkesworth, et al, 2016, concluded that, by a combination of processes, including plate subduction and underplating that the Farallon plate argument was real and that inverted metamorphism was real and that eclogites found in the NVF very probably were, in part, derived from this subducted oceanic slab.[57]

SUMMARY

Kenny Ross would have blown a cork had he known what a major contribution he was witnessing before his own eyes as he and his two sons hiked up and down that damn diatreme as "human mules" hauling backpacks full of exotic rocks they didn't really understand. Rocks that would reveal to the geologic and geophysical world why, at least in part, the Colorado Plateau sat "anomalously" higher than the surrounding geologic provinces. He would have marveled at just how significant the Mule Ear diatreme had become and those hard to find eclogites would be the key to unraveling the mystery. Perhaps the most mysterious and almost laughable reality he would have realized, and for those that followed, was that when one of those small chunks of eclogite was picked up when hiking the Mule Ear diatreme, he would be handling a bit of a subducted terrain that came from over 900 miles west of there. Bits and specks of offshore California lay scattered under his feet in southeastern Utah. Now that was truly mind-boggling!

And all these fundamental concepts and hands-on "data" would be largely deciphered and correlated by his friends, both old and new, who would carry the torch of a new concept, a new paradigm, to the rest of the geological sciences, led by his faithful and oldest amigo – "Big Bill."

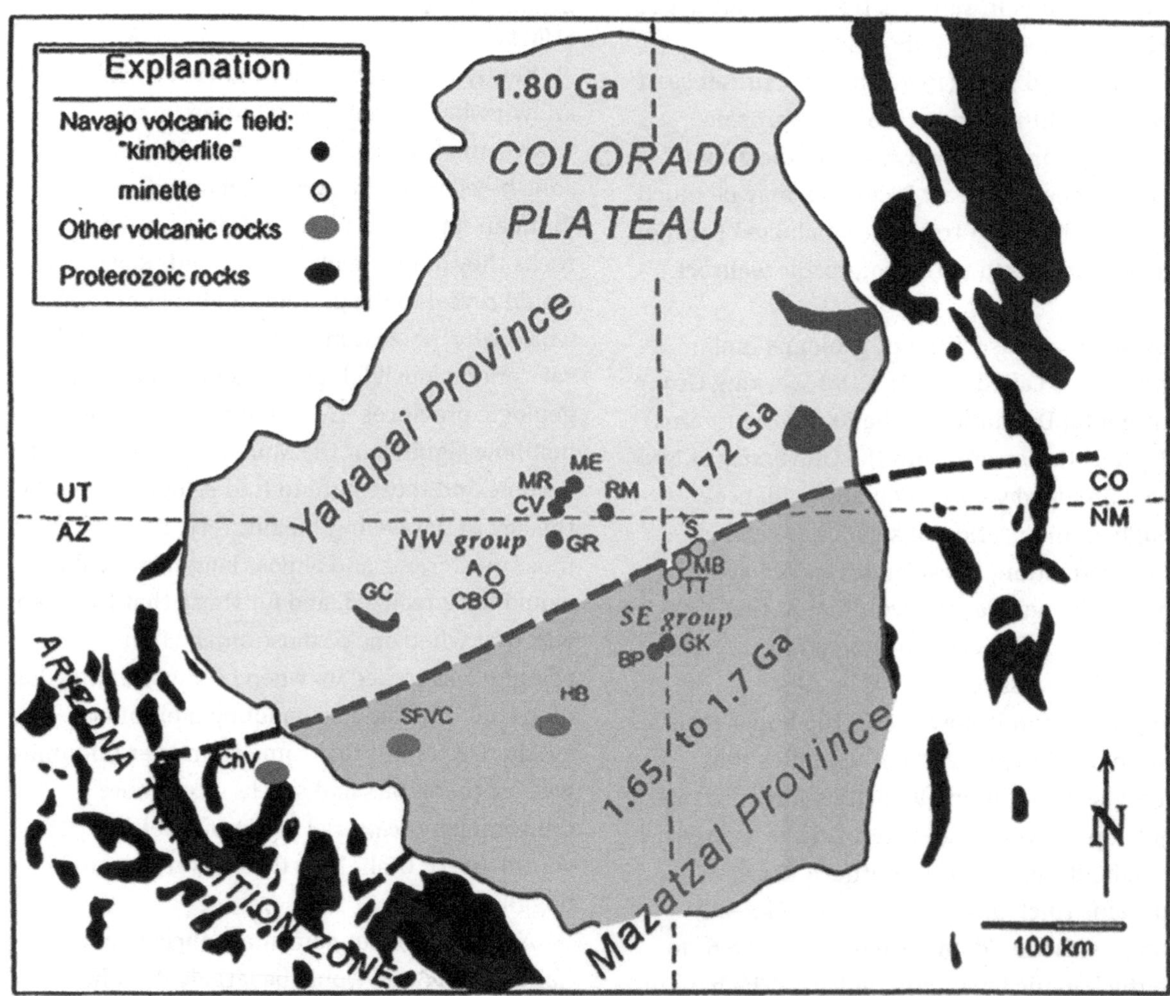

Figure 12.25 Map of the Colorado Plateau showing surrounding exposed Proterozoic rocks; locations of key diatremes within the NVF; and other Tertiary volcanic centers. Diatremes: ME – Mule Ear, MR – Moses Rock, CV – Cane Valley, RM – Red Mesa, GR – Garnet Ridge, GK – Green Knobs, BP – Buell Parks. Minettes: A – Agathla, CB – Chaistla Butte, S – Shiprock, MB – Mitten Rock, TT – the Thumb. Other volcanic centers: SFVC – San Francisco volcanic field, HB – Hopi Buttes, ChV – Chino Valley. Dashed diagonal line defines *best fit* suture boundary between older Yavapai (1.72-1.8 Ga) and younger Mazatzal (1.65-1.7 Ga) crustal provinces. (Modified by GMS/TB from Selverstone, etal, 1999; Condie, 1992; Karlstrom & Bowring, 1988, and Bennett & DePaolo, 1987)

ooooo

13

WILD RIVERS EXPEDITIONS: 1967 to 1976

MAID-O-NEOPRENE

Due to the increased boating activity, both recreationally and in his scientific work, in 1967, Kenny bought a 24 ft inflatable neoprene military pontoon boat, originally classed as "seaplane tender." Ship Tenders were used to shuttle men and/or supplies/gear from ships to shore and were usually hard-hulled boats, but right or wrong Kenny called it a "tender." In keeping with the tradition of naming his boats, Kenny soon named it the "Maid-O-Neoprene" and it was equipped with a drop-in plywood floor and a motor-well. It was used on Cataract Canyon trips chiefly as an equipment carrier, or "Mother Boat." [1] It had twenty-seven-inch tubes and the beam was eight feet. Its first trip was on the San Juan River (Figures 13.1 & 13.2).

In August, 1967, Kenny called Don and said he had a "big Cat trip" and needed his help; Don took time off from bartending at the Diamond Belle Saloon in Durango and went straight to the Bluff boat camp and found Kenny "under the weather." Doug was already at the boat camp rigging for the trip. A local man, Ace Grounds, along with another Bluff resident, Lee Hyde had been working on welding a boat trailer and a steel frame for the Maid-o-Neoprene. Don helped Doug finish getting the boats, gear, food etc together and along with Kenny headed to Moab and out to the Potash landing hauling the Maid and two 10-man LCRs.

The "big Cat trip" actually included five adult married couples, two teenage boys from Pagosa Springs and Gordy Havoner from Salt Lake City. Gordy was a KSL-TV cameraman who Kenny had met in 1966 when Cottonwood Wash flashed and the bridge in Bluff was badly damaged; in fact, it had to be replaced – again. They apparently struck up a friendship witnessing the flash flood and documenting the destruction of the bridge. Gordy had wrangled his way with the TV station into staying in the Four Corners and in 1967 convinced Kenny to include him on the Cataract Canyon trip. He also convinced Kenny that his friend, Bob Goodwin, was a competent boatman who would like to row boats for Kenny. Since Kenny was always on the lookout for qualified rivermen he concurred and Gordy contacted Bob. The plan was to pick up Bob in Moab on the way to the put in at Potash. The ten adults were all mutual friends from out-of-state and were also in Moab. They arranged to fly back to Moab by charter flights from Hite when the river trip was over. The two boys from Pagosa Springs had been dropped off in Bluff, and would ride back to Durango in a Wild Rivers rig when the river trip ended.

Once the Bluff entourage arrived at Potash and began unloading Kenny learned from a BLM representative that a permit was now required by the NPS, so he had to drive back into Moab to the BLM office and obtain a permit. In the meantime, the five couples of paying passengers that was going on this trip had gathered at the Potash launch point. Neither Don nor Doug had met Bob Goodwin until they introduced themselves when they picked him up in Moab. They had gotten to know Gordy Havoner over the past year and thought he was an "OK" kind of guy, but not cut out to be a boatman. Bob was in his mid-forty's and from Alaska and had mountaineering experience as well as some white water boating experience. The next morning Doug launched the group in the three boats and then headed back to Bluff to run the dailies. He had significant transmission/differential problems on his return, but somehow, he finally got there.[2]

Figure 13.1 the "Maid-o-Neoprene" maiden voyage parked at Upper Eight Foot landing; Kenny (white hat) is standing in stern of boat, 1967. (K. Ross collection)

Figure 13.2 the "Maid" in Eight Foot Rapid, 1967. (K. Ross collection)

Kenny ran the Maid-o-Neoprene with a bigger 6 HP Mercury outboard motor and Don and Bob were in the two 10-man boats on oars. But the eight-foot-long two-by-twelve transom board Kenny had designed was bolted across the stern motor-mounts to which a motor could be attached for the long flat-water run down Meander Canyon to the confluence. The river was up a little but when they got to the confluence the combined flow of the Colorado and Green was cooking through Cataract Canyon at about "70,000 cfs" according to Don Ross.[3]

Figure 13.3 aerial view looking west of the new bridge crossing the Colorado River; this bridge and the one crossing the Dirty Devil Gorge (out of view to right) were opened to traffic on June 3, 1966. The Colorado River (when it was a river) flows from bottom of view and forks to left; the mouth of North Wash lies behind low relief point. The new Hite landing is out of view to the left. Air strip is visible in mid-upper right view. (Photo courtesy: Utah Historical Society)

There is no verification of that high a flow for August 1967 based on gage data. The USGS data for the Colorado River at Cisco for August 1967 began the month at 2200 cfs and peaked at 5800 cfs by mid-month and by the end of the month it was down to 500 cfs. The USGS data for the Green River at Green River, Utah for all of August bounced between 3500 to 5000 cfs. When added together the maximum combined flow might have been ~11,000 cfs during the first half of the month of August! [4] However, both gages are many, many miles above the confluence, so it is entirely possible that flash floods could have pumped up the flow to something close to what Don recalled, and in more likelihood had flashed on the Green River since Don made no mention of high flows until they reached the confluence. Big rains on the San Rafael Swell-Green River Desert could certainly have put a lot of water into the Green River by way of the San Rafael River or any number of side canyon washes. It may not have been 70,000 cfs, but anything over 30,000 cfs would make Cataract rapids big and scary!

Anyway, they started down the rapids and Bob lost it going sideways in #2 and Don helped him get the boat to shore. "We go on down in crazy big water and get to Mile Long; Ooh! We decided to line the boats and while in the process at about #15 or #16 Ken Sleight pulled in with a triple rig with a motor. 'Bull Shit' Sleight said, 'gotta go – if I look at this water mess much longer I'll have to line or quit!' And with that he takes off and runs OK." [5] Kenny, Bob and Don lined their way down to the Big Drops – "shit oh dear!" They decided to run #23, #24 and line #25 but at the top of #26 (Satans Gut) Don said "No way; so we portaged the two 10-mans over the boulders, which is a lot of work." [6] Kenny decided to run the Maid on a right-to-left run and Don tried to film "sorta" using the 16 mm KSL camera that belonged to Gordy Havoner. They camped at the bottom of #26, then went on down to Gypsum and camped there the next day. The last day Bob and Don re-rigged their makeshift motor setup and ran on down river following the Maid-o-Neoprene and finally got to the *new* Hite landing. The original Hite at the mouth of White Canyon was now under water.[7]

Doug had led the shuttle team to the marina and pulled the big trailer for the river boats with the red Ford pickup. Ace and Lee had driven the Jeep station wagon. They arrived early enough at the new Hite Marina to rent a small outboard motor boat so they could kill some time water skiing. During this *free* time, Ace proceeded to consume way too much beer in the hot sun.

Nothing of consequence happened to the river group running down the flooded Narrow Canyon to the take out where they unloaded the passengers with their personal belongings. The crew proceeded to deal with the "Maid" and got her onto the trailer. Then they loaded the two heavy 10-man boats on top of the Maid, partially deflated them and tied everything down. The rest of the gear went in the back of the truck leaving some space in back for eight or nine folks to ride the short distance across the newly completed bridge crossing the Colorado River to the air strip (Figure 13.3).[8] They all loaded up and headed to where the charter planes were due to land. Somewhere during all this loading boats and gear, and shuttling folks to the landing strip Ace got all "bent with Kenny's logistics" and was loudly grumbling about the disorganized way he thought things were going, but he was mainly working off his drunkenness. He suddenly "got pissed and took off on foot." [9]

Finally, after the last plane was loaded and took off for Moab, Lee and Bob got in the red Ford pickup truck that pulled the boat trailer and figured they would find Ace along the road. Meanwhile Doug, Don and Kenny were in the old Jeep station wagon with the boys from Pagosa Springs and Gordy Havoner. By then Kenny and Don were both tired and worn out.

Sure enough, they found Ace walking and tried to get him to go with them but he was obstinate and stayed on foot! So they drove away.

At the top of IZ-bell Hill [Mokee Dugway] they met Ace's wife and Chauncey Hall. After explaining the situation about Ace and his drunken obstinacy those two took off to find him. Gordy bailed out of the crowded station wagon and jumped in the truck with Lee and Bob and they followed the station wagon back to Bluff.[10]

Early the next morning Ace showed up at the boat camp and wanted his pistol he had left in the pickup and decided to take the big trailer out of spite. Kenny said "[expletives deleted] forget him – he'll be back." [11] Don and the Pagosa Springs teenage boys that were on the trip went back to Durango and Don left the kids at the Strater Hotel for Betty Feasal to come and take them home. Don said that after all that he had been through that week he just wanted to go back to the little house on 4th Ave. he lived in and sleep for several days.[12] Ace didn't work at Wild Rivers much longer before he faded away, as did Bob and Gordy.

Figure 13.4 Kenny Ross, 1969 the year I met him. (Steve Lawson photo)

That's about all that is known about Kenny for 1967. Kenny's interest in diatremes continued to grow and in 1968 Doug recalled that he spent much of the summer hauling rocks off the Mule Ear diatreme. Kenny had questions about these strange minerals and the new concept of plate tectonics or "continental drift" as it was also referred. He decided to contact his old friend, Bill Dickinson, who was a Geology Professor at Stanford University for some references to read. Bill replied, "Well now, I didn't know you had become a retreaded geologist, but in that case I snatched a grab-bag of things I've written and fired it on to you. If you like the mantle, you should try the Science (1967) and Journal of Geophysical Research (1968) articles on andesites." [13]

He also mentioned that he was divorced from Peggy in 1967 and his two boys, Ben and Ross were twelve and seven years old respectively and "were close to being prime age to see the San Juan." [14] Bill had become recognized as an early proponent of how plate tectonics and shallow slab subduction of the Farallon plate was the principal compressional force allowing the rise of the Colorado Plateau during the **Laramide orogeny**. The geologic community was hardly in agreement about continental plates moving about on Earth's surface and smacking into and/or overriding each other. The mechanism for the apparent anomalous rise of the Colorado Plateau and the large folded monoclinal features such as the Monument upwarp had been debated both in print as well as at professional geological meetings for decades. Consensus regarding the earth's crustal movements was not accepted by the geological or geophysical scientific world for many years, and is still debated!

As for the 1969 river season I know personally that Kenny was still operating Wild Rivers Expeditions because that's when I made my first trip with him, but I have no idea how the season went (Figure 13.4). Charlie DeLorme said his first contact with Wild Rivers was when he swamped a couple of trips for Kenny in 1969. Charlie also worked for a few weeks at Mesa Verde Company with Ansel's son Roger Hall. It was Charlie's connection with the Hall descendants and the interpretive program at Mesa Verde National Park that really made Kenny think that he might work out as a boatman at Wild Rivers.[15]

SNOUT RIGS

In May, 1970 Kenny and Don drove the 1967 Chevy El Camino to Las Vegas to *Buck's War Surplus* store and on May 4th purchased.... three 22 ft snout tubes, "1 extra good for $85.00 and 2 needs repair for $65.00 each," and some rope, patching material etc for a grand total of $255.00 and paid by *Bank of America Travelers checks.*[16] From this purchase the "Gemini" was built and named in honor of the astronaut trainee's that had been on Wild Rivers trips to see the Mule Ear diatreme. Two other boats, the "Mark I" and "Mark II," were both comprised of twin 24 ft snout tubes with steel frames and plywood floors hung between the tubes. Those two were named after Mark Schwindt, who made the frames and floors for all three boats by 1972.[17] When Kenny bought outboard motors they were 3.5 to 6 HP Evinrude or Johnsons.

ANOTHER DIATREME TRIP

In 1970, two boatmen for Kenny, T.J. Knight from Mexican Hat and Bruce Steinhaus from Los Alamos almost became partners with Kenny, but couldn't come up with enough money and just stayed on as boatmen.[18] The war in Viet Nam raged on and Doug had been drafted and was in the Army, stationed stateside in New York. Don had a job tending bar in Durango when not boating for Kenny, but Don couldn't resist driving his Chevy El Camino and launched Kenny on a day trip in the spring (Figure 13.5 & 13.6).

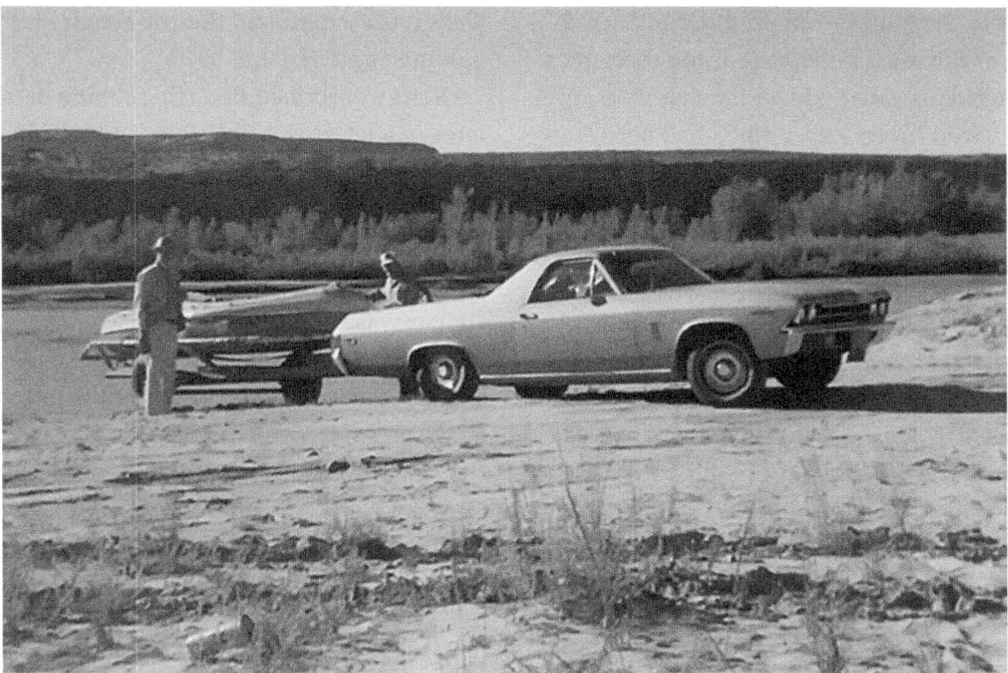

Figure 13.5 Don with his 1967 El Camino launched Kenny at Sand Island for a day trip, 1970. (Don Ross photo)

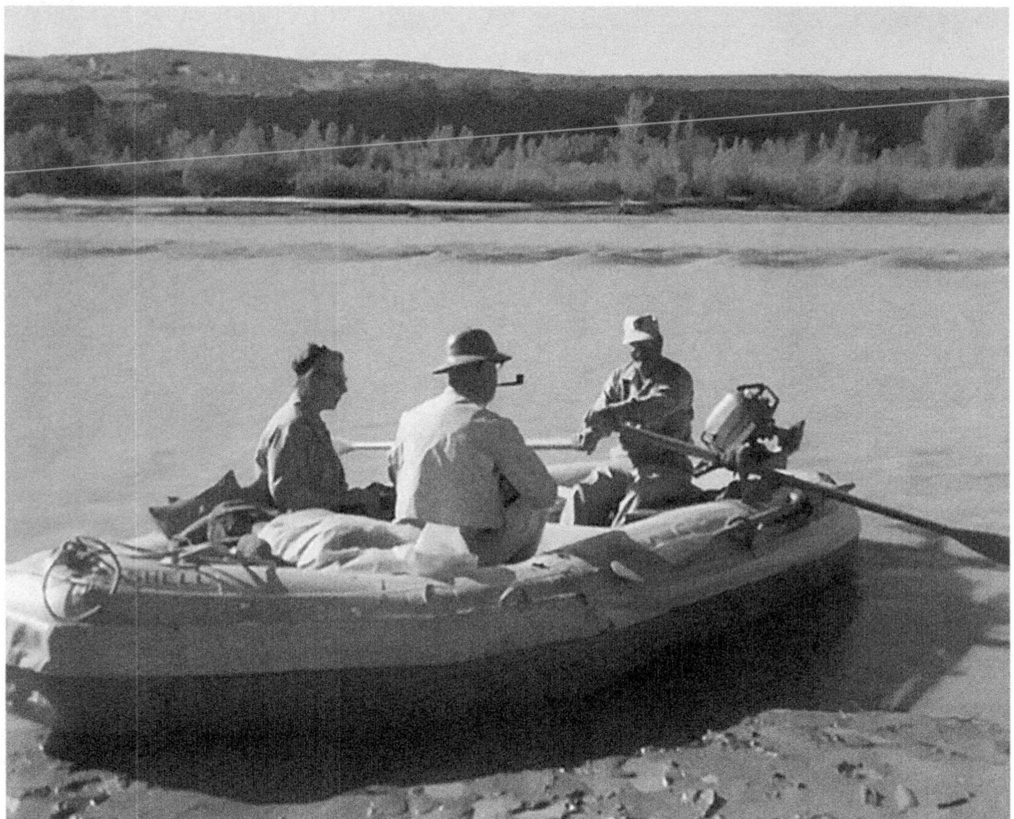

Figure 13.6 Kenny at the oars ready to take a couple on a day run in the "Shell" 10-man boat; note life preservers (horse-collar type) are not being worn; note also small set of sand waves, 1970. (Don Ross photo)

Access to the Mule Ear diatreme, considered to be one of the most important of the diatremes, required a two day boat trip on the San Juan River, and Wild Rivers Expeditions had been selected to assist with the field training of laboratory technicians and "Scientist Astronauts." Several river trips were conducted in this connection, which culminated in 1970, in hosting a two-day San Juan River trip for the "International Committee on the Upper Mantle," that marked the close of the first "International Geophysical Decade." [19] The trip was sponsored by the American Geophysical Union (AGU) and Columbia University. Orson Anderson was the convener of the field conference. Gene Shoemaker was also in the group and brought his own boat (Figure 13.7). "The field party was made up of eighty-three scientists. Seventeen nations were represented and the trip required fifteen boatmen and helpers." [20]

Kenny described this trip in more detail years later in a letter to Bill Dickinson. He said the trip was originally scheduled for fifty-six participants, but the huge Russian delegation brought the number up to eighty-three. The trip was a big hassle but all went well except that supper was served in the dark. The river rose just enough to sweep away sixteen watermelons which had been stashed in the river to cool down by Orson Anderson. "All but one was recovered the next day floating in eddies, all the way to Mexican Hat - - trouble was those in the first few boats got more than their share. Quite naturally, the *Great Watermelon Hunt* became one of the most memorable events of the whole darn trip." [21]

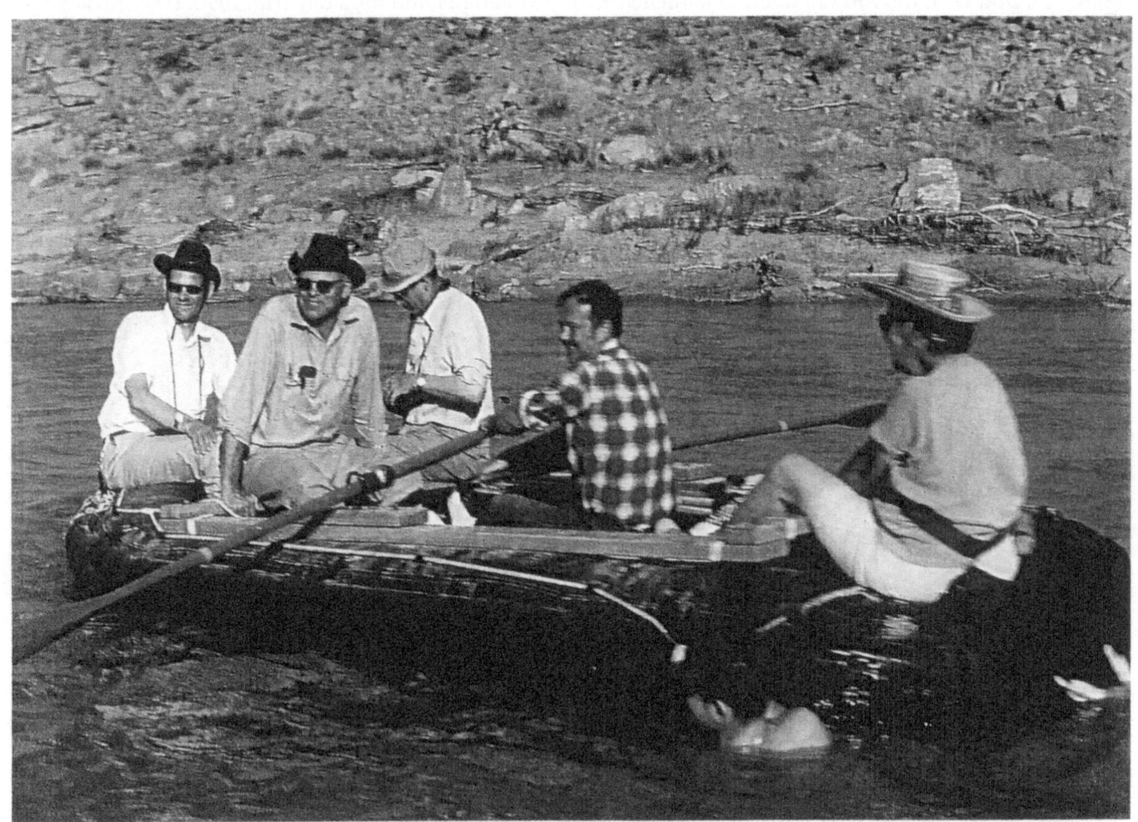

Fig. 13.7 Gene Shoemaker is rowing his own boat on the 1970 Kimberlite trip; Orson Anderson in front (dark hat, khaki shirt & pants), Priscilla Grew in back; note that no one is wearing PFD's. (From O. Anderson's cover photo to Gene Shoemaker Memorial Trip, 1997)

THE LABOR DAY FLOOD OF 1970

Beginning about Thursday, September 3, a major summer monsoon hit the Four Corners region. I was living in Ignacio, Colorado at the time and my sister and her husband came up from Phoenix, Arizona to visit for the Labor Day weekend. We had planned to do some camping and fishing but ended up sitting in my mobile home where we played all kinds of card games as we watched a steady heavy rain fall. By Saturday we heard on the radio that both the Los Piños (Pine) River and Vallecito bridges had washed out above Vallecito Reservoir and had left a number of folks stranded in the various cabins and dude ranch resorts above the bridges. Ignacio was quite small and quaint then (no casino) and I lived only a few hundred yards from the Pine River so we slogged over to see how high the creek was and it was rolling; big and bank full. The Animas was rolling too and I knew the San Juan was going to get enormous. The rain slacked off by Sunday evening, September 6, but my sister and her husband left on Monday, disappointed that we didn't even get into the mountains.

Don Ross was in Bluff that same weekend and recalled the following about the big flood: The State Patrol called Kenny asking for his help in a river rescue upstream at Aneth. He and Kenny took two 7-man boats up to McElmo Creek where the bridge had washed out[22] and they put their boats in McElmo Creek estimated by Don to be running at least 1000 cfs to see if they could latch onto a vehicle that had been washed off the bridge. But the current was too swift and they were immediately flushed out into the San Juan River. Don said that the river had monster sand waves with ten to twelve-foot amplitude crests and they pulled out at Cottonwood Wash, secured their boats and walked to the road. They hitched a ride down to Sand Island where folks were waiting for them. When they got there everyone was excited about "a nine foot tall wave of water" [23] that was supposed to be coming at them, but that warnings had been based on misinformation from Farmington and by the time the "wall of water" got to Bluff there was only a modest two or three foot rise. Soon after, rumors began that the "USGS had gaged the peak flow of the San Juan River at 50,000 cfs at the Mexican Hat gage." [24] As noted earlier in Chapter Ten, the San Juan River had a measured gage height of 26.62 ft with a streamflow of 52,000 cfs. That gaged volume and height remains the highest since Navajo Dam was completed in 1962.

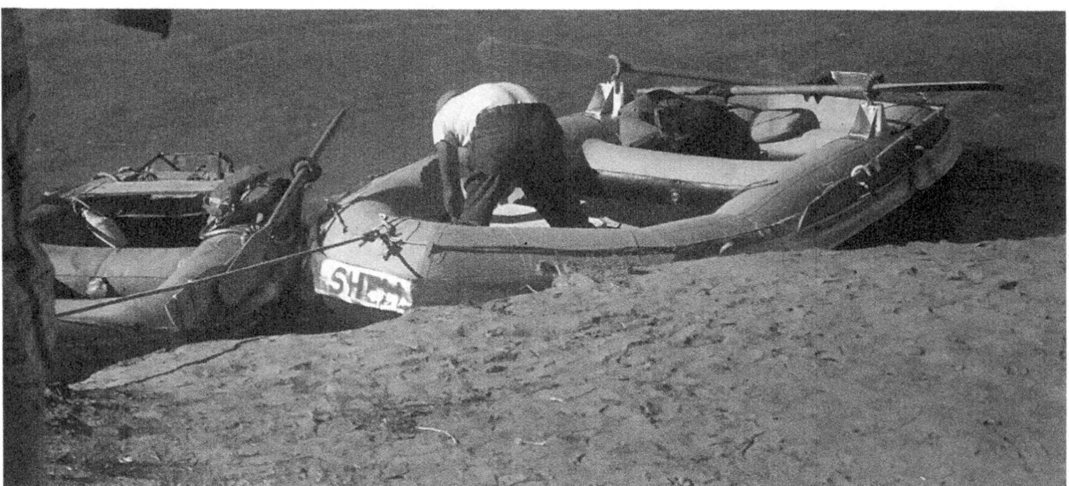

Figure 13.8 Don Ross (in boat) preparing to launch a day trip in the "Shell" and the "Little Bill." Note oar posts (Shell) and welded conduit (Little Bill) shaped to fit boat tubes. (K. Ross collection)

NEW FEDERAL REGULATIONS

Don Ross did numerous trips in spring of 1971 for Kenny (Figure 13.8). Then he received a phone call from Joan Staveley and he went to Grand Canyon and spent the rest of the summer running trips for Canyoneers. In *August, 1971 he took Kenny down Grand Canyon for the first and only time*!

Kenny composed a letter in spring of 1972 that he sent to the Superintendent of Canyonlands National Park which documented all the years he had run river trips down Cataract Canyon, the San Juan and Glen Canyon since 1947 up to 1972. By 1972 the NPS and BLM were getting serious about enforcing and controlling commercial river permits on many of the western rivers. We river runners felt it was a bit of government overreach, but here came the regulations.

For example, I experienced this permit wrangling when I worked for *Cañón Tours*, a river company that Don Baars' started in 1970. He had been issued legal permits (based on user days)[25] for several years by the BLM, but in 1975 he went through some harrowing legal dealings with the BLM for a permit he *thought he had* for Desolation-Gray Canyons on the Green River. I witnessed an Emery County Deputy Sheriff actually draw his revolver out of his holster and point it at Don when we were derigging a trip at Swaseys Campground landing in 1975, with a BLM Ranger standing by. The whole situation was crazy; the BLM Ranger had shown up at the launch point at Sand Wash five days earlier and told Don his permit had been "rescinded" and didn't say why. We had a big group of geologists, including some folks high up in the USGS, and national geological organizations and five boats were loaded including five days' worth of food. Don said "fine" and we launched our trip as the ranger stood there watching us float away. We all laughed and didn't think more about it until we witnessed the situation at Swasey's. When the gun was drawn on Don, all of these bigtime geologists and us grunts were rolling in the sand laughing our heads off and the poor Deputy saw he was just possibly over reacting, and quickly holstered his weapon. Don ended up getting a handful of tickets and turned them over to his attorney when we returned to Durango. The attorney followed up on the violations and told Don to just pay the fine, as the *fines costs less than the permit fees*! So we ran several more trips that summer on Desolation-Gray and just paid the fines; it was cheaper!

Kenny undoubtedly heard about equally bizarre *law enforcement* situations from Grand Canyon outfitters (i.e., all river rules and regulations began in Grand Canyon and migrated upstream) that had passed along their woes regarding permit problems, all of which had led Kenny to document his river trips. His hand-written draft letter of 1972 began:

> Dear Sir,
>
> This refers to future regulation of boat travel thru Cataract Canyon of the Colorado River, by the Nat'l Park Service.
>
> The writer understands and believes that with the growing popularity of boating thru Cataract Canyon and the increasing number of commercial operators offering such boating tours, requires certain regulations be established to insure the safety and convenience of participants. *He is concerned, however, that in initiating regulatory control, especially by limiting the number of commercial operator permits, the rights of some well qualified operators to conduct tours within Canyonlands Nat'l Park could be eliminated.* [Emphasis mine]
>
> Therefore, in the event that the number of commercial operator permits is to be limited, it is respectfully requested that <u>Wild River Expeditions</u> be among the operators permitted to conduct boating tours within the confines of Canyonlands National Park, which includes Cataract Canyon of the Colorado River. Qualifications by experience and historical background and by use of appropriate equipment are briefly set forth in the following paragraphs.[26]

His letter then went into considerable detail of his life experiences in river running from 1933 forward and his first trips in Cataract Canyon in 1949, where he stated that "This was probably the second trip to be accomplished in inflatable crafts but is the first of its kind to be mentioned by the Utah Historical Society in its quarterly reports (article by Otis Marston, date of publication unavailable)." [27] He emphasized that his trips were educational in archaeology, geology and biology. He listed the big FCGS geology trip on the San Juan in 1963, his appointment as a consultant to Lamont Doherty Labs, the 1970 IGU trip hosting eighty-three geophysicists, right up to an April, 1972 trip scheduled to go down the San Juan River for another geological association. He also cited his sons' commercial experience as boatmen. Lastly, he listed all the river equipment he owned and their condition for Cataract Canyon white water trips.[28] Again, from my own experiences with Don Baars and his river company, I know that river operators had to provide *proof of currently paid up liability insurance*, and submit fees for the current river season *in advance of being granted permits for that particular river year.* For small companies, this added burden of having to spend large chunks of money prior to receiving full payment from potential clients was considered extreme and upside down. And controlled flows released from upstream dams were arbitrary and not necessarily tied to natural seasonal flow rates which added to the gamble for commercial river companies. They could no longer rely on nature; now it was the Federal Government and the compliance with the Colorado River Compact to provide water to lower basin states that dictated river flow rates.[29]

SAN JUAN RIVER TRIPS

Anna Gavasci, a geoscience professor from Hunter College in New York was also working at the Lamont-Doherty labs and had been one of the participants on the big AGU field trip in 1970. She wrote Kenny in March, 1972 that she would be visiting the diatremes in the area and specifically wanted to collect garnet-peridotite rocks and asked if Kenny could take her by jeep to Garnet Ridge, Moses Rock and also by boat to the Mule Ear diatreme for further study.[30] He replied with his usual prompt and lengthy letter and stated that it would be necessary to acquire a mineral collecting permit from the Navajo Nation. He said he would file the application in his name because time was too short to allow exchanges of letters between Tribal authorities and Lamont. "Usually the mills of the Tribal Gods grind slowly but the fact that I have had a permit in past years may speed things up a bit." [31] Plans were finalized for her trip from April 2 through April 9.

Later in April 1972, Wild Rivers Expeditions hosted a two-day field trip on the San Juan River following the annual conference of the American Association of Petroleum Geologists (AAPG), which was held in Denver, Colorado. Kenny noted that he took three J-rigs and the Maid-o-Neoprene for a group of forty geologists and charged $30.00 per person (which included meals). His notes also show that he ran a six-day San Juan trip for sixteen Earth Science secondary school teachers and a geologist lead instructor. That river trip went from Aneth to Clay Hills where he used two J-rigs and returned the group to Mexican Hat. The cost was $185.00 per person which included all meals and transportation. At the end of his notes he had calculated his new fare for a "standard three-day trip" from Bluff to Clay Hills would cost $90.00 per person, or $85.00 per person if six or more signed up and boatmen wages were set at $12.00 per day. An extra day on the river would cost an additional $20 per person. Besides actual river running and transportation costs, he was now factoring in the cost for Liability Insurance.[32]

Several trips for large groups of San Juan High School students were booked by Kenneth Topham. Ben Priest, who ran the McElmo Canyon Field School, booked three daily trips with Kenny. Ben's trips usually consisted of twenty or more kids and he continued to run trips with Wild Rivers well into the 1990s and finally ceased when he became too ill to continue.[33]

Robert "Bob" E. Riecker, PhD, Geology Professor at Boston College booked two trips with WRX in 1972 and ran four more trips with Kenny in 1973.[34] Group sizes typically were small, consisting of seven or eight students and Bob, but were always booked for five-day runs from Bluff to Clay Hills. Bob Riecker moved his trips over to Don Baars' trips down Desolation-Gray Canyons on the Green River in 1974 and ended up being one of Baars repeat customers. I recall a memorable Boston College Desolation-Gray trip I did with just me and Don Baars as boatmen in 1975. Bob showed up with seven students who flew in to Sand Wash but required three flights by Redtail Aviation just to handle all the beer and boxes of booze. It was hardly a sober experience, but I do remember that this trip was when I learned how to turn cans of beer into rockets when placed just-so in a hot campfire.

Kenny said that Don and Doug continued as boatmen through the 1972 river season, but both were married by then and in Kenny's own words "they quit; pursuing independent careers of greater economic importance." [35]

The January 29, 1973 letter Kenny received from the newly formed U.S. Environmental Protection Agency[36] which thanked him for San Juan River flow rate data was soon followed by some terribly disturbing news. Orson Anderson wrote a heart-wrenching letter to Kenny whereby he explained in horrific detail how his son, Chester, had committed suicide on February 7; he was just twenty-one years old! Chester had been in the Navy and had been diagnosed with schizophrenia and was sent to the VA hospital in the Bronx, New York for treatment in the fall of 1972. Orson was living in Los Angeles and worked at the University of California Space Science Center: Institute of Geophysics and Planetary Physics. He was divorced and his ex-wife still lived in New York, but he made frequent trips back and forth as Chester's depression intensified. Orson closed: "He was buried in Sacramento. You and Don and Doug can share with me my hurt. We shall not ride again with Chester on the San Juan." [37] Priscilla Grew-Perkins also wrote to Kenny and thanked him for his friendship with Orson. She recounted some good memories of hikes on the Mule Ear diatreme and how Chester had ribbed Orson about his incompetence as a boatman, much to everyone's great amusement at camp on the Upper Mantle trip in 1970. She said that Orson had done everything possible to help Chester and had a clear conscience regarding the suicide and did not have any guilt feelings. She closed: "Orson especially appreciated your letter. I think because you were like an extra father to Ches." [38]

Perhaps Kenny's sadness of this event with Chester was reflected in his comment:

> It became necessary to curtail the activities of Wild Rivers Expeditions after the 1972 river season while the writer endeavored to build a new staff of qualified boatmen who could also -run?—his standards of accurate interpretation of the river scene, its geology, archaeology, and natural history, with appropriate emphasis upon preserving the whole environment. Two such qualified persons have now joined the summer staff, one in 1973 and the other in 1974. Each arrived already trained and experienced at river running and have qualified as "Boatman" under Utah law. Both plan to return for the 1976 season. If otherwise feasible, another such qualified person will be added to the staff as boatman in 1976.[39]

The boatmen Kenny alluded to were John Platt from Mesa, Arizona, "Dick" Dickinson (no address and no relation to Bill Dickinson) and

Bruce Steinhaus from Los Alamos, New Mexico. "Little Bill" Bill Huber, Jr. from Bluff worked as a "trainee" for the 1973 season. The river season included a group of four with Kent Frost aboard as field guide. Kent advertised with fancy letterhead stationary stating "Kent Frost Canyonlands, Inc." with a photo of the Needles Country at the top and "See the Country with Southern Utah's Most Experienced Guide" at the bottom. The group went on a three-day trip from Mexican Hat to Clay Hills.[40]

In May 1973 I drove from Flagstaff to Durango and helped run two back-to-back Sand Island to Clay Hills San Juan River trips with Don Baars' *Cañón Tours* for the FCGS Seventh Field Conference.[41] Some of Kenny Ross's boats and boatmen were on this big trip, but I don't recall who they were. I know that neither Kenny nor Doug was on this trip and Don was working in Durango for Colorado Trails. Kenny may very well have been on a Bluff to Mexican Hat three-day river trip with Geology Professor Donald Smith and his geology students from Idaho State University. Smith later said "they had a great time!" [42] Kenny closed out his May trips by taking a group from the State of Utah Travel Development Board on a "funsey trip." [43] Kenny charged $38.50 per person for this three-day trip from Mexican Hat to Clay Hills.

Anna Gavasci returned in July 1973 with another geology professor, Dennis Darby, and nine students from Hunter College for a two-day river trip. The primary focus of the trip was to collect mineral samples from the Mule Ear diatreme. Then Gene Shoemaker showed up as a guest scholar for a two-day river trip with a student group from the University of Texas led by Professor Dean Presnall on June 11-12. The focus again was the Mule Ear diatreme.[44]

Kenny continued to receive enquiries about river trips costs and logistics and with his usual flare for detail he replied to each and every letter. Some actually ended up booking trips. Trips for 1974 were priced: one-day at $23/person with at least two passengers and $17/person if more than ten passengers. Costs for a two-day trip ranged from $50/person to $37.50 and a three-day ranged from $110 to $80 per person depending on group size.[45] Of equal concern to enquiring potential passengers was the cost and availability of gasoline in the Four Corners region. The "oil embargo of 1973-1974" from Mid-East oil suppliers had created a rapid rise in petroleum prices and a hoarding scare spread across the country. There never was a real shortage, only those created by the public's panic. Demand certainly exceeded supply for at least a year, but the panic finally subsided. However, gasoline prices would never go back to the inexpensive rates prior to the embargo.[46]

The bookings for the 1974 river season continued at a good pace considering global economic concerns. Kenny and Don even "went to Flagstaff to pick up three new J tubes – REALLY good ones" to add to the "San Juan Navy."[47] Kenny had exchanged letters in May, 1973 with Norman Howard from South Australia who had been on a Canyoneers trip with Don in Grand Canyon two years prior and wanted to take a San Juan River trip that Don had recommended. Kenny ended up booking a five-day trip for the Australian group for July, 1974.[48]

Kenny described in a letter to an archaeologist that was interested in going down the San Juan and visiting the numerous petroglyphs when a particular group of petroglyphs were vandalized. These hacked petroglyphs later gained the name "Desecrated Panel" (Figure 13.9). Kenny explained "A few years ago I watched helplessly while a family of Navajos mutilated several of these figures, believing them to be drawings by a "witch-wolf" (werewolf) and the cause of death and serious illness (tuberculosis) within the family." [49]

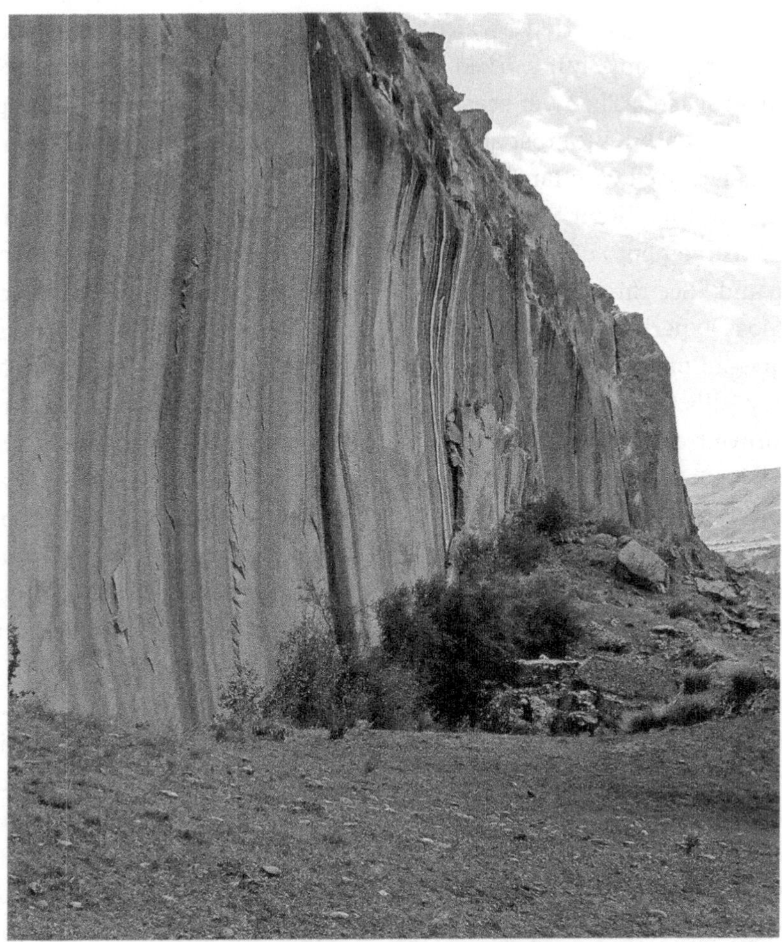

Figure 13.9 the tapestry wall along the San Juan River loaded with petroglyphs later defaced ceremonially by neighboring Navajo family and now called "Desecrated Panel." (G.M. Stevenson photo)

William B. Travers, Geology Professor at Cornell University, Ithaca, New York booked a San Juan trip with his students.[50] Kenny took two groups of thirty-nine down the river June 11 and again June 27 from Education Overland USA, Inc., from Wichita, Kansas.[51] After much hand-wringing regarding her concerns about gasoline rationing, Kenny finally booked a three-day trip from Mexican Hat to Clay Hills in June for Mrs. Cullen Bryant of Kirkwood, Illinois.[52]

Geology Professor William R. Brice, at the University of Pittsburgh, Johnstown, Pennsylvania booked a five-day Bluff to Clay Hills June trip for thirteen students and two instructors. "They wanted to visit the Mule Ear diatreme and everything else." [53] Kenny recommended that they use Don Baars' 1973 Geology book, but Brice also wanted Kenny to compose a "special" detailed eight-page typed geological trip outline for the first two days from Bluff to Mexican Hat. The focus was to hike the Mule Ear diatreme and camp the first night at the landing site on RL near the downstream RM 9.2. Brice was obviously satisfied with the initial geological trip in 1974 as he booked trips again for the same group size for 1975 and again in 1976, 1977, and 1979 using the same notes Kenny prepared in 1974 for Prof. Brice.[54] Kenny gave a student group discounted price of $54 per person for the fifteen passengers on each trip from 1974 to 1979.

For reasons unknown, Jon Lindbergh visited Durango in the fall of 1974 and contacted Kenny. In October, Kenny wrote Jon Lindbergh that he was "mailing a package with the bust of your father which I told you about when you were in Durango earlier this month. To refresh your memory, and for your records, I found the bust in May of 1970, in Harold Buck's Salvage (Junk) Yard in Las Vegas, Nevada, where I was picking up some surplus rubber pontoons to add to my 'San Juan Navy.'" [55] He explained how the bust was entangled in a pile of "better class junk" and that Jon could do what he wished with it. Kenny also said "It is impossible for me to express the pleasure I had from our brief visit of a few weeks ago. I can only say that it was very good to have you near again and to hear from you a little of your experiences and career activities during the intervening years." [56] Jon's mailing address was Bainbridge Island, Washington. He replied in November on stationary letterhead: DOMSEA FARMS, INC., Bremerton, Washington stating that the bust of his father had arrived safely. "It generated considerable interest by various members of the family. 'Those old books are getting pretty valuable!' one of the boys commented. How accurate this is I don't know, but the bust is highly prized." [57] He mentioned the rainy weather and "I've installed two wood stoves to reduce fuel consumption. It keeps me busy on the weekends with a chain saw, but I rather like that kind of work. It was certainly enjoyable to see you again in Durango. You sure haven't changed much over the last 25 years, must be the desert sun and the river." [58]

The 1975 river season was documented with more trip enquiries where Kenny listed the base price of $37.50 per person per day for trips from Bluff to Clay Hills. And, of course, reduced rates based on group size. In an effort to advertise the river business Kenny ordered "emblem patches" from Artcraft Mfg. Co. in Grand Rapids, Michigan (Figure 13.10). Kenny asked that they "send a current catalogue to my son, Donald K. Ross; Colorado Trails Ranch, Box 81301 Durango, Colorado. He is Foods and Supplies Mgr. and trail boss for this 'posh' resort, which handles 75 guests a week, June thru Sept." [59]

He booked a June river trip with Bruce M. Adams of Southwest Safaris, from Santa Fe who wanted to coordinate air tours with the river trip.[60] He took a Geology group on the river from the University of Maine and a group from Wichita, Kansas and several scout groups.[61]

But more importantly, Kenny continued his time-consuming documentation for the NPS and BLM regarding Wild River's commercial status as recorded by his many typed and handwritten notes for the years 1974 – 1976.[62] Kenny wrote another draft letter in 1976 where he stated that "Wild Rivers Expeditions served 769 people for more than 1,000 passenger days on the San Juan River during the 1972 river season" and he had to cancel some seventy-six reservations due to extremely low water conditions between June and late August. He said that was only the fourth time in nineteen years of operation on the San Juan that he had to cancel trips for more than a week or ten days because of impossible water conditions. He also said that conditions in 1974 were similar.[63]

Both Don and Doug were away from the Four Corners area following careers that got them away from Wild Rivers Expeditions. Kenny's mother, Erma, who had lived in California since the early 1950s died in the early 1970s, but only Kenny and Mildred went out for the funeral. Doug said that his grandmother was one lady that had even more mystery to him and Don. He remembered that his grandmother Erma "was a character in the best traditions and kept track of Don and I until we became assholes and ignored her after we were teenagers."[64] He recalled Kenny making trips to California in the '50s and '60s to visit Erma, but provided no other details.

Figure 13.10 the iconic Wild Rivers Expeditions logo was designed by Kenny and Don; the "WR" represents the Goosenecks and the "x" defines a *"prescription for adventure."* (G.M. Stevenson photo)

∞∞∞

14

THE END OF AN EPOCH: 1976 to 1982

BUSY SEASONS

The 1976 Wild Rivers boating season brought the return of T.J. Knight and Bruce Steinhaus as experienced boatmen and Martin Zemitis, who had joined as a swamper in 1974 and boated through the 1976 river season. Kent Green (Art Green's nephew) was a new boatman. Bruce Steinhaus boated for Kenny from 1973 to 1977 and then left for college and attended New Mexico State in Las Cruces. Norman Nevills Reiff, son of Sandra Nevills Reiff began working as a swamper/trainee. Kenny was godfather to Norman and his younger brother Gregory and had the following comment to pass along to the trainee:

> When you join the crew you will have the advantage of starting with professional river boatmen – not as your Grandfather or I did, as amateurs who had to develop our own methods, techniques and attitudes out of sometimes very tough experiences. Adventure boating on the rivers has changed a lot as professionalism has developed. Nowadays all the really good amateurs have learned the basics from the pros. I'm sure that before the summer is over you will take real pride in the professional approach to boating.[1]

It was a good thing he had some experienced boatmen as the 1976-77 river seasons were busy ones. Kenny continued writing confirmations for upcoming trips or answering the usual questions from potential new clients. He confirmed a group trip from Switzerland for an April, 1977 trip.[2] He was thanked for information regarding the "history and settlement of northern San Juan County" from the State of Utah Division of State History.[3] He booked a new client, North American Expeditions, for a river trip from Bluff to Clay Hills. He confirmed a follow-up trip with Bruce M. Adams of Southwest Safaris (Santa Fe) and mentioned that fares had increased to a three-person minimum for two-day trips to $70/person or $62.50 if more than ten participants. He reordered *DuraBorder* Emblems from Artcraft Mfg. Co. and said they were well received by customers. One of Wild Rivers' most successful trips was with the Sierra Club. The trip was a six-day that launched from Sand Island on June 21 and landed at Clay Hills on June 26, 1976. The trip was limited to nineteen Sierra clubbers and the applications filled in record time. Kenny received letters following the trip from several participants who stated that they had a wonderful time.[4]

He confirmed a repeat trip with a geologic group of thirty from the *University of Maine* (Farmington, Maine) but warned the professor that group size limits had begun to be enforced by the BLM. Kenny received a deposit for six people for a three-day trip in June with Robert Amsden; his son scheduled a three-trip for later that year. Kenny quoted the price to each that three-day trips were $135 per person for groups of four to eight. Kenny took Pam Koopman and several other new geology students who worked with Lamont-Doherty Labs in New York on a three-day trip to Clay Hills. Ann Stewart from California was so satisfied with her experience the year before with her school group that she booked a trip with three girl friends that brought their own kayaks for an April run from Bluff to Clay Hills. Kenny replied to a group from Farmington, New Mexico regarding his 1977 rates for a three-day trip from Bluff to Mexican Hat. He replied that it would cost $100 per person or $90 if there were eight or more; A five-day Bluff to Clay Hills would be $225 per person or $200 if more than eight participants.[5]

But, by far, the most important letter came in July from Tom McGetchin's secretary at the Los Alamos Scientific Laboratory "confirming that the dates September 28-29, 1977 for a raft trip from Bluff to Mexican Hat, Utah, with an overnight at Mule Ear, for a group of *fifty-seven or more* geologists. The group consisted of those who would be participating in the International Kimberlite Conference. The conference convener was Joe Boyd, Carnegie Institute of Washington." [6] It was the biggest trip Kenny had booked in years, and he was going to pull it off come hell or low water!

Kenny received a letter from Bill Dickinson in November, 1976 with Bill's introduction "A voice from your misspent youth!" He had heard that Kenny had run into Jon Lindbergh a couple of years ago in Durango. Bill then mentioned he had remarried in 1970 to a lady named Jacqueline (Jackie) and "that all the years are good years now." Bill then suggested a San Juan trip for the 1977 summer and that he would love to see Kenny again.[7] Of course, Kenny immediately replied by explaining that yet "another fire had occurred on October 29, 1976 that had gutted his trailer home/office and destroyed his current files, office equipment and printed materials regarding 1977 trips. The gas-powered hot water tank had blown while he was away and insurance would cover about two-thirds of the loss. His old trailer where his crew stayed and all of the boats and river gear were not affected. The burned trailer house has now been moved away and we will be moving another, larger one to take its place.....even has a fireplace.....will set it up this month." [8]

Kenny then suggested that Bill "might want to consider September 28-29, 1977 for a post-conference field trip following the International Kimberlite Conference." [9] The Mule Ear diatreme would be the primary focus of the field trip. He suggested that Bill could be a guest boatman and that Joe Boyd from the Carnegie Institute would be the conference convener. Tom McGetchin, who was working on the Los Alamos geothermal project, would lead the field trip(s). Kenny wasn't sure about field trip announcements but he thought it would be great fun to see Bill again. He said they had tentatively set a limit of fifty-six participants.[10] To further entice Bill in participating in the field conference he felt that a little name-dropping wouldn't hurt:

> Can't say yet who all will be on the '77 field trip but you can be sure the party will include some of the most notable deep-earth scientists. Besides Boyd and McGetchin we can almost count on Gene Shoemaker (a fine boatman who usually brings along his own pet 10-man raft), Orson Anderson (who at least tries to run a boat and scares hell out of his passengers), probably Bill Muehlberger and Leon Silver. I plan to specially invite Robert Parker, Astronaut (Ground Commander, Skylab Project), for a brief evening discussion of the latest developments in remote (satellite) sensing as may be applied to geo-research (Figure 14.1). Bob is a close friend of my son, Don, and a great guy to have on a river trip. This invitation is already on its way, officially, so that Bob can clear with NASA. And, yes, Don is really all grown up, has his degree in geology, and is an NPS approved Grand Canyon Pilot and now rapidly becoming prominent in the Dude-Ranching business.[11]

Kenny also mentioned that the Hoyt twins (Alfie and Eddie), Frank Thorp and David Scott proposed a reunion trip for next year sometime in August, 1977 for those who had been members of the Explorers Camp. They all had families and wanted to show them the San Juan River from Bluff to Clay Hills. Even though Bill didn't necessarily remember all of them, Kenny would sure like him to join in.[12] Bill wrote back and said he would not be able to make the "kimberlite party" or the reunion trip due to his field camp responsibilities.[13] But, Bill suggested an early July trip; "July 4-8 looks like our best time slot when we are as free as a bird." Bill really wanted Kenny to meet Jackie and closed by saying "Come hell or low water, we are coming to Bluff anyway. It is high time I saw the master river rat face to face again!" [14] Bill and Jackie apparently stopped in Bluff for a brief visit with Kenny but they didn't have time for a river trip and hoped they could arrange a trip for next year.

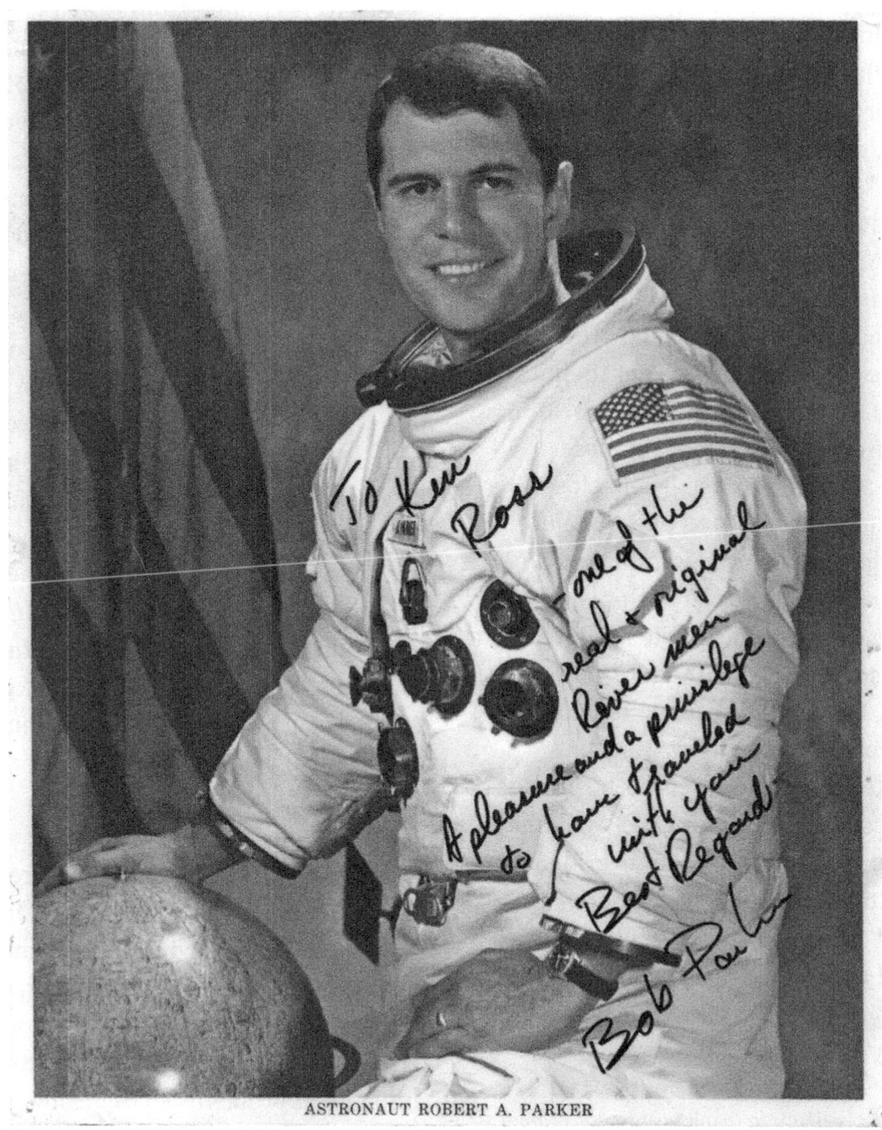

Figure 14.1 Astronaut Robert "Bob" A. Parker was one of many astronauts-in-training at NASA who went on river trips with Kenny and visited the Mule Ear diatreme. Bob remained a long-time friend of the Ross family. (K. Ross collection)

BEER AND ICE LOGISTICS

Joe Boyd was the USA representative as a co-convener of the "Second International Kimberlite Conference" as it was now advertised. His initial contact with Kenny was by letter on March 1, 1977 where he laid out the field trip in detail. He wanted to confirm logistics for a group of about "80 participants, about half of whom will be from abroad. We will be arriving at Bluff by bus a little before sunset and wish a cook-out dinner on the river bank that night. We wish to camp at Comb Wash for lunch and dinner on Wednesday, September 28, proceeding on to Mexican Hat the next morning." [15] He wanted to confirm the raft trip included five meals for a total cost of $57 per person and he assumed they would pay extra for beer and soft drinks and wanted to be sure there would be enough room for these and other supplies on the rafts, "or can you get them in to Comb Wash by truck?" Joe requested a written confirmation from Kenny regarding these arrangements as soon as possible and closed by saying he had been on the 1970 Upper Mantle Symposium trip "and enjoyed it immensely." [16]

Kenny replied in short order with his usual lengthy letter and included the latest information booklet. Boyd soon replied with more comments and questions. He said the absolute maximum participants would be ninety-two and was pleased with Kenny's assurance that he would have plenty of shuttle drivers for the vans that accompanied the buses since a single bus could not handle all the folks. Boyd particularly thanked Kenny for his warning about "Utah beer" and said they would bring beer in a van from Los Alamos and purchase soft drinks through Kenny.

> This group is likely to drink quite a lot of beer if they get the chance. Ideally, I would like to let them blow off a little steam around a campfire in the Canyon and then have them be real quiet in Kayenta. Presumably beer could go into our Wednesday night camp by truck, along with other supplies. That right? Would Wednesday morning be O.K. time to send it in? [17]

Obviously, beer and plenty of it was a major concern! Boyd noted that the participants would arrive by airplane into Cortez Airport and that the buses were coming from Grand Junction that would meet the group and he estimated a two hour drive to Bluff (Sand Island). He was also concerned about dinner being served in darkness and asked if Kenny could provide a big bonfire? He reiterated their arrival would be around 6:30 PM on Tuesday, September 27 and expected to come off the river at Mexican Hat no later than 1:00 PM on Thursday, September 29.

The snowpack over the winter of 1976-77 was one of the lowest on record for the San Juan Mountains which almost guaranteed a miserable runoff for the river season. USGS gage data for the San Juan River from the gage near Bluff (at Mexican Hat) recorded a mid-May peak of 550 cfs then in the second week of June it peaked at approximately 1300 cfs[18] (Figure 14.2). By late June and into early July the river flow gaged less than 200 cfs, and got as low as 80 cfs in mid-July.[19] Kenny knew the river and how ridiculous it might be to try and float boats loaded with adults and camp gear at these flow rates.

There was always a chance for some late summer monsoons, but these were too unpredictable, but Kenny crossed his fingers in hopes of a flash flood or two. By mid-July Kenny sent word out to Gene Shoemaker, Orson Anderson and Tom McGetchin about the fickle river flow. They were all well aware of the impending problems so Gene and Joe Boyd drove to Moses Rock diatreme and in a letter dated August 29, 1977 addressed to Kenneth Wohlentz, a geologist at the University of Arizona, Joe explained:

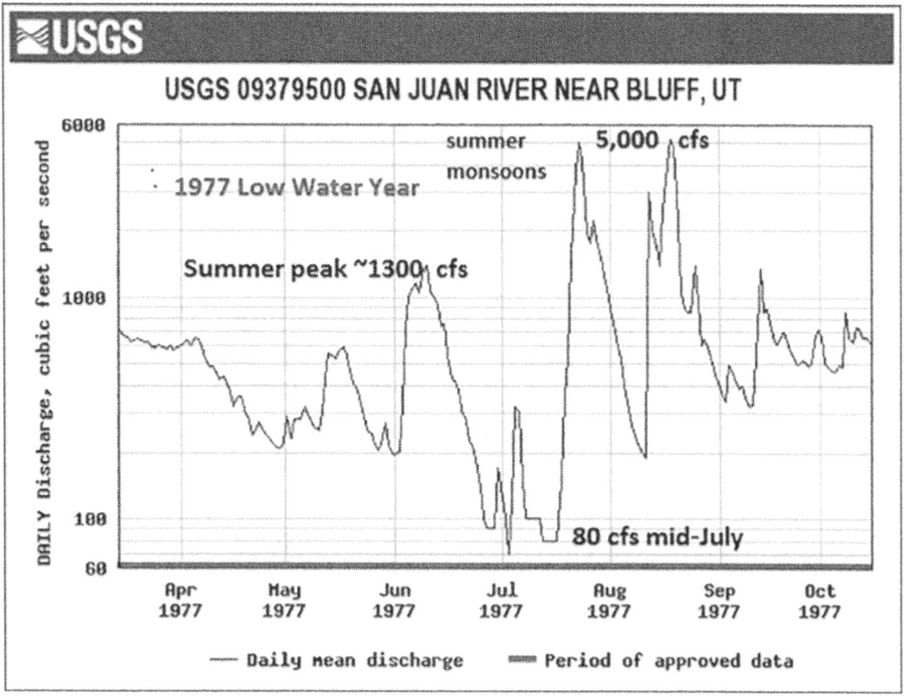

Figure 14.2 river gage chart for 1977 indicated that by late June a super low water season was in the making and the big diatreme river trip was in jeopardy of having to be cancelled but the late summer monsoons saved the day! (USGS water data)

Gene Shoemaker and I worked out a route into Mule Ear from the south. It took us a day and a half, much of which time was spent digging a ramp out of a 10' wash. Later we figured out a way to bypass the ramp! The route we finally established takes one hour from Moses Rock. If we have to give up the river trip we will take all vehicles into Moses Rock and make the run into Mule Ear with 4-wheel drive vehicles only. The Survey vehicles will each take 5-6 additional passengers riding on bed-rolls in the back.[20]

Joe had other concerns too, namely – the beer! He said Kenny wanted to take the beer and food needed for Wednesday, September 28 down river at dawn on Tuesday. That meant the beer had to get to Bluff before then. But the worry now centered on *ice* and the availability thereof!

It is desirable to get calibrated on ice well in advance. I suggest block ice, coarsely chopped. Start with warm beer and experiment by setting a trash can load out in the hot sun – how long will the ice last? You will need ice for Tuesday evening and Thursday night through Sunday noon continuously. Decide how much block ice you need and phone me. I estimated more than 500 lbs. The ice needed for Thursday night and thereafter can be stored in the freezer and/or meat locker of the Kayenta Trading Post. Conceivably the Post would store the beer and pop in their meat locker – in which case it would start cold. Obviously, this is a delicate matter in reference to the beer, but let Lois [Joe's secretary] try to arrange it. It would be nice if participants could have cold beer available in the back of the van on Thursday and Friday evenings in Kayenta. Block ice can be purchased for about $6/100 lbs. The Kayenta Trading Post orders its ice from Page (Lake Powell). Probably the best way of getting the ice is to have the Post order it for us in 50 lb blocks. Lead time needed.[21]

A WORD ABOUT DRAG BAGS

Joe Boyd had been down the San Juan and other rivers and had apparently had unsatisfactory experiences with *drag bags* – burlap sacks within which canned beer and soda was added and then hung by rope over the side of the boat to cool in the river water. This technique was created soon after canned beverages of any sort made it to the river community, but everyone had their own tricks as to how to get the coldest beer (or soda) possible. Some would lower the bag all the way in the river, while some would just wet the bag occasionally and let the dry desert air evaporate the water and thus cool the contents in the cans.

Obviously, river water temperature, air temperature and relative humidity varied by season and by rivers, but the San Juan had one more ingredient to consider, and that was the large volume of suspended silt in the river. Only the novice or foolhardy let the beer bag get fully loaded with canned drinks and then lowered completely into the river. By doing so, the mesh of the burlap sack allowed the moving silty water to slow just enough to allow the sediment to settle out inside the bag thereby creating what was known as a "sea anchor!" And this phenomenon was particularly true when drag bags full of canned drinks was left unattended overnight. Many an unwary boatman or passenger had to spend several minutes digging and prying their bag out from the river bank after being filled with a hundred pounds of silt.

Another phenomenon occurred after the aluminum can was introduced to the public – abrasion! Cans that were in submerged bags tend to rub against each other and the added silt would not only erase all the labeling, but given sufficient time, small holes were worn in the cans such that all the contents would leak out and get displaced by silty river water. Many a soul on river trips unwittingly flipped the tab on a beer can and taken a big gulp of river water, only to spew it out in complete bewilderment of this exchange of fluids in what appeared to be a cold drink. Since most drinks were carbonated the sure sign of a punctured can was to pay attention to the "pszzz" when opening.

∞∞∞

Joe continued: "the Navajo trip will start with 97 people on the river and wind up with 125 at Kayenta." Regarding housing, Joe said he had cancelled their accommodations at Gouldings and had made arrangements with the Holiday Inn and Wetherill Inn at Kayenta. And lunch following the river trip would be provided by "the café by the bridge at Mexican Hat and the Mexican Hat Trading Post (Mr. Knight)." [22]

As the time for the big river trip drew nearer, so came the summer monsoons and by mid-July the "gage near Bluff" had recorded a peak of 5,000 cfs that soon dropped to 200 cfs in early August, followed by another storm where the river peaked again at 5,000 cfs in mid-August (see Figure 14.2). In a letter sent by Kenny to Joe Boyd dated September 9, 1977 Kenny confirmed that Tom Knight would charge $10.00 for the use of his shed for two nights and that five cases of *Utah beer* would be charged at the going rate of $7.60 per case and *Pepsi Cola* at $6.50 per case. Kenny mentioned that the rains had hit the mountains and the river had swollen several times to around 4,000 cfs at Bluff and had not gone below 300 cfs. He hoped that Joe and others in high places could "induce BurRec to increase the release from Navajo Lake in case it is needed." [23]

On August 22, 1977 the Bureau of Reclamation's Assistant Commissioner C. Barrett had informed Joe Boyd with a lengthy letter that ended "since climatic conditions may not improve sufficiently to provide high natural flows by September 28, it would be prudent for you to investigate alternative means of reaching the Mule Ear site." [24] But Kenny needed to commit one way or the other. He needed to find boats and boatmen if he were to run a river trip. Time was too close to wait any longer about which way the trip was going to be pulled off, and Kenny elected to stay with the river plan, but with some modifications as to where and how folks and all that beer and ice got on boats and where the big group camped.

THE SECOND INTERNATIONAL KIMBERLITE CONFERENCE DIATREME TRIP

The big trip was about to happen and Kenny had elected to run it as originally planned – as a river trip. Or, at least, as a field trip supported by boats and following the diatreme field trip, then to run the participants to Mexican Hat by boats.

The trip was just an overnighter from Comb Wash to Mexican Hat. According to USGS discharge data at the Mexican Hat gage, the river ran between 500 to 700 cfs during the field trip – September 28–29, 1977 (Figure 14.3). To accommodate all the expected participants, and to provide sufficient time for them to hike and explore the diatreme, Kenny decided to have the boats floated down to Comb Wash the day before where they would meet passengers brought in by vans and carryalls. J-rigs and anything that floated was used; Mitch Williams from Tag-along Tours out of Moab came down with five boats with crew and they set up to launch the next morning to go the two miles to a "base camp" on the big gravel bar on river right (RR) across from the diatreme.

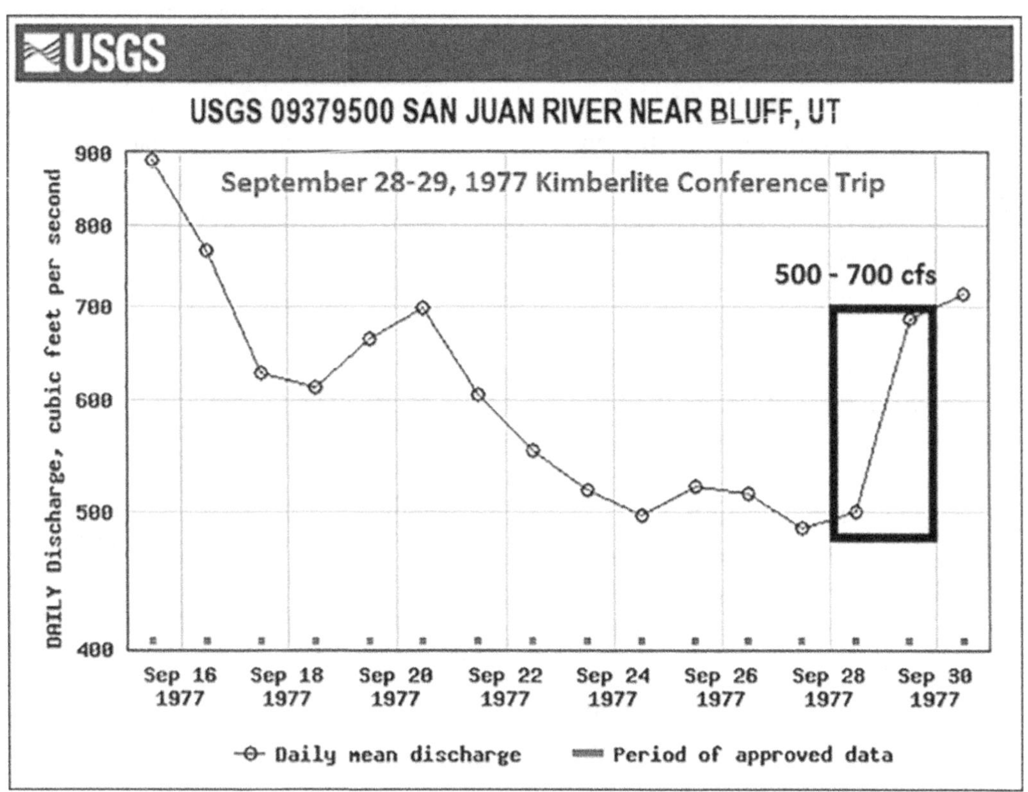

Figure 14.3 River gage chart for the week of the big diatreme trip indicates that the trip was run at a respectable 500 to 700 cfs volume for the period highlighted. (USGS water data)

The conference group flew into Cortez from Denver and then bussed their way to Sand Island on Tuesday, September 27. They all camped at Sand Island the night before the river trip where Johnny Lester and his Navajo wife made a Navajo Taco dinner for everyone and breakfast the next morning. Orson Anderson brought pickup truck loads of block ice in large garbage cans and cases of ice-cold beer and dozens of watermelons for guests but elected to not go on the trip to the Mule Ear diatreme. The next day, Wednesday, September 28, the caravan of vehicles arrived at Comb Wash where *fifteen boats* waited and nearly one hundred participants were floated down to the "base camp." Kenny had rounded up all the folks he could find to run boats. Field trip participants were ferried across the river to the other side in batches where they all went up on the diatreme and returned in small groups back to camp – and cold beer! [25] Boats and boatmen were kept busy most of the day ferrying the participants back and forth across the river.

Kenny had contacted Don Ross in Durango to come over and help with running the trip. Don said he put food together for more than a hundred folks and someone had suggested "par-boiling a ton of chickens so they could finish on the grill at camp." [26] Doug came down from Grand Junction and helped rig the trip, boil chickens, and run one of the boats on the trip, even though he was in the early stage of moving to the Northwest. Brad Dimock, who had been recruited to row one of Kenny's boats, had come from Flagstaff, and he remembered Don and Doug "grilling 110 half-chickens on an eight-foot-long grill for hours!" [27] Like most river camps of that era, the grilling was all done by burning driftwood, and there were plenty of eager hungry spectators. And there was plenty of cold beer. Don said they didn't finish until close to midnight, and all he wanted to do was drink a beer and go to bed. He said he didn't eat roasted chicken for ten years! Doug and Brad didn't figure out they were both on this trip together until a few years ago when I started researching this book.[28]

After an early breakfast the next morning, Don recalled that they finally started down through the San Juan canyon gorge, where they slammed rocks and hung up on gravel bars, but somehow, they made it to Mexican Hat before dark and saw the geoscientists off and returned to the Bluff boat camp and crashed! Actually, Joe Boyd, in a last-minute frantic letter to Gordon Swann with the Center of Astrogeology from Flagstaff, Arizona was contacted to change the "rendezvous point for the rafts from the town of Mexican Hat to the landing at the foot of the Mexican Hat Rock." [29] He spelled out how to get to the new take-out point and also asked:

> Could your drivers pick up some stuff in Mexican Hat for us on your way through? 120 bag lunches will be waiting for us at the Café by the bridge. Just sign for these and bill will be sent to Lois. There will also be 2-3 cases of mixed booze at the Café which will have been pre-paid. A few hundred yards up the hill towards the landing – on your right – is the Mexican Hat Trading Post. It is owned by Mr. Knight. Please stop there for the beer and pop we will drink for lunch. There will be seven cases and it will all be cold. This beer and pop will have been pre-paid by Ken Wohlentz.[30]

One thing was for sure – Joe Boyd knew how to run a field trip for geoscientists! [31] There may have been concerns about logistics of whether the field trip could be conducted as a river trip, or overland, but by golly, there sure as hell wasn't a shortage of beer and booze; and ice!

The next day, Friday, September 30, TJ, Don, Doug and Randy, a wrangler from a Durango dude ranch, launched boats from Sand Island and went back down to the campsite and picked up all the camp gear, trash, beer bottles, and cans. Then they ran out to Mexican Hat and back to Bluff where they cleaned-up all the boats and equipment. Everybody dispersed the following day; Don went back to Durango and looked for a job and Doug returned to Grand Junction to deal with his big move.

Kenny explained how the trip went in a letter to Bill Dickinson in January 1978:

> I feel that the kimberlite Conference trip really did come off very well. Many post-trip remarks make me feel good about it. There were 97 delegates on the trip and there were 12 in our crew. The last few days of preparation were hectic as usual and tension built up right to the moment of launching, after which things went very smoothly. Everybody seemed to be happy at the end of the trip and I was near to total exhaustion as I've ever been. Upon looking back only the personal fun really stands out. I really enjoyed the reunions with a number of people with whom I had worked during the late 60s and early 70s. Especially nice (useful too) was the almost continuous visiting with "Herb" Helmstaedt. He rode all the way in my boat and stayed right at my elbow to be helpful with running the big "J-Rig" – and he was, he is very good "crew." In the evening, after supper, we, with Jeff Harris, formed the nucleus of a campfire bull session, in and out of which nearly everyone wove a way. Discussions ranged from the lofty to the utterly ridiculous as Harris, possibly the funniest man in the deep-earth business, kept conversation current with whoever entered the circle. I suspect that it was neither wit nor wisdom that made us a focus of attention – we had grabbed all the cases of beer to use as seats around the fire and the thirsty had no choice except to join for at least a bottle – or two – or three. Our seats were all collapsed by 11 PM, and all but the Russians hit the sack. The latter broke out their vodka and partied loudly for another couple of hours.
>
> Of course, Helmstaedt took a bit of good-natured ribbing about his subduction – continental over-ride hypothesis to explain widely separated occurrences of Lawsonite-bearing eclogites. He fended these with good humor and a cogency that seemed to get thoughtful attention. At least it seemed to me that some indifference turned into cautious interest – in the informal atmosphere of the field trip.
>
> The two-day trip ended, right on schedule, at noon and I was able to get home to shower and grab about 50 pounds of specimens, then rejoin the conference group at Kayenta in time for supper at the Holiday Inn. Herb and I spent much time over my eclogites and I gave him a selection to take back to the lab. I have a lot of respect for him as a careful and enthusiastic worker. He is an elegant and beautiful person and I've greatly enjoyed working with him from time to time.[32]

Kenny's description of the big kimberlite trip was in response to a short letter from Bill Dickinson in December, 1977 where Bill had asked "Can we try for the San Juan again? Same drill as before!" He suggested the week of "July 4th plus the two weekends on either end, into which to fit a San Juan ride." Bill also noted:

> My agents tell me that the diatreme show came off dandy. George Thompson [a participant] is a Stanford colleague of mine. He and Helmstaedt and I now have a three-cornered correspondence underway about subduction and diatremes. We shall see. Other diatreme folk evidently do not worry much about subduction. So be it. *The fruit is always for those who will reach!* Also, I think I have worked out the Laramide in general terms, and will fire a preprint your way soon.[33] [Emphasis mine]

In Kenny's reply to Bill, he said he was very glad that there was a correspondence going on between Bill and Herb "as the two of you have much in common besides similar geo interests." Kenny suggested that Bill should consider a joint river trip with the Helmstaedt family at any time Bill and Jackie could schedule as Herb was very interested in meeting Bill.[34] Bill quickly replied and thought "a five-day trip sounds dandy. Three days via Mule Ear from Bluff to Mex Hat with the Helmstaedts also sounds dandy." [35] Kenny had promoted the three-day to Mexican Hat as he had stated earlier his dubious thoughts about a Clay Hills take-out:

> It is questionable as to whether or not Lake "Folly" will refill enough to make a landing at Clay Hills Crossing anything but an impractical muddy

> mess but I'm obligated (by the N.P.S.) to set up a tentative schedule of trips anyhow.[36]

William R. Dickinson's seminal paper published in 1978 entitled "Plate tectonics of the Laramide orogeny" and co-authored by Walter S. Snyder from Lamont-Doherty opened the eyes of the geological community that, in all likelihood, the Farallon oceanic plate was the primary "driver" that brought about the rise of the Colorado Plateau. His close colleague George Davis, University of Arizona Regents' Professor Emeritus of geosciences and former head of the UA Department of Geosciences had this to say in an interview following Bill's death in 2015:

> Bill helped in the whole discovery and introduction of plate tectonics — and then proceeded to so tightly integrate tectonics and sedimentology that he created a new field of endeavor. ... I've never known anyone who had such focus when he was going after the solution of the problem — I mean never. This guy was able to put his entire intellectual and field work faculties into just assaulting a geological problem and bringing it to its knees.[37]

The following excerpt from Dickinson and Snyder's Abstract (1978) provides an example of Bill's classic short and to the point style:

> The crustal buckling of the classic Laramide orogeny is marked by fault-bounded, basement-cored uplifts separated by intervening sediment-filled basins. The descending slab of lithosphere slides along under the overriding plate of lithosphere, with which contact is maintained; crustal earthquakes are widespread across the dormant arc massif, within which local block uplifts bounded by reverse faults are prominent, and magmatism is meanwhile suppressed because the asthenosphere is never penetrated by the descending slab. The largely amagmatic Laramide style of deformation can be ascribed to the dynamic effects of an overlapped plate scraping beneath the Cordillera.[38]

Kenny received a preprint from Bill and in a February 1978 letter to him he stated:

> I feel honored by the thoughtfulness that prompted you to give me a preview. I am very much intrigued by the model you and Snyder present and am impressed that this may very well be a landmark work. It engendered "brain-storms" in me and I am sure that it will also in others. To comment further would be pretension to expertise I do not possess. Nevertheless, I am full of topics for informal discussion when we meet next. Oh well; I'm just an interested bystander. To quote a renowned Prof of anthropology of long ago: "Like a boy riding on top of the hearse; I'm just going along for the ride!" No doubt that under a star-spangled sky, by a blazing fire, with a few bottles of beer and thou beside me in the wilderness, you can put me straight.[39]

Bill soon replied that he "wasn't so sure that a beer on the banks of the river would entirely clarify the Laramide, but I am all for giving it a try. You will note anyway that we employ the strategic waffle on a point or two. I do believe, however, that we are looking in the right direction, and *it would be indecent to spoil the fun by solving it all out of hand! Moreover, I have noticed in this game that one man's solution is but another man's problem*; thus, we can go on ad infinitum, rather like the College of Cardinals.[40] [Emphasis mine] Bill concluded by confirming the date of launching on July 5th for a four- or five-day river trip. There is no record of the trip, but it in all likelihood actually happened.

ooooo

In addition to numerous individuals enquiring about river trips, costs and dates the remainder of 1978 and 1979 was documented by Bruce Adams with Southwest Safaris booking two more trips for April and May. Bruce continued booking trips with Kenny through the 1983 river season. Bert Stern, Director of CAMP SCOTMAR that operated from West Covina, California wanted to take a group of older children to which Kenny wrote a lengthy reply and offered reduced prices based on group size and if the Camp provided their own food. Kathy Whitaker, Chief Curator for the San Diego Museum of Man booked a trip for twenty. Kenny did take a group from Saint Andrews School from Boca Raton, Florida in June.[41]

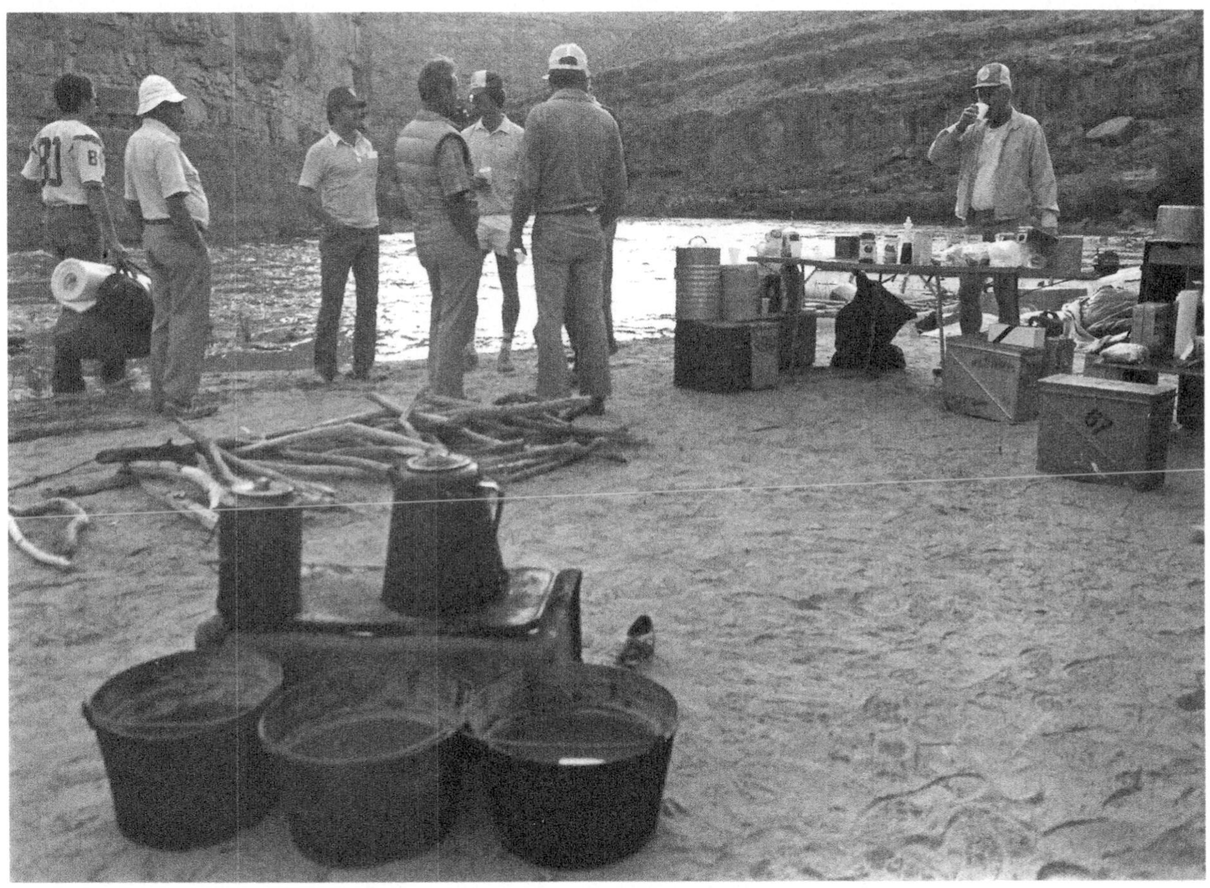

Morning camp scene at upper Eight Foot in 1980s; river camping had changed significantly from the days of John Wetherill in 1933 (see Chapter 2, Figure 2.7); now a three stage set-up of wash buckets set near camp fire (in a metal firebox to control ashes) in foreground with coffee pot and hot water for tea; fires were still made with driftwood as shown by pile of wood; table set above ground for convenience and less chance of sand in the food; water cans with potable drinking water set on small ice chests; passengers drinking from Styrofoam cups. (Ian Thompson photo)

"A Boatman is a peculiar combination of brilliance and "quirkivity". Bronzed masters of the river, at home on the water, in the natural world, able to read his/her surroundings, comfortable in the great outdoors, as in one's own skin. I am not, and have never been, a boatman, but I have sure known a multitude of 'em, loved their stories, and fed most of them at my table, repeatedly. . . . grand folk, those. . . .and man, can they eat!" **(Susan DeLorme, former co-owner, Wild Rivers Expeditions)**

15
END OF THE LINE

CHIEF BOATMAN

Charlie DeLorme had moved to Mancos in 1976 and he would occasionally help Kenny, but Charlie mostly ran his own trips. Charlie met Susan in Mancos and they married in 1981.[1] She taught at the elementary school and she and her three young daughters from a previous marriage became close friends with Mildred. Both Charlie and Susan worked at Mesa Verde Company that was now operated by Ansel Hall's son-in-law Bill Winkler. Susan worked during summers and Charlie had been their purchasing agent. Both Susan and Charlie continued to stop at Kenny and Mildred's home to see how they were doing, but it would be 1982 before Charlie started full time for Wild Rivers Expeditions as "Chief Boatman" as nothing very regular happened for the river company between 1979 and 1982. Charlie noted, "when you're the ONLY Boatman it's pretty easy to be designated 'Chief.'" [2] DeLorme continued; "Kenny was a tough old bird by the 1980s. Many a morning my 06:00 alarm was the sound of a Hamm's beer pop-top opening. And the shopping list for Cortez always included a half dozen bottles of Nyquil that he started hitting at the same time as that 06:00 Hamm's. And when I asked how to prepare or rig something I learned to anticipate 'you *never* do it that way!'" [3]

Figure 15.1 from L to R: Don, Mildred, Kenny and Doug Ross, August, 1982; the last family photo. (K. Ross collection)

ROCKED

The entire Ross family was rocked with bad news in the summer of 1982. Chuck Ziegler Ross, the older half-brother of Don and Doug, the adopted son of Kenny's, the oldest son of Mildred's had died in a hospital bed in Houston, Texas at the age of 53! Mildred was understandably shaken to her knees, and when Don learned about it, he told his folks that he would handle things. Arrangements were made and Chuck's body was sent to Mancos and was buried in Cedar Grove Cemetery. When he was buried, Kenny bought a large enough plot for himself and Mildred. It pretty much took the wind out of Kenny's sails too (Figure 15.1).[4]

That's about the last story known about Kenny and Wild Rivers operations until Gary Matlock, a Durango archaeologist, showed up. Gary Matlock had been Kenny's "partner" in some fashion during that period of time of the late '70s to early '80s but they really didn't have anything formalized on paper. Kenny told Doug that the "partnership" didn't work out as Gary was too tight with his money. Gary paid the insurance a couple of times and thought that earned him a partnership. Kenny said he liked Gary immensely, but things just didn't work out (Figure 15.2).[5]

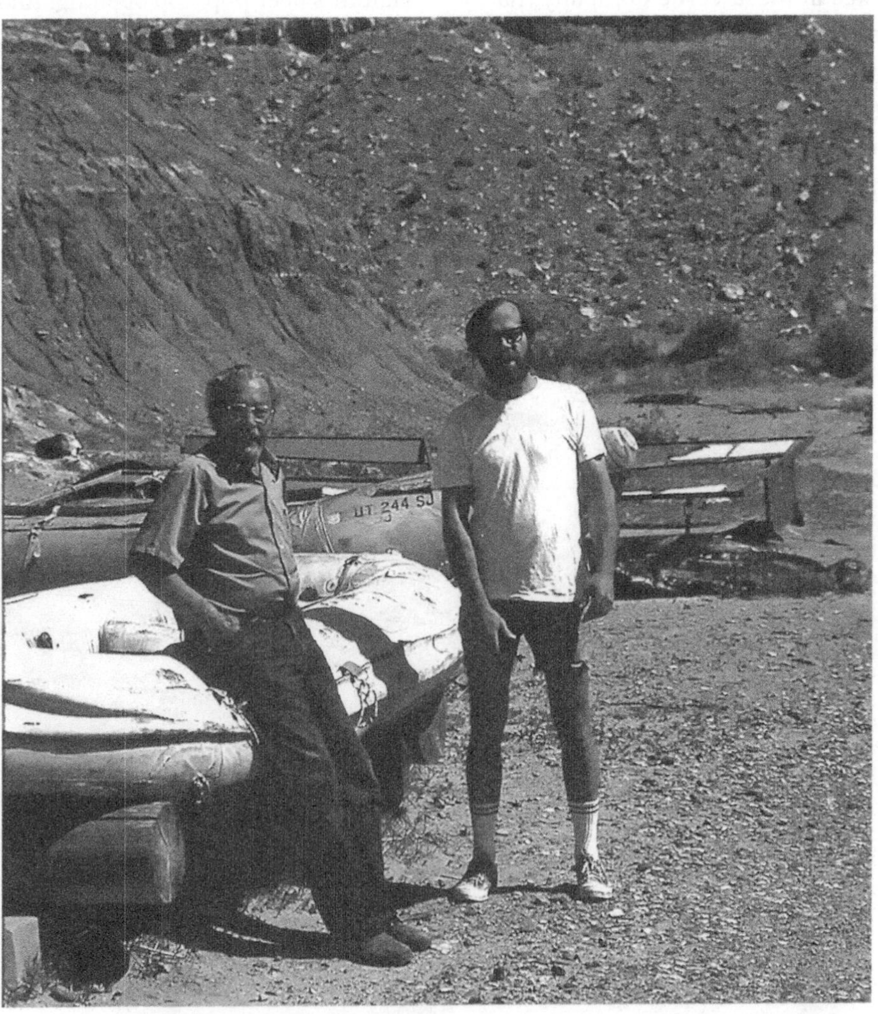

Figure 15.2 Kenny and Gary Matlock at Boat Camp No. 5, 1983. (H. Hoops photo)

The last time Kenny provided prices was in a reply letter in January, 1981 to Dave Thomas, Geology Instructor with Kettering Fairmont West High School from Kettering, Ohio. Thomas booked a one-day trip from Bluff to Mexican Hat for thirty participants. Kenny charged $33 per person but with his usual discount it came to $28.05 per person. He also encouraged a "Fool's Boat" for "motivated students" just like he had provided for me and my three buddies in 1969.

THE 1983 PECOS CONFERENCE

The 46th anniversary of the Pecos Conference was held in Bluff or actually at St. Christopher's Mission east of Bluff, on August 10-13, 1983 and co-sponsored by the new *"Edge of Cedars State Historical Monument"* in Blanding. "Now, on the fiftieth anniversary of J. O. Brew's landmark excavations at Alkali Ridge, in southeastern Utah, the Conference would finally be held in this part of the Southwest." The archaeological program held to tradition: "In keeping with the informal nature of the Pecos Conference, unwritten presentations are encouraged....Since meetings will be held outdoors beneath tent and ramada cover, there will be no provisions for slide presentations." [6]

On the morning the conference kicked off, Kenny Ross gave a rousing welcome address to the attendees and was roundly applauded following his talk. Although 158 names appeared on the registration sign-up sheets, attendance was estimated at 220. A special T-shirt was designed and sold (for $6.00) to commemorate the conference and "All agreed in was a TERRIFIC Conference!" [7] Among all the Who's Who in Archaeology that attended the conference, Kenny's old friend from the early days of the Explorers Camp, Bill Dickinson, made an appearance much to Kenny's surprise and delight. "Big Bill" was definitely a world-famous geologist and a recognized authority on the increasing acceptance of the theory of Plate Tectonics and his explanation of the Laramide Orogeny and the rise of the Colorado Plateau physiographic province (Figure 15.3).

In September 1983 following the Pecos Conference, archaeologist Art Rohn and his wife, Cheri, along with Charlie DeLorme and Gary Matlock ran a Cataract Canyon trip. Kenny declined to go and just did the driving and launched the trip from Potash boat landing.[8] Kenny never went out on another river run. Charlie DeLorme had pretty much taken on all the river running responsibilities by then and in 1983 Rob Rice was hired as a boatman. Rob said: "I came to Bluff in 1982 to work as an SCA (Student Conversation Assistant Ranger) for the BLM. Bill Davis picked me up at the Russian olive tree south of Monticello on the last leg of my hitch-hike to Bluff. He was the first Bluff person I met. I swamped a trip or two for Kenny that summer." [9]

NEW OWNERSHIP OF WRX

Charlie took over as manager of Wild Rivers Expeditions with a purchase contract in 1983. He later found out that Gary Matlock wasn't really aware of that arrangement! Charlie and Kenny completed the sale of WRX in 1985 although Kenny carried a portion of the note which was paid off in 1990. Marcus Coldsmith also began working that year as shop foreman as did Siste O'Malia as office secretary.

It was during the early 1980s that Charlie realized that Kenny had quite a following of well-known and highly respected scientists, scholars and celebrities who had their first river experiences with Kenny as their guide, colleague, and/or mentor. Some of these folks included: Bill Dickinson, Don Baars, David Lavender, Russ Dyer, Walt Zabriski, Al Lancaster, Art Rohn, Alton "Al" Hayes, Bob and Florence Lister, Jo Ben Wheat, David Noble, Polly Schaafsma, Ed Abbey, James A. Peterson, Orson Anderson, Gene Shoemaker, Sherman Wengerd, Dan Murphy,

Georgia O'Keeffe, and Eliot Porter, to name a few. Kenny knew them all and he introduced Charlie to most of them (Figure 15.4).[10]

Charlie was very thankful, and fortunate as he made acquaintances with those interpretive and knowledgeable folks in their particular scholarly endeavors who returned many times during Charlie's tenure as owner of Wild Rivers Expeditions. And when Louis L'Amour stopped by the old boat camp [Boat Camp No. 5] when Charlie was there (about 1984 or 1985) to ask Kenny questions about No Man's Mesa when he was writing *The Haunted Mesa* Charlie knew there was an even longer list of many great personal contacts who knew Kenny.[11]

Charlie said that "his first big break as the new owner of Wild Rivers was when he sold the President of the Board of Directors for the *Crow Canyon Archaeological Foundation* on the idea of an 'endowment' trip for the Crow Canyon Archaeological organization." [12] Funding was provided by Denver oil tycoon Raymond Duncan whereby the Crow Canyon Archaeological Center became independent from the Center for American Archaeology in 1985. As a not-for-profit organization, the Crow Canyon Archaeological Center focused on public education and outreach and their program fit perfectly with the goals that Charlie had set forth for Wild Rivers to provide the experience of boating down the scenic San Juan River with visiting ancient archaeological sites along the river corridor. The trips were soon called educational adventures, or "Ed-ventures." Susan DeLorme thought of the slogan "educational adventures, with an emphasis on pleasure" and the name stuck and remained a part of all the advertisement brochures.[13] Crow Canyon groups became a major client for Wild Rivers the entire time Charlie ran the river company. Wild Rivers Expeditions expanded from a few day trips a year to as many as twenty-eight day trips and numerous multi-day trips throughout the 1990s.[14]

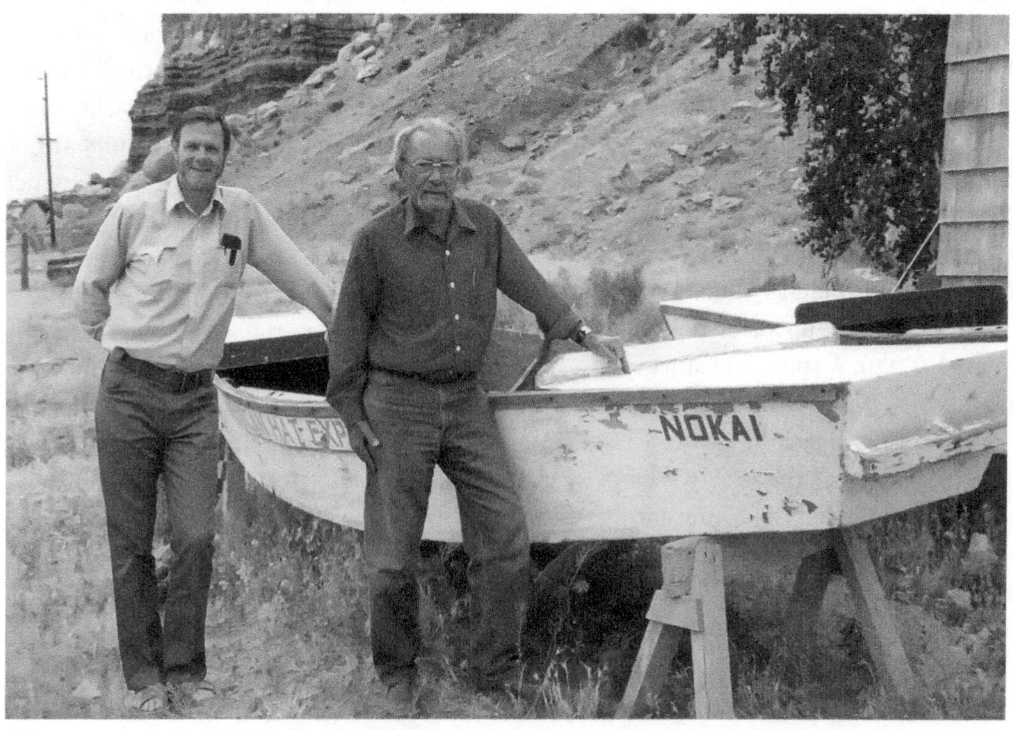

Figure 15.3 Bill Dickinson visited Kenny in 1983. (K. Ross collection)

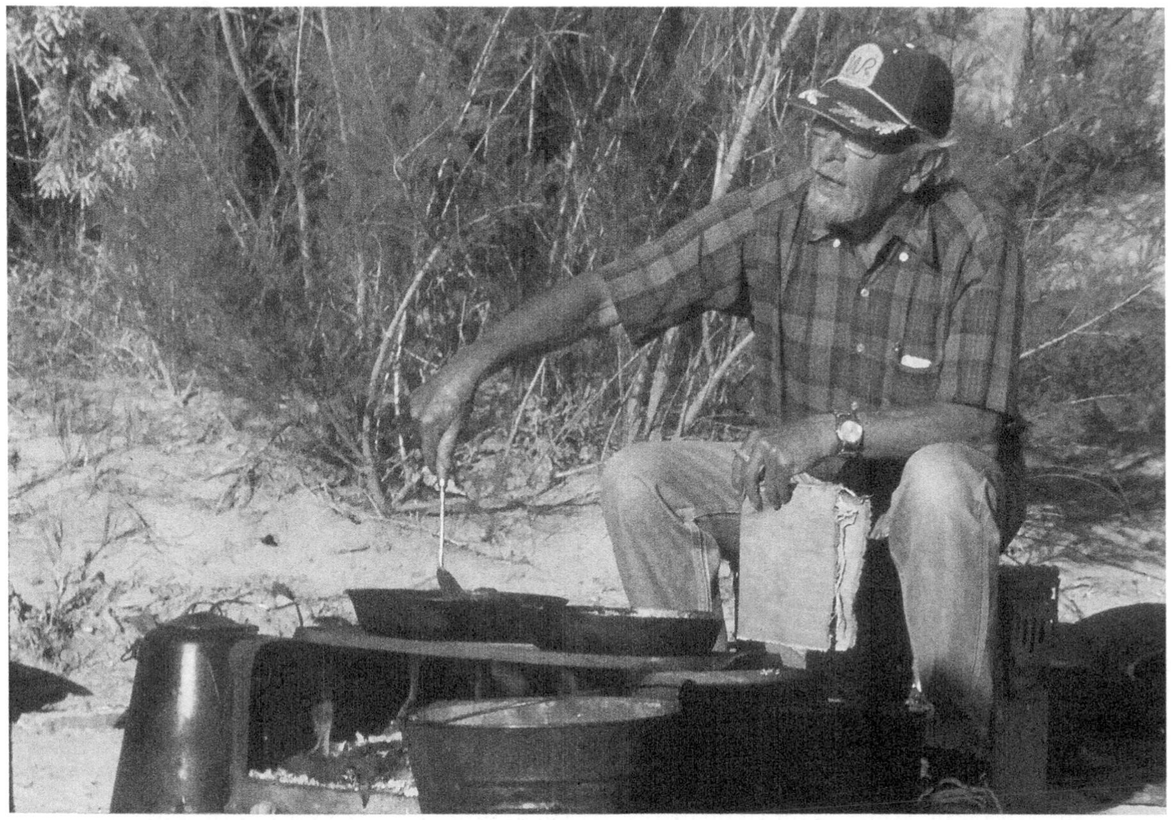

Figure 15.4 "Classic Kenny" in 1983 cookin' on a driftwood fire, cigarette in hand and tellin' a story. (Walt Zabriski photo)

Charlie and Susan located a larger property for sale in Bluff that was adjacent to the Recapture Lodge and moved there in 1986 to accommodate their ever-growing family and increased "family" of river guides. That location became *Boat Camp No. 6*, and remained so until 2012, when the company was sold to the present-day owners and relocated to Gail's old house under the cliffs across from the old Grat Wilson gas station (*Boat Camp No. 5*). In following the tradition in numbering boat camps, the present location would be known as *Boat Camp No. 7*.[15]

Boat Camp No. 6 was the location I remember as the biggest and best of the Wild Rivers days. But Kenny didn't make that move. My first time to stop by the new Wild Rivers office was in August, 1986 when Don Baars and I needed to go down Cataract Canyon from the Green River side to field check a new river guidebook we were making for Cataract Canyon and we needed to launch from Mineral Bottom. That was the first time I met Charlie DeLorme. He ran a J-rig (the "Mark I") on motor for our trip. I had brought my sixteen-foot Rogue with an aluminum frame with adjustable rails and diamond plated sides that caught Charlie's eye. We threw my boat on top of the J-rig and headed north. Marcus Coldsmith drove the truck and we followed in the old Dodge van (the "Nova-burner" as it was called) out on Big Flat Mesa north of Canyonlands National Park entrance and then down the narrow switchbacks of the Horse Thief Trail (my first time).

To help cover the river trip expenses, Charlie brought a family of five along as paying passengers. The river was agonizingly low and it was hot. We camped at Mineral Bottom that night and prepared dinner for the family and us. Then a late evening dust storm swirled through camp and blew the tent instructions away from the family who were in the process of erecting a very large one-size fits all tent. It was already apparent that they had never camped out before, and the instructions getting blown away confirmed that they had never set up the tent – until then. For the rest of the trip one of my funniest memories was to sit out on the J-rig with Charlie and Don in the evening, drinking gin and tonics while watching yet another way the tent would be set up as it was set up differently each day. It certainly made for good laughs.

The river was so low and the mosquitoes so fierce that we camped on exposed mid-river sand bars down to the head of Cataract Canyon. I also recall that it made it tough for much privacy for groover set ups, but we got by with some creative tarping. I made good runs through all the rapids including Mile Long and the Big Drops and when we got to the last night's camp, I rolled up my boat, threw it on the J-rig and we all boarded and made the slow run out together down to Hite Marina. Marcus had driven the "One-ton" pick-up and trailer and was waiting for us at the Hite boat ramp. Someone drove the passenger's car and after exchanging pleasantries – they drove off. We loaded the boats and gear on the trailer and in back of the pickup and headed back to Bluff. Charlie told me years later that he wanted to see if I knew how to boat as he had only heard about me through Don Baars at that point. I hadn't realized I had auditioned, but was happy to know I had passed the test.

THE SCREAMING YELLOW ZONKER

As new ownership of Wild Rivers had taken place along with its relocation into town, Kenny needed to find a buyer for his sixty-five-foot mobile home that set next to *Boat Camp No. 5*. On a fateful August morning in 1987, he closed the mobile home deal with Buck Wilson who had offered to pay cash and was going to haul it away and park it on the land his ex-wife, Inez Wilson, had in Bluff. Kenny had driven over that morning from Mancos in his little 1971 yellow Chevy Vega and was feeling happy about the sale. He went to the Turquoise Café for a celebratory lunch but instead got himself into a big argument with the owners, Bob and Barbara Boot.

There are quite a number of eccentric folks who have lived, or still live in Bluff, but none as caustic as the Boots. They seemed to have always been in a terrible mood and were notorious for taking out their anger on paying customers at the café, or their adjacent gas station. Bob ran the gas station and garage, while Barbara was in charge of the café, but it really didn't matter which business one visited, as the customers were almost surely in for some puckish lambasting. They genuinely disliked people, yet here they were in businesses requiring courtesy and daily contact with paying customers. A conundrum if there ever was one. Several years later they just up and left in the middle of the night to never be seen or heard from again. Strange couple indeed, and what follows can only be told by Doug and Don.

Doug Ross said that he had always been under the impression that Kenny tried to *kill* the Turquoise Café with his *Screaming Yellow Zonker*, "the crap-yellow goofy 70s vintage *Chevy Vega* little car that Kenny drove."[16] He continued:

> It's my understanding that Kenny went to the Turquoise and got into a major quarrel with Barbara (who ever went in there who didn't?) and went storming out the door, got in the car and popped it into gear, stuck his foot in it and hit the wall. I had come out to Mancos on a visit earlier and the old man was complaining to me that the gearshift was tricky because this little car was a three-speed floor-shift manual that had a little squeeze bar thingy (technical term) on the shifter that you held up to get the car into reverse...all the way to the left and down. The pull-up thing was because otherwise you could get the car into first gear (which was

> right next to the reverse) and the lock release thing was to prevent that. If you didn't pull the lever, it wouldn't go into reverse, but went into first [gear]. This was probably so that you couldn't accidentally shift into reverse while the car was moving. With this not working you could get the car into either first gear or into reverse. Well, it wasn't working right and the old man was fussing about it, so I found the problem (a little sheer pin inside the shaft which I replaced) and fixed it. So now after driving the damn thing for so long with the gear shift lock thing not working, Kenny had gotten used to fishing around and hunting for reverse by just pushing far to the left putting it into gear. Well I had fixed it and you had to pull the lever again. But you know how we all are, get into physical habits over time and don't think about it. Add some alcohol (of which there most certainly was) and anger and Kenny comes out of that café cooking along at about 10 over boiling, jumps into the car, slams it into reverse and floors it....only he forgot to pull the lever to put it into reverse and it was in first gear when he gives it the gas. I don't think he ever did it on purpose as the legend has grown to be believed. So, unless I am corrected by further research, (Charlie, Susan, Marcus, or Don) that's the story and I'm sticking to it. On the other hand, the old man could have really been pissed off enough to have done it on purpose and the gearshift had nothing to do with it....doesn't seem like him, alcohol or not, though. See how history gets screwed up? [17]

Of course, Bob Boot called the cops and Sheriff Claude Lacy showed up and arrested Kenny for willful destruction of property as Bob Boot immediately declared $2,000 in damages. The café had some cracks in the mortar of the cinder block building and damages were substantially less than claimed, but nevertheless, Kenny was hauled away to the county jail in Monticello. Doug was living in Portland, Oregon at that time and Don was working at the dude ranch in Durango. Charlie DeLorme called Don and told him what had happened and wanted Don to come over and get Kenny out of jail as Charlie was on his way for a Cataract Canyon trip with paying passengers. Don left work as soon as possible but it was really late so he pulled over on some turnout to get some sleep. The next morning Don bailed Kenny out of jail and they came down to Bluff and met with Buck Wilson who just then paid Kenny the cash for the trailer. The keys were locked in the Zonker, so they had to find the Deputy who unlocked the car by using a slim-jim tool. Kenny got in the Zonker and followed Don out of town and back to Mancos. That was the last time Kenny was in Bluff.[18]

After this ignominious exit Kenny retired to his home in Mancos never to return to Bluff. Doug returned to the Four Corners area via Portland, Oregon in 1988 to help at the Mancos home after Kenny had a stroke. He found a place to live nearby in Hesperus and he worked the Purgatory janitorial night shift until the spring thaw. He then worked two river trips for Steve Glass, and ended up getting *fired* because he was too *old school*. Doug called Charlie and told him he would take the boatman job offer Charlie had made earlier. That was around Memorial Day, 1989 and his first trip was a Crow Canyon six day.[19]

Doug and I did a bunch of trips together that year. That was also the year that Chinle Wash flashed so much silt and mud it actually "laminated" the San Juan all the way to Clay Hills [my definition]! For a week or better, the entire river ran no more than four to eight inches deep from bank to bank. It finally re-established its channels, but it took several weeks to do so. That fall the multi-day trips for Crow Canyon were headliners. But by then the river was so low we had to take boats out near the Mexican Hat rock, at a place one of the Wild Rivers crew had named "Dead Doggie" and we were triple stacking boats and always covered in mud and sweat. That was also the year of the infamous "People from Hell" trip that Jacque Ledbetter and Doug (and later Milt, much to his surprise) endured. But that's another story.[20]

ROSS RAPID & CANYON

But we still boat the old San Juan and love it – most of the time, when the wind isn't howling and there's some water in the creek. Kenny had a special place in the lower canyon he liked. He called it "False John's" and said he liked it because most folks never camped there. He was enamored by a thick bed of bluish-colored cherty limestone that cropped out at the base of the cliffs. He also liked to look at the stack of rocks at the back of the large boulder strewn side canyon that were probably the remnants of walls built by gold prospectors in the 1890s. But the main reason he stopped here so often was to scout, or "conn" the rapid, as there is a big flat rock at the bottom of the narrow rapid that could be a real problem, or even lead to flipping a boat in high water. And best of all, the nice sandy beach at the bottom right side of the rapid made a great camp spot.

Little did Kenny know that Don Baars and I had just published a new waterproof river guidebook for the San Juan River in 1986 and in it, we named his False John's canyon and rapid "Ross Rapid" as Don Baars really wanted to honor Kenny by naming something along the San Juan River after him and we both decided that this rapid should be pointed out to the novice boater, due to the big "surprise" rock at the bottom of the rapid. There aren't any noteworthy significant rapids of concern once leaving Mexican Hat until that point. Sure, there are a lot of small rock-dodging rapids that require paying attention to, but nothing that can capsize a boat – until Ross Rapid. A boater can get lulled into complacency by the straight forward-looking riffles, rapids and rocks to navigate around or between from the Goosenecks and beyond Honaker Trail, but when they reach this particular left bend – a sharp blind bend, this rapid holds a BIG surprise. A very large tilted flat slab of limestone sits at the bottom of the narrow cliff-lined rapid and potential disaster awaits the unwary boatman. So, we named it "Ross Rapid" in honor of Kenny. Unbeknownst to us at the time, the USGS had just completed a whole new set of so-called provisional topographic maps in the 7.5-minute Quadrangle Series and they included our naming the canyon and rapid after Kenny and added it to the official USGS map series. The funny thing is, it was never formally nominated as a name by us, but there it is, on all modern topographic maps – *Ross Rapid*. Don Baars stopped by the Ross home to give Kenny a signed copy of our new river log that summer of 1986, and he was so thrilled to see his name at one of his favorite canyons. It made Don and I feel good too.

THE COMMEMORATIVE TRIP

After making it through several strokes in 1988 and declining health Kenneth Irving Ross passed away on October 2, 1990 at a nursing home in Mancos. By the following year Doug and Don wanted to do something to commemorate Kenny so they decided to have a brass-plated plaque made up that said:

They organized a private river trip to go to the newly designated Ross Canyon where they planned to bolt the plaque on a "top secret, out of the way" limestone. The canyon that Kenny was so fond of and called "False John's," enters on river right and is definitely within the boundary of the Glen Canyon National Recreation Area that had been extended all the way upstream to Honaker Trail. No permits were obtained – they just did it. They scheduled their trip so that the plaque would be placed exactly one year after Kenny's passing. Doug commented:

> "The criminal element" that put up the Kenny plaque on October 2, 1991 was made up of me, Don, and five other old boatmen and friends of Kenny's. A gasoline generator was used to power

the drilling of the holes for the molly bolts with which we secured the illegal plaque, adding environmental insult to NPS/BLM/Federal injury. We were all worried that officialdom would come along and remove it, so we glued in the molly bolts with some sort of super welding glue and ground off the slot on the screws after they had been glued and screwed into the molly anchors. And just in case, before we put the thin brass plate on over the aluminum backing plate that we had made, the artist in the group sketched a raised middle finger on the aluminum and wrote "Well, Fuck you then!" in case somebody managed to pry the plaque loose. It hasn't happened yet as far as I know. I think it took a case of beer and most of a bottle of Scotch whisky to get that plaque up.[21]

The "criminal element" and plaque were duly noted by photographs prior to attaching the plaque to the rock face, alongside a can of Hamm's beer (Figure 15.5). I guess I was committed to taking a group of geologists on a field trip when this illegal act went down or else I would have been there too. I know where the plaque is and have visited it on numerous occasions. It has become a shrine of sorts for those of us who knew Kenny. We have always made the trek to the site and left beers and cigarettes in a protected undercut ledge above the plaque in honor of Kenny. How else does one honor a mentor and fellow boatman?

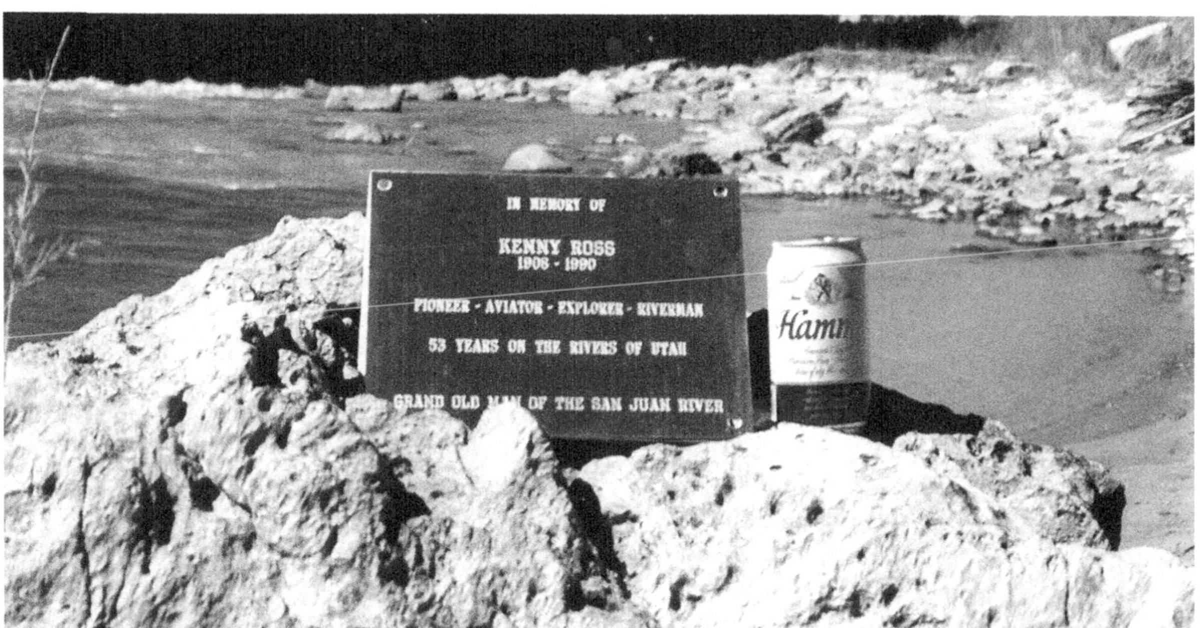

Figure 15.5 the commemorative plaque and can of beer before it was bolted into rock ledge, October 2, 1991. (Doug Ross photo)

IN MEMORY OF
KENNY ROSS
1908-1990
PIONEER-AVIATOR-EXPLORER-RIVERMAN
53 YEARS ON THE RIVERS OF UTAH
GRAND OLD MAN OF THE SAN JUAN RIVER

MILDRED

Mildred wasn't mentioned much in this story, but she has not been forgotten. Mildred, like so many wives of that era, was the glue that kept the family together and financially afloat. She taught school before she met Kenny in Durango in 1938. She taught at Mesa Verde School from 1938 to 1942. She taught off and on at the Mancos Elementary School until she was fired by the crazy school board in 1960, and then went to work for Social Services in Cortez. She was deeply involved in community projects. After her teaching career hit a roadblock, she found other work to help pay the bills beginning with the county social services. She finally found work for the Montezuma County Welfare Office from 1961 to the mid-1970s. She worked under the direction of Maureen McNeil and they became best of friends. Rev. J. Wayne Schwindt, who was a Methodist minister, also worked at the welfare office. He had been asked to transfer to somewhere out-of-state, but he declined the offer and decided to stay in Cortez. He eventually became the head of Social Programs for Montezuma County, but "he still did some preaching."[22] One of his sons, Mark, went to work for Kenny and built (welded) the steel frames for three of the J-rigs in the early 1970s (the Gemini, and the Mark I and II). And, of course, throughout the early years of Kenny's river trips, Mildred was always driving one of the shuttle vehicles with two young boys in tow. After Kenny moved away from the Explorers Camp and set up operations in Bluff, Mildred made grocery runs to Bluff, but ceased doing the shuttles. However, she loved the river, even though she only went from Bluff to Mexican Hat once! She wished she had been able to see more, including Rainbow Bridge, but that never happened. She was always on time (as much as possible considering road conditions) and was always cheery and compassionate with the guests. She was a true supporter of Kenny's endeavors and her boys.

I asked if Susan DeLorme had some thoughts to share about Mildred since they were both "river widows" during river season.

> Mildred was a sweet, sweet generous lady; she was often left by herself on the "back burner," while the more important "business of living" was tended. She and I shared a friendship, and a common history of growing up on the West Slope of Colorado, attending Western State College, and having the privilege of being married to obsessive river runners. We spent many Sunday afternoons and Mother's Days together, and if she was disturbed by the fact that I was the one who was there for her, brought her flowers, or made dinner, she didn't let on.[23]

Susan met Mildred when Doug and Don were college-aged. She continued about her daughters:

> Jen, Erin & Heather were most involved with Mildred and Ivy Jane was a baby. Mildred was long gone from the school in the years I worked there, and the girls were in class. We would have liked having her there, though! She was "proper, precise, and funny." She'd bring the girls little art projects, or take them out in the yard to show them interesting things – a new kind of lily, or bug, or animal. She talked to them as though they were grown-ups, and they liked that.
>
> I think she was also more private than I realized. While we talked about a lot of things, she avoided conversations about Chuck, except for, like Doug & Don, anecdotes about their childhood. In retrospect, I think a lot of what was going on was painful to her, and we might even have been her escape for relief, from a multitude of things that were bothersome. She fiercely loved those boys, but rarely had much to say about Kenny. They seemed to have an understanding, which Kenny gave voice to, more than she, which was to say "Mildred KNOWS where she belongs."
>
> When Kenny died, the boys agreed that I was the one who should be there for Mildred, while they tended to other things. She didn't complain. I love seeing what a beauty she was; she was a funny little

old lady by the time I met her. She still smoked, herself, apologetically, as she was convinced that it was cigarettes that killed Chuck. (Maybe that's just what she wanted to believe, or have me believe . . . doesn't matter . . . that's entirely her business. . .) She shared her version of stories of the boys' childhoods, her days, and Kenny's, at Mesa Verde, and her times as a school marm. She must have been a wonderful teacher. . . she was so good with my girls. . . they loved her, and the funny boxes of craft treasures she unearthed from her house, and shared with them.[24]

I asked Susan if she remembered my mother, Margaret, coming to Bluff over Easter weekend in 1992 and visiting with Mildred in the DeLorme's home at Wild Rivers. At that time my mother was 82, a farm girl from Missouri, another hard-working woman that had experienced the hardships of the Depression years before she met my dad, and then mostly tough, lean years the rest of the way. She was the mother of three daughters and now a riverman/geologist and loved to talk about the good ole days and family. My father was killed in a car crash in 1985, but was just about the same age as Kenny so she could relate to Mildred's loss.

I do remember that visit with your Mom (still a favorite of mine!!!) and Mildred. I had begged Mildred to stay the night with us, but she was well versed that Bluff was not her territory, and that little homing pigeon was determined to return to Mancos. She did possess a willfulness of character, which showed up; right up to the moment she died, after the boys had put her in a nursing home. She did NOT want to be there, and died within *hours* of being there! We always thought Doug got his stubborn nature from Kenny, but I'm not so sure.

I wish Mildred had gotten to know your Mom much sooner. Margaret was a wonderful soothing presence, who would have been such an enhancement in Mildred's lonely life.[25]

Mildred Skinner Ross died in June, 1993. Both she and Kenny are buried in the Cedar Grove Cemetery in Mancos, Colorado, next to Charles.

THE "OLD MAN"

As for Kenny Ross, I'm not sure what kind of legacy he left, but those of us who have grown to love that dirty, lively little old San Juan River, or hiked around these canyons, or the Mule Ear diatreme, or visited some petroglyph sites or Ancient Puebloan ruins, or happen to be aware of the fragile desert flora, or marvel at our incredible skies and canyon scenery just might have a little bit of "the old man" inside us. As far as fame and fortune goes, he had neither. He wasn't *the first* at doing anything, but he was certainly *among the firsts* who did. He was definitely in that pack of early river runners when it moved beyond a personal thrill to one of wanting to share this incredible country with others in perhaps the most spectacular means of getting there – by boat. I suppose in this regard he *was* one of the firsts to emphasize Educational Adventure Trips with knowledgeable and capable guides.

He never published more than a few articles in some boating enthusiasts' magazines, even though he was an incredible writer and prolific researcher. He was a self-made man in every sense of the phrase in developing an anthropologic knowledge of Southwest History – from the earliest Native Americans to the Spanish explorer's right up to those who were his contemporaries. He learned archaeology from the best and brightest. Same for geology, geophysics and his special awareness called naturalism. He was a student of all this and more, because he was also a teacher; a teacher of all things that mattered in life. He mentored and inspired an uncountable number of young men and boys into being respectful and knowledgeable of their surroundings and other people. Just read and listen to Kenny's description here, lost in an old mimeographed Explorers Camp brochure:

> The La Plata Mountains, the San Juan and San Miguel Ranges march in lofty procession up the backbone of the continent. From the top of any of the 13,000 ft peaks which surround the Explorers Gold King base camp one can see almost the whole extent of the Four Corners Country. The view westward is thrilling and unforgettable. From the mountain tops the land drops, at first abruptly, then in long canyon-cut slopes into the Mancos Valley. Beyond, it rises again into the high sage-covered plateaus of western Colorado and on into Utah's purple distances. The north half of the western horizon is rimmed by mountain masses: the La Sals, the Abajos, and Elk Ridge, which hide the Colorado River and its fantastic maze of tributary canyons from view. Southward, the eye slips past these to pick up the towering, colored buttes of Monument Valley, the dark line of Black Mesa: and strains to separate the more distant blue bulk of Navajo Mountain from the brighter blue of the sky. The vertical range of the viewer, from the chilly heights of his mountain peak to the hot depths of the Colorado Canyon at Lee's Ferry, is almost two miles, and the average height above sea level of all the land between is nearly a mile. Even on the clearest, brightest days a shimmering blue light welds the atmosphere to the landscape, thickening about distant buttes and mountains and pouring into the canyon-slashed earth. More often than not, magnificent cloud castles cast moving shadows across the land, their flat bottom planes reflecting the pink, orange and red barren rocks, the grayed purple of the sage seas, and the green of forested mountains. The Four Corners Country is truly a fabulous land of beauty and splendor. Its climates and interests are more varied, its population is smaller, its wilderness is more profound, and it is less explored than any other region of similar size in the United States. – Kenneth I. Ross, 1955

∞∞∞ THE END ∞∞∞

EPILOGUE

The scenic mysterious wonders of the canyon country in the greater Four Corners region of the central Colorado Plateau continue to attract visitors from around the world making tourism the number one industry for the area. National Parks from Grand Canyon to Zion to Arches have reached "overload" capacities during prime visitation periods such that several parks have been forced into considering "reservations" as the parks simply can't handle the increasing influx of visitors. It would have been hard for Kenny Ross to fathom that he would have to wait in vehicle *traffic jams* for lengthy periods just to gain entry into some parks and monuments that were seldom visited during his lifetime – if they were even recognized and named. There's just not enough parking space at visitor's centers, or main attraction sites to handle the throng of visitors eager to see with their own eyes and experience the grandeur of the greater Four Corners region. Most of the roadways Kenny bounced over for years have been paved and repaved and widened to handle the increased traffic. Small towns like Moab or Durango are tourist mecca-centers and provide scores of motels and restaurants of all price ranges and tastes. Even little old Bluff has seen a spurt in growth and like the rest of the region, property values continue to rise at almost exponential rates.

And the popularity of "back country" hiking or travel by four-wheel vehicles of all stripes has led to permits being required more and more to access the remotest of areas that Kenny Ross trail blazed, like Dark Canyon. The unimaginable rules and regulations he escaped from at Mesa Verde in 1946 have been multiplied to almost laughable levels now. As my father used to say, "the mountains were getting so crowded we might have to take our own rock to sit on!" And that was in the 1960s in reference to the Sandia Mountains east of Albuquerque, New Mexico. But it's almost true when it comes to boating down the San Juan River.

Moab and Bluff, are now hubs for river runners either queuing up to go down some section of the Colorado River if in Moab, or the San Juan if in Bluff. Commercial boating companies are particularly popular in the Moab area, while individual, or "private" boaters dominate the San Juan River. River running by private boat owners has exploded since the 1980s as a variety of boat types (inflatable rafts, kata-rafts, hard-hulled dories, canoes and kayaks) have been made affordable by numerous manufacturing companies. Boating down these rivers have become so popular that here, too, reservations must be made. Almost all western rivers now operate on a lottery system, where eager boaters must apply well in advance for the upcoming season's desired time to throw their boats on the water and enjoy the splendors of canyons seldom seen until the late 1940s.

Regarding just the San Juan River, the BLM Monticello office's outdoor recreation representative provided numerical statistics compiled from the time river permits began to be required in 1973 up though 2016 (the last year data had been compiled) and are shown in two graphs to illustrate the increase in river traffic on the San Juan River over this span of forty-three years (see Graphs 1 and 2).

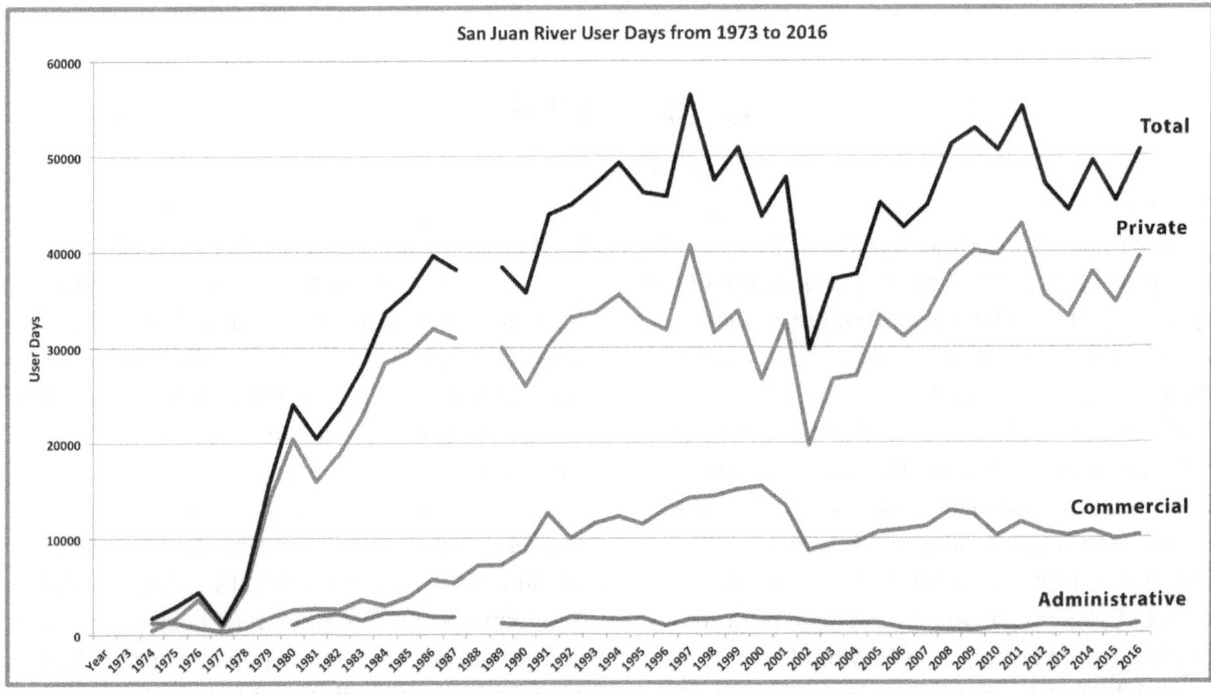

Graph 1 showing "User Days" by groups: Private, Commercial, Governmental [Admin] and Cumulative Total for San Juan River from 1973 to 2016. (Graph by GMS/TB from data provided by Silas Sparks, BLM Monticello office)

The numerical data was tallied by year and broken down into four categories of users: Private, Commercial, Administrative (Administrative includes BLM, Fish & Game, USGS or other governmental agencies) and Total cumulative use. Each user category was further divided into: 1) Trips: recorded launches from Sand Island and/or possibly Mexican Hat; 2) Users: head-count of total number of people leaving on boats from either Sand Island or Mexican Hat, and 3) User Days: tabulation of combined day use and multi-day use multiplied by head-count.

The BLM began tracking commercial launches and user days in 1973 and private launches the following year, but records were hit-and-miss until 1980, when commercial, private and "administrative" numbers were tracked. For that first year in 1973, only commercial trips were recorded. Just 21 trips were recorded with a total of 436 user days. By 1978, 211 private launches were recorded with total user days of 4,822 while commercial users had only 42 launches and 698 user days. Administrative use was scattered during this period and records are incomplete.

The year 1986 marked the first time that all three user categories were recorded and by then private launches (917) and total user days (31,997) far exceeded commercial (150 launches; 5,709 total user days) and Administrative (26 launches; 1,830 total user days). The combined total of user days for these three categories reached 39,536. Data again is incomplete (other than commercial use) from 1987 to 1991. Beginning in 1992 all categories are fully recorded though 2016 (the last year data was tabulated and made available).

Combined total user days for all three categories continued to stay above 35,000 for the 1987–1991 periods, and exceeded 40,000 for the first time in 1991 and reached a peak of 56,351 total user days in 1997 and dropped to under 30,000 in 2002. Charlie DeLorme said that 9/11/2001 had an incredible impact on all tourism and recreation activities in the U.S. that began immediately and certainly hit Wild Rivers with almost zero reservations for the 2002 season. Usage quickly resumed and by 2005 total user days exceeded 45,000. Since 2005 total user days for all three categories has remained well above 40,000 and reached 50,000 or more for almost half of the last twelve years.

Private use has always exceeded commercial or administrative use, and other than the "9/11" dip that affected all categories in 2002, private use has increased to a maximum of nearly 43,000 user days in 2011 (42,914) and over 30,000 for most of the past twelve years.

Actual numbers of launches (Trips) are shown in Graph 2 for all categories and complete data isn't meaningful until 1992 forward. Commercial launches have averaged 298 per year, but private launches have averaged around 993 launches per year, ranging from a high of nearly 1200 in 2011 to a low of 590 in 2002 and have been over 1000 per year since 2008. That's 333% more private trips than commercial trips for the twenty-four-year period 1992 to 2016!

Bottomline: The San Juan River is a popular river for private boaters who outnumber commercial boaters by over 300%. The San Juan has been deemed a river for novices or unskilled boaters and has attracted an ever-increasing number of the inexperienced crowd as a result (see SOCOTWA, Chapter 11). This overall rise in private boating has increased across most western rivers as boats and gear have become available and affordable to the general public. But the lazy little "spirited river" occasionally becomes a raging torrent and the unwary are forewarned. The BLM rangers are there at the Sand Island or Mexican Hat ramps to check the cluster of boaters in and make sure they all meet safety and camping regulations. However, with few rangers on the river and in times of need of assistance the inexperienced boaters will soon realize the San Juan canyon country remains some of the most remote territory in the southwestern United States.

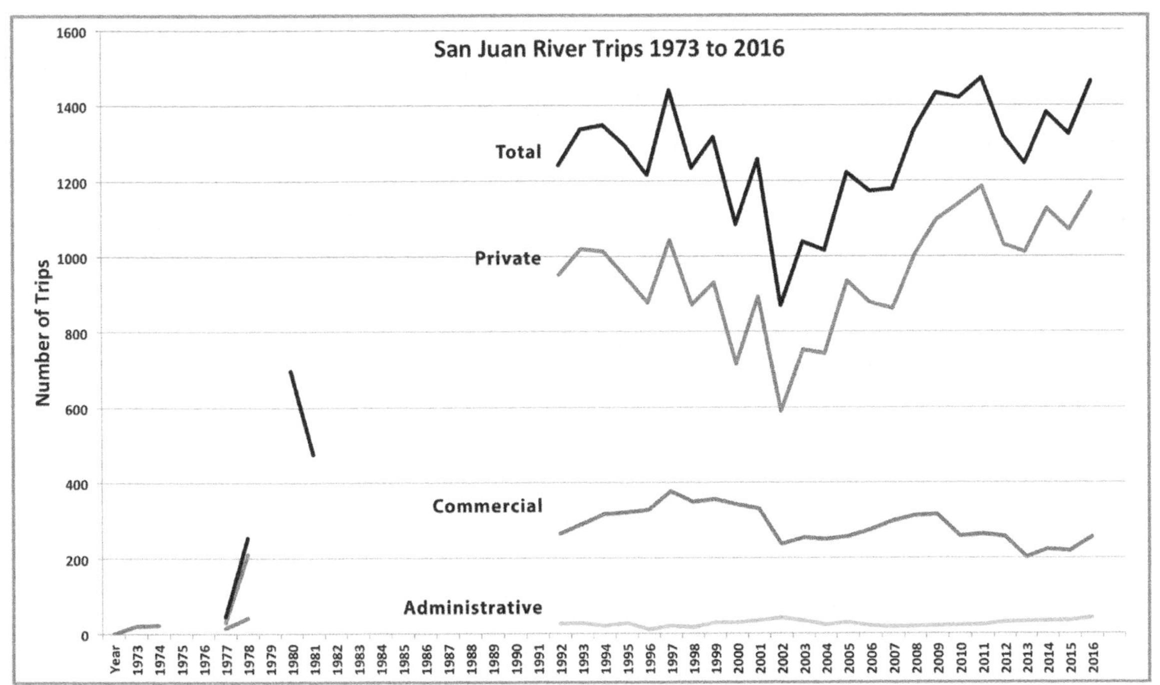

Graph 2 showing number of trips launched down San Juan River by Private, Commercial and Governmental [Admin] groups from 1973 to 2016. (Graph by GMS/TB from data provided by Silas Sparks, BLM Monticello office)

So, what's to become of this relatively small money-making enterprise on the San Juan River? After all, "user fees" are included in what tourists pay commercial outfitters or private groups pay to the BLM and also the Navajo Tribe. As shown on the graphs, commercial use is on a downward cycle driven by ever increasing rules, regulations and liability insurance. Private boating continues on the upswing. But what's the future of the river itself? Climate change combined with increased demands by upstream communities and diversions to meet long ignored water rights issues with Native American tribes continues to strain the deliverable water necessary to enjoy the San Juan, particularly in low flow years. Add to this dilemma the demands for overgrown downstream communities driven by the unrealistic requirements set forth in the ill-designed Colorado River Compact where water is released during non-boating months through the winter to meet downstream requirements. And then, just for fun, don't forget about that last eighteen miles of silted in flat water one must zigzag through and drag boats across constantly shifting silt bars to end their trip at Clay Hills.

Trips in the lower canyon used to be the "treasure" of the San Juan, but with all that muck waiting for the unwary, more and more boaters question whether it's worth the effort. Due to the silt problem in the lower canyon, more boaters are launching farther upstream, at Montezuma Creek or even Four Corners, but zigging around miles of braided stream channels with shorelines blanketed by impenetrable thickets of Russian olive trees just doesn't seem to replace the grandeur of floating through deep canyons of the Goosenecks with river access to Slickhorn Canyon or Grand Gulch.

And where did all those sand waves go? What used to be seen as a near year-round phenomenon is now only seen during big side canyon flash floods, and then they only last a few hours before they are gone. Man-made storage projects like Navajo Dam, and controlled releases have not allowed the river to retain its normal characteristics. The braided reaches of the San Juan have been modified by invasive plants and channelized such that the needed delicate balance of sediment load, gradient, and stream velocity have been destroyed. Continuation of controlled flows has reduced the hydrologic phenomenon to the point that it is only a memory of the past. With all these modifications and increasing demands, the future of an enjoyable boating trip down the San Juan River is rapidly becoming slim at best. Maybe we humans will wake up at some point and realize that building dams on high gradient, silt-laden streams wasn't a very good idea. We have created false hopes and problematical population centers in places that cannot be sustained with water that just isn't there. Islands of humanity built in a desert incapable of sustaining that number is just another example of humanity ignoring natural constraints.

ooooo

This story has relied heavily on documents from the Kenny Ross files. And yet, there are admittedly some discrepancies. Why did Kenny report that he was born in 1908 when his birth certificate clearly shows 1909? Did Kenny really go on two RBMV San Juan River trips in 1934? Available documents provide conflicting numbers of trips. Did he ever really make it to the Yucatan with archaeologist Earl Morris? Was he part of an exploratory group on the Yukon River in 1931 with Bayne Beauchamp? Why did he tell Dock Marston he did a Cataract Canyon river trip in 1951, when his second trip down this section of river following his 1949 adventure was in 1953? We will just never know for sure.

As a reminder to the reader, Kenny was first and foremost a wonderful storyteller – a talent he picked up early in his career listening to Jess Nusbaum's fireside talks. Kenny then refined his art over the years by expounding on his own experiences to interested folks sitting around campfires somewhere on a beach on the San Juan River or in Cataract Canyon.

In reflecting on Kenny's storytelling abilities and witnessing his two son's similar gifts, as well as numerous other river guides tales and my own stories, I am best reminded of my good friend and fellow river guide Hanley Begay, a proud Navajo man, who when asked by a television documentarian about what he had said, replied "DO YOU WANT ME TO TELL YOU THE TRUTH, OR WHAT I TOLD YOU YESTERDAY?"

I suppose that's as good a way as any to end this story of the Riverman - Kenny Ross.

∞∞∞

APPENDICES

APPENDIX I

TABLE 1

SAN JUAN RIVER TO LEES FERRY

Length of San Juan River from headwaters to mouth with Colorado River and from this confluence to Lees Ferry Boat Ramp, AZ; measured by using *Esri ArcGIS* USGS topographic maps. Distance in miles to the nearest 1/10th mile (528 ft); Headwaters of West Fork of San Juan River to confluence with East Fork and Wolf Creek confluence = 17.3 miles; all tributaries listed are from their mouths (pre-dams) with the San Juan River or the Colorado River below the confluence.

	Distance (in miles) Below Headwaters /////	Distance (in miles) Above -	
NAME	CUMULATIVE	SJ&C Confluence	Lees Ferry
Headwaters of SJR (West Fork of SJR)	0.0	406.6	485.6
Pagosa Springs Bridge; U.S. Hwy 160	28.5	378.1	457.1
Navajo River	55.1	351.5	430.5
Piedra River	75.2	331.4	410.4
Pine River	99.3	307.3	386.3
Dam wall (6085' full pool; 1856 m)	102.5	304.1	383.1
Animas River	147.9	258.7	337.7
La Plata River	151.0	255.6	334.6
Shiprock Bridge; U.S. Hwy 491 & 64	182.5	224.1	303.1
Mancos River	212.7	193.9	272.9
NM/CO Stateline	215.0	191.6	270.6
CO/UT Stateline:	218.1	188.5	267.5
McElmo Creek	237.9	168.7	247.7
Montezuma Creek	247.3	159.3	238.3
Swinging Bridge (footbridge)	257.7	148.9	227.9
Launch point across from Mission	260.4	146.2	225.2
Cottonwood Creek (Bluff)	261.8	144.8	223.8
Buck Creek (Sand Island BLM Boat Ramp)	265.2	141.4	220.4
U.S. Hwy 191 Bridge (west of Bluff)	265.7	140.9	219.9
Butler Wash	269.5	137.1	216.1
Comb Ridge @ Wingate SS (RL)	272.3	134.3	213.3
Chinle Wash	*274.1	*132.5	211.5
KGS Drill Site	280.4	126.2	205.2
Eight Foot Rapid	282.7	123.9	202.9
Mexican Hat BLM Boat Landing	292.2	114.4	193.4
Gypsum Creek (Top: Rapid)	292.7	113.9	192.9
Mexican Hat "Goodridge" Bridge; Hwy 163	293.3	113.3	192.3
Honaker Trail (main camp)	310.3	96.3	175.3
Ross Rapid	318.2	88.4	167.4
"Bert Loper's Government Rapid"	324.1	82.5	161.5
Mouth: Johns Canyon	324.5	82.1	161.1
Top: Government Rapid	329.4	77.2	156.2
Top: Slickhorn Canyon	332.2	74.4	153.4
Grand Gulch	336.0	70.6	149.6
Oljeto Wash	341.6	65.0	144.0

TABLE 1 (continued)

	Distance (in miles) Below Headwaters /////	Distance (in miles) Above -	
NAME	**CUMULATIVE**	**SJ&C Confluence**	**Lees Ferry**
Clay Hills boat ramp:	349.2	57.4	136.4
Copper Canyon	360.0	46.6	125.6
Piute Canyon (Top: Piute Rapid)	385.2	21.4	100.4
Desha Canyon (Top: Syncline Rapid)	391.7	14.9	93.9
Cha Canyon (Top: Thirteen Foot Rapid)	395.1	11.5	90.5
Nasja Creek (fresh water spring)	401.0	5.6	84.6
Confluence: SJR & CR	*406.6	0.0	79.0
(*Miser, 1924, surveyed distance from the mouth of Chinle Wash to SJR & CR confluence = 132.5 miles)			
Forbidding Canyon (RL) from south	416.3	9.7	69.3
Kane Creek mouth (RR pre-lake fill)	444.4	37.8	41.2
Padre Canyon (RR) from north	445.1	38.5	40.5
Warm Creek (RR) from NW	457.1	50.5	28.5
Utah-Arizona Stateline	457.2	50.6	28.4
(SWNW Sec 7-T43S-R5E; San Juan Co., UT and nenw Sec 34-T42N-R9E; Coconino Co., AZ); CR turns south)			
Wahweap Creek (RR) from N (bay)	468.2	61.6	17.4
Glen Canyon Dam Wall	469.6	63.0	16.0
Lees Ferry Boat Ramp (RR)	485.6	79.0	0.0

Measured distances and intervals compiled by Gene M. Stevenson

Lees Ferry landing to Bluff Cottonwood Wash (485.6 – 261.8) = **223.8 miles**
[Kenny Ross advertised a 225 mile long trip from Bluff to Lees Ferry in his Explorers Camp, Southwest Explorations brochures written from 1949 to 1955]

River boat takeout below dam site was closed in 1957 & diverted to Warm Creek, then Kane Creek via old uranium miner's road following Crosby Canyon to the southwest or a Jeep trail to northwest on ridge north of Wagon Box Canyon on Alstrom Point. Trails lead to unpaved CR 277 west to Glen Canyon City which is located along east side of U.S. Highway 89 that heads west to Kanab or east back across Glen Canyon Bridge, completed in 1959.

☙ APPENDIX I ❧

TABLE 2

CATARACT & GLEN CANYONS

FROM CONFLUENCE OF GREEN & COLORADO RIVERS TO LEES FERRY

	Distance (in miles) Below Confluence	/////	Distance (in miles) Above-
NAME	INTERVAL	Downstream	Lees Ferry
Confluence GR & CR	0.0	0.0	218.7
Upper Spanish Bottom (RR)	3.1	3.1	215.6
Lower Spanish Bottom (RR)	0.3	3.4	215.3
Lower Red Lake Canyon (RL)	0.4	3.8	214.9
"Y" Canyon (RL)	4.1	7.9	210.8
Cross Canyon (RL)	0.2	8.1	210.6
"Crum Dome" Canyon	1.7	9.8	208.9
Range Canyon (RR)	2.1	11.9	206.8
Teapot Canyon (RR)	2.0	13.9	204.8
Imperial Canyon (RL)	2.6	16.5	202.2
Calf Canyon (RR)	1.6	18.1	200.6
Gypsum Canyon (RL)	1.9	20.0	198.7
3600 ft contour	1.0	21.0	197.7
Palmer Canyon (RL)	0.1	21.1	197.6
Easter Pasture Canyon (RR)	2.0	23.1	195.6
Clearwater Canyon (RR)	1.6	24.7	194.0
Bowdie Canyon (RL)	1.3	26.0	192.7
Cove Canyon (RR)	4.3	30.3	188.4
Dark Canyon (RL)	3.4	33.7	185.0
Sheep Canyon [RL end of Cataract Cyn; last rapid]	**5.9**	**39.6**	**179.1**
Rock Canyon [RR in Narrow Canyon]	4.4	44.0	174.7
Colorado River Bridge [Hite Crossing]	1.8	45.8	172.9
Dirty Devil River (RR) [top: Glen Canyon]	1.1	46.9	171.8
GLEN CANYON [171.8 MILES or ~172.0 miles]			
North Wash (RR)	2.0	48.9	169.8
Farley Canyon (RL)	4.7	53.6	165.1
White Canyon (RL)	0.2	53.8	164.9
Trachyte Creek (RR) [Old Hite]	1.3	55.1	163.6
Twomile Canyon (RR)	2.3	57.4	161.3
Fourmile Canyon (RR)	1.3	58.7	160.0
Scorup Canyon (RL)	3.8	62.5	156.2
Red Canyon (Good Hope Bay; RL)	4.4	66.9	151.8
Tickaboo Creek (mid-delta) (RR)	1.6	68.5	150.2
Sevenmile Creek (RR)	9.4	77.9	140.8
Warm Springs Canyon (RR)	2.6	80.5	138.2
Knowles Canyon (RL)	2.2	82.7	136.0
Forgotten Canyon (RL) Smith Fork (RL)	2.3	85.0	133.7
Crystal Springs Canyon (RL)	1.9	86.9	131.8

TABLE 2: CATARACT & GLEN CANYONS (continued)
FROM CONFLUENCE OF GREEN & COLORADO RIVERS TO LEES FERRY

	Distance (in miles) Below Confluence	/////	Distance (in miles) Above -
NAME	INTERVAL	Downstream	Lees Ferry
Hansen Creek (RR)	0.3	87.2	131.5
Moqui Canyon (RL)	5.0	92.2	126.5
Center-Bullfrog Bay (RR)	4.5	96.7	122.0
Halls Crossing (RL)	1.0	97.7	121.0
Halls Creek (RR)	1.2	98.9	119.8
Lost Eden Canyon (RR)	0.3	99.2	119.5
Lake Canyon (RL)	5.0	104.2	114.5
Annie's Canyon (RR)	5.5	109.7	109.0
Slick Rock Canyon (RL)	3.2	112.9	105.8
Iceberg Canyon (RL)	3.2	116.1	102.6
THE RINCON (RL)	1.7	117.8	100.9
Long Canyon/Navajo Creek (top of Big Bend, RR)	4.3	122.1	96.6
ESCALANTE RIVER (RR)	7.3	129.4	89.3
Ribbon Canyon (RL)	2.7	132.1	86.6
Hole-in-the-rock (RR)	1.3	133.4	85.3
Cottonwood Canyon (RL)	1.4	134.8	83.9
Llewellyn Gulch (RR)	1.0	135.8	82.9
Confluence of SJR & CR	**3.9**	**139.7/0.0**	**79.0**
Reflection Canyon (RR) from north	1.0	140.7	78.0
Hidden Passage (RR) from NW	1.0	141.7	77.0
Music Temple (RL) from SW	0.3	142.0	76.7
Anasazi Canyon (RL) from south	2.2	144.2	74.5
Twilight Canyon (RR) from north	2.8	147.0	71.7
Forbidding Canyon (RL) from south	2.4	149.4	69.3
Cascade Canyon (RR) from north	0.8	150.2	68.5
Driftwood Canyon (RR) from north	1.3	151.5	67.2
Cathedral Canyon (RL) from south	0.6	152.1	66.6
Little Arch Canyon (RL) from south	2.0	154.1	64.6
Balanced Rock Canyon (RR) from north	0.1	154.2	64.5
Mountain Sheep Canyon (RL) from south	0.6	154.8	63.9
Teddys Horse Pasture (RR) north	2.4	157.2	61.5
Cornerstone Canyon (RR) from north	1.3	158.5	60.2
Wetherill Canyon (RL) from south	1.2	159.7	59.0
Grotto Canyon (RL) from south	0.9	160.6	58.1
Dungeon Canyon (RL) from south	0.9	161.5	57.2
Three canyons converge from north (RR) Dry Rock Canyon, Middle Rock Canyon & Rock Canyon			
Rock Creek Bay (RR)	1.2	162.7	56.0
Friendship Cove (RR) from north	1.4	164.1	54.6
West Canyon (RL) S side Cummings Mesa	3.4	167.5	51.2
Last Chance Creek (RR) N Last Chance Bay	1.6	169.1	49.6
River loops S around Gooseneck Pt & on RL is Dominguez Butte & Padre Butte			

TABLE 2: CATARACT & GLEN CANYONS (continued)
FROM CONFLUENCE OF GREEN & COLORADO RIVERS TO LEES FERRY

	Distance (in miles) Below Confluence	/////	Distance (in miles) Above -
NAME	INTERVAL	Downstream	Lees Ferry
Kane Creek mouth (RR pre-lake fill)	8.4	177.5	41.2
Padre Canyon (RR) from north	0.7	178.2	40.5
Labyrinth Canyon (RL) from south	5.5	183.7	35.0
Gunsight Canyon (RR) from north	1.1	185.3	33.4
Warm Creek (RR) from NW	5.4	190.2	28.5
Utah-Arizona Stateline	0.1	190.3	28.4
(SWNW Sec 7-T43S-R5E; San Juan Co., UT and nenw Sec 34-T42N-R9E; Coconino Co., AZ); CR turns south			
Navajo Canyon (RL) from E-SE	2.7	193.0	25.7
Navajo Canyon defines southwestern edge of Rainbow Plateau upon which Cummings Mesa lies			
Antelope Canyon (RL) from SE	5.7	198.7	20.0
Wahweap Creek (RR) from N (bay)	2.6	201.3	17.4
Glen Canyon Dam	1.4	202.7	16.0
Ferry Swale Canyon (RR) from NW	5.0	207.7	11.0
Water Holes Canyon (RL) from SE	7.5	215.2	3.5
Lees Ferry Boat Ramp (RR)	3.5	218.7	0.0

Measured distances and intervals compiled by Gene M. Stevenson

NOTES TO TABLES

NOTE 1: Confluence of Green and Colorado Rivers measured 216.55 miles above Lees Ferry on 1921 USGS Chenoweth Survey; River Miles (RM) referenced in text pertaining to Cataract Canyon compares Kenny Ross Group River log, 1949 to Don Baars, 1987 river map. I have re-measured RM distances above Lees Ferry using *Esri Arc/GIS* topographic maps that reflects an approximate two mile discrepancy;[CR & GR Confluence: GMS 218.7 vs USGS 216.55 or difference of 2.15 miles].

NOTE 2: Cataract Canyon typically measured from confluence of Green and Colorado Rivers to Sheep Canyon in Mille Crag Bend – a distance of 39.6 river miles and commonly rounded to approximately 40.0 miles. Actual distance begins at mouth of Lower Red Lake Canyon to Sheep Canyon – a distance of 35.8 miles or rounded to approximately 36.0 miles.

APPENDIX I

TABLE 3

COLORADO RIVER FROM CONFLUENCE TO DOLORES RIVER

	Distance (in miles) Above Confluence	
NAME	INTERVAL	CUMULATIVE
Confluence GR & CR	0.0	0.0
Elephant Canyon (RL)	3.0	3.0
Salt Creek (RL)	0.5	3.5
Monument Basin (RR)	12.1	15.6
Indian Creek (RL)	1.1	16.7
Dog Leg Canyon (RR)	4.8	21.5
Gooseberry Canyon (RR)	0.5	22.0
Buck Canyon (RR)	1.1	23.1
Lathrop Canyon (RR)	0.8	23.9
Horsethief Canyon (RL)	2.6	26.5
Lockhart Canyon (RL)	0.4	26.9
Little Bridge Canyon (RR)	3.5	30.4
Musselman Canyon (RR)	2.0	32.4
Shafer Canyon (RR)	2.8	35.2
Shafer Basin K-Evap Ponds (RR)	10.8	45-46
Potash Boat Ramp (RR)	2.0	**48.0**
Potash Creek/mill site (RR)	1.1	49.1
Long Canyon (RR)	2.2	51.3
Day Canyon (RR)	2.1	53.4
Gold Bar Canyon (RR)	0.9	54.3
Bootlegger Canyon (RR)	0.7	55.0
Kane Springs Canyon (RL)	4.2	59.2
"The Portal"	**3.1**	**62.3**
Moab: Bridge over Colorado River	2.8	65.1
Upstream boat ramp (RR)	0.7	65.8
Negro Bill Canyon (RL)	2.5	68.3
Jackass Canyon (RL)	1.9	70.2
Salt Wash (RR)	6.0	76.2
Castle Creek (RL) **Whites Rapid**	2.9	79.1
Professor Creek (RL)	5.7	84.8
Onion Creek (RL)	1.7	86.5
Bull Canyon (RR)	6.6	93.1
Pole Canyon (RL)	1.7	94.8
Dewey Bridge	1.3	96.1
Dolores River (RL)	1.6	97.7
Sagers Wash (RR)	2.8	100.5

Measured distances and intervals compiled by Gene M. Stevenson

Meander Canyon is defined by the distance from the GR/CR Confluence to "the Portal" near Moab (~62.3 miles).
[River Miles (RM) average ~1.1 mile discrepancy with Baars, 1987 river log]

⁂ APPENDIX I ⁂

TABLE 4

GREEN RIVER, UTAH TO CONFLUENCE WITH COLORADO RIVER

		Distance (in miles) above -	
NAME	INTERVAL	CUMULATIVE	Lees Ferry
Green River Park (RR) [boat ramp]	0.0	122.0	340.7
Railroad Bridge	0.2	121.8	340.5
I-70 Bridge	0.8	121.0	339.7
Crystal Geyser (RL)	3.7	117.3	336.0
Little Grand Wash (RL)	0.5	116.8	335.5
Salt Wash (RL)	9.6	107.2	325.9
San Rafael River (RR) [begin Labyrinth Canyon]	**8.7**	**98.5**	**317.2**
Red Wash (RL)	2.2	96.3	315.0
Three Canyon Wash (Trin-Alcove Bend) (RR)	5.0	91.3	310.0
Bull Hollow (RR)	5.8	85.5	304.2
Keg Spring Canyon (RR)	5.2	80.3	299.0
Hey Joe Canyon (RL)	3.2	77.1	295.8
Top: Neck of Bowknot Bend (RR)	5.8	71.3	290.0
Spring Canyon (RL)	2.6	68.7	287.4
Two-mile Canyon	6.7	62.0	280.7
Horseshoe Canyon (RR)	1.6	60.4	279.1
Hell Roaring Canyon (RL)	4.0	56.4	275.1
Mineral Canyon (RL)	3.1	53.3	272.0
Horsethief Trail **Mineral Bottom** (RL) **[boat ramp]**	0.5	52.8	271.5
Mouth Upheaval Canyon (RL) [Upheaval Btm]	7.9	44.9	263.6
Mid-loop Fort Bottom [end of Labyrinth Canyon]	**3.6**	**41.3**	**260.0**
	LABYRINTH CANYON [57.2 MILES]		
Potato Bottom Basin (RL)	3.1	38.2	256.9
Queen Anne Btm (RL)	3.7	34.5	253.2
Valentine Btm (RR)	4.7	29.8	248.5
Holeman Spring Basin (RL)	1.3	28.5	247.2
Lwr Tuxedo Btm [Turks Head loop]	4.2	24.3	243.0
Deadhorse Canyon (RR)	4.3	20.0	238.7
Horse Canyon (RR)	5.6	14.4	233.1
Jasper Canyon (RR)	4.7	9.7	228.4
Water Canyon (RR)	5.1	4.6	223.3
Confluence to Water Cyn [end: Stillwater Canyon]	**4.6**	**0.0**	**218.7**
	STILLWATER CANYON [41.3 MILES]		

Measured distances and intervals compiled by Gene M. Stevenson

Labyrinth Canyon (~ 57.2 miles) is defined from the mouth of the San Rafael River to the middle of Fort Bottom.
Stillwater Canyon (~41.3 miles) is defined from the middle of Fort Bottom to GR/CR confluence.

APPENDIX II

Stratigraphic Column of Geologic Formations & Ages in the Four Corners Region

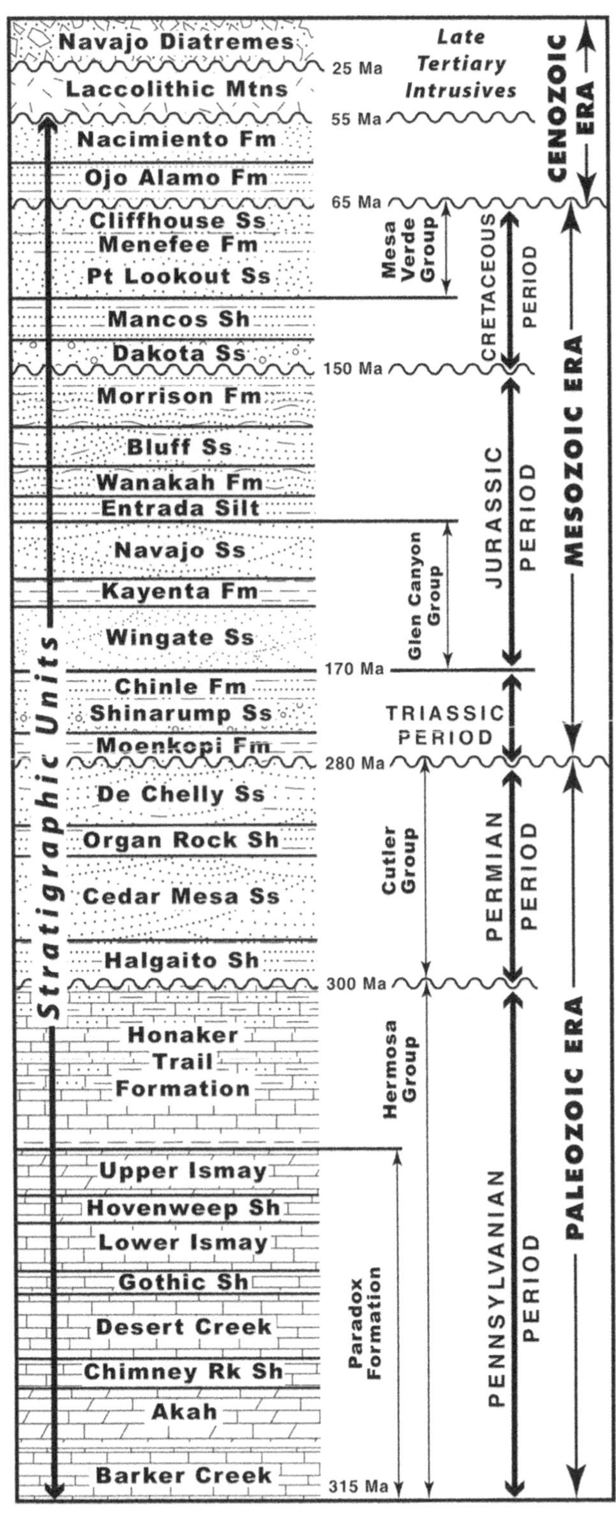

APPENDIX III

Geologic Time:

Ma = Million annuals or millions of years ago; example: expressed as 315 Ma (Pennsylvanian Epoch)

Ga = Giga annuals, or billions of years ago; example: 1.7 Ga or 1750 Ma (Paleoproterozoic Era)

GEOLOGIC TIME SCALE

CENOZOIC

AGE (Ma): 5, 10, 15, 20, 25, 30, 35, 40, 45, 50, 55, 60, 65

PERIOD		EPOCH		PICKS (Ma)
QUATERNARY		HOLOCENE		0.01
		PLEISTOCENE		1.8, 2.6
TERTIARY	NEOGENE	PLIOCENE		3.6, 5.3
		MIOCENE	L	7.2, 11.6
			M	13.8, 16.0
			E	20.4, 23.0
	PALEOGENE	OLIGOCENE	L	28.4
			E	33.9
		EOCENE	L	37.2
			M	40.4, 48.6
			E	55.8
		PALEOCENE	L	58.7
			M	61.7
			E	65.5

MESOZOIC

AGE (Ma): 70, 80, 90, 100, 110, 120, 130, 140, 150, 160, 170, 180, 190, 200, 210, 220, 230, 240, 250

PERIOD	EPOCH	PICKS (Ma)
CRETACEOUS	LATE	65.5, 70.6, 83.5, 85.8, 89.3, 93.5, 99.6
	EARLY	112, 125, 130, 136, 140, 145.5
JURASSIC	LATE	151, 156, 161
	MIDDLE	165, 168, 172, 176
	EARLY	183, 190, 197, 201.6
TRIASSIC	LATE	204, 228, 235
	MIDDLE	241, 245
	EARLY	250, 251.0

PALEOZOIC

AGE (Ma): 260, 280, 300, 320, 340, 360, 380, 400, 420, 440, 460, 480, 500, 520, 540

PERIOD	EPOCH	PICKS (Ma)
PERMIAN	L	251, 254, 260
	M	266, 268, 271
	E	276, 284, 297, 299.0
CARBONIFEROUS	PENNSYLVANIAN	304, 306, 312, 318
	MISSISSIPPIAN	326, 345, 359
DEVONIAN	L	374, 385
	M	392, 398
	E	407, 411, 416
SILURIAN	L	419, 421
	M	423, 426, 428
	E	436, 439, 444
ORDOVICIAN	L	446, 455, 461
	M	468, 472
	E	479, 488
CAMBRIAN*	Furongian	492, 496, 501
	Series 3	503, 507, 510
	Series 2	517, 521
	Terreneuvian	535, 542

PRECAMBRIAN

AGE (Ma): 750, 1000, 1250, 1500, 1750, 2000, 2250, 2500, 2750, 3000, 3250, 3500, 3750

EON	ERA	BDY. AGES (Ma)
PROTEROZOIC	NEOPROTEROZOIC	542, 630, 850, 1000
	MESOPROTEROZOIC	1200, 1400, 1600
	PALEOPROTEROZOIC	1800, 2050, 2300, 2500
ARCHEAN	NEOARCHEAN	2800
	MESOARCHEAN	3200
	PALEOARCHEAN	3600
	EOARCHEAN	3850
HADEAN		

(Modified from Geological Society of America 2009 Geologic Time Scale)

APPENDIX IV

GLOSSARY OF GEOLOGIC AND RIVER RELATED TERMS

RIVER RELATED TERMS

line/lining: if conditions appear too dangerous to run a rapid, an alternative is to walk along the shoreline with lines tied to bow and stern and carefully sneak the boat down the side of the rapid; commonly requires one person to remain on the boat to shove boat clear of rocks while others handle the lines.

portage; portaging: the labor-intensive practice of carrying the boat and all the cargo over land to avoid a rapid considered too dangerous to negotiate with all contents aboard the craft.

quicksand: forms in saturated loose sand when the sand is suddenly agitated. When water in the sand cannot escape, it creates a liquefied soil that loses strength and cannot support weight. The saturated sediment may appear solid until a sudden change in pressure initiates **liquefaction** (like your body weight). The object (you) in the liquefied sand will sink to a level at which the weight of the object is equal to the weight of the displaced sand/water mix and the submerged object floats due to buoyancy.

rapids: are hydrological cascading features between smoothly flowing parts of a river. Virtually all rapids on the San Juan River or the Colorado River through Cataract Canyon were formed by large rocks and boulders carried into the river from side canyons. Typically large summer monsoonal thunderstorms and infrequent winter storms contribute the majority of the debris fans into the river, thereby constricting the river by depositing a boulder strewn fan of debris. As the river has narrowed the debris fan creates a modified dam that backs up the river and the current slows above the rapid. The slowed pool of water then accelerates over and around the scattered boulders forming a rapid before the water carried in the river returns to a widened and unobstructed gradient where the flow slows back down.

ran rapids, running rapids or **shooting rapids:** The act of navigating a boat between and over the large rocks that form the constricted and accelerated volume of river water, or rapids.

sand waves or sand rollers: this phenomenon used to commonly occur in the San Juan River, but is seldom seen due to controlled releases from dams and diversions upstream. Sand waves are uncommon on most rivers around the world. They are the products of a perfect combination of stream bed gradient, suspended clay, silt, and sand particles (load), and water velocity. Sand waves normally develop on stretches of the river where the gradient flattens, thus allowing the coarser particles (sand) to settle out of suspension. The sand grains accumulate and build ripples on the floor of the stream bed that rapidly build into small sand dunes oriented perpendicular to the streams current. These small symmetrically-shaped sand dunes were named *antidunes* by G.K. Gilbert (1914, p. 31-34) and build vertically as well as migrate upstream. As the antidune builds, the amplitude of the surface wave increased up to ten feet or higher on the San Juan River in pre-dam years. Spacing or frequency of the antidunes remain constant, but build upstream. Eventually, the antidunes build too high, become unstable and wash out, only for the cycle to be repeated. This cycle from flat water to maximum amplitude to wash out takes only a few minutes. Due to the dynamics, antidunes are not preserved in the rock record.

GEOLOGIC TERMS:

Primary source: Glossary of Geology, 1997, AGI 4th edition

Geologic Time:

Ma = Million annuals or millions of years ago
Ga = Giga annuals, or billions of years ago

amphibole: a group of dark rock-forming ferromagnesian silicate minerals, closely related in crystal form and composition; characterized by columnar or fibrous prismatic crystals, and by good prismatic cleavage in two directions parallel to crystal faces; colors range from white to black. They constitute an abundant and widely distributed constituent in igneous and metamorphic rocks, and they are analogous in chemical composition to the pyroxene group. Most common mineral name is *hornblende.*

asthenosphere: the layer of Earth below the lithosphere, which is weak and in which isostatic adjustments take place, magmas may be generated, and seismic waves are strongly attenuated. It is part of the *upper mantle.*

biotite: a widely distributed and important rock-forming mineral of the mica group. High in potassium, magnesium and iron; it is generally black, dark brown, or dark green; platy; forms a constituent of crystalline rocks (either as an original crystal in igneous rocks of all kinds or a product of metamorphic origin in gneisses and schists).

breccia: a granular clastic rock, composed of angular broken rock fragments held together by a mineral cement or in a fine-grained matrix. Igneous and metamorphic varieties originate under explosive disturbances in volcanic pipes.

cataclastic: pertaining to the structure produced in a rock by the action of severe mechanical stress during dynamic metamorphism.

crust: the outermost layer of Earth, defined according to various criteria, including seismic velocity, density and composition; that part of Earth above the Moho discontinuity; it represents less than 0.1% of Earth's total volume.

continental crust: that which underlies the rigid continents and continental shelves; It ranges in thickness from about 20 km to 70 km and averages 40 km. The density averages 2.8 g/cm^3 and the velocities of compressional seismic waves through it average ~6.5 km/sec to less than ~7.0 km/sec.

oceanic crust: that which underlies the ocean basins; it averages 7-10 km thick; it has a density of 2.9 g/cm^3, and compressional seismic wave velocities travel through it at 4-7.5 km/sec.

crust-mantle boundary: the crust-mantle boundary is called the Moho discontinuity as defined by a marked jump in seismic wave velocity.

diamond: a cubic mineral, representing a naturally occurring crystalline form of carbon dimorphous with graphite and being the hardest natural substance known. Diamonds form under extreme temperatures and pressures and are found in ultrabasic breccia pipes in igneous rocks.

diapir: a spherical, elliptical, or teardrop-shaped body of magma or flowing ductile solid rock which rises toward the surface through the overlying layers of rock.

diatreme: a breccia-filled volcanic pipe that was formed by a gaseous explosion.

dike/sill: a *dike* is tabular igneous intrusion that cuts across the bedding of the country rock; a *sill* is a tabular intrusion that parallels bedding of the country rock.

diopside: a mineral of the clinopyroxene group, high in calcium and magnesium; contains little or no aluminum and may contain iron. It ranges in color from white to green; transparent to translucent; occurs in some metamorphic rocks and especially found as a contact-metamorphic mineral in crystalline rocks.

dunite: an igneous rock composed almost entirely of the mafic mineral *olivine*, with accessory mineral *chromite* almost always present.

eclogite: a granular mafic metamorphic rock composed essentially of red to pink garnet (almandine-pyrope) in a green matrix of sodium-rich *pyroxene* (omphacite); accessory minerals include: rutile, kyanite, *lawsonite*, coesite, amphibole, zoisite and quartz may also be present. Eclogite typically results from high-pressure metamorphism of mafic igneous rock as oceanic crust is subducted beneath continental crust. Eclogites containing lawsonite are rarely exposed at Earth's surface; the rarity of lawsonite eclogites do not reflect unusual formation conditions but does reflect unusual exhumation processes as seen in the Mule Ear diatreme in southeast Utah as xenoliths of Franciscan oceanic crust.

enstatite: a common rock-forming mineral of the orthopyroxene group (magnesium silicate); color ranges from grayish white to yellowish, olive green, and brown. It is an important primary constituent of intermediate and mafic igneous rocks.

epiclastic rock: rock formed at the earth's surface by consolidation of fragments of pre-existing rocks.

Farallon plate: was an ancient oceanic plate that began subducting under the west coast of the North American plate (then located in western Utah) about 100 Ma. The Farallon plate was completely subducted under southwestern part of North America as a shallow slab by 35 Ma causing, in part, the rise of the central Rocky Mountains and the Colorado Plateau. Magma from a portion of the plate exploded out the vent in the Mule Ear diatreme around 28 Ma.

Feldspar: a group of abundant rock-forming minerals typically occurring as colorless or pale-colored crystals and consisting of aluminosilicates of potassium, sodium, calcium and iron. The general formula is: $M[Al(Al,Si)_3O_8]$ where M = K, Na, Ca, Ba, Rb, Sr, or Fe. Feldspars are the most widespread of any mineral group and constitute 60% of the earth's crust.

garnet: is a brittle and transparent to sub-transparent mineral group, having a vitreous luster, no cleavage, and a variety of colors, dark red being the most common (pyrope garnet). It occurs as an accessory mineral in a wide range of igneous rocks, but is most commonly found as distinctive euhedral cubic crystals in metamorphic rocks (gneiss, mica schist); it may be massive or granular.

gneiss: a foliated rock formed by regional metamorphism, in which bands or lenticles of granular minerals of unequal thickness alternate with bands or lenticles in which minerals having flaky or elongate prismatic forms predominate. The layering forms perpendicular to the direction of higher pressure.

graphite: a naturally occurring form of carbon dimorphous with diamond. It is soft, opaque, lustrous, and greasy to the touch and iron black to steel gray in color. It occurs in veins or bedded masses or as disseminations in metamorphic rocks.

hypabyssal: (of an igneous rock) intermediate in texture between coarse-grained intrusive rocks and fine-grained extrusive rocks.

igneous: a rock or mineral that solidified from molten material; i.e. from magma

kimberlite: an ultramafic igneous rock containing at least 35% olivine, and a groundmass of serpentine, phlogopite and diopside. The name originated for the Kimberley district, South Africa where kimberlite is the host rock for diamonds. *[Author's note: over time, "kimberlite" was correctly changed to* ***serpentinized ultramafic microbreccia*** *for the rocks in the NVF diatremes by petrologists but "kimberlite" has been kept for discussion simplicity here.]*

lamprophyre: a group of dark-colored porphyritic, hypabyssal igneous rocks characterized by a high percentage of mafic minerals (i.e., biotite, hornblende, and pyroxene), which form the phenocrysts, and a fine-grained groundmass with the same mafic minerals in addition to feldspars; most lamprophyres are highly altered.

Laramide Orogeny: is a geologic event that occurred over the course of 30 million years in the Late Cretaceous to Early Tertiary Periods that uplifted the Colorado Plateau from the Cretaceous Sea. In essence The Laramide Orogeny is the birth of The Colorado Plateau. As it is currently understood, the uplift was caused by the subduction of the Farallon Plate under the North American plate 1000 kilometers (or about 620 miles) to the west. This event also uplifted the Rocky Mountains and the western Great Plains.

lawsonite: it is a colorless to grayish-blue metamorphic silicate mineral related chemically and structurally to the *epidote* group of secondary metamorphic minerals. It is close to the ideal composition of $CaAl_2(Si_2O_7)(OH)_2 \cdot H_2O$. The substantial amount of water bound in lawsonite's crystal structure is released during its breakdown to denser minerals during *prograde metamorphism*. This means lawsonite is capable of conveying appreciable water to shallow depths in subducting oceanic lithosphere. Experimentation on lawsonite to vary its responses at different temperatures and different pressures is among its most studied aspects, for it is these qualities that affect its abilities to carry water down to mantle depths, similar to other OH-containing phases.

Lawsonite is a very widespread mineral and has attracted considerable interest because of its importance as a marker of moderate pressure (6-12 kb) and low temperature (300 - 400 °C) conditions in nature. This mainly occurs along continental margins (subduction zones) such as those found in: the Franciscan Formation in California.

lithosphere: the rigid outer shell of the upper mantle that makes up the tectonic plates; lithosphere averages 70 km thick beneath oceans and 125-250 km thick beneath continents; beneath the lithosphere seismic wave speeds abruptly decrease in a plastic low-velocity zone called the asthenosphere.

maar: a low-relief, broad volcanic crater formed by multiple shallow explosive eruptions.

mafic: an igneous rock composed chiefly of one or more ferromagnesian (i.e. containing iron and magnesium), *dark-colored* minerals

magma: naturally occurring molten or partially molten rock material, generated within the earth and capable of intrusion and extrusion, from which igneous rocks are derived through cooling and solidification processes.

mantle: the zone of Earth below the *crust* and above the core, which is divided into the *upper mantle* and *lower mantle*, with a transition zone between. The upper mantle consists of rigid *lithosphere* and plastic *asthenosphere.*

mantle plume: a vertical cylindrical part of the Earth's mantle, hotter than its surroundings, within which larger-than-normal amounts of heat are conducted upward to form a "hot spot" at the Earth's surface.

metasomatism: is the chemical alteration of a rock by hydrothermal and other fluids. It involves the replacement of one rock type by another of different mineralogical and chemical composition. The rock's mineral compositions are dissolved and new mineral assemblages form in their place. Dissolution and replacement occur simultaneously and the rock remains solid. Metasomatism typically occurs through the action of hydrothermal fluids from an igneous or metamorphic source. Because metasomatism is a mass transfer process, it is not restricted to rocks which are changed by addition or deletion of chemical elements or hydrous compounds. Metasomatism is more complicated in the Earth's mantle, because the composition of peridotite at high temperatures can be changed by infiltration of carbonate ($CaCO_3$) and silicate (SiO_2) melts and by carbon dioxide-rich (CO_2) and water-rich fluids (H_2O).

meta-igneous: metamorphosed igneous rock (example: granite altered to gneiss)

metamorphism: the mineralogical, chemical, and structural adjustment of solid rocks to physical and chemical conditions which have been imposed at depth below the surface of weathering or cementation, and differs from the conditions under which the rocks in question originated. **Metamorphic** pertains to the process of metamorphism.

meta-sedimentary: metamorphosed sedimentary rock (example: sandstone altered to quartzite; limestone altered to marble; shale altered to phyllite or slate)

minette: a variety of *lamprophyre* with alkali feldspar more abundant than plagioclase; generally containing biotite and clinopyroxene phenocrysts.

Moho boundary or discontinuity: the boundary surface or sharp seismic-velocity contrast that separates Earth's *crust* from the subjacent *upper mantle.*

olivine: an olive-green to grayish-green ferromagnesium mineral; common rock-forming mineral in mafic to ultramafic, low-silica igneous rocks; it crystallizes early from magma, weathers readily at the earth's surface and metamorphoses to serpentine.

orogeny: the process of formation of mountains. The process by which structures within fold belt mountainous areas were formed, including thrusting, folding and faulting

orthoclase: a colorless, white, cream-yellow, pink or gray mineral of the alkali feldspar group [potassic-aluminosilicate]; remains stable at higher temperatures; a common rock-forming mineral, esp. in granites, crystalline schists; a general term applied to potassium feldspar that appears to be monoclinic (i.e. sanidine, microcline).

peridotite: a coarse-grained plutonic igneous rock composed chiefly of olivine with other mafic minerals such as pyroxene, amphiboles, or micas and contains little to no feldspar; encompasses the more specific term *dunite*; peridotite is commonly altered to serpentine.

petrology: that branch of geology dealing with the origin, occurrence, structure, and history of rock

Phanerozoic: the geologic time period that includes the Paleozoic, Mesozoic and Cenozoic Erathems

plagioclase: a group or series of feldspars ranging in sodium/calcium ratios from $NaAlSi_3O_8$ to $CaAl_2Si_2O_8$; plagioclase minerals are among the commonest rock-forming minerals, have characteristic twinning, and commonly display zoning.

plate tectonics: a theory in which the lithosphere is divided into a number of plates whose pattern of horizontal movement is that of torsional rigid bodies that interact with one another at their boundaries, causing seismic and tectonic activity.

Precambrian: a unit of the geologic time scale comprising that time in which rocks formed before the beginning of the Paleozoic Erathem.

pyroclastic rock: clastic rock material formed by volcanic explosion or aerial expulsion from a volcanic vent.

pyrope: The magnesium-aluminum end-member of the garnet group, characterized by a deep, fiery to "ruby" red color. Found as angular fragments associated with serpentine and olivine basic igneous rocks such as kimberlite.

pyroxene: a group of dark rock-forming silicate minerals with primary composition of calcium, sodium, magnesium, or iron and secondary composition of chromium, manganese or aluminum. It is characterized by short, stout prismatic crystals and good prismatic cleavage in two directions; colors typically dark green to black.

sedimentary rock: a rock resulting from the consolidation of loose *sediment* that has accumulated in layers; e.g. a *clastic rock* (such as sandstone) consisting of mechanically formed fragments of older rock transported from its source and deposited by water (rivers, lakes, and oceans), ice (glaciers), and wind; or a *chemical rock* (such as rock salt or gypsum) formed by precipitation from solution; or *organic rock* (limestones) consisting of the remains or secretions of plants and animals in an aqueous environment.

sedimentology: the scientific study of sedimentary rocks and the processes by which they were formed; the description, classification, origin, and interpretation of sediments.

serpentinized ultramafic microbreccia (SUM): *serpentine* is a group of greenish-gray magnesium and iron rich silicates formed as secondary minerals derived by the process of hydrothermal alteration of highly metamorphosed magnesium-rich silicate minerals (olivine, pyroxene, and other ultrabasic rocks) that form the groundmass for the *microbreccia*: a well indurated, massive rock that has been crushed to very fine grain size through *cataclastic* flow. So-called ***kimberlites*** in the NVF are better defined as "SUMs" due to lack of diamonds, but the kimberlite term has been used here for simplicity in describing diatreme mineralogy.

stratigraphy: the branch of geology concerned with the order and relative position of strata and their relationship to the geologic time scale.

tomography: a method of producing a three-dimensional image of the internal structures of earth by the observation and recording of the differences in effects on the passage of waves of energy impinging on those structures.

tuff ring: *tuff* is very fine-grained volcanic ash; *tuff ring* is a wide, low-rimmed, well-bedded accumulation of volcanic ash accumulated around a volcanic vent.

ultramafic: and igneous rock composed chiefly of mafic minerals (e.g. dunite, peridotite, and pyroxene)

uranium: is a heavy metal that occurs in most rocks at varying concentrations and occurs in relatively high concentrations as ores in several geologic formations on the Colorado Plateau (Mossback and Shinarump members of the Chinle Fm, scattered throughout the Morrison Fm and to some extent in the Cutler Group); most commonly occurs as carnotite and uraninite; production of U_3O_8 (yellowcake) was the most common end-product from the various mills in the greater Four Corners.

vanadium: is a hard, silvery gray, ductile metal that occurs naturally in many different minerals and occurs as a byproduct of uranium mining. It is mainly used to produce steel alloys. Titanium-aluminum-vanadium alloy is used in jet engines and for high-speed aircraft. Vanadium foil is used in cladding titanium to steel. Vanadium pentoxide is used in ceramics and as a catalyst for the production of sulfuric acid.

vents=pipes=necks: **vent**: the opening at the earth's surface through which volcanic materials are extruded; also the channel or conduit through which they pass; **pipe**: a vertical conduit through the earth's crust below a volcano, through which magmatic materials have passed. It is usually filled with volcanic breccia and fragments of older rock; **neck:** a vertical, pipe-like intrusion that represents a former volcanic vent. The term is usually applied to the form as an erosional remnant.

volcanoes, volcanic: occur as vents in the surface of the Earth through which magma and associated gases and ash erupt; volcanic pertains to the activities, structures or rock types of a volcano.

xenoliths: A fragment of country rock enveloped in larger rocks during the latter's development and solidification. They may be engulfed along the margins of a magma chamber, or in the case of an explosive diatreme, torn loose from the walls during the eruption.

≈ NOTES ≈

CHAPTER 1

1. Email from Bill Dickinson; 5/7/2015

2. Ibid.

3. William R. "Bill" Dickinson was a leader in the "plate tectonics revolution" served as the Head of the Geology Department @ University of Arizona (UA) from 1986 to 1991, but came to University of Arizona in 1979. He began his career @ Stanford University where he earned his doctorate in 1958 and was a faculty member until moving to Arizona. He was honored by Stanford's School of Earth, Energy & Environmental Sciences in June, 2015 with its inaugural Distinguished Alumni Award. In presenting the award, *Dean Pamela Matson* called Dickinson "a thought leader in relating plate tectonics to the accumulation of sediment in Earth's major sedimentary basins, and is widely recognized as the father of modern sedimentary basin analysis." He also knew what problems to tackle, said his stepson *Jon Spencer*, senior geologist at the Arizona Geological Survey in Tucson. "He had a really good vision for what problems we needed to understand if we really wanted to understand how the earth works." He was on an archaeological field trip to Fiji and Tonga when he died in his sleep on July 21, 2015. He was 83.

4. Barry, John M., 1997, RISING TIDE: The great Mississippi flood of 1927 and how it changed America: Simon & Schuster Paperbacks; 524 p.

5. Typescript of a taped oral interview of Kenny Ross in Mancos, CO on September 13, 1986 by Herm Hoops; personal communications with Don & Doug Ross in 2015

6. See Barry, 1997, Mississippi River Flood of 1927: The drainage basin of the Mississippi River stretches north into Canada and south to the Gulf of Mexico, east from New York and North Carolina and west to Idaho and New Mexico. Its drainage area is twenty percent larger than that of China's Yellow River, double that of Africa's Nile and India's Ganges, and fifteen times that of Europe's Rhine. Within it lies over 40% of the conterminous United States, including all or part of thirty-one states. No river in Europe, no river in Asia, no river in the ancient civilized world compares with it. Only the Amazon and, barely, the Congo have a larger drainage basin. Measured from the head of the Missouri River, the Mississippi is the longest river in the world, and it pulses like the artery of the American Heartland.

   In August, 1926 a persistent rain began to fall over much of the Midwest. All across the country it rained and as winter fell, so did voluminous amounts of snow, and more rain in lower elevations. The Mississippi was swollen to record flood levels by the first of the year, 1927, but the rains continued. By the early spring tributaries to the Mississippi had already overflowed in record amounts from Oklahoma and Kansas in the west to Illinois and Kentucky in the east; and the Mississippi continued to rise. Levees had been built along the 1100 mile length of the river from the southern end of the Mississippi delta in Louisiana to the mouth of the Ohio River near Cairo, Illinois. But the levee broke at Greenville, Mississippi on April 15, 1927, where the river was estimated to carry in excess of three million cubic feet of water per second!

   President Coolidge had dragged his feet during the increasing emergency situation and finally, and reluctantly, issued an order in late April for all able bodied men to assemble a "rescue fleet" even though rescue operations had long since begun in the lower river delta country. By then, literally tens of thousands of people were clinging to trees or sitting on rooftops. All waited for boats, but there were few to be found that were navigable. Most were only manned by oars as motors were scarce. It was under these circumstances that Kenny Ross first tried his hand at boating, so his comment about rescuing a cat was certainly "tongue-in-cheek" sarcasm.

   The flooding wasn't just in the mid-continent. The second highest peak flow from the Animas River (and largest perennial tributary to the San Juan River) in southwestern Colorado occurred on June 29, 1927 where it was gaged in Durango at 20,000 cfs. All in all, the great floods on the Mississippi River system forced the hand in Washington, D.C. to support the Boulder Canyon project as a result from public reaction to the disastrous flood on the Mississippi River in 1927! The structure was declared necessary to *save the Imperial Valley*. Of course, the water year 1927 was an exceptionally wet year for most of the conterminous

United States and was rapidly followed by an extended drought throughout the 1930s – commonly referred to as the "Dust Bowl Era" but congressional approval for the Boulder Dam was strongly influenced by the Flood of '27.

7. In most of Kenny's job applications he listed his birthdate as 1908, but occasionally the year 1909 was entered. Following Kenny's passing in 1990, the year 1908 was placed on the memorial plaque in the lower San Juan River by his two sons in 1991. But late in the research of this book Don Ross came across a small dusty file folder of Mildred's that contained a few letters and Kenny's birth certificate. It said August 20, 1909! So right off the bat, the question arises – why the dual dates? Since most of the time he claimed 1908, I have stayed with this date throughout this biographical narrative, as the specific date seems non-consequential to the book, other than to open the readers' eyes to Kenny the storyteller.

8. According to family lore, Charley Ross's mother (Kenny's grandmother) was full-blooded Lakota Sioux. The Great Sioux Nation comprises three major divisions based on language variations: the Dakota, Lakota, and Nekota. The "Sioux" Name is derived from the French as a pejorative name meaning "little snakes." Although coaxed many times over the writing of this book, neither Don nor Doug have committed to a DNA test to resolve the rumor.

9. The Homestead Act of 1860 did pass in Congress, but it was vetoed by President James Buchanan, a Democrat. After the Southern states seceded from the Union in 1861 (and their representatives had left Congress), the bill passed and was signed into law by President Abraham Lincoln (May 20, 1862). The Homestead Act of 1862 opened up millions of acres. Any adult, who had never taken up arms against the U.S. government, could apply for 160 acre tracts. Women, blacks, and immigrants were eligible. Several additional laws were enacted in the latter half of the 19th and early 20th centuries.

   An amendment to the Homestead Act of 1862, the Enlarged Homestead Act, was passed in 1909 and doubled the allotted acreage to 320. Between 1862 and 1934, the federal government granted 1.6 million homesteads and distributed 270,000,000 acres (420,000 mi^2) of federal land for private ownership. This was a total of 10% of all land in the United States. About 40 percent of the applicants who started the process were able to complete it and obtain title to their homesteaded land. Because by the early 1900s much of the prime low-lying alluvial land along rivers had been homesteaded, the *Enlarged Homestead Act* was passed in 1909. To enable dryland farming, it increased the number of acres for a homestead to 320 acres (1.3 km^2) given to farmers who accepted more marginal lands, which could not be easily irrigated. The Homestead Acts had few qualifying requirements. A *homesteader* had to be the head of the household or at least twenty-one years old. They had to live on the designated land, build a home, make improvements, and farm it for a minimum of five years. The filing fee was eighteen dollars.

10. Thompson, Ian "Sandy", 1982, "Kenny Ross: River rat and teacher; for Early Man (unpublished manuscript)

11. Doug Ross personal communication; personal stories told to Doug by Kenny following Kenny's stroke in 1988-89

12. Personal communications with C. DeLorme & Gary Matlock in July, 2016

13. Letter from Hank Zuidema to Kenny, 06/08/1949

14. Letter from Kenny to Hank Zuidema, 06/09/1949

15. Sandy Thompson interviews with Kenny, 1982; see also *Yukon River Expedition* pamphlet for summer, 1936. By then "Mr. Beauchamp has organized and led three student exploratory expeditions in northern Canada and Alaska. His parties have built small boats and navigated both the Mackenzie and Yukon rivers from points near their sources."

16. Email from Bill Dickinson 5/31/2015

17. Ibid.

18. There is no question that Kenny and David Lavender were good friends as Kenny asked David to be the special guest on several river trips. By the time David did the trips, Kenny had sold WRX to C. DeLorme who organized trips in 1988-90.

19. Personal communication with Charlie DeLorme confirming comment above

20. Email from Tamara Desrosiers dated Wed 8/3/2016

21. Email from Tom Rice dated Mon 8/1/2016

22. See Lavender, David S., 1943; *One Man's West*; Doubleday & Co., reprinted 1956 & 1977; 316p.

23. For more insight into Marie Ogden and her Home of Truth see: W. Paul Reese; *History Blazer*, April, 1995; Wallace Stegner, *Mormon Country* (Lincoln: University of Nebraska Press, 1970), pp. 331-43; *San Juan Record*, April 4, 11, June 20, 1935; *Times Independent*, June 13, 20, 1935; Leo P. Ribuffo, *The Old Christian Right: The Protestant Far Right from the Great Depression to the Cold War* (Philadelphia: Temple University Press, 1983), pp. 26-27. For details concerning Al Scorup see Lavender, David S., 1943; *One Man's West*; Doubleday & Co., reprinted 1956 & 1977, p. 174. For details about Buck Lee, see Lavender, p. 168.

24. Personal communications with Doug Ross, 2015 relating one of Kenny's favorite stories

25. Information about early years from conversations with Don & Doug Ross; Certificate of Discharge from Civilian Conservation Corps dated 07/28/1935; Numerous applications for Employment at Mesa Verde National Park dated October, 1934 through January, 1944

CHAPTER 2

1. Personal communications with June Head, April 12, 2017; see Robert S. McPherson, 2015, *LIFE IN A CORNER: cultural episodes in southeastern Utah, 1880 – 1950*; 293p.

2. See internet "End of the Frontier in 1890"

3. See internet "Frederick Jackson Turner"

4. Ibid.

5. McPherson, 2015, p. 14

6. Bernheimer, Charles L., 1924, *RAINBOW BRIDGE: Circling Navajo Mountain and Explorations in the "Badlands" of Southern Utah and Northern Arizona: With a New Introduction: Charles Bernheimer: The Tenderfoot and Cliff Dweller from Manhattan*, 1999, by Albert E. Ward; A CAS Reprint; originally published in 1924; Doubleday, Page & Co., Garden City; 187 p.

7. Franklin, Robert and Pamela A. Bunte, 1990; *The Paiute*; Chelsea House, New York, NY; see also Cultural History – San Juan Southern Paiute by Glen Canyon Natural History Association.

8. Ibid.

9. Ibid.

10. Franklin, Robert and Pamela A. Bunte, 1990; *The Paiute*; Chelsea House, New York, NY

11. Christenson, Andrew L., 1987, *The Last of the Great Expeditions: The Rainbow Bridge/Monument Valley Expedition 1933-38:* Museum of Northern Arizona, Plateau 58, no. 4, 32p; see p. 29 Map of Tsegi Canyon.

12. Ibid.

13. Notes regarding RBMV expeditions and Ansel Hall: see Turner, Jack, 1998, *Early Images of the Southwest: Lantern slides of Ansel F. Hall*; published by Roberts Rinehart, Niwot, Colorado, 90p; and Winkler, William C., and Bradley, Bruce, 1999, *Ansel Hall Pueblo: a National Historic Place*; Colorado Historical Society Document submitted November 25, 1997.

14. Ibid.

15. Notes passed along by Don Ross from conversations with Roger Hall. Note: Roger Hall and his siblings have known Don and Doug Ross since their childhood days in Mancos, Colorado circa 1950s.

16. Christenson, Andrew L., 1987, *The Last of the Great Expeditions: The Rainbow Bridge/Monument Valley Expedition 1933-38:* Museum of Northern Arizona, Plateau 58, no. 4, 32p.

17. Hall, Ansel Franklin, 1934; General Report of the Rainbow Bridge-Monument Valley Expedition of 1933; University of California Press, Berkeley, CA, 32p.

18. Email from Harvey Leake; 7/17/2016

19. Email from Harvey Leake; 8/6/2017

20. Email from Andy Christenson; 8/6-8/2017

21. Christenson, Andrew L., 1987, *The Last of the Great Expeditions: The Rainbow Bridge/Monument Valley Expedition 1933-38:* Museum of Northern Arizona, Plateau 58, no. 4, 32p.

22. Crotty, Helen K., 1983, *Honoring the Dead: Anasazi Ceramics from the Rainbow Bridge-Monument Valley Expedition; Museum of Cultural History, UCLA, Monograph Series Number 22,* Los Angeles, Museum of Cultural History.

23. The *Ford Motor Co.* was contacted by Geology Professor Henry Zuidema from Michigan who was later involved in the Explorers Camp program for teenage boys interested in earth science.

24. Cover letter (p.2) from Arthur W. Nelson, Jr. to Andrew L. Christenson dated January 24, 1986 that accompanied a complete copy of his hand-written unpublished journal entitled "My Experiences as a member of the Rainbow Bridge – Monument Valley Expedition summer of 1936."

25. Hargrave, Lyndon Lane, 1935; *Report on Archaeological Reconnaissance in the Rainbow Plateau Area of Northern Arizona and Southern Utah, based upon fieldwork by the Rainbow Bridge-Monument Valley Expedition of 1933.* Berkeley, California: University of California Press.

26. The Sponsors and Advisory Staff of the Expedition listed in Ansel Hall's "General Report of the Rainbow Bridge-Monument Valley Expedition of 1933" included: William Frederick Bade; Professor of Semitic Languages, Pacific School of Religion, organizer of four expeditions to Palestine to excavate the ancient biblical city of Mizpah; Knowles A. Ryerson; Director, Bureau of Plant Industry, Department of Agriculture, Washington, D.C.; Vice-President American Horticultural Society; member Explorers Club; Wm. B. Herms; Chairman, Department of Entomology, University of California; President, Berkeley-Contra Costa Area Council, Boy Scouts of America; Francis P. Farquhar; President, Sierra Club; Vice-President, American Alpine Club; Editor Sierra Club Bulletin; Ralph W. Chaney; Chairman, Department of Paleontology, University of California; member of Roy Chapman Andrews expedition to Mongolia; Duncan McDuffie; Chairman, California State Parks Council; Trustee, Save-the-Redwoods League; formerly President of the Sierra Club; and Robert Sibley; Executive Secretary, University of California Alumni Association. In addition, Jack Turner (1998) cites this list of sponsors: Horace M. Albright, former director

of the NPS; Harold S. Colton, director of the Museum of Northern AZ; Alfred L. Kroeber, anthropologist for the Univ of CA; Jessie L. Nusbaum, archaeologist for the US Dept of Interior; Wallace Atwood, president of Clark University; Herbert E. Gregory, geologist and director of the Bishop Museum; Knowles Ryerson, director of the US Bureau of Plant Industry.

27. Hand-written letter from Jesse Nusbaum to Dock Marston, Feb 7, 1955; Kenny Ross-Dock Marston Library letters, Huntington Library

28. Lister, Florence C, 1997, *Prehistory in Peril: the worst and best of Durango Archaeology*; University Press of Colorado; 196p.

29. Hargrave, Lyndon Lane, 1935; *Report on Archaeological Reconnaissance in the Rainbow Plateau Area of Northern Arizona and Southern Utah, based upon fieldwork by the Rainbow Bridge-Monument Valley Expedition of 1933.* Berkeley, California: University of California Press.

30. Aton, James M. and McPherson, Robert S., 2000, RIVER FLOWING FROM THE SUNRISE: an environmental history of the Lower San Juan; Utah State University Press, 216 p.

31. Hall, Ansel Franklin, 1934; General Report of the Rainbow Bridge-Monument Valley Expedition of 1933; University of California Press, Berkeley, CA, 32p.

32. Ibid., p.17

33. Email note from Allison-Fischer-Olson (agent for E. Kahn, RBMVE-Onward); 12/9/2015 from information she found at Huntington Library and sent to me

34. Ibid.

35. Ibid.

36. Note: a significant number of B&W photos from these flights are in the Kenny Ross collection that are not in the SWC collection at Ft. Lewis College, Durango, Colorado; captions to photos have been added by this author.

37. Beals, Ralph Leon, George W. Brainerd, and Watson Smith, 1945, *Archaeological studies in northeast Arizona: A report on the archaeological work of the Rainbow Bridge-Monument Valley Expedition; University of California publications in American archaeology and ethnology 44, no. 1, 235 p., plus 31 plates;* Berkeley: University of California Press.

38. Email note from Andy Christenson 5/15/2018

39. See Aton & McPherson, 2000, p. 62-64; A. Christenson, 1987; Don D. Fowler, 2011, *The Glen Canyon Country* is an excellent overview of the salvage archaeological efforts in Glen Canyon prior to inundation by Powell reservoir waters.

40. Bernheimer, Charles L., 1924, RAINBOW BRIDGE: Circling Navajo Mountain and Explorations in the "Badlands" of Southern Utah and Northern Arizona: With a New Introduction: Charles Bernheimer: The Tenderfoot and Cliff Dweller from Manhattan, 1999, by Albert E. Ward; A CAS Reprint; originally published in 1924; Doubleday, Page & Co., Garden City; 187 p.

41. Ibid.

42. Bernheimer's map, p.33, showed proven routes to the San Juan River by way of Copper Canyon and overland routes to Rainbow Bridge.

43. Topping, Gary, 1997, *Glen Canyon and the San Juan Country*, Moscow: University of Idaho Press; p. 127; see Gabel Co, Jonathan Patterson Williams who built the Blue Canyon Trading Post and operated a barge with

pumping equipment & worked downstream from Williams Bar located about one mile above mouth of Copper Canyon; also Zahn & Spencer camps but abandoned by 1909; The Red Rock Mining & Expl Co (1910); San Juan Mining Co. (1911).

44. Gregory, Herbert E., 1917, Geology of the Navajo country: a reconnaissance of parts of Arizona, New Mexico and Utah: USGS Professional Paper 93, 161p; see page 139.

45. Aton, James M. and McPherson, Robert S., 2000, RIVER FLOWING FROM THE SUNRISE: an environmental history of the Lower San Juan; Utah State University Press, 216 p.

46. Hall, Ansel Franklin, 1934; General Report of the Rainbow Bridge-Monument Valley Expedition of 1933; University of California Press, Berkeley, CA, 32p.

47. Ibid; Art Nelson's unpublished journal states "I first became aware of the Rainbow Bridge-Monument Valley Expedition through an announcement posted on the bulletin board at the School of Forestry, University of Idaho, Moscow, Idaho during the spring of 1936."

48. Email from A. L. Christenson; 8/6/2017 where he provided all the names of the 1933 RBMV river trip, including Kenny Ross.

49. Letter from Lloyd W. Lowrey to Andrew L. Christenson, December 5, 1988; this comment also leads one to question the caption to Melinda [Malinda] Elliott's reference to same photo shown as Figure 2.7 here and shown on page 201 in her book, *Great Excavations*, 1995, where the caption reads *"John Wetherill preparing his famous hot biscuits at Warm Creek Camp, August, 1933."* The photo was taken by Lowrey, but there is zero indication that Wetherill is "preparing hot biscuits" as there is no fire burning under the grate and firewood sits ready to burn at the side; I also question the location as "Warm Creek" based on geologic formation in background; location probably in lower San Juan or Glen Canyon well above Warm Creek.

50. This story of Kenny's first San Juan River trip in 1933 was recounted by Kenny Ross to C. DeLorme, Don and Doug Ross, Bill Dickinson, Rob Rice and Gary Matlock.

51. Hall, Ansel Franklin, 1934; General Report of the Rainbow Bridge-Monument Valley Expedition of 1933; University of California Press, Berkeley, CA, 32p.

52. Ibid; Photo of boats launching into rapids in lower canyon from RR; General Report Rainbow Bridge-Monument Valley Expedition of 1933, p.11.

53. Email from Bill Dickinson, 5/31/2015

54. Information for specific gaged flows on the San Juan River below Bluff, Utah is provided by USGS Historical Water Data [Gage Number 09379500] for most years since 1914. The gage is actually located at Mexican Hat, Utah near the bridge, twenty-seven river miles downstream from Bluff, but has always maintained the name "The gage near Bluff." (The gaged flow for 1934 is shown on accompanying graph; see text)

55. Email from Andy Christenson, 8/7/2017

56. Email from Andy Christenson, 8/6/2017

57. Andy Christenson provided me with a copy of Art Nelson's journal, including hand-drawn maps and all fifteen photos taken by Torrey Lyons to which I added more details to captions

58. Southwest Explorations *Explorers Camp* 1955 brochure written by Kenneth I. Ross, Director: p.4

59. Email from Andy Christenson, 8/7/2017

60. Letter from Lloyd W. Lowery to Andrew L. Christenson, December 5, 1988

61. Staveley, Gaylord, 2015, *The Rapids and the Roar: a boating history of the Colorado River and Grand Canyon*; Fretwater Press, Flagstaff, AZ; p.113-114; Staveley also misstates the hiking distance from the river to Rainbow Bridge. The hiking distance from the river is four and a half miles, not six as stated here.

62. Beals, Ralph Leon, George W. Brainerd, and Watson Smith, 1945, *Archaeological studies in northeast Arizona: A report on the archaeological work of the Rainbow Bridge-Monument Valley Expedition*; p.7

63. Ibid., p.5; note the mention of a "fourth" trip – implying three prior trips (one in 1933 and two in 1934); but I question any boat launching from "Moonlight Creek" due to topography and lack of accessibility; launch point was most likely from the mouth of Copper Canyon. Furthermore, Lowrey states in his letter to Christenson (see Note 49 and 60 above) that he was on ALL the river trips EXCEPT the 1935 season because he was in Alaska. So Beals information regarding who, what, where, when is questionable too.

64. Ibid. p.7; eleven vs three RBMV river trips? Who's right? Actual river mile distance from Copper Canyon to Lees Ferry is about 125 miles.

65. Letter from Dock Marston to Kenny Ross, Feb 22, 1953

66. Letter from Kenny Ross to Dock Marston, March 3, 1953; after 1950 Kenny began referring to his San Juan River and Glen Canyon of the Colorado River trips to Lees Ferry as the "SJ&C" trips.

67. Letter from Lloyd W. Lowery to Andrew L. Christenson, December 5, 1988

68. Staveley, 2015, p. 111; the photo has no date as to when he actually ran this rapid, but Norm running stern-first suggests this was photographed after the 1935 trip, as stern-first was not his "style" previously

69. During summer, 2016 the entire Kenny Ross photo collection, including four movie reels 1600 ft long of 16 mm film was donated to the Marriott Library, Univ of Utah, that were labeled "1937-RBMVE." The library has not digitized any of the film.

70. Hall, Ansel Franklin, 1934 report; p. 13

71. Ibid. p. 28

72. Letter from Lloyd W. Lowery to Andrew L. Christenson, December 5, 1988

73. For biographies of Norman Nevill's see Webb, Roy, 2005, *High, Wide, and Handsome: The river journals of Norman D. Nevills*; Utah State University Press, 308p, and Staveley, Gaylord, 2015, *The Rapids and the Roar: a boating history of the Colorado River and Grand Canyon*; Fretwater Press, Flagstaff, AZ, 333p;

74. Mexican Hat oil field and Billy Nevill's "topping plant." The oil field was discovered in 1908 and originally called the "San Juan oil field." By 1933 the field had been visited by geologists E.G. Woodruff in 1910, H.E. Gregory in 1911, and reviewed by Hugh Miser, 1921, 1923 and 1925. Much of the information about the oil field is repeated in their geological reports. The oil field received substantial publicity, but production never amounted to much. *The Nevills topping plant was the very crudest in construction.* Typically only condensates, light sweet crude and kerosene would be processed at this type of facility. I am in the process of writing a full updated historical and geological review of this marginal oil field [book in progress].

75. See Webb, Roy, 2005, *High, Wide, and Handsome: The river journals of Norman D. Nevills*; Utah State University Press, 308p.

76. Valle, Doris, 1986, *Looking back around the Hat: a history of Mexican Hat*; 60p.

77. Webb, Roy, 2005, *High, Wide, and Handsome: The river journals of Norman D. Nevills*, p. 15

78. Webb, Roy, 2005, p.2 erroneously states that the air strip was *"the one that he* [Norm Nevills] *had carved out of the dirt with his own hands."*

79. See Staveley, 2015, p. 131 for details about airplane crash

80. See Staveley, 2015, p. 111-112 for details; also see Roy Webb, 2005, or D. Valle, 1989 regarding the "honeymoon trip." They repeat the same stories handed down by the Nevills family without question.

81. Roy Webb, 2005, p. 4; G. Staveley, 2015, p. 110-112; the honeymoon story based on Joan Nevills Staveley's recollections of stories told to her by grandmother "Moe"

82. G. Staveley, 2015, p.111

83. Ibid. p. 111

84. See internet "time and date" to calculate daylight hours

85. See Staveley, 2015, p. 112 where depth of canyon at Honaker Trail is erroneously reported as 1,500 ft

86. Staveley, 2015, p. 111 makes a point of Norm driving out past Johns Canyon with Jack Frost in November to plug an abandoned well at Slickhorn Gulch; but the road doesn't pass close to the rim at Honaker Trail and since the trail had not been in use for several decades, there was little to suggest where the turn-off was to the trailhead.

87. Email from Tamara Desrosiers 11/28/2017; she described how she and fellow river guide Karla Vanderzanden missed the Honaker Trail landing altogether with a group in the spring, 1989 after her having boated this stretch several times previously.

CHAPTER 3

1. W.H. Jackson kept a daily journal of his trip in 1875 which was translated to typescript in 1983 by James Knipmeyer from which the details were ascertained.

2. Hayden, F.V., 1877, *Ninth Annual Report of the United States Geological and Geographical Survey for the Year 1875*; Washington, D.C.; GPO; the Hayden Survey reports, and photographic displays at the Great Exposition in Philadelphia in 1876 opened the public's eye to the Four Corners exquisite landforms. Hayden sent two of his men, W.H. Holmes and W.H. Jackson, to survey and photograph prehistoric ruins in the San Juan drainage. They were part of the USGS Surveys of 1874 and 1875. Hayden had a knack for playing to the expansionist ideas of 19th century America. He turned out popular scientific reports that became an annual geological enticement to the territories. He knew how to use Jackson's photos of Anasazi ruins to generate interest in the region and astounded audiences at the 1876 Exposition in Philadelphia. (see Aton, James M. and McPherson, Robert S., 2000, *RIVER FLOWING FROM THE SUNRISE: an environmental history of the Lower San Juan*; Utah State University Press; p.51;)

3. Snead, James E., 2003, *Ruins and Rivals: the making of Southwest Archaeology*, p.51-52.

4. Snead, James E., 2003, p. 82; also, Smith, Duane A. and Winkler, William C., 2005, *Travels and Travails, Tourism at Mesa Verde*; p. 13.

5. Following the discovery of Mesa Verde in 1888 by *Charlie Mason & Al and Richard Wetherill*, photos of the cliff dwellings were made famous at the Columbian Exposition in Chicago in 1893 and started a stampede. The San Juan drainage basin became known as an archaeological wonderland. A "gold rush" for cliff dweller ruins attracted looters, relic collectors, museum-directed excavations, tourists, and wannabe archaeologists as well as budding archaeologists. Archaeology as a scientific discipline was in its infancy.

Not surprisingly, from 1890 to 1910 most artifacts dug up ended in both the eastern museums and universities or in private hands. The first semi-professional excavations in Utah were probably done by *Charles Cary Graham* and *Charles McLoyd* in Grand Gulch in 1890-91. They were friends of the Wetherill's and had helped with Mesa Verde excavations. But their efforts were amateurish leading *Frederick Putnam* of Harvard's Peabody Museum to organize an expedition to the San Juan area in 1892 and headed up by *Warren K. Moorhead*. He took a boat down the Animas River to Farmington and had a tough time and claimed it was the most dangerous feat since J.W. Powell's trips in Grand Canyon. Moorhead also described *sand waves* but couldn't figure out how they were caused. Their haste and unfamiliarity with Anasazi ruins combined to make the expedition an exercise in ineptitude.

Two scientists who took the time to familiarize themselves with the region were *T. Mitchell Prudden* and *Byron Cummings*. Prudden, a physician, spent summers from 1892 to 1915 exploring the region. Cummings was a professor and dean of arts and sciences at the University of Utah, and another self-taught scientist. He began excavating up Montezuma Creek at Alkali Ridge in 1908 under tutelage of *Edgar L. Hewett*, director of School of American Research out of Santa Fe, NM. Two of his students – *Neil Judd* of Utah and *Alfred V. Kidder* of Harvard later earned distinctions in the field of archaeology and to train and professionalize San Juan archaeologists. (For further reading see Smith, Duane A., 1988, Mesa Verde National Park: Shadows of the Centuries; Smith, Duane A. and Winkler, William C., 2005, *Travels and Travails, Tourism at Mesa Verde;* Snead, James E., 2003, Ruins and Rivals: the making of Southwest Archaeology.)

Cummings, along with *W.B. Douglass* became famous as the official Anglo discoverers of Rainbow Bridge in 1909 located on west side of Navajo Mtn (but led there by John Wetherill). Teddy Roosevelt and Zane Grey were two of the more famous early visitors who wrote about the area which led to increase in tourists. (see Bernheimer, Charles L., 1924, *RAINBOW BRIDGE: Circling Navajo Mountain and Explorations in the "Badlands" of Southern Utah and Northern Arizona*: With a New Introduction: *Charles Bernheimer: The Tenderfoot and Cliff Dweller from Manhattan*, 1999, by Albert E. Ward; A CAS Reprint; originally published in 1924; Doubleday, Page & Co., Garden City; 187 p.)

6. Chapin, Frederick H., 1892, *The Land of the Cliff Dwellers*. Boston: W.B. Clarke & Co.

7. *Alice Eastwood*, (1859 – 1953) was a self-taught botanist. She was born in Toronto, Canada but the family moved to Denver in 1873 where she graduated from high school and then taught at her alma mater for next ten years, foregoing a college education. She was a shrewd investor and bought a house in Durango in the 1880s as an investment property. (Wilson, 1955; Bonta, 1991)

Earlier, in May, she had attended a botanical show at the California Academy of Sciences in San Francisco where she met *Townsend Stith Brandegee* and his wife, Katherine, the Curator of Botany and it was also here that she was encouraged to learn more about the Great Southwest flora. T.S. Brandegee had been the botanist on the Hayden Surveys of the 1870s and many species of flora had his name associated with it.

She lived in an age when the American West was still uncharted territory in some places – like the Four Corners (Wilson, 1955; Bonta, 1991). Because it was considered improper and dangerous for an unmarried single woman to roam about the countryside alone collecting plants, in 1892 she arranged to meet up with Al Wetherill as her guide into "San Juan Country." They met at the D&RG train stop in Thompson Springs, Utah where Al had arrived with three horses – one for each to ride and the other as a pack horse, thus relieving Alice of having to carry the plant press on her back as she was accustomed to doing. They checked in to the only hotel and when asked if they were married she emphatically said "no." Although eyebrows were raised they were allowed to stay the night. Eastwood cared little about convention. The following morning they headed south into San Juan country down Montezuma Creek and up the San Juan River. She shortened her skirts at the ankles making it easier to ride a horse by sitting astride the saddle rather than the proper lady-like side-saddle method which she found uncomfortable and unnecessary. Besides, the shortened skirt made it easier to mount and dismount her horse as well as making it less cumbersome to hike.

In 1895 she met up with Al Wetherill again and this time they headed down river along the San Juan past Bluff all the way to Johns Canyon (which she called Willow Creek (Wilson, 1955, p. 44). She was a dedicated conservationist and her study of plants from the Four Corners area provided the baseline for future work in the field of botany. With three main goals in mind: identification, classification and description, she collected and documented hundreds of varieties of rare native plants from the high desert plateau as she focused on collections from areas that had not been fully studied and areas that were in danger of disappearing. The large cattle herds that spread across the Four Corners arid rangeland were eating and stomping rare native plants into oblivion. She is credited with building the botanical collection at the California Academy of Sciences. She published over 300 scientific articles, several books and edited botanical journals. Alice Eastwood served as an inspiration for all women and published half of her works after she was fifty years old. She never married as her first love was always plants. (Wilson, 1955)

8. Nordenskiöld, Gustaf, 1893, *The Cliff Dwellers of the Mesa Verde*

9. Snead, James E., 2003, Ruins and Rivals: the making of Southwest Archaeology, The University of Arizona Press, Tucson, p166.

10. Ibid. p.79-80; also Lee, Ronald F., 1970, *The Antiquities Act of 1906.*

11. Smith, Duane A., 1988, Mesa Verde National Park: Shadows of the Centuries; p. 149.

12. Smith, Duane A. and Winkler, William C., 2005, *Travels and Travails, Tourism at Mesa Verde:* Durango, Colorado: Durango Herald Small Press; Heriot, Ruthanne, 1987, Finding aide to the Jesse L. Nusbaum papers, 1921-1958 *in* NPS History Collection; 4p.

13. Smith, Duane A. and Winkler, William C., 2005, p. 43-65.

14. Seyfarth, Jill and Ruth Lambert, 2010, *History of La Plata County, Colorado*; pdf, p.101-102.

15. Smith, Duane A., 1988, Mesa Verde National Park: Shadows of the Centuries; p. 105.

16. Ibid, p. 106.

17. Ibid, p. 127

18. Ibid, The Nusbaum Years, p. 105-126.

19. Don Ross, personal communications, 2015

20. Smith, Duane A. and Winkler, William C., 2005, p. 71.

21. Ibid, p.82.

22. Kenny Ross Mesa Verde National Park job application form; Jan 4, 1944

23. Brown, Ronald C. and Smith, Duane A., 2006, *New Deal Days: The CCC at Mesa Verde*: The Durango Herald Small Press, 133p. for details regarding the CCC and the program's involvement in working at Mesa Verde National Park

24. Unedited draft of taped oral interview of Kenny Ross in Mancos, Colorado September 13, 1986 by Herm Hoops (unpublished manuscript)

25. Letter of commendation to Kenny Ross from Emergency Conservation Work; Feb 15, 1935

26. Certificate of Discharge from Civilian Conservation Corps dated 07/28/1935

27. Ibid.

28. Kenny Ross interviewed by Duane Smith, July 29, 1986 *in* Smith, Duane A., 1988, p.136.

29. Smith, Duane A. 1988, Mesa Verde National Park: Shadows of the Centuries, p. 132.

30. See *Louis Jacques Mandé Daguerre* on Internet

31. WILLIAM HENRY JACKSON (1843 – 1942) was an American painter, Civil War veteran, geological survey photographer and an explorer famous for his images of the American West. He was asked by Ferdinand Hayden in 1870-1871 to join Hayden's expedition to explore the Yellowstone River region; Famous painter Thomas Moran was also part of the expedition.

Jackson exhibited photographs and clay models of Anasazi dwellings at Mesa Verde in Colorado in the 1876 Centennial Exposition in Philadelphia. He continued traveling on the Hayden Surveys until the last one in 1878. Jackson came to Bluff and SE Utah as a detachment of the Hayden Survey in hot midsummer of 1875. Jackson followed the San Juan River and came from Colorado via McElmo Canyon and made it as far down the San Juan River to south side of river near Midway Canyon, then went up Chinle Wash and on southwestward to the Hopi Mesa's. He went through Comb Ridge where Highway 163 goes today and missed seeing River House Ruin but found Poncho House. From Hopi he came back via Chinle but then went up Comb Wash.

CHARLES GOODMAN (1843 – 1912) was a traveling photographer and salesman. In the summer of 1893 he moved his studio to Mancos, Colorado where he became the local newspaper's photographer. He followed the "gold excitement" west to Bluff City and took part in the over-promotion of the excitement and the oil boom that followed in 1908. He died on February 13, 1912 in Bluff.

32. Email from Fred Blackburn, 11/15/2016

33. Don Ross, personal communications, 2015

34. Ibid.

35. Ibid.

36. Jill Blumenthal, Mesa Verde NPS Education and Volunteer Coordinator let me and Don Ross see the back of the dioramas in Sept, 2017. The space is incredibly tight; there was barely enough room to squeeze between the back of dioramas and the back wall.

37. Letter to Kenny from MVNPS Acting Chief, Division of Appointments dated May 18, 1936, appointing Kenny a National Park Ranger, Grade 7, at Mesa Verde National Park.

38. Ibid.

39. Don Ross personal communications 2015

40. Kenny Ross MVNPS work file of letters 1935-1946

41. Memo to Kenny Ross from Paul R. Franke, 03/25/1937

42. Letter to Kenny from William B. Newbold; 03/09/1937

43. Job application notes 05/28/1937

44. Letter to Kenny from Earnest Hunter, 06/09/1937

45. Lister, Florence C, 1997, *Prehistory in Peril: the worst and best of Durango Archaeology*; University Press of Colorado; 196p.

46. Letter to Kenny from Editha Berry, 03/08/1937

47. Letter from Kenny to Helen Sloan Daniels, 09/03/1937

48. Mildred Skinner Ross hand-written notes; Ross letter collection

49. Ibid.

50. Ibid.

51. Don and Doug Ross, personal communications, 2015

52. Ibid.

53. Kenny Ross MVNPS work file of letters 1935-1946

54. Mildred Ross notes remembering Skinner family origins

55. Mildred Ross hand-written notes

56. Ibid.

57. Email from Doug Ross, 5/20/15 re: airplanes and Indians

58. Email exchange with Bill Dickinson and his reply 6/6/2015

59. Telephone conversation mid-June, 2015 with Roger Hayes, a pilot friend from Durango who identified the plane as a Stinson; also internet search of 1930s vintage airplanes

60. Email from Doug Ross, 5/25/15

61. Kenny Ross MVNPS work file of letters 1935-1946

62. Ibid.

63. Mildred Ross hand-written notes

64. Don Ross personal communications 2017

65. Kenny Ross MVNPS work file of letters 1935-1946

66. Mildred Ross hand-written notes

67. Ibid.

68. Don Ross, personal communication, 2015 regarding a comment he remembered being told.

69. Doug Ross, personal communications, 2017

70. Kenny Ross MVNPS work file of letters 1935-1946

71. Kenny Ross job application at MVNP dated 01/04/1944

72. The flash of light and earth-shaking noise was an experimental Atomic bomb blast from White Sands Missile Range – 325 miles south of the Colorado-New Mexico stateline

73. Mildred's handwritten notes are from many years later (early 1990s). The Germans surrendered May 7, 1945 and America declared May 8th VE Day. On August 6, 1945 the B-29 Flying Fortress "Enola Gay" dropped the first atomic bomb on Hiroshima, followed by the second bomb dropped on Nagasaki on August 9, 1945. Japan surrendered on August 15, with the formal surrender occurring on September 2, 1945 aboard the USS Missouri; President Harry S. Truman declared September 2 as V-J Day and WWII had ended.

74. Kenny Ross MVNPS work file of letters 1935-1946

75. Mildred Ross hand-written notes

76. Kenny Ross Memorandum Letter of Resignation from Mesa Verde National Park, January 15, 1946

77. Mildred Ross hand-written notes

78. Doug Ross, personal communications, October, 2016

79. Letter from Ansel Hall to Kenny Ross 04/29/1946

80. Letter from Jess Nusbaum in Santa Fe, NM to Kenny At Ross Photographic Studios, Cortez, Colorado 05/07/1946

81. Ibid.

82. Ibid.

83. Ibid.

84. The Denver and Rio Grande Western Railroad provided rail lines across much of southwestern Colorado; most were narrow gauge rails to accommodate the twisting alpine courses required for the region. The railroad company had established concession agreements with national parks as part of their carrying passengers and supplies to the remote southwest.

85. Turner, Jack, 1998, Early Images of the Southwest: Lantern slides of Ansel F. Hall; published by Roberts Rinehart, Niwot, Colorado; 90p.

86. Ibid.

87. Smith, Duane A., 1983; *Rocky Mountain Boom Town: A History of Durango, Colorado*: Boulder, Colorado; Pruett Publishing Company

88. Ibid.

89. Ibid.

90. Ibid., p.176

CHAPTER 4

1. The Sponsors – Advisory Board listed twelve individuals in the 1946 Explorers' Camp for Boys brochure whose achievements were on record in "Who's Who in America" and "American Men in Science."

2. 1944 Memo from Ansel Hall to Col. MacNab and Harvey Stork; 1945 Explorers Camp brochure; 1946 Explorers Camp promotional pamphlet; GMS pdf files

3. Hand-written memo from Ansel Hall to Col. MacNab and Dr. Stork, 1944

4. Ibid.

5. Ibid.

6. Eckel, Edwin B., Williams, J.S. and Galbraith, F.W., 1949, Geology and ore deposits of the La Plata district Colorado, U. S. Geological Survey Professional Paper 219, p. 120.

7. Ibid, p. 120-121: "Gold King, Location and History" The Gold King mine began large-scale production in 1927 from telluride veins in altered redbeds. The Gold King vein (an extension of the Eureka and Bulldozer

mines) was discovered by Basil Caramouzis in 1921. The La Plata Mines Co. bought the property and claim from Basil in 1927. They bought the old Bonnie Girl & Baker Contact mills, which had not been operated since 1908 and rebuilt them, adding flotation machinery to the original stamp-mill equipment. After several years of successful operation the company "fell into difficulties" and from 1933 to the end of 1935 the mine was operated on a cooperative basis under a trusteeship. The mine was taken over in 1936 by a Canadian company – the Fawn mining Co. They worked the mine under several managements until the autumn of 1937 when the developed ore having been exhausted, the mine and mill were shut down.

Production of Gold King Mine, 1921-1941: Gold (ounces): 12,137.45; Silver (ounces): 141,349; Lead (pounds): 440,900

The mill site was purchased by Ansel Hall in 1945 and, "there was one substantial two story building (which became the HQ office and the mess hall) that had been part of the finishing process for the mining. There was a cabin on the hillside above the road (for the Ross family), a couple of shed structures scattered about and the remains of an old flume, long abandoned and falling down. What stands there now, is an old chimney left after the 'mess hall' burned down a year or two after Explorers Camp left the place. The stone fireplace and chimney were added by some Texans after Ansel sold the place. The Texans had bought it for a hunting camp/lodge." (Don and Doug Ross, June, 2017)

8. "A thick wooden box was built out of aspen boards (Jim Cook made the boards out of sawn billet cores leftover from the match making process in Mancos). Kenny probably built it. Then one of the other chores was to drive up the road and find an avalanche that had crossed the road and chop out rock solid pieces of snow and haul them back to the mess hall and toss them in the 'cooler' and cover the blocks of ice/snow with straw. Thus was the refrigeration for things that needed it. Kenny was very talented as a woodworker and did some amazing carving projects for furniture and tables at MVNP and around our house. He definitely liked woodworking. I don't think it was something he sought out much after the CCC, but when it needed to be done around boat camp or in Mancos, he was really good at it." (Doug Ross, June, 2017)

9. 1944, Dr. Harvey E. Stork's seven-page Field Director's Report; p. 1-2.

10. Ibid, p. 3

11. Ibid, p. 3-4

12. Ibid. The Three Programs outlined;, p. 4

13. Ibid, Details about the Mesa Verde Program; p. 4-5.

14. Ibid, The Rancho La Plata Program, p. 5

15. Ibid, The La Plata City Area Program, p.5-6

16. 1945 Explorers Camp four-page glossy promotional pamphlet

17. Ibid.

18. Travel to and from Gold King Camp to Durango was a much different route than today requiring several hours drive time in each direction. Until the late 1950s the dirt road down from Gold King intersected paved road at Hesperus and crossed narrow-gauge railroad tracks. The narrow paved road headed *west* to Mancos or dropped *south* following the La Plata River to Farmington, NM. The route to Durango headed south of Hesperus about 7.5 miles to Breen and then turned east onto the Wildcat Canyon Road that headed east-northeastward into Durango where it crossed the old bridge across the Animas River and mouth of Lightner Creek. Don and Doug Ross recall riding in the old Chevy "woody station wagon" and crossing under railroad trestles along the Wildcat Canyon section. The route of present day U.S. Highway 160 over Hesperus Hill wasn't completed until the early 1960s. The historical bridge crossing the Animas River was replaced in 1968 by a concrete and steel bridge.

19. 1945 Explorers Camp four-page glossy promotional pamphlet

20. Ibid.

21. 1945 Explorers Camp Report of Winslow M. Walker, Archaeologist and Counselor; Summary of Activities; a four-page typed journal

22. Ibid, p. 1

23. Ibid, p. 1

24. Ibid, p. 1

25. Ibid, p. 1; see Arthur Woodward article in the *Ogden Standard-Examiner* on November 19, 1933 where he refers to an Entah as a "mud dance" for the healing or cleansing ceremonies following the taking of scalps. The Entah was a three-day ceremony. It was also tied to a ceremony for the youngest wife of Hosteen Endischi [Endische] – wealthiest Navajo of entire northwestern part of reservation. Endischi land was six miles south of sacred Navajo Mountain. Woodward was the expert archaeologist hired by Ansel Hall for the 1945-46 Explorers Camp season and "discovered" the ancient rock art in Indian Creek under a canopy rock. Randall Henderson wrote an article about these "Glyph Hunters" in the November, 1946 edition of *Desert Magazine*.

26. Ibid. p 1

27. Ibid, p. 1

28. Ibid, p. 2

29. Ibid, p. 2; the artesian water well at Navajo Twin Rocks

30. Ibid, p. 2

31. Ibid, p. 2

32. Ibid, p. 3

33. Ibid, p. 4

34. H.E. Stork eight-page memo recommending Explorers Camp Program changes for the 1946 season; written October 29, 1945 to Ansel Hall

35. Ibid, p. 3

36. Letter from Porter Sargent to Ansel Hall; 03/29/1946

37. Letter from Ansel Hall to Col. Charles A. Lindbergh; 04/27/1946

38. Ibid.

39. 1946 Explorers Camp eight-page glossy promotional pamphlet written by Ansel Hall

40. List of 1946 Explorers Camp Members

41. Magazine article, *Doctors on the Trail*, in *Clinical Medicine*, vol. 54, no.5, May, 1947, p.166-170; reprint

42. Ibid.

43. Ibid.

44. Ibid.

45. Henderson, Randall, 1946, *Glyph Hunters in the Indian Country;* November issue, *Desert Magazine*, p.11-16; a group photo of fourteen boys and four adults is captioned on p. 15 of the article

46. Ibid, a map showing their route is on p. 13

47. *Doctors on the Trail*, p. 168

48. Ibid, p. 168

49. Letter from Ansel Hall to Kenny Ross 04/29/1946

50. Letter from Jess Nusbaum in Santa Fe, NM to Kenny At Ross Photographic Studios, Cortez, Colorado 05/07/1946

51. The Bureau of Land Management (BLM) came into existence during the Truman Administration following WWII as the Reorganization Act of 1945 signed into law on July 16, 1946. The BLM was created through a merger of the General Land Office (GLO) and the U.S. Grazing Service. Originally, BLM holdings were described as "land nobody wanted" because homesteaders had passed them by.

52. Hand-written memo from Ansel Hall to Col. MacNab and Dr. Stork, 1944.

53. 1946 Explorers Camp promotional pamphlet; p. 5

54. Letter from Jess Nusbaum in Santa Fe, NM to Kenny At Ross Photographic Studios, Cortez, Colorado 05/07/1946

55. 1946 Explorers Camp promotional pamphlet; p. 5

56. Kenny Ross, 1951 Southwest Explorations Narrative Report, Explorers Camp, p.19

57. Magazine article, *Doctors on the Trail*, May 1947, Bob Junior quote, p. 169

58. Shanks, Trina R.W., 2005, p. 20-41; Homestead Act and Enlarged Homestead Act of 1909; "About the Homestead Act" National Park Service website.

59. Kenny Ross family records

60. Winkler, William C., and Bradley, Bruce, 1999, Ansel Hall Pueblo: a National Historic Place; Colorado Historical Society Document submitted November 25, 1997.

61. Guthe, Alfred K., 1949, a preliminary report on excavations in Southwestern Colorado: American Antiquity; vol. 15, no. 2, p. 144-154.

62. Kenny Ross, 1951 Southwest Explorations Narrative Report, Explorers Camp, p. 6; Winkler, William C., and Bradley, Bruce, 1999, Ansel Hall Pueblo: Section 7, p.4.

63. Thompson, Ian "Sandy", 1982, "Kenny Ross: River rat and teacher;" for Early Man (unpublished manuscript)

64. Kenny Ross, Director, 1955, Southwest Explorations Explorers Camp Brochure, p. 7.

65. Artifacts from the Ansel Hall Ruin site are now located at the Anasazi Heritage Center in Dolores, Colorado as of December 12, 2000. A discrepancy in reported Longitude was noted in the course of my research that locates the ruin in Section 17 and not Section 18. I spoke with BLM archaeologist Michael Macmillan on

January 19, 2018 to clarify the location and he told me he could not "legally" confirm or deny its' true location. A curious answer considering the ruin is on public land and entered on the National Register of Historic Places. Thus, verification of the actual GPS location of this ruin remains suspect.

The Wilderness Trust Fund requested a grant of $44,900 for the Ansel Hall Ruin (site 5DL.27) in 1999. Reference 25: History Colorado. Retrieved 9-27-2011. County/Location: Dolores / Rural; Applicant Name: The Wilderness Land Trust; Description: Acquisition; ID #: 99-01-024; SITE #: 5DL.27; Property: Ansel Hall Ruin-Cahone Ruin Site No. 1- Great Pueblo Period of the McElmo Drainage Unit

66. Winkler, William C., and Bradley, Bruce, 1999, Ansel Hall Pueblo: a National Historic Place; Colorado Historical Society Document submitted November 25, 1997; Section 7, p.1.

67. Ibid; and Tobin, S.J., 1950, Notes on Site No. 1, Cahone Ruin, Southwestern Colorado: Southwestern Lore, March, vol. XV, No.4.

68. Winkler, William C., and Bradley, Bruce, 1999, Ansel Hall Pueblo

69. Kenny Ross files; Jeep, Chevy and 1.5 ton Truck Titles

70. Randall Henderson, magazine article *"We Explored Dark Canyon"* December 1946, *The Desert Magazine*, p. 5-10)

71. Knowles Hall became sick and did not complete the trip; he is not in any photos in lower canyon

72. Mapping involved using Esri Arc/GIS software to document distances and elevations. All of the Fran Hall and Kenny Ross photographs documenting the trip are part of the Ross Collection at Marriott Library

73. Randall Henderson, 1946, magazine article, p.7

74. Roger Hall comment *in* Gulliford, Andrew, 2010, April 12 Draft manuscript: A column for the Durango Herald newspaper re: overview of Ansel Hall and Explorers Camp; *unpublished*

75. Allen, Steve, 2012, *Utah's canyon country place names: stories of the cowboys, miners, pioneers, and river runners who put names on the land*; Canyon Country Press, Durango, CO; Two Volumes, 985 p; Allen provides three pages (p.193-195) naming various sources of river runners, trappers to early pioneers who may be considered the primary source of when and how Dark Canyon got its name.

76. Randall Henderson, 1946, magazine article, p.7

77. Richard Stultz, 1946 Leader Report; Contribution No. 2, p.1-2

78. Ibid; Contribution No. 8, p.4

79. Ibid; Contribution No. 9, p.5

80. Letter from Ansel Hall to Kenny Ross 10/15/1946; terms of employment

CHAPTER 5

1. Kenny's lengthy letters, memos, and reports have all been scanned and saved as pdf files in my records

2. Bucks War Surplus Store located at 4965 Geist Ave., Las Vegas, Nevada; one of the largest military surplus stores in the southwest

3. Most notable USGS publications Kenny may have read include: Baker, A.A., 1936; Gilbert, G.K., 1911, 1914; Gregory, H.E., 1911, 1916, 1917, 1938; Miser, Hugh D., 1924, 1925; LaRue, E.C., 1916, 1925

4. Evans, Richard T. and Frye, Helen M., 2009, History of the Topographic Branch (Division) of the U.S. Geological Survey Circular 1341, 196p. The earliest topographic maps of Elk Ridge to the Colorado River were made by USGS in 1935 and 1940 at scale of 1:96000 and 1:125000; the best maps for the San Juan River were still plats from the Trimble/Miser U.S. Geol. Survey of 1921 & published in 1924.

5. Staveley, Gaylord, 2015, p. 21; my own personal observations

6. Berg, A Scott, 1999, Charles A. Lindbergh biography

7. Letter from Charles Lindbergh's secretary, Barbara Mansfield, to Ansel Hall 03/05/1947

8. Letter from Kenny to Lindbergh's secretary 05/31/1947

9. Letter from Charles A. Lindbergh's secretary to Kenny 06/16/1947

10. Don Ross did a Grand Canyon trip with Jack Oakes in 1962

11. Personal communications with Don Ross, November, 2016.

12. Ansel Hall Explorers Camp Newsletter, May 1947

13. Ibid; the only direct route to reach Bluff from Cortez, Colorado by automobile in the late 1940s to the late 1950s was to follow the McElmo Canyon graded road westward to the historic Ismay Trading Post near the Colorado-Utah stateline. The route then turned onto a poorly maintained dirt (sand) track where it crossed Yellow Jacket Wash and proceeded north along Ruin Canyon for about two miles and then turned west-northwestward onto the "Old Bluff Road" through Wickiup Canyon, then across Cajon Mesa and down Black Steer Canyon where it intersected the broad sandy Montezuma Creek wash near Hatch Trading Post (Cajon Mesa UT-CO 7.5" 1958 USGS topo map). The route continued westward on a dirt road across McCracken Mesa, crossed Recapture Creek before intersecting the graded State roadway 47 (present day U.S. Highway 191) at the base of White Mesa hill. The route then turned south onto State Road 47 and proceeded south across the Bluff Bench and finally down the steep Cow Canyon road cut into the hamlet of Bluff. *The first sections of these roads from Hatch to Bluff were not graveled until the early 1950s. State Road 47 from Blanding to Bluff wasn't paved until the late 1950s.* The road from Bluff to Mexican Hat was first paved in the early 1960s. Present day route (State Highway 162) that connects the Montezuma Creek Chapter with Bluff was not accessible until bridges were completed in 1983-85 that cross four major washes (Montezuma, Bucket Canyon, McCracken and Recapture creeks) and not paved until 1986 (UDOT Highway records).

14. Ansel Hall Explorers Camp Newsletter, May 1947; it took Ansel and Jim Cook the better part of six hours to make a 25 mile round trip to Mexican Hat. The road cut through Comb Ridge was steep and narrow and the road across Lime Ridge to Mexican Hat was bone jarring and slow going, and of course, unpaved and barely passable in wet weather. There was no bridge crossing Cottonwood Creek immediately west of Bluff and bridge across Comb Wash was not completed until 1966 (earlier bridges may have existed but were washed away); bridges across Lime Creek and some unnamed washes were not completed until 1962-64 (UDOT highway records).

15. Ansel Hall Explorers Camp Newsletter, May 1947

16. Ibid; Barton Trading Post and "Snake House" or "River House Ruin"

17. Dark gray dense limestone beds were mistakenly described as "basalts" by Ansel Hall here and Randall Henderson in his description of hiking down Dark Canyon. Basalt is an **igneous rock**, commonly deposited as molten lava, whereas the dark limestone beds common in the limestone canyons of the San Juan River and Cataract Canyon are **sedimentary** rocks and was originally deposited as seafloor muds and contains marine fossils (see Glossary).

18. Ansel Hall Explorers Camp Newsletter, May 1947

19. Ibid; see Glossary "shooting rapids"

20. Ibid.

21. Letter from *Goodyear Rubber Co.* to Kenny re: repair kit & materials; 05/07/1947
    Lt. Peddicord designed an inflatable boat and brought his plans to the *Goodyear Tire and Rubber Company* who produced the Landing Craft Rubber-Small craft able to hold seven men that was extensively used by the later Naval Combat Demolition Units. Initially the Navy (Marines) and Army worked together on the development of inflatable boats for reconnaissance, special operations and demolition, rescue, assault, carrying cargo and for other purposes. Kayaks and canvas folding boats were also tested but were rejected. The determining criteria for boat selection was that reconnaissance boats needed to fit through the small hatches of fleet submarines while carrying weapons and equipment and be capable of handling related loads. In 1939 Fred Patten had designed and produced small life rafts to be used in planes. The LCRS (Also identified as IBS - Inflatable Boat Small) was an inflatable boat that could transport seven men, used by the U. S. Navy and Marines from 1938 to 1945. During World War II 8,150 LCRSs were made. LCRS were 7-man inflatable rubber boats with a displacement of 210 lb. light, (277.4 lb with motor). length: 12'5"-14', beam: 5'11", draft: 0' and speed: 4.5 knots with 6 ½ HP outboard motor. This boat was the prototype for the Selway Whitewater model designed by Ron Smith and initially manufactured by Rubber Fabricators, Inc. in its Richwood, WV plant (H. Hoops email 6/28/2018).
    On November 10, 1942, the first combat demolition unit (organized in a six-man team of an officer, a petty officer and four seamen using a seven-man LCR-S) succeeded in cutting a cable and net barrier across the Sebou River in northern Morocco during *Operation Torch* in North Africa. Their actions enabled the destroyer USS Dallas to traverse the river under cannon and small arms fire as she plowed her way through mud and shallow water, narrowly missing the many sunken ships and other obstructions, and sliced through a cable crossing the river, to land her troops safely just off the airport. [Dockery, Kevin & Brutsman, Bud, 2007, *Navy SEALS: A History of the Early Years* Berkley; p.16-17] The Explorers Camp acquired four (4) 7-man LCR-S assault boats summer, 1948.
    The first 10-man LCR-L came along in 1951; the EC boys called it "The Monster" since it was so much bigger and heavier than the LCR-S.

22. Ansel Hall Explorers Camp Newsletter, May 5,1947

23. Ibid, p. 4

24. On July 29, 1776, one of the greatest expeditions of the southwest was begun at Santa Fe by *Fray Padre Francisco Silvestre Velez Escalante and Francisco Atanasio Dominguez*, in their search for a route to Monterey. By using *Juan Maria Antonio de Rivera*'s information from his expedition in 1765 Escalante & Dominguez believed a better road existed to Monterey by way of the north than by the middle route, and a further incentive to journey that way was probably the rumors of large towns in that direction. The party went by way of Abiquiu and Chama River and reached the San Juan River (which was named by Rivera) about where it first meets the north line of New Mexico; thence they crossed several tributaries to near the head of the Dolores River, which they descended for eleven days. The party made its way across the Grand River, the Book Plateau, and White River, to the Green (called the San Buenaventura), which was forded apparently near the foot of Split Mountain Canyon. Following the course of the river down some thirty miles, they went up the Uinta (now called Duchesne) and finally crossed the Wasatch Range, coming down the western side, evidently by way of what is now known as Spanish Fork, to Utah Lake, and then called by the natives Timpanogos. Here they heard of a greater lake to the north, but instead of seeking it they turned southwesterly in what they considered the direction of Monterey through Sevier River valley, calling the Sevier the Santa Isabel, and kept down along the western edge of the high plateaus. It was by this time early October and Escalante concluded that it would be impossible to reach Monterey before winter set in; he therefore persuaded his companions that it would be best to strike for the Hopi villages in Arizona.
    Going on southward past what is now Parowan, they came to the headwaters of a branch of the Virgin, in Cedar Valley, and this they followed down to the main stream, which they left flowing southwesterly. The place where they turned from it was probably about at Toquerville. Trying to make their general course southeast, they passed over the country now known as Kanab, Nine-mile Valley, Kaibab Plateau, Horse Rock Valley, and Vermilion Cliffs, and at length struck the Colorado at Marble Canyon. Twice they succeeded in descending to the river but were unable to cross. On November 8, 1776, they reached the ford

by following Padre Creek to what is now known as the *Crossing of the Fathers*, located about forty miles north of Lees Ferry, and about thirty eight miles below the confluence of the Colorado and San Juan Rivers. From this crossing to the Hopi villages Escalante-Dominguez had a plain trail, and on reaching Santa Fe the exploration party had completed a circuit of more than 1,500 miles, mainly through unknown country. This is one of the most remarkable explorations ever carried out in the West (from LaRue, 1916).

Perhaps the most important accomplishment of the expedition was a set of fairly accurate maps of the central Colorado Plateau made by retired engineer *Captain Bernardo de Miera y Pacheco.* [Map from Utah State Historical Society; Aton & McPherson, 2000, p. 44] Pacheco mistakenly identified the upper San Juan as a tributary to the Navajo River rather than the other way around, but he showed it running generally in an east-to-west direction out of the San Juan Mountains and he clearly showed where the San Juan entered the Colorado River. He identified and named the Abajo Mountains, and major tributaries like the Los Piños and Animas, Dolores, and of course, the San Juan River.

25. Ansel Hall Explorers Camp Newsletter, May 5, 1947, p. 4.

26. Richard Van Valkenburgh wrote articles for "*Desert Magazine* about Navajo and prehistoric peoples of the southwest" but was a no-show for the 1947 Explorers Camp.

27. Letter from Kenny to Charles A. Lindbergh 07/23/1947; "Rainbow Lodge was started by the Richardson's near Endische Spring, which is shown on Bernheimer's map. The buildings and corral circled in the referenced photo (Fig. 5.8) are of that. Barry Goldwater once had an interest in the lodge. The trail from there to Rainbow Bridge was put in by John Wetherill and others on the 1922 Bernheimer expedition." (Email from Harvey Leake, April 4, 2018); see Bernheimer trail map, Figure 2.1.

28. Ibid.

29. Ibid.

30. Letter from Kenny to Bill Dickinson 11/12/1948

31. Letter from Charles A. Lindbergh to Kenny 09/05/1947

32. End of 1947 Explorers Camp Report to Charles A. Lindbergh from Ansel Hall

33. See photo, p.24, in A. Christenson, 1987

34. Letter from Hank Zuidema to Ansel Hall 09/12/1947

35. Letter from Ansel Hall to Hank Zuidema 09/23/1947

36. Ibid; also, in 1947 Charles Lindbergh, who was an Honorary Member of the prestigious Explorers Club, NY supported Kenny Ross's full membership in the organization.

37. Letter from A. Hall to H. Zuidema 04/19/1948

38. Letter from Zuidema to Hall 04/26/1948

39. Letter from Jon Lindbergh to Kenny Ross 01/21/1948 Ltr

40. Email from Bill Dickinson 06/15/2015; I had forwarded pdf copies of his correspondences with Kenny and others that were in Kenny's files and Bill replied with commentary about each letter from 1948 to 1983

41. The name **DUKW** comes from the model naming terminology used by GMC

- "**D**", designed in 1942
- "**U**", "utility"

- **"K"**, all-wheel drive
- **"W"**, dual rear axles

The **DUKW** (colloquially known as **Duck**) was a six-wheel-drive amphibious truck used by the U.S. military in World War II. Designed by GMC, the DUKW was used for the transportation of goods and troops over land and water. Excelling at approaching and crossing beaches in amphibious warfare attacks, it was intended only to last long enough to meet the demands of combat. Surviving DUKWs have since found popularity as tourist craft in marine/aquatic environments. The DUKW prototype was built as a cab-over-engine (COE) version six-wheel-drive military truck, with the addition of a watertight hull and a propeller. The final production design was perfected by a few engineers at Yellow Truck & Coach in Pontiac, Michigan. The vehicle was built by the GMC division of General Motors, still called Yellow Truck and Coach at the beginning of the war. It was powered by a 270 in^3 (4,425 cc) GMC straight-six engine. It weighed 6.5 tons empty and operated at 50 miles per hour (80 km/h) on road and 5.5 knots (10.2 km/h; 6.3 mph) on water. It was 31 feet (9.4 m) long, 8 feet 2.875 inches (2.51 m) wide, 7 feet 1.375 inches (2.17 m) high with the folding-canvas top down and 8.8 feet (2.6 m) high with the top up. 21,137 were manufactured. It was not an armored vehicle, being plated with sheet steel between 1/16 and 1/8 inches (1.6–3.2 mm) thick to minimize weight. A high capacity bilge pump system kept it afloat if the thin hull was breached by holes up to 2 inches (51 mm) in diameter. A quarter of all DUKWs held a .50-caliber Browning heavy machine gun in a ring mount. The windshields were provided by GM rival Libbey Glass (Ford).

The DUKW was supplied to the U.S. Army, U.S. Marine Corps and Allied forces. 2,000 were supplied to Britain under the Lend-Lease program and 535 were acquired by Australian forces. 586 were supplied to the Soviet Union, which built its own version after the war. DUKWs were initially sent to the Pacific theatre's Guadalcanal, and were used by an invasion force for the first time during the Sicilian invasion in the Mediterranean. They were used on the D-Day beaches of Normandy and in other battles. Amphibious beachheads were thought to be highly vulnerable to early counterattack as the landing units would deplete their ammunition and the supply system would not yet be established. The principal use was to ferry supplies from ship to shore, and tasks such as transporting wounded combatants to hospital ships or operations in flooded land.

42. DUKW newspaper article 01/21/1948; The *Santa Ana Register* newspaper published an article entitled "Explorers Buy 'Duck' Here to Follow Old Spanish Trail." The promotional article was strongly influenced by Ansel's narrative as it stated the Duck was being "converted into a modern Conestoga wagon that will take a party of nationally-known explorers across a 3000-mile trail blazed by the Spanish explorer Father Escalante in 1776, it was disclosed today to Bascom Rush....who sold the vehicle at his war-surplus lot." The article went to considerable detail with a photo of an employee in the landing craft.

43. Letter from Kenny to Jon Lindbergh 01/28/1948; Bill Winkler personal communication on May 5, 2017 said he cut up the DUKW and turned it into a "winch truck" but could not find photos of the DUKW.

44. Email from Bill Dickinson 06/15/2015

45. Telephone conversation with Bill & Merrie 5/9/2017

46. *Explorers Camp Newsletter*, Part 1 for 1948; by Kenny Ross; formal three-page letter to parents summarizing summer activities through early August

47. Ibid.

48. Ibid; the actual distance in river miles from the Shiprock Bridge to the Mexican Hat Bridge is 110.0 miles

49. Letter from Kenny to Margaret Dickinson 06/25/1948

50. *Excerpts from Explorers' Camp Newsletter (part 1) written by Kenneth Ross: August 3, 1948;* Malcolm Whyte is listed as a member in the Second Group in the DUKW. He contacted Doug after Kenny died in 1990 to talk about the Explorers Camp days and was a super enthusiastic fan of Kenny's. He had become a publisher in San Francisco and had opened a *Comics Museum*; Doug said he was a big deal in San Francisco society.

51. *Explorers Camp Report* Part 2 for 1948, by Kenny Ross, a ten-page draft report by Kenny Ross, where he described the actual summer activities including details re: Beef Basin – Gypsum Canyon hike, p. 3

52. Ibid, p. 4

53. Ibid, p. 5

54. Ibid, p. 4; by following Kenny's notes and tracing his route on topo maps [the earliest topographic maps of Elk Ridge to the Colorado River were made by USGS in 1935 and 1940 at scale of 1:96000 and 1:125000] they drove 25 miles on UT route 95 [present day CR 268] and then turned right (N) onto Forest Road FR0088 past Little Notch, The Notch, Duck Lake, the intersection with Cottonwood Road (FR0095) after 40 miles and proceeded north to the intersection with North Long Point Road (FR0091) at MP 43.5 thence another mile or so to the grove of aspens near Crystal Spring (seswne Sec 27-T33S-R19E; Lat: 37°52'49.9" & Long: -109° 48' 51") where they set up base camp with the DUKW at elevation of 8,640 ft. Total driving distance from Blanding to this spot was approximately 45.0 miles.

55. Ibid, p. 4-5; the 1st day's hike began by following a trail from camp that dropped them into Bull Canyon and they contoured back around and picked up another trail past the junction with Ruin Canyon (@ 6.75 miles) and made it to junction with Beef Basin at about the 10 mile point near Beef Basin Spring.

56. Ibid, p. 5; "passage around a rock point" is at an elevation of ~5500 ft (nwswne Sec 26-T32S-R17E) about 4.5 to 5 miles from mouth of Gypsum Canyon and the Colorado River.

57. Ibid, p. 6; The hike from the DUKW base camp on North Long Point (elev. 8,640 ft) to mouth of Gypsum Canyon was approximately 24.5 miles; elevation at confluence is ~3620 ft, therefore the elevation difference was ~5,020 ft.

58. Ibid, p. 6

59. Ibid, p. 6

60. Letter from Jon Lindbergh to Kenny 02/07/1948

61. Letter from Kenny to Charles A. Lindbergh 06/25/1948

62. Letter from Charles A. Lindbergh to Kenny 07/10/1948

63. Letter from Kenny to Jon Lindbergh 02/07/1949

64. Ibid.

65. 1949 Explorers Camp promotional leaflet, p. 4

66. Letter of recommendation from Kenny to R. Allan Clapp 12/28/1948

67. Ibid.

68. Letter from Maynard Oakes to Allan Clapp 01/09/1949

69. Letter from Stuart Maule to Allan Clapp 01/14/1949

CHAPTER 6

1. 1949 Explorers Camp Brochure with itinerary and Map

2. The U.S. government's only time to guarantee a price for a natural resource occurred during the "uranium frenzy in the post WWII period; see Ringholz, Raye Carleson, 1991, *Uranium Frenzy: Boom and Bust on the Colorado Plateau*

3. Letter from Hank Zuidema to Ansel Hall 01/29/1949

4. Letter from Kenny to Hank Zuidema 03/16/1949

5. Ibid.

6. Letter from Zuidema to Kenny 06/08/1949

7. Letter from Kenny to Zuidema 06/09/1949

8. Letter from Hank Zuidema to Ansel Hall 01/29/1949

9. *Nash-Kelvinator* came into being in 1937 when Nash Motors, an automobile manufacturer in Kenosha, WI since 1916, merged with Kelvinator Appliance, a maker of home appliances in Detroit, MI. The Kelvinator Corporation, pioneers in automatic refrigeration technology, has its roots in 1914 with former General Motors executives Edmund J. Copeland and Arnold H. Goss. That year in Detroit, inventor Nathaniel B. Wales pitched to the entrepreneurs his idea for an automatic refrigeration machine for the home. Within two years, Wales presented them with the first functioning model, and the Electro-Automatic Refrigerating Company was established in 1916. Just two months later, the company was renamed the Kelvinator Corporation in honor of Lord Kelvin, the British physicist who discovered absolute zero and established the Kelvin temperature scale.

   Then in 1954 Nash-Kelvinator merged with Hudson to form what became *American Motors*. Nash-Kelvinator during World War II did not manufacture products related to its pre-war product lines. In fact, it was one of only three American automobile manufacturers to build complete aircraft, in this case the *Sikorsky R-6A helicopter*. Nash-Kelvinator built more helicopters during World War II than Sikorsky and the rest of the aviation industry put together.

   Following the war, normal refrigerator production resumed, and the company expanded by 1952 to manufacture other home appliances like ranges, washers, and driers. In 1954, Nash-Kelvinator Corporation was part of the largest auto-manufacturers merger to that point with the consolidation of Nash and Hudson Motors into the American Motors Corporation. Production continued at American Motors until 1968, when rights to the Kelvinator brand were sold to White Consolidated Industries. (Detroit Historical Society; encyclopedia of Detroit)

10. Fred Black, May 23-28, 1949 "Rio San Juan" Trip Journal, 14p.

11. Packing List for 1949 Shiprock, NM to Mexican Hat, UT San Juan River trip

12. Fred Black, Trip Journal, p. 2

13. A "chaha'oh" means *shadow* or a *summer shade house*; typically constructed from small trees, branches, twig and leaves; (correctly spelled by Navajo linguist Martha Austin-Garrison, a teacher at Navajo College in Tsaile, Arizona; referred to me by Harvey Leake, 2017)

14. Fred Black, Trip Journal, p. 3

15. Ibid, p.4

16. Ibid, p. 5

17. Fred Black didn't send his river buddies his "final" typed journal until almost two years later, so it's quite probable his notes got rearranged.

18. Fred Black, Trip Journal, p. 7

19. Ibid, p. 8

20. Doug Ross, personal communications; "this might be the source of Mildred's prized "pink columbine" that she nourished for many years in the Mancos yard."

21. Fred Black, Trip Journal, p. 8-12

22. Ibid, p. 13

23. Ibid, p. 13-14; end of Fred Black journal

24. Letter from Kenny to Don Hatch 12/15/1956

25. For detailed descriptions of Norman Nevills river adventures and biography see Roy Webb (2005) and Gaylord Staveley (2015).

26. See Crampton, C. Gregory, 1964, "The San Juan Canyon Historical Sites; *in* ANTHROPOLOGICAL PAPERS, Number 70, June, 1964, (Glen Canyon Series Number 22)' Jesse D. Jennings & Carol C. Stout, Eds; p. 21-24. Norm & Doris Nevills second try at a "honeymoon trip" was in March, 1934 as shown in the inscription.

27. See Roy Webb (2005) and Gaylord Staveley (2015) for details concerning his influence on other river runners

28. Staveley, 2015, p. 194-105.

29. See Crampton, 1964, p. 23.

30. Don Ross, personal communication, 2015; also see Staveley, 2015, p.131 about Norms "stunts."

31. Staveley, 2015, p. 112; note: the photo on p. 111 in Staveley book; it's a photo of Nevills running stern first in Gypsum Rapid in a fold flat boat and the narrative leads one to believe this was the pre-Honeymoon test run; but, as Jack Frost stated, it wasn't until <u>after</u> the Honeymoon trip that Nevills accepted this method of 'facing the danger.' I suspect that Norm ran this fold flat boat some years after 1935 'playing' with the old boat and having his photo taken. The photo doesn't fit the narrative about when Nevills began to run stern first.

32. Letter from Kenny to Don Hatch 12/15/1956

33. Letter from Dock Marston to Kenny 03/11/1953

34. Letter from Kenny to Don Hatch 12/15/1956

35. See note 22, Chapter Five re: LCR's

36. Letter from Kenny to Dock Marston 03/07/1953

37. Email from Bill Dickinson, 04/2015

38. A direct quote from Kenny Ross for new boatmen to remember, particularly for the San Juan River; see detailed explanation in note #26, Chapter 10

39. Explorers Camp 1949 promotional leaflet

40. Southwest Explorations Field Program, 1949

41. Ibid, Itinerary for season defined with specific dates for activities

42. Letter from Kenny to Bill Dickinson 03/15/1949

43. Email from Bill Dickinson 06/15/2015; Comments about his old letters

44. Explorers Camp Newsletter; a progress report to parents from Kenny July 28,1949

45. Ibid, p. 1

46. Ibid, p. 1

47. "The Jackson Gulch dam and reservoir was dedicated Sunday, July 3, 1949 before a crowd of nearly 2000 who heard District Judge James M. Noland and Judge Clifford H. Stone suggest that the new $3,850,000 dam near Mancos be renamed for the late Judge John B. O'Rourke, an early proponent of such projects." (1949, July 7 *Montezuma Valley Journal*; p.1 and *Cortez Sentinel*, p.10) The Jackson Gulch Reservoir is located at an elevation of 7,825 ft. Construction of the reservoir was approved by President Franklin D. Roosevelt in 1941. An aqueduct runs nearly seventeen miles from Jackson Gulch Reservoir to Mesa Verde National Park, providing the major source of municipal water to the Far View Annex Visitors Center at the north end of Chapin Mesa as well as the Park Headquarters at Spruce Tree House. The park still receives most of its water from this reservoir.

48. Explorers Camp Newsletter; a progress report to parents from Kenny July 28,1949, p. 1

49. Telephone conversation with Bill Winkler May 9, 2017

50. Explorers Camp Newsletter; a progress report to parents from Kenny July 28,1949, p. 2

51. Ibid, p. 2

52. Newspaper articles with photos in the *Cortez Sentinel*, July 14 and 21, 1949; *Montezuma Valley Journal*, July 21 and 28, 1949

53. Explorers Camp 1955 Newsletter, p.1

54. *Life Magazine's* digitally-archived magazines do not document this event; one poor quality Associated Press (AP) photo of the four governors was shared with numerous newspapers across the country.

55. Explorers Camp Newsletter; a progress report to parents from Kenny July 28,1949, p. 2

56. Ibid, p. 3

57. A comical phrase learned by those who worked at Wild Rivers Expeditions

58. Explorers Camp Newsletter; a progress report to parents from Kenny July 28,1949, p. 3

59. Ibid, p. 3

60. Ibid, p. 3

61. Ibid, p. 3

62. Ibid, p. 3

63. Ibid, p. 3

64. Personal communication with Doug Ross, 2017 who said Kenny told this story when talking about this period in his life.

65. Addendum to 1949 Cataract Canyon Trip Log

66. See R. Nash, 1989; Webb, etal, 2004, p. 204; Dimock, 2007, p. 105, Loper actually included Mile Long with the rapids below and called the whole run "the Big Drops."

67. See Roy Webb, 2005, p.81

68. The term "Graveyard of the Colorado" in reference to Cataract Canyon is attributed to Emery and Ellsworth Kolb following their 1911-12 river trips down this section of the Colorado River (see Allen, 2012, vol 1).

69. The name "Grand" was changed to "Colorado River" above this juncture in 1921; See Baars, 1987, where he defines Meander Canyon & anticline

70. The elevation difference of 102 ft in 63.5 miles = 0.62 feet per mile (fpm) gradient.

71. The elevation difference of 204 ft in 120 miles = 1.7 fpm gradient

72. For excellent overview and history of Cataract Canyon see Webb, et al, 2004; Baars, 1987 and for Glen Canyon see Fowler, 2011

73. See Webb, et al, 2004; Baars, 1987; also see **rapids** in Appendix IV: Glossary

74. Who wrote the river journal for the Cataract Canyon trip? Hand-written field notes were kept by Bill and Jon, but Kenny rewrote the notes and typed them when he got home. Kenny also had duplicate sets of photos made and sent copies of the typed log and photos to both Jon and Bill the following year – 1950; several sets of the typed log were in the Don Ross collection, plus Bill Dickinson sent his copy to me in 2015. As best I can tell, there are at least two slightly different sets of typed logs, but salient information is the same in each copy.

75. River gage flows for this date at Green River (USGS Gage: 09315000) & Cisco (USGS Gage: 09180500) show a combined flow of 5,500 cfs; see USGS graphs for August-September, 1949; both gages are considerable distances above Cataract Canyon and additional flows may have entered below gage points.

76. All quotes are from the Ross River Journal unless otherwise cited; see above note #74: who wrote river journal?

77. Highway number for road from Moab south to Bluff didn't change to U.S. Highway 191 until early 1960s

78. Author's note: myself and cohort boatmen/river guides seemed to always refer to "scouting" a rapid when we have pulled over and checked out the obstacles and discussed our proposed run, however, in all the Kenny Ross journals and letters to other river men of his era, he refers to "conning," an obvious abbreviation for *reconnaissance* or *reconnoiter*. Furthermore, it should also be pointed out, again, that Kenny preferred the two-man stern paddling technique, rather than rowing, but they were certainly "facing the danger."

79. Ross, Dickinson & Lindbergh, 1949, Cataract Canyon River Trip Log; unpublished

80. See Baars, 1987

81. See Huntoon, Peter W., Billingsley, George H., Jr., and Breed, William J., 1982, Geologic Map of Canyonlands National Park and Vicinity, Utah; published by The Canyonlands Natural History Association, Moab, Utah. In 1986, Don Baars and I observed heavy oil seeps occurred at low river level on the left shoreline and I collected samples of these oils in 1988 as part of a geochemical study. The oil was correlated to having been derived from the lower Paradox Formation.

82. Ross, Dickinson & Lindbergh, 1949, Cataract Canyon River Trip Log

83. Ibid.

84. See Baars, 1987; Webb etal, 2004

85. Ross, Dickinson & Lindbergh, 1949, Cataract Canyon River Trip Log

86. See Roy Webb, 2005, p.81

87. Personal *negative* experience in 1986-88 with House Boaters parked at this river camp site.

88. Ross, Dickinson & Lindbergh, 1949, Cataract Canyon River Trip Log

89. Ibid.

90. See Baars, 1987, p.49

91. Ross, Dickinson & Lindbergh, 1949, Cataract Canyon River Trip Log

92. Ibid.

93. Ibid.

94. Ibid.

95. Lengthy quote from 1949, Cataract Canyon River Trip Log; reference to rock cairn and names in the jar in letter from Kenny to Dock Marston 03/17/1956

96. Personal observations; also see geologic discussions in Baars and Stevenson, 1981, 1986b; and Baars, 1987, p.52

97. Email from Bill Dickinson (WRD) with his signature sign-off with "Ciao" June 4, 2015

98. Letter from Kenny to Charles A. Lindbergh 03/16/1950

99. See *The New York Times* Archive, April 19, 1964 "Historic Utah Ferry gets new lease on life"; see McCourt, 2003, p. 26 where he states that Elmer Johnson and later Reed Maxfield leased the ferry from Arth Chaffin. Ferry skipper Woody Edgell was probably employed by either, or both, of these gentlemen ; the ferry was leased - not owned and operated by the State of Utah as mentioned in the NY Times article.

100. See Tom McCourt, 2013, "The King of the Colorado"

101. Ibid.; see also Dimock, 2007 for interactions between Cass Hite and Bert Loper

102. See Tom McCourt, 2003, p. 24

103. Ibid.

104. Ibid., p. 27

CHAPTER 7

1. Letter from Kenny to Jon Lindbergh 01/27/1950

2. Certificate of Title for 1946 CJ2A Willys Jeep sold by Ansel F. Hall to Kenneth I. Ross on 10/17/1949 for purchase price of $800.00 and the Dodge truck purchased on 5/22/1950; no price given

3. Letter from Kenny to Jon Lindbergh 01/27/1950

4. Letter from Charles Lindbergh to Kenny 06/02/1950

5. Letter from Hank Zuidema to Kenny 06/05/1950

6. Letter from Ansel Hall to Hank Zuidema 06/15/1950

7. Letters exchange between George Hall, Sr. and Kenny May 15-22, 1950 (original Ltrs)

8. Ibid.

9. Ibid.

10. In an email exchange with historian/archaeologist Winston Hurst on 6/16/2017 he related a conversation he had with Laverne Powell Tate, custodian of the *San Juan County Historical Society*. "In addition to the 'original' Twin Rocks Trading Post, there were three stores:
    --"Powell Trading Post," the only one still standing in 2017, located across the road east from the present Far Out Expeditions in the lot between the Scorup and Allen houses. Owned and operated by Laverne's father. Opened 1946, sold to (unknown) in 1957.
    --"Bluff Store," a small, white building owned and operated by Kent Nielson until his death, then by his widow Hilda (Oliver) both before and after she was remarried to Ray Perkins, until it finally burned—Laverne does not remember exactly when. Opened same year as Powell's in 1946. Suspicion of robbery associated with the burning. Located on the NE corner of intersection of streets now called Black Locust Ave and 4th East, across the street north from the old Hilda/Olen Oliver house, which is a block west of the old Kumen Jones house ruin in the Bluff Fort block. The store was located right on the corner, next to the Kent Nielson house, which is still standing.
    --Cow Canyon Trading Post, opened by Rusty Musselman, 1955
    --The lodging where George Hall stayed in 1950 may have been in the house that is called the old 'Adams Hotel,' which is the rock house across 4th East from the old Twin Rocks bar/store."

11. Don Ross, personal communication, 2017

12. The actual distance was 225 miles from launch point across from mission, not 230 miles as Ansel mentioned to Hank Zuidema in Note #6 above.

13. Personal communication with Bill Dickinson, May, 2015

14. USGS Historical Water Data [Gage Number 09379500] see gaged flow for summer months, 1950.

15. Letter from Kenny to Jon Lindbergh Dec, 1950

16. See Staveley, 2015, p. 24; infers that round trip was twelve miles

17. Personal communication with Bill Dickinson, May, 2015

18. The Korean 'conflict' began on June 25, 1950 when North Korea invaded South Korea; the United Nations (with the USA as the principal force) came to the assistance of South Korea; China backed the North Koreans. Fighting ended on July 27, 1953 when an armistice was signed where a "demilitarized zone" was established along the 38th Parallel. No peace treaty was ever signed. Harry S. Truman was U.S. President and U.S. involvement was initially called a "police action." The war has also been called the "Forgotten War" or "Unknown War."

19. Letter from Kenny to Jon Lindbergh Dec, 1950

20. Email exchange with Bill Dickinson 6/15-16/2015

21. Letter from Hank Zuidema to Kenny 12/08/1950

22. Ibid.

23. River running "adventure shorts" had become a hot topic in theaters due, in large part, to clips of Norm Nevills and others

24. Letter from Kenny to Zuidema 12/12/1950

25. Ibid.

26. Ibid.

27. Kenny and other river operators were keenly aware of what was being bandied about in Washington, D.C. regarding Federal regulations that would lead to the Colorado River Storage Project and more dams.

28. Letter from Kenny to Zuidema 12/12/1950

29. Letter from Dr. H. Zuidema to Goodyear Rubber Co. 12/14/1950

30. Letter from Kenny to Hank Zuidema 12/16/1950

31. Letter from Zuidema to Kenny 01/17/1951

32. THE GOODYEAR NEWS, *February-March, 1951*; p. 15, p.15.

33. Ibid.

34. Ibid.

35. Ibid.

36. Letter from Kenny to Hank Zuidema 04/14/1951

37. Letter from Zuidema to Kenny 04/23/1951

38. Ibid.

39. Letter from Zuidema to Kenny 06/04/1951

40. Ibid.

41. Letter from Kenny to Hank Zuidema 06/05/1951; note the short turn-around time on these last two letters that were air mailed and compare to U.S. Postal Service turnaround time today

42. Letter from Kenny to Dusty Dustin 05/21/1951

43. Letter from Jon Lindbergh to Kenny 04/09/1951

44. Ibid.

45. Ibid.

46. Ibid.

47. Letter from Kenny to Jon Lindbergh 05/09/1951

48. Letter from Bill Dickinson to Kenny 05/25/1951

49. Letter from Kenny to Col. & Mrs. Lindbergh 05/11/1951

50. Letter from Col. Lindbergh to Kenny 05/24/1951

51. Letter from Kenny to Jon & Bill 04/19/1951

52. Telegram from Bill Dickinson to Kenny 04/24/1951

53. This stretch of the Arkansas River is actually through Brown's Park; Royal Gorge is farther down river and was not run in this race

54. Letter from Kenny to Bill Dickinson 05/22/1951

55. Letter from Kenny to Bill Dickinson 05/28/1951

56. Letter from Bill to Kenny 05/30/1951

57. Buddy Starr was 20 years old or older and later enlisted in the Air Force and was a flight instructor. He was killed flying a jet in 1955

58. Email comments from Bill Dickinson 06/15/2015

59. Smith, Jane S., 1990, *Patenting the Sun: Polio and the Salk vaccine*; William Morrow and Company, Inc., New York, NY, 157p.

60. Letter from Kenny to Hazel H. McClintock aunt of David Wendt 02/13/1951 re: Accident, Health and Polio Insurance: a Group Plan with the Vermont Accident and Life Insurance Company.

61. Seavey, Nina Gilden, Jane S. Smith, & Paul Wagner, 1998, *A Paralyzing Fear: The Triumph over Polio in America*. New York, New York: TV Books; p. 170-171.

62. See SOUTHWEST EXPLORATIONS: Narrative Report – 1951 Expeditions; paper copy and pdf, 40p.

63. Ibid, p. 3

64. See 1951 USGS Historical Water Data [Gage Number 09379500]

65. During Kenny's early years, his favorite launch site was south of St. Christopher's Mission, about 2.0 miles east of Cow Canyon intersection; access is now closed by land owner Roger Atcitty.

66. SOUTHWEST EXPLORATIONS: Narrative Report – 1951 Expeditions; p. 10.

67. Ibid, p. 12

68. Ibid, p. 12

69. The far right "ledge run" was for many years the preferred course to take at Government Rapid in low water, but the ledge collapsed under a rock slide in the late 1990s and has forced all runs in low water to pin-ball through the boulders in the rapid.

70. SOUTHWEST EXPLORATIONS: Narrative Report – 1951 Expeditions; p. 12

71. Ibid, p. 13; Kenny always referred to this section of river with large boulders as "the Boxcars." Some later river runners called it "Freight Train" but the term has been a moot point since Powell Reservoir inundated this section of the river in 1984 when it reached the maximum full pool elevation of 3711 ft above sea level; the section of river has subsequently filled over by silt such that even when lake level dropped, the "Boxcars" and Grand Gulch Rapid have never reappeared.

72. Ibid, p. 13; Moonlight (Oljeto) Canyon was inaccessible from river level in the 1950s, but following the 1984 inundation and subsequent sediment fill the canyon is now at river level – a fill of 80 ft or more of silt.

73. Ibid, p. 13; in later years, Kenny called this "Starr Bar" in honor of Buddy Starr who died crashing an Air Force jet in 1955; a cobble bar from this location was photographed by Eliot Porter in 1961.

74. Ibid, p. 13; the present-day 17 mile long slog from Slickhorn to Clay Hills is similar to the Death march across Paiute Farms that pre-dam river runners frequently experienced. However, the Paiute Farms quagmire was *natural* whereas the current situation is entirely *man-made* due to the impoundment of water (and silt) with the construction of Glen Canyon Dam.

75. See sketch map of Nasja Canyon made by Art Nelson, a member of one of the 1936 RBMV river trips; from his journal courtesy of A. Christensen, 2017

76. The actual canyon named "Redbud Creek" is a northwest-coursing tributary to Bridge Canyon with headwaters in Navajo Mountain. The two drainages converge above Rainbow Bridge and enter the Colorado River as Forbidding Canyon, or Aztec Creek. The "Redbud Canyon" on the San Juan was a minor unnamed declivity in the canyon wall on river left (RL) and only a short distance from the shoreline, making it handy for re-filling water jugs from a natural spring. It's about 2.5 river miles above Nasja Canyon and probably mis-named by Norm Nevills; see Staveley, 2015, p. 21.

77. SOUTHWEST EXPLORATIONS: Narrative Report – 1951 Expeditions; p. 14

78. See Randall Henderson, "Glyph Hunters in the Indian Country" in Desert Magazine 10, November, 1946, p.11-15.

79. Canyonlands became a national park in 1962

80. The Salt Creek drainage is a complex network of intersecting smaller honeycombed tributaries that drain generally northward, where near Cave Springs – several of the larger named tributaries converge and form a single stem for the lower portion of Salt Creek as it enters the Colorado River. From west to east these larger tributaries are: Squaw Canyon, Lost Canyon, the main stem of Salt Creek (it divides into a west and east fork farther south nearer Salt Creek Mesa) and Horse Canyon. Kenny and his Explorers Camp boys headed east at the confluence of Salt Creek and Horse Creek and proceeded south down Horse Creek Canyon.

81. 1951 Kenny narrative; SW Expl Camp: Salt Creek Expedition; p. 31.

82. Ibid.

83. The origin of that chant meaning it is "time to eat" is an authentic Navajo word; see Neil Judd, 1968, p.121 where he spells it "chineago." Martha Austin-Garrison, a Navajo instructor at Dine College, Tsaile, AZ provided the correct spelling and meaning: Ch'iyáán means food; Hágo means come here, or combined - Ch'iyáán Hágo.

84. 1951 Kenny narrative; SW Expl Camp: Salt Creek Expedition; p. 32.

85. They were never in the main upper segments of Salt Creek. The group named an arch they discovered "Explorers Arch" which is known today as Castle Arch, and locate in Horse Canyon. [Location on present day maps: NWSE Sec 20-T31S-R20E; Latitude: 38.065093, Longitude: -109.740275; elevation ~5820 ft. Castle Arch is approximately nine miles south of Cave Springs via 4x4 jeep trail]

86. 1951 Kenny narrative; SW Expl Camp: Salt Creek Expedition; p. 34.

87. Ibid, p. 35.

88. Ibid, p. 35.

89. Various authors have attributed the naming of "Satans Gut" rapid in Cataract Canyon to a river trip Kenny made in 1951; Kenny even mentions this date to Dock Marston in 1956, but Kenny makes absolutely no mention of a Cataract Canyon trip, or naming Satans Gut to Jon Lindbergh in January, 1952. If there is anyone who would have heard about a Cat trip in the late summer of 1951 it would have been to either Jon Lindbergh or Bill Dickinson. There is no documentation that Kenny was in Cataract Canyon in 1951!

90. Letter from Kenny to Jon Lindbergh 01/27/1952; note excitement about Salt Creek and zero information about a Cataract Canyon trip (see above note).

91. Ibid.

92. Ibid.

93. Letter from Kenny to Col. & Mrs. Lindbergh 12/28/1951

94. Letter from Kenny to Land Lindbergh 12/29/1951

95. See 1952 USGS Historical Water Data [Gage Number 09379500]

96. With river flows in the 8,000 to 10,000 cfs range they easily did the full 225 mile run in eight days; the 1952 May Food pack list for eight folks for eight days supports this..

97. Letter from Kenny to Katherine Dumont, mother of Bill Dumont 06/04/1952

98. Quoted from Letter from Mr. Hoyt to Kenny 05/08/1952 and forwarded to Katherine Dumont to alleviate her concerns about science being part of the Explorers Camp experience

99. Letter from David Gorsuch to Kenny 05/11/1952

100. The "Franklins" were a Mancos family known by both the Ross and Lambert families; Apparently Doc Lambert managed to make it out to Colorado for a short period when Explorers Camp was in session – and at least for one of the SJ&C river trips.

101. Letter from Mildred Ross to Doc Lambert 05/24/1952

102. Personal communications, Don Ross, 2015

103. Ibid.

104. Note that, once again, no Cataract Canyon trip materialized for Kenny in 1952, yet river historian, Herm Hoops, wanted to memorialize Kenny following his death and erected a plaque at Ross Canyon but the photo is mislabeled. The photo of Kenny standing in front of a boat says this was the boat he supposedly took down in 1949 (wrong boat) and the date Satans Gut was named as "1952" which is also wrong.

105. Letter from Kenny to Jon Lindbergh 11/16/1952

106. Letter from Kenny to Doc Lambert 12/08/1952

107. Ibid.

108. Ibid.

109. Letter from Kenny to Bill Stitt 12/09/1952

110. Letter from Kenny to Doc Lambert 12/08/1952

111. Ibid; reference to September trip was not panning out: Larry Zuk with *American Canoe Association* hounded Kenny with questions and never did a trip with Kenny as they didn't feel like paying for a guide; just wore him out with a thousand questions! See letter from Kenny to Zuk 04/27/1955, CH 9.

112. Letter from Doc Lambert to Kenny 12/29/1952

113. Letter from Kenny to Doc Lambert 01/08/1953

114. Letter from Kenny to Hank Zuidema 12/23/1952

115. Letter from Hank Zuidema to Kenny 12/31/1952; Hank's observations apply even more so today.

CHAPTER 8

1. Ringholz, Raye Carleson, 1991, *Uranium Frenzy: Boom and Bust on the Colorado Plateau*, p. 59.

2. Letter from Kenny to Bill Dickinson 01/17/1954

3. A "dugway" was originally nothing more than a zigzag route cut by large earthmoving bulldozers with tank treads called "caterpillars"; aka a "cat track"

4. Personal communications, 2015, Don & Doug Ross and other locals over 60 years old

5. See Ringholz, 1991, p.77

6. See Robert McPherson, 1995, p.260

7. Ibid.

8. When the State of Utah DOT hurried to get a new steel bridge constructed, they couldn't tell the public that taxpayer money was used to aid a private industry – namely ore hauling. In reference to the new bridge at Mexican Hat: (UDOT Bridge ID # OC274 on what is now State Hwy 163, Milepost 20.90) it was classified as a Historic Bridge in 1954, even though the bridge was identified and evaluated for an important and direct association related to natural resource extraction and mining operations. While this bridge was in close

proximity to a known mining or extractive operation, investigations into this bridge revealed it *did not* display evidence to demonstrate that the construction of this bridge, individually, played an important role in transporting or processing for the natural resource extraction industry in Utah. This bridge was identified as crossing a major river, gorge, or canyon in the state. Research (conducted before the truck crashed through the river) was said to *not reveal an important and direct association to link the construction, individually, of this bridge to providing a major crossing to substantially improve transportation access or safety in Utah*. The bridge was constructed with a cantilevered span and a pin and hangar connection. The construction of this bridge coincided with the widespread use of that bridge feature nationally and in Utah. As such, the presence of a cantilevered span with a pin and hangar connection was common within this bridge type and this bridge did not represent the early period of use or an important transition in bridge design. The feature was determined *not to be significant*. Later, the bridge was deemed to demonstrate important bridge building practices of an uncommon bridge type in Utah. As such, it was argued by proponents that it illustrated the pattern of features typical of this rare bridge type and was recommended eligible for being claimed "historical." The W. W. Clyde & Company and Utah Crane & Rigging erected the steel bridge in 1953. (See Utah Historic Bridge Inventory)

9. See Allan Kent, 1983, p.237

10. News article in 1952 *Young Earth Scientists*

11. Letter from Hank Zuidema to Kenny 12/31/1952

12. Provides proof that Kenny Ross carried forth the darkroom skills he first learned in a Florida Studio and was very much involved in making the numerous black and white prints that have been preserved in the Ross collection.

13. Letter from Kenny to Zuidema 01/05/1953; also George Pierott magazine article

14. Letter from Kenny to Zuidema 02/03/1953

15. Telegram from Bill Dickinson to Kenny 02/09/1953

16. Letter from Bill Dickinson to Kenny 02/11/1953

17. Ibid.

18. Letter from Kenny to Bill Dickinson 02/20/1953

19. Ibid.

20. Letter from Bill Dickinson to Kenny 03/14/1953

21. Letter from Kenny to Bill Dickinson 03/16/1953

22. Letter from Hank Zuidema to Kenny 03/11/1953

23. Ibid.

24. Ibid.

25. Letter from Kenny to Jon Lindbergh 11/16/1952

26. Letter from Kenny to Hank Zuidema 03/16/1953

27. Letter from Dock Marston to Kenny 02/22/1953

28. This request from Ansel Hall for Kenny to send the journal as well as film from the 1933 RMBV river trip certainly adds credibility that Kenny was, in fact, a participant on this trip.

29. Letter from Dock Marston to Kenny 02/22/1953

30. Letter from Kenny to Dock Marston 03/07/1953;

31. Kenny told Dock Marston that his second Cataract Canyon trip was August 27 to September 7, 1951 although there are absolutely no details documenting that trip and Kenny was certainly a documentarian, leading me to seriously doubt that he ran any Cataract Canyon river trip in 1951 (see previous Chapter, end of Salt Creek Expedition where he began work to close Gold King base Camp on August 18, 1951). Plus, there was definitely *no* Cataract Canyon river trip run by Kenny Ross in 1952.

32. Letter from Kenny to Dock Marston 03/07/1953

33. Letter from Marston to Kenny 03/11/1953

34. Ibid.

35. Letter from Marston to Kenny 07/20/1953

36. See 1953 Announcement of *10th Annual Southwest Explorations* Program; 2-page Leaflet

37. Southwest Explorers Camp four-page letter March, 1953; the new road between Bluff and Mexican Hat was still dirt & gravel and not paved until 1957; see note #5 about new bridge at Mexican Hat.

38. See 1953 USGS Historical Water Data [Gage Number 09379500]

39. Southwest Explorers Camp Promo letter March, 1953; p. 2.

40. Kenny shorthanded and often wrote "Salt Canyon"; the proper name is "Salt Creek Canyon"

41. He was correct about "rough" country, but there is still no approach to the river that is accessible by 4WD vehicles; only hiking trails; see Canyonlands National Park map of Needles District

42. Southwest Explorers Camp Promo letter March, 1953; p. 3.

43. Letter from Kenny to Hank Zuidema 04/29/1953

44. Letter from Herman Thies to Kenny 06/03/1953

45. Art Green was who had the "power boat" as he had built the lodge near Lees Ferry and offered speed-boat up-run overnight trips to those who wanted to hike in and see Rainbow Bridge. There's no doubt it was Art's group who saw the disabled boat(s) at Forbidding Canyon and where some sort of "deal" was worked out to get the Thies group off the river as they had scheduled airplane reservations to return to Ohio. When Glen Canyon Dam became a reality, Art had the foresight to move his boat landing and lodge operation upstream to Wahweap Creek which grew into Wahweap Marina – the largest marina on Lake Powell.

46. Letter from Herman Thies to Kenny 06/03/1953

47. Letters from Herman Thies to Kenny 06/09 & 22/1953; Clayton Lewis the "producer" was an executive with *Ford Motor Co.*, from Marshall, Texas

48. Letter from Herman Thies to Kenny 06/03/1953; these "32 Boys" were probably employees at the Akron, Ohio Goodyear Rubber Co.

49. Letter from Herman Thies to Kenny 06/03/1953

50. Letter from Mildred Ross to Herman Thies 07/16/1953

51. Letter from Kenny to Bill Dickinson 01/07/1954

52. Letter from Mildred Ross to Herman Thies 07/16/1953

53. Ibid; Don Ross said that he and Doug each got a $10 bill that was shoved in Mildred's apron as Herman Thies left

54. *Rocky Mountain News* SJ&C article July 9, 1953; the news article contains a photo of two boys paddling one of the older Air Force life rafts in Glen Canyon. *David Gorsuch* later married *Anne Irene McGill* and their son *Neil*, born in 1968 was appointed a Supreme Court Judge of the United States, filling the seat of deceased Judge Antonin Scalia on February 01, 2017; the appointment was made by President Donald J. Trump.

55. Letters exchanged between Kenny Ross and camp member [name withheld by author] in 1954

56. Ibid.

57. Ibid.

58. Ibid.

59. Letter from Kenny to Bill Dickinson 01/07/1954

60. Letter from Mildred Ross to Frank Thorp, Jr. 08/01/1953

61. Letter from Kenny to Bill Dickinson 01/07/1954 explaining 1953 Cat trip

62. See Baars, 1987 Cataract Canyon River Guide

63. Letter from Kenny to Bill Dickinson 01/07/1954 explaining 1953 Cat trip; the degree of detail and tone of letter definitely confirms that this was Kenny's second trip down Cataract Canyon and his *first time to actually run all the rapids himself* rather than be a passenger or onshore photographer as he was in 1949.

64. See Certificate of Title

65. Letter from Kenny to Bill Dickinson 01/07/1954, detailing his West Elk jeep trek

CHAPTER 9

1. Letter from Kenny to Bill Dickinson 01/07/1954

2. Ibid.

3. Personal communications with Don Ross, 2016

4. Ibid.

5. Letter from Kenny to Bill Dickinson 01/07/1954

6. Ibid.

7. Letter from Kenny to Bill Dickinson 01/17/1954; sadly, the full pool in Powell reservoir combined with the incredible volume of sediment load actually smothered the rapids and reduced river gradients on the San Juan as far upstream as Slickhorn Canyon (74.5 miles above the confluence with the Colorado River); and flooded out the lower two-thirds of the rapids in Cataract Canyon to the foot of Satans Gut (Big Drop #3) in Cataract Canyon (~187 miles above Glen Canyon Dam; see Appendix I, Table 2).

8. Email from Bill Dickinson dated 6/15/2015

9. Letter from Kenny to Doc Lambert 01/08/1954

10. Personal communications with Don & Doug Ross, 2017

11. Letter from Kenny to Doc Lambert 06/05/1954

12. Letter from Kenny to David Stacey, AWW 01/04/1954

13. Letter from Kenny to Gen. Wayne Stacey, AWW 04/26/1954

14. Ibid.

15. See 1954 USGS Historical Water Data [Gage Number 09379500]

16. Letter from Dock Marston to Kenny 02/08/1956; re: first fiber glass kayak on SJ&C run

17. Personal communications with Doug Ross, 2015

18. Ibid.

19. Ibid.

20. Letter from Kenny to Hank Zuidema 04/29/1953

21. Letter from Larry Zuk, ACA to Kenny 05/01/1954

22. Ibid.

23. Letter from Larry Zuk ACA to Kenny 04/22/1955; the phrase "take a guide" shows the ignorance and disregard of what *professionally guided trips* was all about and is still misunderstood in the 21st Century by private boaters. Professional River Guides tend to KNOW (or should know) where they are going, water conditions, weather, emergency situations, where the fresh water springs are and where the scenic/historic places are, etc. This uninformed statement was the beginning of this private boater mentality so abhorred by us lowly "Commercial River guides."

24. Letter from Larry Zuk ACA to Kenny 04/22/1955

25. Ibid.

26. Letter from Kenny to Larry Zuk, ACA 04/27/1955

27. Letter from Kenny to Buddy Starr, USAF 03/31/1955

28. Ibid.

29. Ibid.

30. Personal communications with Doug Ross, 2016

31. Kenny was right, this is the straightest corridor on the whole San Juan River, and in strong westerly winds, making that bend and rowing that last three miles can be a real chore; add zigzagging around all the sand bars formed by the nearly flat gradient due to Powell reservoir impoundment and it can be hellish indeed!

32. See Eliot Porter, 1988, *"The Place No One Knew"* Commemorative Edition, p. 24

33. Kenny Ross records only list seven boys for 1955 camp; March, 2017

34. Personal communications with Don Ross, 2017

35. Letter from Kenny to Mr. & Mrs. Alan Scott 04/06/1955

36. Email from Polly Schaafsma 10/30/2016

37. Letter from Kenny to Larry Zuk, ACA 01/12/1956

38. Letter from L. Zuk, ACA to Kenny 01/25/1956

39. Ibid.

40. Letter from Kenny to L. Zuk, ACA 01/27/1956; although there's no indication that Kenny ever ran Cataract Canyon in June as stated here.

41. Ibid.

42. Ibid.

43. Personal communications with Don Ross, 2017; Kenny's first ice chest was purchased in 1958

44. Letter from Kenny to Frank Thorp, 03/30/1955

45. Southwest Explorations Newsletter for 1956, 4p.

46. Letter from Mrs. Marjory Thorp to Kenny 09/10/1955

47. Letter from Kenny to Dave Stacey, AWW 01/12/1956

48. Personal communications with Don and Doug Ross, 2016

49. Letter from Dock Marston to Kenny 01/14/1956

50. Letter from Kenny to Dock Marston 01/20/1956

51. Letter from Dock Marston to Kenny 02/08/1956

52. See Nash, 1989, p. 79 where he incorrectly says it was August, 1952 when the rapid got its name and there were 46 rapids before Powell reservoir drowned most of them; also see Webb, et al, 2004, for comparison of numbering system. In 2016 river runner Tom Martin questioned Herm Hoops whether the rapid's name should be attributed to Kenny Ross.

53. Letter from Kenny to Dock Marston 03/17/1956

54. Letter from Dock Marston 02/08/1956

55. Ibid.

56. Letter from Kenny to Dock Marston 01/20/1956

57. Letter from Kenny to Clyde Jones, AWWA 01/27/1956

58. Letter from Kenny to Dave Stacey, AWW 02/22/1956; an exquisitely written letter informing the clueless novice about boating Cataract Canyon and warning there is "no way out."

59. Letter from an attorney in Denver [name withheld] to Kenny 02/03/1956; Kenny warned by D. Stacey to not get involved with this "dubious" character

60. Letter from Dave Stacey to Kenny 02/25/1956

61. Ibid.

62. Letter from Kenny to Dave Stacey 04/04/1956

63. See "Cataract Canyon" by Kenneth Ross in 1956 Winter issue of American White Water magazine, p. 9-13.

64. Letter from Don Hatch to Kenny 12/15/1956, p.1

65. Letter #1 from Kenny to Don Hatch 12/22/1956

66. Ibid.

67. Letter from Don Hatch to Dock Marston 12/18/1956

68. Letter from Dock Marston to Kenny in 1956 no month on letter; Key I

69. See all San Juan River guide book logs from 1973 to 2015; the current concrete ramp is at least the third such ramp constructed since the early 1970s and located at the mouth of Buck Draw. The U.S. Highway 191 Bridge was built in 1971 according to UDOT data (Bridge ID # OC616 @ Milepost 20.50)

70. See Miser, Hugh D., 1924, *The San Juan Canyon, southeastern Utah;* the entire length of the San Juan River from its headwaters to its confluence with the Colorado River and the Colorado River from the mouth of the Paria River upstream to the San Juan confluence was remapped in 2016 using Arc/GIS maps by this author. The distances are measured in miles, or tenths of miles, and elevations in feet above mean sea level, both downstream and upstream from either headwaters or confluences, as these points have changed only a few meters, at best, during the last two centuries; see Appendix I: Tables 1-4.

71. See Baars, Don and Stevenson, Gene, 1986a, *SAN JUAN CANYONS: a river runner's guide and natural history of San Juan River Canyons*, p.19.

72. Ibid.

73. See Crampton, 1964; "The San Juan Canyon Historical Sites"; Historical Site 207; p. 19; note his river mileage at Government Rapid is 0.4 mile different than that shown by Baars and Stevenson, 1986a

74. See Miser, 1924, Water Supply Paper 538, Plate XVI, *"View C. View Looking upstream toward rapid between Johns Canyon and Slickhorn Gulch."* Based on the photo and Bert Loper's descriptions (see Dimock, 2007, p. 260-263) the river was running high; the flow in the photo is estimated at >6,000 cfs.

75. See Crampton, 1964; Historical Site 207; p. 19

76. See Miser, 1924, WSP 538, PL XVI, view C

77. See Miser, 1924, WSP 538, p. 51

78. See Baars, Don and Stevenson, Gene, 1986, *SAN JUAN CANYONS: a river runner's guide and natural history of San Juan River Canyons*, p. 18.

79. Based on the narrative of Bert Loper and Hugh Miser, plus my own experience and observations of this stretch of river, I have herein proclaimed that big rock at the bottom of the small gravel bar riffle "Loper's Rock" as graphically depicted in Figure 9.10; for a complete narrative and excellent biography of Bert Loper, see Dimock, 2007, "The Very Hard Way."

80. Bert Loper typed notes by Brad Dimock, 2006, p.8.

81. Randall Henderson, editor of Desert Magazine wrote an article in 1945 about his experience boating with Norm Nevills on the San Juan River and *Government Rapid* was mentioned (the rapid about three miles above Slickhorn Gulch); but not the spot of boat accident in 1921. Wallace Stegner recalled his trip with Norm Nevills in 1947 where he also mentions running Government Rapid (see Stegner, 1969, p.102-103).

82. See Kenny Ross, 1951 Southwest Explorations Report; June 30, 1951, p.12.

83. No other RBMV river trips ran this section; they rest launched from Copper Canyon

84. Kenny hand-written notes for 1/18/1956

85. See Staveley, 2015 description, p. 148-156.

86. Much has been written about the Colorado River Compact (CRC) and the Colorado River Storage Project (CRSP); in its simplest form a two-basin concept proposed by several bureaucrats was adopted and signed into law by Bureau of Reclamation Commissioner Herbert Hoover in 1922. The upper basin included parts of Colorado, New Mexico, Utah, Wyoming, and Arizona, while the lower basin included parts of three of the same states – Utah, New Mexico and Arizona, plus Nevada and California. Since the proposal didn't follow state lines, all subsequent discussions designated Wyoming, Colorado, Utah, and New Mexico as "upper basin" states while the states of Arizona, Nevada and California were designated "lower basin" states. Lees Ferry was determined to be the dividing line. The water-allocation formula was based on total water measured by the Reclamation Service at Laguna Dam near Yuma for the years 1899 to 1920, but these numbers were later found to be falsified. On November 15 Hoover proposed 7.5 million acre feet of water per year as a compromise [7.5 is half of 15 – a completely arbitrary number] to satisfy both upper & lower basin states, and that Arizona would also keep the 1 million acre feet from the Gila River. The Colorado River commissioners approved the compact on the afternoon of November 24, 1922. By 1927 more than four years had passed and still the compact was not ratified. Both Arizona and Utah still had some reservations about the deal. Strong opposition continued from both factions in the two basins, but the bill picked up support in favor of the Boulder Canyon project as a result from public reaction to the disastrous flood on the Mississippi River in 1927 *[and the flooding of the Animas and San Juan Rivers affecting Colorado & Utah]*. On December 21, 1928 President Calvin Coolidge signed the Boulder Canyon bill into law. On June 25, 1929 newly elected President Herbert Hoover proclaimed the Boulder Canyon Act of 1928 effective, but only for six of the seven states. Arizona and California continued to fight over the Gila River/Imperial Valley and other tributary rights. After many years of negotiations and promises, the compact was ratified on February 9, 1944. Inspired by the construction and completion of Hoover Dam in 1936, the Bureau of Reclamation (as it was deemed after 1923) and the Army Corp of Engineers went into a frenzy of engineering feats and dam building. Navajo Dam was completed in 1962; Glen Canyon Dam in 1963 and Flaming Gorge Dam in 1964. And they are not done yet! No one has ever corrected the so-called *average* flow of 15 million acre feet of water in the Colorado River system!

CHAPTER 10

1. "Gas stations" were still called "filling stations" in 1956

2. Boat camp numbers were a tradition started by Kenny and continue to this day according to Don and Doug Ross

3. The original Twin Rocks Trading Post was located at the northwest corner of present day 7th East and Black Locust; some confusion exists regarding names; this may be the Hyde Store; see J. Willian email 4/1/17)

4. See 1957 Southwest Explorations River Trip Plans; first time trips are launched from Sand Island and not two miles upstream; daily trips from Sand Island to Mexican Hat offered on weekends

5. Ibid.

6. Ibid.

7. Ibid.

8. Ibid.

9. Ibid, Kenny's multi-day trips launched from upstream of Bluff to avoid rocky access at Sand Island

10. Ibid.; actual river miles from Potash launch site to White Canyon takeout is 102 miles, not 120 miles

11. Personal communications with Don & Doug, 2016

12. Christmas card & note from Frank Thorp to Kenny and family 01/20/1957

13. Letter from Kenny to Frank Thorp 01/31/1957

14. Kenny stayed with stern dual paddlers until the 1958 river season when he switched to one man on oars. He painted splash tube on 10-man LCR-L's and later began painting oar blades different colors so oars would match. Oars were 8 or 9 ft long.

15. Mrs. June Head (curator of the *Montezuma County Historical Society*) from Cortez said she and her husband Bill and several others came over to Bluff and went down the river on day trips with Kenny several times during this time period. She and Bill were part of the Four Corners Jeep Club and jeeped all over this country then and thought the world of Kenny. She said their group painted the white stripes at Four Corners for the 1949 Governor's dedication and returned every now and then to keep the state lines colored white (actually used dry lime, not paint). (June Head, personal comm 5, 2017)

16. Don Ross personal communications, 2017

17. See Brandt Hart, 2009, "If a bridge could speak" *in* Blue Mtn Shadows Vol 40, p. 56-58.

18. The alcove ruin was first noted and photographed by W.H. Jackson, 1875

19. The USGS Surface Water for Utah: Peak Streamflow Data [Gage Number 09379500] indicates a peak flow of 52,000 cfs on September 6, 1970.

20. See Brandt Hart, 2009; see the USGS Surface Water for Utah: Peak Streamflow Data [Gage Number 09379500] for September 11, 2003 indicating a peak flow of over 23,000 cfs.

21. See Brandt Hart, 2009.

22. Don Ross personal communications, 2017

23. Ibid.

24. Email from Martha Wilson, 4/20/2017

25. Don Ross personal communications, 2017

26. When navigating a boat on a river with rocks and boulders near the surface, a "V" shape or "tongue" in big rapids is readily apparent and the oarsman should follow the V as it points downstream; if it points upstream, then choose either side to avoid running up on the obstacle. Rivers like the San Juan bend, or meander (a lot), forming an arcuate course for the main channel current. If left unattended, the boat will slam into the outer curve, so as one navigates a meander, one should pull away from the outer curve, thus "cutting the "C." And, the San Juan is notoriously shallow and muddy water, so as the boat floats along, it tends to work its way sideways thus requiring the oarsman to not let the downstream oar aimlessly fall into the river or else it will lodge in the streambed and the current will move the boat over the oar and in a matter of seconds – snap! The oar is broken or badly damaged. So "watch your downstream oar!"

27. Life preservers, or jackets, or belts are now called "Personal Flotation Devices, or PFD's.

28. Don Ross personal communications, 2017

29. Kane Wash is shown on Map No. 3 (made by Patricia DeBunch) in Fowler, 2011, p. 253; also noted on map by Crampton, 1964 and Kenny Ross's sketch map in his 1951 Southwest Explorations Report, p.8. But it is not shown as a formally named creek on any USGS topographical maps other than the 1953 Gunsight Butte 1:62500 Quadrangle topographic map. On this 1953 map, Kane Wash is shown to have a Right Fork, Center Fork and Left Fork that comprises the eastern portion of Padre Bay; the 1953 topographic map designated Gooseneck Point as "Kane Point" and "Cookie Jar Butte" is first shown as a named geographic feature on 1958 and later vintages of maps. The left fork of Kane Wash was the route taken to reach the bull-dozed trail that led to Highway 89.

30. Christmas card & note from Frank Thorp to Kenny and family 01/20/1957

31. See Staveley, 2015, p.151

32. See Staveley, 2015, p.156

33. Doug & Don Ross personal communications, 2017

34. CDOT Bridge ID #P-01-G; Hwy Route 160A; Mile Post 00.19; Location: San Juan River (Stateline); completed: 1961

35. See Jon Krakauer, 2003, p.238; in his extraordinary book *Under the Banner of Heaven*, where a significantly different version is well documented indicating that the three were killed by Anglos inside the LDS ware house in Toquerville, Utah.

36. See Wallace Stegner, 1992; J.W. Powell, 1875, report

37. Doug Ross, notes from 2015

38. Herm Hoops transcribed interview with Kenny Ross, 1986

39. Doug Ross, notes from 2015

40. Don & Doug Ross, personal communications, 2017

CHAPTER 11

1. Email from Winston Hurst 6/16/2017

2. Email from Doug Ross, 6/16/2017

3. Email from Winston Hurst 6/17/2017

4. Personal communications in July, 2018 with my neighbor, Jerry Howell, a lifetime resident of Bluff who provided many of these names

5. Don Ross personal communication, 2017

6. Don & Doug Ross, personal communications, 2017

7. Ibid.

8. Don Ross, personal communications, 2018; Mildred was busy working at Social Services in Cortez and Kenny adjusted to having local men drive to Page and out to Kane Creek.

9. Eliot Furness Porter (December 6, 1901 – November 2, 1990) was possibly Ansel Adams most famous student. Eliot moved past black & white photography to color and perfected a lab technique of five-color separation that brought praise to Porter's medium of color photography.

10. Contrary to Eliot's narrative dated 1987, in the beginning of his 1988 book, this trip that launched from Sand Island and proceeded down the San Juan River was <u>not</u> a group trip; it was just the four of them. The photograph labelled "star bar" in *The Place No One Knew,* is actually "Starr Bar" named by Kenny in honor of Buddy Starr and located on RR about three miles above Clay Hills on the San Juan River.

11. Gene Foushee ran overland FWD scenic trips and filled in occasionally for Kenny when he needed a boatman. Gene and Mary Foushee moved to Bluff in 1959 and built the Recapture Lodge. Gene was from North Carolina and had come west as a young geologist working for a vanadium/uranium company. He met Mary in Grand Junction and as the uranium boom gradually became a bust, they decided to stay and make a go of it by opening a *motor hotel* for the ever increasing tourist crowd. At first their lodge *(called Recapture Court)* only consisted of a few rooms, but over the years Gene kept adding rooms and it has become one of the iconic motels in Bluff. It still has the quaint charm and warmth that Gene and Mary endeavored to make beginning in 1959. Both Gene and Mary passed away in May, 2017 – they were both 88 years old.

12. Georgia Totto O'Keeffe (November 15, 1887 – March 6, 1986); her charcoal sketches were exhibited by Alfred Stieglitz, an American photographer and modern art promoter, at an exhibition in New York without her permission in 1918, but their meeting led to their marrying in 1924. Georgia was best known for her rather sensual paintings of enlarged flowers; she has been recognized as the mother of American modernism. Her works are exhibited at the Georgia O'Keeffe Museum in Santa Fe, NM. Todd Webb (September 5, 1905 – April 15, 2000) was an American photographer and developed a strong friendship with Georgia O'Keeffe soon after moving from New York to Santa Fe in 1961. He later moved to Portland, Maine in the 1970s. His estate is managed by Betsy Evans Hunt who serves as the Executive Director of the Todd Webb Archive.

13. See introduction (p. 6-7) *in* Porter, Eliot, 1988, *The Place No One Knew*; Commemorative Edition 1963, Peregrine Smith Books, David Brower, ed; 184 p. There is no mention of Kenny Ross by name as the river guide. In Don Fowler's book *"The Glen Canyon Country"* (2011) he mentions on p.240 that Tad Nicols also took Porter and his family through Glen Canyon on his boat on a photographic trip with reference to an interview of Nicols (see *Boatman's Quarterly Review*, 2000, vo. 13, no. 2), although there are no supportive

photos as illustrated here. If there were other real river guides, then Porter may have simply merged all his guided trips and unfortunately did not mention individual guides by name.

14. Don Ross verified the paper sack drawings were on display when he visited the museum in the late 1980s

15. Three pages of typed notes were provided by the Todd Webb Archivist, Betsy Evans Hunt. The notes were transcribed from his field notebook he had with him for the trip. His earliest entry is dated August, 14, 1961 where he mentions unrelated items and that he was beginning to make preparations for the upcoming river trip. The notes follow day-by-day events from August 21 through August 30, 1961 and a comment dated November 9, where he finally got the notebook back from Georgia who had used his notebook to do some sketches. Days of the week were determined through a website: http://www.daysoftheweek.org

16. All down river float trips had to take their river boats out at Kane Creek landing and then drive an unmaintained rocky road some 25 miles to where it intersected Highway 89 on west side of Glen Canyon Bridge.

17. Don Ross recalled that the "big truck" was a 1947 vintage Dodge flatbed with wooden sideboards; the vehicles also included the old Chevy station wagon (Georgia probably rode in it) and a red GMC Ford pickup truck that Kenny had purchased from a worker at the defunct White Canyon mill site.

18. The White Canyon mill site, store, and town were a short-time enterprise built at the mouth of White Canyon; the old Hite ferry crossing was just downstream from the mill and abandoned houses.

19. Todd mentioned observing *Echo 1* (a bright satellite) and a total eclipse of the moon on two dates – Aug 25 and again on Aug 27. Checking lunar cycles on website and Echo 1, I found the following: actually a partial eclipse happened on the 25th and was visible from Moab, so probably also in Glen Canyon; the Echo 1 satellite was the first experimental passive communications satellite; it was a metalized balloon satellite measuring about 100 ft in diameter and acted as a reflector of microwave signals. The low altitude and metallic composition made for quite visible conditions, particularly if away from ambient city light pollution. And August 26 was a full moon.

20. "Navaho Canyon" is more commonly known as Long Canyon or Navajo Creek located at the top of Big Bend on RR about 68.3 river miles below Hite Ferry launch point.

21. The fact that Georgia and Todd passed up the hike to see Rainbow Bridge suggests their return a few weeks later with the motor boat group, as Todd Webb collection has a number of images in this same batch as the Kenny Ross trip and clearly shows the motor boat group camping at mouth of Forbidding Canyon; no motor boats were noted in the Kenny Ross August trip.

22. He refers to twelve mile hike, but as noted previously, the round trip was only a nine mile hike.

23. It was common practice for Kenny and crew to spend the night in Page, Arizona before making the long drive back to Bluff and would stay at the *Page Boy Motel*. Don & Doug Ross are pretty sure that's where they all spent the night; the Page Boy Motel still exists today at 150 N Lake Powell Blvd, Page, AZ 86040.

24. June Head, age 87 and longtime resident of Montezuma County said she recalled June Hall when she lived in Mancos and she was always "uppity" and did not interact with local women; Ms. Head added that the Hall kids all loved Mancos, but June preferred the big city life. Notes from phone conversation with June Head, May 04, 2017.

25. See 1962 USGS Historical Water Data [Gage Number 09379500]

26. See Staveley, 2015, p.11-12 for descriptions of Norman Nevills boats; Brad Dimock made a replica of the clumsy looking *San Juan punt* and its maiden voyage on the San Juan River was spring 2018.

27. Don Ross personal communication, 2017

28. Internet search; see Wikipedia.org

29. Ibid.

30. Ibid.

31. For insights about Bears Ears National Monument as originally declared and then subsequently reduced in size see Jim Stiles commentary in *The Canyon Country Zephyr* bi-monthly newspaper editions 2016-2018.

32. Roy Webb wrote an article for *The Confluence*, a defunct publication by the Colorado Plateau River Guides Association (CPRG) in 2003 about the history of this organization where he wrote "SOCOTWA had a lot of impact on Glen Canyon."

33. See Roy Webb, 2003, "Set my spirit free" a history of SOCOTWA

34. Ibid.

35. Ibid.

36. Email from Doug Ross, 04/03/2017

37. Kenny Ross handwritten river notes circa 1972

38. See *Shelf carbonates of the Paradox Basin*: a symposium Fourth Field Conference Guidebook, 1963, Ralph O. Bass and Seymour L. Sharps, eds., Four Corners Geological Society, 273p; and map insert.

39. Kenny Ross handwritten river notes circa 1972

40. See 1963 FCGS Guidebook; road logs

41. Kenny Ross handwritten river notes circa 1972

42. Doug Ross personal communication, 2016

43. Don Ross personal communication, 2017

44. Kenny Ross handwritten river notes circa 1972

45. Kenny Ross handwritten river notes circa 1976

46. Based on State of Utah Division of Water Rights data

47. Doug Ross, personal communication, 2016

48. "Ford's ford" is adjacent to the Mexican Hat Rock and is unofficially named after the famous movie director, John Ford, who directed all the John Wayne movies with iconic Monument Valley, Raplee anticline and other recognizable features in the Four Corners in the background. Of course, the storyline was always based in Texas and the Indians were played by Navajo, but called anything from Comanche to Apache. The San Juan River more typically was referred to as the Rio Grande or Rio Concho. No wonder folks are so confused with geography.

49. See C.W. Cross & A.C. Spencer, 1899; H.E. Gregory, 1911, 1916; E.G. Woodruff, 1912; H. Miser, 1924, 1925; A.A. Baker & J.B. Reeside, Jr. 1929; A.A. Baker,1933, 1936

50. See Cross & Spencer, 1899

51. Sherman A. Wengerd and Marvin Matheny conducted first measured sections on Honaker Trail and first publications about Paradox basin and oil potential. Sherman A. Wengerd married Florence Mather in 1940; he served in Navy during WWII; 1940 joined Shell Oil; returned to Shell after war & completed his PhD at Harvard in 1947, then began long career at UNM; President of AAPG 1971-72. Began studying Hermosa section in 1950 with early publications on reef limestones in the Hermosa Fm in 1951. Along with co-author J.W. Strickland, in 1954 – Regional stratigraphy of Paradox basin & in 1958 upgraded Hermosa to Group status and proposed Honaker Trail, Paradox, Pinkerton Trail formation names with co-author Marvin Matheny and finally with E. Szabo.

52. "Paradox Formation" named by Baker, 1933 for rocks exposed in Paradox Valley, Montrose, CO

53. See S.A. Wengerd & Strickland, 1954; S.A. Wengerd & M.L. Matheny, 1958

54. Wengerd, et al; Baars, et al, 1967

55. From 1952-1957 Shell Oil geologists James A. Peterson, Howard Spencer, and John M. Foster conducted field work @ Eight Foot Rapid and Raplee Anticline; Kenny was hired for river support and served as camp nanny. Don Baars was not part of this first group with J.A. Peterson; this was when Baars was in Florida doing modern-carbonate studies with Eugene Shinn! Therefore, D.L. Baars may not have seen algal mounds in San Juan River canyons until 1956-57. He always kidded Kenny about the "SHELL" 10-man LCR being left as one of Kenny's first boats.

56. Geologic terminology that means mixed silica [mostly quartz]-dominated sandstones with limestones and various types of salt

57. See RMAG 2009 SPECIAL PUBLICATION: The Paradox Basin Revisited – New Developments in Petroleum Systems and Basin Analysis, list of major contributor papers & authors, 816p.

CHAPTER 12

1. For early descriptions of diatremes see: Newberry, 1861; Dutton, 1880; Woodruff, 1912; Gregory, 1915-1938; Hack, 1942; For modern descriptions see Stuart-Alexander, D.E., Shoemaker, E.M., and Moore, H.J., 1972; Semken, Steve, 2003; Gonzales, D.A., 2015

2. Gregory, 1917; Williams, 1936; Hack, 1942

3. Semken, 2003 re: number of diatremes; Semken claims there are 80, while Shoemaker says 250

4. Sterrett, 1909, p.825

5. Woodruff, 1912

6. H.E. Gregory (1916, 1917)

7. Miser (1924)

8. Williams, 1936; Hack, 1942

9. Semken, 2003

10. Lorenz, 1973; 1986; Ort, et al, 1998, fig.3

11. Eugene Merle Shoemaker (1928-1997). He received his PhD at Princeton in 1960; helped pioneer field of astrogeology and founded the Astrogeology Research Ctr (USGS) in Flagstaff in 1961 & was first director;

taught astronauts geology (didn't qualify for moon walk as he had Addison's disease, a disorder of the adrenal glands) so Harrison Schmitt was 1st geologist on moon. Shoemaker went on to Caltech in 1969. He died in weird auto collision near Alice Springs, Australia on July 18, 1997; his ashes were carried to the moon by the Lunar Prospector space probe; his are the only human whose ashes have been buried outside of Earth. Most noted for *Comet Shoemaker-Levy* 9, where he & wife Carolyn discovered July 1992 and comet broke into pieces that collided with Jupiter in July, 1994 leaving a noticeable scar. Speed of impact was 216,000 km/h or 134,000 mph. One of the pieces was larger than Earth.

12. Shoemaker, Byers, and Roach, 1962

13. Orson Anderson, Field trip Tutorial #5 September 11, 1997, The Diamond-Graphite Phase Boundary

14. John Deede, 2016

15. Ibid.

16. Ibid.

17. Information available on internet

18. Orson Lamar Anderson: born December 3, 1924; came from a ranching community in Eastern Utah (Kreis, UT); his father acquired a 700 acre homestead out of the Homestead Act; he was a kid when the Great Depression hit (9-10 yrs old). He graduated from high school in Price, Utah in 1942. Orson illegally joined the Army Air Corp at age 17 with his college buddies and went to the South Pacific and flew all sorts of aircraft as a "test pilot" to make sure they had been repaired properly before being reloaded with bombs. He returned to Utah after the war and went to the University of Utah where he received all his degrees and graduated with a Ph.D. in Physics in 1951 under the supervision of famous scientists Henry Eyring and Walter Elsasser. He joined Bell Telephone Laboratories where he spent nine years working in the physical acoustics group of Warren Mason.

    Orson joined the research staff of the Lamont Geological Observatory in 1963; followed by a Visiting Professorship at Cal Tech, and then he was appointed Prof. Geology at Columbia University. During his "Lamont era" he and colleagues and students (including Priscilla Grew) published 75 papers in the new emerging field of Mineral Physics. In 1971 he moved to Los Angeles and served 15 years at UCLA. Orson pioneered work in resonant ultrasound spectroscopy for measuring the elasticity of minerals at high temperature. He retired to Salt Lake City in 1998. Orson is 95; his wife Berneice, 88, lives in Green River, Utah.

19. Lieberman, R. 1966, Kimberlite trip notes

20. Ibid.

21. Ibid.

22. Ibid.

23. Ibid.

24. Letter from Orson Anderson to Kenny 1967; also letter from Orson to Kenny renewing contract dated Nov 11, 1968

25. Ibid.

26. Orson Anderson; see 1997 Gene Shoemaker Memorial trip notes for details.

27. McGetchin, T.R. and Silver, L.T., 1970, Compositional relations in minerals from kimberlite and related rocks in the Moses Rock dike, San Juan County, Utah: American Mineralogist, Vol. 55, p.1738-1771.

28. McGetchin, T.R. and Silver, L.T., 1972, A crustal-upper mantle model for the Colorado Plateau based on observations of crystalline rock fragments in the Moses Rock dike: Journal of Geophysical Research, Vol. 77, p.7022-7037. The first and only geologic map of the Mule Ear diatreme was mapped by Shoemaker and others in the 1960s and published by the USGS as: Stuart-Alexander, D.E., Shoemaker, E.M., and Moore, H.J., 1972, Geologic map of the Mule Ear diatreme, San Juan County, Utah: USGS Misc. Geologic Investigations, Map I-674.

29. Orson Anderson field notes

30. Ibid, and personal communications with Orson in the field, 1997

31. Ibid.

32. Ibid.

33. Anderson & Grew, 1977, AGU paper

34. Ibid.

35. Anderson, O.L., 1979, Diatremes and carbonatites, *in* Kimberlites, Diatremes, and Diamonds: their geology, petrology and geochemistry

36. Ibid.

37. Anderson and Grew, 1977

38. Ibid.

39. Definition to further explain *P-T* measurements. In determining the source depth of a xenolith found at the earth's surface, petrologists use methods bases on the principle that at the point of crystallization from the liquid, the minerals of the rock must satisfy the requirement that the *Gibbs energy** of neighboring minerals be equal. During the process of crystallization, certain species will change so that thermodynamic equilibrium will be maintained. Thus, suites of xenoliths obtained at one collection site, all having the same assembly of minerals, will have a variety of compositions within the minerals, if the xenoliths came from different depths.

    In determining the source depth of a xenolith found at the earth's surface, petrologists compare the compositions of the suite of minerals from a given xenolith to an experimental data set to determine the pressure (*P*) and temperature (*T*) conditions of equilibrium at crystallization. However, during the process of crystallization, certain species will change so that thermodynamic equilibrium will be maintained. Thus, suites of xenoliths obtained at one collection site, all having the same assembly of minerals, will have a variety of compositions within the minerals, if the xenoliths came from different depths. From the pressure, the depth in the earth can be deduced.

    (*) Gibbs energy is a thermodynamic potential that can be used to calculate the maximum of reversible work that may be performed by a thermodynamic system at a constant temperature and pressure. It also defines where the thermodynamic potential that is minimized when a system reaches chemical equilibrium at constant pressure and temperature.

40. Janse, A.J.A., 1984, Kimberlites, where or when, in Kimberlite Occurrences and Origin: a basis for conceptual models of exploration; J.E. Glover and P.G. Harris, eds., publ. by the Geology Department and University extension, The University of Western Australia, Pub. No. 8, Perth, Australia.

41. Orson Anderson Tutorials #1-#5, 1997

42. Comodi, P., and Zanazzi, P.F., 1996, Effects of temperature and pressure on the structure of lawsonite, Piazza University, Perugia, Italy. American Mineralogist 81, p. 833-841.

43. Sbar & Sykes, 1973; Morgan, 1972 as referenced by Orson Anderson Tutorials #1-#5, 1997

44. Orson L. and Perkins, Priscilla C. 1975, A plate tectonics model involving non-laminar asthenospheric flow to account for irregular patterns of magmatism in the southwestern United States; p.113-122.

45. Atwater, T., 1970, Implications of plate tectonics for the Cenozoic tectonic evolution of western North America: Geological Society of America Bull., Vol 81, p.3513-3536.

46. Ibid.

47. Anderson & Perkins, 1975; p.120.

48. Ibid, p. 122.

49. "Big Bill" had become a recognized "mega-thinker" and major contributor to the geologic community's knowledge of plate tectonics; see Dickinson, W.R., and Snyder, W.S., 1978, Plate tectonics of the Laramide orogeny: Geological Society of America Memoir 151, p.355-366; also, Dickinson, W.R., 1989, Tectonic setting of Arizona through geologic time, in Geologic Evolution of Arizona, J.P. Jenny and S.J. Reynolds, eds., Arizona Geological Society Digest No. 17, p.1-16.

50. Dickinson, W.R., and Snyder, W.S., 1978, Plate tectonics of the Laramide orogeny

51. Ibid.

52. Helmstaedt, H. and Doig, R., 1975, Eclogite nodules from kimberlites of the Colorado Plateau – Samples of subducted Franciscan-type oceanic lithosphere; see also Helmstaedt, H., and Schulze, D.J., 1979, Garnet clinopyroxenite-chlorite eclogite transition in a xenolith from Moses Rock: Further evidence for metamorphosed ophiolites under the Colorado Plateau; Helmstaedt, H., and Schulze, D.J., 1988, Eclogite-facies ultramafic xenoliths from Colorado Plateau diatreme breccias: Comparison with eclogites in crustal environments, evaluation of the subduction hypothesis, and implications for eclogite xenoliths in diamondiferous kimberlites; and Helmstaedt, H.H., and Schulze, D.J., 1991, Early to mid-Tertiary inverted metamorphic gradient under the Colorado Plateau: evidence from eclogite xenoliths in ultramafic microbreccias, Navajo Volcanic Field. More recent work by Behr & Smith, 2013 and Hawkesworth, etal, 2016 provide additional evidence of Early Tertiary crustal deformation and evolution of shallow slab subduction beneath the western U.S. continental plate.

53. Selverstone, Jane; Pun, Aurora and Condie, Kent C., 1999, Xenolithic evidence for Proterozoic crustal evolution beneath the Colorado Plateau: GSA Bull., vol. 111, No. 4, p. 590-606.

54. Ibid.

55. Ibid, p. 591; Bennett, Victoria C. and DePaolo, Donald J., 1987, p. 682

56. CD-ROM Working Group, 2002, Structure and evolution of the lithosphere beneath the Rocky Mountains: initial results from the CD-ROM experiment, in GSA Today, vol. 12, No. 3, p. 4-10.

57. CD-ROM Working Group, 2002; Karlstrom, K.E., Whitmeyer, S.J., Dueker, K., Williams, M.L., Bowring, S.A., Levander, A., Humphreys, E.D., Keller, G.R., and the CD-ROM Working Group, 2005, Synthesis of results from the CD-ROM experiment: 4-D image of the lithosphere beneath the Rocky Mountains and implications for understanding the evolution of continental lithosphere; Karlstrom, K.E., 2012, Mantle-driven dynamic uplift of the Rocky Mountains and Colorado Plateau and its surface response: toward a unified hypothesis; Levander, A., etal, 2011, Continuing Colorado Plateau uplift by delamination – style convective lithospheric downwelling; Gonzales, D.A., 2015, New U/Pb zircon and 40Ar/39Ar age constraints of the Cenozoic plutonic record, southwestern Colorado: implications for regional magmatic-tectonic evolution; Schulze, D.J., Davis, D.W., Helmstaedt, H. and Joy, B., 2015, Timing of the Cenozoic "Great Hydration" event beneath the Colorado Plateau.

CHAPTER 13

1. Kenny Ross handwritten notes ~1972

2. Doug Ross, personal communication, 2017

3. Don Ross personal communication; re: Maid-o-Neoprene 1967 Cat trip

4. See USGS river gage files; USGS 09180500 Colorado River near Cisco, UT, 1967; USGS 09315000 Green River at Green River, UT, 1967

5. Don Ross written notes, June, 2017

6. Ibid.

7. By 1967 the old Hite landing was under water, and a "new" Hite marina/landing was moved about five miles upstream nearer the new bridges that cross the Colorado River and the Dirty Devil that were completed in June, 1966; see Figure 6.38.

8. The dirt landing strip lies just north of the new Colorado River Bridge and visible in Figure 13.3; it was finally paved in the 1990s and has a steep slope to the north and used frequently by river guests wanting to return to Moab quickly and avoid a long drive back.

9. Don Ross written notes, June, 2017

10. Ibid.

11. Ibid; Don's notes contain considerable "expletives" I deleted that Kenny had to say about Ace's actions.

12. Don and Doug Ross personal notes, 2017

13. Letter from Bill Dickinson to Kenny 07/23/1968

14. Ibid; nothing was mentioned in this letter, but I find it rather interesting that Bill named one of his boys "Ross" – a sure sign that Kenny meant a whole lot to Bill.

15. Charlie DeLorme personal communication, 2016

16. Buck's War Surplus Store receipt, 1970

17. Personal phone conversation with Mark Schwindt in 2016

18. Don Ross personal communication, 2016

19. Kenny Ross handwritten river notes ~1972

20. Ibid.

21. Letter from Kenny to Bill Dickinson 11/27/1976

22. The McElmo Bridge was not washed out according to UDOT records; see Bridge ID # OD710; Hwy Route 162; Mile Post 22.00; Location: McElmo Creek; Year Built: 1963, but was badly damaged and repaired.

23. Don Ross personal communications, 2016-2017

24. Ibid; see Swinging Bridge, Chapter Ten, note #19: The USGS Surface Water for Utah: Peak Streamflow Data [Gage Number 09379500] indicates a peak flow of 52,000 cfs on September 6, 1970.

25. Example: if five paying passengers go on a five-day trip then that equals twenty-five user days; a large group of 25 or 30 folks could nearly kill the rest of your season, and user days were arbitrarily based on documented numbers of passengers from previous years. As this regulation was in the works, many of the larger outfitters "stuffed the ballot box" by offering extra cheap fares to organizations and college groups to pump up their documented users, knowing full well that once the lines were drawn by the regulators that they would resume or raise the per day fares and have plenty of quota to fill. Unfortunately, small operators who did not or could not document their previous user days were penalized.

26. Kenny Ross handwritten notes ~1972

27. Ibid.

28. Ibid.

29. See Colorado River Compact (CRC) Chapter Nine, note #86

30. Letter from Anna Gavasci to Kenny 03/08/1972

31. Letter from Kenny to Anna Gavasci 03/12/1972

32. Kenny Ross trip cost worksheets for 1972

33. Kenny Ross trip folder of trips run in 1970s

34. Ibid.

35. Kenny Ross handwritten notes ~1976

36. Letter from EPA to Kenny 01/29/1973

37. Letter from Orson Anderson to Kenny 02/11/1973

38. Letter from Priscilla Grew to Kenny 02/13/1973

39. Kenny Ross handwritten notes ~1976

40. Letter from Kent Frost to Kenny 04/08/1973

41. The little white paper guidebook authored by Don Baars, 1973, "Geology of the Canyons of the San Juan River: A river runner's guide by the Four Corners Geological Society" is considered to be the first geologic guidebook to the San Juan River and was used on these and a few other trips. It was a paper book and had only one printing; future guidebooks were all waterproof and covered more than the geological aspects of the river corridor.

42. Letter exchanges Kenny Ross & Prof. D. Smith with Idaho St Univ, 1973

43. Letter from Utah Travel Development Board to Kenny, 1973

44. Letters to/from Kenny - Anna Gavasci, May 3-June 28, 1973 re: trips, sampling

45. See 1974 trip enquiries and prices

46. The Oil Embargo, 1973–1974: During the 1973 Arab-Israeli War, Arab members of the Organization of Petroleum Exporting Countries (OPEC) imposed an **embargo** against the United States in retaliation for the U.S. decision to re-supply the Israeli military and to gain leverage in the post-war peace negotiations. The effects of the embargo were immediate. OPEC forced oil companies to increase payments drastically. The price of oil quadrupled by 1974 to nearly $12 per barrel; US retail gas prices rose from a national average of 38.5 cents/gallon in May 1973 to 55.1 cents in June 1974.

47. Letter from Kenny to Steinhaus 03/10/1974

48. Letter from Kenny to Norm Howard, South Australia, May 1973

49. Letter from Kenny to Kenneth B. Castleton 02/21/1974; Polly Schaafsma expanded on the desecration in an email reply 1/24/2018: "Several thoughts in response to your email—I heard it was connected with the flu epidemic –whether that or TB, it doesn't matter much. But Ross's letter to Castleton is probably accurate. Mark Maryboy and Will Tsosie both explained it to me this way: That during that kind of illness, the blame is put squarely on a witch and that a diviner would be hired to find out where the witch was getting his/her power. In the case of Desecrated [Panel], the power that was making people sick was thought to be resident in the petroglyphs, and to get rid of the power they embody, they would have to be damaged. As you notice this was often done rather systematically with cuts to the head, joints, heart and so forth. Once the images were no longer powerful, then the witch lost its source of power to make people sick. It is interesting that this approach avoids people having to go after the witch him/herself or even having to know whom to blame! Will Tsosie also explained to me that the power thought to be resident in these figures was neither good, nor, evil. It could be used either way. It is simply 'power'."

50. Letter from W.B. Travers Cornell Univ. to Kenny, 1974

51. Letters from Education Overland USA, March 27, 1974

52. Letter from Mrs. Cullen Bryant, 1974 concerned about availability of gasoline

53. Letter from Prof. W.R. Brice, Univ. of Pittsburgh to Kenny 12/19/1974

54. See Kenny Ross "Special Information Sheets" file; copy of trip notes for Prof. W.R. Brice, Univ. Pittsburgh 1974-79, 8p.

55. Letter from Kenny to Jon Lindbergh 10/29/1974

56. Ibid.

57. Letter from Jon Lindbergh to Kenny 11/26/1974

58. Ibid.

59. Letter from Kenny to Artcraft 05/06/1975; the iconic logo was originally designed by Don Ross and Kenny as they were fiddling around trying to come up with a logo in 1970. The loops to the insignia represent the Goosenecks and the idea of the small cross on the "R" was to signify the "prescription for adventure" and only makes sense to those old enough to remember the ubiquitous pharmaceutical signage of times past.

60. Letter from Kenny to Bruce Adams @ Southwest Safaris Jan-April, 1975

61. Kenny Ross files of 1975 letters

62. See Kenny Ross file folder "Permits & Regulations"

63. Kenny Ross handwritten notes ~1976

64. Doug Ross, personal communications, 2015-2017

CHAPTER 14

1. Letter from Kenny to Norman Reiff 02/01/1977
2. November 12, 1976 letter to Switzerland group
3. Letter from Utah Div. of State history to Kenny 02/02/1976
4. Sierra Club brochure mentioning the great time they had on a WRX trip in June, 1976
5. See 1976 letter files
6. Letter from Tom McGetchin to Kenny 07/01/1976
7. Letter from Bill Dickinson to Kenny 11/16/1976
8. Letter from Kenny to Bill Dickinson 11/27/1976
9. Ibid.
10. Ibid.
11. Ibid.
12. Ibid.
13. Letter from Bill Dickinson to Kenny 12/06/1976
14. Ibid.
15. Letter from Joe Boyd to Kenny 03/01/1977
16. Ibid.
17. Ibid.
18. See 1977 USGS Historical Water Data [Gage Number 09379500]
19. Ibid.
20. Letter from J. Boyd to K. Wohlentz 08/29/1977
21. Ibid.
22. Ibid.
23. Letter from Kenny to Joe Boyd 09/09/1977; Kenny was unaware that BurRec had suggested "alternative means" and would not be releasing any extra water from Navajo reservoir.
24. Letter from Bureau of Reclamation to Joe Boyd 08/22/1977 declining to increase river flow
25. The details regarding this big event was recounted to me by Don and Doug Ross, 2016-2017
26. Ibid.

27. Brad Dimock, personal communications, 2015

28. Conversations with Doug, Don & Brad, 2015-2017

29. Letter from Joe Boyd to Gordon Swann 08/29/1977

30. Ibid.

31. See BIG FCGS GEOLOGY RIVER TRIP, Chapter Eleven and compare to James A. Peterson's petroleum geology trip in 1963 with no beer and C-rations for participants.

32. Letter from Kenny to Bill Dickinson 01/08/1978; Herb Helmstaedt who was mentioned by Kenny had just set the geologic world on its heels with his 1975 paper, *Eclogite nodules from kimberlites of the Colorado Plateau – Samples of subducted Franciscan-type oceanic lithosphere* where he suggested that some of the eclogites in the Mule Ear diatreme were derived from a subducted slab of oceanic crust – a radical theory to many at the time.

33. Letter from Bill Dickinson to Kenny 12/08/1977

34. Letter from Kenny to Bill Dickinson 01/06/1978

35. Letter from Bill Dickinson to Kenny 01/17/1978

36. Letter from Kenny to Bill Dickinson 01/06/1978; take-outs at Clay Hills in the late 1970s was incredibly treacherous. As lake level had risen and backed-up the river, the silt bars were not stable; **liquefaction** was very much present and I almost sunk over my head when I jumped out to land a boat there; so I know from personal experience what Kenny was warning Bill about.

37. See University of Arizona obituary of William R. Dickinson

38. From Dickinson, W.R., and Snyder, W.S., 1978, Plate tectonics of the Laramide orogeny: Geological Society of America Memoir 151, p.355; also see Glossary.

39. Letter from Kenny to Bill Dickinson 02/14/1978

40. Letter from Bill Dickinson to Kenny 02/27/1978

41. See Kenny Ross miscellaneous letter file, 1978

42. Letter from E. Velarde to Kenny 03/06/1979

CHAPTER 15

1. Susan DeLorme, personal communications, 2017

2. Email from Charlie DeLorme, 2015

3. Ibid.

4. Don Ross, personal communication, 2017

5. Gary Matlock, personal communications, 2016

6. Notes from Jonathan Till, re: 1983 Pecos Conference in Bluff, Utah

7. Ibid.

8. Charlie DeLorme, personal communications, 2015

9. Email from Rob Rice, 2015

10. Charlie DeLorme, personal communications, 2015

11. Ibid.

12. Ibid, 2016

13. Susan DeLorme, personal communications, 2015

14. Charlie DeLorme, personal communications, 2015

15. Don and Doug Ross, personal communications, 2017

16. Doug Ross, personal communication; the Title to the 1971 Chevy Vega was in Kenny's files; he bought it in July, 1979 for $600 from quality Auto Sales in Cortez, Colorado

17. Email from Doug Ross, 2015, plus personal communications

18. Don Ross, personal communications, 2016-2017

19. Doug Ross, personal communications, 2015

20. During the research for this book and the many conversations I had with Doug & Don Ross and all the old Wild Rivers gang we all thought I should write an Anthology of River Guide stories if I live long enough to get this book out the door.

21. Email from Doug Ross, 2015

22. Gary Matlock, personal communication by phone, July, 2016

23. Emails from Susan DeLorme, May, 2017

24. Ibid.

25. Ibid.

LIST OF REFERENCES

Aitchison, Stewart, 1983, *A Naturalist's San Juan River Guide*; Pruett Publishing Co., Boulder, CO (waterproof edition)

Allen, Steve, 2012, *Utah's canyon country place names: stories of the cowboys, miners, pioneers, and river runners who put names on the land*; Canyon Country Press, Durango, CO; Two Volumes, 985 p.

Anderson, Orson L. and Perkins, Priscilla C., 1974, Runaway temperatures in the Asthenosphere resulting from viscous heating, *in* Journal of Geophysical Research, Vol. 79, No. 14, p.2136-2138.

_________, 1975, A plate tectonics model involving non-laminar asthenospheric flow to account for irregular patterns of magmatism in the southwestern United States, in Publication No. 1241, Institute of Geophysics and Planetary Physics, University of California, p.113-122.

Anderson, Orson L. and Grew, Priscilla C., 1977, Stress corrosion theory of crack propagation with applications to geophysics, *in* Reviews of Geophysics and Space Physics, Vol. 15, No. 1, p. 77-104.

Anderson, O.L., 1979, Diatremes and carbonatites, *in* Kimberlites, Diatremes, and Diamonds: their geology, petrology and geochemistry, F.R. Boyd and H.O.A. Meyer, eds., Proceedings of the Second Kimberlite Conf., Vol II, American Geophysical Union, Washington, D.C.

_________, 1997, Shoemaker Memorial Kimberlite Excursion, Field Tutorials #1-#5 (unpublished)

Aton, James M., 1993, *"The River, the Ditch and the Volcano – Bluff, 1879 – 1884,"* in *Blue Mountain Shadows*: vol. 12, p.15-23.

Aton, James M. and McPherson, Robert S., 2000, RIVER FLOWING FROM THE SUNRISE: an environmental history of the Lower San Juan; Utah State University Press, 216 p.

Atwater, T., 1970, Implications of plate tectonics for the Cenozoic tectonic evolution of western North America: Geological Society of America Bull., Vol 81, p.3513-3536.

Baars, D.L., 1973, Geology of the Canyons of the San Juan River; Four Corners Geological Society 7th Field Conference, 94 p.

Baars, Don, 1987, CATARACT CANYON: a river runner's guide to Cataract Canyon and approaches; Cañón Publishers Ltd., Evergreen, CO (waterproof edition), 80p.

Baars, D.L., J.W. Parker, and J. Chronic, 1967, Revised stratigraphic nomenclature of Pennsylvanian System, Paradox Basin: A.A.P.G. Bull. 51(3), pp. 393-403.

Baars, Don and Stevenson, Gene, 1986a, *SAN JUAN CANYONS: a river runner's guide and natural history of San Juan River Canyons*; Cañón Publishers Ltd., Evergreen, CO (waterproof edition), 64p.

Baars, D.L. and Stevenson, G.M., 1986b, The Paradox: A pull-apart basin of Pennsylvanian age *in* Paleotectonics and Sedimentation in the Rocky Mountains: American Assoc. Petroleum Geologists Mem., no. 41, p. 513-539.

Baker, A.A., C.H. Dane, and J.B. Reeside, Jr., 1933, Paradox Formation of eastern Utah and western Colorado: A.A.P.G. Bull. 17, pp. 963-980.

Baker, A.A., 1936, Geology of the Monument Valley-Navajo Mountain region, San Juan County, Utah: USGS Bulletin No. 965, 106p.

Barry, John M., 1997, RISING TIDE: The great Mississippi flood of 1927 and how it changed America: Simon & Schuster Paperbacks; 524 p.

Beals, Ralph Leon, George W. Brainerd, and Watson Smith, 1945, *Archaeological studies in northeast Arizona: A report on the archaeological work of the Rainbow Bridge-Monument Valley Expedition; University of California publications in American archaeology and ethnology 44, no. 1, 235 p., plus 31 plates;* Berkeley: University of California Press.

Behr, W.M. and Smith, D., 2013, Deformation in mantle wedge associated with Laramide flat-slab subduction; (abs.) American Geophysical Union Annual Meeting, San Francisco, CA.

Bennett, Victoria C. and DePaolo, Donald J., 1987, Proterozoic crustal history of *the* western United States as determined by neodymium isotopic mapping; Geol. Soc. America Bull., v. 99, p. 674-685.

Berg, A. Scott, 1999, Lindbergh, Berkley Books, New York, 628p.

Bernheimer, Charles L., 1924, RAINBOW BRIDGE: Circling Navajo Mountain and Explorations in the "Badlands" of Southern Utah and Northern Arizona: With a New Introduction: Charles Bernheimer: The Tenderfoot and Cliff Dweller from Manhattan, 1999, by Albert E. Ward; A CAS Reprint; originally published in 1924; Doubleday, Page & Co., Garden City; 187 p.

Blackburn, Fred M. and Williamson, Ray A., 1997, Cowboys & Cave Dwellers: Basketmaker Archaeology in Utah's Grand Gulch; School of American Research Press, 188p.

Blair, Bob, 2005, William Henry Jackson's "The pioneer photographer"; with original text from the 1929 edition by William H. Jackson in collaboration with Howard R. Driggs; Museum of New Mexico Press, Santa Fe; 210p.

Bonta, Marcia Myers, 1991, *Women in the Field; America's Pioneering Women Naturalists*; Texas A & M Univ. Press; Includes biographies of Kate Brandegee and Alice Eastwood.

Brown, Ronald C. and Smith, Duane A., 2006, *New Deal Days: The CCC at Mesa Verde*: The Durango Herald Small Press, 133p.

Carrara, Paul E., 2012, Surficial Geologic Map of Mesa Verde National Park, Montezuma County, Colorado: USGS Science Investigations Map 3224, 22p.

CD-ROM Working Group, 2002, Structure and evolution of the lithosphere beneath the Rocky Mountains: initial results from the CD-ROM experiment, in GSA Today, vol. 12, No. 3, p. 4-10.

Chapin, Frederick H., 1892, *The Land of the Cliff Dwellers*. Boston: W.B. Clarke & Co.

Christenson, Andrew L., 1987, The *Last of the Great Expeditions: The Rainbow Bridge/Monument Valley Expedition 1933-38:* Museum of Northern Arizona, Plateau 58, no. 4, 32p.

Cobban, W.A., Walaszczyk, Ireneusz, Obradovich, J.O., and McKinney, K.C., 2006, A USGS zonal table for the Upper Cretaceous Middle Cenomanian-Maastrichtian of the western interior of the United States based on ammonites, inoceramids, and radiometric ages: U.S. Geological Survey Open-File Report 2006–1250, 50 p.

Comodi, P., and Zanazzi, P.F., 1996, Effects of temperature and pressure on the structure of lawsonite, Piazza University, Perugia, Italy. American Mineralogist 81, 833-841.

Crampton, C. Gregory, 1964, "The San Juan Canyon Historical Sites"; *in* ANTHROPOLOGICAL PAPERS, Number 70, June, 1964, (Glen Canyon Series Number 22)' Jesse D. Jennings & Carol C. Stout, eds; [partial report from Brandt Hart, August, 2016]

Crampton, C. Gregory, 1986, GHOSTS OF GLEN CANYON: history beneath Lake Powell; Publishers Place, Inc., 135p.

Cross, C.W. and Spencer, A.C., 1899, USGS La Plata Folio No. 60, p.8.

Crotty, Helen K., 1983, *Honoring the Dead: Anasazi Ceramics from the Rainbow Bridge-Monument Valley Expedition; Museum of Cultural History, UCLA, Monograph Series Number 22*, Los Angeles, Museum of Cultural History.

Deede, John, 2016, Shaking hands with the Devil – the deepest hole ever drilled; Feb 26, Energy Media Group, Eagleford, TX.

Dickinson, W.R., and Snyder, W.S., 1978, Plate tectonics of the Laramide orogeny: Geological Society of America Memoir 151, p.355-366.

Dickinson, W.R., 1989, Tectonic setting of Arizona through geologic time, in Geologic Evolution of Arizona, J.P. Jenny and S.J. Reynolds, eds., Arizona Geological Society Digest No. 17, p.1-16.

Dimock, Brad, 2007, THE VERY HARD WAY: Bert Loper and the Colorado River; Fretwater Press, 457p.

Dockery, Kevin and Brutsman, Bud, 2007, *Navy Seals: A History of the Early Years*; Berkley Publishing; p. 16-17.

Eckel, Edwin B., Williams, J.S. and Galbraith, F.W., 1949, Geology and ore deposits of the La Plata district Colorado, U. S. Geological Survey Professional Paper 219, 179p.

Edwards, Everett E., 1969, The early writings of Frederick Jackson Turner; compiled by E.E. Edwards, Freeport, NT: Books for Library Press.

Elliott, Melinda [Malinda], 1995, Great Excavations, School of American Research Press, 251p.

Evans, Richard T. and Frye, Helen M., 2009, History of the Topographic Branch (Division) of the U.S. Geological Survey Circular 1341, 196p.

Evison, Herb, *Jesse L. Nusbaum: Defender of American antiquities* in the *Courier*; vol. 4, no. 1, January, 1981; National Park Service History eLibrary: npshistory.com/persons-of-the-month

Forsee, Aylesa, 1964, William Henry Jackson: Pioneer photographer of the West; The Viking Press, New York, NY; 205p.

Fowler, Don D., 2011, The Glen Canyon Country: a personal memoir; The University of Utah Press, 424p.

Franklin, Robert and Pamela A. Bunte, 1990; *The Paiute*; Chelsea House, New York, NY.

Friedman, Norman, 2002, *U.S. Amphibious Ships and Craft: An Illustrated Design History*; Naval Institute, p. 490.

Frost, Kent, 1997, My Canyonlands, w/Rosalie Goldman; Canyon Country Publications, 160p.

Gilbert, Grove Karl, 1914, The transportation of debris by running water; U.S. Geological Survey Professional Paper 86, 263p.

Gomez, Arthur R., 1994, Quest for the Golden Circle: the Four Corners and the metropolitan west 1945 – 1970; University of New Mexico Press, 252 p.

Gonzales, D.A., 2015, New U/Pb zircon and 40Ar/39Ar age constraints of the Cenozoic plutonic record, southwestern Colorado: implications for regional magmatic-tectonic evolution: *The Mountain Geologist*, v. 52, no. 2, p. 5-42.

Grammer, G. Michael, Eberli, Gregor P., Van Buchem, Frans S.P., Homewood, Peter and Stevenson, G.M.,1996, Application of high resolution sequence stratigraphy to evaluate lateral variability in outcrop and subsurface -Desert Creek and Ismay intervals, Paradox Basin, *in* M.W. Longman and M.D. Sonnenfeld, eds., Paleozoic Systems of the Rocky Mountain Region, Rocky Mountain Section, SEPM (Society for Sedimentary Geology), p.235-266.

Grand Canyon River Guides, 2000; *Gene Shoemaker*, Quarterly Review vol. 13, no.1, p.28-40.

Gregory, Herbert E., 1911, The San Juan Oil Field, San Juan County, Utah: *in*, Contributions to Economic Geology, 1909, Part II; U.S.G.S. Bulletin 431, p. 11- 25.

_________, 1916, Geology of the Navajo Country: a reconnaissance of parts of Arizona, New Mexico, and Utah: U.S.G.S. Professional Paper 93, 161p.

_________, 1916, The Navajo Country: a geographic and hydrographic reconnaissance of parts of Arizona, New Mexico, and Utah: U.S.G.S. Water-Supply Paper 380, 219p.

_________, 1917, Geology of the Navajo country: a reconnaissance of parts of Arizona, New Mexico and Utah: USGS Professional Paper 93, 161p.

_________, 1938, The San Juan country, a geographic and geologic reconnaissance of southeastern Utah: USGS Prof. Paper 188, 123p.

Gulliford, Andrew, 2010, April 12 Draft manuscript: A column for the Durango Herald newspaper re: overview of Ansel Hall and Explorers Camp; *unpublished*

Guthe, Alfred K., 1949, a preliminary report on excavations in Southwestern Colorado: American Antiquity; vol. 15, no. 2, p. 144-154.

Hack, J.T., 1942, Sedimentation and Volcanism in the Hopi Buttes, Arizona: Geological Society of America Bulletin No. 53, p.335-372.

Hall, Ansel Franklin, 1934; General Report of the Rainbow Bridge-Monument Valley Expedition of 1933; University of California Press, Berkeley, CA, 32p.

Hargrave, Lyndon Lane, 1935; *Report on Archaeological Reconnaissance in the Rainbow Plateau Area of Northern Arizona and Southern Utah, based upon fieldwork by the Rainbow Bridge-Monument Valley Expedition of 1933*. Berkeley, California: University of California Press.

Hart, Brandt, 2009, "If a bridge could speak" *in* Blue Mtn Shadows, Vol 40; p. 56-58.

Hawkesworth, Chris J., Cawood, Peter A., and Dhuime, Bruno, 2016, Tectonics and crustal evolution; in GSA *Today*, v. 26, no.9, p.4-11.

Hayden, F.V., 1877, *Ninth Annual Report of the United States Geological and Geographical Survey for the Year 1875*; Washington, D.C.; GPO.

Head, June, 2017, The 'Dark Corner' and 'Outlaw Capital' of the Southwest, *in* The Cortez Journal, April 12.

Head, June and Joyce Lawrence, 2017, 1911 floods brought havoc to Southwest Colorado, parts I and II, *in* The Cortez Journal, May 5.

Hedden, Bill; *"Towns Angling for Tourism Should Beware of the Great White Shark,"* in High Country News, September 5, 1994. [quoted by Art Gomez]

Helmstaedt, H. and Doig, R., 1975, Eclogite nodules from kimberlites of the Colorado Plateau – Samples of subducted Franciscan-type oceanic lithosphere: Physical and Chemical Earth, Vol., 9, p.95-111.

Helmstaedt, H., and Schulze, D.J., 1979, Garnet clinopyroxenite-chlorite eclogite transition in a xenolith from Moses Rock: Further evidence for metamorphosed ophiolites under the Colorado Plateau, *in* Boyd, F.R., and Meyer, H.O.A., eds., The mantle sample: Inclusions in kimberlites and other volcanics: Washington, D.C., American Geophysical Union, p. 357–365

_________, 1988, Eclogite-facies ultramafic xenoliths from Colorado Plateau diatreme breccias: Comparison with eclogites in crustal environments, evaluation of the subduction hypothesis, and implications for eclogite xenoliths in diamondiferous kimberlites, *in* Smith, D.C., ed., Eclogites and eclogite-facies rocks: New York, Elsevier, p. 387–450.

_________, 1991, Early to mid-Tertiary inverted metamorphic gradient under the Colorado Plateau: evidence from eclogite xenoliths in ultramafic microbreccias, Navajo Volcanic Field: Journal of Geophysical Research, Vol. 96, No. B8, p. 13,225-13,235.

Henderson, Randall, 1945, "Down the San Juan and the Colorado," *in* Sierra Club Bulletin 30; December issue; p.63-70.

_________, 1946, "Glyph Hunters in the Indian Country" in Desert Magazine 10, November, p.11-15.

_________, 1946, "We Explored Dark Canyon" in Desert Magazine 10, December, p. 5-9.

_________, 1952, "Glen Canyon Voyage" in Desert Magazine 15, October, p.7-21.

Heriot, Ruthanne, 1987, Finding aide to the Jesse L. Nusbaum papers, 1921-1958 *in* NPS History Collection; 4p. pdf

Hoops, Herm, 1986, Typescript of a taped oral interview of Kenny Ross in Mancos, CO on September 13, 1986 (unpublished)

Huntoon, Peter W., Billingsley, George H., Jr., and Breed, William J., 1982, Geologic Map of Canyonlands National Park and Vicinity, Utah; published by The Canyonlands Natural History Association, Moab, Utah.

Hurst, Michael T., 1988, "Bluff City, Utah": *in* Blue Mountains Shadows, Issue #2.

Janse, A.J.A., 1984, Kimberlites, where or when, in Kimberlite Occurrences and Origin: a basis for conceptual models of exploration; J.E. Glover and P.G. Harris, eds., publ. by the Geology Department and University extension, The University of Western Australia, Pub. No. 8, Perth, Australia.

Judd, Neil M., 1968, Men met along the trail: adventures in archaeology; University of Oklahoma Press, 162p. [Definition of "*chineago*" (food in Navajo language, p. 121)]

Karlstrom, K.E., Whitmeyer, S.J., Dueker, K., Williams, M.L., Bowring, S.A., Levander, A., Humphreys, E.D., Keller, G.R., and the CD-ROM Working Group, 2005, Synthesis of results from the CD-ROM experiment: 4-D image of the lithosphere beneath the Rocky Mountains and implications for understanding the evolution of continental lithosphere, *in* Karlstrom, K.E., and Keller, G.R., eds., The Rocky Mountain Region: An Evolving Lithosphere (Tectonics, Geochemistry, and Geophysics), Geophysical Monography Series 154, p. 421-441.

Karlstrom, K.E., 2012, Mantle-driven dynamic uplift of the Rocky Mountains and Colorado Plateau and its surface response: toward a unified hypothesis *in* LITHOSPHERE, Vol. 4, No. 1, p. 3-22.

Kearsley, Lisa, 2014, *SAN JUAN RIVER GUIDE: Montezuma Creek to Clay Hills Crossing*; Shiva Press, Flagstaff, AZ; 3rd ed.; (waterproof)

Knipmeyer, James H., 1983, Typescript notes from W.H. Jackson diary, summer 1875.

Krakauer, Jon, 2003, Under the Banner of Heaven: a story of violent faith; Doubleday, 372p.

Lavender, David S., 1943; One Man's West; Doubleday & Co., reprinted 1956 & 1977; 316p.

________, 1986, River Runners of the Grand Canyon; Grand Canyon Natural History Association, 98p.

Lee, Ronald F., 1970, The Antiquities Act of 1906. Washington, D.C.: National Park Service, Office of History and historic Architecture, Eastern Service Center.

Levander, A., etal, 2011, Continuing Colorado Plateau uplift by delamination – style convective lithospheric downwelling in NATURE, Vol. 472, p. 461- 466.

Lewis, Richard Q, Sr., Campbell, Russell H., Thaden, Robert E., Krummel, William J., Jr., Willis, Grant C., and Matyjasik, Basia, 2011, Geologic Map of Elk Ridge and vicinity, San Juan County, Utah: Misc. Publication 11-1DM, Utah Geological Survey; modified from USGS Prof. Paper 474-b, 1965; 12p., 1 plate.

Liebermann, Robert, 1966, Preliminary survey of kimberlite diatremes of southeastern Utah; field notes October 31 to November 4, 1966 (unpublished)

Lister, Florence C, 1997, *Prehistory in Peril: the worst and best of Durango Archaeology*; University Press of Colorado; 196p.

Lister, Florence Cline & Robert Hill, 1968, *Earl Morris & Southwestern Archaeology*; Western National Parks Association pub., 204 p. Reprint edition of this important look at the life and times of one of the true pioneers of Southwest archeology; includes a new preface by Florence C. Lister; includes Historical photos & index.

Lorenz, V., 1973, On the formation of maars: Bulletin *Volcanologique*, Vol. 37, p.183-204.

________, 1986, On the growth of maars and diatremes and its relevance to the formation of tuff rings: Bulletin of Volcanology, Vol. 48, p.265-274.

Macomb, J.N., 1876, Report of the Exploring Expedition from Santa Fe, New Mexico, to the Junction of the Grand and Green Rivers of the Great Colorado of the West in 1859; Washington, D.C., GPO

McGetchin, T.R. and Silver, L.T., 1970, Compositional relations in minerals from kimberlite and related rocks in the Moses Rock dike, San Juan County, Utah: American Mineralogist, Vol. 55, p.1738-1771.

________, 1972, A crustal-upper mantle model for the Colorado Plateau based on observations of crystalline rock fragments in the Moses Rock dike: Journal of Geophysical Research, Vol. 77, p.7022-7037.

________, Smith, D., Ehrenberg, S.N., Roden, M., and Wilshire, H.G., 1977, Navajo kimberlites and minettes field guide: Santa Fe, Second Annual Kimberlite Conference, 40 p.

McCourt, Tom, 2003, White Canyon: remembering the little town at the bottom of Lake Powell; Southpaw Publ., 225p.

________, 2012, King of the Colorado: the story of Cass Hite, Utah's legendary explorer, prospector and pioneer; Southpaw Publ., 202p.

McPherson, Robert S., 1995, *A History of San Juan County, Utah*; State Historical Society, San Juan County Commission; 419p.

_________., 2015, LIFE IN A CORNER: cultural episodes in southeastern Utah, 1880 – 1950; 293p.

Melancon, S.M., Michaud, T.S. and Thomas, R.W., 1979, Assessment of Energy Resource Development Impact on water quality: the San Juan River Basin: EPA Interagency Energy-Environment Research and Development Program Report, EPA-600/7-79-235; 151p. [Fig. 1 Location Map]

Miser, Hugh D., 1924, The San Juan Canyon, southeastern Utah: U.S. Geol. Survey Water Supply Paper 538, p. 1-80.

_________, 1925, Geologic structure of San Juan Canyon and adjacent country, Utah *in* USGS Bull. 751 Contributions to Economic Geology, 1923-24, Part II, p. 115-155

Nash, Roderick Frazier, 1989, *The Big Drops*: Ten Legendary Rapids of the American Southwest; Johnson Books, Boulder; 216 p.

Nelson, Arthur W., 1936, "*My Experiences as a Member of the Rainbow Bridge – Monument Valley Expedition, Summer of 1936*," an unpublished hand-written journal from Andy Christenson, 2017.

Newberry, J.S., 1861, Geological report, in Ives, J.C., Report upon the Colorado River of the West, explored in 1857 and 1858, pt. 3.

_________, 1876, Report of the exploring expedition from Santa Fe, New Mexico, to the junction of the Grand and Green rivers of the great Colorado of the West, in 1859, *in* Capt. J.N. Macomb, Geological report: Washington, D.C., U.S. Army Eng. Dept. p. 9-118.

Noble, David Grant, 1981, revised 1991, Ancient Ruins of the southwest: an archaeological guide, Northland Publishing Co., 218p.

_________, 2006, *The Mesa Verde World: Explorations in Ancestral Puebloan Archaeology*; School of American Research Press; 195p.

Nordenskiöld, Gustaf, 1893, *The Cliff Dwellers of the Mesa Verde*; reprinted 1990 by Mesa Verde Museum Association, 174p, plus Appendices and Plates.

Ort, M., Dallegge, T.A., Vazquez, J.A., and White, J.D.L., 1998, Volcanism and sedimentation in the Miocene-Pliocene Hopi Buttes and Hopi Lake; in Duebendorfer, E.M., ed., Geologic excursions in northern and central Arizona: Flagstaff, Northern Arizona University, p.35-58.

Porter, Eliot, 1988, *The Place No One Knew*; Commemorative Edition 1963, Peregrine Smith Books, David Brower, ed; 184 p.

Powell, Allan Kent, 1983, *San Juan County, Utah – People, Resources, and History*; Utah State Historical Society

Ringholz, Raye Carleson, 1991, *Uranium Frenzy: Boom and Bust on the Colorado Plateau*; University of New Mexico Press, 310p.

RMAG 2009 SPECIAL PUBLICATION: The Paradox Basin Revisited – New Developments in Petroleum Systems and Basin Analysis; edited by W.S. Houston, L.L. Wray and P.G. Moreland, 816p.

Roden, M.F., 1981, Origin of coexisting minette and ultramafic breccia, Navajo volcanic field: Contributions to Mineralogy and Petrology, v. 77, p. 195- 206.

Schulze, D.J., Davis, D.W., Helmstaedt, H. and Joy, B., 2015, Timing of the Cenozoic "Great Hydration" event beneath the Colorado Plateau: Th-Pb dating monazite in Navajo Volcanic Field metamorphic eclogite xenoliths *in* GEOLOGY, Vol. 43, No. 8, p. 727-730.

Seavey, Nina Gilden, Jane S. Smith, & Paul Wagner, 1998, *A Paralyzing Fear: The Triumph over Polio in America*. New York, New York: TV Books; p. 170-171.

Selverstone, Jane; Pun, Aurora and Condie, Kent C., 1999, Xenolithic evidence for Proterozoic crustal evolution beneath the Colorado Plateau: GSA Bull., vol. 111, No. 4, p. 590-606.

Semken, Steve, 2003, Black rocks protruding up: The Navajo Volcanic Field, New Mexico Geological Society Guidebook, 54th Field Conference, Geology of the Zuni Plateau, p.133-138.

Seyfarth, Jill and Ruth Lambert, 2010, *History of La Plata County, Colorado*; pdf, p.101-102.

Shanks, Trina R.W., 2005, "The Homestead Act: A major asset-building policy in American History" *in* Michael Sherraden, ed.; Inclusion in the American Dream: Assets, Poverty, and Public Policy; Oxford University Press, 432p.

Shelf carbonates of the Paradox Basin: a symposium Fourth Field Conference Guidebook, 1963, Ralph O. Bass and Seymour L. Sharps, eds., Four Corners Geological Society, 273p; and map insert.

Shoemaker, E.M., 1953, Collapse origin of the diatremes of the Navajo-Hopi Reservation, Geological Society of America Bulletin No. 64, p.1514 (abs).

________, 1955, Distribution of elements, *in* Geological Investigations of radioactive deposits – Semi-Annual Progress Report, December 1, to May 31, 1955: U.S. G.S. TEI 540, Issued by U.S. AEC Technical Information Service, Oak Ridge, Tennessee, p.76-86.

________, 1956a, Diatremes on the Navajo and Hopi Reservations, Arizona, *in* Geological Investigations of radioactive deposits – Semi-Annual Progress Report, December 1, 1955 to May 31, 1956: U.S. G.S. TEI 620, Issued by U.S. AEC Technical Information Service, Oak Ridge, Tennessee, p.78-85.

________, and H.J. Moore II, 1956b, Diatremes on the Navajo and Hopi Reservations, Arizona, *in* Geological Investigations of radioactive deposits – Semi-Annual Progress Report, June 1, to November 30, 1956: U.S. G.S. TEI 640, Issued by U.S. AEC Technical Information Service, Oak Ridge, Tennessee, p. 197-203.

________, 1956c, Occurrence of uranium in diatremes on the Navajo and Hopi Reservations, Arizona, New Mexico, and Utah (p. 179-185), *in* Contributions to the geology of uranium and thorium by the United States, G.S. and AEC for the U.N. Int'l Conf. on Peaceful uses of Atomic Energy, Geneva, Switzerland, USGS Professional Paper 300, 739p.

________, F.S. Hensley, Jr., and R.W. Halligan, 1957, Diatremes on the Navajo and Hopi Reservations, Arizona, *in* Geological Investigations of radioactive deposits – Semi-Annual Progress Report, December 1, 1956 to May 31, 1957: U.S. G.S. TEI 690, Issued by U.S. AEC Technical Information Service, Oak Ridge, Tennessee, p. 389-398.

________, F.M. Byers, Jr., and C.H. Roach, 1958, Diatremes on the Navajo and Hopi Reservations, Arizona, *in* Geological Investigations of radioactive deposits – Semi-Annual Progress Report, December 1, 1957 to May 31, 1958: U.S. G.S. TEI 740, Issued by U.S. AEC Technical Information Service, Oak Ridge, Tennessee, p. 158-168.

________, C.H. Roach, and F.M. Byers, Jr., 1962, Diatremes and uranium deposits in the Hopi Buttes, Arizona; Petrologic Studies: a volume to honor A.F. Buddington, p.327-366.

Smith, Duane A., 1983; *Rocky Mountain Boom Town: A History of Durango, Colorado*: Boulder, Colorado; Pruett Publishing Company

________, 1988, Mesa Verde National Park: Shadows of the Centuries; University Press of Kansas, 254p.

Smith, Duane A. and Winkler, William C., 2005, *Travels and Travails, Tourism at Mesa Verde:* Durango, Colorado: Durango Herald Small Press

Smith, D., 2000, Insights into the evolution of the uppermost continental mantle from xenolith localities on and near the Colorado Plateau and regional comparisons: Journal of Geophysical Research, v. 105, p. 16769-16781.

Smith, Jane S., 1990, *Patenting the Sun: Polio and the Salk vaccine*; William Morrow and Company, Inc., New York, NY, 157p.

Snead, James E., 2003, Ruins and Rivals: the making of Southwest Archaeology, The University of Arizona Press, Tucson, 226p.

Staveley, Gaylord, 2015, The Rapids and the Roar: a boating history of the Colorado River and Grand Canyon; Fretwater Press, Flagstaff, AZ, 333p.

Stegner, Wallace, 1969, The Sound of Mountain Water; Ballantine Books, New York, 151p; copyright 1946, 1947, 1949, 1952, 1966 and 1969 by Wallace Stegner

________, 1992, *Beyond the Hundredth Meridian: John Wesley Powell and the Second Opening of the West*; New York: Penguin Books, 438p; see Stegner's references to Powell, John Wesley, 1875, *Exploration of the Colorado River of the West and its tributaries*

Sterrett, D.B., 1909, Precious Stones, USGS Mineral Resources of the United States, 1908, part II: Nonmetallic products, p.805-861.

Stevenson, G.M. and Baars, D.L., 1986, The Paradox: A pull-apart basin of Pennsylvanian age *in* Paleotectonics and Sedimentation in the Rocky Mountains: American Assoc. Petroleum Geologists Mem., no. 41, p. 513-539.

Stuart-Alexander, D.E., Shoemaker, E.M., and Moore, H.J., 1972, Geologic map of the Mule Ear diatreme, San Juan County, Utah: USGS Misc. Geologic Investigations, Map I-674.

Stultz, Richard E. "Ted", 1946, Report on Explorers Camp; unpublished thesis for Teachers College, Columbia University, New York City, 116p.

Tanner, Faun McConkie, 1976, The Far Country: A regional history of Moab and La Sal, Utah; Salt Lake City, p. 13-14.

Tate, LaVerne, 2008, Images of America: Early San Juan County; San Juan County Historical Society; Arcadia Publishing; 128p.

Thompson, Ian "Sandy", 1982, "Kenny Ross: River rat and teacher;" for Early Man (unpublished manuscript)

Tobin, S.J., 1950, Notes on Site No. 1, Cahone Ruin, Southwestern Colorado: Southwestern Lore, March, vol. XV, No.4.

Topping, Gary, 1997, *Glen Canyon and the San Juan Country*, Moscow: University of Idaho Press.

Turner, Jack, 1998, Early Images of the Southwest: Lantern slides of Ansel F. Hall; published by Roberts Rinehart, Niwot, Colorado, 90p.

Valle, Doris, 1986, Looking back around the Hat: a history of Mexican Hat; self-published, 60p.

Webb, Robert H., Belnap, Jayne, and Weisheit, John S., 2004, Cataract Canyon: a human and environmental history of the rivers in Canyonlands; University of Utah Press, 268p.

Webb, Roy, 2003, *"Set my spirit free"* a History of SOCOTWA; CPRG web pub online p.12-16; pdf

_________, 2005, High, Wide, and Handsome: The river journals of Norman D. Nevills; Utah State University Press, 308p.

Wengerd, Sherman A., 1951, Reef limestones of the Hermosa formation, San Juan County, Utah: American Association of Petroleum Geologists Bulletin, v. 35, p. 1038-1051.

_________, and Strickland, J. W., 1954, Pennsylvanian stratigraphy of the Paradox salt basin, Four Comers region, Colorado and Utah: American Association of Petroleum Geologists Bulletin, v. 38, p. 2157-2199.

_________, 1958, Pennsylvanian stratigraphy, southwest shelf, Paradox basin: Intermountain Association of Petroleum Geologists Guidebook to the Geology of the Paradox Basin, 9th Field Conference, p. 109-134.

_________, and Matheny, M. L., 1954, Pennsylvanian system of the Four Comers region: American Association of Petroleum Geologists Bulletin, v. 42, p. 2048-2106.

_________, and Szabo, E., 1975, Stratigraphy and tectogenesis of the Paradox basin: Four Corners Geological Society Field Conference Guidebook 8, p. 193-210.

Williams, H., 1936, Pliocene volcanoes of the Navajo-Hopi country: Geological Society of America Bulletin, v. 47, p.111-172.

Wilson, Carol Green, 1955, Alice Eastwood's Wonderland: the adventures of a Botanist; California Academy of Sciences, San Francisco; printed by Lawton Kennedy, 2000 limited copies, 222p.

Winkler, William C., and Bradley, Bruce, 1999, Ansel Hall Pueblo: a National Historic Place; Colorado Historical Society Document submitted November 25, 1997.

Woodruff, E.G., 1912, Geology of the San Juan Oil Field, Utah: *in*, Contributions to Economic Geology, 1910, Part II; U.S.G.S. Bulletin 1103; p. 76 – 104.

CHRONOLOGICAL LISTING OF RIVER LOGS OF THE SAN JUAN RIVER

1973: Baars, D.L.; Geology of the Canyons of the San Juan River; Four Corners Geological Society 7th Field Conference, 94 p; 0.0 begins at Highway Bridge and river miles go downstream

1983: Aitchison, Stewart; *A Naturalist's San Juan River Guide*; Pruett Publishing Co., Boulder, CO (waterproof edition); 0.0 begins at Highway Bridge and river miles go downstream

1986: Baars, Don and Stevenson, Gene; *SAN JUAN CANYONS: a river runner's guide and natural history of San Juan River Canyons*; Cañón Publishers Ltd., Evergreen, CO (waterproof edition); 0.0 begins at Highway Bridge and river miles go downstream

2002: Kearsley, Lisa; *SAN JUAN RIVER GUIDE: Montezuma Creek to Clay Hills Crossing*; Shiva Press, Flagstaff, AZ; 1st ed.; (waterproof); 0.0 begins at Highway Bridge and river miles go downstream

2007: Kearsley, Lisa; *SAN JUAN RIVER GUIDE: Montezuma Creek to Clay Hills Crossing*; Shiva Press, Flagstaff, AZ; 2nd ed.; (waterproof); 0.0 begins at BLM ramp @ Sand Island & river miles go downstream

2009: Whitis, D. and Martin, Tom: GUIDE TO THE SAN JUAN RIVER: Montezuma Creek to Clay Hills Crossing, Utah; 2nd edition: Flagstaff, Vishnu Temple Press, 36p.

2014: Kearsley, Lisa; *SAN JUAN RIVER GUIDE: Montezuma Creek to Clay Hills Crossing*; Shiva Press, Flagstaff, AZ; 3rd ed.; (waterproof); 0.0 begins at BLM ramp @ Sand Island & river miles go downstream.

Made in the USA
Monee, IL
28 May 2023

34148374R00286